International Peacekeeping

The Library of Essays in International Law
Series Editor: Robert McCorquodale

International Peacekeeping

Edited by

Boris Kondoch

University of Peace, South Korea

ASHGATE

Published by
Ashgate Publishing Limited
Wey Court East
Union Street
Farnham
Surrey GU9 7PT
England

Ashgate Publishing Company
Suite 420
101 Cherry Street
Burlington, VT 05401-4405
USA

Ashgate website: http://www.ashgate.com

British Library Cataloguing in Publication Data
International peacekeeping. – (The library of essays in
   international law)
   1.United Nations – Peacekeeping forces 2.Intervention
   (International law) 3.Peacekeeping forces
   4.Internationalized territories
   I.Kondoch, Boris
   341.5'84

Library of Congress Cataloging-in-Publication Data
International Peacekeeping / edited by Boris Kondoch
      p.cm. – (Library of essays in international law)
   Includes bibliographical references.
   1. Peacekeeping forces. I. Kondoch, Boris

KZ6374.I584 2007
341.5'84–dc22

2006049580

ISBN: 978–0–7546–2395–3

Reprinted 2009

Printed in Great Britain by TJI Digital, Padstow, Cornwall

Contents

The Legal Principles of Peacekeeping and the Brahimi Report

PART IV   LAW APPLICABLE TO PEACEKEEPING OPERATIONS

International Humanitarian Law

Human Rights

International Criminal Law

Responsibilities and Liabilities of Peacekeeper

Protection of Peacekeeping Forces

PART V INTERNATIONAL ADMINISTRATIONS

Acknowledgements

The editor and publishers wish to thank the following for permission to use copyright material.

American Society of International Law for the essays: Daphna Shraga (2000), 'UN Peacekeeping Operations: Applicability of International Humanitarian Law and Responsibility for Operations-Related Damage', *American Journal of International Law*, **94**, pp. 406–12. Copyright © 2000 American Society of International Law; Ralph Wilde (2001), 'From Danzig to East Timor and Beyond: The Role of International Territorial Administration', *American Journal of International Law*, **95**, pp. 583–606. Copyright © 2001 American Society of International Law.

Asser Press for the essay: Robert C.R. Siekmann (1998), 'The Fall of Srebrenica and the Attitude of Dutchbat from an International Legal Perspective', *Yearbook of International Humanitarian Law*, **1**, pp. 301–12. Copyright © 1998 R.C.R. Siekmann.

Brill Academic Publishers for the essays: Ola Engdahl (2006), 'Protection of Personnel in Peace Operations', *International Peacekeeping: The Yearbook of International Peace Operations*, **10**, pp. 53–69. Copyright © 2006 Koninkijke Brill; Marcus G. Brand (2001), 'Institution-Building and Human Rights Protection in Kosovo in the Light of UNMIK Legislation', *Nordic Journal of International Law*, **70**, pp. 461–88. Copyright © 2002 Kluwer Law International.

Connecticut Journal of International Law for the essay: Frederick Rawski (2002), 'To Waive or Not to Waive: Immunity and Accountability in U.N. Peacekeeping Operations', *Conneticut Journal of International Law*, **18**, pp. 103–32.

Copyright Clearance Center for the essays: Oscar Schachter (1964), 'The Uses of Law in International Peace-Keeping', *Virginia Law Review*, **50**, pp. 1096–1114; Alexander Orakhelashvili (2003), 'The Legal Basis of the United Nations Peace-Keeping Operations', *Virginia Journal of International Law*, **43**, pp. 485–524.

Denver Journal of International Law and Policy for the essay: Katherine E. Cox (1999), 'Beyond Self-Defense: United Nations Peacekeeping Operations and the Use of Force', *Denver Journal of International Law and Policy*, **27**, pp. 239–73.

Duke University School of Law for the essays: David Wippman (1996), 'Military Intervention, Regional Organizations, and Host-State Consent', *Duke Journal of Comparative and International Law*, **7**, pp. 209–39; Christine Gray (1996), 'Host-State Consent and United Nations Peacekeeping in Yugoslavia', *Duke Journal of Comparative and International Law*, **7**, pp. 241–70.

International Review of the Red Cross for the essay: Bruce M. Oswald (2001), 'The Creation and Control of Places of Protection during United Nations Peace Operations', *International Review of the Red Cross*, **84**, pp. 1013–35.

Kluwer Law International for the essay: Nina Lahoud (2002), 'Rule of Law Strategies for Peace Operations', in Jessica Howard, Bruce Oswald (eds), *The Rule of Law on Peace Operations*, The Hague: Kluwer Law International, pp. 127–45.

Lynne Rienner Publishers for the essay: Leopold von Carlowitz (2004), 'Crossing the Boundary from the International to the Domestic Legal Realm: UNMIK Lawmaking and Property Rights in Kosovo', *Global Governance*, **10**, pp. 307–31. Lynne Rienner Publishers used with permission.

Oxford University Press for the essays: Peter Rowe (2000), 'Maintaining Discipline in United Nations Peace Support Operations: The Legal Quagmire for Military Contingents', *Journal of Conflict and Security Law*, **5**, pp. 45–62; Carsten Stahn (2003), 'The Ambiguities of Security Council Resolution 1422 (2002)', *European Journal of International Law*, **14**, pp. 85–104; Boris Kondoch (2001), 'The United Nations Administration of East Timor', *Journal of Conflict and Security Law*, **6**, pp. 245–65; John Cerone (2001), 'Minding the Gap: Outlining KFOR Accountability in Post-Conflict Kosovo', *European Journal of International Law*, **12**, pp. 469–88.

Springer for the essay: Ray Murphy (2003), 'United Nations Military Operations and International Humanitarian Law: What Rules Apply to Peacekeepers?', *Criminal Law Forum*, **14**, pp. 153–94.

Taylor and Francis for the essays: Nigel D. White (1996), 'The UN Charter and Peacekeeping Forces: Constitutional Issues', *International Peacekeeping*, **3**, pp. 43–63; Heike Spieker (2000), 'Changing "Peacekeeping" in the New Millennium? – The Recommendations of the Panel on United Nations Peace Operations of August 2000', *International Peacekeeping*, **6**, pp. 144–52; Marten Zwanenburg (1999), 'The Secretary-General's Bulletin on Observance by United Nations Forces of International Humanitarian Law: Some Preliminary Observations', *International Peacekeeping*, **5**, pp. 133–39.

Series Preface

Open a newspaper, listen to the radio or watch television any day of the week and you will read or hear of some matter concerning international law. The range of matters include the extent to which issues of trade and human rights should be linked, concerns about refugees and labour conditions, negotiations of treaties and the settlement of disputes, and decisions by the United Nations Security Council concerning actions to ensure compliance with international law. International legal issues have impact on governments, corporations, organisations and people around the world and the process of globalisation has increased this impact. In the global legal environment, knowledge of international law is an indispensable tool for all scholars, legal practitioners, decision-makers and citizens of the 21st century.

The Library of Essays in International Law is designed to provide the essential elements for the development of this knowledge. Each volume contains essays of central importance in the development of international law in a subject area. The proliferation of legal and other specialist journals, the increase in international materials and the use of the internet, has meant that it is increasingly difficult for legal scholars to have access to all the relevant articles on international law and many valuable older articles are now unable to be obtained readily. These problems are addressed by this series, which makes available an extensive range of materials in a manner that is of immeasurable value for both teaching and research at all levels.

Each volume is written by a leading authority in the subject area who selects the articles and provides an informative introduction, which analyses the context of the articles and comments on their significance within the developments in that area. The volumes complement each other to give a clear view of the burgeoning area of international law. It is not an easy task to select, order and place in context essays from the enormous quantity of academic legal writing published in journals – in many languages – throughout the world. This task requires professional scholarly judgment and difficult choices. The editors in this series have done an excellent job, for which I thank and congratulate them. It has been a pleasure working with them.

ROBERT McCORQUODALE
General Series Editor
School of Law
University of Nottingham

Introduction

Most scholars and practitioners in the field of peacekeeping will agree with Alan James that 'the fullest perspective on peacekeeping ... is one which places it firmly in the context of international politics' (James, 1990, p. 13). However, to understand this unique form of conflict resolution, one must also take other factors into consideration – for example, the diplomatic, historical, psychological, military and legal aspects of peacekeeping. The essays collected in this volume look at peacekeeping from the angle of international law, an often neglected and sometimes misunderstood facet of it. Most general textbooks on international law do not cover peacekeeping in great detail and there is no general and updated textbook for students on the subject, which comprehensively addresses the legal issues arising from modern peacekeeping operations. It is hoped that this volume on international peacekeeping can raise greater interest of this subject and contribute to a better understanding of how law applies to international peacekeeping efforts.

This volume covers the traditional legal topics in regard to international peacekeeping, such as the constitutional basis of international peacekeeping, the legal competence to create peacekeeping forces, the legal principles of peacekeeping, the application of humanitarian law to peacekeeping forces, and the responsibilities and liabilities, as well as the legal status of peacekeepers, under international law. It also deals with those legal issues that have moved to the forefront in the last 15 years, such as the legal protection of peacekeeping personnel and the relevance of human rights law and criminal law in peace operations, as well as legal questions arising from the administration of territories.

What is international peacekeeping? There is no generally accepted definition. The United Nations (UN) and its member states, international organizations, political and legal scholars have developed various approaches to define peacekeeping (Diehl, 1993; Katayanagi, 2002). One may follow the definition of the UN, which has defined peacekeeping in various documents by reference to the three key principles: consent of the parties; impartiality; and the non-use of force except in self-defence. According to the *Agenda for Peace*:

> ... peacekeeping is the deployment of a United Nations presence in the field, hitherto with the consent of all parties concerned, normally involving United Nations military and/or police personnel and frequently civilians as well. Peacekeeping is a technique that expands the possibilities for both the prevention of conflict and making of peace (Boutros-Ghali, 1992, para. 20).

This definition provides general guidance, but peacekeeping operations have also been established based on Chapter VII of the UN Charter[1] and in circumstances where force was used beyond self-defence.

---

[1]   Recent examples of Chapter VII peacekeeping operations are the United Nations Mission in the Sudan (UNMIS), the United Nations Stabilization Mission in Haiti (MINUSTAH) and the United Nations Operation in Côte d'Ivoire (UNOCI), which were established in 2004 and 2005. See Security

Instead of peacekeeping, one may also speak of peace operations. UN peace operations may be understood as an umbrella term comprising the various types of peacekeeping mission carried out by the UN. According to the Brahimi Report (2000, para. 10), UN peace operations entail the activities of conflict prevention and peacemaking, peacekeeping and peace-building.

The institution and the concept of international peacekeeping (for early concepts of peacekeeping, see Bellamy, Williams and Griffin, 2004) was invented during the Suez Crisis when the United Nations Emergency Force (UNEF I) was created by the General Assembly in 1956.[2] As an institution, peacekeeping was born out of necessity, because the Security Council was deadlocked during the Cold War and it was the only acceptable practical way for dealing with international and non-international conflicts at that time. Peacekeeping, which involves military, civilian and police personnel, has been the most frequent military operation conducted by the UN. Between 1948 and mid-2007, there have been more than 60 peacekeeping operations conducted by the UN (for a categorization of the different types of peacekeeping operations, see Chapter 20, this volume). These operations have been undertaken in Europe, South America, Asia and Africa. There are currently 100 251 military personnel and civilian personnel serving in 15 peacekeeping operations (UN Department of Public Information, 2007).

Regional organizations or groups of states were rarely engaged in peacekeeping activities during the Cold War. Indeed, most regional organizations did not even provide for peacekeeping or peace-enforcement in their constituent instruments. Since the 1990s this situation has changed, and today peacekeeping operations are conducted by the European Union, NATO and many other regional organizations. These organizations have not only conducted their own operations, but they have also contributed to UN peace operations by mediation in conflicts before the establishment of a UN peacekeeping mission, by providing logistic support and ensuring the safety of the UN missions, and by conducting joint peacekeeping missions (McCoubrey and Morris, 2000).

Since the main actor in the field of international peacekeeping is the United Nations, the focus of this volume is on international law applicable to UN peace operations, but legal issues of peacekeeping-related activities by other actors than the UN are covered as well.

The Role and the Rule of Law in International Peacekeeping

The application of law in peacekeeping operations is complex. The legal framework of peacekeeping can be found in both international law and in national law. If not otherwise regulated – for example, by status of forces agreements – the national law of the host state remains applicable. In cases of violations committed by peacekeepers, the military law and the criminal law of the sending state will come into play. Many states have adopted their own legislation regulating participation in peacekeeping operations. In the case of Germany

---

Council Resolution 1528 of 27 February 2004; Security Council Resolution 1542 of 30 April 2004; and Security Council Resolution 1590 of 24 March 2005.

    [2]   Despite some earlier observer missions (UNTSO and UNMOGIP), the first mission explicitly labelled as peacekeeping was the UN Emergency Force (UNEF I).

and Japan, participation in peacekeeping operations raised controversial issues under the constitutions of both countries (see Stein, 2000).

Law is essential in every mission. As stated by Oscar Schachter in 'The Uses of Law in International Peace-Keeping' (Chapter 1), '[o]ne is the role of legal authority in providing a *locus standi* for third party intervention. ... [T]hird party activity is much less likely to raise objection if it rests on legal authority and is brought within the framework of the United Nations Charter' (p. 5). The law also provides prescribed standards and rules to facilitate settlement, although 'hostilities are not generally called off because legal norms are invoked' (p. 6). Law serves to regulate and guide the international personnel. Only peacekeepers who are acting in conformity with international law are able to gain the trust, respect and cooperation of the local population they are serving. If the various tasks required during a peacekeeping mission are not performed in accordance with international and national legal standards, there can be no legitimacy, and thus no acceptability and credibility, of the mission. Therefore, the understanding of the rule of law[3] and its application is considered to be one of the cornerstones of effective and successful UN peace operations.

In the second chapter of this volume, Nina Lahoud draws the reader's attention to specific rule of law issues in UN peacekeeping operations and how they can be better addressed. As she points out, there are many challenges facing the UN if it is to strengthen the rule of law in post-conflict societies. These range from the establishment of a functioning criminal justice system; addressing property rights; ensuring the rights of the most vulnerable groups such as refugees, internally displaced persons, women and children during the post-settlement phase; and the drafting of constitutions. However, any effort to establish the rule of law must involve local actors and the adherence of the UN to rule of law standards.

The Constitutional Basis of Peacekeeping

When the UN started the first peacekeeping operations, the legality and precise constitutional basis of peacekeeping was widely debated. In the early 1960s, a financial crisis broke out after several member states, including France and the Soviet Union, refused to pay the cost of ONUC and UNEF I. They rejected the principle that the cost of peacekeeping operations had to be shared by the members of the General Assembly according to Article 17(2) of the UN Charter, which provides that 'the expenses of the Organization shall be borne by the members as apportioned by the General Assembly'. In an Advisory Opinion, the International Court of Justice refused the Soviet Union's argument that the forces sent to the Middle East in 1956 and to the Congo in 1960 were illegally created because they were not established in accordance with Article 43 of the UN Charter. The Court held that Article 43 was only applicable to forces designed to take enforcement action, but UNEF and ONUC were not created to take enforcement action (Expenses Opinion, 1962). Since the Court was concerned with the legal duty of the member states to pay for the forces, it only made short remarks in respect of the constitutionality of the forces and left the question open as to which article in the UN Charter could serve as the constitutional foundation for peacekeeping forces.

---

[3]   For a definition of the rule of law, see the Rule of Law Report (Report of the Secretary-General, 2004).

Today, the constitutionality of consensual peacekeeping operations and missions established under Chapter VII is commonly accepted. Although the UN Charter neither explicitly authorizes peacekeeping operations nor mentions peacekeeping, there is a consensus that the legal basis for consensual peacekeeping operations falls between Chapter VI and Chapter VII,[4] which Dag Hammarskjöld referred to as the mythical 'Chapter VI and a half'.

Nonetheless, there is a dispute among international lawyers as to which Charter provisions are exactly the legal basis of international peacekeeping and how to allocate authority among the Security Council, the General Assembly and the Secretariat, represented by the Secretary-General. The essays by Alexander Orakhelashvili, 'The Legal Basis of the United Nations Peace-Keeping Operations' (Chapter 3), and Nigel White, 'The UN Charter and Peacekeeping Forces: Constitutional Issues' (Chapter 4), examine these issues in great detail.

The Security Council, endowed by the UN Charter with the 'primary responsibility for the maintenance of international peace and security' (see Article 24(1)), has established almost all peacekeeping operations. According to Article 29 of the UN Charter, the Security Council may establish peacekeeping forces as its subsidiary organs, and under Article 98 the Council may entrust the Secretary-General with certain functions. However, there is a dispute among international lawyers as to which Charter provisions grant the power to establish peacekeeping operations. Some writers refer to different articles within Chapter VII (Articles 39, 40, 41, 42 and 48), either alone or in conjunction with each other (see, for example, Hufnagel, 1996).

One possible way of solving the dilemma is suggested by Orakhelashvili, who proposes different Charter provisions as the legal authority for the various types of peacekeeping operation. Certain operations may therefore fall under Article 36(1) of the UN Charter as a method of dispute settlement or under Article 39, which grants recommendatory powers to the Council. Peacekeeping operations may also be regarded as provisional measures under Article 40 of the UN Charter. Articles 41 or 42 of the UN Charter can be invoked when an operation has been established under Chapter VII – as in the case of UNTAET[5] and UNMIK. Other authors, such as Nigel White, argue that there is no need to find an express Charter base because either the UN possesses an inherent or implied power[6] to perform activities like peacekeeping or the legal foundation could be a customary rule of the law of the UN. White subsumes peacekeeping under the doctrine of inherent powers, namely as an action which is not expressly forbidden by the UN Charter and which achieves one of the aims of the organization (pp. 89–91).

What are the powers of the General Assembly and the Secretary-General? The General Assembly has only established peacekeeping forces in a few cases. It may be authorized under Article 22 in conjunction with either Article 10, 11 or 14. The Secretary-General has only a limited competence in regard to peacekeeping operations. He can negotiate and conclude

---

[4]   Under Chapter VI the Security Council can adopt various techniques in pursuit of the peaceful settlement of disputes (mediation, negotiation and so on). Under Chapter VII the Security Council may take enforcement measures to maintain or restore international peace and security.

[5]   Another possible approach is to see the legal basis in the implied powers of Security Council. See Ruffert (2001) and De Hoogh (2001).

[6]   As the International Court of Justice stated in the Reparations Opinion: '... under international law, the [UN] Organization must be deemed to have those powers which, though not expressly provided in the Charter, are conferred upon it by necessary implication as being essential to the performance of its duties' (Reparations Opinion, 1949).

agreements in regard to peacekeeping forces or establish and conduct a peacekeeping operation if appropriate functions are delegated to him by the Security Council (for example, in the case of UNEF, the Secretary-General was authorized by the General Assembly to issue all regulations and instructions to the functioning of the force). However, there are two major limitations concerning the powers of the Secretary-General. First, as the majority of international lawyers agree, the Secretary-General cannot launch a peacekeeping force on his or her own, even with the consent of the parties.[7] Second, the Secretary-General has no power to require states to send troops to UN peacekeeping missions because the Security Council itself does not possess this power and is therefore unable to delegate it to him or her.

Regional organizations and group of states are also important actors in the field of peacekeeping. Both may also establish peacekeeping operations based on the consent of the parties but, if they become engaged in enforcement action, the authorization of the Security Council is necessary. With regard to regional organizations, White reminds us that:

> ... [any] enforcement action, whether fully fledged inter-state action or belligerent peacekeeping within a state, does require authorization for legal and practical reason. To accept the practice that seems to have developed in some cases – that this form of peacekeeping falls outside the requirements of Article 53 because it carries the label 'peacekeeping' – would be dangerous, allowing considerable coercive freedom for regional, defence and security organizations, which are, as practice has shown, subject to even greater domination and abuse (p. 103).

Principles of International Peacekeeping

The Consent of Parties

The legal doctrine of consensual peacekeeping operations is based on three principles. First, the presence of a peacekeeping force requires the consent of the host state. Second, the force should be impartial. Third, the use of force is permitted only in the case of self-defence. These key legal principles have been derived from the establishment and operation of UNEF I in 1956, which became a precedent for consensual peacekeeping operations.

Unless the Security Council establishes a peacekeeping mission under Chapter VII, the consent of the parties to a conflict, or at least of the states concerned, is a necessary prerequisite. This follows from Article 2(7) of the UN Charter, which provides that nothing shall authorize the UN 'to intervene in matters which are essentially within the domestic jurisdiction of any state'. Two essays, 'Military Intervention, Regional Organizations, and Host-State Consent' by David Wippman (Chapter 5) and 'Host-State Consent and United Nations Peacekeeping in Yugoslavia' by Christine Gray (Chapter 6) in this volume deal with the question of consent in peacekeeping operations. As a general rule, the continued consent of the governments concerned is required in interstate conflicts. If the consent is withdrawn, the peacekeeping operation can no longer stay in the host state. In civil war situations, although only the consent

---

[7] An exceptional case was the Secretary-General's provisional establishment of the United Nations Good Offices Mission to Afghanistan and Pakistan (UNGOMAP) in 1988, which also comprised 50 military officers. However, the Security Council agreed to the establishment of the mission by Security Council Resolution 622 of 31 October 1988.

of the government is required from a legal point of view, the UN will also try to receive the factual consent of the other parties to the conflict as a matter of practical necessity.

However, these rules are not easily applied in practice. What legal implication does the collapse of internal authority or the loss of control by government have on the requirement of consent? Does the change of the initial mandate require further consent? Which implication does the invocation of Chapter VII have on the consent of the parties? Wippman and Gray discuss these questions by looking at the cases of ECOWAS intervention in Liberia and the deployment of UNPROFOR during the conflict in the former Yugoslavia.

Another important requirement is the principle of impartiality, which means that peacekeepers should not advance the interest of one party over another. Dag Hammarskjöld referred to this principle in the final report on the plan for the establishment of UNEF I of 6 November 1956, by stating that there was no intent 'to influence the military balance in the present conflict and, thereby, the political balance affecting efforts to settle the conflict' (Final Report UNEF I, 1956, para. 8).

Peacekeeping and the Use of Force

The third cornerstone of peacekeeping is the defensive use of force. If not otherwise mandated under Chapter VII, peacekeepers can only use force in self-defence. However, over time, the concept of self-defence has evolved and the UN has occasionally become involved in operations that went beyond self-defence and included robust action. The development and the concept of the use of force is examined by Katherine Fox in her essay 'Beyond Self-Defense: United Nations Peacekeeping Operations and the Use of Force' (Chapter 7). This concept was described by Dag Hammarskjöld as:

> ... [the] rule ... that men engaged in the operation may never take the initiative in the use of armed force, but are entitled to respond with force to an attack with arms, including attempts to use force to make them withdraw from positions which they occupy under orders from the Commander, acting under the authority of the Assembly and within the scope of its resolutions. The basic element involved is clearly the prohibition against any initiative in the use of armed force (Report of the Secretary-General, 1958, para. 179).

In 1964 new elements to this definition were added in respect of UNFICYP, which allowed the use of force where 'specific arrangements accepted by both communities have been or ... are about to be violated, thus risking a recurrence of fighting or endangering law and order ... (or where there were) attempts by force to prevent them from carrying out their responsibilities as ordered by their commanders' (*Aide Mémoire*, 1964, paras. 17c–18c).

The next development was the approach chosen in the case of UNEF II, which was established in 1973. Self-defence also included 'resistance to attempts by forceful means to prevent it from discharging its duties under the mandate of the Security Council' (Report of the Secretary-General, 1973, para. 4a). This formula became applicable to all subsequent missions. But it was only reluctantly and very rarely applied in practice, because it is difficult to reconcile with the principles of consent and impartiality. Fox also considers peacekeeping missions with a robust mandate from the early example of ONUC to certain missions like those established after the end of the Cold War. Peacekeepers were, for example authorized to use force to secure freedom of movement for the delivery of food or to use self-defence in the protection of safe areas and the civilian population. These missions have been criticized for blurring the distinction between peace-enforcement and peacekeeping. She is also critical of the expanded use of force by peacekeepers, but one may wonder whether there are better alternatives or whether the core principles of peacekeeping should be reconsidered as proposed by the *Report of the Panel on United Nations Peace Operations* (the so-called Brahimi Report).

The Legal Principles of Peacekeeping and Brahimi Report

The Brahimi Report is analysed and summarized by Heike Spieker in her essay 'Changing "Peacekeeping" in the New Millenium? – The Recommendations of the Panel on United Nations Peace Operations of August 2000' (Chapter 8). She considers that the Brahimi Report is 'the most incisive and comprehensive analysis of peace operations ever undertaken by the United Nations' (p. 214). The Panel's task was 'to undertake a thorough review of the United Nations peace and security activities, and to present a clear set of specific, concrete and practical recommendations to assist the United Nations in conducting such activities better in the future'.[8] The recommendations focus, to a large degree, on structural and management problems, but the Panel also commented on the doctrine on which peace operations should be conducted. Although the Panel states that the 'consent of the local parties, impartiality and the use of force only in self-defence should remain the bedrock principles of peacekeeping' (Brahimi Report, para. 48), the Report calls for more robust mandates that are also clear, credible and achievable, and does not only question, but also modifies, the traditional approach to peacekeeping concerning the consent of the parties, the principle of impartiality and the non-use of force.

With regard to the use of force, the Panel recommended that:

… rules of engagement should not limit contingents to stroke-for-stroke responses but should allow ripostes sufficient to silence a source of deadly fire that is directed at United Nations troops or the people they are charged to protect and in particularly dangerous situations, should not force United Nations contingents to cede the initiatives to the attackers. … [However,] mandates should specify an operation's authority to use force (Brahimi Report, paras 49 and 51).

This is a clear departure from previous practice where robust mandates were the exception. The rationale for the traditional concept of peacekeeping was explained by UN Secretary-General Boutros Boutros-Ghali in the Supplement to the Agenda for Peace (1995), when he argued that:

… the logic of peacekeeping flows from political and military premises that are quite distinct from those of enforcement; and the dynamics of the latter are incompatible with the political process that peace-keeping is intended to facilitate. To blur the distinction between the two can undermine the viability of the peace-keeping operation and endanger its personnel' (Boutros-Ghali, 1995, para. 35).

---

[8]   See Identical Letters, dated August 2000, from the Secretary-General to the President of the General Assembly and the President of the Security Council in the Brahimi Report (2000).

However, the calls for robust peacekeeping in order to stop and prevent future massacres and genocides, as in Srebrenica and Rwanda, are not new. Therefore, UN Secretary-General Kofi Annan came to different conclusions than his predecessor and stated that 'we learned, the hard way that lightly armed troops in white vehicles and blue helmets are not the solution to every conflict. Sometimes peace has to be made – or enforced – before it can be kept' (Annan, 1998).

Impartiality is no longer understood as the equal treatment of the parties to a conflict under all circumstances but as 'adherence to the principles of the Charter and to the objectives of a mandate that is rooted in those Charter principles' (Brahimi Report, para. 50). Such an understanding of impartiality allows peacekeepers to distinguish between aggressors and victims. Less clear are the recommendations concerning another important requirement: the consent of the parties to a conflict. The Panel observed that 'consent may be manipulated in many ways by the local parties' (para. 48), but draws no conclusion regarding what should happen if consent, once given, authorizes the Security Council to decide upon extensions or enlargements of the initial mandate under certain circumstances or if, in the case of denial of consent, it may be replaced by a decision of another institution. The Panel also fails to address the question of whose consent is necessary in the case of conflicts with many groups of belligerents or where there is a situation of a failed state with no effective government.

It remains to be seen whether the call for more robust peacekeeping and the doctrinal approach proposed by the Brahimi Report will be implemented. As Gray has correctly commented:

> ... it is not clear that the Brahimi Report support for 'robust peacekeeping' will be acceptable to those who support a more limited concept of peacekeeping ... The call for bigger forces, better equipped and more costly, able to pose a credible deterrent, contrasts with the symbolic, non-threatening presence that characterised traditional peacekeeping.(Gray, 2001, p. 270).

Law Applicable to UN Peacekeeping Operations

In general, the legal status of personnel serving in peacekeeping operations refers to their rights and duties under the applicable law, and their terms of service and civil and criminal jurisdiction which are applicable. The legal status is derived from four different bodies of law: a) the national law of the receiving or host state; b) the law of the intergovernmental organization, if the peacekeeping operation is not established by a group of states; c) the law of the sending or participating state; and d) rules of general international law – in particular, international humanitarian law, human rights law and international criminal law.

Part III considers the legal framework applicable to UN peacekeeping operations. UN peacekeepers are generally directed and bound by mission-specific legal sources and internal rules of the organization, such as the mandate, which is laid down in an enabling resolution. These include UN regulations, as used in Kosovo and East Timor, force regulations, which were applied, for example, in regard to UNEF I and ONUC, and status of forces agreements, as well as participation agreements.

It is the mandate, formulated by the Security Council and – exceptionally – by the General Assembly, which provides the legal basis of a UN peace operation. But the mandate can be vague as a result of political compromises. As Peter Rowe writes in 'Maintaining Discipline in United Nations Peace Support Operations: The Legal Quagmire for Military Contingents' (Chapter 11), the mandate 'is likely to be expressed in rather general terms, telling states, where the pitch is, who the players are and the objective of the operation, but providing no clear rules to when a yellow or red card should be shown to the players' (p. 279). Hence it is important that the mandate and the legal duties are implemented into the national structure of the sending states. The mandate can be open to interpretation and there can be a thin line denoting whether the peacekeeper on the ground operates within the UN mandate, as shown by Robert Siekmann in 'The Fall of Srebrenica and the Attitude of Dutchbat from an International Legal Perspective' (Chapter 12).

Status of Forces Agreements (SOFAs) or Status of Mission Agreements (SOMAs), which are concluded between the UN and the host state, regulate the status of the peacekeeping force. They contain provisions on the status of the national contingents, provisions on the freedom of movement within the area of operations, privileges and immunities and jurisdiction, as well as claims and disputes. Participation agreements, which are based on an agreement between the participating states and the UN, contain the specific rights and responsibilities of the force.

General international law is an important source of rights and obligations. International humanitarian law, human rights law and international criminal law are of great relevance in this regard. Furthermore, international law dealing with the protection of peacekeepers and the privileges and immunities, as well as the responsibilities and liabilities, needs to be considered. The UN is not a party to international humanitarian law or human rights conventions, but it does nevertheless possess legal personality and can be bound by customary international law *mutatis mutandis*. In the Reparations Opinion the International Court of Justice stated that the duties of the UN in regard to international law depend on the 'purposes and functions as specified or implied in its constituent documents and developed in practice' (Reparations Opinion, 1949, p. 179). UN peacekeepers may therefore be bound by customary rules of international humanitarian law, human rights law or international criminal law. If the Security Council establishes a peace operation under Chapter VII, it is questionable whether customary international law is applicable. However, one may argue that at least norms regarded as *jus cogens* apply, and Articles 1 and 2 of the UN Charter provide legal limitations (see Chapter 20).

International Humanitarian Law

One of the oldest legal disputes concerning peacekeeping operations is whether international humanitarian law is applicable and to what extent. The question may, for example, arise when peacekeepers become involved in combat-like situations or when they are taken as hostages. Ray Murphy addresses these problems in his essay 'United Military Operations and International Humanitarian Law: What Rules Apply to Peacekeepers?' (Chapter 9). For a long time, the UN argued that UN peacekeepers were under no legal obligations arising from international humanitarian law and that they were only bound by its principles and the spirit. The UN argued that 'United Nations forces act on behalf of the international community, and therefore they cannot be considered a "party" to the conflict, nor a "Power" within the meaning of the Geneva Conventions' (p. 228). Another argument was that only states were parties to the conventions and capable of carrying out certain obligations. The International Committee of the Red Cross (ICRC) maintained that all provisions of international humanitarian law were applicable. From the perspective of the ICRC, it was irrelevant who was holding the gun and for what purpose (p. 254).

According to Murphy, it makes little sense not to apply international humanitarian law to UN forces, since '[a]dherence to these principles will also assist in facilitating a restoration of the peace, a matter that is ultimately the goal of all United Nations forces' (p. 255). In 1999 the Secretary-General promulgated the Bulletin *Observance by United Nations Forces of International Humanitarian Law* (Secretary-General's Bulletin, 1999) and, for the first time, the UN declared itself to the be bound by the fundamental principles and rules of international humanitarian law. However, there are several problems in regard to the Bulletin as pointed out by Marten Zwanenburg in his essay 'The Secretary General's Bulletin on Observance by United Nations Forces of International Humanitarian Law: Some Preliminary Observations' (Chapter 10). The Bulletin is based on, and inspired by, the four Geneva Conventions of 1949 and the Additional Protocols of 1977, but the Bulletin contains far fewer provisions and provides less protection than these instruments.

Human Rights

Peacekeepers should also be aware of human rights standards. The different components in a UN peacekeeping mission may play various roles in the promotion and protection of human rights. Human rights components or units may, for example, monitor and investigate human rights violations, report on human rights violations, assist the host government in developing laws complying with international human rights norms, and train military, police and other government officials. They may also address problems related to vulnerable groups, such as women, refugees, internally displaced people and children. Soldiers may observe and monitor the actions of the armed forces and the civilian population. By their mere presence they can deter human rights violations. The civilian police may monitor and investigate human rights violations as guardians of the law, train and help to establish the local police and prevent criminal activities. Until the 1990s peacekeepers had no specific mandate related to human rights. The common understanding that 'human rights violations are often a cause of conflict and addressing them is a pre-condition for peace' (Kenny, 1996, p. 2) led to the assignment of various human rights functions to second-generation peacekeeping operations and other types of human rights operation.

Human rights played an important role in the performance of the UN administrations in Kosovo and East Timor. Human rights standards were embedded in the same way in all activities of both administrations. According to UNTAET and UNMIK Regulations everybody undertaking public duties or holding public office in East Timor and Kosovo shall recognize international human rights standards as reflected, *inter alia*, in the Universal Declaration on Human Rights of 10 December 1948 and the International Covenants of 1966. By promulgating these regulations human rights became the primary consideration in all activities of both administrations. Even if human rights are not incorporated in the mandate or in UN regulations, peacekeepers serving in consensual peacekeeping operations are bound by human rights rules, which form part of customary international law.[9] In the case of peace operations established under Chapter VII, legal obligations flow at least from those human rights that are regarded as *jus cogens*.

One way of protecting human rights during peacekeeping operations is to establish and control safe havens and humanitarian protected zones. This topic is addressed by Bruce Oswald in 'The Creation and Control of Places of Protection during United Nations Peace Operations' (Chapter 13). The UN established security zones and safe corridors for the protection of civilians in Rwanda and in Bosnia-Herzegovina. From a legal point of view, the creation of such places is unproblematic, if the consent of the parties is given, or in the case of an explicit mandate by the Security Council pursuant to Chapter VII. Oswald argues that authorization might also be implied if 'a Chapter VII enforcement operation that mandates a UN Force "to provide security and protection to civilians at risk" implies that the Force may take necessary and reasonable steps, such as the creation of a place of protection, to discharge that mandate' (p. 317). According to Oswald, places of protection may also be established by UN forces in the absence of consent and without Chapter VII authorization. He argues that legal justification may be derived from several sources: a) the exercise of right of individual and collective self-defence; b) Article 1 of the Convention and Punishment of the Crime of Genocide; and c) the prohibition to target or attack civilian (pp. 318–19). Whether international law has reached the point that would allow the intervention of UN forces to create places of protection in these circumstances, despite Article 2(7) of the UN Charter, is at best unclear.

International Criminal Law

International criminal law plays an increasing role in respect to peacekeeping operations. One may consider the following questions. Which obligations do arise for peacekeepers from international criminal law? What are the obligations of peacekeepers in respect of the prosecution of international crimes? Should there be exceptions for peacekeepers to the principle of individual criminal responsibility? Should the UN develop a transitional criminal code? If yes, under what circumstances would the application of an interim criminal code be lawful? If the UN or any other international organization takes over the administration of a territory, is there a duty to prosecute persons who have been accused of genocide, crimes against humanity or war crimes? Robert Siekmann, in Chapter 12, raises the interesting question as to whether peacekeepers who witness war crimes but do not intervene can be held guilty of war crimes on account of their passive behaviour. However, for this to be possible would require a duty for the individual peacekeeper to assist victims of gross human rights violations, and international law has certainly not developed to that stage.

Peacekeepers may have a responsibility to search for and arrest persons suspected of war crimes. Diane Orentlicher in 'Responsibilities of States Participating in Multilateral Operations with Respect to Persons Indicted for War Crimes' (Chapter 14), discusses these obligations in respect to the Implementation Force (IFOR) and the Stabilization Force (SFOR), which were in charge of security in Bosnia-Herzegovina but were criticized for not arresting indictees

---

[9]   For a detailed analysis of how human rights law becomes applicable to UN peace operations, see Kondoch (2005).

charged by the International Criminal Tribunal for the former Yugoslavia. In general, the legal authority to search for and arrest suspected war criminals can stem from a Security Council resolution under Chapter VII or from the consent of the host state. In addition, as pointed out by Orentlicher, peacekeepers have a legal obligation under international humanitarian law because the Geneva Conventions of 1949 and Additional Protocol I establish such a duty upon the high contracting parties in respect of grave breaches of the conventions (see Geneva Conventions, Arts 49/50/129/146, Additional Protocol I, Article 85). NATO legal advisers and military lawyers of the US government denied this legal obligation. They argued that the Conventions did not apply extraterritorially and that states could only exercise police functions within their own territory (pp. 338–39). Furthermore, NATO and SFOR could not be bound by Geneva Conventions and the Additional Protocols because only states could become parties to the conventions. Orentlicher rejects these arguments with good reasons, since 'both the Dayton Peace Agreement and various U.N. Security Council resolutions make clear that NATO forces may lawfully exercise police powers in Bosnia' (p. 340). Legal obligations arise from Security Council Resolution 827, which requires states to cooperate with the ICTY, the Genocide Convention and international humanitarian law. In her opinion, 'the issue is not whether NATO and SFOR themselves are bound by the conventions' (p. 343); every member state that is party to the Conventions is still bound by its individual obligations when joining a multinational force. It would lead to bizarre results, if 'any state could violate the Geneva Conventions with impunity merely by joining other countries in a military alliance' (p. 343). Taking into account the object and purpose of the grave breaches provisions, she comes to the conclusion that the Geneva Conventions are extraterritorially applicable, because:

> [t]he core aim of the grave breaches provisions ... is to foreclose impunity for such breaches. This aim would be ill served if Contracting Parties' obligations were inapplicable in territories where those states exercise lawful power to arrest persons allegedly responsible for grave breaches (pp. 341–42).

Carsten Stahn in 'The Ambiguities of Security Council Resolution 1422 (2002)' (Chapter 15) addresses the issue of criminal immunities of the peacekeeper by analysing Security Resolution 1422. This controversial resolution was adopted on 12 July 2002 and renewed as Security Council Resolution 1483 in 2003. It granted immunity to personnel from ICC non-state parties involved in UN-established or UN-authorized operations for a renewable 12-month period. The resolution raises questions not only about its compatibility with the ICC statute, but also in regard to the constitutional powers of the Council under the UN Charter to treat the immunity of peacekeepers as a matter of international peace and security. Since Resolution 1422 was adopted under Chapter VII, it requires the existence of a threat to the peace, breach of the peace or act of aggression. Stahn points out that 'the threat to the peace seems to be based less on the existence of a specific conflict situation than on the potential inability of the United Nations to address future threats without US military personnel' (p. 351). However, this hardly seems to be a convincing argument for viewing a situation as a threat to the peace. The important question is 'to what extent the exemption of peacekeeping personnel from criminal jurisdiction lies in the interests of the maintenance of peace and security' (p. 351).

Responsibilities and Liabilities of Peacekeeper

During any peace operation, whether conducted by the UN or by an international organization, damages, such as personal injury or property loss, may be encountered. Who bears responsibility and who can be held liable? Is it the international organization, the individual peacekeeper, the host state or the sending state? Borhan Amrallah, in 'The International Responsibility of the United Nations for Activities Carried out by U.N. Peacekeeping Forces' (Chapter 16), addresses these questions in regard to the UN and also considers the organization's claims practice. In general, the UN bears responsibility for its internationally wrongful acts in the same way as states. There must be the breach of an international obligation either in the form of an unlawful act or by an omission. The unlawful act of the peacekeeper must be imputable to the UN. These principles have also been reaffirmed by the ILC's draft on the responsibility of international organizations.[10] Harmful conduct can be attributed if the peacekeeper was under the UN's military command and control. The UN bears responsibility for two reasons. First, the UN is a legal entity that possesses international rights and duties and, second, the force is considered as a subsidiary organ of the organization. The acts must be undertaken in the performance of the individual's official function. although responsibility may also arise when the official has acted *ultra vires* or *bona fide*. If the unlawful act has been performed outside of the individual's official function, the state of which the individual is a national is responsible. Where the UN has had no control over the forces, as was the case in the Korean War and the Gulf War of 1991, the organization has denied responsibility. Since the early days of peacekeeping, the UN has accepted responsibility for UN peace operations and has, in exceptional cases, also paid compensation for damage that could not clearly be imputed to the organization. In the past, the UN has also settled third-party claims, made by local claims review boards, for personal injury, property loss or damage occurring during peacekeeping operations. As described by Daphna Sharga in 'UN Peacekeeping Operations: Applicability of International Humanitarian Law and Responsibilities for Operations-Related Damage' (Chapter 17), the issue of compensation was reviewed due to the increasing number of claims. Based on two reports by the Secretary-General, the General Assembly decided to impose temporal and financial limitations on third-party liability. In addition, there is no liability in cases of operational necessity.

Protection of Peacekeeping Forces

Another important legal area is related to the protection of the UN personnel. In recent years peacekeepers have become victims of crimes such as killing, kidnapping, hostage-taking and armed robbery, and one of the urgent problems on the UN's agenda is to improve the protection of personnel serving in peace operations. The legal framework analysed by Ola Engdahl in 'Protection of Personnel in Peace Operations' (Chapter 18) can be found in Security Council resolutions, human rights law, international humanitarian law, international criminal law, status of forces agreements, privileges and immunities provided by international law, as well as national law. Engdahl closely examines the Convention on the Safety of UN and Associated Personnel of 1994 (Safety Convention, 1994), which was adopted as a result of assaults on

---

[10]　See Draft Articles 1, 2 and 3 (2003), UN doc. A/CN.4/L.632 of 4 June.

peacekeepers in Somalia, Rwanda and the former Yugoslavia.The Convention, which entered into force in 1999, criminalizes certain acts, such as murder, kidnapping or other attacks against UN and associated personnel (see Article 9).[11] States parties are required to make attacks or threats against UN and associated personnel punishable under their national law and either to prosecute or to extradite alleged offenders. The Convention met with much criticism because of its narrow scope of application. According to Article 2, the Convention applies to UN and associated personnel and UN operations. Article 1(c) defines a UN operation as:

> ... an operation established by the competent organ of the United Nations in accordance with Charter of the United Nations and conducted under United Nations authority and control: where the operation is for the purpose of maintaining or restoring international peace and security, or where the Security Council or the General Assembly has declared for the purposes of this Convention, that there exists an exceptional risk to the safety of the personnel participating in the operation.

The Convention does not apply to a UN operation authorized by the Security Council as an enforcement action under Chapter VII of the UN in which any personnel are engaged as combatants and to which the law of international armed conflict applies. Walter Gary Sharp criticizes the approach chosen by the Convention because it excludes most Chapter VII operations and it blurs the line of demarcation between the law of armed conflict and the Safety Convention. He proposes to apply the Safety Convention to all operations authorized by the UN even if they are not under UN control (Sharp, 1996). The condition that the protection of operations not established for the purpose of maintaining or restoring international peace and security requires a declaration of exceptional risk by the Security Council or the General Assembly has also received much criticism. The scope of the Safety Convention was discussed by the Ad Hoc Committee on the Scope of Legal Protection under the Convention on the Safety of United Nations and Associated Personnel.[12] Consequently, on 8 December 2005, the Optional Protocol to the Convention on the Safety of United Nations and Associated Personnel was adopted. The new protocol expands the legal protection from emergency humanitarian assistance to peacebuilding and the delivery of humanitarian, political and development assistance.[13]

International Administrations

The UN administrations of East Timor and Kosovo raised new questions from the perspective of international law, and they intensified some old legal debates in regard to peacekeeping operations. For this reason, Part V considers the legal issues arising from international administrations. The administration of territories is not a new phenomenon. Territories have been administered by a single state, a group of states or an international organization. International territorial administration as a means of conflict management has been used

---

[11]   The statutes of the ICC and the Special Court for Sierra Leone have also incorporated provisions on crimes committed against peacekeepers. See Article 8(b)(iii) and Article 8, para. 2(e)(iii) of the Rome Statute of the International Criminal Court and Article 4 of the Statute of the Special Court of Sierra Leone.

[12]   Documents and reports can be found at www.un.org/law/UNsafetyconvention.

[13]   See Annex to the General Assembly Resolution (2006), A/RES/60/42, 6 January.

since the League of Nations; examples include the administration of the Saar Territory by the League of Nations (1920–35), the occupation of Germany by the Allied Powers after the Second World War, the mandate system of the League of Nations and the UN trusteeship system. Ralph Wilde in 'From Danzig to East Timor and Beyond: The Role of International Territorial Administration' (Chapter 19) provides the background to these administrations. He identifies two reasons for establishing international territorial administration: 'In the first place, they attempt to address a perceived "sovereignty problem" regarding the identity of those local actors exercising administrative control. In the second place, they attempt to address a perceived "governance problem" regarding the conduct of governance by local actors' (p. 427). Before the establishment of the UN Interim Administration in Kosovo (UNMIK) and the UN Transitional Administration in East Timor (UNTAET) in 1999, the UN had little experience in non-trusteeship administration. These differed from previous UN administrations in places like Cambodia or Eastern Slavonia, because the UN was now authorized to exercise all legislative and executive powers over both territories, including the administration of justice. As Boris Kondoch, who examines the legal issues arising from 'The United Nations Administration of East Timor' (Chapter 20), comments, '[t]he scope of the responsibilities and the range of the mandate were unprecedented in the history of UN peacekeeping operations' (p. 452).

Both administrations faced great difficulties in establishing the rule of law and a functioning justice system on account of the devastating situations in East Timor and Kosovo and the lack of a coherent strategy to develop rule of law institutions. UNMIK and UNTAET were confronted with a collapsed judicial system and escalating violence and crime on the ground. At the same time, the administrations lacked qualified personnel, knowledge and financial resources. Where necessary, UNTAET and UNMIK could issue legislative acts in the form of regulations. The local law remained in force unless it conflicted with international human rights standards. However, there was a lack of review in respect of the applicable law in both territories. The administrations have been criticized for flaws in the law-making process. In general, one may ask, like Leopold von Carlowitz in 'Crossing the Boundary from the International to the Domestic Legal Realm: UNMIK Lawmaking and Property Rights in Kosovo' (Chapter 23), who analyses UNMIK's efforts to regulate property rights in Kosovo 'how far international lawmakers may intrude in the domestic legal realm for the purpose of maintaining (international) peace and security' (p. 539).

Marcus Brand in 'Institution-Building and Human Rights Protection in Kosovo in the Light of UNMIK Legislation' (Chapter 21) takes a critical look at the UN's efforts to create an administration based on the rule of law and in compliance with human rights standards. As Brand writes, '[r]espect for human rights for all people in Kosovo was one of the leading motifs for international efforts' (p. 500). This was explicitly laid down in Security Council Resolution 1244, which mandated UNMIK to protect human rights in Kosovo. In addition, Regulation 1/1999 obliged all persons undertaking public duties or holding public office in Kosovo to observe internationally recognized human rights standards. Part of Brand's criticism is directed against the absence of the separation of powers, because the Special Representative of the Secretary-General exercised the supreme and legislative executive authority in Kosovo at the same time and no court could check the legality of legislative or executive acts. Consequently, UNMIK could not provide adequate human rights protection because '[o]nly a state with a balance of powers and system of mutual checks and balances (i.e.

adhering to the principles of constitutionalism) can effectively provide a rule of law system that protects human rights, and correspondingly, will hold itself responsible and accountable for shortcomings' (p. 500).

John Cerone in 'Minding the Gap: Outlining KFOR Accountability in Post-Conflict Kosovo' (Chapter 22) examines how human rights law and international humanitarian law are applicable to the Kosovo force (KFOR). The international security presence was mandated under Security Council Resolution 1244, among others, to deter renewed hostilities, to establish a secure environment and to ensure public safety and order. Unlike the case of UNMIK, KFOR was not explicitly mandated to promote and protect human rights. However, KFOR was established under UN auspices and was therefore also bound by the purposes of the UN Charter, among which included the promotion of human rights. In addition, Resolution 1244 requires 'that both presences operate towards the same goals and in mutually supportive manner'. Cerone notes that human rights obligations may also be based on the principle of automatic succession for human rights obligation and the individual human rights obligations of the states participating in KFOR.

Another question is whether KFOR was bound by international humanitarian law. Cerone argues that the law of occupation laid down in the regulations annexed to the 1907 Hague Convention No. IV on the Law and Customs of War and the Fourth Geneva Convention was applicable to KFOR, because KFOR exercised public authority and the formal consent of the former Republic of Yugoslavia was possibly lacking. In general, the idea of applying the law of occupation to peacekeeping forces is not a new one (see Chapter 11). However, unlike traditional cases of occupation, the presence of peacekeeping forces is based on a legal authority – namely, on the consent of the parties or on a Chapter VII resolution, as in case of KFOR. According to Cerone, 'this does not directly affect application of the Geneva Conventions, which consciously avoid inquiries into the legality of resort to the use of force' (p. 516). However, there is almost no state practice to support his interpretation, and KFOR itself has not referred to the law of occupation.

In the last decade there has been an increase in reports about human rights abuses by peacekeepers, ranging from torture, sexual violence and assault to involvement in prostitution. In regard to the sexual misconduct of peacekeepers the UN has taken vigorous measures to address this problem by implementing a zero-tolerance policy and through an increase in transparency, investigation and gender training. The human rights violations and cases of misbehaviour by peacekeepers have also led to a debate among international lawyers about the concept of immunity granted to peacekeepers and possible mechanisms to hold them accountable.[14] Frederick Rawski addresses these issues in 'To Waive or Not to Waive:

---

[14]   In general, peacekeepers are granted immunity from criminal proceedings. The UN does not exercise criminal jurisdiction over peacekeepers. If the individual peacekeeper commits a crime, the individual remains under the jurisdiction of the sending state and he or she may be held accountable for their action by the courts of the sending state. Since only a few decisions of court martials and inquiries have addressed the violations of international law by members of UN peacekeeping forces (see Zwanenburg, 2005, pp. 224–34 and, for further references, Kondoch, 2005, fn. 8), academic writers and non-governmental organizations have criticized the United Nations and member states for not providing effective mechanisms of accountability. It will be one of the challenges of the future to create consistent mechanisms to ensure the identification and punishment of law violations committed by UN forces (in regard to the sexual exploitation and abuse by United Nations peacekeeping personnel, see the recommendations of Prince Zeid's Report 2005)..

Immunity and Accountability in U.N. Peacekeeping Operations' (Chapter 24) by considering the cases of East Timor and Kosovo. The purpose of granting privileges and immunities is not to benefit any particular individual but to safeguard the efficient functioning of the peacekeeping operation. Legal privileges and immunities may derive from various legal sources (Article 105 of the UN Charter, the Convention on the Privileges and Immunities of the UN of 1946, status of forces agreements, UN regulations, national law and so on). Four types of immunity need to be distinguished: immunity from criminal, civil, administrative and legal process. Special Representatives of the Secretary-General and his deputies enjoy full diplomatic immunity. Peacekeeping forces under the command and control of the UN are generally granted absolute immunity. Civilian personnel enjoy limited immunity, which can be waived. The UN itself enjoys absolute immunity, unless there is an express waiver.

What kinds of immunity were granted in Kosovo and East Timor? According to UNMIK Regulation 2000/47, KFOR enjoys absolute immunity, while UNMIK and its personnel are immune with respect to all acts performed in their official capacity. With regard to UNTAET, no such regulation was promulgated, but the Convention on the Privileges and Immunities was fully applied. The approach chosen by the UN appears to be questionable. The granting of immunities to a peacekeeping operation is based on the idea that the organizations need to be protected from interference and harassment by local authorities and the government of the host state. However, that is not a convincing argument when a UN administration is vested with executive, legislative and judicial powers and takes over the function of a state. As Rawski points out, '[b]road staff immunity in such cases may violate the principles of democratic accountability and human rights at the core of these missions' mandates' (p. 549). He suggests that 'the UN should narrow immunities to a reasonable definition of "official duty," explicitly excluding serious violations of human rights and criminal law, and only invoke immunity protections when failing to do so would truly endanger the success of the mission' (p. 572). Such a definition could be laid down in a bulletin on the scope of the privileges and immunities of UN staff, which would also regulate 'a consistent procedure for handling questions of immunity in the peacekeeping context, including a clear articulation of the role of Boards of Inquiry, Ombudsperson offices, and UN supervised courts' (p. 575).

Conclusion

Peacekeeping operations do not exist in a legal vacuum and they never did. Many peacekeeping operations nowadays acquire a 'greater legal dimension' than in their early days because of the new and growing tasks undertaken by the peacekeeper (Corell, 2000).

Any actor in the peacekeeping process should understand the conceptual differences between consensual peacekeeping operations based on the consent of the parties and missions mandated under Chapter VII and possibly allowing the use of force beyond self-defence. Every peacekeeper, whether he or she is involved in the planning, training or decision-making process or fulfils functions, such as a soldier, policeman or civilian, should have a basic understanding of his or her rights and duties under international law.

The rule of law is arguably the most important aspect in any peace operation. As shown by the essays collected in this volume, there are many legal controversies and difficulties to implement and enact in accordance with the rule of law during a peacekeeping operation. Addressing these issues will remain a challenging task.

References

Aide Mémoire of the Secretary-General Concerning Some Questions Relating to the Function and Operation of the United Nations Peacekeeping Force in Cyprus (1964), UN doc. S/5653, 10 April.

Annan, K. (1998), *Fifty Years of United Nations Peacekeeping Has Helped Pave Road to Peace, Secretary General Tells Special Commemorative Meeting of Assembly*, UN doc. SG/SM/6732, 6 October.

Bellamy, A.J., Williams, P. and Griffin, S. (2004), Understanding Peacekeeping, Oxford: Polity.

Boutros-Ghali, B. (1992), *An Agenda for Peace: Preventive Diplomacy, Peacemaking and Peacekeeping*, UN doc. A/47/277-S24111, 17 June.

Boutros-Ghali, B. (1995), *Supplement to An Agenda for Peace*, UN Doc. A/50/60-S/1995, 13 January.

Brahimi Report (2000), Report of the Panel on United Nations Peace Operations, UN doc. A/55/305/ S/2000/809, 17 August, reprinted in *International Peacekeeping*, **6**, pp. 186–206.

Corell, H. (2000), *The Role of the United Nations in Peacekeeping-Recent Developments from a Legal Perspective*, at : http://www.un.org/law/counsel/english/washingtonDec00.pdf.

Expenses Opinion (1962), *Certain Expenses of the United Nations (Article 17, paragraph 2 of the Charter*, Advisory Opinion, ICJ Rep.

De Hoogh, A.J.J. (2001), 'Attribution or Delegation of (Legislative) Power by the Security Council? The Case of the United Nations Transitional Administration in East Timor (UNTAET)', in M. Bothe and B. Kondoch (eds), *International Peacekeeping – The Yearbook of Peace Operations*, **7**, pp. 1–41.

Diehl, P. (1994), *International Peacekeeping*, Baltimore, MD: Johns Hopkins University Press.

Final Report UEF I (1956), *Final Report on the Plan for the Establishment of UNEF I*, UN doc. A/3302, 6 November.

Gray, C. (2001), 'Peacekeeping after the Brahimi Report: Is there a Crisis of Credibility for the UN?', *Journal on Conflict and Security Law*, **6**, pp. 267–88.

Hufnagel, F.-E. (1996), *UN-Friedensoperation der zweiten Generation*, Berlin: Duncker und Humblot.

James, A. (1990), *Peacekeeping in International Politics*, Basingstoke: Macmillan.

Katayanagi, M. (2002), *Human Rights Functions of United Nations Peacekeeping Operations*, The Hague: Kluwer Law International.

Kenny, K. (1996), *Towards Effective Training for Field Human Rights Tasks*, Dublin: Human Rights Trust.

Kondoch, B. (2005), 'Human Rights Law and UN Peace Operations in Post-Conflict Situations', in N.D. White and D. Klaasen (eds), *The UN, Human Rights and Post-Conflict Situations*, Manchester: Manchester University Press, pp. 19–41.

McCoubrey, H. and Morris, J. (2000), *Regional Peacekeeping in the Post-Cold War Era*, The Hague: Kluwer Law International.

Reparations Opinion (1949), *Reparations of Injuries Suffered in the Service of the United Nations*, ICJ Advisory Opinion.

Report of the Secretary General (1958), *Summary Study of the Experience Derived from the Establishment and Operation of the Force*, UN doc. A/3943, 8 October.

Report of the Secretary-General (1973), *Implementation of Security Council Resolution 340*, UN doc. S/11052/Rev., 27 October.

Report of the Secretary-General (2004), *The Rule of Law and Transitional Justice in Conflict and Post-conflict Societies*, S/2004/616, 23 August.

Ruffert, M. (2001), 'The Administration of Kosovo and East-Timor by the International Community', *International and Comparative Law Quarterly*, **50**, pp. 613–31.

Safety Convention (1994), *Convention on the Safety of United Nations and Associated Personnel*, UN doc. A/RES/49/59, 9 December.

Secretary-General's Bulletin (1999), *Observance by United Nations Forces of International Humanitarian Law*, UN doc. ST/SBG/1999/13, 6 August.

Sharp, W.G. (1996), 'Protecting the Avatars of International Peace and Security', *Duke Journal of Comparative and International Law*, 7, pp. 93–183.

Stahn, C. (2001), 'International Territorial Administration in the Former Yugoslavia: Origins, Developments and Challenges Ahead', *Zeitschrift für ausländisches öffentliches Recht und Völkerrecht*, **61**, pp. 107–72.

Stein, T. (2000), 'Germany's Constitution and Participation in International Peacekeeping Operations', *Asia-Pacific Review*, 7, pp. 33–40.

United Nations Department of Public Information (2007), *Background Note: 30 April 2007, United Nations Peacekeeping Operations*, at: http://www.un.org/Depts/dpko/dpko/bnote.htm.

Zeid Report (2005), *Comprehensive Strategy to Eliminate Future Sexual Exploitation and Abuse in UN Peacekeeping Operations*, UN doc. A/59/710, 24 March.

Zwanenburg, M. (2005) *Accountability of Peace Support Operations*, Leiden: Martinus Nijhoff.

Further Reading

Bothe, M. (2002), 'Peace-Keeping', in B. Simma (ed.), *The Charter of the United Nations*, Oxford: Oxford University Press, pp. 648–700.

Bothe, M. and Dörschel, T. (eds) (1999), *UN Peacekeeping. A Documentary Introduction*, The Hague: Kluwer Law International.

Bothe, M. and Dörschel, T. (2001), 'The UN Peacekeeping Experience', in D. Fleck (ed.), *The Handbook of the Law of the Visiting Forces*, Oxford: Oxford University Press, pp. 487–506.

Bowett, D.W. (1964), *United Nations Forces: A Legal Study of United Nations Practice*, London: Stevens & Sons.

Cassese, A. (ed.) (1978), *United Nations Peace-Keeping. Legal Essays*, Alphen aan den Rijn: Sitjhoff & Noordhoff.

Challenges Project (2002), *Challenges of Peace Operations: Into the 21st Century – Concluding Report 1997–2002*, Stockholm: Elanders Gotab.

Chesterman, S. (2005), *You the People: The United Nations, Transitional Administration, and Statebuilding*, Oxford: Oxford University Press.

Conflict, Security and Development Group, International Policy Institute, (2003), *A Review of Peace Operations: A Case for Change*, London: King's College London.

Findlay, T. (2002), *The Use of Force in UN Peace Operations*, Oxford: Oxford University Press.

Higgins, R. (1969, 1970, 1980, 1981), *United Nations Peacekeeping 1946–1967, Documents and Commentary, Vol. I: The Middle East, Vol. II: Asia, Vol. III: Africa, Vol. IV: Europe 1946–1979*, London: Oxford University Press.

Howard, J. and Oswald B. (eds) (2002), *The Rule of Law on Peace Operations*, The Hague: Kluwer Law International.

Katayanagi, M. (2002), *Human Rights Functions of United Nations Peacekeeping Operations*, The Hague: Kluwer Law International.

Kelly, M.J. (1999), *Restoring and Maintaining Order in Complex Peace Operations. The Search for a Legal Framework*, The Hague: Kluwer Law International.

Knoops, G.-J.A. (2004), *The Prosecution and Defense of Peacekeepers under International Criminal Law*, Ardsley, NY: Transnational Publishers.

Langholtz, H., Kondoch, B. and Wells, A. (eds) (1994–), *International Peacekeeping – The Yearbook of Peace Operations*, Leyden: Martinus Nijhoff.

McCoubrey, H. and Morris J. (2000), *Regional Peacekeeping in the Post-Cold War Era*, The Hague: Kluwer Law International.

McCoubrey, H. and White, N.D. (1996), *The Blue Helmets: Legal Regulations of United Nations Military Operations*, Aldershot: Dartmouth.

Olonisakin, F. (2000), *Reinventing Peacekeeping in Africa. Conceptual and Legal Issues in ECOMOG Operations*, The Hague: Kluwer Law International.

Ramsbotham, O. and Woodhouse, T. (1999), *Encyclopaedia of International Peacekeeping*, Santa Barbara, CA: ABC-Clio.

Ratner, S.R. (1995), *The New UN Peacekeeping. Building Peace in the Lands of Conflict After the Cold War*, New York: St Martin's Press.

Sarooshi, D. (1999), *The United Nations and the Development of Collective Security*, Oxford: Oxford University Press.

Schmalenbach, K. (2004), *Die Haftung Internationaler Organisationen*, Frankfurt am Main: Peter Lang.

Seyersted, F. (1966), *United Nations Forces in the Law of Peace and War*, Leyden: Sitjhoff.

Sharp, W.G. (1999), *Jus Paciarii. Emergent Legal Paradigms for U.N. Peace Operations in the 21st Century*, Tafford, VA: Paciarii International.

Siekmann, R.C.R. (1989), *Basic Documents on United Nations and Related Peace-Keeping Forces*, Dordrecht: Martinus Nijhoff Publishers.

Siekmann, R.C.R. (1991), *National Contingents in United Nations Peace-Keeping Forces*, Dordrecht: Martinus Nijhoff Publishers.

Sommereyns, R. (2000), 'United Nations Forces', in R. Bernhardt (ed.), *Encyclopedia of Public International Law*, Vol. IV, Amsterdam: North-Holland, pp. 1106–119.

Suy, E. (2000), 'United Nations Peacekeeping System' in R. Bernhardt (ed.), *Encyclopedia of Public International Law*, Vol. IV, Amsterdam: North-Holland, pp. 1143–149.

White, N.D. (1997), *Keeping the Peace: The United Nations and the Maintenance of International Peace and Security*, Manchester: Manchester University Press.

Zwanenburg, M. (2005), *Accountability of Peace Support Operations*, Leiden: Martinus Nijhoff.

Part I
The Role and the Rule of Law
in International Peacekeeping

[1]

THE USES OF LAW IN INTERNATIONAL PEACE-KEEPING

*Oscar Schachter**

Because of the great rapidity with which an inflammable international situation can materialize and become critical, and because of the overtones of world holocaust which accompany such situations, an organization designed to keep peace in our present world must be able to act quickly and positively, and in modes that will not of themselves compound the crisis. Mr. Schachter points out that legal precepts and precedents are essential to effective on-the-spot peace-keeping action by the United Nations. For they, on the one hand, provide a framework within which the peace-keeping agency and its members may operate and, on the other hand, make possible confidence in the legality and impartiality of the agency. He proceeds to examine United Nations peace-keeping operations as occasioned both by frontier conflicts and internal turmoil, tracing the role of legal principles in the evolution of an effective peace-keeping apparatus and drawing to light the importance, over and above the principles themselves, of their impartial, consistent, and reasoned application in a manner characteristic of "law."

THE task of keeping the peace was viewed by the drafters of the United Nations Charter mainly in terms of deliberative, measured, and even protracted procedures. They understood that peace could not be secured by fiat or the mere assertion of authority, and they expected that the processes of settlement and adjustment would require time—time for negotiation, for inquiry, for working out compromises, for diplomacy, and for debate.[1] The more time, as a rule,

---

* Director, General Legal Division, United Nations Secretariat. B.S.S., 1936, College of the City of New York; LL.B., 1939, Columbia University. Visiting lecturer, Yale Law School.

The article is written in Mr. Schachter's personal capacity and the views presented are not to be attributed to the organization with which he is associated. Most of the article is adapted from lectures given by Mr. Schachter at the Hague Academy of International Law in 1963 under the general title "The Relations of Law, Politics and Action in the United Nations."

1. See RUSSELL, A HISTORY OF THE UNITED NATIONS CHARTER 457-64, 657-69 (1958); Jordan, *Handling of Disputes*, 1952 ANNUAL REV. OF UNITED NATIONS AFFAIRS 56, 63 (1953).

the better; "as long as they talk they will not fight." The very delays inherent in the quasi-parliamentary procedures of the General Assembly and the Security Council—the submission and adoption of agenda items, the virtually untrammelled right to speak, the procedural maneuvers—were regarded as virtues as well as necessities.

Actual events did not always fit into this general conception. It soon became evident that the maintenance of the peace could not in every case be left to negotiation or debate; some type of action was required to prevent an outbreak of hostilities or to bring about an end to those which had already begun. Such "action" embraced a variety of measures: most typically, observation and reporting; sometimes administration, technical measures, and public information; and in the most critical cases, the use of armed force.

Moreover, action had to be taken speedily. An apparently minor frontier incident, if unchecked, could set in motion a series of irreversible events. Domestic disorders could quickly bring about foreign military action, with counteraction by a rival state. A show of strength could involve a confrontation by the major powers and subsequent steps to the brink which demanded immediate action. In the past, even in 1945, international conflict was viewed mainly in spatial terms—the movement of troops or vessels over surface areas, the demarcation of boundaries, and the exercise of territorial dominion. Today the significant dimension is more likely to be time. Threats are measured in hours or minutes; relative strength is calculated as much in terms of time-lag as in quantities; the danger of "escalation" is perceived more as a sequence of events in time than as moves through space.[2]

Related to this is the impact that the new technology, especially of weapon systems, has had in fixing the limits of armed conflict. It has become a truism that the major factor influencing governments to refrain from, or at least to limit, armed hostilities is the pervading risk of almost universal destruction, a risk recognized not only in instances of direct confrontation of the great powers but also as implicit in small-power disputes and even in internal disorder likely to have international repercussions. We take it for granted that there can be virtually no aspect of international tension which does not fall under the shadow of nuclear disaster, and when we speak of the common interest of all peoples in preserving peace, that well-worn generality has a sharpness,

---

2. See the Security Council discussion on military aircraft flights carrying atomic and hydrogen bombs, U.N. Doc. Nos. S/PV.813-17 (1958), and on the Cuban situation in October 1962, U.N. Doc. Nos. S/PV.1022-25 (1962). See also McDougal & Lipson, *Perspectives for a Law of Outer Space*, 52 Am. J. Int'l L. 407, 410-11 (1958).

Virginia Law Review

a direct personal impact, which transmutes every far-off conflict into a matter of immediate self-interest.

It is against this background that I shall discuss some aspects of the measures taken by the United Nations to preserve the peace in its most immediate sense, that is to extinguish the local fires that threaten to ignite the rest of the globe. My purpose, in part, is to show that these emergency "fire-brigade" activities are more complicated and subtle than may seem to be the case; they involve more than rushing observers and soldiers to the scene or getting Washington and Moscow to restrain (or perhaps exercise) their influence. "Action" even in times of crisis takes place in the context of political, legal, and institutional determinants, and the significance and effectiveness of such action will usually depend on factors that lie outside of the operation itself and which may not at times be perceptible to those directly engaged in it.

The Function of Law in Peace-Keeping Activities

Before going into particular situations, I should like to present a few general observations about the role that law can perform in the processes of peace-keeping. There are several aspects meriting mention. One is the role of legal authority in providing a *locus standi* for third party intervention by an international organ or individual official. It is true that this may not always be essential; a friendly state may on occasion lend its good offices to bring about a settlement without invoking a juridical basis. But such voluntary conciliatory assistance has its limitations: the mediator's self-interest may be suspected, rival states may harbor resentment, internal factions may be displeased.[3] In general, third-party activity is much less likely to raise objection if it rests on legal authority and is brought within the framework of the United Nations Charter. The fact that an international organ has been granted formal authority, whether by the Charter or an armistice or cease-fire agreement, may in itself be an element in overcoming a ground of resistance to its participation, whether such participation involves good offices or a "presence" or more. Often a prior commitment by a state to rules and procedures laid down in the Charter or another legal instrument removes questionable implications which might be raised by offers

---

3. Thus, it was not surprising that the initial diplomatic role of the United States in seeking a settlement between Indonesia and The Netherlands regarding West New Guinea had to be superseded by the good offices of the United Nations Secretary-General. See Secretary-General, *Annual Report on the Work of the Organization*, U.N. Doc. No. A/5501, at 35-41 (1963).

of assistance from a third-party "volunteer."[4] Even if a state on its own accord assumes the role of "good offices" it may find it useful, as several have, to link its efforts to the pacific settlement provision of the Charter.[5]

The role of law is also manifest in the use of prescribed standards and rules to facilitate settlement and discussion. One must be careful to avoid overstating this aspect; hostilities are not generally called off because legal norms are invoked. There are, nevertheless, situations in which a skilled and perceptive "peace-keeper" will find that persuasion is immensely facilitated by invoking legal obligations and prescriptions.[6] United Nations experience has shown that governments will more easily acquiesce in an unwelcome ruling if it is supported by fairly specific provisions of an armistice agreement or a cease-fire resolution which has been accepted by the parties. Moreover, United Nations troops or military observers will be able to move freely to the scene of a disturbance without the delays of official clearance if they can invoke a "status" agreement with the host government which clearly guarantees freedom of movement.[7] Consequently, in most of the United Nations peace-keeping operations the presence of a legal foundation for the necessary activities has been found to be essential to effective performance.

This legal foundation is essential not only for relations with the host state, but also for regulation and guidance of the international personnel engaged in the operation. The very fact that the Organization is composed of competitive blocs, wary of each other, underlines the importance of ensuring that those who act in the name of the Organization adhere as strictly as possible to the principles and decisions of the political organs. To achieve this, there must be measures of control and supervision by the member states, and to a large extent such measures must take the form of general rules and prescribed procedures. Thus, in each of the emergency peace-keeping operations (ranging from observation to "law and order" functions) there has been a governing body of law consisting of, first, the resolutions of the political organ

---

4. See GOODRICH & SIMONS, THE UNITED NATIONS AND THE MAINTENANCE OF INTERNATIONAL PEACE AND SECURITY 291-306 (1955).

5. For example, the United States invoked this provision of the Charter in the 1946 dispute between France and Thailand. See U.N. Doc. No. S/199 (1946).

6. See Schachter, *Dag Hammarskjold and the Relation of Law to Politics*, 56 AM. J. INT'L L. 1, 5-6 (1962).

7. See Secretary-General, *Summary Study of the Experience Derived from the Establishment and Operation of the Force*, U.N. Doc. No. A/3943 (1958).

responsible for the operation; second, agreements by the states concerned (especially the territorial states) with the United Nations or between themselves; and third, regulations and rules promulgated by the Secretary-General or his representative. Since these legal rules necessarily cannot cover all contingencies, it has been considered appropriate to invoke and rely upon precedents and consistent practice as evidence of the agreed interpretations.

In addition, in certain situations, the required guidance for international officials has to be sought in the recognized precepts of international law and in the general principles of law accepted by states. By utilizing and relying upon well-established principles as well as upon techniques of legal analysis, the international official is enabled to adopt and justify positions which might otherwise seem to be novel and perhaps attributable to personal predilections.[8] Of course, legal precepts and techniques cannot in themselves fully safeguard the interest of the Organization in ensuring the proper performance of its mandates; there are inevitably areas of discretion and judgment left to the administrative official where rule and precept provide but slight, if any, guidance. In these areas, techniques of review and supervision by the member states have assumed importance and have given rise to controversial proposals for new forms of governmental control.[9] Also quite important are the requirements relating to the responsibility and standards of the international civil service. It is especially in the situations we are considering—those involving strife, bitterness, impassioned partisans—that there is a need for the impartiality, dedication, and understanding that are the essential qualities of those entrusted with the task of bringing about peace admidst hostility and distrust.

Surveillance in Frontier Areas and Along Demarcation Lines

The task of peace-keeping, in its most common aspect, has focused on troubled frontier regions where hostility between neighboring coun-

---

8. See comments of Mr. Oscar Schachter in the panel discussion, *Constitutional Developments of the United Nations*, 1961 PROCEEDINGS AMERICAN SOC'Y OF INTERNATIONAL L. 78, 85-86. See also HAMMARSKJOLD, THE INTERNATIONAL CIVIL SERVANT IN LAW AND IN FACT (1961) (lecture given at Oxford University on May 30, 1961).

9. See *Report of the Committee of Experts on the Activities and Organization of the Secretariat*, U.N. Doc. No. A/4776 (1961); U.N. GEN. ASS. OFF. REC. 15th Sess., Plenary 869, at 82-83 (A/PV.869) (1960) (statements of N.S. Khrushchev); U.N. GEN. ASS. OFF. REC. 15th Sess., Plenary 871, at 95 (A/PV.871) (1960) (remarks of D. Hammarskjold); Bailey, *The Troika and the Future of the UN*, Int'l Conc., May 1962, at 36; Stein, *Mr. Hammarskjold, The Charter Law and the Future Role of the United Nations Secretary-General*, 56 AM. J. INT'L L. 9 (1962).

tries has given rise to acts of violence and depredation which have threatened to spread or escalate into outright warfare. In its first year, 1946, the United Nations undertook a field operation to investigate Greek charges of frontier violations. The Security Council, acting under Chapter VI, dispatched to Greece and its neighbors a commission of investigation composed of one representative of each of the Council members. This governmental commission, assisted by a large Secretariat staff, carried on inquiries on the spot, heard more than 200 witnesses, filled three large volumes of evidence, and made findings as to the responsibility for supporting guerilla warfare.[10] In the next year, a similar governmental body, the United Nations Special Committee on the Balkans (UNSCOB), was set up by the General Assembly; it utilized observer teams in Greece (they were not admitted into the neighboring states) and submitted detailed reports to the General Assembly.[11] Thus, the United Nations instituted the prototype of peace-observation activity: a mechanism for inquiry, fact-finding, and reporting. Inquiries were conducted through interviews and submissions by national officials. The Commissions possessed no compulsory powers to elicit testimony or to require the productions of evidence. The only "sanction" consisted of reports and findings to the United Nations organs and such consequential influence as they might have on governmental policy.

In subsequent situations—especially those involving India and Pakistan in the Jammu-Kashmir region and Israel and its Arab neighbors in the Palestine area—the fact-finding inquiry evolved into more extensive and more durable machinery for rapid observation and reporting of incidents and violations. One significant development was that the commission of government representatives was replaced by personnel appointed by and under the authority of the Secretary-General, although of course he and they were subject to the resolutions and decisions of the Security Council. The observers were almost entirely military personnel seconded by their national governments; they were not, strictly speaking, international Secretariat personnel, but they were international "agents" (as the International Court put it in the Reparations opinion) who were responsible to the Organization alone in the performance of their official duties and who did not look to their respective national governments for instructions.[12]

10. See *Report of the Commission of Investigation on Greek Frontier Incidents to the Security Council*, U.N. Doc. No. S/360 (1947).

11. See *UNSCOB Reports*, U.N. Doc. Nos. A/574, A/644 (1948).

12. The military observers for the Kashmir-Jammu area and for the United Nations

Both the Truce Supervision Organization in Jerusalem (UNTSO) and the Military Observers Group in Kashmir (UNMOGIP) received their authority from the Security Council and were to report to the Council on the observance of the respective cease-fire arrangements in each area. In the case of UNTSO, the staff was also assigned to assist in the supervision of the General Armistice Agreements through the Mixed Armistice Commissions established thereunder.[13] However, because UNTSO was also directly responsible to the Security Council for reporting on the observances of the cease-fire order of July 15, 1948, the Chief of Staff was able to act quickly, as General Burns stated, "without the delays and restrictions imposed by the rules of procedure adopted by the parties for the work of the Mixed Armistice Commissions."[14] The Chief of Staff was in a position to send observers instantly to the area of disturbance and to arrange a cease-fire before the investigation machinery of the Armistice Agreement was set in motion. Similarly, in the case of the military observers in the Kashmir area, incidents could be dealt with on the spot and arrangements made to preserve the cease-fire terms without protracted procedures.

While the activities of both these military observer groups gave rise to legal problems, they did not raise substantial constitutional issues; no one doubted that the observation of and reporting on cease-fire arrangements came within the proper scope of the Security Council's authority and those governments directly concerned accepted the arrangements. Constitutional controversy did arise, however, in connection with the next peace-keeping action—the establishment in 1956 of the United Nations Emergency Force (UNEF) on the Egyptian side of the armistice demarcation line. Legal differences arose in the first instance because that Force was established by the General Assembly, not the Security Council.[15] It was described in a statement of the

Truce Supervision Organization (UNTSO), Jerusalem, are appointed by the Secretary-General and are subject to international discipline and control. The Kashmir military observer group was established pursuant to resolutions of the United Nations Commission to India and Pakistan, August 13, 1948, and January 5, 1949, and confirmed by agreement between India and Pakistan on July 27, 1949. The UNTSO military observers were originally formed in 1948 by the Mediator in Palestine and subsequently authorized by the Security Council in its resolution of August 11, 1949, passed after the conclusion of the armistice agreements.

13. See BURNS, BETWEEN ARAB AND ISRAELI 26-27 (1963); Hurewitz, *The Israeli-Syrian Crisis in the Light of the Arab-Israel Armistice System*, 5 INTERNATIONAL ORGANIZATION 459 (1951).

14. BURNS, *op. cit. supra* note 13, at 27.

15. See U.N. GEN. ASS. OFF. REC. 1st Emergency Special Sess., Plenary 567, §§ 291-93,

Secretary-General (concurred in by the General Assembly) as "more than an observers corps" which had for its purposes first, to "secure" and "supervise" the cessation of hostilities and the withdrawal of troops, and second, to maintain quiet during and after the troop withdrawal.[16] Although the Force was established by a resolution adopted without a negative vote, several states abstained on the ground that such action by the General Assembly "by-passed" the Security Council and was therefore contrary to the Charter.[17]

When this issue came before the International Court in the advisory proceeding relating to "certain expenses of the United Nations," the court held that UNEF did not constitute an "enforcement action" within the meaning of Chapter VII, which under the Charter could be undertaken only by the Security Council.[18] In reaching this conclusion, the court observed that the resolutions of the General Assembly were not intended to be binding on states: the troops were contributed voluntarily and the stationing and operation of the Force required the consent of the government of the country in which it was stationed.[19] Moreover, the Force itself could not undertake "coercive" action against a state and in no way "controlled" the territory in which it operated. The court's opinion acknowledged that the Force could be described as "action," but it pointed out that only enforcement action was excluded from the competence of the General Assembly under the terms of the last sentence of Article 11, paragraph 2.[20] The opinion referred to other "actions" of the General Assembly for the maintenance of peace such as the creation of subsidiary organs for observation and supervision, and it also referred to Article 14 which authorizes the Assembly to recommend "measures" for the peaceful adjustment of precarious situations.[21] One of the several dissenting

---

at 127 (A/PV.567) (1956) (statement of U.S.S.R. representative); Chaumont, *La situation juridque des etats membres a l'égard de la force d'urgence des Nations-Unies*, 4 ANNUAIRE FRANÇAIS DE DROIT INTERNATIONAL 399, 424 (1958); Sohn, *The Authority of the United Nations to Establish and Maintain a Permanent United Nations Force*, 52 AM. J. INT'L L. 229, 240 (1958).

16. Secretary-General, *Second Report on Plan for Emergency International Force*, U.N. Doc. No. A/3302, § 12 (1956), approved in Gen. Ass. Res. 1001 (ES-1), U.N. Doc. No. A/RES/395 (1956).

17. See U.N. GEN. ASS. OFF. REC. 1st Emergency Special Sess., Plenary 567 (A/PV.567) (1956) (U.S.S.R.); U.N. GEN. ASS. OFF. REC. 11th Sess., Plenary 592 (A/PV.592) (1956) (Ukraine).

18. Certain Expenses of the United Nations, [1962] I.C.J. Rep. 151.

19. *Id.* at 170-71.

20. *Id.* at 165.

21. *Id.* at 172.

opinions, that of Judge Koretsky, took issue with the court's conclusion on the ground that the Force involved measures of "compulsion" and, therefore, that its activities exceeded the recommendatory power of the General Assembly.[22]

It is true that the Force may be said to have involved compulsion in the sense that it was authorized to seize and detain individuals who attempted to violate the armistice lines and that—although it could not take the initiative in using armed force—it was "entitled to respond with force to an attack with arms, including attempts to use force to make them withdraw from positions which they occupy under orders from the Commander . . . ."[23] However, this qualified right to use armed force against individuals and bands did not extend to action against the armed forces of a state. The Secretary-General had taken the position that action of that sort could not be taken under the authority of the General Assembly, a decision of the Security Council under Chapter VII being required.[24] Nonetheless, it must be recognized that, in spite of the limitations upon the Force's authorization to act, the essential element in reconciling the fundamental limitation on the General Assembly's authority with the use of arms by a United Nations Force lay in the fact that the governments concerned (that of the host territory and those of the states contributing troops) gave their consent and voluntarily responded to a recommendation of the General Assembly adopted in the interest of maintaining peace.[25]

While the requirement of consent was generally accepted, it had implications of a legal character which influenced the policies and arrangements in regard to UNEF and subsequent actions. One question was whether the continued presence and manner of such a force as UNEF was to be dependent upon the functioning of unilateral decision of the host state; or, alternatively stated, whether the acceptance of the force and the relevant resolution implied a limitation on the authority of the host state. This question has never been authoritatively answered by a competent organ; it was partly dealt with in regard to UNEF by an express "understanding" between the Egyptian government and the Secretary-General (approved by the General Assembly on November 24, 1956) which in highly general language affirmed that

---

22. *Id.* at 258-59.

23. Secretary-General, *Summary Study of the Experience Derived From the Establishment and Operation of the Force*, U.N. Doc. No. A/3943, §§ 134-47 (1958) [hereinafter cited as *Summary Study*].

24. See U.N. Doc. No. A/3302, § 12 (1956).

25. See Certain Expenses of the United Nations, [1962] I.C.J. Rep. 151, 171.

both parties would be "guided in good faith" by the General Assembly resolution with respect to the continued presence and functioning of the Force.[26] One could hardly have devised a more delicate legal undertaking. It was not quite an agreement, for the sovereign rights of the Egyptian government were recognized. At the same time, the government formally accepted the General Assembly resolution, and the Secretary-General construed this to mean that the right of unilateral action had been superseded by a recognition of the necessity of collaboration. What is significant for our present discussion is that this gossamer-like formula achieved the purpose for which it was intended: it satisfied both sides that they were maintaining their essential rights and it avoided an impasse on a highly controversial issue of prestige.[27] Two months later it was followed by a detailed agreement on the status, immunities, and facilities of the Force, including provisions on rights of access, freedom of movement, and immunity from local criminal jurisdiction, which were considered essential for the functioning of the Force.[28] A legal foundation was thus laid for the day-to-day activities of an international armed force that was "more than an observers corps" but less than an "enforcement action."

Principles of Action in Frontier Situations

If we examine the normative aspects of United Nations actions in the several international frontier situations considered, we might conveniently distinguish two categories of principles that are significant. One such category concerns the relation of the action to the settlement of problems and the relative positions of the states concerned. The second category includes the principles governing the composition, role, and administration of the United Nations operation. The norms in each of these categories are linked to each other in some degree and exert a reciprocal influence.

In the first of these categories we find three distinct though related principles: (1) that the United Nations operation "should not prejudge the solution of controversial questions involved," (2) that the action should not "change the political balance affecting efforts to settle the conflict," and (3) that the action should not modify the prior *status*

26. See U.N. Doc. No. A/3375, Aide-Memoire (1956), approved in Gen. Ass. Res. 1122 (XI), U.N. Doc. No. A/3572 (1956).

27. See GROSS, THE UNITED NATIONS: STRUCTURE FOR PEACE 30-34 (1962); ROSNER, THE UNITED NATIONS EMERGENCY FORCE 56-58 (1963); Chaumont, *supra* note 15.

28. 260 U.N.T.S. 62, No. 3704 (1957).

juris. These three principles were noted by the Secretary-General in establishing UNEF.[29] He suggested that they were required because of the limitations on the authority of the General Assembly or, as he put it, by the fact that they were not actions taken under Chapter VII of the Charter.[30]

Stated somewhat differently, the point is that in the absence of a decision by the Security Council to take enforcement action, a peace-keeping operation of the kind employed in UNEF and the other border disputes had to be provisional in the sense that it could not settle or decisively affect the rights, claims, or position of the parties concerned. Secretary-General Hammarskjold observed that if the United Nations did not limit its action in this way it would not be in a position to receive the necessary support from the member nations.[31] Thus, the conservatory and self-limiting rules followed in these peace-keeping operations may be said to have been a consequence of the fragility of the Organization's authority and its inability to bring about an imposed solution without obtaining the consent of all the states concerned. At the same time they reflected the general consensus that, under present conditions, priority must be given to the prevention of international violence even if neither party to a dispute considers that the status quo satisfies justice and equity.

When we consider the second category of norms—those relating to the administration of the United Nations operation—we find that the rules of restraint had, perhaps paradoxically, their positive and creative aspects. For the desire to avoid a shift in political balance and an intervention which might prejudice the position of the parties was an important factor in shaping the rules for truly international, non-partisan United Nations action. Thus when UNEF was established, ambiguities of the kind that characterized the Korean operation were eliminated; UNEF was clearly an international force directly and

---

29. See U.N. Doc. No. A/3512, § 5 (1957); U.N. Doc. No. A/3302, § 12 (1956).

30. U.N. Doc. No. A/3512, § 5 (1957); see *Summary Study* §§ 12, 15, 167. In fact, the one Charter provision which perhaps comes closest to expressing these principles is found in Chapter VII: namely Article 40, which authorizes the Security Council to call on states to comply with "provisional measures" which it deems desirable to prevent an aggravation of the situation threatening international peace. Such provisional measures, Article 40 states, "shall be without prejudice to the rights, claims or position of the parties concerned." That this principle is found in Article 40 does not change the essential point in Secretary-General Hammarskjold's analysis, since, in referring to Chapter VII, he evidently had in mind the enforcement action provided for in Articles 41 and 42.

31. *Summary Study* § 167.

wholly under the authority of the United Nations.[32] All of its personnel, including the national military contingents, were subject to international obligations and discipline. They were required to perform their duties solely in support of the aims of the Organization and to abstain from acts in relation to their countries of origin or any other country which might deprive the operation of its exclusively international character.[33] The composition of UNEF was designed to avoid the danger of national involvement; units from the permanent members of the Security Council were excluded as were units from any country which might be considered as having a "special interest" in the situation which gave rise to the United Nations involvement.[34] While the views of the host country were to be taken fully into account with regard to the nationality of troop units, it was made clear that the United Nations would alone have the right to decide on the composition of the Force.[35] The international status of the Force was further assured by the provisions for immunity from national jurisdiction, freedom of movement, and rights of access and communications contained in the status agreement which closely followed its entry into Egypt.[36] Legal principles and rules were an important means of assuring that the United Nations action to maintain "quiet" would not founder on the shoals of national mistrust and rivalry. In short, "law" did not merely impose restrictions; it also contributed in a positive manner to the development of international authority and responsibility in a tense and critical political context.[37]

Peace-Keeping in Internal Conflicts

The evolution of international peace-keeping machinery has not been limited to the classic cases of frontier warfare; it has been carried over—with some adaptation—to troubled areas of internal strife which threatened to turn into international conflict. Although civil wars are not mentioned in the Charter, it could hardly be thought that they would necessarily be outside of its purview. At the time of San

---

32. *Id.* §§ 13-14.

33. *Id.* §§ 19, 127.

34. *Id.* §§ 16, 160-61.

35. *Id.* § 161.

36. See note 28 *supra* and accompanying text. The agreement is analyzed in *Summary Study* §§ 134-47.

37. See Address by U Thant, Harvard University, June 13, 1963, found in United Nations Rev., July 1963, p. 54. See generally Rosner, The United Nations Emergency Force (1963).

Francisco, the "internationalization" of the Spanish Civil War of the nineteen thirties was still of fresh memory, and history could have furnished many other examples of the links between local conflict and international violence.[38] In recent United Nations experience, domestic strife has been the occasion for several important peace-keeping actions—Cyprus, Yemen, and the Congo provide the outstanding examples.

The legal pattern is exemplified in the Congo action, where the danger appeared even before civil war. A breakdown in internal order, especially manifested in the mutiny and depredations of the Congolese Force Publique, had led to armed intervention by Belgium (feeling that its "sacred duty" was to intervene to protect the lives and honour of Belgian nationals) and, in turn, to charges of Belgian aggression by the Congo and a possibility of counter-action by other states.[39] When faced with the request by the Congo for military assistance to protect its national territory against "external aggression" by the Belgian troops, the Secretary-General relied on Article 99 to convene the Security Council on the ground that there existed a possible threat to international peace, a conclusion concurred in by the members of the Security Council and the neighboring African governments.[40] The Secretary-General then proposed military assistance based on the guiding principles derived from the UNEF experience.[41]

These principles, as we have seen, had a dual aspect: on the one side, they asserted the policy of nonintervention in internal political conflicts and they restricted use of force to self-defense alone; on the other side, they stressed the international character and status of the Force and the international responsibility for maintenance of the peace. We have further seen, at least as to the first aspect, that these principles were related to and in part the product of the Charter provisions which

38. See Sohn, *The Rôle of the United Nations in Civil Wars*, 1963 PROCEEDINGS AMERICAN SOC'Y OF INTERNATIONAL L. 208; Wright, *International Law and Civil Strife*, 1959 PROCEEDINGS AMERICAN SOC'Y OF INTERNATIONAL L. 145.

39. A useful summary of the first period of the Congo action is found in *Annual Report of the Secretary-General on the Work of the Organization*, U.N. GEN. ASS. OFF. REC. 16th Sess., Supp. No. 1 (A/4800) (1961), and additional information on the Congo situation is contained in *First Report of the Secretary-General to the Security Council on the Congo*, U.N. Doc. No. S/4389 (1960).

40. See U.N. SECURITY COUNCIL OFF. REC. 15th year, 873d meeting 4 (S/PV.873) (1960).

41. The 1958 action in Lebanon also provided grounds for the development of these principles.

governed UNEF.[42] However, the constitutional character of the Congo action differed significantly from that of UNEF. The Congo action rested both on a request by the Congolese government for assistance in the maintenance of internal law and order and on the Security Council's implied finding that such assistance was necessary to meet a serious threat to international peace.[43] Thus, although involving from the outset a contractual type of arrangement with the Congolese government, the United Nations action was not merely a response to a request for aid; its essential justification lay in the Council's responsibility under the Charter to maintain international peace and security.[44] Nevertheless, in its initial resolution, addressed first to the Belgian government and secondly to the Secretary-General, the Council approved, though by implication only, the restraint in the exercise of its powers inherent in the principles recommended by the Secretary-General.[45]

The second and third resolutions did not go beyond these principles, although they did, in the face of unexpected resistance, turn to the Charter in order to assert the legal force of Council decisions. In the second resolution, that of July 22, 1960, the Council made explicit the connection between the restoration of domestic law and order and the maintenance of international peace. It also authorized the Secretary-General to take "all necessary action" to bring about the withdrawal of Belgian troops—thus introducing a clear element of pressure for implementation—and it requested all states to refrain from action that might tend to impede the restoration of law and order and from action

---

42. See text accompanying notes 29-31 *supra*.

43. See U.N. Security Council Off. Rec. 15th year, Supp. July-September 1960, at 34 (S/4405) (1960).

44. The Security Council did not go beyond this general justification in the Charter: they did not explicitly relate the action to grants of competence specified in the Charter, nor did they employ the "words of art" which could have served to identify the precise constitutional slot into which the members intended the decision to fall and which could have thereby determined the chain of legal consequences. These omissions were not, of course, the result of absent-mindedness or ignorance, but reflected the difficulties and complexities of deciding on a course of action when the members had diverse views as to the causes of the problem and the means of solution. Of course, there was a measure of consensus, and this was expressed in the objectives of the initial resolution—namely, that the United Nations should provide "military assistance" for the maintenance of internal order in the Congo and that the Belgian troops should withdraw.

45. See U.N. Security Council Off. Rec. 15th year, 873d meeting 4 (S/PV 873) (1960); Miller, *Legal Aspects of the United Nations Action in the Congo*, 55 Am. J. Int'l L. 1 (1961).

that might undermine the territorial integrity and the political independence of the Republic of the Congo.[46]

The Council in its resolution of August 9, 1960, followed the line indicated by the Secretary-General. It invoked Articles 25 and 49, called on Belgium to withdraw all its troops from Katanga, and declared the entry of the United Nations into Katanga necessary. It also stated expressly that the "United Nations Force in the Congo will not be a party to or in any way intervene in or be used to influence the outcome of any internal conflict, constitutional or otherwise . . . ." [47] It was this latter provision which became the focus of controversy immediately thereafter and for almost the entire period of the Congo operation.

It was not easy, of course, for the United Nations to maintain a policy of nonintervention in internal politics when it had the tasks of maintaining law and order, of expelling foreign military personnel, and of preventing civil war. This is not the place to recount the numerous dilemmas faced by the United Nations when internal political groups competing for power sought to enlist its support, or when measures to carry out the mandate appeared to help one of the disputing factions. It is, however, pertinent to our theme to draw attention to the function that "law" played in meeting these difficulties. For as both Mr. Hammarskjold and U Thant emphasized, the key to these dilemmas had to be adherence by the United Nations Force to basic principles— that is to say, to the precepts which were authoritatively prescribed by the Security Council and the General Assembly and to those derived from the Charter or contained in applicable international agreements. This was not only a matter of characterizing these precepts as "binding" or as "law" but, more important, of applying them in a manner which is characteristic of "law"—that is, in an impartial, consistent, and reasoned fashion, recognizing their legal force and resisting pressures and temptations to make exceptions which could not be justified by general principles. Thus, in accordance with the resolutions, protection was extended to political leaders regardless of their points of view, and external military intervention outside of the United Nations framework was excluded, whatever its source.

However, it was in connection with the use of armed force by the United Nations that issues of "legality" and propriety were most sharply presented and the necessity of adhering to legal criteria most evident.

---

46. See U.N. SECURITY COUNCIL OFF. REC. 15th year, Supp. July-September 1960 (S/4405) (1960).

47. U.N. Doc. No. S/4426, § 4 (1960).

The initial resolutions, as we have seen, were premised on a restriction of the use of arms to self-defense alone; this was made clear in the Security Council by the Secretary-General in his initial recommendation and early reports; it was also an essential condition in the assignment of national contingents to the Force.[48] But it had already become evident in the UNEF experience that the meaning and scope of self-defense required further clarification. UNEF had been authorized not only to carry arms but to seize and detain individuals who violated the demarcation lines; if resisted or threatened they could respond with arms.[49] No less authority could be granted the troops in the Congo in their task of maintaining law and order. Clearly they had the right to apprehend criminals and to use arms if threatened or attacked. Furthermore, as in the case of UNEF, they had the right to take up certain positions required for their task and to defend such positions with arms against attempts to compel their withdrawal.[50] They could therefore set up check-points to prevent disorder and post guard details at transportation and communication facilities. No one doubted the necessity of these actions to cope with the uncontrolled groups of armed men who defied national and local authority and who had engaged in pillage and violence. When efforts were made by one group or another to dislodge the Force from these essential positions, resistance was considered justified as self-defense under the agreed conditions.

It is important to note (in view of the misunderstandings that have arisen) that the United Nations did not assert an unlimited right to assume positions and then hold them by military means. Positions were assumed only if required to carry out the necessary functions within the agreement with the Congolese government.[51] Airports, rail centers, and roads, for example, were recognized by both parties to be necessary to the "law and order" function. After the resolution of February 21,

---

48. See *First Report of the Secretary-General to the Security Council on the Congo,* U.N. Doc. No. S/4389 (1960); U.N. Security Council Off. Rec. 15th year, 885th meeting 1 (S/PV 885) (1960).

49. See *Summary Study* § 31.

50. See U.N. Doc. No. S/4758, Add. 4 (1961); *First Report of the Secretary-General to the Security Council on the Congo,* U.N. Doc. No. S/4389, § 34 (1960). With regard to the U.N. peace-keeping force in Cyprus, similar principles were laid down by the Secretary-General and specified in greater detail than had been done in the Congo. See Secretary-General, *Function and Operation of United Nations Peace-Keeping Force in Cyprus,* U.N. Doc. No. S/5653, Aide-Memoire (1964).

51. See U.N. Doc. No. S/4775 (1961); U.N. Security Council Off. Rec. 15th year, 896th meeting 14-30 (S/PV.896) (1960).

1961,[52] and prior to the establishment of a central government in August of that year, positions were taken by the United Nations to prevent clashes under the specific authority of the resolution, which in turn had been accepted by the authorities exercising governmental functions, including those in Katanga.[53]

In addition to the defense of positions, the United Nations maintained its right to defend its freedom of movement, which was obviously necessary to carry out its agreed functions. Here, too, it is essential—from the legal standpoint—to note that "freedom of movement" had a clear and precise legal basis. It had been guaranteed by the government of the Congo in the first "basic" agreement of July 1960,[54] an agreement patterned closely on that of UNEF. It had received more explicit specification in the general status agreement with the central government[55] concluded subsequently, and it had also been assured from time to time by the provincial government of Katanga.[56] In view of its legal right to freedom of movement, the United Nations considered that it had been authorized to maintain positions necessary for protection of its freedom of movement and to use force to eliminate restrictions on that freedom of movement. In point of fact, the United Nations never initiated hostilities based on its right to freedom of movement. In each of the cases involving hostilities between the Organization's troops and the Katanga gendarmerie—namely, in September 1961, December 1961, and December 1962—the United Nations did not undertake military operations until armed attacks had been made on its personnel and the security of its Force seriously threatened. In responding to these attacks, the United Nations limited itself to military objectives and to obtaining control of positions necessary to secure freedom of movement. In short, force was used in self-defense and carried through to achieve effective recognition of the Force's right to freedom of movement necessary for its security. Detailed accounts of these actions and their specific objectives have all been made public in the reports of the officer in charge of United Nations operations in the Congo.[57]

52. U.N. Doc. No. S/4741 (1961).

53. See *Report of Officer-in-Charge*, U.N. Doc. No. S/5053, Add. 7 (1962).

54. U.N. Doc. No. S/4389, Add. 5 (1960).

55. U.N. Doc. No. S/5004, A/4986 (1961). A similar agreement was concluded with Cyprus for the United Nations force located there. U.N. Doc. No. S/5634 (1964).

56. See U.N. Doc. No. S/5053, Add. 7 (1962); U.N. Doc. No. S/5053, Adds. 11, 13 (1962).

57. See U.N. Doc. No. S/4940, Adds. 1-9 (1961); U.N. Doc. No. S/5053, Add. 14 (1962). For the Secretary-General's account of the Congo situation, see *Annual Report*

The use of force in a complex and fluid situation such as that of the Congo obviously cannot be governed in every detail by pre-existing rules. There were difficult decisions to be taken in emergency situations which could not be foreseen and as to which reasonable men, especially with the aid of hindsight, might differ. I do not wish to suggest that all such decisions were right or wise, but I think it can be said that every effort was made to conduct the operation on the basis of the restricted objectives and basic rules laid down by the competent organs.

The complexities of preserving national unity and political independence required, of course, much more than legal prescriptions. It became evident very early in the Congo case that declarations in United Nations resolutions favoring the objectives of unity and independence meant little without measures of implementation; and it was not long in becoming apparent that such measures had to involve the whole fabric of the national society, in which the political, economic, social, educational, and psychological factors were all inextricably intertwined. This was not a task to be performed in the spirit of a new Holy Alliance in support of the status quo; it required rather a series of far-reaching institutional innovations in almost every area of national life. Such measures necessarily went beyond the previous patterns of United Nations assistance: they called not merely for a few experts in technical fields, but for building national institutions in almost every phase of public activity. The United Nations could not substitute itself for the government or impose a covert trusteeship. Its legal authority was subordinated to that of the central government. Yet it was required to deal with the most delicate internal issues: constitutional revision, parliamentary procedures, the organization of the armed forces, the establishment of a civil service and judicial administration, and the integration of sectional and national interests.[58]

Conclusion

This is not the place (nor may it be the time) to assess the results in the Congo,[59] but one can at least conclude that it was of some im-

---

of the Secretary-General on the Work of the Organization, U.N. GEN. ASS. OFF. REC. 17th Sess., Supp. No. 1 (A/5201) (1962).

58. See *Report of the Secretary-General to the Security Council,* U.N. Doc. No. S/5420 (1963). Similarly, in the case of Cyprus, the role of the United Nations could not be limited to police functions. See U.N. Doc. No. S/5764, §§ IV-V (1964).

59. An assessment of the results of the U.N. action in the Congo may be found in the report of the Secretary-General. U.N. Doc. No. S/5784 (1964).

portance in that case, as subsequently in Cyprus, that the United Nations had a constitutional foundation and an established legal pattern for furnishing assistance in the maintenance of internal order on an international basis and without taking sides in domestic conflicts. To be sure, many of the actions taken were practical responses to immediate problems; but, as we have seen, these actions were also related to, and in a sense the consequence of, various provisions of the Charter. Intangible as this relation may seem, its influence should not be underestimated. The authority of the Security Council under Chapter VII to meet the threat to the peace, the prohibition against force in Article 2 (4), the conceptions of political independence and nonintervention in Articles 1 and 2, the objectives and procedures for economic and social aid based on Chapters IX and X, the precepts governing international officials in Chapter XV—all of these constitutional norms played their parts, at times amid controversy, but more often inconspicuously. In doing so they provided the common frame of reference and the standards of mutual interest that are necessary for collective effort in today's divided world.

[2]

RULE OF LAW STRATEGIES FOR PEACE OPERATIONS

Nina Lahoud[†]

I   INTRODUCTION

It is a privilege for me to represent the Department of Peacekeeping Operations (DPKO) in this forum among such distinguished speakers and participants, including many veteran peacekeepers from the military, police and civilian ranks – a number of whom I have had the pleasure to serve with in various peace operations over the years. Speaking on behalf of DPKO, I can say that we are most grateful to have this opportunity to contribute to a better understanding of rule of law issues in peace operations and how they can be more effectively addressed. The theme of this particular Conference reflects the fact that the international community has progressively recognised that a major ingredient for building a durable peace in a war torn society is strengthening the rule of law. While it is uplifting that, at the General Assembly's Millenium Summit, Heads of State and Government stood unified in expressing their resolve, in the Millenium Declaration, '[t]o strengthen respect for the rule of law in international as in national affairs', it is obvious that we still have much to do to meet that lofty objective in the context of our peace operations.

In addressing the topic on which I have been asked to speak today, 'Rule of Law Strategies for Peace Operations', let me first attempt to capture what 'rule of law' entails in a post-conflict setting.

II   WHAT 'RULE OF LAW' ENTAILS IN A POST-CONFLICT SETTING

To most laypersons, UN peacekeeping has very little to do with anything other than the act of separating warring armies. Indeed, during the first forty years or so of UN peacekeeping, from 1948 to 1988, this first generation of UN peacekeeping operations was largely restricted (with the notable exception of the Congo in the early 1960s) to the interposition of unarmed military observers and lightly armed military contingents between the armies of warring

---

[†] The views expressed in this paper do not necessarily reflect the views held by the author in her official capacity.

Jessica Howard & Bruce Oswald (eds), *The Rule of Law on Peace Operations* (2002).

states to monitor adherence to ceasefire agreements. The mere presence of these 'traditional' peacekeeping operations raised the political cost of one or more of those armies violating the agreement and thus helped to prolong a ceasefire to give more time and space for diplomatic efforts to be pursued to address the underlying causes of the conflict.

As you all know, however, the end of the Cold War ushered in a new generation of multidimensional UN peacekeeping operations. The presence of peacekeepers was no longer just largely symbolic or restricted to an 'eyes and ears' role on the ground, as they were also asked to assist in and guide the implementation of comprehensive peace agreements that brought protracted civil wars to an end, in such places as Namibia, El Salvador, Cambodia and Mozambique. In those operations, peacekeepers were no longer only military personnel. They were joined by civilian police officers in the thousands, working to monitor, train and restructure local police forces, as well as civilians serving as human rights monitors, election experts helping to supervise and organise elections for new peacetime governments, and humanitarian workers, to name but a few.

The fact that some of these initial multidimensional peacekeeping operations of the late 1980s and early 1990s were relatively successful perhaps gave rise to false expectations that somehow UN peacekeeping could be a panacea for most of the world's conflicts – and, as a result, peacekeepers were also deployed to places like Somalia and the Former Yugoslavia, where no peace agreements or even durable ceasefire agreements were in place and where there was no real consent for the peacekeepers' presence. Perhaps those initial multidimensional operations also gave the misleading impression that the UN had found the 'right model' for addressing the rule of law aspects of post-conflict transition, by focusing on two main tasks: one, creating a secure environment in which elections can be held; and, two, diminishing the incidence of gross abuses of human rights and/or acts of politically or ethnically motivated violence.

Now, a decade later, with the benefit of experience and hindsight, we realise that the accomplishment of just those two tasks alone requires more than the deployment of international civilian police, human rights monitors and/or electoral experts. We have also learned – in some cases the hard way – that the accomplishment of those tasks is just the 'tip of the iceberg' when it comes to addressing the multiplicity of rule of law requirements in a post-conflict setting.

In a post-conflict setting, for even a semblance of rule of law to prevail, there is an obvious need to restore security in a country or region devastated by war, where violent crime, particularly politically or ethnically motivated violence, as well as organised crime, including trafficking in drugs and in human beings, often run rampant. An essential element for the restoration of security and public order – although certainly not the only one – is a functioning criminal justice system. The police, however, are just one part of the criminal justice system, which also includes the judicial and the penal systems. Each of these constituent parts not only needs to be impartial and free of political control, but also requires, in order to function properly, well-trained personnel, the necessary infrastructure, material and equipment, and, of course, the legal framework from which to be guided. That framework must also be able to deal effectively with the unique needs and special circumstances of vulnerable groups who are often the victims of violent crimes, such as women and children. Likewise, that framework should include adequate mechanisms, as part of a juvenile justice system, to deal with instances in which children themselves are the perpetrators of crimes, including those committed when they have been forcibly recruited by armed groups.

While crimes committed after a 'peace' has been reached present one significant challenge for a peace operation, another daunting challenge is dealing with those committed during the war, including genocide, crimes against humanity and other gross violations of human rights – the prosecution and trial of which will undoubtedly have an effect on the peace and reconciliation process. This brings into the fore dilemmas concerning, on the one hand, amnesty to promote peace, and, on the other, the use of tribunals to ensure that peace does not come at the expense of justice – and, in both instances, the challenge of achieving reconciliation. These competing concerns were recently raised by President Xanana Gusmao, on the occasion of the admission of the Democratic Republic of Timor Leste to the UN on 27 September, as he explained:

> We have adopted a policy of reconciliation between all Timorese; reconciliation that will be based on justice. Notwithstanding, to honour justice, our effort is focused on the eradication of all sentiments of hatred and revenge, because a sound reconciliation will only exist when there is a greater social justice in the Timorese society.

The establishment of a functioning criminal justice system, moreover, is only one aspect of the requirements that need to be met for the promotion of rule of law on a broader level. For example, a common feature of post-conflict settings is the need to facilitate the return of traumatised refugees and displaced persons – sometimes in the thousands – to their homes of origin, which is often impeded not only by security concerns but also by disputes over property rights and the destruction of key documentation. There is also the need to reconcile legal concerns of children who have been orphaned and women who have been widowed or whose husbands are missing. And there are issues of citizenship and statelessness as well.

Furthermore, many countries emerging from war often have to rethink and entirely reconstruct the very type of state that they feel will most effectively deliver their national aspirations and reconcile national differences. The challenge of drafting or amending a constitution, determining an electoral system, or re-establishing a process by which critical legislation can be

130   *Rule of Law Strategies for Peace Operations*

promulgated, are all rule of law issues that lie at the core of the transition from war to peace.

I have mentioned only a few of the many rule of law-related issues and related competencies that need to be considered in developing comprehensive rule of law strategies for peace operations. These issues, in fact, have been a priority concern for the Under-Secretary-General for Peacekeeping, Mr. Jean-Marie Guéhenno. Indeed, in March of this year, he turned to the Secretary-General's Executive Committee on Peace and Security – comprised of the heads of UN departments and agencies – to propose the establishment of a Task Force for Development of Comprehensive Rule of Law Strategies for Peace Operations. That proposal was warmly adopted, a Task Force quickly constituted, its Final Report fully endorsed by the Executive Committee, and the General Assembly's Fourth Committee was briefed on it by the Under-Secretary-General on 18 October. In that briefing, the Under-Secretary-General identified the development of comprehensive rule of law strategies in the peacekeeping context as one of six outstanding issues related to previous recommendations of the General Assembly's Special Committee on Peacekeeping Operations and the *Brahimi Report* that warranted particular attention – as well as enhanced dialogue – on the part of the Secretariat and Member States in the upcoming year.

Now, before examining what this Task Force specifically addressed and ultimately recommended, it is important to share some background on what prompted this effort to better coordinate and strategise on rule of law issues arising in peace operations. Then I will turn to some of the larger issues raised and some of the major challenges ahead.

III   GENESIS, OBJECTIVES AND RECOMMENDATIONS OF THE TASK FORCE

The *Brahimi Report* issued in August 2000 drew heightened attention to the problems faced by our peace operations in the rule of law area. This was by no means surprising given that the Report was issued just a few months after the security situation had deteriorated throughout Sierra Leone, placing the UN mission (UNAMSIL) in crisis, and about one year after the UN had launched transitional administration missions in Kosovo (UNMIK) and in East Timor (UNTAET) with unprecedented responsibilities and often unpredictable challenges. In those two transitional administration missions, we were then struggling not only with helping build the nucleus of a local police service, but also with the even more difficult tasks of helping establish judicial and penal systems virtually from scratch – compounded by the fact that much of the pre-existing physical infrastructure had been destroyed. To even begin to make progress in tackling these enormous tasks, we had to first overcome such basic problems as determining the applicable law and obtaining translated texts; converting dilapidated buildings into facilities needed to begin screening and training police candidates; erecting makeshift courtrooms and detention centres, while reconstructing courthouses and prisons that had been destroyed, looted or even mined; identifying qualified candidates to serve as local judges and prosecutors and, once selected, trying to convince them to take on sensitive cases despite threats to their security; obtaining basic furniture, equipment and supplies so that judges and lawyers could discharge their much-needed functions, given that court equipment, furniture, registers, records and archives as well as law books and case files had been dislocated or burned; finding sufficient numbers of trained interpreters, translators and court reporters so that judicial proceedings could be conducted in three to four required languages; and, of course, searching for suitable international judges and prosecutors who would be willing to join the ranks of the local judiciary under such circumstances, and would later have to spend enormous time familiarising themselves with the local legal systems.

To illustrate just one of these difficulties, I would recount when, as Chief of Staff to the Special Representative of the Secretary-General (SRSG) in Kosovo (then Mr. Bernard Kouchner), I had been asked on a Thursday in early 2000 to arrange for interpreters and translators for a sensitive trial to be held in Mitrovica the following Monday involving war crimes charges against a Kosovo Serb for the alleged murder of Kosovo Albanians. After being told by the international Chief of the Language Unit that none of his local staff were willing to serve, I chaired an emergency meeting with all of them to convey the urgency of the need. However, in probing each, I heard a litany of reasons that were difficult to dismiss. Some feared having their faces exposed in such a trial; others feared travelling by car across the Ibar River bridge to the courthouse in Serb-dominated northern Mitrovica; still others feared somehow being associated with the defence of a Serb war crimes suspect. Ultimately, I had to turn to the UNHCR Office in Tirana, Albania to urgently loan one of their local staff, a law student, for that trial.

These situations and problems were well understood by the Brahimi Panel, which had witnessed them firsthand during visits to these mission areas. It is against this backdrop that the Panel recommended a shift in the use of civilian police, other rule of law elements and human rights experts in peace operations in order to reflect an increased focus on strengthening rule of law institutions and improving respect for human rights in post-conflict environments. The Panel also stressed the need for an 'adequately-resourced team approach' to upholding the rule of law and respect for human rights, through policing, judicial, penal, and human rights experts working together in a coordinated manner in those operations. In support of this 'team approach', the Panel recommended that arrangements be established for deploying 'rule of law teams', comprised of civilian police, judicial, penal and human rights specialists, and that 'on-call lists' of these specialists be part of the UN Standby Arrangements System. The Panel also recommended that a new unit be established in DPKO, staffed with criminal law experts, specifically for the purpose of providing advice to the Civilian Police Adviser's Office on those rule of law issues that are critical to the effective use of civilian police in peace operations.

In addressing the Panel's recommendations in his implementation report, the Secretary-General emphasised that there was a critical need for civilian police, human rights experts and related specialists to work more closely together in peace operations in order to achieve the Millenium Declaration's objective of strengthening the rule of law. The Secretary-General highlighted that police are but one part of the solution to strengthening local rule of law capacities, which may also be constrained by weaknesses in or the absence of an independent judiciary and penal system – as has been so vividly seen in our operations in Bosnia, Sierra Leone, Kosovo and East Timor (now independent Timor Leste). The Secretary-General also supported the recommendation to establish standby arrangements for the deployment of rule of law teams to peace operations but indicated that, in order to assist Member States in implementing this recommendation, further work needed to be undertaken on the broader issues related to the rule of law in peace operations. He explained that he had therefore requested DPKO to work with the Office of Legal Affairs, the Office of the High Commissioner for Human Rights (OHCHR) and the United Nations Development Programme (UNDP) to draft guidelines covering the principles and practices of the rule of law sector of peace operations which, he emphasised, should build on the considerable amount of work already undertaken within the UN system as well as lessons learned in the field.

As you know, the Secretary-General also endorsed the recommendation for a new unit with criminal law expertise to be established in DPKO. In explaining why such a unit was needed, the Secretary-General stressed that any concept of deployment for UN civilian police should be developed with the full knowledge of the entire criminal law system of the country concerned. In very straightforward terms, he stated:

> Every police force in the world has the benefit of legal advice during the conduct of its work. The United Nations should not be any different. When the Civilian Police Adviser is asked to propose a concept of operations for the civilian police component of a new mission, (s)he should have the benefit of counsel on the type of judicial system in place, the interrelation between the police and the judiciary in a particular country and the nature of criminal procedures and laws in effect. If the civilian police component is mandated to restructure a local police force, then it is imperative that such restructuring be done with some cognizance of the entire criminal justice system in the country concerned. Before civilian police deploy to a country, they should be properly trained in the applicable criminal and judicial system, so that they have credibility with their local counterparts.[1]

When initially presenting the terms of reference for the establishment of a Criminal Law and Judicial Advisory Unit in October 2000, the Secretary-General proposed that it consist of six staff with judicial and penal expertise,

---

[1] *Report of the Secretary-General on the Implementation of the Report of the Panel on United Nations Peace Operations*, UN Doc A/55/502, 20 October 2000, para 127.

including a director-level Chief, and report directly to an Assistant Secretary-General. He emphasised that this Unit would primarily be of an operational nature and, to avoid duplication, would rely on UN partners engaged in capacity building programmes to strengthen rule of law institutions, such as OHCHR and UNDP, to provide the necessary advice and support to peace operations. However, the proposed Unit became the subject of rather protracted debate within the General Assembly's Special Committee on Peacekeeping Operations and the legislative budgetary bodies, which raised such fundamental issues as what the precise role of a peacekeeping operation should be in this area and whether the peacekeeping support account budget should finance what some considered to be 'peace building' rather than peacekeeping activities. Taking account of these concerns, the Secretary-General subsequently proposed a smaller, three-person Unit as part of the Civilian Police Division, although the General Assembly ultimately approved, in February 2002, a staff of only one Judicial Officer and one Corrections Officer.

Given the legislative mandate of the new Criminal Law and Judicial Advisory Unit (CLJAU) and its resource limitations as configured, DPKO then faced a major challenge: how would it forge an integrated and coordinated team approach to upholding the rule of law and respect for human rights in peace operations, and how would it mobilise the necessary expert advice and resources to achieve that goal? And, in seeking to do so, how would it apply lessons learned and best practices in this process? To tackle these challenges, the Under-Secretary-General for Peacekeeping presented a proposal to the Executive Committee on Peace and Security – which it endorsed on 1 April – to set up a Task Force, comprised of 11 UN departments and agencies, to address four major issues:

1. What existing expertise and resources among *UN departments and agencies* in the criminal law, judicial and penal areas can be made available to assist the CLJAU in providing advice and support to peace operations on rule of law issues;

2. Whether, in view of the UN expertise available, there is a need to identify *entities outside the UN system* which can provide such expertise to the CLJAU and peace operations, particularly among governmental, intergovernmental and non-governmental organisations;

3. What are the most appropriate arrangements for UN partners (and external partners as required) to assist the CLJAU in providing the necessary support to peace operations on rule of law issues; and

4. What further action is needed to draft any additional guidelines to cover the principles and practices of the rule of law sector of peace operations, taking account of work already undertaken and lessons learned in the field.

After working intensively for three months, the Task Force submitted its Final Report in mid August, which the Executive Committee fully endorsed on 30 September. It is the view of DPKO, one widely shared, that not only do the recommendations provide a viable framework for making system-wide progress in this critical area, but the Report itself serves as a depository of valuable information on available rule of law capacities both inside and outside of the UN system. So let me now share some of those recommendations and the vision for moving ahead.

A   Available Rule of Law Expertise among UN Partners and Gaps

At the outset, the Task Force – of which I was a member – grappled with one major substantive issue: what was the exact scope of the term 'rule of law' for purposes of its review? Although the terms of reference required the Task Force to identify expertise and resources among UN partners in the 'criminal law, judicial and penal areas' which could be made available to support the CLJAU and peace operations, the members felt that the scope of review should be expanded to a number of *related* areas that can and do affect the rule of law in most post-conflict situations, such as property disputes, citizenship and statelessness, birth registration, amnesty provisions, customary justice mechanisms and reconciliation efforts. The significant impact of such issues on the overall law and order environment can be witnessed in almost any peace operation theatre: the devastating predicament of a returnee family who, after months of living in refugee camps abroad, finds their house occupied but has no papers to prove ownership; the unemployed mother whose husband is missing and has no birth certificates for her children to claim entitlements because they were seized and burned; and the pressures placed on victims of rape and domestic violence to not pursue any formal redress in the courts but to deal with such matters in more 'traditional' ways to avoid embarrassing the family.

With this broader perspective, the Task Force members decided to focus primarily on identifying the specific competencies and resources of their respective departments and agencies in the 'criminal law, judicial and penal' areas, but also to identify competencies and resources in a second set of 'related' areas that often directly affect those three priority areas. They further agreed to identify the prior experience of their departments and agencies in providing rule of law support to peace operations. The result of this extensive 'stock-taking exercise' was the compilation of a single document providing an overview of available rule of law expertise and relevant experience within the UN system in both the priority and related areas – yielding a valuable reference source for the CLJAU and all UN partners. To obtain a more complete picture, the Task Force also identified, in a separate document, the 'gaps' in UN capacity in key rule of law areas. This process revealed, as the Task Force pointed out, that the available UN expertise in various rule of law areas is not of equal strength: in some areas, there is significant overlap in expertise – so coordination to avoid duplication is essential – while, in others, the expertise is thin or non-existent. To cite but a few of these gaps, the Task Force found that the UN system lacks expertise in undertaking assessments of judicial and penal systems; in providing or developing practical training for judges, prosecutors and prison officials in various areas; in conducting, or providing training in, forensics investigations and advanced investigative techniques essential to modern police work; and assisting in the development of ombudsperson institutions and in building the capacity of traditional justice systems.

The Task Force therefore concluded that the UN should explore how relevant external entities – particularly among governmental, intergovernmental and non-governmental organisations – might provide the required expertise to help fill these gaps and weaknesses. Its members then canvassed their colleagues to identify reliable, experienced external entities using two criteria: first, that their department/agency had previously worked with that entity on rule of law-related issues and, second, that the entity operated internationally. Based on that information, the Task Force prepared a preliminary compilation of relevant external entities with expertise and resources in the priority and related rule of law areas. However, in recognising that such a preliminary listing of entities reflects only a portion of the substantial rule of law expertise that exists outside the UN system, the Task Force recommended that it be augmented and regularly updated, with the assistance of Member States, so as to extend the outreach to a broader geographical range.

Now let me turn to the Task Force's recommendations on appropriate support arrangements to be established for UN partners as well as external entities to assist the CLJAU, starting with our internal partners.

*B   Recommended Support Arrangements to be established with Relevant
     UN Partners*

Throughout its deliberations, the Task Force focused on the need to formulate a more *coordinated approach* in tackling rule of law issues in peace operations, as no single department or agency had the required expertise, experience, resources or mandate to identify and handle all such issues. The Task Force stressed, however, that this coordination would not happen spontaneously, and would require not only a team effort by various UN partners but also enhanced planning and a structured approach. The Task Force pointed out that the two-person CLJAU should be the *catalyst of coordination efforts*, but that it alone could not possibly develop comprehensive rule of law strategies for peace operations. After considering various options for establishing support arrangements between the CLJAU and UN partners, the Task Force proposed a three-pronged approach that largely builds on existing institutional arrangements.

1st: The Task Force proposed the **designation of 'Rule of Law Focal Points'** by each of the 11 departments and agencies represented, who would ensure that they respond, to the fullest extent possible, to specific requests from the CLJAU and lead department for advice and support on rule of law issues. The CLJAU would also be able to 'mobilise' this network of focal points, when needed, to address broader rule of law-related issues arising within peace operations.

2nd: The Task Force recommended the **implementation of a 'Coordination Framework for Addressing Rule of Law-Related Issues Linked to the Planning for and Deployment of a Peace Operation'**, which would apply whenever a new operation is being launched or when an existing operation's mandate is being renewed or modified. This Coordination Framework outlines a process through which the lead department and other relevant UN departments/agencies will systematically address rule of law issues at each critical stage of the planning and deployment of an operation when appropriate in view of its mandate: starting with mission planning within an Integrated Mission Task Force (another outgrowth of the Brahimi Report), to in-theatre assessments, to formulation of a mission's concept of operations and mandate, to preparation of the mission's budget, to recruitment of staff and, finally, to support for the operation of rule of law-related offices within a mission once deployed. Under this Framework, a 'Rule of Law Working Group' – comprised of representatives of the CLJAU and other UN partners concerned – would be established for individual operations, either as part of an Integrated Mission Task Force or under the lead department if no Task Force is formed, to assist in developing a comprehensive rule of law strategy for each operation. The Framework also recognises that local experts are indispensable to the success of implementing a coherent rule of law strategy, as it calls for the UN to consult such experts early in the mission planning process as well as in all subsequent phases.

3rd: The Task Force proposed the **establishment of support arrangements between DPKO's Personnel Management and Support Service and relevant UN departments and agencies for the recruitment and rapid deployment of rule of law specialists** for peace operations, including for assessment teams. The Task Force presented four possible support arrangements that could be implemented, ranging from the sharing of rosters of rule of law specialists – which DPKO is particularly eager to pursue – to providing vacancy announcements for specific rule of law-related posts in particular operations.

As was apparent in the early days of our deployment in Kosovo and East Timor, the UN lacked a clear strategy on how to approach the panoply of rule of law-related issues that we faced, including on how best to establish functioning judicial and penal systems in parallel – and at a commensurate pace – with building a local police service. The SRSG of UNMIBH, Mr. Jacques Klein, described this predicament in Bosnia, in May of this year, as follows:

> The legacy of UNMIBH when it completes its core mandate in December is that police reform will be much more advanced than other rule of law

initiatives. The UNMIBH mandate focuses on the improvement of the local police, while the Office of the High Representative and other international community actors are primarily responsible for judicial reform and related rule of law initiatives. Upon conclusion of the UNMIBH mandate, the mission will have succeeded in establishing local police forces that meet all the basic international standards. However, the local police remain constrained by the weaknesses and inadequacies of the judicial system ...

DPKO is optimistic that the Coordination Framework – under which it has a central coordinating role as a 'lead department' – will now provide an effective mechanism for ensuring that such rule of law-related issues in a peace operation are addressed in a systematic, comprehensive and timely way. With this early collaboration with UN and external partners as well as relevant local actors, we will reduce the risk of rule of law issues being dealt with in an ad hoc or fragmented manner – and often too late in the process to make real headway.

We are also hopeful that, with the support arrangements for the recruitment of rule of law specialists, we will be able to show how the UN system can pool its energies to achieve quicker deployment of such high-quality experts. We should never again have to encounter the crises that plagued UNMIK and UNTAET in recruiting sufficient numbers of judicial officers and corrections officers as well as international judges and prosecutors, which further contributed to delays in implementing much-needed judicial and penal programmes and the processing of serious crimes cases. In Kosovo, these recruitment problems were compounded by the fact that the initial operational plan and budget for UNMIK did not include posts for international judges and prosecutors – or for the interpreters, support staff and close protection personnel they would need – which meant that, when the decision was made in January 2000 to utilise them, we then had to seek exceptional funding arrangements pending the General Assembly's approval of such posts. I can tell you that it was not easy to find a suitable candidate willing to serve as the first international judge to hear sensitive cases in Mitrovica that January. I still remember sitting in my office in Pristina trying, for hours, to convince a judge who was then working in the Department of Judicial Affairs why it was worthwhile to accept the function for a trial scheduled 10 days from then, even though the conditions were certainly not optimal: he would have to live in the French military barracks for security purposes; he would have to be accompanied by close protection officers 24-hours a day; the case files had not yet been translated; we were still trying to identify qualified translators and interpreters for the trial; and he would have to rely on an UNMIK secretary as a court reporter.

C   Recommended Support Arrangements to be established with External Entities

As I have mentioned, the Task Force recognised the need to tap into the expertise of experienced external entities in order to supplement the UN's rule of law capacities, which are limited or non-existent in certain areas. In assessing the most appropriate arrangements for external entities to provide such rule of law-related support to the Civilian Police Division and peace operations, the Task Force concluded that no single option could be prescribed for all situations. It recommended that <u>at least four options be considered,</u> subject, of course, to legal review to ensure compliance with UN rules and procedures.

1st: The Task Force proposed that an **exchange of letters** could be concluded between DPKO and an external entity, setting out the nature of the rule of law-related assistance to be provided in a particular peace operation and the applicable terms and conditions.

2nd: The Task Force recommended that the Under-Secretary-General for Peacekeeping consider proposing, after consulting with Member States, the establishment of a '**UN Rule of Law Standby Arrangements Initiative**' and related database, which would include Member States and external entities that are prepared, in principle, to render rule of law-related assistance to the CLJAU and peace operations.

3rd: The Task Force proposed the establishment of **support arrangements** between DPKO and relevant external entities **for the recruitment and rapid deployment of rule of law specialists** for peace operations, including for assessment teams. The Task Force considered that four practical options, similar to those proposed for UN partners, could be implemented with such entities.

4th: In noting that rule of law initiatives in peace operations are often hampered by the host country's lack of sufficient human and financial resources to strengthen its basic rule of law institutions, the Task Force proposed that DPKO and the Department of Political Affairs (DPA), in consultation with the Controller's Office, spearhead a '**Rule of Law Support Initiative**'. This Initiative would offer two mechanisms – a '**Rule of Law Trust Fund**' and '**Partnership Arrangements**' – for Member States and external entities to provide voluntary funds and resources to 'jumpstart' the development of these critical institutions. Under the proposed Partnership Arrangements, it is envisaged that DPKO or DPA – as the lead department – and the peace operation concerned would consult with the host country on its priority rule of law requirements. Once identified, they would then approach Member States and relevant external entities which might be willing to enter into partnership with that government to provide human or financial resources to strengthen a particular rule of law institution – such as through the refurbishment of courts, the development of police and judicial training programmes, or, for that matter, the provision of such basics as office equipment and legal reference materials for judges and prosecutors. I will never forget how shocked and rather embarrassed I was during my first visit to the districts in East Timor in August 2001, when nearly every single judge and prosecutor we met, when asked what assistance they most needed, requested such fundamental things as law books and translated copies of the regulations which UNTAET had promulgated.

In proposing these various modalities to reach out to external entities, the Task Force also recognised that many UN departments and agencies – particularly those which are field-based such as UNHCR and UNICEF – have had longstanding relationships with many of these entities. They emphasised that this existing web of relationships should be viewed as a very useful framework to be capitalised on rather than needlessly duplicated. The overriding objective, they indicated, should now be for the UN to approach outside entities in a more focused and manageable manner on rule of law issues, which should lead to better results and a more efficient use of resources for all concerned.

The Department of Peacekeeping Operations fully supports the Task Force's conclusion that it is time to extend our outreach to experienced external entities – from a broad geographical range – which might be able to provide much-needed rule of law expertise to fill some of the UN system's gaps and weaknesses. As the Task Force noted, this outreach offers a compelling example of an area in which we can give flesh to the Secretary-General's reform vision to promote partnerships between civil society and the Organisation to better respond to some of today's complex challenges. To offer just one example of how this type of outreach produced positive results in one of our peace operations, I would recall the assessment mission undertaken to East Timor in December 2001 by a team of lawyers and judges from the International Legal Assistance Consortium (ILAC) – a Sweden-based non-profit organisation comprised of bar associations and councils from over 150 countries. Following intensive discussions over the course of one week with East Timorese and international UNTAET managers sitting together, which regretfully had not frequently happened in the past, the ILAC team reached a consensus with the then Second Transitional Government and UNTAET on potential assistance to be provided in five priority legal and judicial areas. This instance of outreach was truly the product of collaboration with relevant local actors, as every aspect of the assessment team visit was arranged and undertaken in close consultation with both East Timor's Chief Minister and the Justice Minister. In fact, the Justice Minister, Ms. Ana Pessoa, established the criteria for and cleared the selection of the ILAC team members; identified the legal/judicial areas to be examined by the team; led most of the discussions with the team; and agreed on the potential types of assistance needed in each priority area. The outcome of this outreach was not only the submission of the team's written assessment and recommendations, but also ILAC's follow-up assistance to the government – ranging from the submission of candidates to serve as international judges and prosecutors to the identification of donors to fund the establishment of a legal defence centre.

The Under-Secretary-General for Peacekeeping also looks forward to consulting with Member States on the recommended launching of a Rule of Law Support Initiative. The establishment of Partnership Arrangements and a Rule of Law Trust Fund could serve as practical mechanisms for Member States and external entities to provide – in a hopefully more coordinated and timely manner – voluntary resources to help strengthen critical rule of law institutions of host countries. As can be vividly seen in a number of peace operation theatres, including in Bosnia, East Timor and Sierra Leone, the host country often lacks adequate funding to strengthen core rule of law institutions and, consequently, progress in strengthening local police forces is rarely matched by progress in strengthening judicial and penal institutions. To illustrate the myriad of problems that can be encountered on this front, let me refer to the stark views of the Chairman of the Sierra Leone Bar Association, Mr. J.B. Jenkins-Johnston, when addressing the Conference on 'Creating an Enabling Environment for the Consolidation of the Rule of Law' in February 2001:

> ... [I]t is my view that before we can talk meaningfully about consolidating the rule of law, the machinery and system by which justice is administered must be completely overhauled as it is now in disarray. Thus far I have not addressed the fact that we do not have enough judges and magistrates; that there is no High Court sitting outside Freetown; that several prisoners are forgotten on remand and many die in prison; that the Under Sheriff's Office which has the responsibility to serve process and to enforce judgments of all the courts is a den of inequity and corruption and needs to be totally reformed and re-orientated. Bailiffs need to receive proper training, uniforms, identification, vehicles, storage space and police protection at all times so that the public will take them seriously. Furthermore, I have not thus far addressed the sad fact that law reports have not been published in Sierra Leone since 1973. All the judgments delivered in all our courts since 1973 are gathering dust somewhere, lost to the development of case law in Sierra Leone forever. Indeed there is a lot to talk about ...

By liaising early with host country authorities on their rule of law-related needs (which, in post-conflict settings, are invariably numerous), peace operations could assist in identifying the priority requirements for rule of law institutions that could most benefit from such partnership support and trust fund financing. Through such Partnership Arrangements, the host country obviously benefits as the recipient, but the donor partner also benefits from assisting the government in a very tangible and identifiable way. As an encouraging precedent, one can look to the positive results achieved by the partnership support offered in UNMIK through the OSCE-sponsored 'Assembly Support Initiative', a multi-agency program supporting the Assembly of Kosovo elected in November 2001. This Initiative, the members of which include organisations and institutes from a number of countries, seeks to support and strengthen the Assembly by, among other things, arranging working visits to parliaments of other countries; holding conferences, seminars and workshops with Assembly members; and providing training for the Assembly's legislative staff and interpreters as well as infrastructure support. And I would also mention the 'sister city' arrangement forged by an UNMIK Regional Administrator between the city in Sweden where he had worked and the war-ravaged town of Prizren. This resulted in funding and assistance on a number of projects, including, within only weeks, the introduction of a modern traffic plan and road signs that not only gave a noticeable 'facelift' to the town but an encouraging sense of a gradual return to a more normal life.

I would now like to briefly discuss the last set of the Task Force's recommendations on rule of law-related guidelines.

D   *Recommendations on Rule of Law-Related Guidelines Needed for Peace Operations*

After canvassing the 11 departments and agencies represented, including their field presences, the Task Force identified a *broad range* of existing rule of law-related guidelines, manuals and training modules that deal with various aspects of rule of law activities in peace operations in the priority criminal law, judicial and penal areas as well as in the other related areas. As reflected by the bibliography compiled, the Task Force found that the rule of law areas in which there are no such guidelines developed or endorsed by the UN largely correspond to the gaps in internal competency areas. The Task Force also noted that DPKO is preparing a 'Handbook on Multi-Dimensional Peacekeeping', which will include guidance on civilian police, judicial and corrections programs in the context of UN peace operations. Given the extent of existing guidelines, as well as DPKO's forthcoming Handbook, the Task Force recommended that no further action be undertaken at this stage for developing *general guidelines* for rule of law activities in peace operations, but suggested that the issue be revisited in the future.

The Task Force recognised, however, that the lead department may sometimes have an operational need for *guidelines to be developed for a particular rule of law area* and recommended that, in such instances, assistance be sought from relevant departments or agencies and, if needed, from external entities. In this connection, I would refer to a recent example where an NGO and experts from a broad range of Member States collectively worked to help fill a gap in the corrections area where no comprehensive UN guidelines had been produced, as we discovered so quickly in our operations in Kosovo and East Timor. The International Corrections and Prisons Association (ICPA) – a Canada-based organisation with 400 members from 65 countries – recently produced 'Practical Guidelines for the Establishment of Correctional Services within United Nations Peace Operations' with the participation of corrections and peacekeeping experts from around the globe, including from the UN.

142   *Rule of Law Strategies for Peace Operations*

E   Involvement of Local Actors

Finally, let me turn to the one area that the Task Force focused on that transcends any one specific issue set out in its terms of reference – and that is the need to *meaningfully involve* local actors in formulating and carrying out rule of law initiatives in peace operations, rather than imposing a rule of law strategy on them. Let me not try to paraphrase the Task Force's strong views on this, but instead read a passage from their report:

> ... [T]he Task Force wishes to emphasize that the UN should make it a high priority to engage local actors (eg government officials, local NGOs and community organizations) in a meaningful way in undertaking rule of law initiatives in peace operations. Local experts on the judiciary, police, corrections system, criminal law – as well as on such issues as property disputes, amnesty provisions and traditional justice – are precious assets and indispensable to the success of implementing a coherent rule of law strategy. The UN should consult with such experts as early as possible in the mission planning process as well as in all subsequent phases. For example, local experts should participate in any review of local laws; local lawyers and police should be trained as trainers for judicial or police training projects and help design the curricula; and civil society leaders should be consulted on what the priority rule of law issues are from their perspective as potential 'beneficiaries' of a fair and impartial justice system and a rights-respecting police force. Simply put, the goal of all UN personnel working in the rule of law area should be to reinforce the capacities of, and not replace, local actors whenever possible...

IV   THE IMPORTANCE OF WIDE PARTNERSHIP AND NATIONAL OWNERSHIP: CHALLENGES AHEAD

Now, in reflecting on this broad-reaching set of recommendations put forth by the Task Force, I think that one recurring message emerges very clearly: While the nature of a rule of law strategy for a specific peace operation will largely depend on its mandate and the prevailing circumstances, real progress in formulating and implementing that strategy can <u>only be achieved if the lead department is able to rely on the full support of partners within the UN system, Member States, relevant external entities and, perhaps most importantly, the crucial local actors from those war-stricken theatres</u>. At the same time, I should stress that, in undertaking this initiative, the members of the Task Force – and the departments and agencies they represent – fully appreciated that the UN system is not, nor should be, the main actor in developing a *national* rule of law strategy for a country emerging from conflict. Nor should bilateral donors or international NGOs, for that matter.

Simply put, the primary responsibility for developing a comprehensive rule of law strategy for a country emerging from conflict, as well as the responsibility for its long-term implementation, ultimately rests with the men and women of the country concerned. It is they who need to craft and live with the system of rule of law that will regulate the behaviour of their citizens as well as safeguard their interests and freedoms. It is they who will have to determine what system of law is best suited to their local culture, traditions and norms. It is they who, when a UN operation closes, will continue to steer the rule of law process and operate the police stations, the courts and the prisons, often with limited resources and funding. And it is they who have the most at stake, particularly given that the role played by the rule of law in a society has a tremendously formative influence on shaping a national identity as a whole. The fundamental stake that the people of a country have in the rule of law process is perhaps best captured by the moving words of President Gusmao when closing his address before the General Assembly in September:

> The international community, politicians and academics often mention our country 'as a UN success story'…. At the core of this success, were, above all, our People. By rejecting to embark on the path of violence, even when provoked, by exercising their rights in a democratic and civic manner, even if it meant risking their own lives, by looking towards the future hoping for the certainty of freedom, our people proved to the world to be worthy of the respect that we all owe and know, and thus gain the credibility and admiration of all.

While promoting national ownership and capacity building is one of the most important goals of international involvement in undertaking rule of law initiatives in a post-conflict environment, I must admit that our experience shows that it is easier said than done in the peacekeeping context. I need only recall that Sunday in early August 1999 in Kosovo when SRSG Bernard Kouchner held an emergency meeting to address the large group of newly-appointed Kosovo Albanian judges and prosecutors who had submitted a resignation letter that previous Friday because they had not been consulted prior to his signing the first regulation on 25 July 1999, which set out the applicable law. That Regulation[2] provided, among other things, that the laws that had been applied in the territory prior to the adoption of Security Council resolution 1244 would apply, *mutatis mutandis*, insofar as they conformed with internationally recognised human rights standards and did not conflict with the mission's mandate or any regulations promulgated by the mission. Had it not been for Mr. Kouchner's outright apology for not consulting on such an important issue and his pledge to establish a mechanism for future consultation on all proposed regulations, as well as the eventual issuance on 12 December of Regulation 1999/24 which provided that the law in force in Kosovo on March 22, 1989 (ie before the revocation of its autonomy status within Serbia) would serve as the applicable law for the duration of the UN administration, we would have undoubtedly faced a prolonged standstill on the judicial – and perhaps also the political – front.

---

[2] Regulation No 1999/1.

Hopefully, we will get closer to achieving the goal of promoting national ownership and capacity building through implementation of the Task Force's recommendations, including the Coordination Framework – which allows us to address rule of law issues in the peacekeeping context in a more holistic and systematic way, at each critical stage in the planning and deployment of an operation, and in close consultation and partnership with other UN players, national actors and relevant external entities. Even with the implementation of the Task Force recommendations, however, the constraints of time itself will remain a major and perennial challenge. Valuable opportunities can be lost on the ground and confidence in the peace process can start to erode if the international community is unable to act in a timely manner – hence, the importance of forging partnerships and collaborating on an integrated rule of law strategy for a given peace operation early on in the process, and of sequencing and prioritising efforts in light of short and long-term objectives. For example, had we, at the very start in both Kosovo and East Timor, given urgent priority to planning for and obtaining sufficient resources for the provision of the necessary professional training and mentoring programmes and facilities for newly-appointed judges and prosecutors and for the immediate establishment of an adequate prison infrastructure, we would have obviously accelerated the development of operational judicial and correctional systems.

Given these considerations and variables, it is clear that, in planning a rule of law strategy for an operation, a fundamental challenge is to figure out what needs to be done urgently, in what order, and by whom – including during the critical initial days on the ground. The scope of the mandate is a pivotal factor in this regard, as sometimes the peace operation will carry a huge share of the burden, particularly where the Organisation has transitional administration responsibilities, as in the case of Kosovo or East Timor. We must remember, however, that those cases have been the exception and not the norm. In most cases, civilian administrative functions and legislative and executive powers are vested with a national authority, even if with an interim national administration, as in the case of Afghanistan. In most cases, the UN peacekeeping operation does not have executive law enforcement authority. And, in most cases, the UN is not the only major international actor on the ground. Nevertheless, in all cases, there has to be a recognition – by the UN peacekeeping operation and all other players involved – that the promotion of the rule of law must feature prominently throughout all stages of the peace process and that each must do its part. We recently heard this message forcefully conveyed by the SRSG in Bosnia, Mr. Klein, at DPKO's tenth anniversary celebration on 29 October, when he stated:

> ... We need to ask ourselves why BiH has now received more per capita assistance than Western Europe under the Marshall Plan, but still remains weak and unsustainable requiring several years more of intensive international attention?

The Rule of Law on Peace Operations 145

One reason is that we have failed to prioritize the priorities, particularly with respect to rule of law. I have no doubt that rule of law must be placed as the centerpiece of practically every peacekeeping mission. Without it, a credible exit strategy is inconceivable – international military forces cannot leave, the economy cannot recover, democracy remains a façade, and corruption and criminalization become entrenched.

V CONCLUDING REMARKS

I have mentioned but a few of the many challenges that lie ahead of us as we move forward with the Task Force's recommendations in seeking to strengthen rule of law in the context of our peace operations. That having been said, it would also seem fair to say that there are a few key ones that we have overcome as well, starting with the basic recognition of the following:

First, rule of law issues have not been given the attention that they deserve in the peacekeeping context.

Second, what is meant by the rule of law in the peacekeeping context, and the related scope of issues which need to be addressed to build a durable peace, is much broader than we had previously thought to be the case.

Third, DPKO must cast its net much wider, and forge its partnerships much deeper, with those both within and outside the UN system, in planning and implementing any rule of law strategy.

Fourth, whatever we do in the rule of law area must be done closely together with local actors, including civil society, so as to maximise national ownership and develop local capacity, in the interests of promoting a durable and self-sustaining peace.

I realise, however, that the path between the recognition of these basic premises and their application on the ground – so that we see real differences and concrete achievements in our field operations – is not necessarily a short or simple one. While the Executive Committee's full endorsement of the Task Force recommendations advances the UN system in a unified direction, we need to think collectively, with Member States, as well as local actors and external partners in forums like this, about how to make progress on all of these fronts. I thus genuinely look forward to taking your questions and getting your thoughts on these issues during the remainder of this session and in our group discussions.

Part II
The Constitutional Basis
of Peacekeeping

[3]

The Legal Basis of the United Nations Peace-Keeping Operations

ALEXANDER ORAKHELASHVILI*

TABLE OF CONTENTS

---

* LLM (Leiden); PhD Candidate, Jesus College, Cambridge.

486   VIRGINIA JOURNAL OF INTERNATIONAL LAW   [Vol. 43:485

I. INTRODUCTION

At the early stages of the United Nations' existence, it was already clear that the UN and its member states did not succeed in concluding agreements under Article 43 of the United Nations Charter, which would have provided for the delivery of military units to the United Nations for the enforcement of its decisions. This circumstance limited the UN's capability to a "narrow security role" in international conflicts. In general, the UN's use of enforcement powers has always been dependent on the consensus among the members of the Security Council. The peace-keeping operations have therefore been considered an alternative to the collective security.[1] This factor is important in determining the legal basis of the peace-keeping operations. In the absence of the "Article 43 agreements," the UN must find a legal basis for every concrete peace-keeping operation. This task involves the interpretation of the UN Charter (Charter) in order to make it clear which organs of the UN are competent to establish the peace-keeping forces and which powers they may use in doing so.

Two principal elements of the legal basis of the peace-keeping operations are the competence of the relevant organs of the UN and the consent by the affected parties.[2] With respect to the peace-keeping operations that are based on consent given by parties, it may be questioned whether the issue of powers and functions of the principal organs is relevant at all. The parties to a conflict may negotiate—on a bilateral basis or under involvement of a third State—the establishment of a peace-keeping force with a view to maintain the peace and prevent the aggravation of a given conflict. The role of the principal organs may, in a formalistic sense, seem to be superfluous.[3] On the other hand, the United Nations, as well as

1. HILAIRE MCCOUBREY & NIGEL D. WHITE, THE BLUE HELMETS: LEGAL REGULATION OF UNITED NATIONS MILITARY OPERATIONS 2-3, 11-12 (1996); John F. Murphy, *Force and Arms, in* 1 UNITED NATIONS LEGAL ORDER 292 (Oscar Schachter & Christopher C. Joyner eds., 1995).

2. Michael Bothe, *Peace-Keeping, in* THE CHARTER OF THE UNITED NATIONS: A COMMENTARY 684, 692 (Bruno Simma ed., 2002).

3. Establishment of the ad hoc independent peace-keeping forces has been practiced without the mandate of international organizations, mainly in the conflicts of the Middle East and Indo-China. For an overview of such operations, see Henry Wiseman, *The United*

several regional organizations, consider the establishment of peace-keeping forces to be an integral element of their efforts to maintain peace and security. Moreover, the establishment of the peace-keeping forces under the auspices of the UN may involve an increased degree of legitimacy because the decision-making process within the UN is characterized by transparency and balance between the conflicting political interests. These factors similarly increase the likelihood of impartiality of the peace-keeping forces thus established. Also, in an institutional sense, the peace-keeping forces established by the United Nations are the subsidiary organs of this organization based on Articles 7, 22 and 29 of the Charter.

Peace-keeping forces are uniformly established by a resolution of a principal organ of the UN. In this context, the relevant organs are the Security Council, the General Assembly, and the Secretary-General. However, there is no consensus as to which power of which organ may serve as a basis for the establishment of peace-keeping operations. The International Court of Justice, which could clarify this issue by way of an *obiter dictum*, refuses to specify which articles of the UN Charter may serve as the basis of the peace-keeping operations.[4]

The Charter of the United Nations does not contain an express authorization for any principal organ to establish peace-keeping forces. Therefore, the relevance of any principal organ in establishing peace-keeping forces should be assessed in light of functions and powers entrusted to that organ under the Charter. As Finn Seyersted explained,

> even if it is determined that the Organization as a whole has the inherent power to establish and operate military forces with the consent of the Member States concerned, the organ making a decision to this effect can only do so within its field of competence as laid down in the Charter.[5]

This circumstance makes it necessary to examine the place of the peace-keeping operations in the context of powers and functions of the principal organs and, to a certain extent, of regional organizations.

It is conventional wisdom that the implied or inherent powers of international organizations may provide the basis for actions that are not expressly warranted under their constituent instruments. This

---

Nations and International Peacekeeping: A Comparative Analysis, in THE UNITED NATIONS AND THE MAINTENANCE OF INTERNATIONAL PEACE AND SECURITY 315-30 (United Nations Institute for Training and Research ed., 1987).

4. Certain Expenses of the United Nations, 1962 I.C.J. 151, 177 (Advisory Opinion of July 20) [hereinafter *Certain Expenses*].

5. FINN SEYERSTED, UNITED NATIONS FORCES IN THE LAW OF PEACE AND WAR 170 (1966).

488   VIRGINIA JOURNAL OF INTERNATIONAL LAW   [Vol. 43:485

concept is relevant to the peace-keeping operations, particularly since it has gained substantial support in doctrine[6] and in the jurisprudence of the International Court of Justice (ICJ).[7] It is not the purpose of this article to challenge the relevance of the implied powers doctrine. It is nevertheless submitted that although frequent references are made to the implied, inherent, and general powers of the principal organs as to a basis for the establishment of the peace-keeping operations, the provisions of the Charter relating to the maintenance of peace and security may provide more clear guidance than frequently inferred from its text by the commentators.

As Professor Suy has argued, a distinction should ˙be drawn between the distribution of powers between the principal organs relating to the establishment of the peace-keeping forces and the distribution of powers concerning the continuing authority over the operations already established.[8] This article will focus primarily on the authority to establish the peace-keeping forces because it is the core issue of the legal basis of the peace-keeping operations.

This article analyzes the legal bases for United Nations peace-keeping operations, arising from the UN Charter, and from general international law. Parts II-IV analyze the legal authority available to principal organs of the U.N. Part V evaluates the legal basis for the establishment of peace-keeping operations by regional organizations, instead of by the UN itself. Part VI focuses upon the relevance of consent of affected parties as a basis of peace-keeping operations. Finally, this article concludes by drawing conclusions about the legal bases for the establishment of peace-keeping operations under the UN Charter and general international law.

---

6. Seyersted notes that limiting the powers of international organisations to those enumerated in their constitutive instruments is not supported by the practice of intergovernmental organisations because they enact regulations, conclude treaties, exercise territorial jurisdiction, establish organs although the constitutive instruments do not specifically confer relevant powers on them. *Id.* at 144-50. Seyersted holds that it is a principle of well-established customary international law that the powers of an organisation are not confined to those enumerated in their constitutive instruments. *Id.* at 151

7. Reparation for Injuries Suffered in the Service of the United Nations, 1949 I.C.J. 174, 182, 184 (Advisory Opinion of Apr. 11); Effect of Awards of Compensation Made by the United Nations Administrative Tribunal, 1954 I.C.J. 47, 57 (Advisory Opinion of July 13); *Certain Expenses*, 1962 I.C.J. at 167-68; Legality of the Threat or Use of Nuclear Weapons, 1996 I.C.J. 226, 240 (Advisory Opinion of July 8); Difference Relating to Immunity From Legal Process of a Special Rapporteur of the Commission on Human Rights, 1999 I.C.J. 62, 82 (Advisory Opinion of April 29). For a skeptical approach, see the dissenting opinion by Judge Hackworth in the *Reparation* case, stating that "[p]owers not expressed cannot freely be implied" due to the delegated nature of the powers of the United Nations. 1949 I.C.J. at 198 (Advisory Opinion of Apr. 11) (Hackworth, J., dissenting).

8. Erik Suy, *Peace-Keeping Operations, in* A HANDBOOK OF INTERNATIONAL ORGANIZATIONS 545 (René-Jean Dupuy ed., 2d ed. 1998).

II. THE SECURITY COUNCIL

A. General Remarks

Since the Security Council (Council) is vested with the primary responsibility for the maintenance of international peace and security,[9] its role must be analyzed first. A natural difficulty, however, is that Chapters V, VI and VII of the Charter, which relate to the powers of the Security Council, contain no explicit basis for peace-keeping operations. The absence of clear authorization is important in an analysis of the role of the Council, whose Charter-based powers vary in their substance and legal force. Therefore, it may be assumed that the nature of peace-keeping operations and their role in furthering the purposes of the UN provide necessary guidance for determining the suitability of a particular power of the Council to establish peace-keeping forces.

On the basis of this assumption, it is possible to focus on the Security Council's specific powers. In order to assess their relevance in the present context. The various provisions of Chapters VI and VII sometimes are referred to as a legal basis of a particular peace-keeping operation. This is helpful, but sometimes may also be confusing. Therefore, the best approach is to examine the particular provisions of the Charter in light of the nature and function of the peace-keeping operations. Such an approach may help clarify whether, and to what extent, those provisions may serve as a legal basis of the peace-keeping operations.

In examining the Security Council's powers and its authority to establish peace-keeping forces, one must keep in mind that the Council's powers are discretionary in nature. Of course, the Council is limited by the purposes and principles of the United Nations,[10] but within those limits, this organ is empowered to act according to its discretion. The Council possesses wide discretion in assessing situations in which it is called upon to act. It may decide which measures would be necessary and effective in a given context. This context may involve not only the factual situations, but also the specific powers of the Council. Thus, the Council may decide which of its powers, as considered in conjunction with other powers and the factual circumstances, may be useful and necessary for performance of its primary responsibility in the area of peace and security. This general conclusion provides a necessary basis to understand the role of the Council's specific powers in the area of

---

9. U.N. CHARTER art. 24, para. 1.

10. U.N. CHARTER, art. 24, para. 2; Legal Consequences for States of the Continued Presence of South Africa in Namibia (South West Africa) notwithstanding Security Council Resolution 276 (1970), 1971 I.C.J. 3, 52 (Order of January 26).

490   VIRGINIA JOURNAL OF INTERNATIONAL LAW   [Vol. 43:485

the peace-keeping.

B. Powers Under the Charter

1. Chapter VI of the Charter

Since Chapter VI of the Charter deals with the procedures of the pacific settlement of disputes, certain authors believe that the provisions of this Chapter are unsuitable for the establishment of the peace-keeping forces. For example, Rosalyn Higgins has expressed discomfort with the proposition that the peace-keeping forces may be established on the basis of Chapter VI.[11] Further, according to Dan Ciobanu, it is impossible to find a constitutional basis for the peace-keeping operations in Chapter VI, because these operations may, to a certain extent, involve the use of force, which is in no way an element of the pacific settlement of disputes.[12]

However, under Chapter VI, the Council's powers deal not only with disputes in a strict sense, but also with situations that may endanger international peace and security.[13] According to Article 36(1) of the Charter, the Council may "recommend appropriate procedures or methods of adjustment" for such situations.[14] In *Certain Expenses*, the International Court of Justice described the United Nations Emergency Force (UNEF) in Egypt as an operation "to promote and to maintain a peaceful settlement of the situation."[15]

At first glance, it may seem unclear how a provision dealing with the adjustment of situations, as understood narrowly within the dispute settlement perspective, may provide a legal basis for peace-keeping operations, which do not fall within the category of methods of dispute settlement. The ICJ, however, has not interpreted the "appropriate procedures or methods of adjustment" of Article 36 so narrowly. The ICJ in *Certain Expenses* affirmed that Article 11(2) and Article 14 of the Charter provide for powers to the General

---

11. 4 ROSALYN HIGGINS, UNITED NATIONS PEACEKEEPING 144 (1981).

12. Dan Ciobanu, *The Power of the Security Council to Organize Peace-Keeping Operations, in* UNITED NATIONS PEACE-KEEPING: LEGAL ESSAYS 15, 17, 40 (Antonio Cassese ed., 1978). The official UN-edited handbook also states that the peace-keeping operations "go beyond purely diplomatic means or those described in Chapter VI of the Charter" and emphasizes the notion of "Chapter 'Six and a Half.'" THE BLUE HELMETS: A REVIEW OF UNITED NATIONS PEACE-KEEPING 5 (United Nations ed., 2d ed. 1990).

13. HANS KELSEN, THE LAW OF THE UNITED NATIONS: A CRITICAL ANALYSIS OF ITS FUNDAMENTAL PROBLEMS 401 (1950).

14. U.N. CHARTER art. 36, para. 1. For references to this provision in context of the peace-keeping operations, see Suy, *supra* note 8, at 544; *see also* Murphy, *supra* note 1, at 294.

15. *Certain Expenses*, 1962 I.C.J. at 172. The fact that UNEF was established by the General Assembly does not prejudice our conclusion. As an element of the peaceful settlement, peace-keeping forces may be established both by the General Assembly and Security Council.

Assembly, similar to those powers given to the Council under Article 36, and may serve as a basis for establishment of the peace-keeping operations. Therefore, the Security Council—the organ with the primary responsibility for maintaining international peace and security—may exercise a power which may also be exercised by the General Assembly. However, the Assembly's responsibility in this area is secondary and residual.

Hans Kelsen correctly observes that the recommendations made by the Security Council on "procedures or methods of adjustments" under Article 36(1) do not relate to a substantive settlement of a dispute or a situation, but merely to the procedural aspects thereof.[16] With regard to *disputes*, he concludes that "procedures or methods" under Article 36(1) are identical to means of settlement of disputes under Article 33(2).[17] Kelsen, however, does not clarify what the content of recommendations under Article 36(1) could be if they relate to *a situation* and not to a dispute.[18] Obviously, the Council may recommend all methods of adjustment that it considers appropriate to prevent the continuance of a situation which is likely to endanger the international peace and security. Peace-keeping operations, which do not relate to the substantive terms of settlement, but constitute only the methods of adjustment, naturally fall within this category. Peace-keeping operations may thus be initiated on the basis of recommendations under Article 36(1).[19] Therefore, Chapter VI of the UN Charter may provide a legal basis for establishment of the peace-keeping forces.

Finally, once peace-keeping operations are established under Chapter VI, they can be empowered to use force.[20] As it follows from the conclusions reached by the ICJ in *Certain Expenses*, any peace-keeping force not involving the use of force against a *State* may be established outside the context of Chapter VII.[21] The Charter, taken in isolation, may leave open the question which forcible actions may be performed exclusively under Chapter VII.

---

16. KELSEN, *supra* note 13, at 402.

17. *Id.* Article 33 of the Charter obliges the States to settle their disputes by negotiation, conciliation, arbitration or judicial methods. The Council may "call upon the parties to settle their dispute by such means." U.N. CHARTER art. 33, para. 2.

18. KELSEN, *supra* note 13, at 402.

19. Recommendations concerning substantive settlement or adjustment of a dispute or of a situation is the subject-matter of article 37(2) of the U.N. Charter. *See id.* at 401. *See also* S.C. Res. 186, U.N. SCOR, 19th Sess., 1098th mtg. at 12, U.N. Doc. S/5575 (1964) (establishing the United Nations Force in Cyprus (UNFICYP) and clearly designating its recommendations as the basis of establishment of that force).

20. It must not be forgotten that Chapter VI of the Charter governs peaceful settlement of *disputes only*, but neither its title nor any provision of it may justify an assumption that settlement or adjustment of a *situation* under Chapter VI shall necessarily be peaceful.

21. *Certain Expenses*, 1962 I.C.J. at 177. *See also* the Written Statement by the Government of Netherlands in the *Certain Expenses* case, reaching analogical conclusions, *ICJ Pleadings*, 1962, 173.

492   Virginia Journal of International Law   [Vol. 43:485

However, the ICJ's authoritative interpretation of the relevant provisions of the Charter concluded that Chapter VII exclusively governs only enforcement actions taken against a State.[22] Thus, non-State secessionist or separatist entities may be subject to the use of force by the Security Council even outside the context of Chapter VII.

2. *Chapter VII of the Charter*

a. Article 39

According to Article 39, the Security Council may either take coercive measures or make recommendations with a view of maintaining or restoring international peace and security. Recommendations under this article may undeniably provide a legal basis for the peace-keeping operations.

b. Articles 41 and 42

In *Certain Expenses*, the International Court of Justice emphasized that peace-keeping operations are not enforcement actions.[23] Therefore, some argue that Articles 41 and 42 of the Charter cannot provide the legal basis for establishment of the peace-keeping forces.[24] Since Articles 41 and 42 deal with enforcement actions,

> there would be a *contradictio in subiecto* to designate, as their [the peace-keeping operations'] constitutional basis, a legal rule which regulates precisely that kind of actions [enforcement].... [I]t is not certain that under that legal rule [Article 39] the Security Council may take other measures than those provided in Article 41 and 42.[25]

The text of Article 39, which empowers the Council not only to take enforcement actions, but also to make recommendations, illustrates the incorrectness of such an approach. Moreover, the wording of Articles 41 and 42, which contains a merely illustrative

---

22. Indeed, the ONUC has been authorized to use force without a reference to Chapter VII. S.C. Res. 161, U.N. SCOR 16th Sess., Supp. for Jan.-Mar. 1961, at 40, U.N. Doc. S/4741 (1961).

23. *Certain Expenses*, 1962 I.C.J. at 166, 171.

24. The official UN-edited handbook of UN peace-keeping operations emphasizes that the peace-keeping operations "fall short of the provisions of Chapter VII...which deal with enforcement." THE BLUE HELMETS, *supra* note 12, at 5. "The international force in Korea was not a United Nations peace-keeping operation in the current sense of the term since the enforcement action was not carried out by the Organization, was not based on the consent of the parties, and involved the use of force." *Id.* at 9. Reference to the *Certain Expenses* case is made in this regard by Ciobanu, *supra* note 12, at 18.

25. Ciobanu, *supra* note 12, at 18. For a similar skepticism, see *id.* at 35-36.

but not exhaustive list of enforcement actions, does not *a priori* exclude establishment of the peace-keeping forces as a part of the action by the Council under Chapter VII. According to Articles 41 and 42, the Council can exercise wide discretion in choosing the measures it will apply.[26] There are no Charter-based limitations on the powers of the Council as to the nature of measures under Chapter VII, and these measures are not strictly limited to the enforcement.[27] Therefore, peace-keeping operations may constitute part of an enforcement action taken by the Security Council pursuant to Articles 41 and 42.

It has been suggested that the Council, "acting solely under Article 39 of the Charter, may not take other actions than the enforcement measures provided for in the two legal provisions that the said legal rule specifically mentions."[28] However, the limitations imposed by the Charter on the Council through Article 39 are of a negative, rather than positive, nature. Specifically, Article 39 merely implies that the enforcement measures may not be taken unless a determination under Article 39 is made. It does not mean that the Council's role after making a determination under Article 39 is limited solely to enforcement measures. The Council may adopt every measure it deems appropriate for the restoration of international peace and security.

Furthermore, the conclusions reached by the ICJ in *Certain Expenses* do not justify the assertion that Chapter VII may not provide a legal basis for peace-keeping operations. Rather, the Court's conclusions have a negative, rather than a positive, importance for the issues under consideration. Specifically, the ICJ's treatment of UNEF and the United Nations Operation in Congo (ONUC) as non-enforcement actions demonstrated that the establishment of those forces was not exclusively within the powers of the Security Council. The General Assembly, of course, may also assume responsibility in the area of peace and security, provided that it only takes non-enforcement measures. But the court's opinion in

---

26. According to Article 41, "The Security Council may decide what measures not involving the use of armed force *are to be employed* to give effect to its decisions." U.N. CHARTER art. 41 (emphasis added). Under Article 42, the Council "may take such action by air, sea, or land forces *as may be necessary* to maintain or restore international peace and security." U.N. CHARTER art. 42 (emphasis added).

27. Secretary-General Hammarskjold held that Article 41 of the Charter could serve as a basis for UN operations in Congo, although it involved no enforcement measures. R. SIMMONDS, LEGAL PROBLEMS ARISING FROM THE UNITED NATIONS MILITARY OPERATIONS IN THE CONGO 62 (1968). Moreover, the International Criminal Tribunal for the Former Yugoslavia is established under Article 41. Although this is not expressly provided for in the text of the article, the Tribunal held in the *Tadic* case that this article may serve as the legal basis of its establishment. Prosecutor v. Tadic, Case IT-94-1-AR72, 35 I.L.M. 32, 44-45 (I.C.T.Y 1995).

28. Ciobanu, *supra* note 12, at 22.

494 VIRGINIA JOURNAL OF INTERNATIONAL LAW [Vol. 43:485

Certain Expenses has not prejudiced the powers of the Council to establish peace-keeping forces as part of an action under Chapter VII. This was simply not within the framework of the advisory opinion.

Particular skepticism has been expressed as to the suitability of Article 41 for the establishment of peace-keeping forces because it relates only to non-military enforcement measures.[29] However, the only kind of action excluded from the ambit of Article 41 is *military enforcement measures*. Peace-keeping operations cannot fall under that category. The fact that the peace-keeping forces may use force in self-defense does not place them in the category of enforcement measures directed against a State or a non-State entity.

Recent developments in UN practice have demonstrated the necessity of an extended notion of peace-keeping on the agenda. In particular, United Nations Operation in Somalia II (UNOSOM II) and the United Nations Protection Force (UNPROFOR) in former Yugoslavia are referred to as instances where peace-keeping was combined with enforcement measures under Chapter VII, bearing in mind that some support for the powers of those missions may be found in resolutions of the Council adopted under Chapter VII.[30]

Nevertheless, it is still possible to distinguish peace-keeping and enforcement by their legal bases. The Council may establish non-enforcement peace-keeping forces with the consent of parties to the conflict without resorting to its Chapter VII powers. But if the Council comes to the conclusion that a given situation constitutes a threat to the peace under Article 39, it may add certain enforcement elements to the powers of a peace-keeping force already established. Such a subsequent enlargement of powers of an existing peace-keeping force may be effected only by reference to Chapter VII, as evidenced in the cases of UNPROFOR[31] and UNOSOM.[32] If the element of enforcement (including a possible enforcement against a State) is present, it must be based on a decision under Chapter VII. By adopting the Chapter VII decisions, the Council may utilize the units and entities established by its earlier decisions (including the non-Chapter VII decisions) for the purpose of enforcement measures. This accords with the wide discretion the Council enjoys in deciding the measures to be taken under Chapter VII. But again, this discretion does not empower the Council to add enforcement powers to the mandate of a peace-keeping force without formally

---

29. *See supra* notes 24-25.

30. CHRISTIAN WALTER, VEREINTE NATIONEN UND REGIONALORGANISATIONEN 327-29 (1996).

31. S.C. Res. 836, U.N. SCOR 48th Sess., 3228th mtg., at 14, U.N. Doc. S/25825 (1993).

32. S.C. Res. 837, U.N. SCOR 48th Sess., 3229th' mtg., at 83, U.N. Doc. S/25493 (1993).

resorting to Chapter VII.

Therefore, a peace-keeping mission may be transformed into a peace-enforcement mission. This transformation takes place without requiring the consent of the parties. The difference between peace-keeping and peace-enforcement missions is also crucial for determining the allocation of powers between the UN and regional organizations. The latter are empowered to establish the peace-keeping missions, but not to perform the enforcement actions.[33]

c.   Provisional Measures under Article 40

According to the prevailing view, the most proper legal basis for the peace-keeping operations may be Article 40 of the Charter.[34] It empowers the Council to "call upon the parties concerned to comply with such provisional measures as it deems necessary or desirable."[35] This follows from the nature of the peace-keeping operations, which have been described as follows: "Peacekeeping is not the same as peaceful settlement; it is simply a provisional measure aimed at stopping the fighting—it does not, at least in its basic form, sort out the underlying problem."[36]

While this is generally true, the scope of applicability of Article 40 is also relevant. Provisional measures taken under Article 40 may be ordered: (1) after the existence of a threat to the peace under Article 39 is determined; and (2) before the Council decides to make recommendations under Article 39 or take enforcement actions under Articles 41 and 42. Therefore, although Article 40 is generally very suitable for establishment of the peace-keeping forces, in practice its applicability depends on fulfilment of these two conditions. This must be remembered when trying to invoke Article 40 as a legal basis of a particular peace-keeping operation.

Within the above-mentioned limits, there seems to be no Charter-based limitation on using Article 40 as a basis for establishing peace-keeping forces. On the other hand, the nature of provisional measures may preclude the establishment of peace-keeping forces as a provisional measure under Article 40. By way of analogy, it has been argued that as far as provisional measures indicated by international tribunals focus on actions by States exclusively and not

---

33. U.N. CHARTER art. 53, para. 1.

34. HIGGINS, *supra* note 11, at 144; Ciobanu, *supra* note 12, at 19 (emphasizing the "strong resemblance between the operations here under consideration and the provisional measures which are provided for in Article 40"). According to the official UN-edited handbook, "peace-keeping operations are intended to be provisional and thus temporary measures." THE BLUE HELMETS, *supra* note 12, at 8. *See also* Murphy, *supra* note 1, at 294; Karin Rudolph, *Peace-Keeping Forces, in* 2 UNITED NATIONS: LAW, POLICIES AND PRACTICE 963 (Rüdiger Wolfrum ed., 1995).

35. U.N. CHARTER art. 40.

36. McCOUBREY & WHITE, *supra* note 1, at 5.

496   Virginia Journal of International Law   [Vol. 43:485

on actions by the tribunals, the Council may not order provisional measures which go beyond requiring an action or omission by States. Thus, the provisional measures cannot comprise an action by the UN itself.[37]

The nature and extent of the limits of provisional measures depends not on the essence of provisional measures (as reflected in the Charter or in the statute of a relevant tribunal), but on the limits of competence of the organ ordering those measures. The powers of the Council are relatively wide in this regard: It may not only deal with a dispute or situation, but also take independent action for its resolution. Therefore, the provisional measures may include orders directed at parties to a conflict which require them to act in a certain way or to abstain from certain action, or may consist of orders to comply with the action taken by the Council itself, such as the establishment of a peace-keeping operation.[38] International tribunals do not possess adequate powers for an independent unilateral action to prevent aggravation of a dispute. However, the Council does possess such powers by virtue of operation of Article 29 of the Charter, which enables it to create subsidiary organs for the fulfilment of its functions.

Jochen Frowein expresses a somewhat sceptical view of Article 40 of the Charter as a basis for peace-keeping operations, arguing that the establishment of a peace-keeping force under Article 40 would go beyond the scope of Article 40 and constitute an action· under Article 42.[39] As with the example of Article 41, peace-keeping operations do not constitute military enforcement measures and do not belong exclusively to the ambit of Article 42.

A question may arise in this regard whether the establishment of a peace-keeping mission under Article 40 requires determination by the Security Council according to Article 39 of the Charter, which is the basis of operation of other Chapter VII decisions including indication of provisional measures under Article 40. In other words, this question asks whether the Council may indicate provisional measures outside the context of Chapter VII. Frowein argues that the systematic position of Article 40 clearly supports the view that this provision is applicable after the prerequisites for application of Article 39 have been fulfilled. In certain cases, the Council has made formal determinations under Article 39 in order to make the

---

37. Written Statement by South Africa in the *Certain Expenses* case, *ICJ Pleadings*, 1962, 261ff.; Ciobanu, *supra* note 12, at 20-21.

38. It seems, therefore, that such a limited perspective on provisional measures by the Security Council is not justified in the light of Article 40 of the Charter which, according to its natural and plain meaning, may contemplate the actions and omissions by States as well as the compliance with actions taken by the Security Council. U.N. CHARTER art. 40.

39. Jochen Abr. Frowein & Nico Krisch, *Article 40*, in THE CHARTER OF THE UNITED NATIONS: A COMMENTARY 732 (Bruno Simma ed., 2002).

application of Article 40 possible.[40]

d. An Interim Conclusion

The preceding discussion demonstrates that both Chapter VI and Chapter VII provide a legal basis for peace-keeping operations. In this regard, a question may arise as to which criteria determine whether a given peace-keeping operation should be considered as established under either Chapter VI or Chapter VII powers. The answer may be offered by analyzing the Charter itself, which contemplates action by the Council in different contexts. Chapter VI deals with disputes or situations "the continuation of which is likely endanger the maintenance of international peace and security."[41] Chapter VII, on the other hand, deals with the "existence of any threat to the peace, breach of the peace, or act of aggression."[42] The Council may decide that the establishment of a peace-keeping force is necessary to avoid continuance of a situation which is likely to endanger international peace and security. The Council may equally decide that the establishment of a peace-keeping force may be appropriate in response to a threat to the peace which already exists. In the first case, the Council may act under Chapter VI, in the second case, under Chapter VII. The power to make appropriate determinations forms part of the Council's discretionary powers in the area of international peace and security.

Likewise, the Security Council may face a circumstance that Article 2(7) of the UN Charter prohibits—the United Nations interfering in the domestic jurisdiction of States. Nevertheless, if the Council considers that the maintenance of peace and security so requires, it may adopt a decision on the establishment of a peace-keeping force under Chapter VII and thereby escape the operation of Article 2(7). This may happen if the establishment of a peace-keeping force is decided in the context of or in conjunction with the enforcement measures. For instance, if the Council uses its enforcement powers in order to achieve the stationing of a peace-keeping force on a given territory. Otherwise, the Council must respect the domestic jurisdiction of States.

It must be concluded, therefore, that the Council's powers, as based on the relevant Charter provisions, may empower it to effectively discharge its primary responsibility in the area of peace and security by choosing between the different legal bases for establishment of a given operation, and by adapting its actions to the nature and level of aggravation of a given conflict, as well as to the

---

40. *Id.* at 731.
41. U.N. CHARTER art. 33, para. 1.
42. U.N. CHARTER art. 39.

498   VIRGINIA JOURNAL OF INTERNATIONAL LAW   [Vol. 43:485

level of a political consensus within the Council itself. Only such an
approach enables the Council to exercise its "primary responsibility
in the peace-keeping to the fullest extent possible."[43]

C.   Case Studies

1.   United Nations Operation in Congo

The United Nations Operation in Congo (ONUC) is probably the
most complicated peace-keeping operation initiated by the United
Nations, and thus deserves a separate examination. The absence in
UN resolutions of a reference to a concrete Charter provision as a
legal basis of ONUC, as well as the dynamic development of that
operation leading to its evolution into an operation empowered to
use force and to engage in hostilities, has given rise to the radical
divergence of opinions of the ONUC's legal basis. Seyersted, for
instance, argues that ONUC was based on Article 42 of the
Charter.[44] Other commentators, such as Schachter,[45] Higgins,[46] and
Simmonds[47] argue, on the other hand, that ONUC was established as
a provisional measure under Article 40 of the Charter.

Simmonds' suggestion that Articles 41 and 42 cannot have
formed the legal basis of ONUC is correct and in accordance with
the approach endorsed by the ICJ in *Certain Expenses*. The ICJ held
that ONUC was neither a preventive nor enforcement measure under
Chapter VII.[48] Nevertheless, the line of reasoning chosen by
Simmonds to justify his conclusion can hardly explain the legal
basis of ONUC. Schachter, Higgins and Simmonds all find that
ONUC was based on Article 40 with an implicit determination by
the Council under Article 39.[49] Simmonds reaches this conclusion by
excluding in this case (1) the operation of Articles 41 and 42 and (2)
the relevance of recommendations under Article 39.[50] Therefore, he
concludes that ONUC could not have been established but as a

---

43. Suy, *supra* note 8, at 545.

44. Finn Seyersted, *United Nations Forces: Some Legal Problems*, 37 BRIT. Y.B. INT'L
L. 351, 446 (1961). *See also* John Halderman, *Legal Basis for United Nations Armed Forces*,
56 AM. J. INT'L L. 971, 985-86, 990 (1962) (sharing the same view). *But see* 3 ROSALYN
HIGGINS, UNITED NATIONS PEACE-KEEPING 56-57 (1980) (arguing that Article 2(7) of the
U.N. Charter was applicable to the situation in Congo and therefore that ONUC was not an
enforcement measure in the sense of Chapter VII).

45. Oscar Schachter, *Legal Aspects of the United Nations Action in the Congo*, 55 AM. J.
INT'L L. 1 (1961).

46. HIGGINS, *supra* note 44, at 55.

47. SIMMONDS, *supra* note 27, at 63. *See also* MCCOUBREY & WHITE, *supra* note 1, at
53 (designating Article 40 as a basis of ONUC).

48. *Certain Expenses*, 1962 I.C.J. at 177.

49. Schachter, *supra* note 45, at 4 (arguing that the explicit determination under Article
39 is not a prerequisite for all Chapter VII decisions). *See also* HIGGINS, *supra* note 44, at
56; HIGGINS, *supra* note 11, at 144; SIMMONDS, *supra* note 27, at 59-61.

50. SIMMONDS, *supra* note 27, at 63.

provisional measure under Article 40.[51] Simmonds' approach has several shortcomings which render it inadequate to explain the ONUC's legal basis.

Simmonds gives sufficiently detailed reasoning why Articles 41 and 42 may not be considered as ONUC's legal basis, but he does not give any explanation as to why he excludes the relevance of recommendations under Article 39.[52] Such a hesitation is understandable because Simmonds finds that the establishment of ONUC involved implicit determination of a threat to the peace under Article 39.[53] But the controversy in Simmonds' reasoning still stands: if he finds that the provisional measures under Article 40 can be based on an implicit determination under Article 39, it is unclear why recommendations under Article 39 itself are not. The focus upon this issue destroys Simmonds' line of reasoning. The Council cannot issue recommendations under Article 39 without clarifying that it is acting under that article. Nor can the Council act under Article 40 unless a clear determination is made under Article 39.

An express determination of a threat to the peace is a requirement for action under Chapter VII. Under Article 39, recommendations shall be made or coercive actions shall be taken only after a determination of a threat to the peace has been made. The text is clear on this point. Moreover, Article 40 of the Charter stipulates that provisional measures should be ordered before making a decision on the recommendations or coercive measures under Article 39. This circumstance makes it impossible to order the provisional measures before explicit determination under Article 39 has been made. Even the title of Chapter VII suggests that Article 40 is an "action with respect to threats to the peace" which shall be determined under Article 39. Therefore, the ONUC could not have been based on Article 40 without an explicit determination under Article 39.

Notwithstanding the dogmatic prerequisites as considered above, the approach of Schachter, Higgins and Simmonds fails to account for the nature of ONUC, as well as the practical circumstances surrounding the operation. By declaring that ONUC was not a *preventive* or enforcement measure under Chapter VII, the ICJ excluded this operation from the ambit of Chapter VII completely. Provisional measures under Article 40 are clearly preventive, as they shall be indicated "in order to *prevent an aggravation of the situation*."[54] This clarifies why ONUC could not be based on recommendations under Article 39, despite the suitability of this

---

51. *Id.*
52. *Id.* at 62-63.
53. *Id.*
54. U.N. CHARTER art. 40 (emphasis added).

500   VIRGINIA JOURNAL OF INTERNATIONAL LAW   [Vol. 43:485

option, or under Article 40—it was established completely outside Chapter VII.

Furthermore, by its very nature, ONUC could not be considered a provisional measure. Resolutions 143 and 161, among others by the Security Council, make it clear that the intention of the Council was to assist the government of Congo in fighting with secessionist Katanga.[55] Therefore, ONUC itself was not in accordance with the requirements of Article 40 because the operation was not "without prejudice to the rights, claims or the position of the parties concerned." The development of ONUC, resulting in its engagement in hostilities against the military units of Katanga, is practical evidence in this regard. Moreover, by Resolution 169, the Council authorized the Secretary-General "to take vigorous action, including the use of the requisite measure of force, if necessary, for the immediate apprehension, detention pending legal action and/or deportation of all foreign military and paramilitary personnel and political advisers not under the United Nations command...."[56] Taken together, this evidence supports the view that the Council, from the moment of commencing its action concerning Congo, (1) was not determined to take provisional action and (2) clearly designated its measures as supporting the Government of Congo.

Therefore, the views of Schachter, Higgins, and Simmonds on Article 40 as the legal basis of ONUC fail to reflect the proper legal basis of this operation. ONUC's legal basis was outside Chapter VII. Instead, its legal basis was Article 36(1) of the Charter. ONUC was established, as the ICJ mentioned, with a view to maintain international peace and security,[57] in a situation which might have endangered the maintenance of international peace and security and thus fall within the scope of Article 36(1). The establishment of ONUC was a *method of adjustment* of the situation under Article 36(1). The fact that ONUC involved the use of force did not prejudice the fact that it was based on Chapter VI, under which only *disputes* shall be settled exclusively by peaceful means and this limitation does not extend to the adjustment of *situations*. As discussed above, Chapter VI does not obligate the Council to undertake only peaceful actions with regard to situations, as distinguished from disputes. Lastly, by resolutions establishing and developing ONUC, the Security Council did not intend to bind either Congo or other States, including those delivering troops for this operation. Moreover, these resolutions were fully *recommendatory*, which makes it possible to consider them as based

---

55. S.C. Res. 161, *supra* note 22; S.C. Res. 143, U.N. SCOR 15th Sess., 873rd mtg., at 5, U.N. Doc. S/4387 (1960).

56. S.C. Res. 169, U.N. SCOR 16th Sess., 982nd mtg., at 3-5, U.N.Doc. S/5002 (1961).

57. *Certain Expenses*, 1962 I.C.J. at 175.

on Article 36(1).

Therefore, for a peace-keeping operation to be considered as established under a given provision of the UN Charter, at least two conditions : (1) by its nature, a peace-keeping operation must be suitable for being established under that provision, and (2) the formal criteria of applicability of a Charter provision which is claimed to be the legal basis of a given peace-keeping operation must be fully met.

2. *United Nations Protection Force*

In 1992, Security Council Resolution 743 established the United Nations Protection Force.[58] Its establishment was based on the determination of a threat to the peace under Article 39. Although no other provision of Chapter VII was invoked by the Council,[59] the establishment of UNPROFOR was clearly an action with regard to a threat to the peace under Chapter VII. In its original state, UNPROFOR may be considered to have been established as a provisional measure under Article 40. Paragraph 6 of Resolution 740 emphasized that the UN peace-keeping plan and its implementation was in no way intended to prejudge the terms of political settlement.[60] The same approach has been expressed by the Secretary-General in his report to the Council[61] and further reaffirmed by the Council in paragraph 10 of Resolution 743.[62] The functions of UNPROFOR were limited to good offices, observation, and monitoring[63] and were thus preventive rather than coercive. While the Security Council has the power to establish peace-keeping forces under Articles 41 and 42, in this case, UNPROFOR's original mandate falls within the scope of provisional measures under Article 40.

Generally, after finding a threat to the peace under Article 39, the Council may establish peace-keeping forces either as a provisional measure or under Articles 41 and 42. The selection of the appropriate article depends on the intention of the Council. If the Council intends to establish a peace-keeping force for the protection

---

58. S.C. Res. 743, U.N. SCOR 47th Sess., 3055th mtg., at 8-9, U.N. Doc. S/RES/743 (1992).

59. WALTER, *supra* note 30, at 328.

60. S.C. Res. 740, U.N. SCOR 47th Sess., 3049th mtg., at 7-8, U.N. Doc. S/RES/740 (1992).

61. "It is to be emphasized that these arrangements will be of an interim nature, pending the negotiation of an overall settlement." *Further Report by the Secretary-General pursuant to Security Council Resolution 721 (1991)*, at 5, U.N. Doc. S/23592 (Feb. 15, 1992).

62. S.C. Res. 743, U.N. SCOR 47th Sess., 3055th mtg., at 8-9, U.N. Doc. S/RES/743 (1992). Therefore, the Council's intention was not to prejudge rights, claims or positions of parties concerned, as required by Article 40 of the Charter.

63. Report of the Secretary-General (Feb. 15), 1992 U.N.Y.B. 332 (1992).

of rights or positions of one of the parties, it may resort to Articles 41 and 42. But if the Council wishes to act without prejudice to those rights, claims, and positions, as well as to a final settlement, as in the case of UNPROFOR, Article 40 may be invoked as a legal basis.

Resolution 836 extended the mandate of UNPROFOR.[64] In particular, paragraph 5 authorized UNPROFOR "to deter attacks against the safe areas, to monitor cease-fire, to promote the withdrawal of military or paramilitary units other than those of the Government of the Republic of Bosnia and Herzegovina and to occupy some key points on the ground."[65] Paragraph 9 empowered UNPROFOR to use force in carrying out the mandate as defined in paragraph 5.[66]

This case is a clear illustration of a peace-keeping force being transformed into a peace-enforcement one. Paragraph 5, in conjunction with paragraph 9, empowers UNPROFOR to use force against military units of States other than Bosnia-Herzegovina. Therefore, Resolution 836, has transformed UNPROFOR into a peace-enforcement force, acting under Article 42 of the Charter, and empowered it to take enforcement measures against *States*. This transformation made it possible to consider UNPROFOR a Chapter VII enforcement measure, in accordance with the criteria developed by the ICJ in *Certain Expenses*.

3.   Kosovo Force

The legal basis of the Kosovo Force (KFOR) in Yugoslavia was Security Council Resolution 1244, which established the international security presence in Kosovo.[67] This resolution was adopted under Chapter VII and made an explicit determination under Article 39, following a similar determination in Security Council Resolution 1199.[68] Under paragraph 9 of Resolution 1244, the KFOR is authorized to take actions "[d]eterring renewed hostilities, maintaining and where necessary enforcing a ceasefire, and ensuring the withdrawal and preventing the return into Kosovo of Federal and Republic military, police, and paramilitary forces."[69]

Therefore, although KFOR shares many similarities with the traditional peace-keeping forces (being based on the consent of the Federal Republic of Yugoslavia (FRY) and empowered to maintain ceasefire), its initial mandate as enshrined in Resolution 1244

64. S.C. Res. 836, U.N. SCOR 48th Sess., 3228th mtg., U.N. Doc. S/RES/836 (1993).
65. *Id.* at para. 5.
66. *Id.* at para. 9.
67. S.C. Res. 1244, U.N. SCOR 54th Sess., 4011th mtg., U.N. Doc. S/RES/1244 (1999).
68. S.C. Res. 1199, U.N. SCOR 53rd Sess., 3930th mtg., U.N. Doc. S/RES/1199 (1998).
69. S.C. Res. 1244, *supra* note 67, at para. 9.

supports an assumption that KFOR is a Chapter VII enforcement measure established under Article 42. By being empowered to deter the renewed hostilities and to prevent the return into Kosovo of the FRY's military forces, KFOR is in fact authorized to use coercion against a *State*. Therefore, according to the ICJ's criteria, KFOR is an enforcement force. It differs, however, from UNPROFOR in that the KFOR has been designated as an enforcement force from the moment of its establishment, whereas UNPROFOR was transformed from a peace keeping force into a peace-enforcement force.

D. *Institutional Prerequisites: Article 29 of the Charter*

Article 29 of the Charter enables the Security Council to "establish such subsidiary organs as it deems necessary for the performance of its functions."[70] The Council, as an organ enjoying *Kompetenzkompetenz*, that is, the competence to decide on its competence, may itself determine whether such a necessity exists.

Article 29 of the Charter may provide merely an institutional or procedural background for the establishment of peace-keeping operations. Alone, Article 29 is insufficient to explain the legal basis for a peace-keeping operation, as the justification for a peace-keeping operation transcends questions of procedure.[71] Therefore, recourse should necessarily be made to one of the powers of the Security Council analyzed above.

E. *General Conclusions*

The legal bases of the peace-keeping operations established by the Security Council are provided for in the UN Charter by virtue of the operation of:

- the recommendatory power under Article 36(1) in conjunction with Article 29;

- the recommendatory power under Article 39 in conjunction with Article 29;

- the provisional measures under Article 40 in conjunction with Article 29; and

- the power to take measures under Articles 41 or 42 in conjunction with Article 29.

Because of the need for peace-keeping forces in particular situations, as well as the need to determine their functions and

---

70. U.N. CHARTER art. 29.

71. Andreas Paulus, *Article 29*, in THE CHARTER OF THE UNITED NATIONS, A COMMENTARY 554 (Bruno Simma ed., 2002). *See also* SIMMONDS, *supra* note 27, at 64.

powers (taking into account the need for effectiveness and successful performance), the various bases explicitly or implicitly provided for in the UN Charter should be considered as mutually supportive and not as mutually exclusive legal preconditions. As each operation is unique, both by the circumstances of its establishment and by the environment in which it operates and develops, the consideration of various elements of legal basis in a mutually complementary way contributes towards the viability of each peace-keeping force.

III. THE GENERAL ASSEMBLY

A. *The Recommendatory Powers*

As the International Court of Justice has confirmed, the primary responsibility of the Security Council in the area of international peace and security is not the exclusive one. The functions of the General Assembly (Assembly) are not confined to discussion, consideration, initiation of studies and making of recommendations.[72] Rather, the General Assembly assumes an important role in maintaining peace and security, subject only to the express limitations imposed on its powers under the Charter. The only relevant limitation in this regard is Article 12, which proscribes the Assembly from addressing issues which are under consideration by the Security Council. This limitation is obviously in accordance with the Council's primary responsibility for the maintenance of peace and security.

The General Assembly's first step to assert its own role in the area of peace and security was Resolution 377, "Uniting for Peace" (UfP), adopted in 1950. The resolution concerned the situation in Korea and dealt with the residual role of the Assembly in the maintenance of international peace and security. According to paragraph A of that Resolution,

> if the Security Council, because of lack of unanimity of the permanent members, fails to exercise its primary responsibility for the maintenance of international peace and security...the General Assembly shall consider the matter immediately with a view to making appropriate recommendations to Members for collective measures, *including* in the case of a breach of the peace or act of

---

72. *Certain Expenses*, 1962 I.C.J. at 163 (rejecting the conclusion made by Kelsen that the General Assembly has been established merely as a "town meeting of the world" but rather finding it to be a deliberative and criticizing organ). *See* KELSEN, *supra* note 13, at 199-200.

aggression the use of armed force when necessary.[73]

This provision makes it clear that the Assembly did not consider its residual competence in the area of peace and security as limited to coercive measures. Indeed, if the Assembly asserts its power to recommend forcible measures, it shall naturally be considered as asserting its power to organize the peace-keeping operations on the basis of consent given by the parties.

For the purposes of organizing the peace-keeping operations, the resolution "Uniting for Peace" accords not only with the purposes of the Charter, but also with its textual context of distribution of competences among the principal organs of the UN.[74] First, it should be mentioned that the resolution assigns the respective role to the General Assembly only if "the Security Council, because of lack of unanimity of the permanent members, fails to exercise its primary responsibility."[75] This means that the resolution fully takes into account the operation of Article 12 of the Charter and is thus not designed to obstruct the work of the Security Council. Secondly, in the UfP resolution, the General Assembly did not assert the power to bind the member states. This power is exclusively reserved for the Council. Thirdly, the role of the Assembly, as reflected in the UfP resolution, is only a residual one. In this sense, it has a remedial nature. The primary responsibility is delegated to the Security Council in order to ensure prompt and effective action by the United Nations. When the Council is prevented from acting promptly and effectively—as required by the Charter—it reflects not only the failure of the Council, but also the failure of the Organization as a whole.[76] This factor enhances the political accountability of the Security Council for not properly exercising its responsibilities in the area of concurrent jurisdiction of the Assembly and Council.[77]

The text of the Charter, as interpreted by the International Court of Justice, may also support such an approach. In *Certain Expenses*, the court directly referred to Article 11(2) of the Charter, which

---

73. G.A. Res. 377, U.N. GAOR, 5th Sess., Supp. No. 20, at 10, UN Doc. A/1775 (1950) (emphasis added).

74. Rudolph, *supra* note 34, at 962 (suggesting that the UfP resolution is not in itself the sufficient basis for establishment of the peace-keeping forces and that forces must adhere to the general Charter regulations). *See also* KELSEN, *supra* note 13, at 959 (emphasizing that the constitutionality of the UfP resolution depends on the interpretation of Articles 10, 11, and 14 of the Charter); *id.* at 960 (suggesting that the UfP resolution is an interpretation of the Charter).

75. G.A. Res. 377, *supra* note 73.

76. As already emphasized, these observations relate only to the relevance of the UfP resolution in the area of peace-keeping and are without prejudice as to the acceptability of that resolution as a basis of the enforcement measures.

77. *See* MALCOLM SHAW & KAREL WELLENS, FIRST REPORT BY THE ILA-COMMITTEE ON ACCOUNTABILITY OF INTERNATIONAL ORGANIZATIONS (1998) (discussing the notion of political accountability).

506 VIRGINIA JOURNAL OF INTERNATIONAL LAW [Vol. 43:485

deals with the power of the Assembly to issue recommendations to States concerning the "questions relating maintenance of international peace and security."[78] The ICJ indicated that this provision empowers the General Assembly to organize, by means of recommendations, the peace-keeping operations. The Assembly could act unless the enforcement measures against a *State* are involved.[79] As illustrated by UNEF, the ICJ indicated that the Assembly may establish the peace-keeping operations either under Article 11 or under Article 14.[80]

Articles 10, 11(2) and 14 of the Charter substantially overlap in scope with one another. They all foresee that the General Assembly may make recommendations on any matter within the scope of the Charter or on any question of peace, security, and general welfare.[81] Equally, all three articles are limited by the operation of Article 12. However, there are some differences: Article 14 encompasses only measures of a peaceful nature, while Articles 10 and 11(2) provide a basis for *all* recommendations, except those relating to enforcement measures.

The General Assembly, as implicitly confirmed in *Certain Expenses*, may not authorize forcible actions against a *State*. However, the peace-keeping forces established by the General Assembly may take forcible action against non-State secessionist or separatist entities. Following the reasoning of the ICJ, the Security Council thus has the force monopoly only in enforcement actions against *States*. However, the peace-keeping forces authorized by the General Assembly to use force against the non-State actors shall necessarily be established under Article 11(2) and not under Article 14, for the latter relates only to *peaceful* adjustment of situations or disputes.

---

78. *Certain Expenses*, 1962 I.C.J. at 164; U.N. CHARTER art. 11, para. 2.
79. *Certain Expenses*, 1962 I.C.J. at 164. *See also* KELSEN, *supra* note 13, at 204-05 (conforming with the I.C.J. interpretation of the meaning of "action" under Article 11, paragraph 2 of the Charter).

> In Article 11, paragraph 2, the term "action" can hardly mean "discussion" and "recommendation by the General Assembly".... For if the term "action" includes "discussion" and "recommendation by the General Assembly" the previous sentence is meaningless.... "Action" can only mean "enforcement action." This is the specific function which is reserved to the Security Council.

Id. at 204-05. On the basis of several provisions of the Charter, Kelsen correctly observes that the enforcement measures against a *State* may be taken only by the Security Council. *Id.* at 973-74. The contextual analysis of Articles 5, 50, 53, and 99 may provide appropriate evidence for assuming that the Charter envisages only the role of the Security Council in taking coercive measures against States. *Id.*
80. *Certain Expenses*, 1962 I.C.J. at 172.
81. KELSEN, *supra* note 13, at 202 (noting that these notions enshrined in various articles are more or less identical)..

B. *Institutional Prerequisites: Article 22 of the Charter*

Article 22 empowers the General Assembly to establish subsidiary organs for performance of its functions. This power may be used for establishment of a peace-keeping force. UNEF, in particular, has been established under this article.[82] Similar to the Security Council, the General Assembly may (1) by virtue of its *Kompetenzkompetenz*, determine if the necessity to establish a peace-keeping force exists, and (2) invoke Article 22 only in conjunction with one of its substantive powers—Articles 10, 11 or 14.

IV. THE SECRETARY-GENERAL

A. *Establishment of Peace-Keeping Forces under the UN Charter*

The undisputed areas of competence of the Secretary-General in organizing peace-keeping operations include reporting to the Security Council and General Assembly on situations likely to endanger international peace and security,[83] as well as the negotiation and conclusion of agreements concerning the peace-keeping force.[84] The Secretary-General may also establish and conduct a peace-keeping operation if appropriate functions are delegated to it by the Security Council.[85] But this undisputed competence says little about the independent role of the Secretary-General because it relates only to the its powers vis á vis those of the Security Council or of the General Assembly.

According to Higgins, there is a general consensus that the Secretary-General is not empowered to establish peace-keeping forces, even with the consent of the parties.[86] Further, it has been

---

82. *See* Bothe, *supra* note 2, at 665-66, 685-86.

83. U.N. CHARTER, arts. 12, 99.

84. SEYERSTED, *supra* note 5, at 99 (referring to the regulations of the various peace-keeping forces).

85. U.N. CHARTER art. 98. *See also* DANESH SAROOSHI, THE UNITED NATIONS AND THE DEVELOPMENT OF COLLECTIVE SECURITY 64 (1998); DICKE & RENGELING, DIE SICHERUNG DES WELTFRIEDENS DURCH DIE VEREINTEN NATIONEN 145 (1975): "Er ist insoweit nicht Träger einer selbstständigen Initiative, sondern bedarf zu seiner Tätigkeit der Ermächtigung durch andere Organe. Eben hierin findet die Stellung des Generalsekretärs als eines den übrigen Organen der Organisation der Vereinten Nationen dienstbaren Hilfsorgans ihren Ausdruck." ("In this respect he is not a bearer of an independent initiative, but needs the authorization by other organs for his activity. Herein finds the position of the Secretary-General its expression as an auxiliary organ serving the remaining organs of the United Nations.") *Id.*

86. *See* Rosalyn Higgins, *A General Assessment of United Nations Peace-Keeping, in* UN PEACE-KEEPING: LEGAL ESSAYS 1, 7 (Antonio Cassese ed., 1978) ("The Secretary-General's powers under Articles 97-99 of the Charter, even when taken with the consent of

508   VIRGINIA JOURNAL OF INTERNATIONAL LAW   [Vol. 43:485

suggested that the Secretary-General may act in this area only on the basis of the powers delegated to it. The power to provide a legal basis for peace-keeping operations is therefore considered to be exclusively reserved for the Security Council and General Assembly.[87]

Higgins' suggestion is tantamount to arguing that the Secretary-General is not empowered to commit the UN; or, in other words, that the Secretary-General is not a proper organ for expression of its will. However, this suggestion is inconsistent with the ICJ's position in *Certain Expenses*, where the ICJ emphasized that "obligations of the Organization may be incurred by the Secretary-General."[88] Moreover, even the action taken by an organ not properly empowered thereto is nevertheless an action by the Organization, because "[b]oth national and international law contemplate cases in which the body corporate or politic may be bound, as to third parties, by an *ultra vires* act of an agent."[89] In addition, the consent by the host State may validate the allegedly *ultra vires* decisions by an international organ which establishes a peace-keeping force.[90] Therefore, the Secretary-General's decision in response to an initiative by the parties concerning the establishment of a peace-keeping force must be considered as a decision taken by the United Nations. At least two reasons may be advanced in favor of such reasoning. First, neither the Charter nor any other UN document contemplate any division or distribution of the powers relative to establishment of the peace-keeping forces among the UN bodies. Second, there is no explicit provision that this area belongs to the exclusive competence of the Council and/or the Assembly.

Furthermore, the argument that the Secretary-General lacks the power to establish peace-keeping forces with the consent of the parties fails to reflect the policy considerations surrounding the establishment of such forces. When the Council and Assembly fail to act, they fail to respond to the need to end hostilities or large-

---

the host State and all parties concerned, apparently are not a sufficient basis for a United Nations peace-keeping mission."). *See also* SAROOSHI, *supra* note 85, at 123-24; Suy, *supra* note 8, at 385; MCCOUBREY & WHITE, *supra* note 1, at 53; Bothe, *supra* note 2, at 592; Rudolph, *supra* note 33, at 961.

87. *See* SAROOSHI, *supra* note 85, at 124; DICKE & RENGELING, *supra* note 85, at 141 (stating that the Secretary-General is not a principal organ of the U.N.); Nabil Elaraby, *The Office of the Secretary General and the Maintenance of International Peace and Security, in* THE UNITED NATIONS AND THE MAINTENANCE OF INTERNATIONAL PEACE AND SECURITY 182 (United Nations Institute for Training and Research ed., 1987). *But see* SIMMONDS, *supra* note 27, at 71 (citing Alf Ross and considering the characterization of the U.N. Secretariat as a non-principal organ as unwarranted).

88. *Certain Expenses*, 1962 I.C.J. at 169.

89. *Id.* at 168.

90. *Cf.* ILC Articles on Responsibility of States for 'Internationally Wrongful Acts, art. 20 (formerly art. 29), A/CN.4/L.600, *available at* http://www.law.cam.ac.uk/rcil/ILCSR/Statresp.htm (last visited Oct. 12, 2002).

scale human suffering. In the case of inaction by the Council and/or Assembly, the Secretary-General could be an appropriate body for ensuring that the effectiveness and credibility of the Organization is not undermined. For example, if the Secretary-General negotiates a cease-fire and establishment of a peace-keeping force with the parties of a conflict, as well as the provision of military units with third States, the absence of a decision by the Council or Assembly should not preclude the establishment of a peace-keeping mission. A necessary reservation is, of course, that the Secretary-General's power is limited exclusively to non-coercive operations because the Charter clearly allocates the exclusive responsibility for coercive operations to the Security Council.

The Secretary-General thus has secondary responsibility for the maintenance of international peace and security. Such a secondary responsibility is not exclusively reserved for the General Assembly, according to the relevant Charter provisions. The only condition contained in the Charter is that the primary responsibility in this field is assigned to the Security Council. Other organs, including the Secretary-General, may thus assume secondary responsibility if the achievment of the purposes of the Organization so require.

The need for organizing preventive peace-keeping forces might be referred to as a basis for the Secretary-General's powers to establish such forces. As the majority of conflicts require rapid response before or after they break out, the Secretary-General might be an appropriate body to respond because it can act quickly. For instance, if a State feels that an armed invasion of its territory is being prepared and is expected to occur, it may ask the UN for its mandate for stationing a preventive peace-keeping force at its border. Deliberations in the Council or Assembly may require a significant amount of time and the response, even if made, may be belated and ineffective. By contrast, if the Secretary-General manages—in cooperation with an affected State—to secure the necessary military units, he shall be empowered to grant the UN mandate to such units for the purpose of preventing an alleged expected invasion. In such a case, the affected States will not have to wait for approval by the permanent members of the Security Council, one of which will very likely have political affiliation or geopolitical interest in a region concerned. This is the only interpretation of the Secretary-General's powers that conforms with the fact that the United Nations, as an international organization, shall possess the capacity of independent decision-making in the area of peace and security. More precisely, decisions in the area of peace and security shall be taken not only by bodies composed of member states and expressing their compromised will, but also by the Secretary-General as a person representing the United Nations and being the chief administrative officer thereof.[91] Recognition of the Secretary-General's power to organize peace-keeping forces is a necessary constructive step in establishing the primacy of common interests in prevention of conflicts over the self-interests of member States. In addition, such recognition does not affect the powers of any other principal organ of the UN because it does not involve the elements of an enforcement action.

The peace-keeping forces established by the Secretary-General in cooperation with the interested States may, however, be authorized to use force against non-State entities. Insofar as such forces are based on the consent of and do not use force against a given State, they may not be considered as established in contravention of primary responsibility of the Security Council in the area of peace and security. This line of reasoning is similar to that developed above in the example of the General Assembly.

B.   Establishment of Peace-Keeping Forces under the Law of Treaties

An additional basis of the Secretary-General's power to establish peace-keeping forces is his treaty-making power. As a rule, the peace-keeping operations are based on treaties between the UN and the host State or States delivering military units. According to Article 6 of the Vienna Convention on the Law of Treaties concluded between States and International Organizations or between International Organizations, the capacity to conclude treaties on behalf of an international organization is governed by the relevant rules of that organization.[92] In adopting this provision at the drafting stage, the International Law Commission (ILC) refused to elaborate a universal approach applicable to all international organizations (comparable to the treaty-making powers of State agents and representatives.[93]

In practice, the Secretary-General represents the UN in

---

91. U.N. CHARTER art. 99.

92. Vienna Convention on the Law of Treaties Concluded Between States and International Organizations or Between International Organizations [hereinafter Vienna Convention], Mar. 21, 1986, art. 6, *available at* http://www.un.org/law/ilc/texts/trbtstat.htm (last visited Dec. 13, 2002).

93. *Draft Articles on the Law of Treaties Between States and International Organizations or Between International Organizations Adopted By the International Law Commission at its Thirty-Fourth Meeting*, U.N. Doc. A/CONF.129/4, *reprinted in United Nations Conference on the Law of Treaties Between States and International Organizations or Between International Organizations* (Feb. 18–Mar. 21, 1986), at 11, U.N. Doc. A/CONF.129/16/Add.1 (Vol. II) (commentary to Article 6). For the treaty-making power of State agents, *see* article 7 of the Vienna Convention on the Law of Treaties of 1969, *available at* http://www.un.org/law/ilc/texts/treatfra.htm. Article 6 of that convention suggests that "Every State possesses capacity to conclude treaties." This is a formulation substantially different from Article 6 of the 1986 Convention.

concluding agreements concerning the peace-keeping forces. Article 7(3) of the Vienna Convention states,

> [a] person is considered as representing an international organisation for the purpose of...expressing the consent of that organization to be bound by treaty if: (a) that person produces appropriate full powers; or (b) it appears from the circumstances that it was the intention of the States and international organizations concerned to consider that person as representing the organization for such purposes, in accordance with the rules of the organization, without having to produce full powers.[94]

From this practice, it appears that the Secretary-General, as the chief administrative officer, may conclude agreements on behalf of the UN. This power has never been disputed. As the ILC determined, in this case it is the acquiescence by other organs that produces the Secretary-General's power to conclude treaties. The abstention by other organs of an organization to limit such a solution signifies that the practice in question has acquired its legal standing.[95]

Generally, if a treaty is concluded by the Secretary-General in violation of the rules of an organization, Article 8 of the Vienna Convention provides that the violation may be cured through the subsequent confirmation by the relevant organization.[96] Article 46 of the same Convention, dealing with the invalidity of treaties concluded in violation of the rules of an organization, does not envisage any limitation on the rule embodied in Article 8.[97]

Which organ of the UN is required to validate an unauthorized entry into treaty relations by the Secretary-General? As the ILC explained, there are no general guidelines or standards to identify which organs are empowered to conclude a treaty on behalf of an international organization: "The titles, competence and terms of reference of the agents responsible for the external relations of an international organization differ from one organization to another."[98]

---

94. Vienna Convention, *supra* note 92, art. 7, para. 3.

95. *Draft Articles on the Law of Treaties Between States and International Organizations or Between International Organizations Adopted By the International Law Commission at its Thirty-Fourth Meeting*, U.N. Doc. A/CONF.129/4, *reprinted in United Nations Conference on the Law of Treaties Between States and International Organizations or Between International Organizations* (Feb. 18–Mar. 21, 1986), at 14, U.N. Doc. A/CONF.129/16/Add.1 (Vol. II) (commentary to Article 7).

96. Vienna Convention, *supra* note 92, art. 8.

97. *Id.*, art. 46.

98. *Draft Articles on the Law of Treaties Between States and International Organizations or Between International Organizations Adopted By the International Law Commission at its Thirty-Fourth Meeting*, U.N. Doc. A/CONF.129/4, *reprinted in United Nations Conference on the Law of Treaties Between States and International Organizations or Between International Organizations* (Feb. 18–Mar. 21, 1986), at 35, U.N. Doc.

512   VIRGINIA JOURNAL OF INTERNATIONAL LAW   [Vol. 43:485

Bearing this in mind, two prerequisites must be clarified. First an organ whose confirmation is allegedly required must itself, according to the rules or practice of the UN, possess the treaty-making capacity. Second, the area within which the Secretary-General enters into the treaty commitments must belong to the exclusive competence of that organ. Therefore, the Secretary-General acting in pursuance of his implied powers and concluding agreements concerning the peace-keeping forces may not be considered to have exceeded its powers unless the limits on these powers are identified. The Charter does not reserve the exclusive competence relating to the peace-keeping operations for the Security Council or General Assembly. These organs may not be considered as indispensable for confirming the allegedly unauthorized commitments made by the Secretary-General. Therefore, the refusal by these organs to validate the allegedly *ultra vires* peace-keeping agreements concluded by the Secretary-General does not render those agreements invalid.

Moreover, as a practical matter, in order to interfere with or stop the peace-keeping operation based on an allegedly *ultra vires* action of the Secretary-General, the Security Council or General Assembly must adopt a decision to that effect. Without prejudice to the juridical aspect outlined above, the practical problem here is the same as in the case of the establishment of the peace-keeping forces by the Council or Assembly. In adopting a decision against the peace-keeping operation initiated by the Secretary-General, the interested States must secure either the two-thirds majority in the Assembly or the qualified majority in the Council, including the votes of all permanent members. Unless these conditions are met, the Council or the Assembly may not be considered as even expressing their position, regardless of whether this position would have a definitive impact on the legal consequences of the Secretary-General's decision to organize the peace-keeping operations.

A final observation extending beyond the ambit of the law of treaties should also be made. The regime governing the possible peace-keeping initiatives of the Secretary-General is radically different from the issue of the so-called validation of the forcible actions undertaken by the regional organizations in violation of Article 53 of the Charter, which is sometimes inferred from the fact of the non-condemnation of such actions by the Security Council, as in the case of Kosovo. At least two differences may be observed. First, a forcible action by a regional organization undertaken without the authorization of the Security Council violates both conventional and customary international law, while the decision by the

---

A/CONF.129/16/Add.1 (Vol. II) (commentary to Article 46).

Secretary-General to establish a peace-keeping force would not offend international law. Second, such forcible actions by the regional organizations would encroach upon the exclusive competence of the Security Council, while a peace-keeping initiative of the Secretary-General would not encroach upon the exclusive competence of any principal organ of the United Nations.

C. Institutional Prerequisites: Article 7 of the Charter

The Charter does not explicitly empower the Secretary-General to establish the subsidiary bodies of the United Nations, as it empowers the General Assembly and Security Council.[99] Article 7 of the Charter, however, does contain a general authorization to establish subsidiary organs.[100] This general authorization, as evidenced by the practice, warrants the establishment of subsidiary organs beyond the scope of concrete authorizations, as contained in Articles 22 and 29. According to Gunther Jaenicke, "the better interpretation of Art. 7(2) seems to be that authority to establish subsidiary organs may also be inferred from it, *either directly* or in combination with other articles of the Charter".[101] The general nature of the power under Article 7(2) is also affirmed by Kelsen.[102]

It could be questionable to what extent this circumstance may influence the existence of the Secretary-General's power to establish a force on its own initiative. However, the need to advance the purposes of the United Nations provides justification for the Secretary-General's action, insofar as this is not prohibited under the Charter. The establishment of subsidiary organs is allowed by Article 7 "in accordance with" the Charter and not "as provided for by" the Charter. The wording of Article 7, therefore, permits the establishment of a subsidiary organ as long as it is not prohibited by the Charter.

Lastly, the provisions of the constituent instruments of international organizations should be interpreted "in a way which is considered to be most likely to advance the particular objectives of the Organization."[103] This is also true for Article 7. The primary purpose of the United Nations—the maintenance of international peace and security—will be better served if the decision-making process is not unduly delayed and if political controversies have less influence on the process of establishing peace-keeping operations.

99. U.N. CHARTER arts. 22, 29.

100. *Id.* art. 7, para. 2.

101. Gunther Jaenicke, *Article 7, in* THE CHARTER OF THE UNITED NATIONS, A COMMENTARY 224 (Bruno Simma ed., 2002) (emphasis added).

102. KELSEN, *supra* note 13, at 138.

103. E. Lauterpacht, *The Development of the Law of International Organization by the Decisions of International Tribunals, in* RECUEIL DES COURS IV 376, 421 (1976).

514 VIRGINIA JOURNAL OF INTERNATIONAL LAW [Vol. 43:485

V. REGIONAL ORGANIZATIONS

There is a trend towards a decentralized approach to establishing peace-keeping operations. The UN, acting in situations endangering peace and security, is subject to financial, political, and, in certain cases, legal constraints. This circumstance leads to the consideration of the role of regional organizations in the establishment of peace-keeping forces which would be stationed within the region concerned.

A. Legal Principles and Policy Considerations

Regional organizations are empowered to establish peace-keeping forces without authorization by the United Nations.[104] Peace-keeping operations do not constitute enforcement actions, and hence they do not fall within the scope of Article 53 of the UN Charter.

The preferability of the regional organizations' role in establishing peace-keeping operations may be explained by reference to the following factual, political, and legal conditions:

- Article 52 of the UN Charter endorses the role of regional organizations in adjusting disputes or situations arising in their respective regions. It could even be inferred from the text of this article that regional organizations possess the primary competence for dealing with such disputes and situations;[105]

- The decision-making process within the regional organizations is less complicated than in the UN. There is no danger of the use of veto, as in the UN Security Council. Generally, the members of the regional organizations are relatively more like-minded when dealing with issues of peace and security than members of the Security Council or General Assembly;

- The involvement of regional organizations in peace-keeping operations may help avoid severe financial problems present

---

104. WALTER, *supra* note 30, at 334-35. On the contrary, it has been argued by Errki Kourula that the regional organizations are not empowered to establish peace-keeping forces without approval by the Security Council. If the Security Council refers a dispute or situation to a regional organization, it does so because of convenience and effectiveness and not because of a legal obligation. Errki Kourula, *Peace-keeping and Regional Arrangements, in* UNITED NATIONS PEACE-KEEPING: LEGAL ESSAYS 95, 117 (Antonio Cassese ed. 1978). Even the host State's consent does not change the situation. *Id.* at 118. Consent under certain circumstances may not be genuine. *Id.*

105. For instance, the primacy of the Arab League over the UN was asserted by Arab States in the Lebanon crisis, where they opposed involvement of the UN Security Council. WALTER, *supra* note 30, at 337.

within the UN. Governments are generally more reluctant to spend within the UN than within the regional organizations;

- Peace-keeping operations by regional organizations are without prejudice to the powers of the principal organs of the UN;

- According to Articles 52 and 54 of the Charter, the Security Council possesses the residual competence with regard to the peace-keeping operations initiated by the regional organizations. This circumstance opens the door for the accountability of regional organizations to the UN;

- Peace-keeping operations by regional organizations, since they do not involve the elements of enforcement, do not affect the force monopoly of the Security Council; and

- Peace-keeping operations are based on the consent of the parties. Whether the forces are mandated by the UN or by a regional organization is not decisive for the legal nature or legal basis of a peace-keeping operation.

Taken together, these factors may bring us to the conclusion that the role of regional organizations in peace-keeping operations is necessary and appropriate. Yet, this still begs the question concerning the limits of this necessity and appropriateness. Consideration of the UN's role in peace-keeping operations undertaken by regional organizations is crucial for understanding this problem.

Under certain circumstances, the involvement of a regional organization in peace-keeping operations may serve to undermine, rather than to strengthen, the role, purposes, and functions of the UN. Within the Security Council different geopolitical interests are present. The clash between those different interests is characteristic of the work of the Security Council and General Assembly and the balance (although an imperfect one) between the different geopolitical aspirations is thereby maintained.

Regional organizations, on the other hand, which are dominated by one or more Great Powers having far-reaching geopolitical interests, do not offer the same opportunity for checks and balances as provided by the UN. After a peace-keeping force is mandated by a regional organization, it becomes practically impossible to hold a regional organization accountable before the UN because of the possible involvement of permanent members of the Security Council. The purposes and functions of the UN may therefore suffer

516   VIRGINIA JOURNAL OF INTERNATIONAL LAW   [Vol. 43:485

to an important and irreparable extent.

The use of regional organizations by Great Powers for maintaining or enlarging their own spheres of influence has become a usual practice in international relations.[106] An obvious consequence of this practice is that the functions and powers of the UN in the area of peace and security become paralyzed in the region or area concerned. The Great Powers prefer to have the presence of regional organizations, where their interests dominate, rather than the presence of the UN within which the conflicting geopolitical interests have to be balanced. These circumstances support the survival and effective operation of the old doctrines concerning the division of the spheres of influence between the Great Powers. The dominant role of a regional organization, including in the area of peace-keeping operations, may strengthen the assertions of regional dominance. Examples of such as the Monroe Doctrine with its modern ramifications,[107] as well as the Brezhnev Doctrine, which is being currently succeeded by the Russian conception of the "near abroad."[108] The procedural technicalities of asserting and enforcing these assertions are very simple: after a regional organization acts (in a proper or improper way), a permanent member of the Security Council may—using its right to veto—prevent an effective response or supervision by the UN.

B.   Case Study: CIS Forces in Abkhazia (Georgia)

The practice of regional organizations may offer many examples of when the old doctrines of regional hegemony are revived in the context of the modern peace-keeping by regional organizations, as seen with the peace-keeping practice of the Commonwealth of Independent States (CIS).[109] This organization, established in 1991[110] in order to fill the political vacuum that emerged after the dissolution of the Soviet Union, maintained the Russian political and military hegemony over the area of the former Soviet Union. Although the CIS, according to its founding instruments, is an association "of Independent States," in practice, as well as in its

---

106. *See, e.g.,* Antonio F. Perez, *On the Way to the Forum: The Reconstruction of Article 2(7) and the Rise of Federalism under the United Nations Charter,* 31 TEX. INT'L L.J. 353, 443 & nn.441-42.

107. For an example of one such modern ramification, see GEORG NOLTE, EINGREIFEN AUF EINLADUNG 269 (1999).

108. *Id.* at 440 (emphasizing, in particular, that political interests of Russian Federation contribute to preventing involvement of peace-keeping activities in conflicts in States of the former Soviet Union). For further elaboration on the "near abroad" doctrine, see *id.* at 475.

109. *Id.* at 440.

110. The Charter of the CIS was adopted in 1993. For an unofficial translation of the Charter, see Charter of the Commonwealth of Independent States (John Fowler trans.), *available at* http://www.therussiasite.org/legal/laws/CISCharter.html (last visited Oct. 12, 2002).

underlying conceptual background, this organization merely serves to limit in political terms the sovereignty of its member states in the sense of the Warsaw Pact and Brezhnev-doctrine.[111] This has resulted in the CIS asserting its primacy in conflict resolution involving territories of former Soviet republics over organizations like the UN and OSCE.[112] The peace-keeping activities of the CIS are an integral part of this enterprise.

After the large-scale atrocities and crimes against humanity in Abkhazia (Georgia) committed in 1992 and 1993 against the Georgian population and involving tens of thousands of killings and hundreds of thousands of displacements and expulsions, the resistance by the Russian Federation prevented the establishment of a UN peace-keeping force for Abkhazia. The UN involvement in the management of this conflict was limited to the deployment of the small United Nations Observers Mission in Georgia (UNOMIG) and the Human Rights Office in Sukhumi.[113] In 1994, in accordance with Russia's geopolitical interests, the CIS peace-keeping troops, composed exclusively of Russian personnel, were stationed in the region. UN involvement was limited to the approval of the CIS peace-keeping force by Security Council Resolutions 934 and 937.[114] The Security Council even indicated that the establishment of the CIS peace-keeping force took place "in accordance with the established principles and practices of the United Nations."[115]

This peace-keeping operation by the CIS as a regional organization was based on consent by the parties and did not involve enforcement action to be approved, or authorized, by the UN. An important point regarding the legal background, as well as the legal consequences, of the UN approval of a regional action is that such approval was not required under the law in force.

As far as the political context is concerned, the approval of deployment of CIS troops may be characterized as entrusting the outcome of the conflict to a directly interested State, while the peace-keeping function was originally considered to be impartial.[116] This approval was most probably part of a broader "package deal" between the United States and the Russian Federation, both of which needed the UN mandate for the presence of their troops in Haiti and

---

111. *See generally* NOLTE, *supra* note 107.

112. NOLTE, *supra* note 107, at 475.

113. *See* http://www.un.org/Depts/DPKO/Missions/unomig/unomig_body.htm (last visited Nov. 11, 2002).

114. NOLTE, *supra* note 107, at 472-73. *See also* S.C. Res. 934, U.N. SCOR, 49th Sess., 3398th mtg., U.N. Doc. S/RES/934 (1994); S.C. Res. 937, U.N. SCOR, 49th Sess., 3407th mtg., U.N. Doc. S/RES/937 (1994).

115. S.C. Res. 937, U.N. SCOR, 49th Sess., 3407th mtg., U.N. Doc. S/RES/937 (1994).

116. NOLTE, *supra* note 107, at 468.

518   VIRGINIA JOURNAL OF INTERNATIONAL LAW   [Vol. 43:485

in Georgia, respectively.[117] The role of the Security Council was limited to giving the mandate to the assertion of spheres of influence by the Great Powers, respectively in the Americas and the Caucasus.

The mandate of the CIS force in Abkhazia described the objectives of that force as "to exert its best efforts to maintain the cease-fire and to see. that it is scrupulously observed" and "to promote the safe return of refugees and displaced persons."[118] The troops, however, lacked the willingness and, to a certain extent, the resources to meet these requirements. They lacked, for instance, anti-landmine capability. In fact, they perpetuated the separatist regime and failed to promote the return of refugees.[119] In the period after CIS peace-keeping forces were deployed in Abkhazia, several thousands of killings and deportations of the Georgian population took place in the region, including the zone of the immediate responsibility of CIS forces. The CIS forces failed to respond to that.

The CIS considers itself a regional organization under Chapter VIII of the UN Charter. Under Article 54 of the UN Charter, the CIS is bound to report to the UN concerning its peace-keeping operations.[120] Moreover, the UN supervises the activities of the CIS forces through UNOMIG. Nevertheless, the organs of the United Nations have shown no willingness to determine the consequences of the CIS's failure to meet the requirements of their mandate.

VI. CONSENT BY THE AFFECTED PARTIES

A. *General Remarks*

Consent is an instrument for the creation of international obligations. It is even a factor capable of validating behavior which would otherwise be illegal. Therefore, consent is an inevitable element in the legal basis of peace-keeping forces.[121] There is another aspect to the requirement of consent by States to the establishment of a peace-keeping force: continuing consent, as seen from a dynamic perspective, is a precondition of the effective accomplishment of a peace-keeping mission in a practical sense.

---

117. *See, e.g.,* Percz, *supra* note 106, n.442 (citing Lally Weymouth, *Yalta II*, WASH. POST, Jul. 24, 1994; Daniel Williams, *Powers Assert Influence in Peacekeeping Roles; Independent Missions Lack UN's Idealism*, WASH. POST, Jul. 30, 1994, at A12).

118. *Annex I to Letter Dated 17 May 1994 from the Permanent Representative of Georgia to the United Nations Addressed to the President of the Security Council*, U.N. SCOR, 49th Sess., U.N. Doc. S/1994/583 (1994).

119. Ruth Wedgwood, *The Promise of and Obstacles to Effective Peace-Keeping by the CIS, NATO, OSCE, WEU and UN (remarks)*, in CONTEMPORARY INTERNATIONAL LAW ISSUES: NEW FORMS, NEW APPLICATIONS – PROCEEDINGS OF THE FOURTH HAGUE JOINT CONFERENCE HELD IN THE HAGUE, THE NETHERLANDS, 2-5 JULY 1997 57, 69 (1998).

120. WALTER, *supra* note 30, at 361.

121. *Id.* at 321-22.

For the actual deployment of a peace-keeping force into the territory of a State, the consent of the latter is indispensable. If UN forces are stationed in the territory of a State without its consent, they necessarily involve use of force against that State, thus being *peace-enforcement* and not peace-keeping forces. The necessity of consent in peace-keeping operations does not prejudice the power of the Security Council to make binding decisions under Chapter VII. The Council must simply make a choice as to which means would be appropriate for maintaining or restoring international peace and security in a given situation. If the establishment of a peace-keeping force is considered by the Council to be an appropriate option, the consent by the host State shall be necessarily sought.[122]

Chapter VII decisions are expected to be involved in the establishment of peace-keeping operations only if a sufficient consensus is reached within the Security Council for making a determination under Article 39. Thus, consent remains a usual part of this enterprise. Higgins considers that even in the event of Chapter VII action, the consent by affected parties is necessary. Although this conclusion may not be reached by way of a textual interpretation, practice supports the necessity of consent also in the case of Chapter VII decisions.[123] Several examples may be referred to where—notwithstanding the legal force of the Chapter VII decisions—the consent of a host/target State has been requested for the initiation of the respective measures, whether peace-keeping or peace enforcement. UNPROFOR was established on the basis of the request by Yugoslavia.[124] Similarly, the consent of Indonesia was requested when the decision was made to establish (again under Chapter VII) United Nations Transitional Authority in East Timor (UNTAET); likewise, Federal Republic of Yugoslavia consented to the deployment of KFOR in Kosovo.[125] The relevance of consent by the host State in the case of peace-keeping operations established within the framework of Chapter VII therefore depends not on the nature and legal force of Chapter VII decisions, but on the nature of the peace-keeping operations.

Consent may be expressed in an organ establishing a given peace-

---

122. However, it should be mentioned that the refusal of consent may, in certain situations, lead to the adoption of coercive measures under Articles 41 and 42. This assumption finds its basis in the Charter. See U.N. CHARTER arts. 41-42.

123. Higgins, *supra* note 86, at 5.

124. *See, e.g., Letter Dated 26 November 1991 from the Permanent Representative of Yugoslavia to the United Nations Addressed to the President of the Security Council*, U.N. SCOR, 46th Sess., U.N. Doc. S/23240 (1991); S.C. Res. 743, U.N. SCOR, 47th Sess., U.N. Doc. S/RES/743 (1992).

125. S.C. Res. 1272, U.N. SCOR, 54th Sess., U.N. Doc. S/RES/1272 (1999); S.C. Res. 1264, U.N. SCOR, 54th Sess., U.N. Doc. S/RES/1264 (1999); S.C. Res. 1244, U.N. SCOR, 54th Sess., U.N. Doc. S/RES/1244 (1999).

520   VIRGINIA JOURNAL OF INTERNATIONAL LAW   [Vol. 43:485

keeping force and also through an agreement between the UN and relevant States.[126] In practice, the consent by a host State is inferred from the exchange of notes between the Secretary-General of the UN and the host State. It is hardly disputable that such an exchange of notes constitutes an agreement under international law governed by the law of treaties, in particular, the Vienna Convention on the Law of Treaties of 1986.[127]

According to Article 2 of the Vienna Convention of 1986, a treaty is an agreement concluded between States and organizations or between organizations, governed by international law, embodied in one or more related instruments and whatever its particular designation. The exchange of notes is in fact a treaty, based on the free will of the host State. This is evidenced by Article 13 of the Vienna Convention, which provides that the exchange of instruments constituting the treaty expresses the consent by parties to be bound by a treaty.

B.   The Specific Dimensions of Consent

1.   Consent ratione personae

The general assumption of consent *ratione personae* is that the consent of a host State is requested because of its sovereignty over the territory into which the peace-keeping forces have to be deployed. Consent by a State, as represented by its government, is necessary even when the government is in exile. This means that consent is requested from a State not merely because it is in effective control of the territory but also because it is sovereign over the territory in a juridical sense.

It might be suggested that in the case of the so-called "failed States," due to the absence of an effective government, no consent of the parties is necessary. In a purely legal sense, this might be true. Also, the need for the maintenance of international peace and security may require UN intervention in a situation where the absence of an effective government may endanger the international peace. However, the nature and function of peace-keeping operations make the consent by the parties necessary. Non-consensual peace-keeping operations are subject to the risk of being unsuccessful.[128] Peace-keeping operations are, by their very nature,

---

126. Antonietta Di Blase, *The Role of the Host State's Consent with Regard to Non-Coercive Actions by the United Nations, in* UNITED NATIONS PEACE-KEEPING: LEGAL ESSAYS 55, 55-56 (Antonio Cassese ed., 1978).

127. This Convention embodies the customary international law on the rules and principles governing treaties concluded by international organizations. Vienna Convention, *supra* note 92.

128. MCCOUBREY & WHITE, *supra* note 1, at 72.

consensual and the presence of consent is a prerequisite for ensuring that nothing will interfere with the deployment and operation of a peace-keeping force. The conclusion is that situations involving the absence of an effective government shall be addressed not through peace-keeping, but through peace-enforcement operations in conjunction with the establishment of transitional authorities.

It is widely accepted that in inter-State conflicts, the deployment of a peace-keeping force requires consent of both States.[129] The majority of contemporary conflicts are, however, not inter-State, but internal. This begs the question how the practice could be explained where the consent is requested not only from the host State, but also from other parties to the conflict, including rebels or separatists. A sovereignty-based approach to the principle of consent is obviously not in position to explain this scenario. It may be asked whether the requirement of consent by parties other than host States is based on juridical imperatives or merely on considerations of expediency.

The functional nature of peace-keeping operations may explain why the consent of parties other than States is frequently requested. This functional nature consists of the maintenance of international peace and security in the area concerned, subject to the respect for the territorial integrity and sovereignty of a host State.[130] The fact that the host State has consented to the stationing of forces means that its territorial sovereignty has been respected. But once this requirement is satisfied, the core function of peace-keeping operations is the maintanance of peace in the area (respect for territorial sovereignty being the limitation on this function). For the successful performance of that function, the consent by all affected parties is necessary. This circumstance is entirely without prejudice to territorial sovereignty or to the settlement of a controversy in question.

There is no legal requirement necessitating consent of non-State actors for the establishment of a peace-keeping force, although the requirement of consent emanates from the nature of peace-keeping operations. Consent by non-State actors is sought as a matter of expediency[131] and not as a legal imperative. The United Nations Force in Cyprus (UNFICYP), for instance, was established on the basis of consent by the government of Cyprus only.[132]

---

129. WALTER, *supra* note 30, at 322. UNEF, for instance, was located only on the territory of Egypt because Israel had not consented to the stationing of troops on both sides of the armistice line. *Id.*

130. S.C. Res. 1272, *supra* note 125 (establishing UNTAET and acknowledging the territorial sovereignty of Indonesia); S.C. Res. 1244, *supra* note 123, at para. 10, Annex II (establishing KFOR and respecting the territorial integrity and sovereignty of the FRY).

131. Walter refers to the relevance of the influence of parties in a civil war in this context. WALTER, *supra* note 30, at 324.

132. MCCOUBREY & WHITE, *supra* note 1, at 70.

522   VIRGINIA JOURNAL OF INTERNATIONAL LAW   [Vol. 43:485

In the *Certain Expenses* case, the ICJ acknowledged the difference between the measures taken against States and those taken against non-State entities, including secessionist ones. The Operation of the United Nations in Congo has been considered by the ICJ to be a peace-keeping operation, not a Chapter VII enforcement measure.[133] The ICJ reached this conclusion notwithstanding the fact that the Security Council, by Resolution 161, extended the mandate of ONUC by authorizing it to take "all appropriate measures to prevent the occurrence of civil war in the Congo," including "the use of force, as a last resort, if necessary."[134] The decisive point for the ICJ was that ONUC was "not authorized to take military action against any State."[135]

Therefore, it must be assumed that the UN military operations not involving the forcible action against a State cannot be regarded as enforcement actions, but rather, fall within the notion of peace-keeping. As far as they may involve the use of force against non-State entities, including secessionist ones, the requirement of consent by such non-State entities is not legally imperative.[136] When such a consent is sought, it is based simply on convenience and the need to prevent aggravation of a conflict.

2. *Consent* ratione materiae

There may be differing views on whether consent of a host State shall extend not only to the establishment of a peace-keeping force but also to the scope of its mandate and its composition. The power to determine the composition of a mission belongs in principle to the Security Council or Secretary-General.[137] In practice, however, "the records of the discussions in connection with [peace-keeping] decisions amply show the large degree of concern for the constant fulfilment" of the consent of concerned parties.[138] Such a practice is no doubt reasonable because a host State may always make its

---

133. *Certain Expenses*, 1962 I.C.J. at 177.

134. S.C. Res. 161, *supra* note 22, at para. 1.

135. *Certain Expenses*, 1962 I.C.J. at 177.

136. Nolte considers that as far as States are the regular subjects of international law and represented by their respective governments, these governments may meet rebellion movements with force and may therefore avail themselves of the appropriate assistance by foreign States. NOLTE, *supra* note 107, at 133. By way of analogy to approach of Nolte, we conclude that States may also use assistance by international organizations while dealing with rebellion movements, including secessionist and separatist units.

Our conclusion is supported by the practice of the Security Council, which, in the case of the Congo, expressly stated that its aim was to support Congolese government in fighting against secessionist Katanga and to enable national security forces to fully meet their tasks. S.C. Res. 161, *supra* note 22, at para. 2.

137. SAROOSHI, *supra* note 85, at 65. For details regarding consent in connection with composition of forces, see Di Blase, *supra* note 126, at 58-69.

138. Suy, *supra* note 8, at 550.

consent to the deployment of a peace-keeping force dependent on conditions regarding the mandate and composition of such a force.

Nevertheless, an exception to that circumstance may occur if the peace-keeping forces are established under Chapter VII. If the UN is ready to support its proposals regarding the composition of a peace-keeping force by a further enforcement action, the host State may decide to accept the composition of a force as proposed by the UN.

3. *Consent* ratione temporis

Peace-keeping operations are always considered temporary measures. Therefore, as a rule, the duration of their mandate is stated in the resolutions which establish them. Generally, in practice, the mandates of peace-keeping forces are limited to a certain period (usually up to six months) and are periodically prolonged. Such a periodic prolongation of the mandate may be considered a tool for maintaining the empirical viability of consent given by the parties. However, this does not prejudice the juridical quality of consent already given by a State.

VII. CONCLUDING REMARKS

To examine the legal basis of peace-keeping operations within the limits of one contribution is a hard and complex task. Nevertheless, an attempt has been made here to analyze several legal bases provided for in the UN Charter and in general international law. Some tentative general conclusions may be formulated in this regard as follows: First, the provisions of the Charter of the United Nations governing the maintenance of international peace and security confer on the UN the powers sufficient to establish peace-keeping operations, as well as to adapt the existing peace-keeping forces to particular needs following from a situation in which the peace-keeping forces operate and purposes they serve. In particular, the peace-keeping forces may be transformed into peace-enforcement ones.

Second, several bases provided in the Charter for the establishment of a peace-keeping operation should be interpreted and applied in a mutually supportive and not in a mutually exclusive way. Such an approach may guarantee the effective realization of the political discretion conferred upon the principal organs of the United Nations and support the performance of their powers to the fullest possible extent.

Third, the consensual nature of peace-keeping operations, in conjunction with the purposes and principles of the United Nations, may contribute to empowering the organs of the UN—in our case the Secretary-General—to establish the peace-keeping forces when

524   VIRGINIA JOURNAL OF INTERNATIONAL LAW   [Vol. 43:485

the need of maintenance of peace and security so requires. The need for effective application of the Charter provisions should also be borne in mind. It should be emphasized that such an approach does not intend to encroach upon the exclusive competences of any other UN principal organ.

Finally, the consensual nature of peace-keeping operations shall be a necessary criteria for the United Nations in order to decide which situations involving dangers to peace may be addressed through peace-keeping operations. The need to maintain peace and security and the suitability of a particular situation for establishing a peace-keeping force shall be considered as equally significant factors in each case.

[4]

The UN Charter and Peacekeeping Forces: Constitutional Issues

NIGEL D. WHITE

The inconclusive formalist debate on the constitutional basis of peacekeeping can lead to scepticism over the relevance of law to peacekeeping. A contextual approach to the law based on an understanding of the shaping and ultimate dependence of law on politics frees the international lawyer from dry and circular discussion. In this light constitutional issues about the origins and the control of peacekeeping operations are seen to be of paramount importance in the understanding and development of peacekeeping. The potentially restrictive formalist doctrine of implied powers is shown to be a sham behind which the reality is that of a wider, but not unlimited, doctrine of inherent powers. Such a doctrine enables the United Nations to create a wide variety of peacekeeping forces, though the creation and control of such forces is shown to be subject to the constitutional structure of the UN. As regards peacekeeping, the division of competence between the Security Council, the General Assembly and the Secretary-General has grown up in practice. The centralist tendencies of this practice have been undermined in recent years by the growth in quasi-enforcement actions. It is questionable whether the looser constitutional restraints on these operations is desirable.

United Nations peacekeeping has grown with the organization, but its peacekeeping role was not envisaged by the founders. It became a useful, arguably necessary, element of the restricted Cold War collective security function of the UN. Its constitutionality has not really been in doubt since the World Court's decision in the *Expenses* case in the early 1960s, although debates have continued as to the exact constitutional basis of this power. Such issues will be considered in this article, but it will be seen that the desire to find an express Charter base for that power is unnecessary in the light of the doctrines of implied, or perhaps more accurately, inherent, powers. For external purposes there appears to be no doubt that the UN can create peacekeeping forces. The internal question of which organ is empowered to create and control the force is less clear, with both the Security Council, the General Assembly and the Secretary-General involved in the area.

In addition to considering these issues, this article will consider the growing issue of the UN 'sub-contracting' peacekeeping operations to other organizations/bodies, as well as the undertaking of such operations by

Nigel White is a Senior Lecturer in Law, Department of Law, University of Nottingham, UK.

outside bodies with no express UN approval or authorization. The rather uneasy legal relationship between the UN and other organizations whether they be regional, defence or security organizations, will be considered.

Implied Powers

An international organization has to respond to events to be able to fulfil its functions effectively. Even the most prescient founders of an organization established in 1945, or even 1985, cannot have foreseen the developments that have occurred since the establishment of the institution. To restrict organizations to the express provisions of their constituent treaties would therefore consign many organizations to a peripheral role in world affairs. Most organizations have a degree of legal personality or autonomy, which means that they have a certain flexibility in interpreting their powers as contained in their constituent documents.

The problem facing international lawyers is how far have organizations progressed in divorcing their activities from the institution's treaty base and, more importantly, whether this has been accepted in the law of international organizations. It appears to be accepted, in the practice of such institutions, the decisions of judicial institutions, and the comments of international jurists, that the doctrine of implied powers is valid in international law. Early in the life of the United Nations, the World Court accepted such a doctrine in the *Reparation* case when it stated:

> Under international law, the Organization must be deemed to have those powers which, though not expressly provided in the Charter, are conferred upon it by necessary implication as being essential to the performance of its duties.[1]

The Court deemed that it was necessary for the UN to be able to bring a claim on behalf of its employees, though it did not state from which express power this implied power derived. It appeared to be derived more from the general nature and purposes of the UN as a body aimed at securing international peace and security, an aim requiring the extensive use of personnel in dangerous situations. Judge Hackworth, in his dissenting opinion, pointed to the problem with the Court's approach:

> Powers not expressed cannot freely be implied. Implied powers flow from a grant of expressed powers, and are limited to those that are 'necessary' to the exercise of powers expressly granted. No necessity for the exercise of power here in question has been shown to exist. There is no impelling reason, if any at all, why the Organization should become the sponsor of claims on behalf of its employees.[2]

The difference between the approach of the majority and Judge Hackworth embodies the doctrinal confusion of what exactly is meant by implied powers, in particular what is 'necessary' to make the express powers work.[3]

The International Court of Justice has adopted a very generous view of the doctrine of implied powers, not only in the *Reparation* case but in the *Expenses* and *Namibia* cases. In the latter case, the International Court found that the General Assembly's termination of South Africa's mandate over South West Africa was within its competence, although it pointed to no specific Charter provisions empowering the Assembly so to act.[4] As to the legal basis of Security Council Resolution 276 (1970), which affirmed the General Assembly's decision, and declared that the presence of South Africa was illegal, the Court stated that:

> Article 24 of the Charter vests in the Security Council the necessary authority to take action such as that taken in the present case. The reference in paragraph 2 of this Article to specific powers of the Security Council under certain chapters of the Charter does not exclude the existence of general powers to discharge the responsibilities conferred in paragraph 1. Reference may be made in this respect to the Secretary-General's Statement, presented to the Security Council on 10 January 1947, to the effect that 'the powers of the Council under Article 24 are not restricted to the specific grants of authority contained in Chapters VI, VII, VIII and XII....[T]he Members of the United Nations have conferred upon the Security Council powers commensurate with its responsibility for the maintenance of peace and security. The only limitations are the fundamental principles and purposes found in Chapter I of the Charter'.[5]

The Court's approach is liberal and functionalist 'so that powers *relating* to the purposes and functions specified in the constitution can be implied', rather than narrow and formalist whereby 'one can imply only such powers as arise by necessary intendment from the constitutional provisions'.[6]

The fact that in these opinions the World Court has accepted that the UN can imply powers, not solely as arising by necessity from the express powers of the Organization, but as enabling it to fulfil its functions more effectively, means that consensual peacekeeping operations which facilitate a ceasefire or a withdrawal must be within the powers of an organization such as the UN, the primary concern of which is collective security. This reasoning is followed in the *Expenses* case, an advisory opinion directly concerned with the constitutionality of peacekeeping.

Certain Expenses Case

In the *Expenses* case a financial crisis over payment for the UN's peacekeeping operations in the Middle East (UNEF I) and in the Congo (ONUC), led the UN General Assembly to request an advisory opinion from the Court on the question of whether these expenditures constituted 'expenses of the Organization' within the meaning of Article 17(2) of the UN Charter. The request raised the question of whether the General Assembly was entitled to authorize peacekeeping operations, or whether exclusive competence in the field of peace and security lay with the Security Council, given that the Assembly had created UNEF I and had taken over the mandating of ONUC when the Security Council was deadlocked.

After analysing the structure and powers of the two principal UN organs and finding that the General Assembly was indeed empowered to create and mandate peacekeeping forces, the Court then tested whether the expenditures were compatible with the purposes of the UN. The Court then summarized the broad purposes set out in Article 1 of the Charter and stated:

> These purposes are wide indeed, but neither they nor the powers conferred to effectuate them are unlimited. Save as they have entrusted the Organization with the attainment of these common ends, the Member States retain their freedom of action. But when the Organization takes action which warrants the assertion that it was appropriate for the fulfilment of one of the stated purposes of the United Nations, the presumption is that such action is not *ultra vires* the Organization.[7]

It must be stressed that the Court is prepared only to *presume* that the action is *intra vires* and that it leaves itself the option of being able to declare future actions *ultra vires*, if given the opportunity. The difficulty is that it rarely has the opportunity, hence the presumption. It would make for a totally inefficient security system if every resolution of the Security Council or General Assembly, on peacekeeping or other matters, had question marks as to its legality hanging over it. States wanting to deny their obligations to the UN would simply maintain opposition to the resolutions on the basis of their alleged illegality, as France and the Soviet Union had done over the expenses crisis, and very little could be done to prevent this. However, if the decisions are presumed to be lawful until declared otherwise, States are under an undeniable obligation to comply.

Furthermore, it must be emphasized that in the *Expenses* case, the World Court was prepared to examine the legality of the General Assembly's action in terms of its competence under the UN Charter; it did not abdicate its responsibility as the judicial organ of the UN in deference to the political power of the Assembly. However, what it did do was to adopt a very liberal attitude to Charter interpretation. In effect the approach was to assert its ability to examine the actions of the Assembly but to do so in a very lenient way with the end result being the General Assembly was found competent. Perhaps this lenient approach is an inevitable consequence of the presumption against *ultra vires*. Indeed, it could be said that the presumption against *ultra vires* and the liberal doctrine of implied powers, are two sides of the same coin.

The liberal approach to implied powers is exemplified in the *Expenses* case when the Court did not stop to consider whether the development of a power to create and mandate peacekeeping forces by the General Assembly was *necessary* for the fulfilment of the express provisions of the Charter.[8] On the issue of the General Assembly's power, the Court stated that 'the provisions of the Charter which distribute functions and powers to the Security Council and to the General Assembly give no support to the view that such distribution excludes from the powers of the General Assembly the power' to adopt measures designed to maintain peace and security. The emphasis is not on the implication of powers necessary to make an express provision effective as in the *Reparation* case, but on the absence of any provision in the Charter prohibiting the exercise of such a power. The only limitation on the powers of the General Assembly in the field of peace and security is that, according to the Court, only the Security Council can 'order coercive action'.[9] In effect, the General Assembly's powers are only limited by provisions in the Charter which clearly prohibit such acts; in the case the restriction was that only the Security Council could order enforcement action under Chapter VII. Furthermore, in discussing the creation of the Congo force (ONUC) by the Security Council, the Court did not feel it necessary to identify the provisions of the Charter from which peacekeeping could be derived; it simply stated that 'the Charter does not forbid the Security Council to act through instruments of its own choice', and that ONUC was not a 'preventive or enforcement' action under Chapter VII and therefore did not come within the sole ambit of the Security Council but could be mandated by the General Assembly.[10]

Peacekeeping as an Inherent Power

The Court, in the *Expenses* case, certainly seemed to accept the British view on the creation of UNEF, contained in a Minister's response in the House of Commons to the question of which Article of the Charter had the Force been created under. The response was in terms of it not being created under any express provisions, but under a resolution of the General Assembly which was not prohibited by the Charter. The narrow view of the Soviet Union, that the only express mention made of the creation of any type of armed forces in the Charter was in Chapter VII, where only the Security Council was authorized to act, was rejected.[11] With the emphasis on UN organs having the power to undertake any action within the UN's purposes as long as the Charter does not expressly prohibit it, the Court, in many ways, seemed to have moved away from the doctrine of implied powers to that of inherent powers as argued for by Professor Seyersted.

> Indeed, it appears that while intergovernmental organizations, unlike States, are restricted by specific provisions in their constitutions as to the aims for which they shall work, such organizations are, like States, in principle free to perform any sovereign act, or any act under international law, which they are in a factual position to perform to attain these aims, provided that their constitutions do not preclude such acts. While a minority of the members will always have the right to challenge the legality, from an internal point of view, of acts performed to attain aims other than those defined in the constitution, the minority cannot challenge acts performed in order to attain aims covered in the constitution merely on the basis that such acts were not 'essential' or 'necessary' to attain these aims. Thus it is not necessary to look for specific provisions in the constitution, or to resort to strained interpretations of texts and intentions, or to look for precedents or constructions to justify legally the performance by an intergovernmental organization of a sovereign or international act not specifically authorized in its constitution. As an intergovernmental organization it has an *inherent power* to perform such acts.[12]

Seyersted's view is very powerful and seems to be supported by the ICJ's approach, particularly in the *Expenses* case, although the Court still uses the traditional, more accepted, terminology of 'implied' powers. Seyersted's approach certainly seems to be suitable for the creation of peacekeeping forces by the UN in that it may be difficult to argue that such forces are 'necessary' or 'essential' for the achievement of express powers.

More generally, the doctrine of inherent powers has two clear advantages over the doctrine of implied powers. First, it satisfies the functionalist agenda by allowing an organization to fulfil its aims and not be hidebound by the legal niceties of its individual, and often obscurely drafted, provisions; and second, it enables Courts and commentators to review the actions of the organizations quickly and accurately since there are only two real legal controls on the actions of the organization – that the action in question aims to achieve one of the purposes of the organization, and that it is not expressly prohibited by any of the provisions of the constitution. Only if either of these legal thresholds is crossed can an international court, jurist or member State claim that the action is *ultra vires*. On this basis peacekeeping is clearly lawful.

Furthermore, as the following sections show, there are ample express provisions of the Charter which peacekeeping enhances, though it cannot be said that peacekeeping is necessary to make these provisions work. It will be quite useful to quickly review these provisions and explain their importance as well as attempting to delineate the peacekeeping competencies of the General Assembly, the Security Council and the Secretary-General which have arisen in practice.

The Competence of the General Assembly

The World Court in the *Expenses* case clearly stated that the UN General Assembly had the power to create peacekeeping forces. It did not feel the need to recognize any particular Charter provision, an approach which itself supports the doctrine of inherent powers. However, it is relatively simple to point to Charter provisions which give the Assembly a significant secondary competence in the field of collective security, sufficient enough for it to mandate peacekeeping forces. Article 10 of the Charter allows the Assembly to make recommendations on any matter 'within the scope of the present Charter'. If Article 10 is insufficient to grant the Assembly the full range of recommendatory powers, Article 14 re-emphasizes its potentially wide jurisdiction with specific reference to international security by providing that 'the General Assembly may recommend measures for the peaceful adjustment of any situation, regardless of origin, which it deems likely to impair the general welfare or friendly relations among nations'.

However, to prevent any clash between the work of the Security Council – which according to Article 24 is the primary organ in such matters – and the General Assembly, Article 14, as well as Article 10, are subject to the limitation contained in Article 12 which states that:

> While the Security Council is exercising in respect of any dispute or situation the functions assigned to it in the present Charter, the General Assembly shall not make any recommendations with regard to that dispute or situation unless the Security Council so requests.

Article 12 is probably the most difficult provision, in constitutional terms, to reconcile with the practice of the General Assembly. The Assembly often adopts resolutions on a matter at the same time that the Security Council is considering the question.[13] Although disregarded in general, it will be seen that in the area of peacekeeping the Assembly, when it has created forces, has not infringed the requirements of Article 12, in that it has created forces only when the Council has desisted from dealing with the matter or has not touched the matter in a deliberate effort to enable the Assembly to deal with it.

Furthermore, the creation or mandating of peacekeeping forces does not infringe the requirements of Article 11(2) which provides that 'any...question on which action is necessary shall be referred to the Security Council by the General Assembly either before or after discussion'. As we have seen when looking at the World Court's judgment in the *Expenses* case, Article 11(2) only forbids the Assembly from *ordering* member states to adopt coercive measures, whether military or economic. This certainly does not prohibit the Assembly from creating a consensual peacekeeping force, nor, although this is more contentious, does it prevent the Assembly from recommending enforcement action.

This interpretation of the UN Charter is in line with the limited practice of the Assembly in the area of enforcement action. The Assembly has not only made recommendations for the adoption of economic sanctions against states, but it has also adopted a resolution, the Uniting for Peace resolution of 1950, which recognizes that the Assembly possesses the power to make 'appropriate recommendations to members for collective measures, including in the case of a breach of the peace or act of aggression the use of armed force when necessary'.

The Soviet Union stated that the resolution was *ultra vires*, arguing that collective action was solely within the province of the Security Council.[14] However, the resolution recognized the primary responsibility of the Security Council and only granted the Assembly the power to *recommend* collective measures. Such a power appears to be *intra vires*, which with the current expansion of peacekeeping by the Security Council into the area of quasi-enforcement, signifies that the Assembly could also, if the political circumstances so permit, recommend a quasi-enforcement peacekeeping force along the lines of that sent to Somalia in 1993.

Paradoxically, the Uniting for Peace resolution, while being accepted in practice as a procedure of moving items from the Security Council's agenda to the General Assembly's (meeting in Emergency Special Session), has failed to make the intended impact in the realm of collective security in its proper sense. No UN enforcement action has been authorized by it, although it was used to authorize the first UN peacekeeping force, the United Nations Emergency Force (UNEF I) in Sinai in 1956.[15]

Beyond the creation of UNEF I, the General Assembly has rarely exercised its inherent power to create a significant peacekeeping force. It did approve in 1962 of the creation of a UN Temporary Executive Authority (UNTEA) and a UN Security Force (UNSF) in West Irian as requested by the Netherlands and Indonesia as part of their agreement to end the conflict over the territory.[16] Furthermore, it did take over the control of ONUC in the Congo in September 1960, at a time when the Security Council, having placed ONUC in an impossible position, then ceased to deal with the conflict due to deadlock between the superpowers. In the Security Council the United States proposed that the matter be transferred to the General Assembly under the auspices of the Uniting for Peace resolution.[17]

Although opposed by the Eastern bloc the Assembly adopted a resolution on 20 September 1960. This resolution stated, *inter alia*, that to safeguard international peace it was 'essential for the United Nations to continue to assist the Central Government of the Congo' and to this end requested the Secretary-General to take 'vigorous action' to restore law and order and to preserve the unity, integrity and political independence of the Congo.[18] Although the World Court thought that the actions of ONUC in the Congo did not constitute enforcement action,[19] the Assembly certainly, by recommending 'vigorous action', seemed to be taking a quasi-enforcement approach to peacekeeping which, although controversial, seems to be within the powers of the Assembly.

Although the Assembly's practice in the field of peacekeeping is limited, its contributions have had much wider significance. First, it created the paradigm inter-state peacekeeping force in the form of UNEF I; second, it contributed to the concept of peace enforcement by peacekeeping forces in civil wars when it took over the mandating of ONUC; and finally, its creation of UNTEA and UNSF was the forerunner of the combination of peacekeeping and peaceful settlement, successfully used by the Security Council after the Cold War. In many ways, the Assembly, which was not constrained by the veto, gave birth to several aspects of peacekeeping which were nurtured by the Security Council as it re-asserted supremacy in peacekeeping matters.

The Competence of the Security Council

The competence of the Security Council in the area of peacekeeping is much less controversial. Although there is no express power granted in the UN Charter allowing for the creation of peacekeeping forces, the arguments for recognizing that the Council has an implied or inherent power to create a peacekeeping force are much clearer than those put forward for the Assembly.

First of all there are the general powers granted to the Security Council under Article 24(1) to maintain or restore international peace and security. Second, an examination of the specific powers granted to the Security Council indicates that peacekeeping falls somewhere between Chapter VI, 'Pacific Settlement of Disputes', and Chapter VII, 'Action with Respect to Threats to the Peace, Breaches of the Peace, and Acts of Aggression'. Peacekeeping constitutes a concrete military presence and therefore does not simply consist of mere recommendations for settlement or the establishment of basic fact-finding missions as is found in Chapter VI.[20] However, peacekeeping is not pure military enforcement action as envisaged under Chapter VII. Sometimes peacekeeping is closer to or linked to pacific settlement and therefore can be seen as a power linked to Article 36(1) of Chapter VI which provides that 'the Security Council may, at any stage of a dispute...recommend appropriate procedures or methods of adjustment'.

On other occasions peacekeeping is solely concerned with overseeing provisional measures (ceasefires, withdrawals) in which case the nexus is Article 40 which contains the power to call for provisional measures. Generally peacekeeping forces are created to facilitate the observance of such measures, when they have been accepted by the parties to the conflict. Furthermore, the nature of traditional peacekeeping based on the UNEF I model remains consensual and non-offensive whether or not the call for provisional measures is mandatory.[21]

However, the Security Council has occasionally used peacekeeping forces to enforce provisional measures – a practice which dates back to the Congo in 1960. This is still reconcilable with Article 40 in that the provision goes on to say that 'the Security Council shall duly take account of failure to comply with provisional measures'. In these instances then, although it is arguable that the peacekeeping force is not taking enforcement action in the full-blown sense of Article 42, it is taking action which is closer to Chapter VII action, in that it is enforcing provisional measures. This type of action has been much more readily taken in the post-Cold War era (Somalia, Haiti, Rwanda).[22]

In many ways the enforcement of provisional measures is similar to enforcement action under Article 42, particularly when the provisional or interim measures are so widely drawn as to include the maintenance of the integrity of a nation as in the Congo or, perhaps less obviously, 'to use all necessary means to establish as soon as possible a secure environment for humanitarian relief in Somalia'.[23] This has led Professor Bowett to describe ONUC's constitutional base as being somewhat wider than Article 40, seeing it as a force 'for the purpose of supervising and enforcing compliance with the provisional measures ordered under Article 40 and for other purposes which were consistent with the general powers of the Council under Article 39'.[24] This involves recognizing that ONUC had gone beyond Article 40, but not as far as Article 42, by suggesting that the general powers of Article 39 were utilized. It must be pointed out, however, that the provisions of Article 39 have been used as authority for the recommendation of enforcement action in the Korean War.[25]

It would be best to summarize ONUC's actions as having as their constitutional base the enforcement of provisional measures under Article 40, but since these measures were increasingly widely drawn so as to cope with an ever-deteriorating crisis, despite the judgment of the World Court in the *Expenses* case, they amounted to at least *de facto* enforcement action. It could be argued that ONUC was acting in defence of its purposes. However, this is a wide interpretation of self-defence, going far beyond that authorized for other peacekeeping operations, which are only allowed to use self-defence when fired on. Allowing a force to take positive action in defence of its purposes is little different from allowing it to enforce them. A similar argument can be made as regards the mandate and activities of UNOSOM II in Somalia in 1993 where the actions taken against General Aideed's faction in particular constituted an offensive, not defensive, operation.[26]

The near disaster of the peacekeeping operation in the Congo in the 1960s led to a return to consensual, non-offensive peacekeeping operations, tightly controlled by the Security Council. The end of the Cold War has seen a continuation of close control, or 'micro-management',[27] of consensual peacekeeping operations by the Security Council. For example the small UN Observer Mission in Georgia (UNOMIG) was established in August 1993 by the Security Council to supervise the ceasefire in the secessionist conflict in Abkhazia.[28] Despite breaches in the ceasefire and the deadlock in talks, UNOMIG's limited mandate is renewed on a three or six monthly basis.

However, a contrast can be drawn between non-offensive peacekeeping operations which are kept on a short rein, and the quasi-enforcement operations which have arisen with the end of the Cold War. The constitutional link between the Security Council and this type of operations is normally less strong, despite the fact that these operations represent a much greater use of force with potential to embroil the United Nations in a continuing, and possibly escalating, conflict. Those states contributing to the more aggressive 'peacekeeping' operation are unwilling to submit their actions to continuous, and potentially debilitating, UN review. In particular, the United States, although willing to seek UN authorization for its military actions, is not willing to have them placed under the command and control of the UN.[29] Political realities have meant that the greater the level of UN-sanctioned military involvement, the less control the UN has over it.

The Security Council's patience with the military rulers in Haiti finally ran out in July 1994 when, under Chapter VII of the Charter it authorized:

> Member States to form a multinational force under unified command and control and, in this framework, to use all necessary means to facilitate the departure from Haiti of the military leadership, consistent with the Governor's Island Agreement, the prompt return

of the legitimately elected President and the restoration of the legitimate authorities of the Government of Haiti, and to establish and maintain a secure and stable environment that will permit the implementation of the Governor's Island Agreement, on the undertanding that the cost of implementing this temporary operation will be borne by participating Member States.

The resolution then stated that the multinational force would be replaced by an expanded and strengthened UNMIH on a renewable six monthly mandate.[30] Whereas the multinational force has a flexible mandate allowing its US commanders to use any means it considers necessary, with no time limits specified, the UN peacekeeping force is subject to stricter review and control by the Security Council. The only obligation on member states contributing to the multinational force, and the UN Secretary-General, was to provide regular reports to the Security Council on its progress. In theory, if the Council thought that after considering these reports the force was going beyond its mandate then it could terminate the force. However, with the main contributor and leader of the force being the United States, a permanent member, once the force was mandated by the Security Council, it was effectively up to the United States to determine when its task was completed.

The lack of control over such military actions is an inevitable consequence of the decentralization of enforcement action under Chapter VII of the Charter. The failure to implement Article 43 and the delegation of command and control to states rather than the Military Staff Committee has resulted in a similar constitutional approach to quasi-enforcement peacekeeping-type operations as found in Rwanda, Haiti and Somalia, as has been used as regards full-blown enforcement actions in the Gulf and Korea. Nevertheless, the bridge between the Security Council and the multinational force used in quasi-enforcement operations is sometimes strengthened by the Secretary-General who is required to provide detailed, objective reports on the action of the force, as in the case of Haiti and Rwanda.[31] However, on other occasions the reporting requirement is placed mainly on the contributing states, although a supplemental reporting function is placed on the Secretary-General, as in the authorization of the NATO-led Implementation Force (IFOR) following the Dayton Peace Accords of November 1995.[32] Nevertheless, the constitutional bridge is stronger than in the case of full enforcement actions, were the reporting obligation is on the contributing states alone.[33] Indeed, in the case of Somalia, although UNITAF was given a relatively free rein,[34] UNOSOM II was subjected to much closer political control and review by the Security Council and the Secretary-General.[35]

The Role of the Secretary-General

From the relatively narrow provisions of the UN Charter concerning the office of Secretary-General, the various holders of this post have developed an impressive set of powers to be used in the peaceful settlement of disputes and situations. Article 97 states that the Secretary-General 'shall be the chief administrative officer of the Organization'. However, unlike the Secretary-General of the League of Nations, who was simply a 'civil servant', the Secretary-General is granted somewhat wider powers in the Charter. Article 98 provides that the Secretary-General 'shall perform such other functions as are entrusted to him' by the Security Council, General Assembly, Economic and Social Council and the Trusteeship Council. Under this provision the Secretary-General carries out the mandates granted to him by the Security Council or the General Assembly. This may range from sending a fact-finding mission, to offering his good offices, to the organization and emplacement of a peacekeeping force.

The only autonomous power granted to him in the Charter is contained in Article 99 which provides that '[t]he Secretary General may bring to the attention of the Security Council any matter which in his opinion may threaten international peace and security'. Given the importance of the concept of a 'threat to the peace' in the workings of the Security Council, particularly as regards internal conflicts, this is potentially a very important provision. However, it has been little used by the office holders, although one notable exception was when Secretary-General Hammarskjöld brought the deteriorating situation in the Congo to the attention of the Security Council in 1960 explicitly relying on Article 99.[36]

Nevertheless, despite the fact that the Charter explicitly only grants the Secretary-General the autonomous power to bring to the attention of the Security Council threats to international peace, over the years the office holder has developed an impressive set of inherent powers, such as good offices, mediation, even arbitration and fact finding. These powers have developed either with the acquiescence of the Security Council and General Assembly, or sometimes with their active encouragement in the sense that it has been recognized that the Secretary-General has inherent powers not dependent on a specific mandate from one of the other principal organs of the United Nations.[37]

The Secretary-General's inherent powers seem to have stretched as far as to allow the office holder, on his own authority, to send a fact-finding mission to a conflict; they have not formally extended as far as the authorization of an observer force or peacekeeping force – that still has to be mandated by the Security Council.[38] However, greater activity by the United Nations in the late 1980s as the Cold War came to an end did see the possible extension of the Secretary-General's powers to at least the negotiation and emplacement of an observer force in exceptional circumstances as in the initial deployment of UNGOMAP to Afghanistan following the Geneva Accords of 1988, retrospectively endorsed by the Security Council.[39] Normally, however, although the Secretary-General may be heavily involved in the negotiations about a possible peacekeeping force, Security Council, or exceptionally General Assembly, authorization must be forthcoming before the force is emplaced.

The Secretary-General's powers in the field of peacekeeping have expanded over the years from the holder of the office simply being the administrator of forces to becoming the instigator and executive commander of the forces within the overall framework of the Security Council's mandate.[40] It must be noted that this only applies to traditional peacekeeping forces and the new generation of integrated pacific settlement missions as found in Namibia and Cambodia. In the quasi-enforcement operations in Haiti, Rwanda and Somalia, and now with IFOR in Bosnia, the Secretary-General does not have any political control over the forces. In general, they are commanded, both politically and militarily, by a state or a group of states, operating under a loose Security Council mandate, although generally, as with consensual peacekeeping forces, the Secretary-General is required by the Council to provide regular reports on the progress of the force.

The UN and Regional Organizations

A genuinely consensual peacekeeping operation undertaken by an organization outside the UN does not require the permission of the UN before it is undertaken. The constitutional link between the UN and other organizations is to be found in Chapter VIII of the UN Charter. Article 52 actually encourages regional organizations or arrangements to 'make every effort to achieve peaceful settlement of local disputes...before referring them to the Security Council', as long as their activities in this field are consistent with the Purposes and Principles of the United Nations. Consensual, neutral peacekeeping conforms with the UN Charter and is a mechanism developed to facilitate the settlement of disputes.

A good example of a genuine peacekeeping operation undertaken outside the UN by another international body was the Commonwealth Monitoring Force (CMF) in Southern Rhodesia, which was part of the peace process established by the Lancaster House Agreement of 15 December 1979. The ceasefire agreement entered into by the parties to the conflict stated that the British government was responsible for the establishment of a monitoring force under the Command of the Governor's Military Adviser,

THE UN CHARTER AND PEACEKEEPING FORCES 57

'to assess and monitor impartially all stages of the inception and maintenance of the cease-fire by the forces'.[41] In a statement accompanying the ceasefire agreement the Chairman of the conference, Lord Carrington, stated that the CMF's role was one of peacekeeping not enforcement.[42]

However, when the activities or mandate of the force include enforcement, then the constitutional position is changed, for Article 53(1) of the UN Charter provides:

> The Security Council shall, where appropriate, utilize such regional arrangements or agencies for enforcement action under its authority. But no enforcement action shall be taken under regional arrangements or by regional agencies without the authorization of the Security Council.

This provision is effective in asserting the constitutional superiority of the UN over regional bodies in the field of enforcement action because of the near universal membership of the UN and because regional organizations, in their constituent documents, themselves do not claim superiority, or indeed sometimes recognize UN superiority in this matter.[43]

Nevertheless, there are several instances where the relevant regional organization has, in practice, undertaken enforcement action under the guise of a peacekeeping mandate, without authorization from the Security Council. The Arab League's creation of Arab Deterrent Force (ADF) October 1976 in response to the civil war in Lebanon[44] is such an example. Although there were aspects of the mandate of the ADF which appeared to be based on the peacekeeping concept, such as supervision of a ceasefire, withdrawal of troops and the collection of the weaponry belonging to the parties in the internal conflict, other aspects seemed to grant the force much wider powers of enforcement, such as maintaining internal security and assisting Lebanese authorities in taking over public utilities.[45] Although it is possible to argue that the UN gave a similarly wide mandate to ONUC in the Congo, as we have seen, that operation in reality became one of enforcement. In addition, if the performance of the Arab League Force is examined it can be seen that it became increasingly ruthless in its actions and was unafraid to use military coercion beyond that required in strict self-defence. Furthermore, even when the Lebanese government withdrew its consent to the ADF in 1982, the Force, which was by then entirely composed of Syrian troops, remained and increasingly aligned itself with the pro-Syrian factions in Lebanon.[46]

On another occasion the Security Council has retrospectively endorsed a regional organization's quasi-enforcement peacekeeping operation. This was the case of Liberia, where the overtly aggressive, Nigerian dominated ECOWAS Monitoring Group (ECOMOG), which had operated in the country since August 1990, mainly against the NPFL faction, was endorsed by the Security Council in 1992.[47] Furthermore, the Contonou peace agreement of July 1993 contained provisions for the involvement of UN observers in the disarmament and elections process. UNOMIL's presence in Liberia has not led to a peaceful solution; indeed in September 1994 the Security Council requested that ECOMOG protect UNOMIL personnel.[48]

During its long involvement in Liberia, ECOMOG has overstepped the boundary between neutral peacekeeping and military enforcement action. The UN Security Council has apparently retrospectively endorsed the action as coming with the provisions of Chapter VIII of the UN Charter, illustrating a dangerously relaxed approach to the constitutional requirement that such actions must be prospectively endorsed. The danger in allowing greater unauthorized regional enforcement action as opposed to consensual peacekeeping is that, as these two examples clearly show, they are likely to be abused by the regional superpower. Nevertheless, practice is not settled and in other instances, the Security Council has, in accordance with Article 53, prospectively authorized organizations to undertake enforcement action alongside a UN peacekeeping operation.

This 'sub-contracting' to other organizations is a new development caused by the need to back up, or replace, peacekeeping operations by the use of force. This coincides with another post-Cold War development in the shape of the changing role of the NATO from defence pact to a form, or component, of collective security.[49] Despite the fact that the NATO Treaty of 1949,[50] has not been altered to reflect this emerging role, this does not appear to have prevented the Security Council calling on NATO to undertake certain enforcement tasks in Bosnia.[51] The Security Council has thus treated NATO as a regional arrangement within the meaning of Article 53, while the defects in the NATO treaty, which does not permit enforcement action, can be overcome if the authorization is seen as being directed at the individual members of NATO rather than the organization itself. In this way the authorization is no different from that given to the United States and other countries to form a multinational force to restore democracy in Haiti.

Initially, limited coercion was used by NATO under these provisions: NATO threatened air strikes against the Bosnian Serbs surrounding Sarajevo in February 1994 if they failed to withdraw their heavy weapons; NATO planes shot down four Serb warplanes above Bosnia in the same month; and NATO planes bombed Serb airbases in Croatia in November 1994,[52] and Serb ammunition dumps near Pale, the Bosnian Serb 'capital', in May 1995. In this limited enforcement period, with UNPROFOR vulnerable on the ground, there was a considerable amount of control over NATO operations by the UN Secretary-General's representative and

UNPROFOR commanders, with NATO air strikes only taking place at the request, or with the consent of, UNPROFOR – the so-called 'dual key' approach.[53] A greater use of air power by NATO, in consultation with the Secretary-General, and the emplacement of a Rapid Reaction Force on the ground at end of August 1995, followed Bosnian Serb attacks against the UN safe areas of Srebrenica and Zepa.[54]

The peace agreements secured at Dayton, Ohio in November 1995,[55] in part as a result of NATO actions, provided for UNPROFOR in Bosnia to be replaced by the NATO-led IFOR, which has the power to oversee and enforce the agreements, without the need to seek further approval from the Secretary-General. The London Peace Implementation Conference on Bosnia of 9 December 1995 summarized the primary functions of IFOR as ensuring compliance with the ceasefire, ensuring withdrawal and separation of forces, and secondary functions such as the creation of conditions in which humanitarian tasks could be performed by other organizations and bodies, the prevention of interference with the return of refugees, and the clearance of minefields.[56]

The UN Security Council endorsed the creation and emplacement of IFOR, in what amounted to a greater degree of delegation to NATO than had occurred in Bosnia before, but which was little different from the delegation to member states to undertake potentially offensive military operations in Rwanda, Haiti and Somalia. Resolution 1031 of 15 December 1995 authorizes IFOR 'to take all necessary measures to effect the implementation of and to ensure compliance with [the agreement], stresses that the parties shall be held equally responsible for compliance...and shall be equally subject to such enforcement action by IFOR as may be necessary to ensure implementation...and takes note that the parties have consented to IFOR's taking of such measures'. Although IFOR has been consented to by the various parties it is not a traditional form of peacekeeping. IFOR is performing a traditional peacekeeping role while the accords are being complied with but, significantly, it will become an offensive operation if the accords are broken. Indeed, even while IFOR is performing a basic peacekeeping function, the threat of enforcement action if the peace is broken, combined with its greater military capacity, makes it a much more capable military operation than UNPROFOR, which was limited to a basic peacekeeping mandate.

It appears from this situation that the Security Council can use NATO, if its members are willing, to carry out enforcement measures. Constitutionally, Article 53 states that NATO could not initiate enforcement action by itself, only action in collective self-defence. NATO members and others contributing to IFOR (including the Russian Federation) also require Security Council authorization under Chapter VII (Articles 39 and 42) since they are not simply acting in self-defence. Nevertheless, despite having brought the NATO-led operation under the umbrella of the UN Security Council, it is clear that IFOR is under the command and control of NATO leaders, not the UN. As with enforcement actions by *ad hoc* military coalitions, the centralization of coercion in the hands of the Security Council is purely formal. In practical terms the operation is outside the control of the United Nations.

Conclusions

Impartial and consensual peacekeeping, whether in the form of a buffer force or more generally as a mechanism to facilitate peaceful settlement, remains firmly anchored in the UN Charter, despite the lack of an express provision. An impartial military presence in fulfilment of the inherent competence of the UN remains an important feature of the Organization's work. Although the legal competence for the creation of such forces is divided between the Assembly and the Council, it is the latter which, for political reasons, is now the mandating body. Such forces are generally authorized by the Security Council in furtherance of peaceful settlement under Article 36 or pursuant to the acceptance of provisional measures called for under Article 40. Within a renewable mandate, the Secretary-General is delegated with the overall control of the force. Discounting the absence of a fully fledged standing UN peacekeeping force,[57] impartial and consensual peacekeeping possesses many of those constitutional features of a centralized security system, features distinctly lacking in UN military enforcement actions in Korea and the Gulf. Despite the presence of centralizing provisions in the UN Charter (Articles 42–9), UN military enforcement action to date has consisted of the delegation of authority to prosecute a war to a state or group of states.

With the erosion of the line between peacekeeping and enforcement occurring at pace,[58] there is a need for the UN Security Council to adopt a more consistent approach to what can be labelled quasi-enforcement peacekeeping operations.[59] Its tendency to follow the line of loose authorization as with pure enforcement actions is an unwelcome, though predictable, development. However, there are some centralist tendencies to be discerned with the greater involvement of the Secretary-General in some of the quasi-enforcement operations. It is submitted that the development of constitutional controls over such operations is to be encouraged in that it would help to prevent charges of western domination or, if undertaken by a regional organization, domination by the regional power, as well as curbing excessive uses of force. However, greater control would not be without its dangers; in particular, the increase in UN involvement in these military operations might endanger the credibility of the UN as a neutral peace broker and keeper.

Furthermore, greater centralization of quasi-enforcement operations would require the Security Council to exercise its constitutional supremacy over regional bodies, not only to ensure that they are mandated before enforcement action is taken, but also to develop in practice greater constitutional control over the military operation as it is occurring. Traditional impartial and consensual peacekeeping does not require UN authorization; indeed its autonomous development should perhaps be encouraged to take some of the burden off the UN. However, enforcement action, whether fully fledged inter-state action or belligerent peacekeeping within a state, does require authorization for legal and practical reasons. To accept the practice that seems to have developed in some cases – that this form of peacekeeping falls outside the requirements of Article 53 because it carries the label 'peacekeeping' – would be dangerous, allowing considerable coercive freedom for regional, defence and security organizations, which are, as practice has shown, subject to even greater domination and abuse.[60]

Political pressure has inevitably led to considerable decentralization of military enforcement measures. This signifies a lack of constitutional checks and balances which have developed in the area of impartial consensual peacekeeping. It is this writer's opinion that greater control of the new belligerent peacekeeping operations, whether undertaken in a genuinely collective action or by states or other organizations, is essential if the UN is going to protect and enhance its peacekeeping function.

NOTES

1. *ICJ Rep.* 1949, p.182.
2. Ibid., p.198.
3. See further H.G. Schermers and N.M. Blokker, *International Institutional Law*, The Hague: Martinus Nijhoff, 3rd edn, 1995, pp.158–63; D.W. Bowett, *The Law of International Institutions*, London: Stevens, 4th edn, 1982, p.337.
4. *ICJ Rep.* 1971, pp.46–7,49–50. See GA. Res. 2145, 21 UN GAOR (1971).
5. Ibid., p.52.
6. Bowett, (n.3 above), pp.337–8.
7. *ICJ Rep.* 1962, p.168.
8. Bowett, (n.3 above), p.338.
9. *ICJ Rep.*, 1962, pp.163–4.
10. Ibid., p.177.
11. F. Seyersted, *United Nations Forces*, Leyden: A.W. Sijthoff, 1966, pp.133–4.
12. Ibid., p.155. But see M. Rama-Montaldo, 'International Legal Personality and the Implied Powers of International Organizations', *British Yearbook of International Law*, Vol.44, 1970, pp.118–22.
13. See N.D. White, *Keeping the Peace: The United Nations and the Maintenance of International Peace and Security*, Manchester: Manchester University Press, 1993, pp.140–57. See further, B. Simma (ed.), *The Charter of the United Nations: A Commentary*, Oxford: Oxford University Press, 1994, pp.254–64.

14. GA 299 mtg, 5 UN GAOR (1950).
15. SC Res. 119, 11 UN SCOR (1956) transferred the matter to the Assembly despite the negative votes of the UK and France. See further, M. Ghali, 'The United Nations Emergency Force I', in W.J. Durch (ed.), *The Evolution of UN Peacekeeping*, London: Macmillan, 1994, pp.104–30.
16. GA Res. 1752, 17 UN GAOR (1962). See further, R. Higgins, *United Nations Peacekeeping: Documents and Commentary, Vol.2: Asia 1946–1967*, Oxford: Oxford University Press, 1980, pp.61–86.
17. SC Res. 157, 15 UN SCOR (1960), again adopted by a procedural vote unaffected by the negative vote of the Soviet Union.
18. GA Res. 1474, 2 UN GAOR ESS (1960).
19. *ICJ Rep.* 1962, p.151 at p.166, p.177; Higgins (see n.16 above), p.54; G. Abi-Saab, *The UN Operation in the Congo*, Oxford: Oxford University Press, 1978, p.105.
20 Fact-finding and peacekeeping are often combined, and occasionally an observer force simply performs the function of fact-finding – see UNOGIL created by SC Res. 128, 13 UN SCOR (1958).
21. See further D.W. Bowett, *United Nations Forces*, London: Stevens, 1964, pp.274–312.
22. E. Clemons, 'No Peace to Keep: Six and Three Quarters Peacekeepers', *New York University Journal of International Law and Politics*, Vol.26, 1993, p.107.
23. SC Res. 794, 47 UN SCOR (1992).
24. Bowett, (n.21 above), p.180.
25. Sir Gladwyn Jebb (UK), SC 477 mtg, 5 UN SCOR (1950). See further, J. Kunz, 'Legal Aspects of the Situation in Korea', *American Journal of International Law*, Vol.44, 1950, p.709.
26. P.F. Diehl, *International Peacekeeping*, Baltimore: Johns Hopkins University Press, 1994, p.188.
27. Secretary-General in *Supplement to An Agenda for Peace*, UN doc. A/50/60, S/1995/1, para.39.
28. SC Res. 854, 48 UN SCOR (1993).
29. T. Stein, 'Decentralized Law Enforcement: The Changing Role of the State as Law Enforcement Agent', in J. Delbrück (ed.), *Allocation of Law Enforcement Authority in the International System*, Berlin: Duncker & Humblot, 1995, p.125.
30. SC Res. 940, 49 UN SCOR (1994).
31. SC Res. 929, 49 UN SCOR (1994) (Rwanda).
32. SC Res. 1031, 50 UN S/PV (1995).
33. See for example SC Res. 678, 45 UN SCOR (1990) re Kuwait. See further, A. Parsons, 'The UN and the National Interests of States' in A. Roberts and B. Kingsbury (eds.), *United Nations, Divided World*, Oxford: Clarendon Press, 2nd edn, 1993, p.121.
34. SC Res. 794, 47 UN SCOR (1992).
35. SC Res. 814, 48 UN SCOR (1993). See further Secretary-General (n.27 above), para.80.
36. SC 873 mtg, 15 UN SCOR (1960). See further, B. Simma (ed.), (n.13 above), pp.1044–57.
37. See the General Assembly's 'Declaration on the Prevention and Removal of Disputes and Situations which may Threaten International Peace and Security and the Role of the United Nations in this Field', GA Res. 43/51, 43 UN GAOR (1988).
38. See R. Lavalle, 'The "Inherent" Powers of the UN Secretary General in the Political Sphere: A Legal Analysis', *Netherlands International Law Review*, Vol.37, 1990, p.22.
39. SC Res. 622, 43 UN SCOR (1988).
40. Secretary-General (n.27 above), para.38. Command in the field is in the hands of the chief of mission.
41. *International Legal Materials*, Vol.19, 1980, pp.401–3.
42. Ibid., p.404.
43 See H.G. Schermers and N.M. Blokker (n.3 above), pp.1068–70. See also Article 103 of the UN Charter.
44. For a thorough review see I. Pogany, *The Arab League and Peacekeeping in the Lebanon*, Aldershot: Avebury, 1987.
45. Ibid, Appendix 3.

THE UN CHARTER AND PEACEKEEPING FORCES 63

46. Ibid, Ch.8.
47. SC Res. 788, 47 UN SCOR (1992). See generally M. Weller (ed.), *Regional Peace-Keeping and International Enforcement: The Liberian Crisis*, Cambridge: Cambridge University Press, 1994.
48. Presidential Statement S/PRST/1994/53. UN doc. S/1994/1167.
49. See generally C.L. Glaser, 'Future Security Arrangements for Europe: Why NATO is Still Best' in G.W. Downs (ed.), *Collective Security beyond the Cold War*, University of Michigan Press, 1995, p.217. On 'sub-contracting', or what has been called 'franchising', see N.D. White, 'The Legitimacy of NATO action in Bosnia', *New Law Journal*, Vol.144, 1994, pp.649–50; T.M. Franck, 'The United Nations as Guarantor of International Peace and Security', in C. Tomuschat (ed.), *The United Nations at Age Fifty: A Legal Perspective*, The Hague: Kluwer, 1995, pp.31–3.
50. 34 UNTS 243.
51. SC Res. 770, 47 UN SCOR (1992); SC Res. 816, 836 48 UN SCOR (1993).
52. SC Res. 958, 49 UN SCOR (1994).
53. Security Council resolutions authorizing NATO air strikes simply required 'close coordination' with the UN Secretary-General and UNPROFOR. They did not explicitly state that UN consent was necessary before each strike, though this was the interpretation put on them in practice.
54. UN doc. S/1995/987.
55. UN docs. S/1995/999, S/1995/1021, S/1995/1029; *International Legal Materials*, Vol.35, 1996, pp.73–183.
56. UN doc. S/1995/1029.
57. Though the stand-by peacekeeping arrangements in member states seems to be developing – see the Secretary General's report UN doc. S/1995/943.
58. Though the Secretary General has warned against this (n.27 above), para.34.
59. N.D. White, 'U.N. Peacekeeping: Development or Destruction?', *International Relations*, Vol.XII, 1994, p.149.
60. Secretary-General, (n.27 above), para.88.

Part III
Principles of International
Peacekeeping

The Consent of the Parties

[5]

MILITARY INTERVENTION, REGIONAL ORGANIZATIONS, AND HOST-STATE CONSENT

DAVID WIPPMAN[*]

I. INTRODUCTION

That consent may validate an otherwise wrongful military intervention into the territory of the consenting state is a generally accepted principle. When a government is both widely recognized and in effective control of most of the state, this principle affords a clear alternative to Security Council authorization as a basis for justifying external intervention, whether by states acting unilaterally, or by states acting under the auspices of the United Nations (U.N.) or a regional organization.

In many cases, however, consent is often a highly controversial justification for military intervention. In some cases, it is doubtful whether the consent at issue is voluntary.[1] In other cases, the individual purporting to give consent may lack the legal authority to do so.[2] But these issues, although they may prove difficult to resolve in particular cases, are usually at least nominally susceptible to resolution under generally accepted principles of treaty law dealing with coercion and the representation of states.[3] More difficult problems

---

* Associate Professor of Law, Cornell Law School. The author would like to thank Professor John H. Barcelo, III, for helpful comments on a prior draft of this Article.

1. As Judge (then Special Rapporteur) Roberto Ago observed in his report to the International Law Commission on state responsibility, consent may be "*expressed* or *tacit, explicit* or *implicit,* provided however that it is *clearly established*," and is not "vitiated by 'defects' such as error, fraud, corruption or violence." Eighth Report on State Responsibility, Document A/CN.4/318 and Add.1-4, 2 Y.B. INT'L L. COMM'N 3, 35-36 (1979).

2. To be valid, "consent . . . must be *internationally attributable to the State*; in other words, it must issue from a person whose will is considered, at the international level, to be the will of the State and, in addition, the person in question must be competent to manifest that will in the particular case involved." *Id.* at 36.

3. *See id.* ("The principles which apply to the determination of the validity of treaties also apply with respect to the validity of consent to an action which would, in the absence of such consent, be internationally wrongful."); John Lawrence Hargrove, *Intervention by Invitation and the Politics of the New World Order, in* LAW AND FORCE IN THE NEW INTERNATIONAL ORDER 113, 119 (L. Damrosch & D. Scheffer eds., 1991) (legal issues regarding the genuine-

210   DUKE JOURNAL OF COMPARATIVE & INTERNATIONAL LAW   [Vol. 7:209

arise when the authority of a particular government purporting to consent to intervention on behalf of the state is subject to challenge, either because the government has lost control of a substantial portion of the state, or because the government's international legitimacy is otherwise subject to doubt.

The theoretical basis for the rule that consent may validate an otherwise wrongful intervention is not entirely clear. In a study of state responsibility for wrongful conduct, the International Law Commission concluded that consent to intervention acts as a form of bilateral agreement between the consenting and intervening states that suspends the normal operation of the legal rules that would otherwise govern their relationship.[4] It seems more plausible, however, to conclude simply that consent or its absence is central to the definition of wrongful intervention in the first place. In other words, prohibited intervention should be understood as intervention against the will of the state. In Oppenheim's formulation, it is "dictatorial interference" in a state's internal affairs that is impermissible, not external involvement per se.[5]

Consistent with this understanding, many states have attempted to justify military intervention in other states on the basis of consent. In some cases, the justification was relatively persuasive, and the interventions met with general acquiescence. During the Cold War both France, and to a lesser extent the United Kingdom, relied on consent to justify periodic interventions in former colonies to support friendly governments against small-scale rebellions or palace coups.[6] Most states accepted such interventions, even when the invitations at

---

ness of invitations to intervene "are resolvable on the basis of familiar concepts drawn straightforwardly from other areas of the law than those having to do directly with restraints on the exercise of force, for example, the law of treaties."); *see also* Vienna Convention on the Law of Treaties, U.N. Doc. A/CONF. 39/27 (1969), art. 51 (rejecting the validity of consent based on coercion of a state's representative); *id.* art. 52 (rejecting the validity of consent based on coercion of the state itself); *id.* art. 7 (identifying individuals presumptively capable of expressing a state's consent to be bound to a treaty).

4. *See* Roberto Ago, Eighth Report on State Responsibility, *supra* note 1, at 31-32.

5. 1 L. OPPENHEIM, INTERNATIONAL LAW 305 (H. Lauterpacht ed., 8th ed. 1955) (defining prohibited intervention as "dictatorial interference . . . in the affairs of another State for the purpose of maintaining or altering the actual condition of things.").

6. In 1964, Britain intervened in Tanganyika, Uganda, and Kenya to help incumbent governments quell local disturbances and mutinies in the armed forces. *See* Louise Doswald-Beck, *The Legal Validity of Military Intervention by Invitation of the Government*, 1985 BRIT.Y.B. INT'L L. 189, 189 n.4 (1986). France intervened more than a dozen times in its African colonies, usually, though not always, to assist beleaguered governments to retain or to resume control in the face of attempted military coups. *See* John Darnton, *The World: Intervening with Elan and No Regrets*, N.Y. TIMES, June 26, 1994, § 4, at 3.

issue arguably came after the inviting officials had already lost their hold on power.[7] Similarly, the 1982 deployment of United States, French, Italian and British forces to assist the Lebanese government in restoring order met with little international opposition, at least at the outset.[8]

In other cases, reliance on consent proved unpersuasive. For example, when the Soviet Union invoked the principle of state consent to justify invasions of Hungary in 1956, Czechoslovakia in 1968, and Afghanistan in 1979, it met with widespread criticism on the ground that the invitations at issue were either manufactured or coerced.[9] Similarly, when the United States sent troops to the Dominican Republic in 1965 and to Grenada in 1983, it was condemned by many states which questioned the legal authority of the officials who issued the invitations to intervene.[10] Still, in these cases, as in those described above, the principle that voluntary consent from proper state authorities can validate intervention was not in dispute.

In most cases, the real issue was, and remains, who is entitled to express the will of the state concerning intervention? Although it is the consent of the state itself that is ultimately at issue, states are abstract entities and cannot by themselves give or withhold consent to intervention.[11] In general, international law presumes that when a government exercises effective control over the territory and people of the state, the government (and more particularly, the authorized

---

7. When France intervened *against* an incumbent government, however, it met with more international criticism than approbation. In 1979, when French troops forcibly deposed the head of state of the Central African Empire, various countries criticized the French action as a violation of the non-intervention principle, despite Bokassa's atrocious human rights record. *See* W. Michael Reisman, *Humanitarian Intervention and Fledgling Democracies*, 18 FORDHAM INT'L L.J. 794, 800 (1995).

8. *See* Doswald-Beck, *supra* note 6, at 241-42. Not long after arrival, however, U.S. (and to some extent French) forces were drawn into the conflict in a way that exceeded their status as peacekeepers. As a result, the intervention eventually attracted considerable criticism from other states. *See id.*

9. *See* U.N. SCOR, 14th Sess., 746th mtg. at 4, U.N. Doc. S/PV.746 (1956) (Hung.); U.N. SCOR, 23d Sess., 1441st mtg. at 1, U.N. Doc. S/PV.1441 (1968) (Czech.); U.N. SCOR, 35th Sess., 2185th mtg. at 2, U.N. Doc. S/PV.2185 (1980) (Afg.). The interventions were generally deemed invalid. *See* Rein Müllerson, *Intervention by Invitation*, *in* LAW AND FORCE IN THE NEW INTERNATIONAL ORDER 127, 128-29 (L. Damrosch & D. Scheffer eds., 1991).

10. *See* Doswald-Beck, *supra* note 6, at 228, 237 (noting that "[d]iplomatic reaction to the [U.S.] intervention [in the Dominican Republic] was generally unfavourable" and that "the vast majority of States, including the traditional allies of the U.S., characterized the intervention [in Grenada] as illegal.").

11. *See* Quincy Wright, *United States Intervention in the Lebanon*, 53 AM. J. INT'L L. 112, 120 (1959).

officials of that government) possesses the exclusive authority to express the will of the state in its international affairs.[12] This presumption derives from a mix of practical and theoretical considerations.
As a practical matter, states cannot ignore an effective government,
whatever its origin or political leanings. Moreover, reliance on effective control as the test for a government's capacity to represent the
state offers a reasonably objective and externally verifiable basis for
determining governmental authority, thus "inhibiting intervention"
by outside states.[13] As a theoretical matter, effective control serves as
a rough proxy for the existence of some degree of congruity between
the government and the larger political community of the state,
which supports the government's claim to represent the state as a
whole. To the extent that the government is unrepresentative, this
assumed congruity may be largely fictitious.[14] But it is nonetheless
widely accepted as the only viable basis on which states can conduct
international relations in a decentralized system.

In some cases, however, the presumption that the government
speaks for the state may break down. In particular, when the government's control over the state is effectively challenged by an internal, armed opposition, the presumption that the government represents the state may become untenable.[15] Indeed, it is precisely the
authority of a particular government to speak for the state as a whole
that is called into question by an internal conflict.

Arguably, the U.N. Charter prohibits aid to either government
or rebel forces in a civil war, since aid to one side might disrupt the
internal play of forces, and thereby violate the political independence
of the state and the right of its people to determine their own political future.[16] During the Cold War, however, most states acted as if

---

12. *See, e.g.,* Tom J. Farer, *Panama: Beyond the Charter Paradigm,* 84 AM. J. INT'L L. 503,
510 (1990) (noting "the virtually uniform practice in international relations of treating any
group of nationals in effective control of their state as constituting its legitimate government");
RESTATEMENT (THIRD) OF FOREIGN RELATIONS § 210 cmt. d (1985).

13. *See* Farer, *supra* note 12, at 511.

14. *Cf.* Fernando Tesón, *Collective Humanitarian Intervention,* 17 MICH. J. INT'L L. 323,
332 (1996) (arguing that "[a] rule requiring democratic legitimacy in the form of free adult universal suffrage seems the best approximation to actual political consent and true representa-
tiveness").

15. *See generally* David Wippman, *Change and Continuity in Legal Justifications for Military Intervention in Internal Conflicts,* 27 COLUM. HUM. RTS. L. REV. 435 (1996)

16. *See, e.g.,* Oscar Schachter, *International Law: The Right of States to Use Armed Force,*
82 MICH. L. REV. 1620, 1641 (1984); John Norton Moore, *Legal Standards for Intervention in
Internal Conflicts,* 13 GA. J. INT'L & COMP. L. 191, 196 (1983); *see also* U.N. CHARTER, art.
2(4).

international law permitted military aid to an incumbent government, at least when the government could plausibly claim that such aid was needed to offset external assistance given illicitly to opposing forces.[17] Conversely, most states viewed aid to rebel forces as a violation of the non-intervention principle, even if the rebels portrayed themselves as freedom fighters opposing a dictatorial regime.[18]

Although easy to state, these general rules are often exceptionally difficult to apply.[19] Moreover, it is not yet clear whether the end of the Cold War will bring about any significant modifications in these rules. Among the issues yet to be resolved are the following: (1) the point at which an incumbent government loses its authority to request external military assistance; (2) the extent to which the collective character of an intervention may alter the applicable legal analysis; (3) whether multiple warring factions may jointly consent to external military intervention; (4) what happens when one or more of those factions wishes to revoke its consent; and (5) whether a state may bind itself in advance to accept military intervention in specified circumstances. These issues are considered below primarily in the context of a regional organization contemplating intervention in a civil conflict.

II. CONSENT AND ITS PROBLEMS

In considering the issues noted above, it may be helpful to characterize invitations to intervene by the relative standing of government and rebel forces at the time an invitation to intervene is issued. A review of past cases suggests the following division: (1) cases in which a recognized government exercises control over most of the state; (2) cases in which the government and rebel forces reach a rough equilibrium, with each in control of a substantial portion of the state; (3) cases in which the incumbent government is merely one of

---

17. *See* Tom J. Farer, *A Paradigm of Legitimate Intervention, in* ENFORCING RESTRAINT: COLLECTIVE INTERVENTION IN INTERNAL CONFLICTS 316, 319 (L. Damrosch ed., 1993) (during the Cold War, many states "consistently acted as if recognized governments had an unfettered right to seek foreign assistance in crushing domestic rivals").

18. In keeping with this view, the International Court of Justice held that U.S. aid to rebel forces seeking to overthrow the Government of Nicaragua was illegal, noting that the principle of nonintervention "would certainly lose its effectiveness as a principle of law if intervention were to be justified by a mere request for assistance by an opposition group in another State." Military and Paramilitary Activities (Nicar. v. U.S.), 1986 I.C.J. 14, 126 (June 27).

19. *See* Müllerson, *supra* note 9, at 127 (noting that application of the rules governing provision of external assistance at the request of a government, though "perfectly clear from the juridical point of view, is in practice nonetheless fraught with dangers from misapplication").

several warring factions; and (4) cases in which all semblance of internal order disappears.

A. Government Control

From a legal standpoint, the simplest cases to analyze are those in which a recognized, incumbent government controls the political apparatus and most of the territory of the state. In such cases, the government ordinarily retains full authority to request external assistance, or even military intervention, to assist it in maintaining control of the state.[20] The government may seek such assistance from the United Nations, from regional organizations, or from individual states. As the International Court of Justice observed in *Nicaragua v. United States,* intervention is generally "allowable . . . at the request of the government of a State . . . ."[21]

In some respects, this position is difficult to reconcile with the principle of self-determination. It can be argued that any government forced to call in external military assistance to maintain itself against internal opposition is not genuinely in a position to speak for the state, and that the provision of such assistance by outside states constitutes an impermissible interference with internal political processes.[22] Further, provision of external aid, even to the government, runs the risk of internationalizing a previously internal conflict. Nonetheless, most states appear to accept the authority of an effective incumbent government to invite external intervention.[23]

Conversely, neither states nor international organizations may lawfully intervene against the will of an effective, incumbent government. In *Nicaragua v. United States,* the International Court of Justice concluded that intervention at the request of opposition forces, even those characterizing themselves as "freedom fighters," violated

---

20. *See* IAN BROWNLIE, INTERNATIONAL LAW AND THE USE OF FORCE BY STATES 327 (1963); Schachter, *supra* note 16, at 1641-42; Louis Henkin, *Use of Force: Law and U.S. Policy, in* RIGHT V. MIGHT: INTERNATIONAL LAW AND THE USE OF FORCE 37, 63 (2d ed. 1991). Indeed, aid to the government in such cases does not constitute intervention in the technical sense, since it does not amount to unlawful interference in the state's internal affairs. *See* Müllerson, *supra* note 9, at 127.

21. *Nicaragua,* 1986 I.C.J. at 126.

22. *See, e.g.,* WILLIAM E. HALL, A TREATISE ON INTERNATIONAL LAW 344-47 (8th ed. 1924); Wright, *supra* note 11, at 121-122; Müllerson, *supra* note 9, at 132.

23. *See, e.g.,* Henkin, *supra* note 20, at 63 ("[U]pon authentic invitation, a state may introduce military forces into the territory of another to assist the government for various purposes, including maintaining internal order."); Farer, *supra* note 17, at 319.

the non-intervention principle.[24] For the same reason, the U.S. invasion of Panama was widely condemned even though the invasion ousted a dictatorial regime and replaced it with a democratically elected one.[25]

In general, an effective government's right to seek or oppose external intervention does not depend on the manner in which the government acquired power or the manner in which the government exercises power.[26] But, there are several existing or potentially emerging exceptions to this general rule. First, a government may not authorize external military intervention against a national liberation movement opposing racist or colonial domination.[27] This exception represents a specific application of the more general principle that a state may not lawfully authorize a foreign state to take any action that would be illegal under international law if undertaken by the authorizing state itself.[28] As the process of decolonization accelerated in the 1960s and 1970s, a majority of states in the United Nations concluded that action against national liberation movements constituted a violation of the principle of self-determination.[29] As a result, the usual presumption that the effective government constitutes the sole representative of the state in international affairs was at least partially reversed.[30] Although the incumbent government could

24. *Nicaragua*, 1986 I.C.J. at 126.

25. A large majority of the U.N. General Assembly criticized the U.S. invasion as "a flagrant violation of international law and of the independence, sovereignty and territorial integrity of States." G.A. Res. 44/240, U.N. GAOR, 44th Sess., Supp. No.49, 88th plen. mtg. at 52, U.N. Doc. A/44/L.63 and Add. 1 (1989). *See generally* Louis Henkin, *The Invasion of Panama Under International Law: A Gross Violation*, 29 COLUM. J. TRANSNAT'L L. 293 (1991); Ved Nanda, *The Validity of United States Intervention in Panama Under International Law*, 84 AM. J. INT'L L. 494 (1990).

26. *See* Brad R. Roth, *Governmental Illegitimacy Revisited: 'Pro-Democratic' Armed Intervention in the Post-Bipolar World*, 3 TRANSNAT'L L. & CONTEMP. PROBS. 481, 482 (1993).

27. *See* HEATHER A. WILSON, INTERNATIONAL LAW AND THE USE OF FORCE BY NATIONAL LIBERATION MOVEMENTS 91-136 (1988).

28. *See* Hargrove, *supra* note 3, at 116-17 (asserting that state consent cannot validate "activities which would have been unlawful by the [consenting] state if acting alone").

29. *See, e.g.*, Declaration on Principles of International Law concerning Friendly Relations and Co-operation among States in accordance with the Charter of the United Nations, G.A. Res. 2625 (XXV), U.N. GAOR 6th Comm., 25th Sess., Supp. No. 28, 1883 of plen. mtg. at 123, U.N. Doc. A/8082 (1970) (adopted without a vote) ("Every State has the duty to refrain from any forcible action which deprives peoples referred to in the elaboration of the principle of equal rights and self-determination of their right to self-determination and freedom and independence."); WILSON, *supra* note 27, at 99-100, 135.

30. *See* Rein Müllerson & David J. Scheffer, *Legal Regulation of the Use of Force, in* BEYOND CONFRONTATION: INTERNATIONAL LAW FOR THE POST-COLD WAR ERA 125-26 (L. Damrosch, G. Danilenko, & R. Müllerson eds., 1995); W. Michael Reisman, *Allocating Com-*

216   DUKE JOURNAL OF COMPARATIVE & INTERNATIONAL LAW   [Vol. 7:209]

continue to represent the state in most aspects of its international relations, it could not lawfully invite external aid in suppressing the efforts of a liberation movement to overthrow the government.[31] To the contrary, the liberation movement alone possessed the right to seek external assistance, although there is considerable controversy over whether such assistance could entail aid amounting to a use of force.[32]

Second, it is at best unclear whether a de jure government overthrown in violation of domestic constitutional law may authorize external intervention to re-establish its authority.[33] The situation arises most commonly in the case of a palace coup, that is, when a small group of military officers engineers the abrupt and forcible ouster of the incumbent head of state. On its face, external military intervention to reinstate the ejected incumbent would seem to constitute impermissible interference in the state's internal affairs. Nonetheless, a number of countries periodically send troops to help ousted leaders return to the presidential palace. In 1964 for example, the United Kingdom came to the aid of President Julius Nyere of Tanganyika.[34] Nyere headed an elected government that lost control of the capital to mutinous army troops. At Nyere's request, British troops intervened to restore order. The British action went largely unremarked in the United Nations. Similarly, France has frequently intervened militarily in its former colonies to restore de jure governments to power following internal military coups without attracting much adverse comment from other states.[35]

---

petences to Use Coercion in the Post-Cold War World: Practices, Conditions, and Prospects, in LAW AND FORCE IN THE NEW INTERNATIONAL ORDER 26, 32-34 (L. Damrosch & D. Scheffer eds., 1991).

31. *See generally* Wilson, *supra* note 27, at 91-136 (discussing pertinent U.N. resolutions and state practice).

32. *See id.*

33. *See* Domingo Acevedo, *The Haitian Crisis and the OAS Response: A Test of Effectiveness in Protecting Democracy,* in ENFORCING RESTRAINT: COLLECTIVE INTERVENTION IN INTERNAL CONFLICTS 119, 139 (L. Damrosch ed., 1993) ("It is unclear . . . whether a de jure government that has only *formal* but not actual power may invite foreign 'military intervention' for the purpose of removing the de facto regime.").

34. *See* Reisman, *supra* note 7, at 796.

35. *See* Darnton, *supra* note 6, at 3. In 1996, French paratroopers helped the democratically elected but corrupt government of the Central African Republic force mutinous army troops back into their barracks. Although the French intervention was highly unpopular within the Central African Republic itself, most other states paid little attention. *See* Jim Hoagland, *Does Anyone Care About Africa?,* DENV. POST, June 2, 1996, at F4. Some states even commended the French action, including a U.S. official who praised the French intervention as "very efficient," and who described France as a "force for stability in Africa." Gus Constantine, *France Keeps a Hand in Ex-Colonies: Bangui Mutiny Latest Example of Intervention,*

Several factors appear to account for the apparent acquiescence of most states in actions of this nature. So long as the interventions at issue are swift and small in scale, most states seem willing to ignore the brief discontinuity in the de jure government's effective control of the state. In effect, states treat the coup makers as temporary usurpers whose actions do not fundamentally alter the de jure government's power to speak for the state. This attitude may be attributable in part to a general recognition that political constraints usually preclude the U.N. Security Council from authorizing intervention in such cases, and in part to a sense that the former colonial powers should be allowed leeway to assist their former colonies in maintaining order, even at the cost of some inconsistency with international legal principles.

A third possible exception is a variant of the previous exception, limited, however, to intervention to restore a democratically elected government subjected to an unconstitutional seizure of power by internal forces. The overthrow of the popularly elected government of Haitian President Aristide presents the paradigmatic contemporary example. Aristide became President of Haiti in 1990, following his victory in an internationally monitored and supervised election.[36] Some months later the Haitian military, alarmed by Aristide's populist rhetoric and reformist policies, staged a military coup and forced Aristide to flee the country.[37] Had Aristide immediately invited external military intervention, it might conceivably have fallen within the second exception. Aristide, however, was reluctant to invite foreign military forces into Haiti. He did so, grudgingly and obliquely, only after it became clear that months of economic sanctions and diplomatic pressure would fail to dislodge the military junta.[38] In any event, Aristide's ouster was not the typical palace coup. The officers in charge had substantial support throughout the military and also in a significant, although minority, segment of Haitian society.[39] Ac-

---

WASH. TIMES, June 6, 1996, at A12.

36. *See* Acevedo, *supra* note 33, at 129-30.

37. *See id.*

38. *See* Melita M. Garza, *Aristide Can Only Hint He'd Like Armed Help*, CHI. TRIB., June 1, 1994, § 1, at 12. Aristide's reluctance to invite intervention openly may be attributable in part to the fact that Haitian law, reflecting unhappy prior experience with foreign intervention, made it illegal for a Haitian government official to invite such intervention. *See id.*; *see also* Deborah Zabarenko, *Aristide Thanks U.S., Gets Assurances on Haiti*, REUTER, Sept. 21, 1994 (cited in Tesón, *supra* note 14, at 360 n. 150) (describing Aristide's ambivalent and shifting views on inviting foreign intervention).

39. *See* Acevedo, *supra* note 33, at 131 (noting that "traditionally entrenched groups that had always represented the power of wealth, privilege, and violence in Haiti—particularly the

cordingly, the usurpers could not be summarily dismissed as transient occupants of the Presidential palace whose ouster would have little impact on the Haitian people's right to self-determination.

The argument in favor of permitting intervention based on an invitation from Aristide was simple. As the elected head of state, Aristide represented the people of Haiti as a whole. Following the coup both the United Nations and the Organization of American States (OAS) continued to recognize Aristide as the legitimate head of state, and both repeatedly demanded his reinstatement.[40] Accordingly, Aristide had a strong claim that he alone was entitled to speak for the state on questions of intervention.[41] By contrast, the military junta achieved its position by force and maintained that position by terrorizing much of the country. It had no legitimacy, domestic or international, and therefore should have had no authority to speak for the state or to oppose an intervention to restore democracy.[42] Intervention in this context, goes the argument, would further Haitian self-determination and fulfill the much-heralded, but still emerging, right to democratic governance.[43]

This argument is a powerful one. But, when the U.N. Security Council finally authorized military intervention to restore Aristide to power, it relied primarily on its authority to maintain international peace through coercive measures under Chapter VII of the Charter.[44] The authorizing resolution implicitly took note of Aristide's consent to intervention,[45] but the Security Council was evidently unwilling to treat that consent as sufficient in and of itself to permit military ac-

---

upper classes and the army—viewed Aristide's popular approach as a threat"); Roth, *supra* note 26, at 511-512 (noting that the "coup leadership ha[d] support in the elected legislature").

40. *See, e.g.,* William M. Berenson, Joint Venture for the Restoration of Democracy in Haiti: The Organization of American States and United Nations Experience: 1991-1995 (unpublished manuscript, on file with author); Tesón, *supra* note 14, at 355-56.

41. *See* Roth, *supra* note 26, at 511-12.

42. *Cf. id.* (noting that Aristide's elected status and the military's "violent conduct and unsavory history" combined to create a situation in which there was "no contest over the mandate to articulate the will of the 'legitimate' government").

43. As Brad Roth observed prior to the U.N. authorization of military intervention in Haiti, "in all likelihood, fulfillment of requests for armed assistance would not in this case be deemed a violation of international law." *Id.* at 511.

44. *See* S.C. Res. 940, U.N. SCOR, 49th Sess., 3413th mtg. at 2, U.N. Doc. S/RES/940 (1994) ("[d]etermining that the situation in Haiti continues to constitute a threat to peace and security in the region," and, "[a]cting under Chapter VII of the Charter," authorizing "Member States . . . to use all necessary means to facilitate" the restoration of the Aristide government).

45. The resolution cited two letters, one from Aristide (S/1994/905, annex), and another from Haiti's Permanent Representative to the United Nations (S/1994/910). Both letters implicitly supported U.N.-authorized military intervention. *Id.*

tion.[46] Thus, it seems clear that no right of forcible pro-democratic intervention has yet emerged. International law continues to place considerable importance on effective control as an indicator of a government's authority to act in the name of the state.[47]

At the same time, however, intervention to restore or install a democratic government is likely to receive much more sympathetic treatment than most other forms of military intervention, at least if it appears that the intervenors are not motivated by hegemonic or ideological ambitions. In a number of recent cases, both international organizations and individual states have objected vigorously to military coups against elected governments, and have taken limited steps to oppose such coups.[48] Moreover, both the Organization for Security and Cooperation in Europe (OSCE) and the OAS have pledged to take action against the unconstitutional overthrow of a democratic government within their respective regions.[49] While the growing consensus on the importance of democratic governance has

---

46. In adopting Resolution 940, the Security Council considered the options outlined in the *Report of the Secretary-General on the United Nations Mission in Haiti,* U.N. Doc. S/1994/828 (1994). In that report, the Secretary-General states that an expanded U.N. force should operate with the consent of the legitimate authorities in Haiti, but also notes that such a force "would have to use coercive means in order to fulfill its mandate," and that it would therefore "be necessary for the Security Council to act under Chapter VII of the Charter in authorizing its mandate." *Id.* para. 8. During the debate on Resolution 940, several states' representatives noted that Aristide's consent to intervention was an important factor supporting the decision to intervene, but no one identified it as either a necessary or a sufficient legal basis for intervention. *See* U.N. SCOR, 49th Sess., 3413th mtg. at 17, 19, 23, 24, U.N. Doc., S/PV.3413 (1994) (statements of the representatives of Argentina, Spain, the Russian Federation, and the Czech Republic).

47. Thus, few states considered Endara's consent legally significant when the United States invoked the support of Panama's President-elect, Guillermo Endara, as one of several grounds allegedly justifying U.S. military intervention in Panama. *See* Abraham D. Sofaer, *Remarks, Panel on The Panamanian Revolution: Diplomacy, War and Self-Determination in Panama,* 84 AM. SOC'Y INT'L L. PROCEEDINGS 182, 183 (1990).

48. *See* Acevedo, *supra* note 33, at 141 (noting OAS criticism of "the coup in Suriname in December 1990, the attempted coup in Venezuela in February 1992, and the so-called autogolpe by the constitutional president of Peru in April 1992 and of Guatemala in May 1993"); Reisman, *supra* note 7, at 797-98.

49. *See* Document of the Moscow Meeting of the Conference on the Human Dimension of the CSCE, 30 I.L.M. 1670, 1677 (1991) (pledging "to make democratic advances irreversible," and to "support vigorously" any democratic government subject to an unconstitutional overthrow); The Santiago Commitment to Democracy and the Renewal of the Inter-American System, O.A.S. General Assembly, 3d plenary sess. (adopted June 4, 1991), at 1, O.A.S. Doc. OEA/Ser.P/XXI.O.2 (1991) (declaring democracy to be the only acceptable form of government for the hemisphere and mandating prompt consideration of collective measures to restore democracy in any member country subject to an illegal seizure of power); Resolution on Representative Democracy, O.A.S. General Assembly, 5th plen. sess. (adopted June 5, 1991), AG/RES. 1080 (XXI-0/91), O.A.S. Doc. OEA/Ser.P/XXI.O.2 (1991).

220   DUKE JOURNAL OF COMPARATIVE & INTERNATIONAL LAW   [Vol. 7:209

not translated into acceptance of military intervention in most cases, it does make it easier to employ non-coercive sanctions, and in rare cases, as in Haiti, to obtain Security Council authorization for more coercive measures.

B. Equilibrium Between the Government and Its Adversaries

In many cases of internal conflict, the Government and its adversaries may achieve a rough balance of power with each controlling a significant portion of the state and its population. Juridical opinion and state practice in such cases are varied and often contradictory.[50] In theory, external assistance to either side, particularly through military intervention, may violate the right of the people of the state to determine the outcome of the conflict themselves.[51] This theory is problematic, since it privileges an outcome based on the relative strength of the combatants over an outcome determined by the popular support each faction holds or the type of regime each faction is likely to establish should it gain full control of the state. Nonetheless, other approaches may be even more problematic, requiring as they do subjective evaluations by potentially biased external actors of the human rights credentials or democratic prospects of contenders for power in another country.

In practice, most states continue to accord substantial deference to the will of a recognized, incumbent government, even after it arguably lost control of a substantial portion of the state, so long as the government retains control over the capital city and does not appear to be in imminent danger of collapse.[52] In virtually all such cases, however, it is possible for the government to allege that the opposition forces are receiving substantial external assistance from third states in violation of the non-intervention principle. Accordingly the government can claim a right to receive outside assistance, including troops, as a form of counter-intervention.[53] This claimed right is related to but independent of any authority the government might otherwise have to consent to foreign military intervention. It rests on the premise that aid in such circumstances is not a form of intervention requiring legitimation, but rather a means to neutralize an unlawful, prior intervention, thus returning control over the state's po-

---

50. *See* Brownlie, *supra* note 20, at 326-27.

51. *See, e.g.*, Schachter, *supra* note 16, at 1641; Moore, *supra* note 16, at 196.

52. *See* Doswald-Beck, *supra* note 6, at 197-98.

53. For a discussion of the right of counterintervention, see generally John A. Perkins, *The Right of Counterintervention*, 17 GA. J. INT'L & COMP. L. 171 (1986).

litical future to internal actors to the extent that is possible.[54] Alternatively, aid may be characterized as a form of collective self-defense against external aggression directed by third states against the state of the requesting government.[55]

Unfortunately, the ease with which individual states may invoke asserted rights of counterintervention or collective self-defense makes it difficult to assess the relative significance of consent as an independent justification in most instances of intervention on behalf of embattled but still functioning incumbent governments. This is particularly true for the many cases in which discussions of legal justification were openly colored by Cold War tensions. The 1958 U.S. intervention in Lebanon provides a case in point. The Lebanese government, which was facing a substantial and growing insurrection, alleged that the United Arab Republic was unlawfully supporting the insurrectionists. The United States sent troops to assist the Lebanese government, at its request. The United States, supported by other western countries, argued that it was entirely in accordance with the United Nations Charter to provide such assistance in the face of "an insurrection stimulated and assisted from outside . . ."[56] The Soviet Union, however, with support from a number of states in the General Assembly, characterized the insurrection in Lebanon as "a popular movement against the 'reactionary government'" of the Lebanese President, and attacked U.S. involvement as a violation of the non-intervention principle.[57]

In most such cases, it is difficult to ascertain with any certainty the facts surrounding a government's claim that its internal armed opposition is receiving significant external support. Even in cases where the facts were reasonably clear, Cold War constraints and concerns about intruding on a state's domestic jurisdiction typically precluded the United Nations from taking any effective action against external intervention. As a result, states commonly acted as if incumbent governments had a virtually unlimited right to obtain help from third states in seeking to suppress internal rebellions.[58] With the

---

54. *See* Schachter, *supra* note 16, at 1642; Henkin, *supra* note 20, at 63-64.

55. *See* OSCAR SCHACHTER, INTERNATIONAL LAW IN THEORY AND PRACTICE 159 (1991) (noting that if aid to rebel forces amounts to an armed attack, a counterinterventionary response may be an instance of legitimate collective self-defense).

56. U.N. SCOR, 13th Sess., 827th mtg. at 6, U.N. Doc. S/PV.827 (1958); *see* Doswald-Beck, *supra* note 6, at 214-15.

57. *See* Doswald-Beck, *supra* note 6, at 216.

58. *See* Farer, *supra* note 17, at 319.

222   DUKE JOURNAL OF COMPARATIVE & INTERNATIONAL LAW   [Vol. 7:209

end of the Cold War, the members of the Security Council now peri- odically find it possible to agree on the undesirability of external intervention in particular cases. When such agreement is possible, the Council often imposes mandatory arms embargos on all parties to the conflict.[59] But for the most part, the Council only adopts coercive measures when the incumbent government disappears or becomes simply one of many warring factions.[60] Until that point is reached, third states continue to act as if they have a broad right to aid incumbent governments, provided those governments can plausibly allege that the rebels are receiving external assistance.

Unlike individual states, however, international organizations generally prefer not to rely on counterintervention or collective self-defense as a justification for military intervention in internal conflicts. Instead, both the United Nations and regional organizations usually proclaim that they are neutral with regard to the merits of the underlying conflict. They strive, at least publicly, to avoid siding openly with either the government or its opposition. In general, they seek to play a mediating or peacekeeping function.[61]

Accordingly, such organizations often face a number of problems specific to intervention under this posture. The first issue they must confront is whose consent must be obtained for intervention. As a prudential matter, both the United Nations and regional organizations will ordinarily seek the consent of each of the primary warring parties before sending troops into the middle of an internal conflict.[62] The applicable legal requirement, however, is consent of the territorial state. In some cases that requirement may be satisfied by the consent of the incumbent government, even if its authority has been substantially undermined by a significant armed rebellion. In evaluating the incumbent government's authority in this context, even wide-spread recognition of a government is not by itself disposi-

---

59. *See, e.g.*, S.C. Res. 788, U.N. SCOR, 47th Sess., 3138th mtg. at 3, U.N. Doc. 3/RES/788 (1992) (imposing a mandatory embargo on "all deliveries of weapons and military equipment to Liberia" except deliveries to West African peacekeeping forces); S.C. Res. 713, U.N. SCOR, 46th Sess., 3009th mtg. at 3, U.N. Doc. S/RES/713 (1991) (imposing a weapons embargo on the former Yugoslavia).

60. *See* Wippman, *supra* note 15, at 473.

61. *See, e.g.*, Tom J. Farer, *Intervention in Unnatural Humanitarian Emergencies: Lessons of the First Phase*, 18 HUM. RTS. Q. 1, 4-7 (1996); Wippman, *supra* note 15, at 25-26, 34-35.

62. *See* Lori Damrosch, *Introduction, in* ENFORCING RESTRAINT: COLLECTIVE INTERVENTION IN INTERNAL CONFLICTS 1, 11 (L. Damrosch ed., 1993) ("obtaining the effective consent of all the combatants has seemed the best way to ensure that they can carry out a feasible mission.").

tive. States and international organizations are slow to withdraw recognition from an incumbent government, even when that government has lost control of much of the state.[63] Indeed, premature withdrawal of recognition might be seen as illicit support for the rebel forces.[64] But, the failure to withdraw recognition does not automatically translate into acceptance of the recognized government's authority to invite external military intervention on its own behalf. As a legal matter, whether a government is entitled to give unilateral consent to the deployment of troops, even for peacekeeping purposes, depends more on the extent of the government's control of the state than on the breadth of its recognition in the international community. As enunciated by the British Foreign Secretary, the test is whether the regime in power "exercise[s] effective control of the territory of the State concerned, and seem[s] likely to continue to do so."[65]

Again, however, the question of control is complicated by the common existence of illicit foreign intervention. In Cyprus, for example, the resolutions authorizing the continued deployment of U.N. peacekeeping forces cite only the consent of the recognized Greek Cypriot dominated Government, even though Turkish Cypriots have long controlled more than one third of the state.[66] The U.N.'s formal reliance on government consent reflects not only the fact that the Government still controls most of Cyprus, but also the fact that the government would control the entire state but for Turkish military intervention.[67]

In general, when a government faces substantial armed opposition, both the U.N. and regional organizations, more so than individual states, appear to have considerable leeway in determining whether to rely on the consent of the government as a sufficient legal basis for intervention. For example, in 1981 the Organization of Af-

---

63. *See* Doswald-Beck, *supra* note 6, at 197-98.

64. *See* 1 L. OPPENHEIM, *supra* note 5, para. 74, at 134-37.

65. *See* Speech of the British Foreign Secretary, Lord Carrington to the House of Lords, 408 PARL. DEB., H.L. (5th sev.) 1121-22 (1980), *cited in* Doswald-Beck, *supra* note 6, at 194. The Foreign Secretary was discussing Britain's decision to dispense with formal recognition in favor of a policy that allows recognition of regimes that take power unconstitutionally to be determined by the nature of the United Kingdom's dealings with those regimes. However, the de facto control test he described is equally applicable to determinations of a regime's authority to invite external military intervention. *See* Doswald-Beck, *supra* note 6, at 194-96.

66. *See, e.g.,* S.C. Res. 723, U.N. SCOR, 46th Sess., 3022nd mtg., S/RES/723 (1991).

67. For a discussion of Turkish military intervention and the legal issues surrounding it, see David Wippman, *International Law and Ethnic Conflict on Cyprus,* 27 TEX INT'L L.J. 1 (1995).

rican Unity (OAU) dispatched an Inter-African Force to conduct peacekeeping operations in Chad on the basis of a request from the Chadian Government, even though that Government's position was so precarious that the rebel forces overthrew the Government the following year.[68]   Similarly, the Arab League relied on Lebanese Government consent as the basis for intervening in that country's civil war, even though the Government's authority in much of the country was tenuous at best.[69] In such cases most states seem willing to defer to the judgment of the appropriate regional organization.[70]

C. Government As Warring Faction

In some civil wars the government loses control over most of the country, ceases to exercise any substantial administrative or governmental functions, and becomes in effect simply one among a number of warring factions. For example, President Samuel Doe's government in Liberia lost control of most of the state to rebel forces following a rebellion that began on December 24, 1989.[71] By the summer of 1990, most government ministers had fled the country, and all state institutions had ground to a halt. The rebels exercised military but not administrative control over most of Liberia, with the exception of a portion of the capital still in the hands of what remained of Doe's military.[72]

Liberia's neighbors watched the growing chaos with some dismay, fearing it might spread throughout the region. Nigeria, the dominant regional power and a supporter of the Doe government, pressed for regional military action to restore order in Liberia.[73] Doe welcomed the Nigerian initiative, as did Prince Johnson, the leader of the smaller of the two rebel factions then battling Doe's forces for control of the capital. However, Charles Taylor, the leader of the

---

68. *See generally* Amadu Sesay, *The Limits of Peace-Keeping by a Regional Organization: The OAU Peace-Keeping Force in Chad,* CONFLICT Q. (Winter 1991).

69. *See generally The Legal Basis of the Arab League in Lebanon, in* ISTVAN POGANY, THE ARAB LEAGUE AND PEACEKEEPING IN THE LEBANON at 93-107 (1987).

70. Some of the possible reasons for such deference are discussed at text accompanying note 92 *infra.*

71. For a more detailed treatment of the Liberian civil war, see David Wippman, *Enforcing the Peace: ECOWAS and the Liberian Civil War, in* ENFORCING RESTRAINT: COLLECTIVE INTERVENTION IN INTERNAL CONFLICTS 157 (L. Damrosch ed., 1991).

72. *See id.* at 158.

73. *See* Anthony Chukwukaa Ofodile, *The Legality of ECOWAS Intervention in Liberia,* 32 COLUM. J. TRANSNAT'L L. 381, 383-84 (1994).

main rebel force, strongly opposed external intervention.[74] Taylor believed that given time his forces could take control of the entire state, and that any regional intervention led by Nigeria would support the failing Doe regime at Taylor's expense.[75]

Although Liberia's U.N. representative sought to place the Liberian crisis on the Security Council's agenda, the Council took no action.[76] In August 1990, five states, operating under the auspices of the Economic Community of West African States (ECOWAS), sent several thousand troops into Monrovia. The troops were instructed to act as a peacekeeping force, to the extent possible. In keeping with this ostensible mission, the "peacekeepers" were designated as the Economic Community of West African States Monitoring Group (ECOMOG).[77] Taylor did not view ECOMOG as a neutral peacekeeping force, however, and his forces attacked ECOMOG on its arrival. ECOMOG then launched a military offensive to expel Taylor's forces from Monrovia and to secure the capital.[78]

This action and subsequent offensives against Taylor's forces are not easy to reconcile with international law. ECOWAS did not have Security Council authorization when it sent troops into Liberia. It did not have the consent of the dominant warring faction, which stated in advance that it would treat an ECOWAS military intervention as an illegal foreign invasion. Thus, this was not a classic peacekeeping operation in which the intervening force obtains the advance consent of the primary warring parties.

At least one author, Professor Georg Nolte, has argued forcefully that President Doe's consent to the intervention was sufficient legal authority for it.[79] Nolte contends that it is "irrelevant" that Doe had been reduced to a "minor contender for power" at the time he gave his consent to the intervention.[80] His government was still the recognized government of Liberia, and was "capable, by agreeing to a cease-fire with an otherwise rival faction, of paving the way for entry

---

74. *See* Wippman, *supra* note 15, at 167; Ofodile, *supra* note 73, at 384-85.

75. *See* U.N. GAOR, 45th Sess., 27th mtg. at 61, U.N. Doc. A/45/PV. 27 (1990).

76. *See* U.N. GAOR, 45th Sess., 27th mtg. at 61, U.N. Doc. A/45/PV.27 (1990); U.N. SCOR, 2974 mtg. at 3, U.N. Doc. S/PV. 2974 (1991).

77. *See* Wippman, *supra* note 15, at 167-68.

78. *See id.* at 168-69.

79. Georg Nolte, *Restoring Peace by Regional Action: International Legal Aspects of the Liberian Conflict*, 53 ZEITSCHRIFT FÜR AUSLÄNDISCHES ÖFFENTLICHES RECHT UND VÖLKKERRECHT 603 (1993).

80. *Id.* at 625.

of the intervention forces into his country."[81] Nolte recognizes that such a rule, allowing an essentially defunct government to invite external military intervention to prevent an adversary from taking power, might be abused by neighboring states with hegemonic aspirations, and might lead to an internationalization of a domestic conflict. Nolte argues, however, that the regional framework for intervention provides "the necessary degree of impartiality and the chance of containment of the conflict," and that in situations comparable to Liberia's, it is necessary to balance the goals served by the non-intervention principle with the need to further humanitarian aims.[82]

Thus, Nolte's position is that Doe's consent was sufficient legal justification for regional intervention in Liberia, especially in light of the humanitarian aims of that intervention. This position is logically consistent with the Security Council's reaction to the ECOWAS intervention. Although the Council never formally authorized military action, months after the initial intervention it did issue statements commending ECOWAS for its efforts to restore peace in Liberia.[83] Since the conventional view is that only prior authorization will suffice to legitimize a regional enforcement action, the Council's post hoc approval suggests that the Council considered the ECOWAS intervention to be a consent-based peacekeeping operation. Moreover, during debate on a later resolution authorizing sanctions against Taylor's forces, various members of the Council expressly characterized ECOMOG as a "peacekeeping force."[84] Since peacekeeping, by definition, is an operation undertaken with the consent of the territorial state, and since Taylor did not consent, one could read this characterization of ECOMOG as an implicit claim that Doe acting alone had the legal authority to consent to ECOMOG's deployment.

Nonetheless, it is difficult to conclude from the facts of this case that a government, reduced to the status of one among several warring parties, can unilaterally consent to an external intervention, even when the intervention is carried out under the auspices of a regional or subregional organization. ECOWAS itself did not cite Doe's con-

81. *Id.*
82. *Id.* at 623-24.
83. *See* Note by the President of the Security Council, S/22133, January 22, 1991; Note by the President of the Security Council, S/23886, May 7, 1992.
84. *See generally* Security Council, Provisional Verbatim Record of the Three Thousand One Hundred and Thirty-eighth Meeting, S/PV.3138, November 19, 1992; Wippman, *supra* note 15, at 185.

sent as a legal basis for intervention,[85] nor did individual states. Given the abysmal nature of the Doe regime, the breadth of opposition to it throughout the country, and the personal ties between Doe and the Nigerian President, reliance on Doe's consent would have been politically intolerable. It would also have run contrary to ECOMOG's claim to be a neutral interposition force. That claim was never entirely credible, since ECOMOG from the start was forced into an adversarial posture with Charles Taylor. But even though ECOMOG intervened against Taylor, it did not intervene for Doe. It made no effort to restore Doe to power. Instead, ECOMOG, and ECOWAS more generally, sought from the outset to arrange internationally monitored elections as the basis for resolving the conflict, and deliberately excluded Doe as a possible candidate in such elections.[86] Indeed, it was precisely because ECOWAS pursued a strategy of national reconciliation through democratic elections that the intervention attracted international support.

By itself, this does not mean that ECOWAS could not rely on Doe's consent as the legal basis for intervention.[87] When the United Nations first intervened in the Congo, it relied in large part on the beleaguered government's consent, even though the U.N. claimed to be neutral as between the internal warring factions.[88] But in the Congo, as in other cases where a multinational intervention force relied on a teetering government's consent, an illicit prior intervention (in that case by Belgium) arguably justified external aid to the government.[89] A similar argument could have been made in Liberia since Taylor received substantial support from Libya, Burkina Faso, and Côte d'Ivoire.[90] But ECOWAS chose not to take that position, preferring to rely instead on a humanitarian justification.

Overall, there are good reasons why Doe's consent should be deemed insufficient as a legal justification. Unlike Aristide, Doe lacked the legitimacy that comes with the acquisition of power through internationally monitored elections. Accordingly, once Doe

---

85. In fact, ECOWAS stressed that its intervention was not designed "to save one part." *See* U.N. SCOR, Annex 1, at 3, U.N. Doc. S/21485 (1990).

86. *See* Christopher J. Borgen, *The Theory and Practice of Regional Organization Intervention in Civil Wars*, 26 N.Y.U. J. INT'L L. & POL. 797, 817 (1994).

87. *See* Nolte, *supra* note 79, at 626.

88. *See* S.C. Res. 143, U.N. SCOR, 15th Sess., 873d mtg., U.N. Doc. S/4387 (1960).

89. For a brief description of events in the Congo, see THOMAS M. FRANCK, NATION AGAINST NATION: WHAT HAPPENED TO THE U.N. DREAM AND WHAT THE U.S. CAN DO ABOUT IT 174-77 (1985).

90. *See* Wippman, *supra* note 15, at 188.

was effectively reduced from head of state to head of a minor warring faction, his authority to speak for the state was nominal and purely formal. Doe's authority rested on the tenuous prop of external recognition. Though not withdrawn, such recognition says little in this context about outside states' views of Doe's authority, and nothing at all about the relationship between effective control and political community that normally underpins a government's claim in international law to be able to invite intervention on behalf of the state.

In the end, Doe's invitation adds only a thin patina of legitimacy to the force of the humanitarian arguments for intervention.[91] If those arguments are not sufficient in and of themselves to warrant intervention, it is difficult to conclude, as a matter of law or policy, that the invitation of one faction, even if it is the faction that previously controlled the government, should materially alter the legal calculus.

This is not to say that regional organizations should not have a substantial margin of appreciation when determining whether a government's political and military position has deteriorated to the point that it no longer possesses sufficient authority to invite outside intervention. States typically do, and should, accord substantial deference to judgments by regional organizations with regard to the standing of a particular government within their region. There are several reasons why such deference is appropriate. First, as noted earlier, the process of multilateral decision-making, which requires achievement of a consensus among states with diverse interests, acts as a screen for purely self-interested interventions. Second, the member states of regional organizations have assented, at least to some degree, to the decision-making procedures at issue. Third, the member states are likely to have a greater expertise on the issues driving the conflict and greater familiarity with the warring parties than extra-regional actors. Regional organizations may thus be in a better position to evaluate and choose among available courses of action than states operating from a greater cultural and political distance.

There are, of course, some countervailing considerations. In particular, the very proximity that affords regional organizations a better understanding of local conditions than more distant states may also generate a greater degree of bias or self-interest than might be expected in other states. Moreover, it is possible in particular cases

---

91. *Accord* Borgen, *supra* note 86, at 818 ("Since ECOWAS marginalized the Doe government and forged a future for Liberia that did not envision Doe at all, the legitimacy of its action cannot be argued to be based on the consent of the parties.").

that a regional organization may simply act as a vehicle to conceal the driving interests of the organization's most powerful state. Most important, regional organizations typically lack the will, the resources, or both to intervene effectively in large-scale internal conflicts.[92]

The dangers of biased or hegemonic interventions are real, but they are probably less significant now than during the Cold War when the United States undermined the perceived utility of regional collective decision making processes through its efforts to use the OAS (and on one occasion, the Organization of Eastern Caribbean States) as vehicles to legitimize ideologically motivated interventions in Latin America and the Caribbean.[93] Moreover, these dangers can be mitigated through careful U.N. oversight of regional interventions.[94] The larger problem is one of capabilities. Only a few subglobal organizations, NATO in particular, have the logistical and financial capacity to conduct effective large-scale military operations in distant countries. But the member states in those organizations seldom see a vital national interest at stake in contemporary internal conflicts, and thus lack the will to engage in the sustained peacekeeping, peace enforcement, and peacebuilding measures needed to stabilize war-torn countries. Fears of regional instability and weaker structures of public accountability may give smaller regional and subregional organizations (such as ECOWAS) the political will to intervene in internal conflicts, and an ability to take casualties well past the point that would drive out less motivated intervenors. But such organizations seldom have the resources, experience, or credibility with the warring parties to intervene effectively.[95]

The obvious response to this dilemma is for the better endowed international organizations to assist the weaker but more motivated

---

92. *See* Jeffrey Laurenti, The Regionals and the U.N.: Keystone Cops?, Address at the conference on "The United Nations, Regional Organizations, and Military Operations" hosted by the Center on Law, Ethics, and National Security, Duke University School of Law, April 12-13, 1996 (on file with the *Duke Journal of Comparative & International Law*).

93. *See, e.g.*, Farer, *supra* note 17, at 333-35.

94. The United Nations dispatched peacekeepers to Liberia in part because of concerns over the neutrality of ECOWAS forces. *See* S.C. Res. 866, U.N. SCOR, 48th Sess., 3281st mtg. at 2, U.N. Doc. S/RES/866 (1993); Binaifer Nowrojee, *Recent Developments: Joining Forces: United Nations and Regional Peacekeeping—Lessons from Liberia*, 8 HARV. HUM. RTS. J. 129 (1995). The United Nations has also sent peacekeepers to the Caucasus, in part to keep watch over peacekeeping actions conducted by forces from the Commonwealth of Independent States. *See* James Meek, *Peacekeeping: U.N. Rules Out Special Status for Russians*, THE GUARDIAN (Manchester, Eng.), April 5, 1994, at 9.

95. *See* Laurenti, *supra* note 92.

regional organizations to intervene constructively. That approach has been attempted in various conflicts. In Liberia, for example, the United Nations and individual states have provided various forms of assistance to ECOWAS, while leaving to ECOWAS the dominant role in attempting to establish peace. To date, the support given to ECOWAS has been far less than the organization needed to compensate for its own limited resources.[96] But as the international community acquires more experience in ending internal conflicts using coordinated efforts by various international organizations, the record in this area may improve.

On balance, it seems appropriate as a legal matter to continue to accord regional organizations a reasonable margin of appreciation in evaluating the authority of particular governments to invite intervention in close cases. Even so, justifications other than governmental consent should be sought when no single faction can credibly claim to speak for the state. One possibility, of course, is consent from all of the principal warring factions. To the extent that international law treats control of the state as a sufficient basis for expressing the state's consent to external military intervention, it seems reasonable to conclude that the collective consent of the various warring factions, which together control the state as a whole, constitutes the best available alternative to consent by a recognized, effective government.[97] In many cases, it may be politically or morally unattractive to accord substantial legal significance to the will of one or more faction leaders, particularly if such leaders command no significant popular allegiance, rule by terror, and exercise no real governmental functions in their areas of military predominance.[98] Unfortunately, external actors wishing to end a protracted and bloody internal conflict often have no choice but to accept such leaders as speaking for the territory and population under their control.[99]

---

96. *See* Nowrojee, *supra* note 94, at 147-48.

97. *See* ANN VAN WYNEN THOMAS & A. J. THOMAS, JR., NON-INTERVENTION: THE LAW AND ITS IMPORT IN THE AMERICAS 215, 221 (1956) (if all parties to an internal struggle request intervention, "the legality of the intervention would then be based upon the total consent of the state").

98. *See* David Wippman, *Treaty-Based Intervention: Who Can Say No?*, 62 U. CHI. L. REV. 607, 657 (1995).

99. *See, e.g.*, Statement of Roy S. Lee, 28 CORNELL INT'L L. J. 643 (1995) ("Essentially you have to negotiate with somebody in power.").

D. Collapse of Internal Authority

In some cases, conflict reaches a level of intensity in which the forces of the incumbent government are routed, and no other internal source of authority exercises any meaningful administrative or governmental functions. It is doubtful that this situation presents a significantly different legal posture than a situation in which the government becomes simply one among a number of warring factions. Some authors have suggested, however, that in a situation of complete breakdown of internal authority, regional organizations have a special competence to intervene to restore order.[100]

It could be argued that in such a case military action by a regional organization to restore order falls within the bounds of regional authority to deal with problems "appropriate for regional action" pursuant to Chapter VIII of the Charter.[101] Absent any viable internal authority, the argument goes, intervention designed to restore conditions under which the population of the state can establish a government of its choosing would not be action against a state, and so would not constitute enforcement action of the sort that would have to be authorized by the Security Council pursuant to Article 53 of the Charter.[102] Accordingly, consent in such cases might be treated as unnecessary. Alternatively, consent in such cases might be presumed. Under this approach, the assumption would be that intervention in such circumstances would be so clearly in the interest of the affected state that the state, or the people of the state, would certainly consent to such intervention if they could.[103] Either way, interventions to restore order could be deemed to fall within the gray area between Article 52's peaceful dispute resolution mechanisms and Article 53's enforcement action.

A variation on this argument would be that in a situation of complete internal breakdown, the highest surviving official of the

---

100. *See* John Norton Moore, *Grenada and the International Double Standard*, 78 AM. J. INT'L L. 145, 154-56 (1984) ("there is substantial authority that regional peacekeeping actions undertaken in a setting of breakdown of authority are lawful under the Charter."); *see also* 20 U.N. SCOR, 1220th mtg. at 15, 16-17, U.N. Doc. S/PV.1220 (1965); 20 U.N. SCOR, 122d mtg. at 3, 4-5, U.N. Doc. S/PV.1222 (1965) (statements of U.S. Ambassadors Stevenson and Yost).

101. Article 52 of the U.N. Charter provides: "Nothing in the present Charter precludes the existence of regional arrangements or agencies for dealing with such matters relating to the maintenance of international peace and security as are appropriate for regional action, provided that such arrangements or agencies and their activities are consistent with the Purposes and Principles of the United Nations."

102. *See* Moore, *supra* note 100, at 154.

103. *See* Ago, *supra* note 1, at 36.

232 DUKE JOURNAL OF COMPARATIVE & INTERNATIONAL LAW [Vol. 7:209

vanished government should have the authority to invite external intervention to restore order.[104] This situation arguably differs from the situation where a government's status is reduced to one of several warring factions, because the surviving official supposedly speaks against a background of anarchy rather than as the representative of one of several factions each claiming the right to speak for the state.

The United States invoked both variations of the argument in support of its 1983 invasion of Grenada. The United States claimed that anarchy reigned at the moment of intervention, and that swift action was necessary to restore order and to protect U.S. nationals resident in Grenada.[105] To support its decision, the United States invoked, inter alia, the authorization of the Organization of Eastern Caribbean States, claiming that it had authority under Chapter VIII of the U.N. Charter to respond to disorder in a member state.[106] The United States also relied on an invitation to intervene issued by the Governor-General of Grenada.[107] Even though the Governor-General's authority within Grenada was largely ceremonial,[108] the United States argued that his consent carried substantial weight in the absence of colorable claims by other internal actors to speak for the state. However, neither of these justifications, either individually or in tandem with the alleged threat to U.S. nationals, proved persuasive to most states.[109]

The notion that states may intervene to substitute an orderly democratic process for anarchic violence as a means to reorder a state's internal political structures is an attractive one, at least on the surface. In theory, an intervention of that sort, if effective and accomplished at a reasonable cost to the affected state, could only benefit the people of that state.[110] Under the conventional under-

---

104. *See* Moore, *supra* note 100, at 153 n. 26, 159-61 (arguing that the Governor-General of Grenada had more authority to speak for Grenada than any other official at the time of the U.S. invasion of Grenada).

105. *See* Statement of the Honorable Kenneth W. Dam, Deputy Secretary of State, before the Committee on Foreign Affairs, U.S. House of Representatives 2 (Nov. 2, 1983), *reprinted in* 78 AM. J. INT'L L. 200, 200-02 (1984).

106. *See id.* at 203.

107. *See id.*

108. *See* Christopher Joyner, *The United States Action in Grenada: Reflections on the Lawfulness of Invasion*, 78 AM. J. INT'L L. 131, 139 (1984).

109. The U.S. invasion was condemned by a substantial majority of the U.N. General Assembly. *See* G.A. Res. 38/7, U.N. GAOR, 38th Sess., Supp. No. 47, U.N. Doc. A/38/47 (1983).

110. *See, e.g.,* Malvina Halberstam, *The Copenhagen Document: Intervention in Support of Democracy*, 34 HARV. INT'L L.J. 163, 167 (1993) (arguing that pro-democratic intervention is not against "but in support of the 'territorial integrity' and 'political independence' of a state");

standing of the U.N. Charter, however, any uninvited military intervention that is not undertaken in self-defense or authorized by the Security Council is illegal.[111] Moreover, the risks of abuse associated with a broad license to restore order are substantial, since there will often be a significant, though temporary, vacuum of authority between the overthrow of the incumbent government and the establishment of a successor government.

It might be appropriate, however, to create an exception for cases of protracted anarchy, in which all government functions cease for an extended period, and the warring factions are unable or unwilling to exercise any administrative functions even within the territory they control.[112] Possession of a government is an element and arguably a duty of statehood.[113] The temporary absence of a government cannot by itself suffice to trigger intervention, because internal actors must be given some opportunity to reestablish order on their own terms.[114] At some point, however, the prolonged absence of any government may constitute an abdication of the responsibilities of statehood sufficient to warrant external intervention designed to enable the citizens of the state to resume control over their affairs, and to put an end to destructive and pointless conflict.[115]

One problem, of course, is determining when that point is reached. The Security Council can decide at any time that the effects of anarchy are intolerable and authorize military intervention simply by finding that the "magnitude of the human tragedy" created by such conditions constitutes a threat to international peace. That, af-

---

Anthony D'Amato, *The Invasion of Panama Was a Lawful Response to Tyranny*, 84 AM. J. INT'L L. 516 (1990); W. Michael Reisman, *Coercion and Self-Determination: Construing Charter Article 2(4)*, 78 AM. J. INT'L L. 642, 644-45 (1984) (The critical question in a decentralized system is not whether coercion has been applied, but whether it was applied in support of or against community order and basic policies . . . .").

111. *See generally* Louis Henkin, *Use of Force: Law and U.S. Policy*, in RIGHT V. MIGHT: INTERNATIONAL LAW AND THE USE OF FORCE 37 (2d ed. 1991).

112. *See* THOMAS & THOMAS, *supra* note 97, at 220-21.

113. *See id.* at 220 ("It is the duty of a population to provide itself with a government."); *see also* 1 RESTATEMENT OF THE FOREIGN RELATIONS LAW OF THE U.S. § 201 cmt. f, at 73 (1987) ("A state need not have any particular form of government, but there must be some authority exercising governmental functions and able to represent the entity in international affairs.").

114. *See* THOMAS & THOMAS, *supra* note 97, at 220-21.

115. *See id.* at 221 ("[I]n the event a nation falls into anarchy, intervention is legal only where there is a prolonged entire absence of government."). *But see* Francis Boyle, et al., *International Lawlessness in Grenada*, 78 AM. J. INT'L L. 172, 173 (1984) ("Even when it actually exists, chronic disorder in a country does not permit neighboring states to intervene for the purpose of reestablishing minimum public security, let alone imposing a democratic form of government.").

ter all, was the basis for the U.N. authorized military intervention in Somalia.[116]

The question is whether regional organizations should have a similar margin of appreciation, either under a theory of presumed consent, or under the view that action to restore order in such cases does not constitute enforcement action under Chapter VIII of the U.N. Charter. Acceptance of a presumed consent theory, unless based on the terms of a regional organization's charter or some other treaty arrangement, would necessarily validate a similar intervention by a state acting unilaterally. That is a dangerous prospect since decisions by individual states are not subject to the checks and balances of a collective decision-making process.[117] Accordingly, it seems better to conclude that such interventions, to the extent they are permissible at all without Security Council authorization, fall within the bounds of appropriate action by a regional organization.

III. CONSENT AND ITS REVOCATION

What happens when a state consents to intervention and then withdraws that consent? In the ordinary case, the answer is simple. Intervention by consent must remain within the bounds of that consent. Accordingly, if a generally effective incumbent government revokes its prior consent to an external military intervention, the intervenors must withdraw.[118] Failure to do so amounts to an intervention against the will of the state.

There are circumstances, however, in which a different result might be reached. First, there is some uncertainty about the conditions under which even an effective government can lawfully revoke consent to the deployment of an international peacekeeping force. In 1967, Egypt withdrew its consent to the presence of the United Nations Emergency Force on Egyptian territory, thus paving the way for an Egyptian attack on Israel.[119] The Secretary-General, after studying the legal aspects of the Egyptian position, concluded that the United Nations had no legal option but to withdraw. In his view, the deployment of peacekeepers required the continuous affirmative consent, or at least acquiescence, of the state in which the troops were

---

116. *See* S.C. Res. 794, U.N. SCOR, 46th Sess., 3145th mtg., U.N. Doc. S/RES/794 (1992).

117. *See* Ago, *supra* note 1, at 36 (arguing against acceptance of a theory of presumed consent on the ground that "cases of abuse would be too common").

118. For examples, see *id.* at 32-33.

119. *See* FRANCK, *supra* note 89, at 87-88; STEVEN R. RATNER, THE NEW U.N. PEACEKEEPING: BUILDING PEACE IN LANDS OF CONFLICT AFTER THE COLD WAR 38 (1995).

placed.[120]

The Secretary-General's decision provoked considerable controversy.[121] Some critics felt that Egypt's consent to the deployment, and its acceptance of a status of forces agreement with the U.N., created a legal obligation to permit the force to carry out its mission in accordance with the parties' prior agreement.[122] To confer on any state the right to force a unilateral withdrawal of international peacekeepers at any time could stimulate strategic behavior, permitting one party to use peacekeepers as a means to buy time until that party is ready to resume a conflict previously suspended by agreement between the warring parties. On the other hand, deployment of military forces in a state's territory without its actual, contemporaneous consent impinges so directly on the autonomy of the state that the state presumably must retain, by virtue of its sovereignty, the right ultimately to revoke its consent and to force the intervenors to withdraw. The solution to this particular dilemma may lie in simply reading a requirement of reasonable notice into a state's right to revoke consent, thus giving all parties time to prepare for the peacekeepers' departure.

A similar problem arises when consent to intervention comes from two or more warring factions in an internal conflict, rather than from an effective government acting unilaterally. In such cases, states can reasonably rely on the consent of the various factions as collectively constituting the state's consent.[123] Unfortunately, consent obtained in such fashion is often fragile.[124] Almost inevitably, one faction may come to believe that the presence of external forces benefits the other side, even if the forces act as neutral peacekeepers. At that point, the faction perceiving itself as disadvantaged by intervention may withdraw consent, and even attack the would-be peacekeepers. Clearly, the peacekeepers have the right to defend themselves, but do they have the right to pursue their mission against

---

120. FRANCK, *supra* note 89, at 88-91; RATNER, *supra* note 119, at 38.

121. *See* FRANCK, *supra* note 89, at 88-93; RATNER, *supra* note 119, at 38.

122. In a 1957 Aide Memoire, Secretary-General Dag Hammarskjöld recorded his understanding that Egypt had agreed to constrain its right to revoke consent to the deployment of UNEF. According to Hammarskjold, Egypt agreed that UNEF could stay until its mission was completed, as determined by *both* Egypt and the U.N. *See* Aide Memoire, *reprinted in* 6 I.L.M. 595 (1967).

123. *See* THOMAS & THOMAS, *supra* note 97, at 215, 221.

124. *See* RATNER, *supra* note 119, at 38-41 (analyzing problems with "decaying" consent in international peacekeeping operations).

236   DUKE JOURNAL OF COMPARATIVE & INTERNATIONAL LAW   [Vol. 7:209]

internal opposition?[125]

If one assumes that any coercive actions and even the continued presence of the peacekeepers requires either the contemporaneous consent of the state as a whole or Security Council authorization, then withdrawal of consent even by one among a number of factions may amount to the termination of consent as a legal basis for intervention.[126] But if one assumes that the withdrawal of consent is as much an act of state will as the grant of consent in the first place, one could argue that revocation requires a collective decision, and that no single faction is entitled to revoke consent unilaterally.

Even if one follows the latter approach, however, consent may still prove to be a dubious basis for intervention, since some of the factions that gave their consent originally may splinter, disappear, or be replaced by new factions. On occasion, factions may reconstitute themselves under new names, precisely in order to escape any obligations they may previously have assumed. At some point, the continued presence of external forces will ordinarily require either renewed consent emanating from the new constellation of warring factions or Security Council authorization.[127]

When consent broke down as a basis for intervention in Somalia, the Security Council switched to enforcement action under Chapter VII.[128] It did the same in the former Yugoslavia.[129] By contrast, the consent of various warring factions to ECOWAS peacekeeping in Liberia has come and gone with some frequency over the last six years. Nonetheless, ECOWAS acts as if it has always had full consent, with

---

125. *See* OSCAR SCHACHTER, INTERNATIONAL LAW IN THEORY AND PRACTICE 408 (1991) (noting that U.N peacekeepers sometimes "stretch" the self-defense principle "far beyond its usual legal meaning," in part by combining a right to freedom of movement with a claimed "right to use arms in defense of positions occupied").

126. In many cases, parties dissatisfied with the activities of peacekeeping forces may simply engage in obstructionist tactics rather than explicitly withdraw consent. *See* RATNER, *supra* note 119, at 38. In such cases, peacekeepers may be forced to consider not simply the technical existence of consent, but also the "quality" of that consent, that is, the extent to which the principal parties to the conflict can be considered on balance committed to the peacekeeping process. *See Id.* at 39-41.

127. *Cf.* RATNER, *supra* note 119, at 39 (arguing that the United Nations cannot force parties to comply with a peacekeeping agreement without impermissibly blurring the distinction between peacekeeping and enforcement).

128. *See* Lee, *supra* note 99, at 643; Jeffrey Clark, *Debacle in Somalia: Failure of the Collective Response, in* ENFORCING RESTRAINT: COLLECTIVE INTERVENTION IN INTERNAL CONFLICTS 205, 221-23 (1993).

129. *See* James B. Steinberg, *International Involvement in the Yugoslavia Conflict, in* ENFORCING RESTRAINT: COLLECTIVE INTERVENTION IN INTERNAL CONFLICTS 27, 50-55 (1993).

the apparent blessing of the United Nations. In the end, this may be yet another area in which both the United Nations and regional organizations should be deemed to have a considerable margin for appreciation, that is, some leeway to decide whether a single faction's withdrawal of consent by itself fatally undermines the authority of the operation as a whole.[130]

Finally, there is considerable uncertainty over whether and under what conditions states may authorize external military intervention by treaty, even in the absence of any contemporaneous consent to the intervention.[131] The issue is particularly intriguing as it relates to the intervention authority possessed by regional organizations or ad hoc coalitions of states. In a series of thoughtful articles, Professor Tom Farer urges us to consider the following hypothetical. Suppose that a group of democratic states in the Caribbean enters into a treaty with interested NATO members to protect democracy in the signatory states. In the event of an unconstitutional seizure of power in any one of those states, the other parties to the treaty are authorized to intervene militarily to restore the elected government, either at the request of the ousted elected officials, or by a two-thirds vote if communication with those officials proves impossible. Professor Farer's conclusion is that an intervention carried out pursuant to such a treaty would be lawful "[s]ince such an action is carried out with the previously expressed consent of the target state."[132]

It could be argued, of course, that only the contemporaneous consent of the effective government can satisfy the peremptory norm against the use of force in international relations embodied in Article 2(4) of the U.N. Charter. But if the forces seizing power unconstitutionally have not yet consolidated their control over the country, or if, as in Haiti, the international community continues to recognize the former government as the legitimate state government, it seems fair

---

130. *Cf.* RATNER, *supra* note 119, at 40-41 (noting that in many cases of "decaying consent", states "neither insist upon enforcement authority from the Security Council to respond to many types of violations nor demand the termination of missions facing lack of compliance").

131. For a more detailed treatment of this subject, see Wippman, *supra* note 71, at 187-89.

132. Farer, *supra* note 17, at 332; *see also* Tom J. Farer, *The United States as Guarantor of Democracy in the Caribbean Basin: Is There a Legal Way?*, 10 HUM. RTS. Q. 157 (1988). For similar proposals, see Morton H. Halperin, *Guaranteeing Democracy*, 91 FOREIGN POL'Y 105, 121 (1993) (urging adoption of an "international guarantee" clause permitting forcible intervention to protect democracy upon "consensus of a group of guaranteeing powers designated in an agreement with a particular country"); Halberstam, *supra* note 110 (arguing that the Copenhagen Document can be construed to permit military intervention to protect democracy).

to conclude that the usurpers acting alone should not be entitled to revoke the state's prior consent to intervention.

The question Professor Farer poses is not entirely hypothetical. A number of recent agreements designed to end protracted civil wars have come very close to authorizing outside states to employ force against any party that violates the agreement.[133] It is too soon to tell, however, whether in the future such agreements might serve as a useful adjunct to existing legal mechanisms for the use of force in internal conflicts.

IV. CONCLUSION

Despite its apparent simplicity, the principle that a state may validly consent to external military intervention turns out in practice to be fraught with difficulty. Once we move beyond the paradigm case of a recognized and effective government inviting intervention for sharply limited ends, it is extremely difficult to define precisely the cases in which invited interventions will be generally accepted. Previous state practice in this area is of only limited utility, since in most cases the reaction of states was strongly colored by Cold War considerations.

Nonetheless, it may be possible to offer a few generalizations, none of which are likely to prove surprising. In keeping with the traditional approach to intervention in internal conflicts, most states are strongly influenced by the extent to which an inviting authority exercises control of the state at the time an invitation to intervene is issued. Increasingly, however, states are prepared to consider the democratic legitimacy of an inviting authority as a counterbalance to considerations of power and effective control. Finally, in close cases,

---

133. *See, e.g.*, Cotonou Agreement (July 25, 1993), art. 8, § 3, attached to Letter Dated 6 August 1993 from the Chargé d'Affaires A.I. of the Permanent Mission of Benin to the United Nations Addressed to the Secretary-General 7, U.N. Doc. S/26272 (1993), *reprinted in* REGIONAL PEACE-KEEPING AND INTERNATIONAL ENFORCEMENT: THE LIBERIAN CRISIS 343, 347 (Marc Weller ed., 1994) (authorizing ECOMOG to "resort to the use of its peace-enforcement powers" against violators of the agreement under specified circumstances); Agreement on a Comprehensive Political Settlement of the Cambodia Conflict (October 30, 1991), art. 6, attached to Letter Dated 30 October 1991 from the Permanent Representatives of France and Indonesia to the United Nations addressed to the Secretary-General 10, U.N. Doc. A/46/608, S/23177 (1991), *reprinted in* 31 I.L.M. 180, 184 (1992) (delegating to the U.N. "all powers necessary to ensure the implementation of this Agreement"); General Framework for Peace in Bosnia and Herzegovina (December 14, 1995), Annex I, Art. 1, *reprinted in* 35 INT'L LEGAL MATERIALS 75, 92 (1996) (inviting the U.N. Security Council to establish a multinational military Implementation Force authorized to undertake "such enforcement action . . . as may be necessary to ensure implementation" of the parties' agreement).

states are likely to defer to the judgment of regional organizations, at least in those cases in which the United Nations itself is reluctant to get involved.

[6]

HOST-STATE CONSENT AND UNITED NATIONS PEACEKEEPING IN YUGOSLAVIA

CHRISTINE GRAY[*]

I. INTRODUCTION

The conflict in the former Yugoslavia highlights some problems that arise when the ostensibly simple principle that host-state consent is necessary for U.N. peacekeeping is put into practice.[1] The difficulty of applying this principle, especially when no generally recognized government has effective control of the entirety of a state's territory, is discussed elsewhere in this Symposium.[2] Such a division of effective control existed in the former Yugoslavia and was compounded by the lack of clarity and consensus in the Security Council mandates which authorize military intervention.[3]

The following account of events in the former Yugoslavia is partly a description of the difficulties that arose there and partly a demonstration that the notion of consent in this context is a complex one. This examination of efforts to reach agreement on foreign military presence reveals that the issue of consent arose at several different times and in different forms. In Part II below, the various forms of consent are discussed—not only is initial consent to the establishment of a force required, but consent to the scope of its mandate and to the composition of its forces is also sought. Obtaining this formal consent to deployment of an armed force is only the starting point of

* Fellow in Law, St. Hilda's College, Oxford University, and Reader in Law, Oxford University

1. On host-state consent in general, see Davis Brown, *The Role of the United Nations in Peacekeeping and Trust Monitoring: What are the Applicable Norms?*, 27 REV. BELGE. D.I. 559 (1994); 1-4 ROSALYN HIGGINS, UNITED NATIONS PEACEKEEPING (1972); N.D. WHITE, KEEPING THE PEACE 202-4 (1993); David Wippman, *Treaty-Based Intervention: Who Can Say No?*, 62 U. CHI. L. REV. 607 (1995); David Wippman, *Military Intervention, Regional Organization and Host-State Consent*, 7 DUKE J. COMP. & INT'L L. 209 (1996) [hereinafter Wippman, *Military Intervention*].

2. *See generally* Wippman, *Military Intervention, supra* note 1.

3. *See generally* Mats R. Berdal, *The Security Council, Peacekeeping and Internal Conflict After the Cold War*, 7 DUKE J. COMP. & INT'L L. 71 (1996) (discussing the latter problem in detail).

a peacekeeping operation. Thereafter, consent to detailed rules on the rights of the peacekeeping force by means of a Status of Forces Agreement (SOFA) allows the force to assert its rights against a recalcitrant host state. Difficulties in securing SOFAs in the former Yugoslavia are discussed in Part III.

In complex peacekeeping operations, the perception of what mandate is necessary to bring about resolution of the conflict often changes. Changes to the initial mandate for the peacekeeping force in the former Yugoslavia are discussed in detail in Part IV. Regardless of what formal agreements are concluded, it is cooperation on the ground that is crucial to the success of a peacekeeping mission. Where this is not forthcoming the Security Council may turn to Chapter VII of the U.N. Charter to make stronger the obligation to comply with its resolutions and to cooperate with the peacekeeping force; this practice is discussed in Part V.

Such references to Chapter VII, of course, do not alter the fact that the presence of the peacekeeping force still depends on host-state consent. Moreover, efforts to obtain consent, and even references to Chapter VII, were not enough to ensure cooperation by the parties in the former Yugoslavia with the United Nations Protection Force (UNPROFOR), since the parties saw UNPROFOR as an obstacle in the way of a favorable military solution rather than as an impartial force. This failure to ensure cooperation and reach agreement with respect to the mandate and status of U.N. forces led to the activation of a Rapid Reaction Force, discussed in Part VI, and ultimately to the withdrawal of UNPROFOR from Croatia and to the establishment of the United Nations Confidence Restoration Operation (UNCRO), discussed in Part VII.

As the world community witnessed in the case of the former Yugoslavia, sometimes the inherent limitations on a peacekeeping force, including the legal requirement of host-state consent and the practical requirement of cooperation from all significant parties involved, are at odds with expectations for what the U.N. force might achieve. U.N. Secretary-General Boutros Boutros-Ghali, well aware of the resulting political difficulties, reaffirmed the appropriate role of a peacekeeping force when he welcomed Croatian President Tudjman's announcement that he would accept the establishment of UNCRO in Croatia:

> As the Council is considering the question of maintaining a U.N. peacekeeping presence in Croatia, it is timely for me to restate the basic principles of such a presence. A U.N. peacekeeping force can

operate effectively only with the consent and full cooperation of the parties. It is an interim measure whose purpose is to help the parties to find a durable peace based on agreement between the parties themselves. It is not intended nor equipped to impose a solution on the parties.[4]

II. INITIAL CONSENT TO THE ESTABLISHMENT AND DEPLOYMENT OF UNPROFOR

A. Consent to Establishment and Deployment

The statement that host-state consent is necessary for U.N. peacekeeping is usually made in the context of the establishment and deployment of the peacekeeping force. In the past it has generally, and not surprisingly, been assumed that the necessary consent is that of the host-state government. Recently certain writers have tried to challenge the orthodoxy, at least with regard to what the law *should* be.[5] However, events in Yugoslavia tend to confirm the traditional position.

Certain points emerge from an examination of the initial consent to the deployment of UNPROFOR in the former Yugoslavia. First, the Security Council resolutions and the Secretary-General's reports on Croatia and Bosnia-Herzegovina refer to the consent of all concerned parties, not simply of the host state. This was consistent with the Secretary-General's *Agenda for Peace* where he said that the consent of "all the parties concerned" in a conflict is necessary to establish a peacekeeping force.[6] Further, the practice of referring to the consent of all the parties in the Yugoslav conflict follows, to some extent, earlier practices in Angola,[7] Namibia,[8] Cambodia[9] and Mozam-

---

4. *Report of the Secretary-General Submitted Pursuant to Security Council Resolution 994*, U.N. SCOR, 50th Sess., at 5, U.N. Doc. S/1995/467 (1995) [hereinafter S/1995/467].

5. *See, e.g.*, Wippman, *Military Intervention, supra* note 1, at 224-34. For the opposing view, see Georg Nolte, *Restoring Peace by Regional Action: International Legal Aspects of the Liberian Conflict*, 53 ZEITSCHRIFT FÜR AUSLANDISCHES ÖFFENTLICHES RECHT UND VÖLKERRECHT 603 (1993).

6. *Further Report of the Secretary-General Pursuant to Security Council Resolution 721*, U.N. SCOR, 47th Sess., at 2, U.N. Doc. S/23513 (1992) [hereinafter S/23513]; *See also Further Report of the Secretary-General Pursuant to Security Council Resolution 721*, U.N. SCOR, 47th Sess., at 6, U.N. Doc. S23363 (1992) [hereinafter S/23363]; *Report of the Secretary-General Pursuant to Security Council Resolution 721*, U.N. SCOR, 46th Sess., at 7, U.N. Doc. S/23280 (1991) [hereinafter S/23280].

7. In Angola, a trilateral agreement among Angola, Cuba and South Africa led to the establishment of a United Nations force. *See* UNITED NATIONS DEPARTMENT OF PUBLIC INFORMATION, THE BLUE HELMETS: A REVIEW OF UNITED NATIONS PEACEKEEPING 325-38, U.N. Doc. DPI/1065, U.N. Sales No. E.90.I.18 (1990) [hereinafter THE BLUE HELMETS]. Resolution 626, establishing UNAVEM, noted Ango-

bique[10] where U.N. peacekeeping operations were created in order to help secure a political settlement for civil conflicts. Of these operations, however, it was only with reference to Mozambique that a Security Council resolution expressly referred to consent by a nongovernment party to the conflict to establishing a peacekeeping force.[11]   In Somalia it was the consent of the government, even though it was no longer in effective control of the whole territory, that was relied on in the Security Council resolutions establishing and deploying the United Nations Operation in Somalia (UNOSOM I) peacekeeping force.[12]

It seems clear that the requirement that all the parties should consent to the establishment and deployment of the force was not a *legal* requirement.   Rather, it was only the host state's consent, as expressed by its government, that formed the legal basis for the peacekeeping force first in Yugoslavia and subsequently in its former republics.[13]   This can be seen from the fact that later in the Yugoslav conflict it was the withdrawal of consent by the government of the host state Croatia that meant the peacekeeping force had to be with-

---

lan and Cuban requests for a U.N. force. *See Letter Dated 17 December 1988 from the Permanent Representative of Cuba to the United Nations Addressed to the Secretary General*, U.N. SCOR, 43rd Sess., U.N. Doc. S/20337 (1988); *Letter Dated 17 December 1988 from the Permanent Representative of Angola to the United Nations Addressed to the Secretary-General*, U.N. SCOR, 43rd Sess., U.N. Doc. S/20336 (1988).

8. The situation in Namibia was unique because of the U.N.'s legal responsibility for Namibia, which was effectively but illegally occupied by South Africa. *See* THE BLUE HELMETS, *supra* note 7, at 341. The U.N. Transition Assistance Group (UNTAG), whose mandate was to ensure the early independence of Namibia through U.N.-supervised elections, was established following a trilateral agreement among Angola, Cuba and South Africa (referred to in Resolution 628). The South West African People's Organization (SWAPO), a major political party in Namibia, was not a party to these Geneva Protocols of August 1988, which provided for a ceasefire. However SWAPO did inform the Secretary-General that it would abide by the ceasefire. *See id.*

9. After the four Cambodian parties in the civil war had made a draft agreement for a comprehensive political settlement and had created a Supreme National Council, the President of the Council invited the United Nations to send peacekeeping forces to Cambodia. *See* UNITED NATIONS AND CAMBODIA at 63-64, U.N. Doc. DPI/1450, U.N. Sales No. E.95.I.9 (1995). Security Council Resolution 717, establishing an advance U.N. mission (UNAMIC), expressly referred to this invitation. *Id.*

10. After the government and the opposing side, RENAMO, concluded a general peace agreement, the government formally requested the establishment of a U.N. force. Security Council Resolution 782 also expressly referred to a joint declaration by the government and RENAMO accepting the creation and deployment of a U.N. force. S.C. Res. 782, U.N. SCOR, 47th Sess., U.N. Doc. S/RES/782 (1992). Resolution 797 subsequently established the United Nations Operation in Mozambique (UNOMOZ). S.C. Res. 797, U.N. SCOR, 47th Sess., U.N. Doc. S/RES/797 (1992).

11. *See id.*

12. S.C. Res. 775, U.N. SCOR, 47th Sess., at 2, U.N. Doc. S/RES/775 (1992); S.C. Res 767, U.N. SCOR, 47th Sess., at 1, U.N. Doc. S/RES/767 (1992); S.C. Res. 751, U.N. SCOR, 47th Sess., at 1, U.N. Doc. S/RES/751 (1992); S.C. Res. 733, U.N. SCOR, 47th Sess., at 1, U.N. Doc. S/RES/733 (1992).

13. *See supra* note 5.

drawn from its territory.[14] The consent of other parties involved in the conflict is important as a matter of *practical* necessity. The peacekeeping force would not be able to function without the cooperation of the parties on the ground.

It would, however, be going too far to assert that existing international law *already* looks beyond the government to groups within the state for consent to U.N. intervention, even if the government no longer has control over the whole territory.[15] Requiring consent by all the parties may be a practical policy at the stage of initial consent, and one that increases the chances of success of the peacekeeping operation. However, as recounted below, subsequent developments in Yugoslavia with regard to changes in the mandate, questions of composition, and the withdrawal of consent show the Security Council and Secretary-General consistently giving decisive weight to the wishes of the governments of Croatia and of Bosnia-Herzegovina rather than to other parties involved in the conflict.

The Security Council made the controversial decision to send a peacekeeping force to Yugoslavia after much hesitation and extensive consultation. It asked the Secretary-General to investigate the prospects for successful deployment of a peacekeeping force. In his reports to the Security Council, the Secretary-General repeatedly insisted that he needed the full and explicit acceptance by the parties directly involved of the concept for a U.N. peacekeeping operation, and a commitment on their part to ensure full cooperation with such a peacekeeping force.[16] He emphasized the need for all the Yugoslav parties concerned to consent to the establishment and deployment of the force.[17]

At first the prospects for consent looked promising. The Secretary-General reported to the Security Council in November 1991 that each of the Yugoslav participants had stated that they wanted to see the deployment of a peacekeeping operation as soon as possible, and that they welcomed the concept of the operation, its mandate, its organization and the areas where it would be deployed, put forward in preliminary form by the Secretary-General's Special Envoy.[18] These

---

14. *See infra* Part VII.

15. Some, however, have asserted that this ought to be the case. *See, e.g.*, Wippman, *Military Intervention*, *supra* note 1, at 224-34.

16. *See* S/23513, *supra* note 6, at 2; S/23363, *supra* note 6, at 6; S/23280, *supra* note 6, at 7.

17. S/23513, *supra* note 6, at 2.

18. *Letter Dated 24 November 1991 from the Secretary-General Addressed to the President of the Security Council*, U.N. SCOR, 46th Sess., at 2, U.N. Doc. S/23239 (1991).

'participants' at a series of meetings to discuss the deployment of peacekeeping forces were President Milosevic of Serbia, President Tudjman of Croatia, and General Kadijevic, Secretary of State for National Defence of the Socialist Federal Republic of Yugoslavia. The statement by the Secretary-General that the participants had consented was followed by a letter from the Federal Republic of Yugoslavia to the Security Council formally requesting the establishment of a peacekeeping operation in Yugoslavia. It read, "I have been instructed by my Government to request the establishment of a peacekeeping operation in Yugoslavia which reflects at the same time the expressed desire of the principal parties to the present conflict."[19]   The Security Council in Resolution 721 explicitly took account of these expressions of consent in urging the Secretary-General to continue to pursue the possible establishment of a peacekeeping force.[20] It said,

> *Considering* the request by the Government of Yugoslavia for the establishment of a peacekeeping operation in Yugoslavia,
>
> *Considering further* the fact that each one of the Yugoslav participants in the meeting with the Personal Envoy of the Secretary-General stated that they wanted to see the deployment of a U.N. peacekeeping operation as soon as possible . . . .[21]

Following these statements, problems over consent began to emerge. The Secretary-General's reports to the Security Council under Resolution 721, from December 1991 to February 1992, refer to difficulties in obtaining and keeping the consent to the U.N. peacekeeping operation in Yugoslavia of Milan Babic, a leader of the Serbian community in Croatia, and of President Tudjman of Croatia.[22] All concerned Yugoslav parties had indicated full acceptance of the U.N. peacekeeping concept, but there had been recent public statements by some of the leaders suggesting that further clarification was needed. Babic was unhappy with any reference to the U.N. peacekeeping forces operating in protected areas "in Croatia" as he sought independence for the Serb-populated areas. President Tudjman was not willing to accept arrangements that seemed to take con-

---

19. *Letter Dated 26 of November 1991 from the Permanent Representative of Yugoslavia to the United Nations Addressed to the President of the Security Council*, U.N. SCOR, 46th Sess., at 1, U.N. Doc. S/23240 (1991).

20. S.C. Res. 721, U.N. SCOR, 46th Sess., at 1, U.N. Doc. S/RES/721 (1991) (passed unanimously).

21. *Id.*

22. *See* S/23513, *supra* note 6, at 5; S/23363, *supra* note 6, at 5; S/23280, *supra* note 6, at 5.

trol of local government and public order in the proposed U.N.-protected areas in Croatia out of Croatia's authority.[23]

After the Secretary-General had reported these problems over consent, President Tudjman wrote to the Security Council on February 6, 1992. His letter read, "In order to avoid any misunderstanding I inform you that I accept, fully and unconditionally, the United Nations Secretary-General's concept and plan which defines the conditions and areas where the United Nations force would be deployed."[24] Security Council Resolution 740 noted this:

> [T]aking note that the letter of President Franjo Tudjman of 6 February 1992, in which he accepts fully the Secretary-General's concept and plan which defines the conditions and areas where the U.N. force would be deployed, removes a further obstacle in that respect . . . expresses its concern that the U.N. peacekeeping plan has not yet been fully and unconditionally accepted by all in Yugoslavia on whose cooperation its success depends.[25]

However, President Tudjman subsequently equivocated about his consent in such a way as to cast doubt on the validity of his commitment. The Secretary-General's Special Envoy, Cyrus Vance, wrote expressing dismay and seeking reassurance.[26] President Tudjman reconfirmed his acceptance, but in distinctly ominous terms. President Tudjman stated that the U.N. peace plan envisaged status of forces agreements and that these would have to resolve what he referred to as "technical questions" such as matters to do with traffic, trade, banking, currency, the maintenance of law and order, and the return of refugees.[27] However, as the Secretary-General pointed out, these were not in fact technical issues. Rather they were substantive matters relating to the extension of Croatia's sovereignty over U.N.-protected areas. Nonetheless, the Secretary-General said he would accept in good faith President Tudjman's positive assurances, and similarly would discount Babic's resistance.[28] He therefore recommended the establishment of UNPROFOR. Its initial mandate was

---

23. *See* S/23513, *supra* note 6, at 5.

24. *Further Report of the Secretary-General Pursuant to Security Council Resolution 721*, U.N. SCOR, 47th Sess., Annex I, U.N. Doc. S/23592 (1992) [hereinafter S/23592].

25. S.C. Res. 740, U.N. SCOR, 47th Sess., at 1, 2, U.N. Doc. S/RES/740 (1992) (passed unanimously).

26. *See* S/23592, *supra* note 24, at Annex II.

27. *See id.* at Annex III.

28. *See id.* at 3.

to "create the conditions of peace and security required for the nego-tiation of an overall settlement of the Yugoslav crisis."[29]

The Secretary-General did note the potential danger to the im-plementation of the peacekeeping plan[30] and these fears turned out to be justified. When the conflict in Yugoslavia threatened to spread to Bosnia-Herzegovina, the government of Bosnia repeatedly requested the establishment of a U.N. force.[31] The Secretary-General again in-vestigated the feasibility of deploying such a force and, as with Croa-tia, repeatedly stressed the need for the agreement of all the hostile parties.[32] This was eventually given in a limited form when the par-ties came to a ceasefire agreement in June 1992. The agreement in-cluded a provision that UNPROFOR would be deployed in Bosnia-Herzegovina in order to secure the operation of Sarajevo airport.[33] The Security Council noted in Resolution 758, which enlarged the strength and mandate of UNPROFOR to allow it to deploy in Bos-nia-Herzegovina, "the agreement of all the parties in Bosnia-Herzegovina to the reopening of Sarajevo airport for humanitarian purposes, under the exclusive authority of the United Nations, and with the assistance of UNPROFOR."[34] With regard to Macedonia, the process of establishing consent to the deployment of UNPROFOR as a preventive force proved more straightforward. In November 1992, the government of Macedonia made a request to the Security Council for the deployment of UNPROFOR on its terri-tory.[35] This request was acknowledged in Security Council Resolu-tion 795[36] and a small force was deployed inside its borders with Al-bania and Yugoslavia (Serbia and Montenegro) with the preventive mandate of monitoring any developments which could undermine stability.[37]

---

29. S.C. Res. 743, U.N. SCOR, 47th Sess., U.N. Doc. S/RES/743 (1992) (passed unanimously).

30. *See* S/23592, *supra* note 24, at 3.

31. *See Further Report of the Secretary-General Pursuant to Security Council Resolution 749*, U.N. SCOR, 47th Sess., at 4, U.N. Doc. S/23900 (1992) [hereinafter S/23900]; *Report of the Secretary-General Pursuant to Security Council Resolution 749*, U.N. SCOR, 47th Sess., at 3, U.N. Doc. S/23836 (1992) [hereinafter S/23836]; S/23363, *supra* note 6, at 4.

32. *See* S/23900, *supra* note 31, at 8; S/23836, *supra* note 31, at 6.

33. *See Report of the Secretary-General Pursuant to Security Council Resolution 757*, U.N. SCOR, 47th Sess., at 1, U.N. Doc. S/24075 (1992).

34. S.C. Res. 758, U.N. SCOR, 47th Sess., at 1, U.N. Doc. S/RES/758 (1992) (passed unanimously).

35. *Letter Dated 23 November 1992 from the Secretary-General Addressed to the President of the Security Council*, U.N. SCOR, 47th Sess., U.N. Doc. S/24851 (1992).

36. S.C. Res. 795, U.N. SCOR, 47th Sess., at 1, U.N. Doc. S/RES/795 (1992).

37. *See Report of the Secretary-General on the Former Yugoslav Republic of Macedonia*, U.N. SCOR, 47th Sess., at 1, U.N. Doc. S/24923 (1992).

B. Consent to Mandate

It is also clear from the negotiations between the parties and the Secretary-General leading up to the creation of UNPROFOR and its deployment in Croatia, Bosnia-Herzegovina and Macedonia that consent is sought by the United Nations not just for establishment of the force, but also for the details of its mandate. Thus, in Croatia detailed discussions were held on the U.N. peace plan and on the exact regime in the U.N.-protected Areas.[38] Again, with regard to Bosnia-Herzegovina the conflicting parties were involved in working out the precise mandate of UNPROFOR.[39]

C. Consent to Composition

The question of consent to the composition of the peacekeeping force has given rise to debate as to who has the final say in determining the nationality of the troops of the force. The issue whether the host state, the Security Council or the Secretary-General has the final say arose with regard to the United Nations Emergency Force (UNEF) in the Middle East and the United Nations Operation in the Congo (ONUC).[40] In both these instances, the host state tried to assert control but was resisted by the United Nations. It seems, as a matter of principle, that the United Nations itself, through whatever organ has established the peacekeeping force, should determine the composition of the force. Any other solution would be incompatible with the impartial status of the force. However, it is clear that, in reality, behind-the-scenes discussions take place between members of the Security Council, the host state and troop contributing states. This pattern was followed again in the former Yugoslavia.

In Yugoslavia, the issue of composition did not give rise to much public discussion. The more serious problem was getting hold of any troops at all, rather than the question of the troops' nationality.[41] Although in the *Concept for a United Nations Peacekeeping Operation in Yugoslavia* the Secretary-General recommended that "[t]he contributing states would be approved on the recommendation of the

---

38. *See* S/23592, *supra* note 24; S/23513, *supra* note 6; S/23363, *supra* note 6; S/23280, *supra* note 6.

39. *See* S/23900, *supra* note 31; *see also* 1992 U.N.Y.B. 349, U.N. Sales No. E.93.I.1.

40. *See* 1 HIGGINS, *supra* note 1, at 367-68; 3 HIGGINS, *supra* note 1, at 135.

41. *See, e.g., Report of the Secretary-General Pursuant to Resolution 844 (1993)*, U.N. SCOR, 49th Sess., U.N. Doc. S/1994/555 (1994); *Former Yugoslavia: Increased Sanctions Weighed*, U.N. CHRON., Dec. 1994, at, 26, 27; *Yugoslavia: Situation Far From Stable*, U.N. CHRON., June 1994, at 22, 26.

Secretary-General after consultation with the Yugoslav parties,"[42] such approval, if it was sought and given, seems to have taken place mainly in private. The early U.N. practice of not accepting troops from the permanent members of the Security Council or from states with interests in the host state[43] was not followed in Yugoslavia. Troops were supplied by the United Kingdom, Russia, France, Germany and Turkey among others. The question of the nationality of peacekeeping troops was not raised publicly by any host state (except in passing and informally in the notorious episode when a Croatian official responsible for relations with the U.N. called for "all-'European' forces").[44] Other concerned parties did, however, express some reservations about the composition of the force. For example, the participation by troops from Turkey, a state with historic interests in the region and sympathies with the government of Bosnia-Herzegovina, was challenged when Turkish troops were sent to UNPROFOR in Bosnia-Herzegovina in March 1994. The Secretary-General had recommended that Turkey's offer to contribute be accepted[45] and the Security Council concurred.[46] The Bosnian Serbs expressed concern,[47] Greece and Bulgaria wrote to the Security Council in opposition,[48] and Yugoslavia (Serbia and Montenegro) also complained, stating that

> [t]he complex nature of the civil, inter-ethnic and religious conflict in Bosnia-Herzegovina and its deep historical roots and underlying causes make it necessary that no former occupying power of the territories of the former Yugoslavia or any neighbouring state should be involved with their forces in peacekeeping efforts . . . . Though it is commendable that the United Nations has so far respected the historical sensitivities on the ground, it is indeed dis-

---

42. S/23280, *supra* note 6, at 15.

43. *See generally* Sally Morphet, *U.N. Peacekeeping and Election-Monitoring*, in UNITED NATIONS, DIVIDED WORLDS 183, 187-88 (Adam Roberts & Benedict Kingsbury eds., 2d ed., 1993); BROWN, *supra* note 1, at 599. For comparison, see 1 HIGGINS, *supra* note 1, at 300; 3 HIGGINS, *supra* note 1, at 84; 4 HIGGINS, *supra* note 1, at 159 (noting that this practice of avoiding participation by the permanent members of the Security Council in peacekeeping forces had already been abandoned in Cyprus and Lebanon).

44. *Croatian Call For All-'European' Force, News Digest for April 1995*, 41 KEESING'S RECORD OF WORLD EVENTS 40512 (1995).

45. *See* Letter Dated 22 March 1994, from the Secretary-General Addressed to the President of the Security Council, U.N. SCOR, 49th Sess., at 1, U.N. Doc. S/1994/330 (1994).

46. *See Letter Dated 23 March 1994 from the President of the Security Council Addressed to the Secretary-General*, U.N. SCOR, 49th Sess., at 1, U.N. Doc. S/1994/331 (1994).

47. *See UN Call For Troop Reinforcements—UK Response—Planned Despatch of Turkish Contingent, News Digest for March 1994*, 40 KEESING'S RECORD OF WORLD EVENTS 39, 926 (1994).

48. *See id.*

turbing that these basic principles of peacekeeping have now been disregarded and that the United Nations has succumbed to pressure to engage a Turkish force within UNPROFOR.[49]

Later, when Germany contributed troops to UNPROFOR in Bosnia-Herzegovina in June 1995, Yugoslavia (Serbia and Montenegro) again protested partly because of German involvement in the region during World War II and because Germany was seen as favoring the Croats.[50] Yugoslavia said that the participation by Germany provoked understandable disquiet and serious concern.[51] This marked yet another breach of the United Nations' principle that neighbouring states which had occupied territory of the former Yugoslavia in the past should not contribute to troops there.[52]

III. CONSENT AND COOPERATION: THE PROBLEMS IN SECURING STATUS OF FORCES AGREEMENTS

The Secretary-General made it clear from the outset that it was not enough merely to secure formal consent of the parties to the establishment and deployment of UNPROFOR; promises of cooperation with the U.N. force were also needed.[53] This cooperation requirement can be seen as a necessary extension of the principle of consent. Based on the principles of effectiveness and good faith, consent should not be interpreted as a purely formal requirement. Given that host-state consent means that the host state has agreed to the presence and mandate of U.N. forces, consent by the host state also necessarily implies that it has undertaken to cooperate with those forces.

In the former Yugoslavia lack of cooperation was the main factor that made it impossible for UNPROFOR to fulfil its mandate. One aspect of the parties' reluctance to give real cooperation was the delay or outright refusal of host states to conclude SOFAs with UNPROFOR. Such agreements govern the rights, duties, and privileges and immunities of U.N. forces and are commonly concluded

---

49. U.N. SCOR, 49th Sess., 3370th mtg., at 33, U.N. Doc. S/PV.3370 (1994); *see also* U.N. SCOR, 49th Sess., at 2, U.N. Doc. S/1994/350 (1994).

50. This information was obtained from a confidential British government document which refers to a Public Statement of Foreign Ministry of Yugoslavia on June 30, 1995. Further details can be obtained by contacting the author.

51. *See id.*

52. *See Provision of Artillery to UNPROFOR—Vote to Deploy German Forces, News Digest for June 1995,* 41 KEESING'S RECORD OF WORLD EVENTS 40607 (1995).

53. *See* Wippman, *Military Intervention, supra* note 1.

with host states.[54] In 1990, at the request of the General Assembly, the Secretary-General produced a Model SOFA. The Model SOFA provided for freedom of movement and freedom of communication for U.N. forces, prohibited the imposition of tolls for roads, bridges, canals, ports and airfields, allowed the import of materiel for the U.N. force free of duty and provided for the freedom to recruit local personnel without government interference.[55] In an ideal world, it would be compulsory for a SOFA to be approved by a host state before a U.N. peacekeeping force could be deployed. However, owing to the realities of international politics, such approval is not compulsory. For example, in Yugoslavia, the United Nations was only able to receive equivocal consent from the host state; it would not have been possible for the United Nations to receive approval for a SOFA from the host state as well.

At the beginning of the conflict in the former Yugoslavia, the Secretary-General was optimistic about prospects for the conclusion of such SOFAs. In April 1992, he reported that the final text of an agreement had been agreed to by Bosnia-Herzegovina, a tentative agreement had been reached with Croatia, and protracted negotiations were being conducted with Yugoslavia (Serbia and Montenegro). He said that the primary difficulties related to the provision of goods and services to UNPROFOR by the various Yugoslav parties either free of charge or on the most favorable terms.[56] In fact, the agreement with Bosnia-Herzegovina was not concluded until May 1993.[57] No agreement was made with Croatia on UNPROFOR, although Croatia did conclude an agreement on the successor to UNPROFOR in Croatia, UNCRO.[58] Further, no agreement was concluded with Yugoslavia (Serbia and Montenegro).[59] A SOFA was

---

54. *See* 1 HIGGINS, *supra* note 1, at 372; Morphet, *supra* note 43, at 187-88.

55. *See Comprehensive Review of the Whole Question of Peacekeeping Operations in All Their Aspects*, U.N. GAOR, 45th Sess., at 5,7, Agenda Item 76, U.N. Doc. A/45/594 (1990)

56. *See Further Report of the Secretary-General Pursuant to Security Council Resolution 749 (1992)*, U.N. SCOR, 47th Sess., at 2-3, U.N. Doc. S/23844 (1992) [hereinafter S/23844].

57. *See Report of the Secretary-General Pursuant to Security Council Resolution 947 (1994)*, U.N. SCOR, 50th Sess., para. 56, U.N. Doc. S/1995/222 (1995) [hereinafter S/1995/222].

58. *See* S/1995/467, *supra* note 4, at 5.

59. *See* S/1995/222, *supra* note 57, para. 58. The Secretary-General reported in March 1995 that no progress had been made on the conclusion of the necessary arrangements with Yugoslavia (Serbia and Montenegro). However, he found that in practice the absence of a SOFA had not caused problems. There was a satisfactory level of cooperation with the authorities. But it was important that the government extend to the U.N. force, its personnel, property funds and assets, the necessary privileges and immunities deriving from Article 105(1) of the Charter, the Convention on the Privileges and Immunities of the United Nations, to which the Federal Republic of Yugoslavia (Serbia and Montenegro) is a party, and the custom-

made with Macedonia on March 13, 1995.[60]

The Security Council repeatedly called on the states to conclude SOFAs.[61] For example, in Resolution 947 it expressed concern that SOFAs had not been concluded with Croatia, Macedonia or Yugoslavia (Serbia and Montenegro) and called on them to make such agreements.[62] The Secretary-General also regretted the difficulties in securing SOFAs.[63]

The mere conclusion of a SOFA, however, cannot guarantee cooperation by the host state with the U.N. force. This is clearly illustrated by events in Bosnia-Herzegovina *after* the conclusion of the SOFA on May 15, 1993. UNPROFOR was not provided the various premises it required free of cost, as was called for by the agreement. Further, the government of Bosnia demanded that the United Nations surrender some facilities it already occupied, pay for other new facilities, and reopen negotiations on the terms of employment for local staff. The United Nations was concerned about the taxation of local employees, their forcible mobilization and detention by government authorities.[64] Thus, while the existence of a SOFA does not mean cooperation by the host state, the Security Council thought it worthwhile to press for its conclusion. A SOFA's existence is not only of symbolic importance as a sign of commitment by the host state; it also provides specific standards which the U.N. force can invoke in dealing with the host state. Further, it improves the bargaining position of the U.N. forces in demanding cooperation from the host state.

The prolonged absence of a SOFA contributed to the difficulties experienced by UNPROFOR in Croatia. The Secretary-General reported on the difficulties and expenses incurred by UNPROFOR in Croatia stating that "[w]hile the Croatian authorities were most cooperative and generous during the initial phase of the mission, there have been recent indications that UNPROFOR's continuing use of

---

ary principles and practices applicable to United Nations peacekeeping or similar operations.

60. *See id.*

61. *See* S.C. Res. 908, U.N. SCOR, 49th Sess., 3356th mtg., at 3, U.N. Doc. S/RES/908 (1994) [hereinafter S/RES/908]; S.C. Res. 947, U.N. SCOR, 49th Sess., 3434th mtg., at 2-3, U.N. Doc. S/RES/947 (1994) (passed unanimously) [hereinafter S/RES/947]; S.C. Res. 981, U.N. SCOR, 50th Sess., 3512th mtg., at 4, U.N. Doc. S/RES/981 (1995).

62. S/RES/947, *supra* note 61, at 2-3.

63. *See Report of the Secretary-General Pursuant to Paragraph 4 of the Security Council Resolution 947 (1994)*, U.N. SCOR, 50th Sess., at 7, U.N. Doc. S/1995/38 (1995); S/1995/222, *supra* note 57. at 16-17.

64. *See* S/1995/222, *supra* note 57, para. 55.

Croatian facilities is being approached on a commercial basis."[65] Thus, UNPROFOR was charged $8.6 million in fuel tax for the period July to December 1994 and $2.5 million airport tax in 1994.[66] Such charges are inconsistent not only with the U.N.'s Model SOFA, but also with the 1946 Convention on the Privileges and Immunities of the United Nations.[67] By mid-1995 the Secretary-General had become more openly critical of Croatia's failure to conclude a SOFA with regard to UNCRO, the force that had replaced UNPROFOR. He referred to "[d]ifficulties [that] have arisen as a result of demands by Croatian authorities which are incompatible with the model status-of-forces agreement."[68] When Croatia finally concluded an agreement, the Secretary-General welcomed the signing of the long-delayed SOFA on May 15, 1995 as a positive step that was expected to reduce obstructions to the functioning of the peacekeeping operation.[69] However, the Secretary-General later reported disappointment:

> Although the conclusion of the agreement was welcomed as a positive step, I regret that, at the time of writing, the Government of Croatia has yet to implement fully various of its provisions such as making available the necessary premises free of rent and making arrangements to exempt the United Nations forces and operations from various taxes and tolls .... Despite repeated requests at various levels, the Government of Croatia has not so far honoured its commitments in this regard.[70]

IV. SUBSEQUENT CHANGES TO THE INITIAL MANDATE OF UNPROFOR: IS FURTHER CONSENT NECESSARY?

It is well known that the initial mandate of UNPROFOR was expanded many times. Over thirty Security Council resolutions directly concerning UNPROFOR were passed out of a total of over eighty-five resolutions on the Yugoslav conflict. UNPROFOR's mandate was gradually altered through incremental additions to the

---

65. *Id.*

66. *See id.*

67. *Convention on the Privileges and Immunities of the United Nations*, Feb. 13, 1946, 21 U.S.T. 1418, 1 U.N.T.S. 15.

68. *Report of the Secretary-General Submitted Pursuant to Paragraph 4 of Security Council Resolution 981 (1995)*, U.N. SCOR, 50th Sess., at 9, U.N. Doc. S/1995/320 (1995).

69. `See S/1995/467, supra note 4, at 5.

70. *Report of the Secretary-General Submitted Pursuant to Security Council Resolution 1009 (1995)*, U.N. SCOR, 50th Sess., at 10, U.N. Doc. S/1995/730 (1995).

original functions, reflecting in part a response to events and the need for the Security Council to be seen as acting, and in part the absence of any agreement between members of the Council as to long term strategy and short term tactics. The issues here are (1) whether the consent of the host states and of other parties to alterations in the mandate is legally necessary, and (2) whether this consent was in fact sought and given to the subsequent changes to UNPROFOR's initial mandate.

With regard to the issue of principle, no categorical answer is possible at this stage. Earlier U.N. practice, such as that in the Congo, does not provide any clear precedent that would cover the type of situation that arose in the former Yugoslavia. Nevertheless, given that the host state's consent to the initial mandate has invariably been sought in practice, it could be argued that its consent to subsequent changes is also necessary. Even if this is not already a legal requirement, the government of the host state retains ultimate control through its power to withdraw consent to the presence of the peacekeeping force on its territory.[71] However, the situation with regard to the consent of the host state to changes in the initial mandate changes when the alterations are made under Chapter VII of the Charter.[72]

With regard to the issue of whether consent to the subsequent changes in UNPROFOR's mandate was actually sought and given in the former Yugoslavia, the answer is complex. Some of the resolutions altering the mandate do expressly refer to consent by all the concerned parties. Resolution 762 contains an apparent reference to consent when it gives UNPROFOR a new role in monitoring Serb-occupied zones (the so-called pink zones) outside the U.N.-protected areas in Croatia—it states that UNPROFOR is to carry out its functions "with the agreement of the government of Croatia and others concerned."[73] Again, in Resolution 781, establishing the no-fly zone over Bosnia-Herzegovina,[74] the Security Council recalls the Agreement arrived at between the interested parties at the London Conference to establish such a zone, noting as well the letter by Bosnia-Herzegovina to the Security Council calling for the enforcement of

---

71. *See infra* Part VII.
72. *See infra* Part V.
73. S.C. Res. 762, U.N. SCOR, 47th Sess., 3088th mtg., para. 7, U.N. Doc. S/RES/762 (1992) (passed unanimously).
74. S.C. Res. 781, U.N. SCOR, 47th Sess., 3122d mtg., U.N. Doc. S/RES/781 (1992).

the no-fly zone agreed to at the London Conference.[75] Other resolutions altering UNPROFOR's mandate refer specifically to government consent. Thus, Resolution 824 on the establishment of safe areas takes into consideration "the formal request submitted by Bosnia-Herzegovina" with regard to Zepa.[76] This request stated, "we suggest the Security Council declare . . . Zepa as a United Nations protected area and send a company of blue helmets to defend this area and the civilian population there."[77]

Except for these resolutions, the many resolutions expanding UNPROFOR's mandate do so without any express reference to consent.[78] These expansions led to problems with consent of the parties. As the Secretary-General said in the *Supplement to the Agenda for Peace*:

> Three aspects of recent mandates, in particular, have led peacekeeping operations to forfeit the consent of the parties, to behave in a way that was perceived to be partial or to use force other than in self-defence. These were the task of protecting humanitarian operations during fighting, the protection of civilian populations in safe areas, pressing parties to accept national reconciliation at a pace faster than they were ready to accept. In Bosnia, as in Somalia, the Security Council gave existing peacekeeping operations ad-

---

75. *See Letter Dated 2 November 1992 From the Permanent Representative of Bosnia and Hercegovina to the United Nations Addressed to the President of the Security Council*, U.N. SCOR, 47th Sess., U.N. Doc. S/24750 (1992); *Letter Dated 23 October 1992 From the Permanent Representative of Bosnia and Hercegovina to the United Nations Addressed to the President of the Security Council*, U.N. SCOR, 47th Sess., U.N. Doc. S/24709 (1992); *Letter Dated 5 October 1992 From the Permanent Representative of Bosnia and Hercegovina to the United Nations Addressed to the President of the Security Council*, U.N. SCOR, 47th Sess., U.N. Doc. S/24616 (1992).

76. S.C. Res. 824, U.N. SCOR, 48th Sess., 3208th mtg., at 1, U.N. Doc. S/RES/824 (1993) (passed unanimously).

77. *Letter Dated 4 May 1993 From the Permanent Representative of Bosnia and Hercegovina to the United Nations Addressed to the President of the Security Council*, U.N. SCOR, 48th Sess., Annex, at 2, U.N. Doc. S/25718 (1993); *see also Letter Dated 31 October 1992 From the Permanent Representative of Bosnia and Hercegovina to the United Nations Addressed to the Secretary-General*, U.N. SCOR, 47th Sess., U.N. Doc. S/24749 (1992).

78. *See* S.C. Res. 815, U.N. SCOR, 48th Sess., 3189th mtg., U.N. Doc. S/RES/815 (1993) [hereinafter S/RES/815]; S.C. Res. 807, U.N. SCOR, 48th Sess., 3174th mtg., U.N. Doc. S/RES/807 (1993) [hereinafter S/RES/807]; S.C. Res. 802, U.N. SCOR, 48th Sess., 3163d mtg., U.N. Doc. S/RES/802 (1993); S.C. Res. 779, U.N. SCOR, 47th Sess., 3118th mtg., U.N. Doc. S/RES/779 (1992); S.C. Res. 776, U.N. SCOR, 47th Sess., 3114th mtg., U.N. Doc. S/RES/776 (1992) [hereinafter S/RES/776]; S.C. Res. 769, U.N. SCOR, 47th Sess., 3104th mtg., U.N. Doc. S/RES/769 (1992). In fact, some of these resolutions were passed with the consent of the host-state government. For example, Resolution 769 allowing UNPROFOR to operate immigration controls in the U.N.-protected areas was passed after Croatia had expressed support for it. *Letter Dated 7 August 1992 from the Chargé d'Affaires A.I. of the Permanent Mission of Croatia to the United Nations Addressed to the President of the Security Council*, U.N. SCOR, 47th Sess., U.N. Doc. S/24390 (1992).

ditional mandates requiring the use of force and therefore they could not be combined with existing mandates requiring the consent of the parties, impartiality and the non-use of force.[79]

Because the peacekeeping forces were authorized to go beyond limited monitoring of a ceasefire, and because they were authorized to use force to carry out their mandate, there was an obvious possibility that they would become involved in conflict with the various parties, including the host state government. Although the force was originally established on the basis of host-state consent, the extension of its mandate meant that it could no longer rely on that consent to its operations. This leads to a discussion of the use by the Security Council of Chapter VII of the U.N. Charter.

V. BLURRING THE DISTINCTION BETWEEN PEACEKEEPING AND ENFORCEMENT ACTION: THE USE OF CHAPTER VII OF THE U.N. CHARTER AND THE IMPLICATIONS FOR HOST-STATE CONSENT

UNPROFOR was beset by operational difficulties from the start of its operations. At the least, UNPROFOR met with non-cooperation and interference with its freedom of movement. This escalated to offensives across UNPROFOR positions in violation of the U.N. peacekeeping plan in Croatia and of local ceasefires in Bosnia, and to attacks on U.N. forces and hostage taking. All the parties were responsible for this non-cooperation.[80] Partly in response to these difficulties, the Security Council not only authorized member states to use force under Chapter VII to secure the implementation of its resolutions,[81] but also turned to Chapter VII in its resolutions

79. *Supplement to an Agenda for Peace: Position Paper of the Secretary-General on the Occasion of the Fiftieth Anniversary of the United Nations*, U.N. SCOR, 50th Sess., paras. 34-35, U.N. Doc. S/1995/1 (1995).

80. *See* S/1995/222, *supra* note 57; *Report of the Secretary-General Pursuant to Paragraph 4 of Security Council Resolution 947 (1994)*, U.N. SCOR, 50th Sess., U.N. Doc. S/1995/38 (1995); *Report of the Secretary-General Pursuant to Security Council Resolution 908 (1994)*, U.N. SCOR, 49th Sess., U.N. Doc. S/1994/1067 (1994); *Letter Dated 26 July 1994 From the Secretary-General Addressed to the President of the Security Council*, U.N. SCOR, 49th Sess., U.N. Doc. S/1994/888 (1994); *Report of the Secretary-General Pursuant to Resolution 871 (1993)*, U.N. SCOR, 49th Sess., U.N. Doc. S/1994/300 (1994); *Report of the Secretary-General Pursuant to Security Council Resolution 815 (1993)*, U.N. SCOR, 48th Sess., U.N. Doc. S/25777 (1993); *Report of the Secretary-General Pursuant to Security Council Resolution 762 (1992)*, U.N. SCOR, 47th Sess., U.N. Doc. S/24353 (1992); S/23900, *supra* note 31; S/23844, *supra* note 56; *See* Brown, *supra* note 1 (providing a rather one-sided account); *see generally* Charles G. Boyd, *Making Peace with the Guilty: The Truth about Bosnia*, 74 FOREIGN AFF. 22 (1995).

81. *See* S.C. Res. 958, U.N. SCOR, 49th Sess., 3461st mtg., U.N. Doc. S/RES/958 (1994); S/RES/908, *supra* note 61; S.C. Res. 836, U.N. SCOR, 48th Sess., 3228th mtg., U.N. Doc. S/RES/836

258   DUKE JOURNAL OF COMPARATIVE & INTERNATIONAL LAW   [Vol. 7:241

on UNPROFOR. Chapter VII empowers the Security Council to make decisions authorizing enforcement action by member states or by U.N. forces, and these decisions are binding on all member states. Thus, although UNPROFOR was originally established as a peacekeeping force whose deployment depended on the consent of the host state, the Security Council subsequently turned to Chapter VII in order to impose binding obligations on member states, including the host state, to comply with its resolutions and to cooperate with the peacekeeping force.

The first sixteen resolutions on UNPROFOR made no reference to Chapter VII; such reference was rare in the context of peacekeeping operations.[82] The institution of peacekeeping developed outside the context of Chapter VII and indeed outside the formal framework of the U.N. Charter through the practice of the U.N. and its member states. Peacekeeping traditionally operated by host-state consent and with the cooperation of all concerned parties; it typically involved lightly armed forces which were impartial and which used force only in self-defense.[83]

In the early days of the Yugoslav conflict, the Security Council made express reference to Chapter VII only in its resolutions on sanctions[84] and then in Resolution 770 authorizing member states to use force to secure the delivery of humanitarian aid by the United Nations.[85] China abstained in the vote on this resolution and in the vote on Resolution 776 which authorized UNPROFOR to use force to secure the delivery of humanitarian aid.[86] It did this precisely be-

---

(1993) [hereinafter S/RES/836]; S.C. Res. 816, U.N. SCOR, 48th Sess., 3191st mtg., U.N. Doc. S/RES/816 (1993); S.C. Res. 787, U.N. SCOR, 47th Sess., 3137th mtg., U.N. Doc. S/RES/787 (1992); S.C. Res. 770, U.N. SCOR, 47th Sess., 3106th mtg., U.N. Doc. S/RES/770 (1992) [hereinafter S/RES/770].

82. At the end of the Iran-Iraq war, the U.N. observer team created to monitor the ceasefire was established under Resolution 598, which passed under Chapter VII. S.C. Res. 598, U.N. SCOR, 42d Sess., 2750th mtg., U.N. Doc. S/RES/598 (1987). Similarly, the United Nations Iraq-Kuwait Observation Mission (UNIKOM), the observer mission established at the end of the Iraq-Kuwait conflict, was created by Resolution 689, which passed under Chapter VII. S.C. Res. 689, U.N. SCOR, 46th Sess., 2983d mtg., U.N. Doc. S/RES/689 (1991).

83. *See generally* HIGGINS, *supra* note 1; WHITE, *supra* note 1.

84. These early resolutions on sanctions were: S.C. Res. 760, U.N. SCOR, 47th Sess., 3086th mtg., U.N. Doc. S/RES/760 (1992); S.C. Res. 757, U.N. SCOR, 47th Sess., 3082d mtg., U.N. Doc. S/RES/757 (1992); S.C. Res. 724, U.N. SCOR, 46th Sess., 3023d mtg., U.N. Doc. S/RES/724 (1991); S.C. Res. 713, U.N. SCOR, 46th Sess., 3009th mtg., U.N. Doc. S/RES/713 (1991).

85. S/RES/770, *supra* note 81 (twelve members voting in favor; China, India and Zimbabwe abstaining).

86. S/RES/776, *supra* note 78 (twelve members voting in favor; China, India and Zimbabwe abstaining).

cause of the invocation of Chapter VII. China said that it opposed the use of Chapter VII in Resolution 770 and it sought a diplomatic solution to the conflict. Although Resolution 776 did not itself refer to Chapter VII, it did refer to Resolution 770, thereby linking UNPROFOR to Chapter VII. According to China, this changed the nature of the peacekeeping force:

> The resolution just adopted by the Security Council aims at en-
> larging the mandate of UNPROFOR in an effort to provide mili-
> tary support for the delivery of humanitarian assistance to Bosnia-
> Herzegovina. In principle, the Chinese delegation does not object
> to the strengthening of humanitarian-assistance activities, but the
> resolution at issue established a link between the enlargement of
> the mandate of UNPROFOR and the implementation of Security
> Council resolution 770 (1992). This is something we cannot accept.
> It is a well-known fact the the Chinese delegation abstained in the
> vote on resolution 770 (1992), which authorizes countries to use
> force in Bosnia-Herzegovina. Therefore, we cannot endorse any
> actions related to the implementation of this resolution. At the
> same time, we believe that UNPROFOR should, as a United Na-
> tions peacekeeping operation, follow the generally recognized
> guidelines established in past United Nations peacekeeping opera-
> tions in implementing its mandate.

> However, in this resolution, which provides for the new mandate of
> UNPROFOR, there are disturbing elements which depart from
> these guidelines. It must be noted that Security Council Resolution
> 770 (1992) is a mandatory action taken under Chapter VII of the
> United Nations Charter. We are concerned that linking this resolu-
> tion with resolution 770 (1992) will change the non-mandatory na-
> ture of UNPROFOR as the United Nations peacekeeping opera-
> tion.   On the one hand, this resolution recognizes that
> UNPROFOR should observe the normal rules of engagement of
> United Nations peacekeeping operation in implementing its new
> mandate, namely to use force only in self-defence. On the other
> hand, the resolution approves the use of force in self-defence when
> troops are blocked by armed force. We are concerned that
> UNPROFOR will run the risk of plunging into armed conflict.[87]

China also was not happy that mandate enlargement of UNPROFOR had not received the express consent of the parties concerned in Bosnia-Herzegovina.[88]

From February 1993 the Security Council began expressly using

---

87. *Provisional Verbatim Record of the Three Thousand One Hundred and Fourteenth Meeting*, U.N. SCOR, 47th Sess., 3114th mtg., at 11-12, U.N. Doc. S/PV.3114 (1992).

88. *See id.* at 12.

260   DUKE JOURNAL OF COMPARATIVE & INTERNATIONAL LAW   [Vol. 7:241

Chapter VII as the basis for its resolutions on UNPROFOR. It did this for the first time in Resolution 807.[89] In the debate leading to this resolution's adoption, only France and China expressly discussed the reference to Chapter VII.[90] France regretted that UNPROFOR's mandate was being extended for only six weeks:

> But even for a brief interim period, it was unthinkable to us that we extend the present mandate in its current form. It was in that spirit that my delegation proposed a substantive and ambitious draft resolution that places UNPROFOR within the framework of Chapter VII of the Charter and suggested a series of concrete measures aimed at ensuring greater stability in the areas where UNPROFOR is deployed. As to the reference to Chapter VII, I reiterate once again that our idea is not to change the nature of the force, that is to move from peacekeeping to peacemaking. We are moved solely by considerations of preventive security. Indeed, this is reflected in the text of the draft resolution before us.[91]

The resolution made it clear that the invocation of Chapter VII was motivated by the need to secure the protection of UNPROFOR. The relevant parts provide:

> *Deeply concerned* by the lack of cooperation of the parties and others concerned in implementing the United Nations peacekeeping plan in Croatia (S/23280, Annex III),
> *Deeply concerned* also by the recent and repeated violations by the parties and others concerned of their cease-fire obligations,
> *Determining* that the situation thus created constitutes a threat to peace and security in the region, . . .
> *Determined* to ensure the security of UNPROFOR and to this end, acting under Chapter VII of the Charter of the United Nations ....[92]

China supported the resolution, although it expressed some reservation about the invocation of Chapter VII. China shared the concern regarding the security of UNPROFOR and would vote in favor "considering that the sponsor country has repeatedly stated that the purpose of invoking Chapter VII of the United Nations Charter in this draft resolution is to take measures to increase appropriately

---

89. S/RES/807, *supra* note 78 (passed unanimously).

90. *See Provisional Verbatim Record of the Three Thousand One Hundred and Seventy-Fourth Meeting,* U.N. SCOR, 48th Sess., 3174th mtg., U.N. Doc. S/PV.3174 (1993) [hereinafter S/PV.3174].

91. *Id.* at 14-15 (comments of Mr. Mérimée, France).

92. S/RES/807, *supra* note 78.

UNPROFOR's self defence capability."[93] However, China pointed out that UNPROFOR was a peacekeeping operation and that Chapter VII was not invoked in Resolution 743 establishing UNPROFOR or subsequent resolutions. Nor had the current report of the Secretary-General requested any reference to Chapter VII. "With regard to the safety of UNPROFOR personnel, the question could be settled through the expanded concept of self-defense and by taking other appropriate measures without invoking Chapter VII . . . ." "We should therefore like to put on record the understanding that the practice of invoking Chapter VII in this draft resolution is an exceptional case and therefore does not constitute a precedent for future U.N. peacekeeping operations."[94]

Having invoked Chapter VII, Resolution 807 then

> 1. Demands that the parties and others concerned comply fully with the United Nations peacekeeping plan in Croatia and with the other commitments they have undertaken and in particular with their cease-fire obligations;
>
> 2. Demands further that the parties and others concerned refrain from positioning their forces in the proximity of UNPROFOR's units in the United Nations Protected Areas (UNPAs) and in the pink zones;
>
> 3. Demands also the full and strict observance of all relevant Security Council resolutions relating to the mandate and operations of UNPROFOR in the Republic of Bosnia-Herzegovina;
>
> 4. Demands also that the parties and others concerned respect fully UNPROFOR's unimpeded freedom of movement, enabling it *inter alia* to carry out all necessary concentrations and deployments, all movements of equipment and weapons and all humanitarian and logistical activities.[95]

Thus, the resolution imposes binding duties on the parties to cooperate with UNPROFOR in its performance of its mandate. Even absent any reference to Chapter VII, there is such a duty on the host state based on its consent to the establishment and deployment of the peacekeeping force. Chapter VII simply strengthens this duty. The reference to Chapter VII does not by itself give UNPROFOR any extra powers, nor does it amount to a blanket authorization to use

---

93. S/PV.3174, *supra* note 90, at 21 (Mr. Chen Jian, China).

94. *Id.*

95. S/RES/807, *supra* note 78, at 1, 2.

force as some writers have mistakenly asserted.[96]   UNPROFOR's powers to use force depend on express provision in Security Council resolutions such as Resolution 776 on humanitarian aid and Resolution 836 on safe areas, and on its inherent right to use force in self-defense.

Almost all the subsequent resolutions on UNPROFOR follow Resolution 807 in invoking Chapter VII.[97]   In fact, the Security Council, having once invoked Chapter VII, found itself almost trapped into continuing to make such references.   France acknowledged this in the Security Council debate on Security Council Resolution 900[98] on the restoration of normal life in Sarajevo:

> I should like to stress, moreover, that we have adopted this resolution under Chapter VII of the Charter of the United Nations, as the other resolutions on Bosnia and Herzegovina have been since August 1992.   In this context, not to have resorted to Chapter VII would for the parties have been the worst of signals, at the very time when the international community has just successfully demonstrated its determination to bring about a halt to the bombing of Sarajevo.   Beyond that, application of Chapter VII, which does not imply an automatic resorting to force, will give UNPROFOR the authority it needs to surmount the obstacles that might be placed in the way of the execution of its mandate.[99]

China again expressed reservations about the invocation of Chapter VII.[100]

Although this series of resolutions imposed binding obligations not only on states but also on all the parties to the conflict, cooperation with UNPROFOR did not improve.   UNPROFOR continued to be obstructed by all sides; its convoys were impeded, its forces were taken hostage, and the safe areas where U.N. troops were posted were subject to attack.[101]   In response to these difficulties facing

96. *See* Paul C. Szasz, *Peacekeeping in Operation: A Conflict Study of Bosnia*, 28 CORNELL INT'L L.J. 685, 696-697 (1995).

97. *See, e.g.*, S.C. Res. 871, U.N. SCOR, 48th Sess., 3286th mtg., U.N. Doc. S/RES/871 (1993); S.C. Res. 870, U.N. SCOR, 48th Sess., 3285th mtg., U.N. Doc. S/RES/870 (1993); S.C. Res. 869, U.N. SCOR, 48th Sess., 3284th mtg., U.N. Doc. S/RES/869 (1993); S.C. Res. 859, U.N. SCOR, 48th Sess., 3269th mtg., U.N. Doc. S/RES/859 (1993); S.C. Res. 847, U.N. SCOR, 48th Sess., 3248th mtg., U.N. Doc. S/RES/847 (1993); S.C. Res. 844, U.N. SCOR, 48th Sess., 3241st mtg., U.N. Doc. S/RES/844 (1993); S/RES/836, *supra* note 81; S/RES/815, *supra* note 78.

98. S.C. Res. 900, U.N. SCOR, 50th Sess., 3527th mtg., U.N. Doc. S/RES/900 (1995).

99. U.N. SCOR, 49th Sess., 3344th mtg., at 14, U.N. Doc. S/PV.3344 (1994).

100. *See id.* at 11.

101. *See, e.g.*, U.N. CHRON., Sept. 95, at 29-32; U.N. CHRON., Dec. 1994, at 27, 29, 30; U.N.

UNPROFOR, the Rapid Reaction Force was created.

VI. THE CREATION OF THE RAPID REACTION FORCE

Further problems with consent arose with the creation of the Rapid Reaction Force (RRF) in June 1995. States were divided as to the nature of the force; as to whether it was a peacekeeping force whose establishment was based on host-state consent or an enforcement force established without the need for host-state consent; and whether it was intended to be impartial or operate against one of the parties involved in the conflict.[102] In fact, the RRF was not given any powers beyond those of UNPROFOR. Additionally, the establishment of the RRF led to further problems over the conclusion of SOFAs with the host states. The host states argued that the RRF was a new force separate from UNPROFOR and demanded the negotiation of a new SOFA.[103] The Security Council justifiably rejected this claim.[104]

France, the Netherlands and the United Kingdom proposed the establishment of the RRF to provide military relief for UNPROFOR to reduce the vulnerability of its personnel and to enhance its capacity to carry out its existing mandate.[105] The RRF was to be a well-armed, mobile force and to operate under the existing mandate and rules of engagement of UNPROFOR. When the Security Council discussed the proposal for an RRF, divisions between member states were apparent.[106] China argued that the force would constitute a de facto change in the peacekeeping status of UNPROFOR. It said that the force was being established for enforcement action and thus UNPROFOR would become a party to the conflict.[107] Russia also said that the resolution did not avoid the impression that the RRF was intended to operate against one party to the conflict, the Bosnian Serbs.[108] But the United Kingdom and France insisted that no change

---

CHRON., Sept. 1994, at 29; U.N. CHRON., June 1994, at 26; U.N. CHRON., March 1994, at 64; U.N. CHRON., Dec. 1993, at 32; U.N. CHRON., Sept. 1993, at 17, 19; *see also* 1993 U.N.Y.B. 487, 489; 1994 U.N.Y.B. 488, 491, 513.

102. *See infra* note 107 and accompanying text.

103. *See infra* note 117 and accompanying text.

104. *See infra* note 119 and accompanying text.

105. *See Letter Dated 9 June 1995 From the Secretary-General Addressed to the President of the Security Council*, U.N. SCOR, 50th Sess., U.N. Doc. S/1995/470 (1995).

106. *See* U.N. SCOR, 50th Sess., 3543d mtg., U.N. Doc. S/PV.3543 (1995) [hereinafter S/PV.3543].

107. *See id.* at 13-14.

108. *See id.* at 10.

in the nature of UNPROFOR was intended.[109] The United States offered limited support, stating "[w]e vote in favour of this draft on the
clear understanding that by doing so we are not incurring any direct
financial obligation."[110] Accordingly, the resolution establishing the
force was passed by 13-0-2 (China and Russia voting against).[111] The
resolution specifically noted a letter from Bosnia-Herzegovina wel-
coming the reinforcement of UNPROFOR.[112]

Serious problems arose regarding the attitude of the host states,
Croatia and Bosnia-Herzegovina.   Bosnia-Herzegovina had expressed its consent to the establishment and deployment of the force
during the Security Council debate.[113] Croatia had been rather less
forthcoming at that stage, but did say that it would consent on the basis that the force would operate in Bosnia alone and that it would sta-
tion only command and logistic facilities in Croatia. Any operational
use of the RRF in Croatia could only proceed after consultation with
the government of Croatia and with its approval and consent.[114] Both
states subsequently wrote to the Security Council promising to cooperate with the force.[115]

However, both states were determined that the RRF would operate in such a way as to support their own particular aims. They
now demanded new SOFAs, claiming that existing agreements did
not cover the RRF as it was not part of UNPROFOR. They wanted
to impose new restrictions on the RRF limiting its freedom of movement. They also wanted to impose less favorable terms than the existing SOFAs with regard to use of premises and payment for services.[116] The Secretary-General rejected these claims. He said that the

---

109. *See id.* at 18-19.

110. *Id.* at 16-17.

111. S.C. Res. 998, U.N. SCOR, 50th Sess., 3543d mtg., U.N. Doc. S/RES/998 (1995).

112. *See Letter Dated 14 June 1995 From the Chargé d'Affaires A.I. of the Permanent Mission of
Bosnia and Hercegovina to the United Nations Addressed to the President of the Security Council*, U.N.
SCOR, 50th Sess., Annex, U.N. Doc. S/1995/483 (1995).

113. *See* S/PV.3543, *supra* note 106, at 3.

114. *See id.* at 7.

115. *See Letter Dated 14 August 1995 From the Chargé d'Affaires A.I. of the Permanent Mission of
Bosnia and Hercegovina to the United Nations Addressed to the President of the Security Council*, U.N.
SCOR, 50th Sess., U.N. Doc. S/1995/691 (1995); *Letter Dated 11 August 1995 From the Permanent Rep-
resentative of Croatia to the United Nations Addressed to the President of the Security Council*, U.N.
SCOR, 50th Sess., U.N. Doc. S/1995/684 (1995).

116. *See Letter Dated 17 August 1995 From the Secretary-General Addressed to the President of the
Security Council*, U.N. SCOR, 50th Sess., U.N. Doc. S/1995/707 (1995) [hereinafter S/1995/707]. Also,
the Croats in Bosnia demanded a separate SOFA with the Federation established under the framework
agreement creating a Federation in the Areas of the Republic of Bosnia and Hercegovina with a majority

RRF was part of UNPROFOR and therefore covered by the existing SOFAs; SOFAs naturally covered variations in size of peacekeeping forces.

On the ground, both states obstructed the RRF's deployment of troops. In July 1995, the Secretary-General reported on these problems to the Security Council.[117] In response, the Council issued a statement:

> The Security Council is deeply concerned at the implication of the continued impediments to the functioning of the RRF for the effectiveness of the United Nations mission in the Republic of Bosnia-Herzegovina. It calls upon the Government of the Republic of Croatia and the Republic of Bosnia-Herzegovina immediately to remove all impediments and to give clear undertakings concerning the freedom of movement and provision of facilities for the RRF, in order that it may perform its tasks without further delay. It further calls upon them to resolve forthwith within the framework of the existing SOFAs any outstanding difficulties with the relevant United Nations authorities.[118]

This episode illustrates Bosnia-Herzegovina and Croatia attempting to take advantage of the creation of the RRF to secure the negotiation of SOFAs more favorable to them, that is, SOFAs which would offer them greater control over the operations of UNPROFOR on their territories. Although both states formally consented to the deployment of the RRF, they did not fulfil their duties to cooperate with it on the ground.

VII. CROATIA'S WITHDRAWAL OF CONSENT FROM UNPROFOR AND THE ESTABLISHMENT OF UNCRO

The termination of Croatia's consent to the presence of UNPROFOR on its territory shows clearly that it was the consent of the host-state government that was essential for the continued deployment of the U.N. force. Croatia used this power to secure the removal of UNPROFOR and the creation of a new peacekeeping force with a mandate more acceptable to it. In so doing, Croatia jeopardized the hopes of peaceful settlement and the entire

---

Bosnian and Croatian population. *See Letter Dated 3 March 1994 From the Permanent Representatives of Bosnia and Hercegovina and Croatia to the United Nations Addressed to the Secretary-General*, U.N. SCOR, 49th Sess., U.N. Doc. S/1994/255 (1994).

117. S/1995/707, *supra* note 116.

118. *Statement by the President of the Security Council*, U.N. SCOR, 50th Sess., 3568th mtg., para. 4, U.N. Doc. S/PRST/1995/40 (1995).

266   DUKE JOURNAL OF COMPARATIVE & INTERNATIONAL LAW   [Vol. 7:241

peacekeeping operation.

Even at the time UNPROFOR was created, Croatia expressed reservations in giving its consent.[119] Croatia was concerned with maintaining its sovereignty over the U.N.-protected areas, and keeping the U.N. peace plan from perpetuating the division of Croatia. From June 1993 Croatia expressed reservations about the renewal of UNPROFOR's mandate,[120] and the Security Council from this time regularly called on the Secretary-General to report on the reconsideration of the mandate "taking into account the position of the Government of Croatia."[121] The Secretary-General regularly reported that UNPROFOR played an indispensable role in Croatia; even if it was not able fully to carry out its mandate, it helped to prevent the renewal of conflict.[122] Croatia also indicated concern about the name of UNPROFOR. It called for a new name from which it would be prima facie evident that the peacekeeping force was located on the territory of Croatia.[123]

Finally, in January 1995, Croatia formally gave notice of the withdrawal of its consent to the deployment of UNPROFOR on its territory.[124] The Security Council interpreted this to mean that

---

119. *See* S/1995/467, *supra* note 4, at 5.

120. *See, e.g., Leter Dated 26 September 1994 From the Permanent Representative of Croatia to the United Nations Addressed to the President of the Security Council,* U.N. SCOR, 49th Sess., U.N. Doc. S/1994/1095 (1994); *Letter Dated 16 March 1993 From the Charge d'Affaires A.I. of the Permanent Mission of Croatia to the United Nations Addressed to the Secretary-General* U.N. SCOR, 49th Sess., Annex, U.N. Doc. S/1994/305 (1994); *Letter Dated 24 September 1993 From the Permanent Representative of Croatia to the United Nations Addressed to the President of the Security Council,* U.N. SCOR, 48th Sess., Annex, U.N. Doc. S/26491 (1993); *Letter Dated 30 July 1993 From the Permanent Representative of Croatia to the United Nations Addressed to the Secretary-General,* U.N. SCOR, 48th Sess., Annex, U.N. Doc. S/26220 (1993) [hereinafter S/26220]; *Letter Dated 25 June 1993 from the Permanent Representative of Croatia to the United Nations Addressed to the Secretary-General,* U.N. SCOR, 48th Sess., Annex, U.N. Doc. S/26002 (1993).

121. *See, e.g.,* S.C. Res. 847, U.N. SCOR, 49th Sess., U.N. Doc. S/RES/847 (1993) (passed unanimously).

122. *See, e.g., Report of the Secretary-General Pursuant to Paragraph 2 of Security Council Resolution 847 (1993),* U.N. SCOR, 48th Sess., paras. 2-5, U.N. Doc. S/26310 (1993); *Further Report to the Secretary-General Pursuant to Security Council Resolution 815 (1993),* U.N. SCOR, 48th Sess., paras. 3-4, U.N. Doc. S/25993 (1993); *Further Report to the Secretary-General Pursuant to Security Council Resolution 743 (1992),* U.N. SCOR, 48th Sess., para. 15, U.N. Doc. S/26470 (1993).

123. *See* S/26220, *supra* note 120, at 1. A similar debate about the name of the peacekeeping force had arisen earlier regarding UNDOF.

124. *See Letter Dated 12 January 1995 From the Permanent Representative of Croatia to the United Nations Addressed to the Secretary-General,* U.N. SCOR, 50th Sess., at 4, U.N. Doc. S/1995/28 (1995); *Letter Dated 18 January 1995 From the Permanent Representative of Croatia to the United Nations Addressed to the President of the Security Council,* U.N. SCOR, 50th Sess., Annex, U.N. Doc. S/1995/56 (1995).

UNPROFOR would have to be withdrawn, that is, despite the many resolutions referring to Chapter VII, the presence of UNPROFOR in Croatia still depended on the consent of the host state. The Secretary-General expressed regret at the withdrawal of consent and said that there was a serious risk of renewed hostilities if UNPROFOR withdrew. He hoped that the Croatian government would reconsider its position before the expiry of UNPROFOR's current mandate.[125] In a later report of March 1995 the Secretary-General said that there had indeed been a significant escalation of military activity and tension. There was an increased lack of cooperation with UNPROFOR and both sides had made tactical deployment of their forces in preparation for wide-scale conflict after the withdrawal of UNPROFOR.[126] The Security Council also expressed grave concern about the risk of renewed hostilities and called for negotiations to secure the continued presence of a peacekeeping force.[127]

President Tudjman then relented and agreed to the continued presence of a smaller peacekeeping force with a new mandate and a new name. UNPROFOR was to be divided into three forces, with forces in Bosnia-Herzegovina and Macedonia continuing as before.[128] In Croatia, substantial alterations were made to the mandate. There were detailed discussions between the United Nations and both the Government of Croatia and the Croatian Serbs over the nature, size and functions of the force.[129] As to the name, President Tudjman said in letters to the Security Council that if the resolution did not allow the official name of the operation to be the United Nations Confidence Restoration Operation in Croatia (UNCRO), Croatia would not give its consent for the establishment of the new force.[130] During

125. *See Report of the Secretary-General Pursuant to Paragraph 4 of Security Council Resolution 947 (1994)*, U.N. SCOR, 50th Sess., para. 31, U.N. Doc. S/1995/38 (1995) [hereinafter S/1995/38].

126. *See* U.N. Doc. S/1995/222, *supra* note 57, paras. 3-5.

127. *See Statement by the President of the Security Council*, U.N. SCOR, 50th Sess., 3491st mtg., U.N. Doc. S/PRST/1995/2 (1995).

128. *See Letter Dated 17 March 1995 From the Permanent Representative of Croatia to the United Nations Addressed to the Secretary-General*, U.N. SCOR, 50th Sess., Annex, U.N. Doc. S/1995/206 (1995). Resolution 982 noted Bosnia's consent expressed in the *Letter Dated 29 March 1995 From the Permanent Representative of Bosnia-Herzegovina to the United Nations Addressed to the Secretary-General*, U.N. SCOR, 49th Sess., U.N. Doc. S/245 (1995). Resolution 983, on the force in Macedonia, does not contain any express reference to consent. S. C. Res. 983, U.N. SCOR, 50th Sess., U.N. Doc. S/RES/983 (1995).

129. *See* S/1995/222, *supra* note 57; *Yugoslav Crisis, A Climate of Uncertainty*, U.N. CHRON., June 1995, at 24-26.

130. *See* S/26220, *supra* note 120; *Letter Dated 30 March 1995 From the Permanent Representative of Croatia to the United Nations Addressed to the President of the Security Council*, U.N. SCOR, 49th

268   DUKE JOURNAL OF COMPARATIVE & INTERNATIONAL LAW   [Vol. 7:241]

the Security Council debate leading to the resolution, Croatia claimed that this name implied that the operation was not merely a static peacekeeping force but an active, task-specific operation.[131] The Krajina Serb Assembly subsequently criticised the name UNCRO, saying that it prejudged a political solution and ignored the sovereign rights of the Serbs in Krajina.[132]

The new force was to support and facilitate the implementation of the March 1994 cease-fire and the December 1994 economic agreement between the parties in Croatia, to assist in controlling military crossing of the borders of Croatia, to help the delivery of humanitarian aid in Bosnia-Herzegovina, and to monitor the demilitarization of the Prevlaka Peninsula.[133] But the Secretary-General reported that the plan for the deployment of UNCRO did not have the full acceptance of the Croatian Government or of the Serb local authorities:

> As was to some degree the case in February 1992 when UNPROFOR was originally established, the plan set out above does not have the full acceptance and full support of either the Government of Croatia or the local Serb authorities. The risk therefore remains that either or both sides will fail to cooperate with the U.N. in its implementation. In these circumstances it is not without misgivings that I present these proposals to the Council. On the other hand, the plan provides for the pragmatic implementation of Security Council Resolution 981 and the alternative to its adoption would be withdrawal of the U.N. forces and the resumption of war.[134]

The Secretary-General recommended that the Security Council authorize the deployment of UNCRO. He set out the proposed composition of the force (and of the forces in Bosnia-Herzegovina and Macedonia) in his report to the Security Council.[135]

Again Croatia proved reluctant to conclude a SOFA. It had

Sess., Annex, U.N. Doc. S/1995/246 (1995).

131. *See Report of the Secretary-General Pursuant to Paragraph 4 of Security Council Resolution 947 (1994)*, U.N. SCOR, 49th Sess., 3512th mtg., at 6, U.N. Doc. S/PV.3512 (1995).

132. *See* S/1995/467, *supra* note 4, para. 18.

133. *See Report of the Secretary-General Submitted Pursuant to Paragraph 4 of Security Council Resolution 981 (1995)*, U.N. SCOR, 49th Sess., paras. 11-28, U.N. Doc. S/1995/320 (1995) [hereinafter S/1995/320].

134. *Id.* Subsequently, Croatia expressly accepted the principles in the mandate of UNCRO. *See Letter Dated 28 April 1995 From the Permanent Representative of Croatia to the United Nations Addressed to the President of the Security Council*, U.N. SCOR, 49th Sess., U.N. Doc. S/1995/339 (1995).

135. S/1995/222, *supra* note 57, paras. 3-5; *Letter Dated 5 May 1995 From the Secretary General Addressed to the President of the Security Council*, U.N. SCOR, 49th Sess., U.N. Doc. S/1995/386 (1995).

never finalized a SOFA for UNPROFOR despite a pledge given by President Tudjman in September 1994.[136] Negotiations on a SOFA for UNCRO progressed very slowly.[137] The Security Council, in the resolution establishing UNCRO, had stressed the need for a SOFA,[138] and Resolution 990 also expressed concern that a SOFA had not been signed and called on Croatia to conclude an agreement.[139] The Secretary-General also reported on the difficulties that had arisen as a result of demands by Croatian authorities incompatible with the U.N. model SOFA.[140] It was only after an offensive by Croatian government forces in May 1995 that Croatia finally concluded a SOFA on 15 May 1995.[141]

On the political level the Krajina Serbs accepted the deployment of UNCRO, but the Secretary-General reported a lack of cooperation on the ground and the occurrence of hijackings and robbery of UNCRO forces.[142] The Croatian government overran UNCRO positions in offensives of May and August 1995.[143] After the first May offensive, both sides asked UNCRO to stay and complete its deployment, but the Secretary-General said that "more than words are required to justify the continuation of this expensive and dangerous mission."[144] Nevertheless UNCRO was deployed in a modified form. Later, in the fourth August offensive the Croatian government drove UNCRO out of all the U.N.-protected areas except Sector East and UNCRO subsequently remained only in Eastern Slavonia in a much reduced form.[145]

---

136. *See* S/1995/38, *supra* note 125.

137. *See* S/1995/320, *supra* note 133.

138. S.C. Res. 981, U.N. SCOR, 49th Sess., U.N. Doc. S/RES/981 (1995) (passed unanimously).

139. S.C. Res. 990, U.N. SCOR, 49th Sess., U.N. Doc. S/RES/990 (1995) (passed unanimously).

140. *See* S/1995/320, *supra* note 133.

141. *See* S/1995/467, *supra* note 4.

142. *See id.*

143. *See Yugoslav Crisis, U.N. Role in Question,* U.N. CHRON., Sept. 1995, at 32-33.

144. U.N. Doc. S/1995/467, *supra* note 4, at 13.

145. *See Report of the Secretary-General Pursuant to Security Council Resolutions 981 (1995), 982 (1995), and 983 (1995),* U.N. SCOR, 50th Sess., U.N. Doc. S/1995/987 (1995); *Letter Dated 10 October 1995 From the President of the Security Council Addressed to the Secretary-General,* U.N. SCOR, 50th Sess., U.N. Doc. S/1995/859 (1995); *Further Report of the Secretary-General Pursuant to Security Council Resolution 1009 (1995),* U.N. SCOR, 50th Sess., U.N. Doc. S/1995/835 (1995); *Letter Dated 29 August 1995 From the President of the Security Council Addressed to the Secretary-General,* U.N. SCOR, 50th Sess., U.N. Doc. S/1995/748 (1995); *Report of the Secretary-General Submitted Pursuant to Security Council Resolution 1009 (1995),* U.N. SCOR, 50th Sess., U.N. Doc. S/1995/730 (1995); *Letter Dated 7 August 1995 From the Secretary-General Addressed to the President of the Security Council,* U.N. SCOR, 50th Sess., U.N. Doc. S/1995/666 (1995).

270   DUKE JOURNAL OF COMPARATIVE & INTERNATIONAL LAW   [Vol. 7:241

CONCLUSION

The early problems in securing the consent of "the concerned parties" to the deployment of UNPROFOR in Yugoslavia were ominous, and the Secretary-General's fears that the force would not be able to operate effectively without the cooperation of all those involved proved prophetic. The initial consent to the establishment of UNPROFOR was grudgingly given by some of the parties, and the formal consent of the host-state governments, even though accompanied by consent to the details of the initial mandate of UNPROFOR, was not sufficient to guarantee cooperation. The lack of active support for UNPROFOR on the ground was made manifest when host-state governments were reluctant to conclude SOFAs to protect the forces' rights and freedom of movement.

The subsequent expansion of UNPROFOR's mandate demonstrated uncertainties as to the law on consent, and led to conflict between the warring parties and UNPROFOR when the parties came to see UNPROFOR as an obstacle to the achievement of their military goals. Even though the Security Council eventually resorted to Chapter VII of the U.N. Charter in order to stress the binding nature of the duty to cooperate with UNPROFOR and to secure the protection of UNPROFOR troops, this did not lead to increased cooperation on the ground. When the Security Council tried to increase the UNPROFOR's effectiveness by creating a Rapid Reaction Force, the host-state governments sought to take advantage of this and to negotiate SOFAs which would give them greater control over the operations of UNPROFOR. Croatia finally withdrew its consent to the deployment of UNPROFOR in its territory and consented to its replacement by UNCRO only on its own restrictive terms.

This sequence of events not only shows the practical problems encountered by the U.N. peacekeeping forces in Yugoslavia with regard to consent, it also vividly illustrates the complexity and multifaceted nature of the concept of consent in the context of peacekeeping.

Peacekeeping and the Use of Force

[7]

BEYOND SELF-DEFENSE: UNITED NATIONS PEACEKEEPING OPERATIONS & THE USE OF FORCE

KATHERINE E. COX[*]

TABLE OF CONTENTS

* Presidential Fellow, Association of the Bar of the City of New York; LL.M. 1998, Columbia University School of Law; LL.B. (Hons.) 1994, University of Adelaide, Australia; B.A. 1990, Flinders University of South Australia, Australia. I would like to thank Professor Lori Fisler Damrosch of Columbia University Law School for her helpful comments on this paper, and Ms. Leila Benkirane, who supervised me during my internship at the United Nations, and provided me with an insight into the practical and legal aspects of United Nations peacekeeping operations.

I. INTRODUCTION

Since the end of the Cold War, the role of United Nations (UN) operations in the area of international peace and security has increasingly become a topical issue for the different nations of the world. In particular, the use of force by, and in support of, peacekeeping has raised questions concerning the future role of UN peacekeeping operations in the resolution of international and internal conflict. During the Cold War there were two accepted forms of United Nations operations: peacekeeping and peace-enforcement. Since the end of the Cold War, however, despite increasing difficulties faced by UN peacekeeping operations, no accepted mode of action beyond these two operations has emerged. This has become problematic as the UN has consistently chosen to use peacekeeping forces as its primary tool in its effort to restore peace and security; despite the fact that peacekeeping, in itself, is not always an effective means to achieve these ends.

Why did peacekeeping come to be used in situations that increasingly necessitated the use of coercive force? Primarily because peacekeeping provided a legal and 'palatable' form of intervention in intrastate conflicts, which have erupted with greater frequency in recent times. The use of UN peacekeepers to intervene and resolve conflict was acceptable to Member States and met with their growing demands and expectations that action be taken to contain State fragmentation and resolve humanitarian crises. Due to their acceptability, such forces were authorized and implemented. The circumstances into which the UN intervened, however, were often volatile and not conducive to effective peacekeeping: situations where, for example, the consent of the warring factions could only be obtained conditionally or where there was no governmental authority in existence with whom the UN could negotiate and work. The Security Council authorized the use of force by and in support of some of these UN peacekeeping operations to enable their mandates to be achieved. Ultimately this has meant that UN peacekeeping has moved beyond the three main legal principles upon which it was originally based, notably the principles of consent, impartiality and non-use of force except in self-defense. Arguably, peacekeeping has outstripped its original doctrinal justifications and as a result now flounders without guidelines and with ill-defined purpose.

The use of force by and in support of UN peacekeeping operations has narrowed the gap that previously existed between peacekeeping and coercive peace-enforcement. Yet the use of force in such instances is controversial, primarily because there is no universally accepted agreement as to how and when force should be used. This gives rise to many legal issues. For example, how broad is a peacekeeper's inherent right to self-defense? When does force used in 'self-defense' become an enforcement measure? When does peacekeeping become coercive peace-enforcement? One way to address these questions is to clarify the legal issues that have emerged due to these developments. Their clarification is not only of theoretical interest, it is of great practical importance. Determining the legal basis for the use of force enables a conceptual framework to be built up regarding its use. A sound legal understanding of this issue would provide the basis for comprehensive policies to be formulated concerning the way in which force is used by UN peacekeepers. It will help address the current problems facing United Nations peacekeeping by ensuring that Security Council resolutions are translated into clear and effective rules of engagement, which will be adhered to by troops in the field.

Not surprisingly, if a peacekeeping operation's mandate is not clear, its rules of engagement will not be clear. Lack of clarity in a mandate or its legal basis invariably gives rise to problems in interpreting or implementing the objectives of the operation. Thus, the criteria for using force are important to define. Sound reasons are needed to explain and justify why force may be used in one situation and not in another. Furthermore, such criteria must be accepted by all the parties involved in the peacekeeping operation — the parties involved in the conflict and the countries who have donated troops. By using legal reasoning to justify the use of force, a consensus among Member States is more likely to emerge as to when and how force should be used by the United Nations. The future credibility of the United Nations depends on successful peacekeeping operations. Operations that have clearly defined mandates and legally obtainable objectives are more likely to succeed than those that do not. Clearly therefore, it is most important to concentrate on resolving the legal difficulties underpinning these operations.

This paper focuses on the extent to which UN peacekeeping operations can use force in self-defense. Clearly this is just one of the areas regarding peacekeeping and the use of force which needs to be clari-

242   DENV. J. INT'L L. & POL'Y   VOL. 27:2

fied.[1] It is an area that warrants particular attention, however, due to the fact that self-defense is the one 'legitimate' way in which peace-keepers can use force.[2] The first part of this paper gives an overview of UN peacekeeping operations and the legal principles governing these operations. Part two examines the history and development of the use of force by UN peacekeeping operations. In particular, the idea that self-defense, in the context of peacekeeping, may include using force 'in defense of one's mandate' is examined. Part three details some recent examples of Security Council resolutions which authorized, either explicitly or implicitly, the use of force in a way that arguably expands this concept of self-defense even further. Finally, I discuss the legal and practical implications this development has for the future of peacekeeping.

This paper focuses on the use of force *by* peacekeeping forces, as opposed to the use of force *in support of* peacekeeping forces. The reason for this limitation is not only space constraints, but the fact that the issues raised by these different uses of force are in fact quite distinct and are not necessarily ideally dealt with together. The use of force as an enforcement measure under Chapter VII of the Charter is legal where the Security Council has found a threat to international peace and security and has authorized the use of force.[3] In the context of a peacekeeping operation the use of force raises different issues. Whilst it may be argued that it is legal for the Security Council to authorize the use of force by UN peacekeeping operations under Chapter VII, this flies in the face of one of the fundamental legal principles governing peacekeeping operations: the principle of non-use of force. If it is accepted that peacekeeping operations can only use force in self-defense, as is generally agreed, one must question whether the concept can be stretched to include more forceful measures, the likes of which have been authorized in recent times. This paper seeks to answer some of these questions.

---

1. Another area, for example, might be to what degree the use of force by Member States in support of peacekeeping operations is compatible with the underlying principles of peacekeeping.

2. As distinguished from a "lawful" use of force authorized under Chapter VII of the UN Charter. This is due to the fact that one of the principles of traditional peacekeeping was that force only be used in self-defense. U.N. CHARTER arts. 42-43. See discussion below concerning the legal principles governing United Nations peacekeeping operations.

3. Article 42 of the U.N. Charter reads:

Should the Security Council consider that measures provided for in Article 41 would be inadequate or have proved to be inadequate, it may take such action by air, sea, or land forces as may be necessary to maintain or restore international peace or security. Such action may include demonstrations, blockade, and other operations by air, sea or land forces of Members of the United Nations.

U.N. CHARTER art. 42.

II. AN OVERVIEW OF UNITED NATIONS PEACEKEEPING OPERATIONS

The purpose of this section is to give a broad overview and some background to UN peacekeeping operations, their legal underpinnings and core characteristics. No attempt is made to give a detailed critique of the subject matter. Indeed, there is a vast array of scholarly writings available on the topic, which highlight the complex and controversial nature of these operations.[4] For the purposes of this paper, however, a few general comments about the nature of peacekeeping operations, are appropriate.

A. *Definition of "United Nations Peacekeeping Operations"*

No two UN peacekeeping operations are alike.[5] Each operation is distinguished by the environment in which it operates and the extent to which it is authorized to carry out various peacekeeping functions. Furthermore, each operation builds upon the experience of past operations. Thus by definition UN peacekeeping operations are evolutionary in nature. For the purposes of delineating the scope and character of such operations, however, it is possible to make some general observations about their distinguishing features and thereby formulate a broad definition of the concept.

Peacekeeping operations are an invention of the United Nations. They were developed in response to the political realities of the Cold War, brought about by the need to address conflicts which occurred after entry into force of the UN Charter and for which the mechanisms provided for in Chapters VI and VII of the Charter could not be used.[6]

---

4. *See, e.g.*, D.W. BOWETT, UNITED NATIONS FORCES: A LEGAL STUDY (1964); Dan Ciobanu, *The Power of the Security Council to Organize Peace-Keeping Operations, in* UNITED NATIONS PEACEKEEPING: LEGAL ESSAYS (A. Cassese ed., 1978); John W. Halderman, *Legal Basis for United Nations Forces*, 56 AMER. J. INT'L L. 971 (1962); Rosalyn Higgins, *A General Assessment of United Nations Peace-Keeping, in* UNITED NATIONS PEACEKEEPING: LEGAL ESSAYS (A. Cassese ed., 1978); Georg Schwarzenberger, *Problems of a United Nations Force, in* 12 CURRENT LEGAL PROBLEMS 247 (George W. Keeton & Georg Schwarzenberger eds., 1959).

5. Indeed, Bowett lists nine different categories of peacekeeping being (1) cease-fire, truces and armistice functions entrusted to "observer" groups; (2) frontier control; (3) interpositionary functions (undertaken to "secure a cessation of hostilities"); (3) defense and security of UN zones or areas placed under UN control; (5) the maintenance of law and order in a State; (6) plebiscite supervision (undertaken in order to "determine the status of a territory disputed between two sovereign States"); (7) assistance and relief for national disasters (undertaken in order to provide humanitarian relief); (8) prevention of international crimes; and (9) disarmament functions: *See* BOWETT, *supra* note 4, at 268-74. Schachter lists eight different categories along similar lines. Oscar Schachter, *Authorized Uses of Force by the United Nations and Regional Organizations, in* LAW AND FORCE IN THE NEW INTERNATIONAL ORDER 65, 80 (Lori Fisler Damrosch & David J. Scheffer eds., 1991).

6. For a discussion of the development of peacekeeping and the early operations, see:

244   DENV. J. INT'L L. & POL'Y   VOL. 27:2

The means provided for in Chapter VI, concerning the pacific settlement of disputes, were inadequate. The means provided for in Chapter VII, concerning the enforcement measures, could not be agreed upon by Members of the Security Council due essentially to the profound ideological differences that prevailed during the Cold War. Peacekeeping emerged as a mode of international intervention other than those provided for in Chapters VI and VII of the Charter.

Peacekeeping operations have been defined broadly as:

> [O]peration[s] involving military personnel, but without enforcement powers, undertaken by the United Nations to help maintain or restore international peace and security in areas of conflict. These operations are voluntary and are based on consent and cooperation. While they involve the use of military personnel, they achieve their objectives not by force of arms, thus contrasting them with the 'enforcement action' of the United Nations under Article 42.[7]

Generally speaking, peacekeeping operations consist of either: (1) unarmed observer missions; or (2) forces which have the function of sustaining peacemaking efforts by helping to create conditions in which negotiation between warring parties can take place.[8] The latter type of operation is typically armed and may use force in limited circumstances that are discussed below. Given that the theme of this paper concerns the use of force by peacekeeping operations, peacekeeping operations are defined here to cover the latter type of operation only.

BOWETT, *supra* note 4; UNITED NATIONS, BLUE HELMETS: A REVIEW OF UNITED NATIONS PEACE-KEEPING, U.N. Doc. DPI/1800, U.N. Sales No. E.96.I.14 (3d ed. 1996) [hereinafter BLUE HELMETS I]; 1 ROSALYN HIGGINS, UNITED NATIONS PEACEKEEPING, THE MIDDLE EAST 1946-1967: DOCUMENTS AND COMMENTARY (1969); 2 ROSALYN HIGGINS, UNITED NATIONS PEACEKEEPING, ASIA 1946-1967: DOCUMENTS AND COMMENTARY (1970); 3 ROSALYN HIGGINS, UNITED NATIONS PEACEKEEPING, AFRICA 1946-1967: DOCUMENTS AND COMMENTARY (1980); 4 ROSALYN HIGGINS, UNITED NATIONS PEACEKEEPING, EUROPE 1946-1979: DOCUMENTS AND COMMENTARY (1981); Marrack Goulding, *The Evolution of United Nations Peace-Keeping*, 69 INT'L AFF. 451 (1993).

7. UNITED NATIONS, THE BLUE HELMETS: A REVIEW OF UNITED NATIONS PEACE-KEEPING at 4, U.N. Sales No. E.90.I.18 (2d ed. 1990) [hereinafter BLUE HELMETS II].

8. *See* Jon E. Fink, *From Peacekeeping to Peace Enforcement: The Blurring of the Mandate for the Use of Force in Maintaining International Peace and Security*, 19 MD. J. INT'L L. & TRADE 1, 10 (1995); Goulding, *supra* note 6, at 457. Note, however, that peacekeeping operations can be divided up into many more categories. For example, both Bowett and Schachter list many different categories of peacekeeping. *See supra* note 5. Given that each peacekeeping operation tends to be designed for the unique situation into which it must operate, it is not surprising that many different categories exist.

B. The Legal Principles Governing United Nations Peacekeeping Operations

As the concept of peacekeeping evolved, UN peacekeeping operations developed core legal principles that became fundamental to their operation. These principles are contained in various legal documents concerning peacekeeping operations, such as the Status of Forces Agreements (SOFAs) and rules of engagement.[9] They embody the essence of peacekeeping and permeate all aspects of an operation.[10] The three main legal principles underlying peacekeeping are: (1) consent of all parties concerned and the competent organ of the UN, usually the Security Council;[11] (2) impartiality; and (3) non-use of force except in self-defense.

These principles developed over time and are based on sound legal and practical reasoning. For example, Article 2(7) of the UN Charter prohibits the United Nations from intervening in the domestic affairs of a Member State except where Chapter VII enforcement measures are involved.[12] Thus, a UN peacekeeping force can only intervene into the domestic affairs of a State if the State concerned has consented to that intervention and to the peacekeeping operation as a whole.[13] Similarly,

---

9. *See infra* note 32 and accompanying text discussing rules of engagement.

10. When a peacekeeping operation is set up, various agreements are drawn up between the United Nations and the Host State (Status-of-Forces Agreement) and between the United Nations and contributing State(s). Model agreements of this nature have been approved of by the General Assembly. *See Comprehensive Review of the Whole Question of Peace-Keeping Operations in All Their Aspects: Model of Status of Forces Agreement for Peace-Keeping Operations: Report of the Secretary-General*, U.N. GAOR, 45th Sess., Agenda Item 76, U.N. Doc. A/45/594 (1990); *Comprehensive Review of the Whole Question of Peace-Keeping Operations in All Their Aspects: Model Agreement Between the United Nations and Member States Contributing Personnel and Equipment to United Nations Peace-Keeping Operations: Report of the Secretary-General*, U.N. GAOR, 46th Sess., Item 74 of the Preliminary List, U.N. Doc. A/46/185 (1991).

11. Peacekeeping operations, unlike enforcement measures, can be authorized by the General Assembly (GA), but the GA has only done this on two occasions: UNEF 1 (United Nations Emergency Force) which was established to secure the withdrawal of troops from Egyptian territory and to serve as a buffer between Egypt and Israel; and UNSF (United Nations Security Force) which was created to maintain peace and security in the West Irian territory, *UN Peacekeeping History*, 1 INT'L PEACEKEEPING 1, 9 (1994).

12. Article 2, paragraph 7 reads as follows:

Nothing contained in the present Charter shall authorize the United Nations to intervene in matters which are essentially within the domestic jurisdiction of any State or shall require the Members to submit such matters to settlement under the present Charter; but this principle shall not prejudice the application of enforcement measures under Chapter VII.

U.N. CHARTER art. 2, para. 7.

13. Although it is worth noting that previously the majority of peacekeeping opera-

246   DENV. J. INT'L L. & POL'Y   VOL. 27:2

if the UN is to effectively "keep the peace," it must be impartial and un-biased in its operations. It is obvious that it would be extremely diffi-cult, if not impossible, for the UN to engage in coercive force and still be regarded as a neutral body. For this reason the use of force by UN peacekeeping forces has been limited to that used in self-defense.

In more recent times a "second generation" of peacekeeping has evolved.[14] These operations, occurring principally since the end of the Cold War, have increasingly involved civilian personnel and have been given more complex and challenging mandates, such as helping to pro-mote human rights and national reconciliation and organizing and monitoring elections.[15] Whilst the fundamental characteristics of these peacekeeping operations have not changed from those of earlier opera-tions as enumerated above, there is no doubt that all three of the main legal principles underlying peacekeeping have been strained by the new demands placed upon these operations. For example, it has become in-creasingly difficult to gain the consent and cooperation of all parties in-volved in UN peacekeeping operations. This has necessitated, at times, an increased use of force by peacekeepers in carrying out UN mandates. The perceived impartiality of operations has similarly become more dif-ficult to maintain for this reason.

However, the legal principles upon which peacekeeping was founded and evolved must be taken seriously. In particular (given the focus of this paper) it is important to emphasize that the UN has been very unwilling to go "beyond self-defense as the touchstone of the right to use force" with respect to peacekeeping operations.[16] Indeed, the Secretary-General and the Members of the United Nations "considered

---

tions have involved interstate disputes as opposed to intrastate disputes. It is only more recently that peacekeeping operations have been involved in disputes contained within a single State. *See* STEVEN R. RATNER, THE NEW UN PEACEKEEPING: BUILDING PEACE IN LANDS OF CONFLICT AFTER THE COLD WAR 23 (1995).

14. Boutros-Ghali acknowledges this development in his introduction to the United Nations publication, THE BLUE HELMETS. *See* BLUE HELMETS I, *supra* note 6, at 5. Ratner similarly discusses these developments in his book. RATNER, *supra* note 13. *See also* NEW DIMENSIONS OF PEACEKEEPING (Daniel Warner ed., 1995); Mats R. Berdal, *The Security Council, Peacekeeping and Internal Conflict After the Cold War*, 7 DUKE J. COMP. & INT'L L. 71 (1996); Kelly A. Childers, *United Nations Peacekeeping Forces in the Balkan Wars and the Changing Role of Peacekeeping Forces in the Post-Cold War World*, 8 TEMP. INT'L & COMP. L.J. 117 (1994); Fink, *supra* note 8, at 1; Roy S. Lee, *United Nations Peacekeep-ing: Development and Prospects*, 28 CORNELL INT'L L.J. 619 (1995); Ruth Wedgwood, *The Evolution of United Nations Peacekeeping*, 28 CORNELL INT'L L.J. 631 (1995).

15. BLUE HELMETS I, *supra* note 6, at 3. Ratner describes the new breadth of respon-sibility of UN peacekeepers as having fallen into ten categories: (1) military matters, (2) elections, (3) human rights, (4) national reconciliation, (5) law and order, (6) refugees, (7) humanitarian relief, (8) governmental administration, (9) economic reconstruction, and (10) relationships with outside actors. He describes the depth of responsibility as covering (1) monitoring, (2) supervision, (3) control, (4) conduct, (5) technical assistance, and (6) public information. RATNER, *supra* note 13, at 42-43.

16. Schachter, *supra* note 5, at 84.

it essential from a political and legal standpoint to distinguish peacekeeping from enforcement by *restricting the use of force to self-defense.*"[17] This point cannot be over-stressed as it indicates why conceptually and in practice, the UN has been reluctant to move away from the non-use of force by peacekeeping operations, and towards a more forceful kind of peace-making operation (as distinguished from peace-enforcement). A more thorough examination of the use of force by UN peacekeeping forces is discussed below.[18]

C. *The Constitutional Basis of United Nations Peacekeeping Operations*

The constitutional basis of United Nations peacekeeping operations is the broad mandate of Article 1 of the Charter, under which one of the purposes of the United Nations is to maintain international peace and security.[19] There is considerable debate amongst commentators as to where the UN gets its more specific mandate within the Charter,[20] although there is now little doubt that the UN does have the power to authorize such operations.[21] This was not always the case. Initially, some States protested the establishment of such operations. They argued that because peacekeeping operations were not specifically provided for in the UN Charter it was beyond the power of the Security Council to establish them.[22] On these grounds, and due to disputes over the constitutional basis within the Charter for such actions, certain States (including the former USSR and France) refused to pay their

---

17. *Id.* (emphasis added).

18. See discussion below on the use of force in self-defense and the use of force in defense of one's mandate.

19. Article 1(1) reads as follows:

The Purposes of the United Nations are: (1) To maintain international peace and security, and to that end: to take effective collective measures for the prevention and removal of threats to the peace, and for the suppression of acts of aggression or other breaches of the peace, and to bring about by peaceful means, and in conformity with the principles of justice and international law, adjustment or settlement of international disputes or situations which might lead to a breach of the peace.

U.N. CHARTER art. 1, para. 1.

20. One issue, for example, is whether the legal basis to establish such operations is found under Chapter VI of the Charter or under the various articles of Chapter VII. There are numerous articles and books discussing this issue. *See, e.g.,* BOWETT, *supra* note 4; Higgins, *supra* note 4; Halderman, *supra* note 4; Schwarzenberger, *supra* note 4; Finn Seyersted, *Can the United Nations Establish Military Forces and Perform Other Acts Without Specific Basis in the Charter?* 37 BRIT. Y.B. INT'L L. 351 (1961), *reprinted in* 12 ÖSTERREICHISCHE ZEITSCHRIFT FÜR ÖFFENTLICHES RECHT 188 (1962); Louis B. Sohn, *The Authority of the United Nations to Establish and Maintain a Permanent United Nations Force,* 52 AMER. J. INT'L L. 229 (1958).

21. *See* HILAIRE McCOUBREY & NIGEL WHITE, THE BLUE HELMETS: LEGAL REGULATIONS OF UNITED NATIONS MILITARY OPERATIONS 50-55 (1996); RATNER, *supra* note 13 at 58; Schachter, *supra* note 5, at 82.

22. *See* Schachter, *supra* note 5, at 80.

248   DENV. J. INT'L L. & POL'Y   VOL. 27:2

share of the early peacekeeping bills. These States argued that such actions were not "expenses of the Organization" within the meaning of Article 17(2) of the Charter.[23] The matter went to the International Court of Justice (ICJ) in the *Certain Expenses of the United Nations Case*, in which the Court confirmed *obiter* the constitutionality of the UN peacekeeping operations UNEF I and ONUC.[24] The ICJ stated that: "[W]hen the Organization takes action which warrants the assertion that it was appropriate for the fulfilment [sic] of one of the stated purposes of the United Nations, the presumption is that such an action is not ultra vires the Organisation."[25]

The ICJ stressed that although peacekeeping operations were not to be regarded as "enforcement measures" within the domain of Chapter VII of the Charter,[26] there was no doubt that because the Security Council had those enforcement powers it was within the power of the Security Council to implement less forceful measures.[27] However, whilst it was made clear that the Security Council had the legal capacity to establish peacekeeping operations, no opinion was given as to where the constitutional sources of such operations lay.[28]

However, insofar as UN peacekeeping forces are entitled to use force in self-defense they cannot be regarded as purely pacific means of dispute settlement under Chapter VI. It is for this reason that Chapter VII is usually thought to provide the general legal basis for UN peacekeeping operations, although such operations are not Chapter VII enforcement measures and should not be regarded as such. Considerable debate still exists as to which Articles of Chapter VII have actually been used to authorize the various operations.[29] As it is not essential to determine the exact legal basis for UN peacekeeping operations for the purpose of this paper, I will not enter into a detailed discussion. It is enough to say that the legality of UN peacekeeping under Chapter VII

---

23. Article 17(2) states that "[T]he expenses of the Organization shall be borne by the Members as apportioned by the General Assembly." U.N. CHARTER art. 17, para. 2.

24. Certain Expenses of the United Nations Case, 1962 I.C.J. 151, 167. *See infra* notes 36, 37, and 40 and accompanying text for background information on UNEF I and ONUC.

25. Certain Expenses Case, 1962 I.C.J. at 168.

26. The I.C.J. stated that the "operations known as UNEF and ONUC were not enforcement actions within the compass of Chapter VII. . . ." *Id.* at 166.

27. *Id.* at 167. The idea presumably being that the power to implement forceful measures encompasses the power to implement less forceful measures. This principle, ("qui peut le plus peut le moins" which is loosely translated as the "greater encompasses the lesser") is acknowledged by Georges Fischer. *See* Georges Fischer, *Article 42, in* LA CHARTE DES NATIONS UNIES 705 (Jean-Pierre Cot & Alain Pellet eds., 1985).

28. Certain Expenses Case, 1962 I.C.J. at 166-67.

29. The five main Articles which have been put forward as providing the possible legal basis for peacekeeping operations under Chapter VII of the Charter are Articles 39, 40, 41, 42 & 48(1) and various combinations thereof. For a discussion on possible constitutional bases for peacekeeping operations, see *supra* note 20.

is generally acknowledged, even if the precise source of that legality cannot be agreed upon. On this point, however, it is worth noting that peacekeeping operations have been described as falling conceptually between Chapter VI and Chapter VII of the Charter and, accordingly, have been referred to as Chapter "Six and a Half" operations.[30] This is due to the fact that peacekeeping operations have traditionally involved the use of military personnel (*i.e.* they have gone beyond a purely diplomatic settlement of disputes outlined in Chapter VI of the Charter) but not Chapter VII enforcement measures. Although this is a symbolic analysis, it is nonetheless a legal fiction. A peacekeeping operation cannot find its constitutional basis in a non-existent Article of the Charter.

III. THE HISTORY AND DEVELOPMENT OF THE USE OF FORCE BY UNITED NATIONS PEACEKEEPING OPERATIONS

As described above, one of the three main legal principles of peacekeeping is that force is only to be used in self-defense. Indeed, the right of UN peacekeeping operations to exercise force in self-defense is one of the authorized legal categories for the use of force by the United Nations and may be thought of as an 'inherent right' of the peacekeepers.[31] There is considerable practice that supports this view and the right to self-defense has been consistently provided for in the rules of engagement established for each peacekeeping operation since their inception.[32] Evidently, under the rules of engagement, instructions on the use of force in self-defense in a peacekeeping operation may vary considerably from those designed to suit a Chapter VII enforcement operation.[33] This leads one to ask what constitutes self-defense within the

---

30. Dag Hammarskjold, former United Nations Secretary-General, described peacekeeping as being authorized by Chapter "Six and a Half." *See* BLUE HELMETS II, *supra* note 7, at 5.

31. Schachter lists six legal categories for the use of force by the United Nations, which he describes as: (1) Armed force as an enforcement measure taken by the Security Council under Chapter VII, particularly Article 42; (2) Collective self-defense in accordance with Article 51; (3) Individual self-defense under Article 51; (4) Enforcement measures under regional arrangements or by regional agencies under Article 53; (5) Peacekeeping forces of the United Nations authorized by the Security Council or General Assembly and deployed in agreement with the States concerned; and (6) Joint action by the five permanent Members pursuant to Article 106 of the Charter. *See* Schachter, *supra* note 5, at 65.

32. When the Security Council authorizes a UN operation to use force, the way in which force may be exercised is set out in the rules of engagement. The rules of engagement "specify the circumstances in which armed force may be used by a military unit and its permissible extent and degree." *See* MCCOUBREY & WHITE, *supra* note 21, at 146.

33. Indeed, the importance of the rules of engagement should not be underestimated. Rowe has stated, "In reality the mandate given by the Security Council is no real indication of how much force has been authorized by the Council for those engaged in enforcing it. Rather, it is the rules of engagement which set out the degree of force that may be

250   DENV. J. INT'L L. & POL'Y   VOL. 27:2

realm of a UN peacekeeping operation? Certainly it differs from its usual legal meaning.[34] The concept of self-defense in the context of peacekeeping evolved over time and in response to the changing needs of peacekeepers in different operations. Initially, a narrow approach was taken: force could only be used in defense of the peacekeeping operation itself and strictly in response to an armed attack ('personal self-defense'). Gradually, a much broader view evolved: force could be used 'in defense of one's mandate.' In other words, force could be used to 'defend' the objects and purposes of the peacekeeping operation. The evolution of self-defense in the context of peacekeeping and the scope of this broader approach is discussed in more detail below.

A. Use of Force in Self-defense ('Personal Self-Defense')

In the first armed UN peacekeeping operation, UNEF 1,[35] peacekeepers were instructed never to initiate the use of force, although they could respond to armed attacks with force and could resist attempts to make them withdraw from their positions.[36] In his report on UNEF I, Dag Hammarskjold wrote:

> [T]he rule is applied that men engaged in the operation may never take the initiative in the use of armed force, but are entitled to respond with force to an attack with arms, including attempts to use force to make them withdraw from positions which they occupy under orders from the Commander . . . The basic element involved is clearly the prohibition against any *initiative in the use of armed force.*[37]

This definition of self-defense was narrow and yet adequate for the UNEF I operation because the UN troops involved in UNEF I were maintaining a cease-fire on a front line between two orderly armed forces. Furthermore, there was only a small civilian population living in the area.[38] Thus, the amount of force which UNEF I was authorized to use was sufficient for the purposes of fulfilling its mandate.

---

used." Peter Rowe, *The United Nations Rules of Engagement and the British Soldier in Bosnia*, INT'L & COMP. L.Q. 946, 947 (1994).

34. Schachter, *supra* note 5, at 84.

35. United Nations Emergency Force I.

36. UNEF I operated from November 1956 - June 1967. Its function was to "secure and supervise the cessation of hostilities, including the withdrawal of the armed forces . . . from Egyptian territory, and after the withdrawal, to serve as a buffer between Egyptian and Israeli forces." UNITED NATIONS, UN PEACEKEEPING BOOKLET 9 (1996) [hereinafter UN PEACEKEEPING BOOKLET].

37. *United Nations Emergency Force, Summary Study of the Experience Derived From the Establishment and Operation of the Force: Report of the Secretary General*, UN GAOR, 13th Sess., Agenda Item 65(c) ¶ 179, U.N. Doc A/3943 (1958) (emphasis added).

38. Marrack Goulding, *The Use of Force by the United Nations*, in MOUNTBATTEN-TATA MEMORIAL LECTURE AT THE UNIVERSITY OF SOUTHAMPTON 8 (1995).

The same was not true of ONUC in the Congo, where circumstances eventually compelled the UN to authorize the peacekeeping operation to use more extensive force.[39] ONUC was deployed in the summer of 1960 to essentially assist the Government of the Congo in carrying out tasks related to the maintenance of law and order. Initially, the establishment of the force was based upon the principles of UNEF I, including the principle that there should be no initiative in the use of armed force by UN troops. This is made clear in the *First Report of the Secretary-General on the Implementation of Security Council Resolution S/4387 of 14 July 1960*[40] in which Hammarskjold reiterated his earlier comments made in the UNEF I Report regarding the limits on the use of force by UN troops. In this report he again emphasized the prohibition of any initiative by UN forces in the use of armed force.[41]

The original mandate of the operation emphasized the restoration of law and order in the Congo.[42] Soon after the deployment of ONUC, opposition and secessionist movements in the Congo brought about disorder and violence and the peacekeeping operation started to face difficulties. It became evident that ONUC could not achieve its objective of halting the civil war whilst it was limited to the use of force within the confines of 'personal self-defense.'[43] If ONUC were to act effectively it would need to be able to exercise a more expanded use of force. Under

---

39. United Nations Operation in the Congo. ONUC operated between July 1960 - June 1964. Its initial function was to "ensure the withdrawal of Belgian forces, to assist the Government in maintaining law and order and to provide technical assistance." Later this function was modified to include "maintaining the territorial integrity and political independence of the Congo, preventing the occurrence of civil war and securing the removal from the Congo of all foreign military, paramilitary and advisory personnel not under the UN command and all mercenaries." UN PEACEKEEPING BOOKLET, *supra* note 36, at 19.

40. *First Report by the Secretary General on the Implementation of Security Council Resolution S/4387 of 14 July 1960, United Nations Emergency Force, Summary Study of the Experienced Derived From the Establishment and Operation of the Force: Report of the Secretary-General*, U.N. SCOR, U.N. Doc. S/4389 (1960).

41. He stated as follows:

> In my initial statement I recalled the rule applied in previous United Nations operations to the effect that the military units would be entitled to act only in self-defence. In amplification of this statement I would like to quote the following passage from the report to which I referred. '[M]en engaged in the operation may never take the initiative in the use of armed force, but are entitled to respond with force to an attack with arms, including attempts to use force to make them withdraw from positions which they occupy under orders from the Commander', acting under the authority of the Security Council and within the scope of its resolution. 'The basic element involved is clearly the prohibition against any *initiative* in the use of armed force.

Id. ¶15 (emphasis in original).

42. S.C. Res. 143, U.N. SCOR, 873d mtg., U.N. Doc. S/4387 (1960).

43. BOWETT, *supra* note 4, at 201.

252   DENV. J. INT'L L. & POL'Y   VOL. 27:2

the circumstances the Security Council revised the mandate of ONUC to enable it to use force as a last resort to prevent civil war in the Congo.[44] It is hard not to view this authorization for the use of force as going beyond self-defense. As Bowett has stated, "[I]t is difficult to avoid the conclusion that the Security Council by this Resolution [S/RES/161(1961)] abandoned a strict reliance on the principle of self-defence."[45] However it is interesting that the Secretary-General continued to express the opinion that troops should only engage in defensive action, or they would risk becoming a party to the conflict.[46] Bowett regards this statement as "clinging to the 'self-defence' concept."[47]

In many ways the UN's experience in the Congo was a premonition of the difficulties that came with the evolution of the more complex second generation of peacekeeping operations. Although it is generally agreed that ONUC was a peacekeeping operation, there is no doubt that it involved some enforcement elements.[48] In the operation's aftermath,

---

44. In Security Council Resolution 161, paragraph 1, the Security Council urged, "that the United Nations take immediately all appropriate measures to prevent the occurrence of civil war in the Congo, including arrangements for cease-fires, the halting of all military operations, the prevention of clashes, and *the use of force*, if necessary, in the last resort." S.C. Res. 161, U.N. SCOR, 942d mtg. ¶ 1, U.N. Doc. S/4741 (1961) (emphasis added). In Security Council Resolution 169, paragraph 4, the Security Council authorized the Secretary-General "to take vigorous action, including *the use of the requisite measure of force*, if necessary, for the immediate apprehension, detention pending legal action and/or deportation of all foreign military and paramilitary personnel and political advisers not under the UN Command, and mercenaries. . ." S.C. Res. 169, U.N. SCOR, 982d mtg. ¶ 4, U.N. Doc. S/5002 (1961) (emphasis added).

45. BOWETT, *supra* note 4, at 201-02.

46. *See Report of the Secretary-General on Certain Steps Taken in Regard to the Implementation of the Security Council Resolution Adopted on 21 February 1961*, U.N. SCOR, 942d mtg., U.N. Doc. S/4752, Annex 7 (1961).

47. BOWETT, *supra* note 4, at 202.

48. There has been dispute about whether or not ONUC was actually a peacekeeping operation because it was couched in language of Chapter VII of the Charter and authorized the use of force. The consensus is that ONUC was not an "enforcement action." This was the determination of the ICJ in the Certain Expenses Case. Certain Expenses of the United Nations Case (Art. 17, Para. 2 of the Charter), 1962 I.C.J. 151, at 177. Certainly, the purposes for which ONUC was created "were essentially different from those for which, at San Francisco, forces used under Article 42 were contemplated." *See* BOWETT, *supra* note 4, at 176. The United Nations force in the Congo was present with the consent of the government of Congo and the measures authorized by the Security Council were specifically aimed at implementing the Security Council peacekeeping mandate. Furthermore, as Higgins points out, "even though the circumstances in which ONUC was permitted to use force was [sic] enlarged, the action was still not a sanction against the Congo[, and] there is ample evidence that the UN still regarded itself as bound by the domestic jurisdiction requirements. . . ." For example, the Article 2(7) restraint operated so that intervention into the internal affairs of a State was not permissible without the consent of that State. 3 HIGGINS, *supra* note 6, at 58. Most commentators express the view that the constitutional basis of ONUC lay in Article 40, Chapter VII of the Charter. This was the view of the Secretary-General and has been described as the "official" view of

and as a result of the UN's experiences in the Congo, the narrow definition of self-defense was revised. It was thought that a broader definition of self-defense would make peacekeeping operations more viable and would enable the United Nations to effectively carry out peacekeeping mandates without the need to resort to 'enforcement measures.' Thus ONUC, while not the definitive peacekeeping operation of the Cold War period due to its expansive use of force, played a notable role in the development of the use of force within the realm of peacekeeping.[49]

B. Use of Force in Defense of One's Mandate

When the UN peacekeeping operation was set up in Cyprus the situation with regards to the use of force in self-defense was more clearly defined by the Secretary-General.[50] In an *Aide-Memoire of the Secretary-General Concerning Some Questions Relating to the Function and Operation of the United Nations Peacekeeping Force in Cyprus, 10 April 1964*[51] the Secretary-General outlined an expanded definition of self-defense. The traditional principles were confirmed (for example, the principle that troops should never take the initiative in the use of armed force) but additional elements were included in the definition.[52]

---

the United Nations. *See* BOWETT, *supra* note 4, at 177; 3 HIGGINS, *supra* note 6, at 54-60; Schachter, *supra* note 5, at 82.

49. Fink has written, "The concept of self-defense, as well as the principles of non-intervention and sovereignty, were loosely defined and greatly modified in the Congo operation." *See* Fink, *supra* note 8, at 15.

50. The United Nations Peace-Keeping Force in Cyprus (UNFICYP) has operated from 1964 to the present. Its initial mandate was to "prevent a recurrence of fighting between Greek Cypriot and Turkish Cypriot communities and to contribute to the maintenance and restoration of law and order and a return to normal conditions." Since 1974 its mandate has been expanded and UNFICYP has "supervised the cease-fire and maintained a buffer zone." UN PEACEKEEPING BOOKLET, *supra* note 36, at 17-18.

51. *Note by the Secretary-General*, U.N. SCOR, U.N. Doc. S/5653 (1964).

52. *Id.* ¶¶ 17(c), 18 (c). The full text of the *Principles of Self-Defence* read as follows:
    16. Troops of UNFICYP shall not take the initiative in the use of armed force. The use of armed force is permissible only in self-defence. The expression "self-defence" includes:
        (a) The defence of United Nations posts, premises and vehicles under armed attack;
        (b) The support of other personnel of UNFICYP under armed attack.
    17. No action is to be taken by the troops of UNFICYP which is likely to bring them in to direct conflict with either community in Cyprus, except in the following circumstances:
        (a) Where members of the Force are compelled to act in self-defence;
        (b) Where the safety of the force or of members of it is in jeopardy;
        (c) Where specific arrangements accepted by both communities have been or in the opinion of the commander on the spot are about to be, violated, thus risking a recurrence of fighting or endangering law and order.
    18. When acting in self-defence, the principle of minimum force shall al-

254   DENV. J. INT'L L. & POL'Y   VOL. 27:2

Thus while troops were not to take the initiative in the use of armed force, they could use force in "self-defense" where:

> specific arrangements accepted by both communities have been or ... are about to be violated, thus risking a recurrence of fighting or endangering law and order ... [or where there were] attempts by force to prevent them from carrying out their responsibilities as ordered by their commanders.[53]

The most significant expansion to be noted here, and one that definitively moves way from the idea that self-defense only includes the defense of the peacekeeping force itself, is the premise that peacekeepers could use force in response to attempts by force to prevent them from carrying out their responsibilities or where agreements agreed to by both sides were not honored. Interestingly, it seems that force could even be used in 'anticipatory self-defense' where such agreements were about to be violated.

This interpretation of self-defense, although expressed more generally, was reapplied in 1973 when UNEF II was established.[54] In the *Report of the Secretary-General on the Implementation of Security Council 340 (1973)*, Kurt Waldheim, the then Secretary-General, wrote

---

ways be applied, and armed force will be used only when all peaceful means of persuasion have failed. The decision as to when force may be used under these circumstances rests with the commander on the spot, whose main concern will be to distinguish between an incident which does not require fire to be opened and those situations in which troops may be authorized to use force. Examples in which troops may be so authorized are:

(a) Attempts by force to compel them to withdraw from a position which they occupy under orders from their commanders, or to infiltrate and envelop such positions as are deemed necessary by their commanders for them to hold, thus jeopardizing their safety;
(b) Attempts by force to disarm them;
(c) Attempts by force to prevent them from carrying out their responsibilities as ordered by their commanders;
(d) Violation by force of United Nations premises and attempts to arrest or abduct United Nations personnel, civil or military.

19. Should it be necessary to resort to the use of arms, advance warning will be given whenever possible. Automatic weapons are not to be used except in extreme emergency and fire will continue only as long as is necessary to achieve its immediate aim.

Id. ¶¶ 16-19.

53. *Id.* ¶¶ 17(c)–18 (c).

54. United Nations Emergency Force II. UNEF II operated from October 1973 to July 1979. Its function was to "supervise the cease-fire between Egyptian and Israeli forces and, following the conclusion of agreements. . . [and] to supervise the redeployment of Egyptian and Israeli forces and to man and control the buffer zones established under those agreements." UN PEACEKEEPING BOOKLET, *supra* note 36, at 10. *See also* Goulding, *supra* note 38, at 9; Adam Roberts, *From San Francisco to Sarajevo: The UN and the Use of Force*, 37 SURVIVAL 7 (1995).

that self-defense included "resistance to attempts by forceful means to prevent it from discharging its duties under the mandate of the Security Council."[55] In other words, self-defense included situations in which peacekeepers needed to use force to fulfil their mandate. This is a significantly broadened definition of self-defense when compared to the definition that applied in UNEF I, and may be regarded as covering all subsequent UN peacekeeping operations.[56] Indeed, Boutros-Ghali made it clear in 1993, that at least at that point in time, "existing rules of engagement allow [United Nations soldiers to open fire] if armed persons attempt by force to prevent them from carrying out their orders."[57]

C. Conclusion

As discussed above, one of the legal principles of peacekeeping is that the use of force is restricted to that used in self-defense. The fact that this is a legal principle which the UN considers to be binding upon itself can be gauged from the way it responded to difficulties encountered whilst operating within this self-imposed limit. Instead of doing away with the principle, it remained, as Schachter has described, the "touchstone" of peacekeeping and the use of force was justified by adopting an expanded and somewhat artificial definition of self-defense.[58] The actual scope of this expanded notion of 'self-defense,' and the extent to which it applies, and has applied, in various peacekeeping operations, is not clear. If self-defense is interpreted broadly to mean 'in defense of one's mandate' in all operations, it would presumably mean that if any operation is hindered (by the use of force) from carrying out any part of its mandate, its inherent right to 'self-defense' entitles it to use force in order to fulfil its duties. The ability of a peacekeeping operation to use force would then largely depend on how broad its mandate was. The broader the mandate, the more occasions in which the peacekeeping operation might find itself not only needing to use force but also legally 'permitted' to do so.

However, interpreting self-defense in this manner, comes perilously close to enforcement measures. Such an approach leads one to ask to what extent force can be used in self-defense to fulfil a mandate and still remain consistent with the principles of consent and impartiality underlying peacekeeping operations? The answer lies in the fact that in practice and for many years, commanders in the field have very rarely

---

55. *Report of the Secretary-General on the Implementation of Security Council Resolution 340 (1973)*, U.N. SCOR ¶ 4(d), U.N. Doc S/11052/Rev. 1 (1973). UNEF II was set up on the basis of Security Council resolution 340 of October 25, 1973.

56. Goulding, *supra* note 38, at 9; Roberts, *supra* note 54, at 14.

57. Boutros Boutros-Ghali, *Empowering the United Nations*, 71 FOREIGN AFF. 89, 91. (1992)

58. Schachter, *supra* note 5, at 84.

applied the expanded definition of self-defense.[59] Instead, negotiation and persuasion have been used. In reality the use of force in the context of peacekeeping is a perilous activity which does not rest easily along side the concepts of consent and impartiality. The reluctance to use force in self-defense by commanders in the field is essentially intended to secure the impartiality of peacekeepers and ensure the continued cooperation of the parties concerned. Thus, while theoretically the concept of self-defense was broadened, in practice the expanded doctrine has remained, at least until more recent times, largely unused.

Clearly, UN peacekeeping operations have an inherent right to use force in self-defense; at least in so far as they have a right to use force to protect themselves and seemingly to defend at least some aspects of their mandate. The issue remains, however, what is the scope of self-defense in the context of peacekeeping? To what degree can force be used in defense of one's mandate? Is the use of force limited to what is necessary and proportionate? Where does anticipatory self-defense fit into the picture? Do some uses of force in 'self-defense' need to be explicitly authorized by the Security Council or risk being considered an illegal use of force? Some of the recent resolutions authorizing the use of force have been couched in terms of "self-defense," indicating that at least in some instances, the Security Council still takes the view that force must be explicitly authorized, even if it is in 'self-defense.' In contrast, there are other resolutions that tend to indicate that no such authorization is necessary. In this regard, the Security Council has been inconsistent, or at least given confusing signals, with respect to the extent to which the use of force by peacekeeping operations is possible. After an examination of recent UN peacekeeping operations, I will discuss some possible answers to the above questions and also reflect on whether or not such a use of force, whilst possibly legitimate, is desirable.

IV. BEYOND SELF-DEFENSE: AN EXAMINATION OF RECENT USES OF FORCE BY UNITED NATIONS PEACEKEEPING OPERATIONS

Since the end of the Cold War the number of peacekeeping operations authorized by the Security Council has outstripped the previous operations not only in number but also in complexity and size.[60] Many of the peacekeeping operations established since 1989 have gone beyond the traditional peacekeeping role of monitoring cease-fires and controlling buffer zones between belligerent States. Although peacekeeping operations continue to carry out such tasks, they have been entrusted additionally with mandates as varied as the monitoring of troop with-

---

59. Roberts, *supra* note 54, at 14.

60. During the Cold War there were 15 peacekeeping operations. Since 1989 there have been 26 established. *See* BLUE HELMETS I, *supra* note 6, at 3.

drawals, elections and human rights violations.[61] Peacekeeping forces have also provided assistance in the resettlement of refugees and displaced persons, the rebuilding of political and administrative structures and the protection of deliveries of humanitarian relief supplies. Certain peacekeeping operations, such as those deployed in Cambodia, Mozambique, and Angola, required an integrated program in which most of the above mentioned tasks were included.[62]

During the Cold War, the concept of self-defense, as elaborated above, remained static and force was not widely used in practice by UN peacekeeping forces.[63] Since then, as peacekeeping itself became more complicated and difficult, peacekeepers have been authorized to use force more liberally and have increasingly resorted to the use of force. Both the authorization and use of force has come about for several reasons: first, due to the number of attacks against civilian and military personnel engaged in peacekeeping operations; secondly, in order to more effectively carry out difficult mandates; and thirdly, due to more complex conflict situations in which peacekeepers are engaged. Given the limited scope of this paper, it is not possible, or desirable, to undertake a detailed examination of all the peacekeeping operations that have taken place since 1989. However, such an analysis is not necessary for the purpose of illustrating the increasing tendency of the Security Council to authorize the use of force by peacekeepers and in so doing to give them more "muscle."[64] In order to illustrate this trend I will give examples of recent Security Council resolutions which explicitly authorize peacekeepers to use force. I will also argue that the use of force may have been implicitly sanctioned in other Security Council resolutions. This can be shown by examining the language of these resolutions and related United Nations reports.

It should be understood that this study is complicated by the fact that in recent times the Security Council has "authorized Member States to use all necessary means to achieve specific goals in operations in Somalia, Rwanda, and Haiti, separate from United Nations peacekeeping missions."[65] This kind of support was also authorized in

---

61. Ratner describes second generation peacekeeping in the following way: (1) Second generation operations aim primarily at assisting a State or group of States in executing an agreed political solution to a conflict; (2) Second generation peacekeeping operations are limited to an exclusively military mandate, but can have a substantial or predominantly nonmilitary mandate and composition; (3) Second generation peacekeeping has complex agendas; (4) The new peacekeeping is as likely to respond to an ostensibly internal conflict as an interstate conflict; (5) Second generation operations involve numerous types of actors; (6) The new peacekeeping is a fluid phenomenon. *See* RATNER, *supra* note 13, at 21-24.

62. *See* BLUE HELMETS I, *supra* note 6.

63. Except in the case of the Congo.

64. Goulding, *supra* note 6, at 461

65. BLUE HELMETS I, *supra* note 6, at 6.

258   DENV. J. INT'L L. & POL'Y   VOL. 27:2

the former Yugoslavia, in the UNPROFOR, UNCRO and UNTAES peacekeeping operations.[66] Such measures, for the purpose of this paper, are characterized as enforcement measures and are not within its scope.[67] Instead, this paper focuses on examples where the peacekeeping force itself was authorized to use force. It is acknowledged, however, that it is becoming harder to distinguish, legally speaking, between peacekeeping and enforcement measures.[68] Indeed, considerable controversy exists in some instances as to how to characterize particular operations. UNOSOM II,[69] for example, is alternatively described as a peacekeeping operation,[70] or as the first "peace-enforcement operation authorized and commanded by the United Nations."[71] This confusion as to characterization is borne in mind in undertaking this analysis.

Finally, it is important to emphasize the common theme that runs through the peacekeeping operations discussed below, as it is this theme which underlies the expanded use of force by peacekeepers. The use of force, whether its specific purpose be to ensure freedom of movement or protect a safe area, is primarily geared towards the ultimate goal of alleviating human suffering. In this respect, I argue, that a significant expansion of the use of force by peacekeepers has occurred. Force, in these instances, has been used for the protection of civilians and the protection of humanitarian activities. This use of force goes beyond self-defense, in even the broader sense of the meaning, because although it might be termed as being in 'defense of a mandate', the mandate now involves the protection of third parties, as distinct from the protection of peacekeepers themselves (albeit in pursuit of their duties). In the context of UNPROFOR, Marrack Goulding has stated that this

---

66. United Nations Protection Force, United Nations Confidence Restoration Operation in Croatia & United Nations Transitional Administration for Eastern Slavonia, Baranja, and Western Sirmium respectively. *See* S.C. Res. 1037, U.N. SCOR, 3619th mtg. ¶ 14, U.N. Doc. S/RES/1037 (1996) (UNTAES); S.C. Res. 981, U.N. SCOR, 3512th mtg. ¶ 6, U.N. Doc. S/RES/981 (1995) (UNCRO); S.C. Res. 836, U.N. SCOR, 3228th mtg. ¶ 10, U.N. Doc. S/RES/836 (1993) (created safe areas which Member States could protect through air power); S.C. Res. 781, U.N. SCOR, 3122d mtg., U.N. Doc. S/RES/781 (1992) *revised by* S.C. Res. 816, U.N. SCOR, 3191st mtg., U.N. Doc. S/RES/816 (1993) (created no-fly zone and gave Member States authority to use all necessary measures to enforce the ban).

67. I use the term "enforcement measures" to encompass measures outlined in Article 42 of the Charter which can be exercised once the Security Council has determined the existence of a threat to the peace, breach of the peace or act of aggression, *i.e.*, a more active and aggressive use of force than that involved in peacekeeping. Thus, enforcement measures are not undertaken with the consent of the State involved (in fact such measures are used 'against' the State) and the use of such force is offensive as opposed to defensive. *See* U.N. CHARTER art. 42.

68. For a discussion on this point see Fink, *supra* note 8.

69. United Nations Operation in Somalia II.

70. UNOSOM II is included in the U.N.'s review of United Nations peace-keaping. *See* BLUE HELMETS I, *supra* note 6.

71. UNITED NATIONS, THE UNITED NATIONS AND SOMALIA 1992-1996 at 43, U.N. Sales No. E.96.I.8 (1996) [hereinafter UNITED NATIONS AND SOMALIA].

use of force, under the "fig leaf of 'self-defence'", was incompatible with the operation's peacekeeping role.[72] It is for this reason that such an expansion of the concept of self-defense should be considered carefully before being adopted.

In the examination below I will trace the development of this broader interpretation of self-defense. I have divided the analysis into three categories: force authorized to deliver humanitarian assistance and relief, force authorized to secure the freedom of movement of UN personnel and force authorized to protect safe areas and protected sites and populations. These are not watertight categories and, as will become evident, there are frequent overlaps between the first two in particular.[73] It is also worth noting that events in the former Yugoslavia dominate this analysis. Indeed, it has been said that the "performance of UNPROFOR in former Yugoslavia will doubtlessly form a prototype for successor peacekeeping forces assigned with a mission that involves the use of force beyond self-defense."[74]

A. Force Authorized to Ensure Delivery of Humanitarian Assistance & Relief: UNOSOM II, UNPROFOR, UNCRO & UNAMIR

The UN's involvement in the Somalia is long and complicated: it consisted of three operations (and phases) being UNOSOM I, UNITAF and UNOSOM II. UNOSOM I can be regarded as essentially a traditional peacekeeping operation that failed primarily because the situation into which in went was not conducive to peacekeeping. UNITAF, a US-led multinational operation, followed UNOSOM. Its mandate, under Chapter VII of the Charter, was to use force to establish a secure environment for humanitarian relief operations.[75] Upon restoration of peace (albeit of a precarious nature) in southern and central Somalia, a second peacekeeping operation, UNOSOM II, took over operational responsibility for the area. This operation is sometimes described as a peacekeeping force, and yet was "deployed without the consent of the parties, [and had] the right to use all necessary measures to carry out its mandate – including the right to the use of force."[76] Such use of force was authorized because UNITAF's task of establishing a secure environment in all of Somalia was "far from complete" when UNOSOM

---

72. Goulding, *supra* note 38. Marrack Goulding is the Under-Secretary-General for Political Affairs of the United Nations.

73. Indeed, Goulding merely divides the new uses of force into two categories: force authorized to protect civilians; and force authorized to protect humanitarian activities. *See id.*

74. Fink, *supra* note 8, at 31.

75. S.C. Res. 794, U.N. SCOR, 3145th mtg., U.N. Doc. S/RES/794 (1992).

76. Serge Lalande, *Somalia: Major Issues for Future UN Peacekeeping*, in NEW DIMENSIONS OF PEACEKEEPING 69, 77 (Daniel Warner ed., 1995).

II took over.[77] In this respect, UNOSOM II must be regarded as an enforcement measure, albeit under the control and command of the United Nations. While, for this reason, UNOSOM II does not truly fit within the scope of this paper, it is worth mentioning the operation because it forged a path for the use of force to deliver humanitarian assistance. The mandate of UNOSOM II was to "take appropriate action, including enforcement measures, to establish throughout Somalia a secure environment for humanitarian assistance."[78] Although UNOSOM II had many other purposes and duties,[79] this was the driving force behind the operation.

This theme has been picked up in subsequent peacekeeping operations. The role of UNPROFOR in delivering humanitarian relief was confirmed in numerous Security Council resolutions.[80] Although the use of force was not explicitly authorized for this purpose in these resolutions, it is interesting to note that the Secretary-General was of the opinion that force could be used. In September 1992 the Secretary-General stated that, *in the context of ensuring the delivery of humanitarian aid and protecting humanitarian convoys,* "self-defence is deemed to include situations in which armed persons attempt by force to prevent United Nations troops from carrying out their mandate."[81] Clearly the Secretary-General was of the opinion that self-defense could include situations involving the protection of third parties. The fact, however, that the operation was later explicitly authorized to use force to secure their freedom of movement in resolution 871 (primarily to en-

---

77. UNITED NATIONS AND SOMALIA, *supra* note 71, at 42.

78. S.C. Res. 794, *supra* note 75. *See also* S.C. Res. 814, U.N. SCOR, 3188th mtg., U.N. Doc. S/RES/814 (1993) (establishing UNOSOM II); BLUE HELMETS I, *supra* note 6, at 722.

79. These duties included, through disarmament and reconciliation, the restoration of peace, stability, law and order. Its main responsibilities included monitoring the cessation of hostilities, preventing resumption of violence, seizing unauthorized small arms, maintaining security at ports, airports and lines of communication required for delivery of humanitarian assistance, continuing mine clearing and assisting in repatriation of refugees in Somalia. *See* S.C. Res. 814, *supra* note 78; *Further Report of the Secretary-General Submitted in Pursuance of Paragraphs 18 and 19 of Resolution 794* (1993), U.N. SCOR, 48th Sess., Addendum 1, U.N. Doc. S/25354/Add.1 (1993); *Further Report of the Secretary-General Submitted in Pursuance of Paragraphs 18 and 19 of Resolution 794* (1993), U.N. SCOR, 48th Sess., Addendum 2, U.N. Doc. S/25354/Add.2 (1993) (proposing that the mandate of UNOSOM II cover the whole country and include enforcement powers under Chapter VII of the Charter).

80. *See* S.C. Res. 776, U.N. SCOR, 47th Sess., 3114th mtg., U.N. Doc. S/RES/776 (1992); S.C. Res. 770, U.N. SCOR, 47th Sess., 3106th mtg., U.N. Doc. S/RES/770 (1992); S.C. Res. 764, U.N. SCOR, 47th Sess., 3093 mtg., U.N. Doc. S/RES/764 (1992); S.C. Res. 761, U.N. SCOR, 3087 mtg., U.N. Doc. S/RES/761 (1992); S.C. Res. 749, U.N. SCOR, 47th Sess., 3066th mtg., U.N. Doc. S/RES/749 (1992); S.C. Res. 743, U.N. SCOR, 47th Sess., 3055th mtg., U.N. Doc. S/RES/743 (1992).

81. *Report of the Secretary-General on the Situation in Bosnia and Herzegovina,* U.N. SCOR, 47th Sess. ¶ 9, U.N. Doc. S/24540 (1992).

sure delivery of humanitarian assistance) seems to indicate that the Security Council did not regard UNPROFOR as being able to use such extensive force without explicit authorization.[82] This interpretation is supported by a later resolution which similarly explicitly authorized the use of force *in self-defense* in the safe areas, in the event of any obstruction in or around the areas which interfered with the freedom of movement of protected humanitarian convoys.[83]

UNCRO's mandate also included "facilitating the delivery of international humanitarian assistance" and other humanitarian tasks.[84] Although the use of force was not explicitly authorized in Resolution 981, the resolution under which UNCRO was established, the operation's mandate included "facilitating the implementation of all relevant Security Council resolutions."[85] In the *Report of the Secretary-General Submitted Pursuant to Paragraph 4 of Security Council Resolution 981 (1995)* the Secretary-General stated clearly that the resolutions referred to in resolution 981 included "those relevant to the functioning of UNCRO (freedom of movement, security, self-defense, including close air support)."[86] This implies that force could be used in 'self-defense' where it was necessary to ensure freedom of movement and the delivery of humanitarian aid. As part of the implementation of UNCRO's mandate was to protect and escort humanitarian convoys,[87] and given that the use of force in self-defense to ensure freedom of movement had previously been explicitly authorized, it is plausible to argue that force could be used in self-defense to protect humanitarian convoys and ensure assistance was delivered.[88]

In Rwanda, the Security Council "recognized" that the United Nations Mission for Rwanda (UNAMIR) might need to take action in self-defense "against persons or groups who threaten[ed] . . . the means of delivery and distribution of humanitarian relief."[89] Interestingly, there was no explicit authorization to use force in this regard and no reference made to Chapter VII. This implies that, in this instance, the Security Council did not believe it was necessary to explicitly authorize such

---

82. See discussion below on the use of force to secure freedom of movement of UN personnel.

83. S.C. Res. 836, *supra* note 66 ¶ 9. See discussion below on the use of force to secure freedom of movement of UN personnel.

84. S.C. Res. 981, *supra* note 66 ¶ 3(c), (e). United Nations Confidence Restoration Operation in Croatia (UNCRO) was one of the three peacekeeping operations which replaced UNPROFOR.

85. *Id.* ¶ 3(c).

86. *Report of the Secretary-General Submitted Pursuant to Paragraph 4 of Security Council Resolution 981 (1995)*, U.N. SCOR, 50th Sess. ¶ 18, U.N. Doc. S/1995/320 (1995).

87. *Id.* ¶ 24(c).

88. S.C. Res. 871, U.N. SCOR, 48th Sess., 3286th mtg., U.N. Doc. S/RES/871 (1993).

89. *See* S.C. Res. 925, U.N. SCOR, 49th Sess., 3388th mtg. ¶ 5, U.N. Doc. S/RES/925 (1994); S.C. Res. 918, U.N. SCOR, 49th Sess., 3377th mtg. ¶ 4, U.N. Doc. S/RES/918 (1994).

a use of force. This interpretation is supported by the *Report of the Secretary-General on the Situation in Rwanda*. In this report it was made clear that UNAMIR was expected to provide security assistance to humanitarian organizations in their programs for distribution of relief supplies.[90] Although the rules of engagement were not to envisage enforcement action, it was acknowledged that UNAMIR might have to take action in self-defense against persons who threatened the means of delivery and the distribution of humanitarian relief.[91] As before, no explicit mention is made of the use of force in this report, however, because 'rules of engagement,' by definition, cover the use force it is clear that forceful measures were contemplated. Furthermore, the Secretary-General was of the opinion that for UNAMIR to successfully execute its mandate it had to be "composed of a credible, *well-armed* and highly mobile force" indicating that the operation had to be suitably armed for such a role.[92]

B. Force Authorized to Secure the Freedom of Movement of UN Personnel: UNPROFOR, UNCRO & UNTAES

Freedom of movement is deemed to be essential to the functioning of all peacekeeping operations and is generally provided for in the Status of Forces Agreements establishing an operation.[93] The right to use force in self-defense to defend one's freedom of movement has existed since ONUC. Bowett has stated that:

> In simple terms, it may be said that ONUC was entitled to assert its freedom of movement and to resort to self-defence against any action constituting a denial of freedom of movement: this would not have meant abandoning the principle, then operative, that ONUC could not take the initiative in military action.[94]

Schachter has likewise recognized that a "significant extension of self-defense resulted from granting the ONUC freedom of movement throughout the country."[95]   UNPROFOR, however, was the first peacekeeping operation to be explicitly authorized to use force in *self-defense* to ensure freedom of movement and some commentators regard this authorization as significantly expanding the concept.[96]

---

90. *Report of the Secretary-General on the Situation in Rwanda*, U.N. SCOR, 49th Sess., ¶ 12, U.N. Doc. S/1994/565 (1994).

91. *Id.* ¶ 15.

92. *Id.* ¶ 16 (emphasis added).

93. Bowett states that "the right to freedom of movement should be acknowledged by the host State as early as possible [and] recognized in the basic agreement, but the details of the right should be worked out in the SOFA." *See* BOWETT, *supra* note 4, at 434.

94. *Id.* at 204.

95. Schachter, *supra* note 5, at 85.

96. Certainly Fink is of the view that "the peacekeeper's mandate to use force for self-defense in Bosnia is greatly expanded by their authority to secure 'free movement,'

What distinguishes the use of force to secure freedom of movement in recent operations from past operations is that recently it has been closely linked to the delivery of humanitarian aid. Not surprisingly then, there is a fair degree of overlap between the force authorized to secure free movement and that authorized to ensure delivery of aid. The main difference between the two is that force here is being used to secure the freedom of movement of UN personnel, as opposed to humanitarian convoys. For example, in order to carry out their humanitarian objectives, UNPROFOR was authorized under Chapter VII of the Charter, "in carrying out its mandate in the Republic of Croatia, *acting in self-defence*, to take the necessary measures, including the use force, to ensure its security and freedom of movement."[97] This new resolution was passed primarily to enable the operation to ensure that humanitarian assistance was provided in compliance with earlier Security Council resolutions.[98] Arguably, this explicit authorization indicates that the Security Council was in some way expanding the operation's original self-defense mandate.[99] The Security Council's determination to ensure the freedom of movement of UN personnel was reaffirmed in many subsequent Security Council resolutions.[100]

The trend allowing peacekeepers to use more forceful measures to secure their freedom of movement in order to deliver humanitarian aid, was implicitly followed in two subsequent former-Yugoslavia operations. In Security Council Resolution 981, in which UNCRO was established,[101] the Security Council reaffirmed its "determination to ensure the security and freedom of movement of the personnel of United Nations [p]eace-keeping operations in the territory of the former Yugoslavia."[102] The peacekeeping operation was established under Chapter VII

---

thereby facilitating the delivery of humanitarian aid." *See* Fink, *supra* note 8, at 37.

97. S.C. Res. 871, *supra* note 88 ¶ 9 (emphasis added). Fink likens the mandate of the peacekeepers in Bosnia to that of the ONUC peacekeepers in the Congo. Fink, *supra* note 8, at 31.

98. S.C. Res. 836, *supra* note 66 ¶ 9.

99. The language of this authorization followed that used in the earlier Security Council Resolution 836, which had authorized peacekeepers to use force in self-defense to ensure their freedom of movement within certain 'safe areas.' See discussion below concerning the authorized use of force to protect 'safe areas' and 'protected sites and populations.'

100. *See generally* S.C. Res. 1026, U.N. SCOR, 3601st mtg., U.N. Doc. S/RES/1026 (1995); S.C. Res. 998, U.N. SCOR, 3543d mtg., U.N. Doc. S/RES/998 (1995); S.C. Res. 987, U.N. SCOR, 3521st mtg., U.N. Doc. S/RES/987 (1995); S.C. Res. 982, U.N. SCOR, 3512th mtg., U.N. Doc. S/RES/982 (1995); S.C. Res. 947, U.N. SCOR, 3434th mtg., U.N. Doc. S/RES/947 (1994); S.C. Res. 941, U.N. SCOR, 3428th mtg., U.N. Doc. S/RES/941 (1994); S.C. Res. 914, U.N. SCOR, 3369th mtg., U.N. Doc. S/RES/914 (1994).

101. United Nations Confidence Restoration Operation in Croatia.

102. S.C. Res. 981, *supra* note 66. This determination was reaffirmed in Security Council Resolutions 990, 994, 1009, and 1025. *See* S.C. Res. 1025, U.N. SCOR, 3600th mtg., U.N. Doc. S/RES/1025 (1995); S.C. Res. 1009, U.N. SCOR, 3563d mtg., U.N. Doc. S/RES/1009 (1995); S.C. Res. 994, U.N. SCOR, 3537th mtg., U.N. Doc. S/RES/994 (1995);

of the Charter. As stated above, in the Secretary's report on the operation he made it clear that the previous resolutions relevant to the functioning of UNCRO applied to the operation. This included resolutions relating to freedom of movement and self-defense.[103] As UNPROFOR had previously been authorized to use force in self-defense to secure freedom of movement in Croatia, there seems to be no reason why UNCRO would not also be covered by this authorization.

The operation that took over from UNCRO, UNTAES, was established under Security Council Resolution 1037.[104] In this resolution the Security Council again stated that it was "determined to ensure the security and freedom of movement of the personnel of the United Nations peace-keeping operation in the Republic of Croatia."[105] As with UNCRO, the peacekeeping operation was established under Chapter VII of the Charter. Although the use of force is not explicitly authorized in this operation it was made clear by the Secretary-General in his *Report Pursuant to Security Council Resolution 1025 (1995)*, that the operation implemented should be able to use force, at least in self-defense. He stated, in advising the UN on the type of force to be implemented, that:

> The force deployed must. . . have a mandate under Chapter VII of the Charter, must have the capacity to take the necessary action to maintain peace and security, must be sufficiently credible to deter attack from any side and must be capable of defending itself. Anything less than a well-armed division-sized force would only risk repeating the failures of the recent past.[106]

It is not clear what the scope of this use of force is and whether or to what extent it included the use of force to ensure freedom of movement. The absence of an explicit authorization allowing force to be used in this manner indicates, however, that unlike the UNPROFOR and UNCRO operations, the scope of the right to self-defense with regards to UNCRO should be interpreted more narrowly. There does not appear to be any reason, however, why force could not be used to secure movement required to carry out its mandated tasks, such as facilitating the return of refugees.[107]

S.C. Res. 990, U.N. SCOR, 3527th mtg., U.N. Doc. S/RES/990 (1995).

103. *Report of the Secretary-General Submitted Pursuant to Paragraph 4 of Security Council Resolution 981* (1995), *supra* note 86 ¶18.

104. United Nations Transitional Administration for Eastern Slavonia, Baranja and Western Sirmium.

105. S.C. Res. 1037, *supra* note 66.

106. *Report of the Secretary-General Pursuant to Security Council Resolution 1025*, U.N. SCOR ¶ 22, U.N. Doc. S/1995/1028 (1995).

107. S.C. Res. 1037, *supra* note 66 ¶ 11(d).

C. *Force Authorized to Protect 'Safe Areas' & 'Protected Sites & Populations:' UNPROFOR & UNAMIR*

In 1993, the critical situation in Bosnia and Herzegovina led the Security Council to adopt two resolutions under Chapter VII creating six 'safe areas' primarily aimed at protecting the civilian populations in those areas. Under Security Council Resolution 836 of 4 June 1993, the Security Council decided to ensure full respect for these areas.[108] For this purpose the Council extended the mandate of UNPROFOR to enable it to deter attacks made against the areas. It further authorized UNPROFOR:

> *[A]cting in self-defence,* to take the necessary measures, including the use of force, in reply to bombardments against the safe areas, in reply to bombardments against the safe areas by any of the parties or to armed incursion into them or in the event of any deliberate obstruction in or around those areas to the freedom of movement of UNPROFOR or of protected humanitarian convoys.[109]

The Security Council also authorized Member States, acting nationally or through regional organizations or arrangements, to take through the use of air power in and around the safe areas and in close coordination with the Secretary-General and UNPROFOR, all necessary measures to support UNPROFOR in the performance of its mandate.[110] Subsequently NATO enforced the use of air power authorized by the Security Council for "close air support" to protect UNPROFOR personnel and for "air strikes" to enforce respect for the safe areas. However, it is clear that UNPROFOR, in its own right as a peacekeeping operation, was authorized to use force in self-defense.

A parallel can be drawn in Rwanda where 'protected sites' were to be established, patrolled and monitored by UNAMIR. In Resolution 918, the Security Council recognized that "UNAMIR may be required to take action in self-defence against persons or groups who threaten *protected sites and populations.*"[111] Interestingly, as described above, no reference is made to Chapter VII or the use of force in this context. It is possible to argue that the "action" described does not include the use of force, however, this seems unlikely. More likely is that the Security Council did not believe it was required to explicitly authorize such a use of force. As discussed above, support for this interpretation can be

---

108. Established under Security Council Resolutionw 819 and 824. *See* S.C. Res. 824, U.N. SCOR, 3208th mtg., U.N. Doc. S/RES/824 (1993); S.C. Res. 819, U.N.SCOR, 3199th mtg., U.N. Doc. S/RES/ 819 (1993).

109. S.C. Res. 836, *supra* note 66 ¶ 9 (emphasis added).

110. *Id.* ¶ 10.

111. *See* S.C. Res. 918, *supra* note 66 ¶ 4; S.C. Res. 925, *supra* note 89 ¶ 5 (emphasis added).

found in the Secretary-General's report on Rwanda.[112] He stated that the rules of engagement would not cover enforcement measures, but acknowledged that UNAMIR might have to take action in self-defense to protect sites and populations.[113] There is no reason why the use of force would not be included in this "action."

Later, in a letter from the Secretary-General addressed to the President of the Security Council, in which he reports on the breakdown of the peace process in Rwanda,[114] the Secretary-General recommends that a French-commanded multinational operation take place in Rwanda under Chapter VII of the Charter. Interestingly, in this letter he states that:

> [I]t would be necessary for it to request the Governments concerned to commit themselves to maintain their troops in Rwanda until UNAMIR is brought up to the necessary strength to take over from the multinational force and the latter has created conditions in which a *peace-keeping force operating under Chapter VI of the Charter* would have the capacity to carry out its mandate.[115]

This indicates clearly that the Secretary-General did not regard any use of force in self-defense by UNAMIR as requiring authorization under Chapter VII of the UN Charter. In fact he seems to regard UNAMIR as an operation falling squarely within Chapter VI of the Charter.

D. Conclusion

As discussed above, there is clear evidence that 'self-defense' has been, or is in the process of being, expanded to include the defense of third parties: namely, civilian populations. and humanitarian convoys. Force has also been authorized to ensure the freedom of movement of UN personnel. Although on its face this does not appear to be an expansion of the concept of self-defense, the purpose for which such force is authorized in fact brings this use of force within the rubric of protecting humanitarian activities, and thus indirectly third parties. This expanded use of force can be traced from the explicit authorizations for the use of force in self-defense in UNPROFOR, to the implicit acknowledgment that such force may be used in self-defense in UNAMIR. It is not clear, with regards to future operations, what kind of authorization or acknowledgement would be required (if any) to enable an operation to legitimately use force in this manner.

---

112. *Report of the Secretary-General on the Situation in Rwanda*, *supra* note 90.
113. *Id.* ¶ 15.
114. *Letter Dated 19 June From the Secretary-General Addressed to the President of the Security Council*, U.N. SCOR, U.N. Doc. S/1994/728 (1994).
115. *Id.* ¶ 12 (emphasis added).

It is true that the uses of force outlined above can all be described as being in 'defense of a mandate'. The use of force to secure freedom of movement was to enable humanitarian aid to be delivered,[116] the use of force to protect safe areas was to enable the civilian population to be protected,[117] and the use of force to protect humanitarian convoys fulfilled, in an even more direct way, the mandate to provide humanitarian relief.[118] Indeed, it is not clear why the Security Council regarded it as necessary to explicitly authorize the use of such force in 'self-defense' in the first place, given that such force would have presumably could have come within the already established inherent right to 'defend one's mandate.' Whether the Security Council did so because it felt legally bound to, or whether it did so merely because it wanted to make it unequivocally clear that peacekeeping operations could use such force, is not evident. France, for example, was of the opinion that bringing the UNPROFOR operation under Chapter VII, was in itself enough to strengthen the peacekeeping's operation traditional right to self-defense, without the need for explicit authorization.[119]

Ultimately it is not clear on what basis force can and cannot be used by peacekeeping operations. Nor is it clear how far the concept of self-defense can be pushed. At the moment it is apparently limitless, able to encompass even the defense of others so long as a legitimate mandate is being pursued. This, in effect, means that the use of force is dependent on an operation's mandate, not on any clear and fixed rules as to how force may and may not be used. The confusion and vagueness that results from this approach must prevail in all operations where clear authorization for the use of force is not set. The main problem with this is that too much is left to chance. Troops are left to apply force haphazardly, with authority to use that force being drawn, not from a mandate, or any concept of an inherent right to defend third parties, but through guesswork and reading between the lines. This is not a desirable state of affairs: it leads to misunderstandings and possible recriminations. Furthermore, while such use of force may come within the concept of 'defending one's mandate,' that is not to say that it should. There are many implications to allowing a peacekeeping operation to use more forceful measures in carrying out its mandate. Some of these are discussed below.

---

116. In Bosnia-Herzegovina and Croatia for example.
117. In Bosnia-Herzegovina and Rwanda for example.
118. In Somalia, Bosnia-Herzegovina, Croatia, and Rwanda for example.
119. *Provisional Verbatim Record of the Three Thousand One Hundred and Seventy Fourth Meeting*, U.N. SCOR, 3174th mtg., at 13-15, U.N. Doc. S/PV.3174 (1993) (remarks of Ambassador Merimée of France).

268   DENV. J. INT'L L. & POL'Y   VOL. 27:2

V. WHAT ARE THE IMPLICATIONS OF THE EXPANDED USE OF FORCE BY UNITED NATIONS PEACEKEEPING OPERATIONS?

> *Creating this kind of grey area between peace-keeping and peace enforcement can give rise to considerable dangers. In political, legal and military terms, and in terms of the survival of one's own troops, there is all the difference in the world between being deployed with the consent and cooperation of the parties to help them carry out an agreement they have reached and, on the other hand, being deployed without their consent and with powers to use force to compel them to accept the decisions of the Security Council.*[120]

As the above passage indicates, there are many implications involved in having a peacekeeping operation that can exercise a more extensive amount of force than was traditionally the case. The problems that arise have two root causes. First, the use of force is unpredictable because there is no understanding regarding the basis on which force is used by peacekeeping operations or how force can and cannot be used. Secondly, the use of force undermines the fundamental principles of peacekeeping and confuses the concepts of peacekeeping and peace-enforcement. As Fink has stated, the "blurring of peacekeeping 'guiding principles' and peace-enforcement standards for use of force . . . jeopardizes the safety of the peacekeepers and hampers the effectiveness of their mission."[121] Thus there are two issues that need to be dealt with by the international community. First, when and how force is used by peacekeeping operations needs to be clarified. It appears that the United Nations has recognized this need and is currently undertaking the complex project of revising guidelines for rules of engagement for future peacekeeping operations. This is being done in light of the fact that the use of force in peacekeeping operations and 'Chapter VII operations' is no longer distinct and separate. However, these guidelines are unlikely to be completed for quite some time.[122]

Secondly, the international community needs to determine whether it is in fact desirable to 'blur' the notions of peacekeeping and peace-enforcement. Certainly once a peacekeeping operation uses force beyond that required for self-defense, the line between defensive and offensive force becomes harder to distinguish. Indeed, if a peacekeeping operation has a broad mandate, it is possible to argue that any force used is exercised in defense of the operation's purpose. Yet it is not hard to see how far removed this is from acting in strict self-defense.

---

120. Goulding, *supra* note 6, at 461.

121. Fink, *supra* note 8, at 31.

122. I have been given this information by a senior legal officer in the Office of the Legal Counsel, United Nations Secretariat, New York. I was also told that the current model rules of engagement, the mission specific rules of engagement and the revised rules of engagement are confidential.

For example, it is possible to argue that UNOSOM II was a peacekeeping operation acting in defense of its widely drawn mandate, rather than an 'enforcement measure.' Clearly, almost any forceful action taken by a UN operation can be described as a 'peacekeeping operation defending its mandate' if the mandate is wide enough. The danger with this approach is that "once you allow a peacekeeping force to use force in defence of its purposes instead of simply in defence of its personnel, the action becomes an enforcement action."[123] This is even truer if force is used in defense of third parties. Because peacekeeping operations and enforcement actions are so different, the legal significance of merging the two operations should not be underestimated.[124] Some of the problems and implications that have emerged due to the unpredictability and confusion regarding the use of force by peacekeepers are discussed below.

A. Legal Implications

The most fundamental problem with authorizing peacekeepers to use force is that the use of force is not compatible with consent and impartiality. This problem has legal and practical implications. If force is authorized in order to allow peacekeepers to implement part of their mandate, ultimately it tends to jeopardize other parts of the mandate, which rely upon the consent and cooperation of the parties. Although technically such force would only be used to support a peacekeeping mandate under threat, the practical reality is that the use of such force could not be carried out without endangering the peacekeeping operation as a whole. As the Secretary-General put it in his supplement to the *Agenda for Peace*: "To blur the distinction between the two [peacekeeping operations and enforcement measures] can undermine the viability of the peacekeeping operation and endanger its personnel."[125] Ironically, therefore, a mandate designed to protect such personnel under the banner of "self-defense" may ultimately do more harm than good.

Aside from the legal difficulty of distinguishing between peacekeeping and peace-enforcement operations, there are other legal issues which arise in this context. One such issue derives from the need to have a clear legal understanding as to the nature of peacekeeping. Ralph Zacklin, Director and Deputy to the Under-Secretary-General, Office of the Legal Counsel of the United Nations, has explained,

---

123. McCOUBREY & WHITE, *supra* note 21, at 87.

124. Some of the practical implications of merging the two operations are outlined below.

125. *Supplement to An Agenda for Peace: Position Paper of the Secretary-General on the Occassion of the Fiftieth Anniversary of the United Nations*, U.N. GAOR ¶ 35, U.N. Doc. A/50/60 – S/1995/1 (1995).

270   DENV. J. INT'L L. & POL'Y   VOL. 27:2

Insistence on clarifying the nature of meaning of peacekeeping is not merely a lawyer's obsession with clarity and legal definition; it is necessary because the legal character and nature of the operation has a direct bearing on the legal issues which arise and their resolution.[126]

As emphasized in the introduction to this paper, lack of clarity in an operation's mandate will give rise to legal difficulties when drafting peacekeeping agreements between the parties (such as SOFAs) and giving advice on the interpretation and implementation of such agreements. More specifically, with regards to the use of force, if it is not clear what authority there is for the use of force, difficult questions arise about what the acceptable levels and uses of force are. As stated above, it is the rules of engagement that govern the use of force in the field.[127] If the mandate of the Security Council is not clear, then the rules of engagement cannot accurately reflect the degree of force that has been authorized by the Council. The importance of specifying the authority for the use of force in order that it can be articulated in the rules of engagement is crucial to establishing an operation with a clear, purposeful, and attainable mandate.[128]

Other more probing issues arise in this context: for example, can the peacekeepers use force in "anticipatory" self-defense when the use of force against them while carrying out their mandate is foreseeable? Do the customary requirements of necessity and proportionality apply to an expanded form of self-defense in the context of peacekeeping?[129] These questions should not be left unresolved only to be 'answered' by chance through future uses of force in the field. As sound reasons are needed to explain and justify why force may be used in one situation and not in another it is preferable to clarify the instances in which force can be used before, rather than after, the event. Furthermore, it is better to use legal reasoning to justify the use of force, rather than appealing to ad hoc and random arguments in any given situation. Such legal reasoning is more likely to enable a consensus among Member States to develop with regards to the use of force. As the future credibility of the United Nations depends on successful peacekeeping operations the utmost attention must be given to these legal issues, and the sooner the better.

---

126. Ralph Zacklin, *Managing Peacekeeping from a Legal Perspective, in* NEW DIMENSIONS OF PEACEKEEPING 159, 159 (Daniel Warner, ed. 1995).

127. MCCOUBREY & WHITE, *supra* note 21, at 146-47.

128. Fink, *supra* note 8, at 46.

129. Oscar Schachter, *The Right of States to Use Armed Force*, 82 MICH. L. REV. 1620, 1635-38 (1984).

B. *Political and Military Implications*

While expanding the concept of self-defense to include a more offensive use of force may be legitimate and cannot be regarded as illegal or intrinsically 'bad,' such an expansion may lead to great political and military difficulties when conducting operations. This is particularly so if the differences between peacekeeping and peace-enforcement become blurred. Some of these problems are outlined below.[130]

It may be harder to get a host State or States to consent to a peacekeeping operation if the "operation is perceived as liable to be transformed into a peace-enforcement operation against one party which initially accepted the deployment."[131] Thus, peacekeeping may, as a result, become an increasingly ineffective and useless tool of the UN, with peace-enforcement left as the primary measure of resolving conflict in the world. If this were to happen the UN would arguably find itself less able to resolve disputes via conciliatory means.

It may be harder to get States to contribute troops to peacekeeping operations if they may be involved in the use of coercive force. This may be due to constitutional reasons. For example, neutral countries or countries with constitutional limitations on getting involved in foreign military involvement, may find it difficult to reconcile involvement in such a force with their constitutional values or limitations.[132] Alternatively States may be reluctant to contribute troops for political reasons. Clearly, there is a huge political difference between becoming involved in a peacekeeping operation with the consent of a host State and working with the cooperation of the parties as opposed to taking sides in a conflict and imposing Security Council resolutions by the use of force. States will have to pay much greater regard to their domestic and foreign policies before deciding to become involved in operations that may entail forceful measures. This is primarily because a State could only justify risking the lives of its military personnel if it had a significant national interest in the conflict.

It follows then, that in an enforcement operation States with a vested interest in the matter are more likely to get involved than neutral States. Thus, not only are peacekeeping operations that use force less likely to retain the consent and impartiality of the parties (principles they traditionally espoused), but they may no longer attract the neutral States that they want and need for an operation to be viewed as

---

130. *See also* Lalande, *supra* note 76; Connie Peck, *Summary of Colloquium on New Dimensions of Peacekeeping, in* NEW DIMENSIONS OF PEACEKEEPING 181 (Daniel Warner ed., 1995).

131. Lalande, *supra* note 76, at 78.

132. Neutral countries include Austria, Switzerland, Finland or Sweden. Countries with constitutional limitations on foreign military involvement include Japan and Germany.

impartial by the host State. The national make-up of operations may inadvertently aggravate the conflict, where for example it is a dispute based on ethnic or religious grounds.

In military terms there is a vast difference between a peacekeeping operation and peace-enforcement measures. This is particularly true of the military conduct and command structure of the operation and how it is equipped. For example, the way in which force can be used and the rules of engagement vary greatly according to the type of operation that is undertaken. Furthermore, a peacekeeping operation may be authorized to use force but, in reality, not be equipped to do so. Thus if it does try to use force it may leave itself exposed to more forceful attacks to which it cannot reply. Leaving the use of force to Member States who can 'support' the peacekeeping operation using 'all necessary measures' is unlikely to resolve the problem. Peacekeepers are still more likely bear the brunt of any forceful retaliation.[133]

The relations between all the parties in peacekeeping operations, as opposed to the relations in an enforcement operation, are different. In a peacekeeping operation everyone works together in a conciliatory atmosphere of cooperation. In peace-enforcement all parties are adversaries and the mission is in a position of authority. It is not realistic to expect that a peacekeeping operation based on consent and impartiality would be able to retain those qualities if force was used against parties in a conflict. The very basis upon which peacekeeping is founded is undermined by allowing an expansive use of force to take place.

On a more theoretical level, conflicting concepts of peacekeeping and peace-enforcement may "lead to confusion, uncertainty and ambiguity in the minds of policy makers currently designing the shape of their countries' involvement in future peacekeeping operations."[134] For example, policies may be designed which limit a country's involvement in future peacekeeping operations because of concern about what kind of operations are being instigated by the UN. A good example of this is in the U.S. where, in response to the events in Somalia, President Clinton issued a Presidential Decision Directive which severely limited the future role of U.S. troops in peacekeeping operations.[135]

A more ethereal effect of the lack of a clear-cut distinction between a peacekeeping operation and peace-enforcement is that it makes it ex-

---

133. Goulding, *supra* note 38, at 10.

134. Lalande, *supra* note 76, at 80.

135. *See Statement by the Press Secretary on Reforming Multilateral Peace Operations*, 30 WEEKLY COMP. PRES. DOC. 998 (May 5, 1994). The United States will now only participate where there have been grave threats to international peace and security, major disasters which require relief, or gross violations of human rights. U.S. troops would most likely be under U.S. command. *See* Fink, *supra* note 8, at 46; Steven J. Lepper, *The Legal Status of Military Personnel in United Nations Peace Operations: One Delegate's Analysis*, 18 HOUS. J. INT'L L. 359, 366 (1996).

tremely difficult for the press and the general public at large, to comprehend the role, nature and purposes of future UN peacekeeping operations. The importance of this problem should not be underestimated. Public opinion, which is sharply influenced by the press, may be decisive in determining whether action is taken in a humanitarian crisis and in determining whether a State gets involved or not.

VI. CONCLUSION

The erosion of the fundamental principles of peacekeeping occurs when force is authorized to such a degree that it can be used to protect third parties and carry out any part of a broad mandate. Such use of force threatens the basis of successful peacekeeping and does not necessarily lead to better results. While the concept of self-defense has been deemed to include 'defense of one's mandate', the continued expansion of this concept, in order to give peace-keepers even greater enforcement powers, is not a good idea for the legal, political and military reasons described above. It is time for the United Nations to accept that it must "either maintain a neutral role with consent of parties to the conflict in future peacekeeping operations, or be prepared to encounter increasing threats to the safety of its peacekeepers and be ready to exercise a level of force beyond the traditional legal meaning of self-defense."[136] In other words, it must choose between peacekeeping and peace-enforcement as its two major methods of conflict resolution.

However, if recent uses of force (as discussed in this paper) are to be regarded as a legitimate expansion of the concept of self-defense, it is essential that the legal basis for such force and the extent to which it can be used, be definitively clarified. It is in the interest of everyone, the UN, the host and contributing States, the troops who risk their lives, and the public at large, that the extent to which peacekeeping troops may become involved in a conflict is made clear. It is only with this kind of clarification that an extensive use of force by a peacekeeping body will remain, in any sense, palatable with the goals and purposes of peacekeeping. The fundamental principles of peacekeeping were developed and based on sound legal and practical reasoning. They should not be done away with without serious reflection about what the possible consequences might be.

---

136. Fink, *supra* note 8, at 45.

The Legal Principles of Peacekeeping
and the Brahimi Report

[8]

Changing "Peacekeeping" in the New Millennium? – The Recommendations of the Panel on United Nations Peace Operations of August 2000

Dr. Heike Spieker

I. The Background of the Recommendations

Since the first peacekeeping operation in 1948 in Palestine, United Nations peace operations have undergone substantive, maybe even dramatic changes. Though peacekeeping in the strict sense constitutes only a sector of all peace operations conducted by the United Nations, the term is often used referring to any such mission. Today, in order to foster the purposes of the United Nations as set in Article 1 of the UN Charter,[1] i.e. to maintain international peace and security, to develop friendly relations among nations and to take appropriate measures to strengthen universal peace, the United Nations engages in a whole variety of missions, operations and actions. These missions, operations and actions may have different legal bases, different compositions and designs and different mandates and aims. Yet, their common feature is that they are established as a tool to pursue the task of the United Nations to promote and secure international peace and to pursue the founding States' motivation "to save succeeding generations from the scourge of war".[2] According to the recent approach, the term "peace operations" comprises the three principal activities of conflict prevention and peacemaking, peacekeeping and peace-building.[3]

As environments of and challenges to such United Nations peace operations have changed over the last 53 years since the first mission of that kind in 1948,[4] their mandates, designs and institutional backing have been adjusted and the perception by the international community has changed accordingly. It is at the end of the twentieth century that the United Nations have undertaken a major review of context and framework of their operations and committed themselves to a new initiative for the future prospect of United Nations peace operations.

On the background of deficiencies which had been revealed by past experience, the Secretary-General of the United Nations in March 2000 set up a high-level panel in order to evaluate the whole range of United Nations activities in the area of peace and security.[5] The Panel was composed of individuals experienced in various aspects of conflict prevention, peacekeeping and peace-building.[6] Its task has been twofold, i.e. firstly, to assess the shortcomings of the existing system of UN peace operations and, secondly, to make frank, specific and realistic recommendations for change.

II. Problems of the 1990s

With the change of the global political climate by 1990 demands on the United Nations, not only to become active in conflict situations, but to become so effectively and efficiently, were raised. Paralysing the Security Council by exercising the right to veto was less and less accepted, and the international community expected the Security Council and the United Nations to guarantee international peace and security in a truly effective manner. Concrete demands on the United Nations focused on resolving the issues that had led to conflict, i.e. on peacemaking as well as on preserving peace through peacekeeping. In parallel, the United Nations was also expected to engage in conflicts at the earliest possible stage in terms of

International Peacekeeping   July–December 2000   145

Articles

preventive action and to provide assistance and support in peace-building measures such as for example rebuilding institutions and infrastructures.

These new, or at least more concrete expectations on the United Nations were accompanied by two factors which confronted the organization with new challenges: In the 1990s both awareness and concern of the international community with regard to international crises, emergencies and disasters grew considerably. More information on such situations became available and was received with greater interest and attention. Awareness and concern of governments and civil societies were focused both on the political environment as on the humanitarian aspect of conflict situations. The armed conflicts of the second Gulf War and in former Yugoslavia on the one hand opened the door for new activities and new roles of the Security Council and United Nations and on the other hand put the burden of success of such activity on the organization.

This burden moreover was especially challenging due to the fact that the nature of conflict situations had changed or at least that armed conflicts not of an international character had very much became the centre of international concern. Non-international armed conflicts *per se* are very likely to result in chaos and anarchy and thereby rendering more difficult to regulate the situation in any kind. Taking only into account the various internal actors of armed groups, governmental armed forces, internally displaced people and political actors as well as the variety of external actors of international governmental and non-governmental providers of humanitarian assistance, regional organizations, neighbouring states especially when hosting refugees and arms traders amounted to what is referred to as "complex emergencies". These were in particular aggravated in situations where certain structures of the state that

was stricken by the conflict were hardly existent, i.e. in the so-called disintegrating or disintegrated states.

These conditions of complex emergencies and disintegrating states mounted to new challenges to the United Nations because the organization had to respond to these quickly and efficiently on the basis that neither the organization nor in particular the Member States had substantive experience in such a role. Organization and Member States had to establish, consolidate and adapt political conditions, legal frameworks, institutional procedures, logistic structures and financial resources. The political conditions have been characterized by a doubtful interplay of high expectations *vis-à-vis* the United Nations and its organs, and an often doubtful political will of Member States. The legal framework has been centring around the criteria for the lawfulness of peace operations, only to mention the question of the legal basis for peacekeeping of the fourth generation, the use of force beyond self-defence and the mixture of traditional peacekeeping mandates with mandates under Chapter VII of the UN Charter. Practical problems of the logistic structures have focused on the efficiency of peacekeeping procurement, and financial resources have been threatened by hardly sufficient supplies furnished by Member States.

III. Addressing the Challenges of the Future of UN Peace Operations

The Report of the Panel is the most incisive and comprehensive analysis of peace operations ever undertaken by the United Nations. It focuses on conflict prevention and peacemaking, peacekeeping and peace-building as the three principal activities in the framework of UN peace operations. In sum, definition and concept of such peace operations are based on former definitions used by UN institutions and do not differ substantially from those found e.g. in the Agenda for Peace[7] and the Supplement[8]

to it. Both documents understand preventive action or peacemaking as aiming at resolving the issues that have led to conflict, peacekeeping and peace-building as principal UN activities in the context of international peace and security.

Conflict prevention is understood as a long-term approach, addressing the structural sources of conflict and aiming at building a solid foundation for peace. The related peacemaking approach refers to conflicts in progress and seeks to bring such conflicts in progress to a halt by using the tools of diplomacy and mediation. The term peacekeeping comprises a variety of types of missions, ranging from the military surveillance of cease-fire agreements to mixed tasks including civil components such as in particular, election monitoring, and to complex mandates authorizing to implement humanitarian, human rights and humanitarian law issues. Peace-building, finally, defines activities undertaken on the far side of conflict management including rehabilitation and reconstruction measures as, besides others, the reintegration of former combatants into civilian society, the strengthening of the rule of law, the monitoring, investigation of human rights abuses, education in the field of human rights, the provision to technical assistance to democratic development as well as the promotion of conflict resolution and reconciliation techniques.[9]

1. Analysis of Shortcomings and Failures

Analyzing completed and ongoing UN peace operations, the Panel identified shortcomings and failures with respect to prevention and peacemaking, peacekeeping and peace-building, as well as with regard to the Secretariat of the UN, the procurement of peacekeeping missions, the capacities of the United Nations High Commissioner for Refugees and the financial support

Articles

given to UN peace operations by the Member States. Only one particular and concrete, but revealing example for such deficiencies is the experience that very often Security Council Resolutions specify certain troop levels for a specific operation without the actual provision of troops and personnel as well as their equipment having been committed by UN Member States.[10] In more general terms, past UN peace operations have often not been deployed into postconflict situations, but operations have had to try to create such situations.

It is not only in the view of United Nations' critics – including the UN Secretary-General in a less sharp wording[11] – that United Nations' performance in peace operations reveals major deficiencies. For example already in 1995 the lacking political will of one or another of the parties to a conflict to accept assistance and support by the United Nations as well as the provision of deficient financial resources had been perceived as the greatest obstacle to preventive diplomacy and peacemaking.[12]

The Secretary-General of the United Nations, in his assessment of the fall of Srebrenica[13] identified the major mistakes of the UNPROFOR mission for which both United Nations and its Member States were responsible. The effort to keep the peace and to apply the rules of peacekeeping when there was no peace to keep[14] and when none ·of the conditions for the deployment of a peacekeeping mission was met, constituted the cause for the mass slaughter of unarmed victims in the safe areas as did the inadequate reaction of Member States. The international community refrained from decisive and forceful measures and responded to policies of "ethnic cleansing" and attempted genocide by imposing an arms embargo, providing humanitarian assistance and deploying a peacekeeping force.[15] The criteria of non-use of violence and impartiality of a peacekeeping mission which were applied, were "wholly unsuited"[16] to the conflict in Bosnia-Herzegovina.

Both a deficient mandate and deficient equipment have been identified as the major reasons why the United Nations force in Rwanda, UNAMIR, at the time of the genocide had been unable to prevent the disaster.[17] These reasons are inherent in the system of the United Nations.[18] In sum, the "lack of capacity of the United Nations peacekeeping mission in place to deal with the realities of the challenge it was faced with" was qualified as the overriding failure in the activities of UN organs and Member States.[19] In particular, both the mandate of the mission and its implementation were inadequate.

The Agenda for Peace in 1992[20] and the Supplement to it in 1995[21] had already identified evident deficiencies in UN peace operations. The 2000 Report of the Panel summarizes the most devastating analysis one could imagine: "Meeting this challenge [i.e. to save succeeding generations from the scourge of war; introductory paragraph of the Preamble to the Charter of the United Nations] is the most important function of the Organization, (…). Over the last decade, the United Nations has repeatedly failed to meet the challenge; and it can do no better today."[22] The basic reason for this failure is that "too often operations are planned on 'best case assumptions', where 'worst case' outcomes are likely to prevail".[23] Main obstacles to an at least sufficient UN performance were the interrelated gaps between the traditional UN peacekeeping ethos, the reluctance of the international community to use military force, and the striking lack of resources and political commitment.

2. Recommendations for Future Action

The Recommendations of the Panel cover both major aspects of UN peace operations, i.e. politics and strategy, on the one hand, as well as operational and organizational areas, on the other hand. Yet, it is apparent that the main interest does not lie on legal and or political bases of operations, but on

their organization and logistics. The Recommendations emphasize three elements of UN peace operations. The first of these elements is missions' mandates in general and the principle of non-use of force in the framework of peacekeeping missions in particular. The second important issue is the relationship between UN peace operations and rule-of-law elements and the inclusion of such rule-of-law elements in UN missions. The third aspect to which the Panel assigns great importance is the impact of information, information technology and information availability on the success of peace operations.

The Panel's Recommendations strongly focus on the question of how operations are to be equipped and deployed. The if and when of such deployment are not substantially covered, i.e. conditions and requirements for peace activities of the United Nations and the necessary or suitable environment of a deployment are hardly elaborated. The same is true for the appropriateness of various elements of a mission. With respect to addressees, the recommendations given are not restricted to the United Nations and its institutions. At least the same emphasis is being laid on UN Member States as addressees of the Recommendations and as those actors who are to implement them.

a) PREVENTIVE ACTION

In the last decade, United Nations peace operations covered only about one-third of all conflict situations. The demand for more preventive action is thus obvious. According to the Panel, the lack of effective prevention strategies has proved to be the prevalent shortcoming of past UN peace operations. In order to respond to this deficiency it makes three main recommendations: First, the Panel endorsed the recommendations of the Secretary-General contained in particular in the Millennium Report and his appeal to "all who are engaged in conflict prevention and development [to] address these challenges in a more integrated fashion".[24] Addressees of

International Peacekeeping   July–December 2000   147

Articles

this appeal were the United Nations, the Bretton Woods institutions, Governments and civil society organizations. Second, fact-finding missions should be used more frequently.[25] This means that Governments on the one hand will have to set aside their national sovereignty concerns and on the other hand will have to prove their commitment to prevention strategies by investing in political and financial support of such missions. The third recommendation emphasizes the obligation of UN Member States to give "every assistance" to such activities of the United Nations according to Article 2 No. 5[26] of the UN Charter.

Although the evidence of the Panel's postures is hardly to deny, it is also undeniable that one of the major obstacles of effective conflict prevention is the lack of efficient, reliable, "hard" prevention strategies and instruments. Political science and sociology do provide prevention theories and practices that in fact have an impact on the prevention of conflicts in certain situations and under certain conditions. The problem is that – as in traditional diplomacy – one always has to try a whole series of instruments and mechanisms, and yet the result is more than uncertain. The mere application of preventive action is anything but the guarantee that such action will result in success. The sober conclusion is that as essential and crucial conflict prevention may be, as uncertain, dependent on a whole variety of hardly controllable factors and unpredictable is the possible outcome. And yet it should be self-evident that this realization must not prevent the international community from giving conflict prevention the highest priority and must not provide any pretext for not becoming active in conflict prevention.

b) Peacekeeping

Recommendations on future peacekeeping form the most substantive political and legal part of the Panel's approach; the Panel itself refers to this

part as doctrine, strategy and mandates. Identified deficiencies focused on the three criteria for lawfulness of traditional peacekeeping missions and formulated a need for "sufficiently robust" Rules of Engagement. Key issues are peacekeeping mandates, human resources, civil administration and technical aspects of deployments.

aa) Missions' Mandates

The question for peace operation's mandates is the basic legal problem in the context of today's United Nations missions. This is especially due to the fact that as political demands on UN activities raised, the United Nations have tried to fulfil increasing tasks. These tasks include in particular relief-escorts guaranteeing the deliverance of humanitarian assistance and thereby strengthening the safety of relief items and the safety of the personnel, protection of civilian victims of conflict, control of heavy weapons in possession of armed groups and managing civil administration. Given such mandates, their exercise becomes particularly risky in complex environments and they need to be protected by the United Nations.

(1) Consent of the Parties to the Conflict

The basis of all observations of the Panel in this context is the affirmation that the consent of the parties concerned, the impartiality of the mission's conduct and the principle of non-use of force except in cases of self-defence remain the "bedrock principles of peacekeeping".[27] Yet, all three criteria are modified or at least restricted in their practical application. The importance of the criterion of consent is limited in so far as it is stressed that consent may be manipulated or at least only partially consistent with the real interests of the parties concerned.[28] Yet, no direct consequences are drawn from this conclusion. The Recommendations do not clarify if consent once given authorizes the Security Council to

decide upon extensions or enlargements of the initial mandate under certain circumstances or if, in case of denial of consent, this missing consent may be replaced by a decision of another institution. Nor do the Recommendations give any indication as to what might be the yardstick for such replacements.

(2) Impartiality

The criterion of an impartial conduct of UN peace operations has traditionally been understood as acting without adverse distinction, in particular as to nationality, race, religious beliefs, class or political opinions. In other words, impartiality is traditionally understood as basically equal treatment,[29] putting it close to the principle of neutrality.[30] In case one agrees with the finding that one of the major failures of past operations has been not to distinguish between victim and aggressor,[31] it is consistent to redefine the impartiality criterion if not to abandon it. The Panel defined the criterion of impartiality as "adherence to the principles of the Charter and to the mandate that is rooted in those Charter principles".[32] In other words, "impartiality" might lead to partial conduct of the mission when necessitated by aim and objective of the deployment of the mission.

(3) Non-use of Force

The principle of non-use of force beyond self-defence is not directly questioned in the Recommendations. The Report on UN action in Rwanda had clearly questioned the requirement of additional mandates authorizing any use of armed force by peacekeeping troops.[33] Whereas a "robust peacekeeping" or a "peacekeeping of the fourth generation" had been discussed with respect to the lawfulness of a use of force without an additional mandate under Chapter VII of the UN Charter, this problem is now addressed by the Panel in the framework of "robust Rules of Engagement".[34] The Recommendations take peacekeepers' ability

Articles

to carry out their mandates professionally and successfully as the starting point and yardstick for means necessary in order to achieve this goal. From this yardstick they conclude that peacekeepers have to be able to defend themselves, other mission components and the mission's mandate. It is therefore demanded that mandates should specify an operation's authority to use force. If such a specification entails the request for larger forces, better equipped members of these forces and more costly operations, this has to be accepted in order to enable missions to be a "credible deterrent".

The most concrete finding in this context is the commitment of the Panel to use armed force beyond self-defence in specific situations. Basing on the suggested redefinition of the criterion of impartiality, peacekeepers should, in case of violence against civilians, be presumed to be authorized to stop this violence within their means.[35] It is quite remarkable that this presumption of authorization to use armed force beyond self-defence is not limited to member of the armed forces but extended to police forces. The Recommendations are not clear in this respect as to whether in such cases where the situation is escalating and violence is used against civilians by any party to the conflict the Security Council will have to become active and to enlarge a mission's mandate under Chapter VII of the UN Charter. The wording of the Recommendations surely does not exclude this understanding. On the other hand, the emphasis on a presumption of the authorization to use armed force does not make much of a sense if such a presumption would have to be stated by the Security Council before it could become effective. It is more convincing to understand the Recommendations as favouring an inclusion of an authorization to used armed force beyond self-defence in the initial mandate established by the Security Council. The fact that the Recommendations do not use the term "robust mandate" but "robust Rules of Engagement" is of minor importance in this respect. It

takes into account the practical approach of the Panel, giving preference to the rules of engagement directly governing the behaviour of the personnel involved compared to the more indirectly effective mandate included in a Security Council resolution. Supplementary is the request that United Nations operations given a broad and explicit mandate for civilian protection must be given the specific resources needed to carry out that mandate.[36] Self-understood as this may sound, especially the past experience of the fall of Srebrenica[37] has shown how poor reality might be in specific situations.

The question of non-use of force beyond self-defence is one of the few points where the Panel's Recommendations depart from previous approaches on UN peacekeeping by a rather evident way. In 1995 the Secretary-General of the United Nations had still been explicitly strict, stating that "peacekeeping and the use of force (other than in self-defence) should be seen as alternative techniques and not as adjacent points on a continuum, permitting easy transition from one to the other".[38] On the basis of an incompatible "logic"[39] of peacekeeping on the one hand and enforcement on the other hand, the use of military armed force in the framework of the UN operation necessitated an additional mandate. The report on UN action in Rwanda still adhered to this concept when it advised that "specific provisions related to the protection of civilian populations should be included in the mandates of peacekeeping operations wherever appropriate and ensure the necessary resources for such protection".[40] In case the Recommendations in that regard will be accepted and implemented in their strict sense, a use of armed force without an explicit additional mandate will have to be tolerated under certain circumstances.

In sum, the presumption to use armed force in order to stop armed violence against the civilian population is probably the most dramatic change in future

peace operations of the United Nations as indicated by the Recommendations of the Panel – at least in legal terms. If it not only indicates an important change but also a major progress in UN peace operations, remains questionable and will have to be proved in future situations of violence against civilians. It has the undeniable disadvantage of lacking considerably clear criteria for such a presumption and practicable conditions of its application by commanders in the field.

Apart from a partly redefining of the three criteria of lawful peacekeeping, the Panel emphasizes the demand for "clear, credible and achievable" mandates.[41] It thereby combines substantive with management criteria. The recommendation that the Security Council should assure itself that the cease-fire or peace agreement to be implemented meets certain "threshold conditions" as in particular consistency with international human rights standards concerns the mandate of a mission and its contents. The further recommendation that the Council should also see to it that specified tasks and set out timelines are practicable references to management aspects of a mandate. The latter approach is further elaborated in the supplementary recommendation that in deploying a mission the Security Council should leave the authorising resolution in draft form until UN Member States firmly commit troops and other support elements which are deemed to be critical to the mission. Finally in this context, the Security Council is recommended to establish a clear chain of command and a "unity of effort" in every resolution authorizing a peace operation of whatever kind.[42]

bb) Personnel

With regard to the personnel of peacekeeping operations the Recommendations differentiate between military and civilian personnel. Common to all personnel is the suggestion to systematize the method of selecting mission

Articles

leaders and to assemble the entire leadership of a mission at the UN headquarters as early as possible. The principal recommendation concerning military personnel is addressed to the Member States of the United Nations. They are to be encouraged to enter into partnerships with one another to form adequate forces for effective rapid deployment – 'rapid deployment' generally meaning a deployment within 30 days of the adoption of a Security council resolution in traditional situations and within 90 days in complex situations.[43] The second major recommendation is addressed to the Secretariat, recommending as a standard practice to send a team to confirm the preparedness of each potential troop contributor. These teams are to verify that contributors meet the provisions of the memoranda of understanding on the requisite training and equipment requirements, and this prior to any deployment.[44] In case the team finds a potential troop contributor not fulfilling these requirements the contributor may not send its troops. This demand refers to the issue of military personnel, but in substance approaches procurement and management of peacekeeping operations.

Regarding civilian personnel the main recommendations are again addressed to the Member States. They are encouraged to establish a pool of civilian police officers for deployment on short notice. In support of this approach Member States should create regional training partnerships with a view to a common level of preparedness, knowledge and skills in the area of rule-of-law elements in peacekeeping missions. In order to be able to develop civilian police components into "collegial rule of law teams", Member States are to take the same approach with respect to judicial, penal, human rights and other relevant specialists.

cc) Civil Administration

The emphasis on a rule-of-law approach in future UN peace operations is further detailed with regard to a number of specific rule-of-law elements. Particularly identified are the development of an interim criminal code, possibly including regional adaptations, and the establishment of local rule-of-law and local law enforcement capacities. Their feasibility and utility with a view to transitional civil administration mandates should be examined and elaborated.

This recommendation reinforces the trend of 1990s peacekeeping not only to endow missions with certain civil, human rights and humanitarian tasks, but to replace substantial local and regional governmental structures issues by "international governance" within the framework of peacekeeping missions. This trend is supplemented by the rather modern and popular emphasis on law enforcement mechanisms in general and criminal law in particular to support and contribute to the effectiveness of peace operations.

In today's international community, criminal law is widely seen as an effective remedy to guarantee the observance of international rules and regulations by its deterrent effect. The establishment of the International Criminal Tribunals for Former Yugoslavia and Rwanda in 1993 and 1994, the plans of the United Nations to establish an *ad hoc* Tribunal for Sierra Leone,[45] as well as the overwhelming adoption of the Draft Statute for an International Criminal Court in 1998 bear witness of this attitude. While deterrence is one of the undeniable effects of criminal law, both national and international criminal law, one should not ignore the limits of such approach. Although already the mere existence of criminal law and the more so its application contribute to the observance of existing legal rules, the cases where criminal sanctions have actually prevented the violation of laws are few. This is obvious in national law and national legal systems and in international law it is not different. As important rule-of-law elements in general and criminal sanctions in particular are for the effectiveness of civil administration and as crucial as they might be in specific peace operations, their added value should not be over-estimated with respect to future peacekeeping missions of the United Nations.

dd) Technical Aspects of Deployments

The following Recommendations focus on technical aspects of the deployment of an operation. Only the main issues are referred to here. A number of recommendations seem to be at least as a matter of course, if not superfluous. Yet, experience has shown that such issues are often clear and uncontroversial in theory, but hardly implemented in practice.

With respect to the timeframe of deployments, the Panel proposes as a key issue the "rapid and effective deployment capacities". In defining such capacities it differentiates between traditional and complex peacekeeping operations. Traditional operations are to be deployed within 30 days after the adoption of a Security Council resolution, complex ones within 90 days. Concerning logistics support and expenditure management it sounds ridiculous that the preparation of a global logistics support strategy – to enable rapid and effective mission deployment within the timelines and corresponding to planning assumptions – is not self-evident. The UN General Assembly is called upon to decide on the maintenance of at least five mission start-up kits to be stationed in Brindisi whereas the UN Secretariat should undertake a review of the entire procurement policies and procedures. The fact that these matters are the object of Recommendations of the Panel and not a self-evident everyday business is rather embarrassing for nowadays UN peace operations.

c) REFORMS WITHIN UN ORGANS

Taking into account substantive and technical recommendations with respect to peacekeeping operations, the basic demand is addressed to both the United

Articles

Nations and its organs as well as to UN Member States, i.e. to treat Head-quarters' support for peacekeeping as a core activity of the United Nations. A "substantial increase in resources for Headquarters support of peacekeeping operations"[46] is then a necessary and consistent consequence. The same is true for the recommendation to under-take structural adjustments in the Secretariat's Department of Peace-keeping Operations (DPKO)[47] and to establish so-called Integrated Mission Task Forces (IMTFs) as "standard vehicle for mission-specific planning and support".[48]

Apart from the Secretariat the Office of the United Nations High Commissioner for Human Rights is also the addressee of proposals. It is suggested to "sub-stantially enhance" its "field mission planning and preparation capacity".

d) Peace-Building

The Panel's observations on peace-building in past missions qualify peace-building as crucial to the success of peacekeeping operations in general and of operations in complex situations in particular. In that respect, five key issues are identified: All peace operations should have the capacity to make a demonstrable difference in the lives of the people in their mission area and "free and fair" elections should be viewed as part of a broader process of democratization and civil society build-ing, including effective civilian gover-nance and respect for human rights. Moreover, if situations so require, civil-ian police elements of peace operations have to reform, train and restructure local police forces according to international standards for democratic policing and human rights. They need to respond effectively to civil disorder. At least as important as civil police components are human rights components, and human rights issues and provisions have to be disseminated and included in the training programmes of all other com-ponents of peace operations. Finally, disarmament, demobilization and

reintegration of former combatants have been a feature of at least 15 peacekeeping operations in the 1990s and contribute directly to public secu-rity and law and order.[49]

Aiming at a strategy on peace-building in future complex operations the Recommendations promote a "doctrinal shift" in the use of civilian police, other rule-of-law elements and human rights experts. Rule-of-law institutions should be strengthened and respect for human rights in post-conflict environments should be improved.[50] The Recom-mendations further demand to incor-porate demobilization and reintegration programmes already in the first phase of complex situations, in order to facil-itate the rapid disassembly of fighting factions and reduce the likelihood of resumed conflicts. These activities should be based on strengthening the capacities of the United Nations to develop peace-building strategies accordingly.[51] The Executive Com-mittee on peace and Security (ECPS) is to develop a plan for such strategies and for the implementation of pro-grammes supporting those strategies. Support for peace-building activities should be focused in the Secretariat's Department of Political Affairs which should be tasked to build a pilot Peace-building Unit.[52]

f) Information Processing

Considerable emphasis is attached to the problem of gathering, systematizing and implementation of information on conflict potentials. The Secretary-General's assessment of the fall of Srebrenica had already identified a major failure of intelligence sharing as a major source of the desaster.[53] The fail-ure to act was due to both the absence of an intelligence-gathering capacity on the side of the UN Secretariat as well as to the reluctance to share sensitive information with the United Nations on the side of its Member States.[54] A "lack of capacity for intelligence analysis" was also qualified as an important factor contributing to the failure of the United Nations to stop

the genocide in Rwanda[55] and an "effective flow of information needs to be ensured within the UN system".[56]

The Panel's Recommendations are quite detailed and technical on this matter. Essential points within this issue are the need for a "responsibility centre to devise and oversee the imple-mentation of common information technology strategy and training for peace operations",[57] a more extensive use of geographic information systems technology[58] to meet specific informa-tion technology needs of specific mis-sion components such as civilian police and human rights units,[59] and Member States are called on to devote additional resources in mission bud-gets to information technology and public information in order to build effective communication links.[60]

IV. Prospects for a Change

The Recommendations of the Panel were received positively by the Secretary-General who on 21 August 2000 "urged all Member States to join [him] in considering, approving and supporting the implementation of those recommendations".[61] On the one hand, he informed the General Assembly and Security Council on the beginning implementation of the Panel's Recom-mendations. On the other hand, he elab-orated on specific Recommendations and added to these, e.g. in the frame-work of conflict prevention strategies,[62] a consistent peace-building concept,[63] an increased role of rule-of-law and civil administration elements,[64] rapid and effective deployment of missions,[65] human resources management[66] and logistics support management.[67] A major part of the report is the detailed indication where additional financial resources will have to be provided by UN Member States,[68] e.g. in particular in the context of human resources,[69] management of operations[70] and infor-mation technology.[71] The Secretary-General concluded by urging Member States not to hold the implementation of the Recommendations "hostage to the resolution"[72] of a reform of the

International Peacekeeping   July–December 2000   151

Articles

Security Council and the scales of assessment for Member States.

The General Assembly in the United Nations Millennium Declaration[73] resolved, first, "to strengthen respect for the rule of law in international as in national affairs (...)" and, second, "to make the United Nations more effective in maintaining peace and security by giving it the resources and tools it needs for conflict prevention, peaceful resolution of disputes, peacekeeping, post-conflict peace-building and reconstruction." The General Assembly was requested "to consider its recommendations expeditiously".[74]

After having addressed the matter already on 7 September 2000,[75] the Security Council on 13 November 2000 reaffirmed its "determination to strengthen United Nations peacekeeping operations" and stressed that "peacekeeping operations should strictly observe the purposes and principles of the Charter of the United Nations".[76] The Council endorsed a number of Recommendations, partly with minor modifications. These include in particular the Recommendations on rapid deployment of operations,[77] adequate training and equipment of troops and personnel[78] and appropriate consultation mechanisms.[79]

With regard to the question of mandates and rules of engagement, the Secretary-General had stressed that the Panel's Recommendations were not to be understood as to "turn the United Nations into a war-fighting machine or to fundamentally change the principles according to which peacekeepers use force", but constituted practical measures.[80] On that basis the Security Council resolved to "give peacekeeping operations clear, credible and achievable mandates" with a view to assign a "credible deterrent capability".[81] The Council undertook to "ensure that the mandated tasks of peacekeeping operations are appropriate", including *inter alia* the potential need to protect civilians.[82] Concerning the principle of non-use of force beyond self-defence the Council's commitment is less

far-reaching than the Recommendations. It was rather reluctant to accept a 'presumption of authorised use of armed force for the protection of civilians'. It took a more conservative position and emphasized that rules of engagement "should be fully consistent with the legal basis of the operation" and should "clearly set out the circumstances in which force may be used to protect all mission components and personnel, military and civilian". Rules of engagement should not *per se* bear an authorization to use armed force for the sake of protecting civilians but should "support the accomplishment of the mission's mandate".[83] The Council thereby denied an inherent authorization to use force and reinforced the existing legal bases and criteria of lawfulness of United Nations peacekeeping operations. This existing concept requires additional and explicit mandates authorizing the use of armed force, and the Secretary-General was requested to prepare a comprehensive operational doctrine for the military component of operations.[84]

The Security Council emphasized its commitment to the importance of promoting a sustainable development and a democratic society, based on a strong rule of law and civic institutions as well as on adherence to civil, political, economic, social and cultural rights.[85] This commitment is explicitly comprising strategies on the prevention of armed conflicts and the willingness to actively deploy such missions.[86] The need to improve the information gathering and analysis capacity within the Secretariat is also recognized,[87] as well as the necessity to strengthen peace-building capacities and strategies.[88]

In summarizing the Recommendations of the Panel and the reactions of UN organs, it appears that the recent initiative in improving the performance of the United Nations in peace operations concentrates on the manner how missions are structured and managed. Conditions of deployment are not further detailed and elaborated on. From a legal point of view, the retention of

the present doctrine on the (non-)use of force is probably the most important issue in the context of UN peace operations. If and when the Security Council will abandon the traditional concept of additional mandates under Chapter VII of the UN Charter, and follow the direction indicated by the Panel, will be proven by future development in this context. However, the Panel's Recommendations have re-opened the discussion.

*Dr. Heike Spieker**

*International Legal Adviser, German Red Cross; Lecturer in International Law, IFHV, Ruhr-Universität Bochum, Germany

Notes

1. Article 1 Charter of the United Nations The Purposes of the United Nations are:
   1. To maintain international peace and security, and to that end: to take effective collective measure for the prevention and removal of threats to the peace, and for the suppression of acts of aggression or other breaches of the peace, and to bring about by peaceful means, and in conformity with the principles of justice and international law, adjustment or settlement of international disputes or situations which might lead to a breach of the peace;
   2. To develop friendly relations among nations based on respect for the principles of equal rights and self-determination of peoples, and to take other appropriate measures to strengthen universal peace;
   3. To achieve international co-operation in solving international problems of an economic, social, cultural or humanitarian character, and in promoting and encouraging respect for human rights and for fundamental freedoms for all without distinction as to race, sex, language, or religion; and
   4. To be a centre for harmonizing the actions of nations in the attainment of these common ends.
2. Charter of the United Nations, Preamble, para. 1.
3. Report of the Panel on United Nations Peace Operations of August 2000 (further referred to as Report of the Panel), II.A.10.
4. UNTSO United Nations Truce Supervision Organization of June 1948.
5. Report of the Panel, I., para. 2.
6. It was chaired by former Algerian Foreign Minister Lakdhar Brahimi and the Panel's Report is therefore also referred to as the "Brahimi Report".
7. A/47/277, para. 15.
8. A/50/60, paras. 26, 35, 47.
9. Report of the Panel, II.A., paras. 10–14.
10. Report of the Panel, III.C., paras. 102–106.
11. Report of the Secretary-General on the implementation of the Report of the Panel

Articles

on United Nations peace operations of 20 October 2000, A/55/502, I., para. 7(d).

12. Supplement to An Agenda for Peace: Position Paper of the Secretary-General on the Occasion of the Fiftieth Anniversary of the United Nations, A/50/60 – S/1995/1 of 3 January 1995; paras. 27 and 31.

13. Report of the Secretary-General pursuant to General Assembly resolution 53/35, A/54/549 of 15 November 1999.

14. A/54/549, para. 488; 'Knowing that any other course of action would jeopardize the lives of the troops, we tried to create – or imagine – an environment in which the tenets of peacekeeping – agreement between the parties, deployment by consent, and impartiality – could be upheld'.

15. A/54/549, paras. 490 and 491.

16. A/54/549, para. 499.

17. United Nations Secretary-General, Statement on Receiving the Report of the Independent Inquiry into the Actions of the United Nations During the 1994 Genocide in Rwanda of 16 December 1999.

18. Report of the Independent Inquiry into the Actions of the United Nations During the 1994 Genocide in Rwanda of 15 December 1999, I.

19. Report of the Independent Inquiry into the Actions of the United Nations During the 1994 Genocide in Rwanda of 15 December 1999, III.1.; "UNAMIR, (…), was not planned, dimensioned, deployed or instructed in a way which provided for a proactive and assertive role (…)."

20. An Agenda for Peace: Preventive diplomacy, peacemaking and peace-keeping; Report for the Secretary-General pursuant to the statement adopted by the Summit Meeting of the Security Council on 31 January 1992, A/47/277 – S/24111 of 17 June 1992; paras. 47–54.

21. Supplement to An Agenda for Peace: Position Paper of the Secretary-General on the Occasion of the Fiftieth Anniversary of the United Nations, A/50/60 – S/1995/1 of 3 January 1995; paras. 25–56.

22. Report of the Panel, I., para. 1.

23. Report of the Panel, II.B., para. 20, and III.E., para. 51.

24. Report of the Panel, II.C., para. 34(a).

25. Report of the Panel, II.C., para. 34(b).

26. Article 2 Charter of the United Nations The Organization and its Members, in pursuit of the Purposes stated in Article 1, shall act in accordance with the following Principles.
…
5. All Members shall give the United Nations every assistance in any action it takes in accordance with the present Charter, and shall refrain from giving assistance to any state against which the United Nations is taking preventive or enforcement action.

27. Report of the Panel, II.E., para. 48.

28. On examples from past experience of peace operations and international politics *see ibid.*

29. A/RES/46/182 of 19 December 1991.

30. Report of the Independent Inquiry into the Actions of the United Nations During the 1994 Genocide in Rwanda of 15 December 1999, III.3.

31. 'Where one party to a peace agreement clearly is violating its terms, continued equal treatment of all parties by the UN can in the best case result in ineffectiveness and in the worst may amount to complicity with evil.'; Report of the Panel, Executive Summary, Implications for peacekeeping.

32. Report of the Panel, III.E., para. 50.

33. Report of the Independent Inquiry into the Actions of the United Nations During the 1994 Genocide in Rwanda of 15 December 1999, III.19.: 'Whether or not an obligation to protect civilians is explicit in the mandate of a peacekeeping operation, the Rwandan genocide shows that the United Nations must be prepared to respond to the perception and the expectation of protection created by its very presence.'

34. Report of the Panel, III.E., para. 53.

35. Report of the Panel, III.E., paras. 49–51 and 62.

36. Report of the Panel, III.F., para. 63.

37. A/54/549.

38. A/50/60, para. 36; para. 35: 'To blur the distinction between the two can undermine the viability of the peace-keeping operation and endanger its personnel'.

39. A/50/60, para. 35.

40. Report of the Independent Inquiry into the Actions of the United Nations During the 1994 Genocide in Rwanda of 15 December 1999, IV. recommendation No. 5.

41. Report of the Panel, III.F., paras. 56–64.

42. Report of the Panel, III.F., paras. 64.

43. Report of the Panel, III.A., para. 88.

44. Report of the Panel, III.F., para. 63.

45. S/RES/1315 (2000).

46. Report of the Panel, IV.A., para. 197.

47. Report of the Panel, IV.C.1., para. 225; 4. para. 233.

48. Report of the Panel, IV.C.1., para. 218.

49. Report of the Panel, II.D., paras. 37–42.

50. Report of the Panel, II.D., para. 47(b).

51. Report of the Panel, II.D., para. 47(c).

52. Report of the Panel, II.D., para. 47(d).

53. A/54/549, para. 474.

54. A/54/549, para. 486.

55. Report of the Independent Inquiry into the Actions of the United Nations During the 1994 Genocide in Rwanda of 15 December 1999, III. Report of the Independent Inquiry into the Actions of the United Nations During the 1994 Genocide in Rwanda of 15 December 1999, III.9.

56. Report of the Independent Inquiry into the Actions of the United Nations During the 1994 Genocide in Rwanda of 15 December 1999, IV., recommendation No. 8.

57. Report of the Panel, V.A., paras. 247–251.

58. Report of the Panel, V.B., para. 252.

59. Report of the Panel, V.B., para. 257.

60. Report of the Panel, VI., paras. 277–280.

61. Transmittal letter of the Secretary-General of 21 August 2000, A/55/305-S/2000/809.

62. A/55/502, paras. 14–18.

63. A/55/502, paras. 21–26.

64. A/55/502, paras. 27–35.

65. A/55/502, paras. 67 and 68.

66. A/55/502, paras. 69–76; 80; 111.

67. A/55/502, paras. 112–118; 131; 154.

68. A/55/502, paras. 6; 7(h).

69. A/55/502, paras. 7(c), 62.

70. A/55/502, paras. 40, 112 and 113.

71. A/55/502, para. 154.

72. A/55/502, para. 8.

73. A/RES/55/2 of 18 September 2000.

74. A/RES/55/2 of 18 September 2000, para. 9.

75. S/RES/1318 (2000), Annex, II and III.

76. S/RES/1327 (2000), paras. 2 and 3.

77. S/RES/1327 (2000), Annex, I and IV.

78. S/RES/1327 (2000), Annex, I.

79. S/RES/1327 (2000), Annex, I.

80. Transmittal letter of the Secretary-General of 21 August 2000, A/55/305-S/2000/809, para. 7 (e).

81. S/RES/1327 (2000), Annex, I., paras. 1 and 2.

82. S/RES/1327 (2000), Annex,, II., para. 1.

83. S/RES/1327 (2000), Annex,, II., para. 2.

84. S/RES/1327 (2000), Annex,, II., para. 3.

85. S/RES/1327 (2000), Annex, V., paras. 1 and 2.

86. S/RES/1327 (2000), Annex, V., paras. 3–5.

87. S/RES/1327 (2000), Annex,, III.

88. S/RES/1327 (2000), Annex,, VI.

Part IV
Law Applicable to
Peacekeeping Operations

International Humanitarian Law

[9]

UNITED NATIONS MILITARY OPERATIONS AND INTERNATIONAL HUMANITARIAN LAW: WHAT RULES APPLY TO PEACEKEEPERS?

RAY MURPHY*

Since the end of the Cold War, the willingness of the United Nations to pursue its role in the maintenance of international peace and security by the adoption of military solutions has increased significantly. Recent United Nations operations have had more in common with the operation conducted in Korea, or the enforcement measures carried out in the Congo during the 1960s, than with the more traditional peacekeeping forces prevalent during the 1970s and 1980s.[1] This article sets out to examine the applicability and relevance of international humanitarian law (humanitarian law) to all types of military action undertaken by or on behalf of the United Nations.[2]

Owing to the controversy surrounding action by the United Nations Operation in Somalia (UNOSOM), the question of respect for the principles of humanitarian law by United Nations forces has been the subject of controversy and debate.[3] Although the reasons for this turn of events are a source of regret, the actual result in heightened awareness is welcome. The less controversial traditional peacekeeping missions can also involve important issues of humanitarian law, especially when the situation that the United Nations Interim Force in Lebanon (UNIFIL) found itself in

---

* Senior Lecturer, National University of Ireland, Galway and Irish Centre for Human Rights; B.A. (NUI Galway, 1979); LL.B. (NUI Galway, 1981); B.L. (Kings Inns, Dublin, 1984), M.Litt. (Trinity College, Dublin, (1991); Ph.D. (Nottingham, 2001).

[1] For an overview of peacekeeping see M. Bothe, *Peacekeeping* in THE CHARTER OF THE UNITED NATIONS 648 (Bruno Simma, ed., 2nd ed. 2002).

[2] Humanitarian law denotes the whole body of law applicable during armed conflict, often referred to as the law of armed conflict (*jus in bello*). See Christopher Greenwood, *Historical Development and Legal Basis*, in HANDBOOK OF HUMANITARIAN LAW IN ARMED CONFLICTS 8 (Dieter Fleck, ed., 1995).

[3] See for example, SYMPOSIUM ON HUMANITARIAN ACTION AND PEACEKEEPING OPERATIONS REPORT (1994); Martin Meijer, *Notes on the Conference on The United Nations and International Humanitarian Law, Geneva, 19–20 October 1995*, 2(6) INT'L PEACEKEEPING 136, 137 (1995); and *Report on the International Workshop: Towards a Future for Peacekeeping: Perspectives of a new Italian/German Co-operation, Pisa, 17–18 November 1995*, 2(6) INT'L PEACEKEEPING 138 (1995).

after the Israeli invasion of 1982 is considered. One of the major stumbling blocks for peacekeeping troops is that the relevant principles are enshrined in international instruments governing the conduct of combatants engaged in armed conflict of an international or non-international character. To use a military metaphor, the target of these rules is the combatant or participant, not the peacekeeper or observer.

Although originally there was some doubt about the applicability of humanitarian law to United Nations forces, it is now generally accepted that United Nations forces are bound by humanitarian law, whether performing duties of a peacekeeping or enforcement nature.[4] The United Nations has declared its commitment to the application of humanitarian law to peacekeeping operations, but it has consistently taken the position that United Nations forces act on behalf of the international community, and therefore they cannot be considered a "party" to the conflict, nor a "Power" within the meaning of the Geneva Conventions. To accept that peacekeepers were parties to a conflict would at the very least mean a loss of impartiality. The mere presence of United Nations peacekeeping soldiers in an area of conflict or a theatre of war, while performing a humanitarian or diplomatic mission, does not necessarily mean that humanitarian law binds these troops.[5]

The United Nations, as an international organisation, is not in a position to become a party to the Geneva Conventions or Additional Protocols. This would entail binding the Organisation to detailed provisions that are aimed at states, and do not fit the role and function of an international organisation. Notwithstanding its international legal personality, the United Nations is not itself a state and thus it does not possess the juridical or administrative powers to discharge many of the obligations laid down in the Conventions.[6] It also lacks the legal and other structures for dealing

---

[4] Christopher Greenwood, *Scope of Application of Humanitarian Law*, in Fleck, *supra* note 2, pp. 39–49, at p. 46. This is not just a practical necessity, but may arise from obligations of states "to respect and ensure respect" for the Geneva Conventions and Protocols "in all circumstances". See also Brian D. Tittemore, *Belligerents in Blue Helmets: Applying International Humanitarian Law to United Nations Peace Operations*, 33 STAN. J. INT'L L. 61, 107 (1997).

[5] This position has not altered with the Secretary-General's Bulletin on Observance by United Nations forces of international humanitarian law, UN Doc. ST/SGB/1993/3.

[6] *Reparation for Injuries Suffered in the Service of the United Nations*, [1949] ICJ Reports 174. From a formal point of view, the United Nations cannot become a party to the Conventions because their final clauses do not provide for participation of international organisations, such as the United Nations; SYMPOSIUM ON HUMANITARIAN ACTION, *supra* note 3, p. 43. In addition, "[t]he UN, as such, had no judiciary [*sic*] system, no legal basis on which it could try individuals" (B. Miyet, Under-Secretary-General for peacekeeping Operations, quoted in XXXIV (3) UNITED NATIONS CHRONICLE 39 (1997). As

with violations of humanitarian law. Nor does it possess the competence to recognise that an armed conflict invoking the application of the Geneva Conventions exists.[7] However, this does not mean that the conduct of hostilities by United Nations forces will be free from humanitarian constraint or that humanitarian law considerations do not apply.[8]

In addition, another serious obstacle confronting those charged with ensuring compliance with humanitarian law norms is to make the rules establishing such norms accessible and relevant to those most responsible for their implementation, *i.e.*, the soldiers on the ground. The language of the international instruments in question is often obtuse and unintelligible. The principles enshrined in these instruments, when combined with a "dumb down" approach for classroom instruction, are often presented in a half hearted and "touchy feely" way that makes the instructors and principles involved appear out of touch with reality. Best has described the situation as follows:

> It cannot be said that books in this field are lacking. The international law of war ... has become something of a boom industry in the legal realm and raises a regiment of professional experts. The way in which those experts write about it and debate it among themselves, however, is not often directly communicable to all the others who also have pressing interests of their own in the subject and who, some of them, also write and confer increasingly about it, conscious that, beyond the legal experts they may happily have contact, are many from whom they are cut off.[9]

In considering the applicability of humanitarian law to United Nations operations, a number of questions arise for consideration. What international law applies to the conflict or situation in the country where the United Nations force is deployed? What international law regulates the conduct of the United Nations force itself and how is this determined? And what can or should the United Nations force do when it becomes aware that parties in the country where it is deployed are violating applicable international law? (The answer to this question will be dependent in part on the mandate of the force.) The question may also be posed as to whether there is any useful purpose served in applying humanitarian law to peacekeeping and similar forces whose mission is to restore or maintain

---

a result, United Nations soldiers involved in child prostitution while part of the United Nations operation in Mozambique were repatriated.

[7] Susan L. Turley, *Keeping the Peace*, 73 TEX. L. REV. 158 (1994).

[8] It is widely accepted that the "laws of war remain directly relevant to such forces", DOCUMENTS ON THE LAWS OF WAR 721 (Adam Roberts & Richard Guelff, eds., 3rd ed., 2000).

[9] GEOFFREY BEST, WAR AND LAW SINCE 1945 10 (1994). An example of a more accessible read is the A.P.V. ROGERS, FIGHTING IT RIGHT, MODEL MANUAL OF THE LAW OF ARMED CONFLICT FOR ARMED FORCES (1999).

a peaceful environment in a crisis area? And if these principles of law have a role, how can this be evaluated and improved to make it an accepted part of the conduct of all those involved, even if not actually participating in, armed conflict that may be either international and non international in character.

The answer to these questions will determine the standards that peacekeeping forces will be required to uphold in order to comply with the relevant international obligations.[10] There is also the issue of the appropriate use of force and rules of engagement, and in what circumstances could the use of force constitute a grave or other breach of the Geneva Conventions and/or Additional Protocols. These are real problems confronting today's peacekeepers, but especially those participating in the so-called "robust" peacekeeping operations similar to that of the United Nations Operation in Somalia II (UNOSOM II) in Somalia. A failure to comply with applicable humanitarian law could result in a soldier being tried by an appropriate national court, a foreign national court or an international tribunal on criminal charges or for war crimes, irrespective of the categorisation of the conflict as internal or international in character.[11]

I. HUMAN RIGHTS AND HUMANITARIAN LAW

Human rights and humanitarian law have different historical and doctrinal origins.[12] Previously, scholars assumed that in conflict situations, one or other of the regimes was applicable, depending on the categorisation.[13] However, Meron has pointed to a dangerous lacuna that may exist if and when the applicability of both regimes is denied.[14] Although humanitarian

---

[10] See James M. Simpson, Law Applicable to Canadian Forces in Somalia 1992/93, a study prepared for the Commission of Inquiry into the Deployment of Canadian Forces to Somalia, 1997, p. 23.

[11] See Institute of International Law, *The application of international humanitarian law and fundamental human rights, in armed conflicts in which non-state entities are parties*, Fourteenth Commission, Berlin Session 1999, p. 3, (25 August 1999).

[12] See Theodor Meron, *The protection of the human person under human rights and humanitarian law*, 91(1) UNITED NATIONS BULLETIN OF HUMAN RIGHTS 33–45 (1992). See also Louise Doswald-Beck & Sylvain Vite, *International Humanitarian Law and Human Rights Law*, 293 INT'L REV. RED CROSS 94–119 (1993); *Minimum Humanitarian Standards, Report of the Secretary-General*, UN Doc. E/CN.4/1998/8.

[13] See Theodor Meron, *On the Inadequate Reach of Humanitarian and Human Rights Law and the Need for a New Instrument*, 77 AM. J. INT'L L. 580, 602 (1983).

[14] *Ibid.*; see also THEODOR MERON, HUMAN RIGHTS IN INTERNAL STRIFE: THEIR INTERNATIONAL PROTECTION 3–49 (1987); Theodor Meron & Allan Rosas, *A Declaration of Minimum Humanitarian Standards*, 85 AM. J. INT'L L. 375 (1991); *Commission*

law was originally intended to govern situations of armed conflict between states, it has become increasingly important in the regulation of internal armed conflict.[15] Human rights, on the other hand, originated in the intra-state relationship between the government and the governed, and are intended to protect the latter against the former, regardless of nationality.[16] But humanitarian law is also concerned with protecting basic human rights in armed conflict and other situations of violence. Humanitarian law does not just bind state armed groups; other armed groups and individuals belonging to them are also bound by its provisions.[17] The application of such principles in non-international armed conflicts is not linked to the legitimacy of armed groups.[18] The position of the International Committee of the Red Cross (ICRC) is that humanitarian law principles, recognised as part of customary international law, are binding upon all states and all armed forces present in situations of armed conflicts.[19]

In recent years, various Security Council resolutions have called upon "all the parties to the conflict" to respect humanitarian law.[20] The United Nations Secretary-General has also issued a Bulletin to the effect that the fundamental principles and rules of humanitarian law are applicable to United Nations forces when in situations of armed conflict they are actively

---

on *Human Rights, Minimum humanitarian standards – Report of the Sub-Commission on Prevention of Discrimination and Protection of Minorities*, UN Doc. E/CN.4/1998/87.

[15] On the issue of internal and international armed conflict, see *infra*. See also Christopher Greenwood, *supra* note 4, pp. 39–49, and D. Schindler, *The Different Types of Armed Conflicts According to the Geneva Conventions and Protocols*, 163 RECUEIL DES COURS 153–156 (1979).

[16] Theodor Meron, *supra* note 14, p. 29.

[17] See *Armed Conflicts Linked to the Disintegration of State Structures, Preparatory Document for the First Periodical Meeting on International Humanitarian Law*, Geneva: International Committee of the Red Cross, 8 (19–23 January 1998); and Christopher Greenwood, *International Humanitarian Law and United Nations Military Operations*, 1 Y.B. INT'L HUMANITARIAN L. 3–34, esp. 7–9 (1998).

[18] It is the identification of the relevant legal prescription in the given context that is of central concern. See HILAIRE MCCOUBREY & NIGEL WHITE, INTERNATIONAL ORGANIZATIONS AND CIVIL WARS 67 (1995).

[19] Daphna Shraga & Ralph Zacklin, *The Applicability of International Humanitarian Law to United Nations Peacekeeping Operation: Conceptual. Legal and Practical Issues*, in SYMPOSIUM ON HUMANITARIAN ACTION, *supra* note 3, p. 40. See also Frits Kalshoven, *The Undertaking to Respect and Ensure Respect in all Circumstances: From Tiny Seed to Ripening Fruit*, 2 Y.B. INT'L HUMANITARIAN L. 3–66 (1999); and ICRC Resolution XXXVII of the XXth International Red Cross Conference (Vienna, 1965) in THE LAWS OF ARMED CONFLICTS, A COLLECTION OF CONVENTIONS, RESOLUTIONS AND OTHER DOCUMENTS 259 (D. Schindler & J. Toman, eds., 3rd ed., 1988).

[20] For example, see S.C. Res. 814 (1993), para. 13 (Somalia), and S.C. Res. 788 (1992), para. 5 (Liberia).

engaged therein as combatants.[21] However, in situations where that law does not apply, the international accountability of such groups for human rights abuses remains unclear (though such acts would be criminal under domestic criminal law). Since the establishment of the International Criminal Court (ICC), in certain circumstances peacekeepers will be subject to the jurisdiction of the Court.[22]

The International Court of Justice, in the *Advisory Opinion on Nuclear Weapons*, looked at the relationship between humanitarian law and human rights law.[23] The Court affirmed that they are two distinct bodies of law, and that human rights law continues to apply in time of war unless a party has lawfully derogated from it. It went on to state the relevance of humanitarian law:

In principle, the right not arbitrarily to be deprived of one's life applies also in hostilities. The test of what is an arbitrary deprivation of life, however, then falls to be determined by the appropriate *lex specialis*, namely, the law applicable in armed conflict.[24]

The effect of this is that humanitarian law is to be used to interpret a human rights rule, and, conversely in the context of the conduct of hostilities, human rights law may not be interpreted differently from humanitarian law.[25] In this way there has been a significant overlap and convergence in humanitarian and human rights law, and the strict separation of the two is not always conducive to providing the maximum protection to victims.

---

[21] *Supra* note 5.

[22] For a discussion of the ICC and related issues, see *infra*, and also Daryl Robinson & Herman von Hebel, *War Crimes in Internal Conflicts: Article 8 of the ICC Statute*, in 2 Y.B. INT'L HUMANITARIAN L. 193–209 (1999). When the United States threatened to veto the renewal of mandates for UN operations in 2002, the Security Council adopted Resolution 1422 of 12 July 2002, which effectively exempts officials and personnel part of UN authorised or established operations and from a State not a party to the ICC Statute, from the jurisdiction of the ICC for twelve months. This was renewed by Security Council Resolution 1487 of 12 June 2003. Furthermore, article 1 of the Statute of the Special Court for Sierra Leone provides that peacekeepers and related personnel shall be within the primary jurisdiction of the sending State.

[23] *Legality of the Threat or Use of Nuclear Weapons*, [1996] ICJ Reports 226. See generally INTERNATIONAL LAW, THE INTERNATIONAL COURT OF JUSTICE AND NUCLEAR WEAPONS (L. Boisson de Chazournes & P. Sands, eds., 1999); and a number of articles in 316 INT'L REV. RED CROSS (1997), esp. Christopher Greenwood, *The Advisory Opinion on nuclear weapons and the contribution of the International Court of Justice to international humanitarian law*, at pp. 65–75.

[24] *Ibid.*; para. 25

[25] Louise Doswald-Beck, *International humanitarian law and the Advisory Opinion of the International Court of Justice on the legality of the threat or use of nuclear weapons*, 316 INT'L REV. OF THE RED CROSS 35–55, esp. 45 (1997).

Unfortunately, there is now ample evidence that United Nations forces in Somalia did perpetrate or engage in conduct and practices that were contrary to humanitarian law.[26] Human rights are a key issue in guaranteeing consistent and effective peacekeeping.[27] Nothing can be more contradictory that a United Nations force transgressing international humanitarian law standards that have been gradually and painstakingly agreed upon during the last sixty years.

II. LEGAL FRAMEWORK FOR PEACE SUPPORT OPERATIONS

The status of a United Nations or similar force depends on the underlying authority upon which the force is present in the receiving state, and on the nature and mission of the force.[28] Under existing law, a United Nations peacekeeping operation is considered a subsidiary organ of the United Nations, established pursuant to a resolution of the Security Council or General Assembly. As such it enjoys the status, privileges and immunities of the Organisation provided for in article 105 of the Charter of the United Nations, and the United Nations Convention on the Privileges and Immunities of the United Nations of 13 February 1946.[29] The legal framework for United Nations forces is usually made up of the following:

[26] See Dishonoured Legacy, Report of the Commission of Enquiry into the Deployment of Canadian Forces to Somalia (1997), also available at <http://www.dnd. ca.somaliae.htm> (English version); and Africa Rights Report, *Somalia – Human Rights Abuses by the United Nations Forces* (1993) and Mark Huband, THE GUARDIAN, 31 December 1993, p. 6. The Africa Rights report documents a number of grave breaches of the Geneva Conventions by a number of contingents in Somalia. Most disturbing is the conclusion that these were "not cases of undisciplined actions by individual soldiers, but stem from the highest echelons of the command structure" (p. i). Italy and Belgium also established inquiries into the conduct of their respective armed forces in Somalia. See Amnesty International, *AI Concerns in Europe: January–June 1997*, AI Index EUR 01/06/97, p. 1 (1997); and *Italy: A Briefing for the United Nations Committee Against Torture*, AI Index EUR 30/02/99, p. 10 (1995).

[27] Diego Garcia-Sayan, *Human Rights and Peace-Keeping Operations*, 29 U. RICH. L. REV. 41, 45, (1995). This article deals primarily with the United Nations mission to El Salvador (ONUSAL). See also David Forsythe, *Human Rights and International Security: United Nations Field Operations Redux*, in THE ROLE OF THE NATION STATE IN THE 21ST CENTURY 265 (Castermans, van Hoof and Smith, eds., 1998).

[28] See Walter G. Sharp Sr., *Protecting the Avatars of International Peace and Security*, 7 DUKE J. COMP. & INT'L L. 92, 112–43 (1996).

[29] In addition, the Secretary-General endeavours to conclude status of force agreements (SOFAs) with the host state governments. This is not always possible; *e.g.*, none was concluded in Somalia, and it took nearly twenty years to conclude a SOFA in respect of UNIFIL. See generally D. Fleck & M. Saalfeld, *Combining efforts to improve the legal*

160   RAY MURPHY

— The resolution of the Security Council or the General Assembly;
— The status of force agreement between the United Nations and the host state;
— The agreement by exchange of letters between each of the participating states and the United Nations;
— The regulations for the force issued by the Secretary-General.

However, as United Nations forces are more often than not deployed in situations of conflict, determining what situations constitute "conflict" under international law, and the laws governing United Nations and other forces present or participating as combatants in such situations, is a vital issue. Humanitarian law will also provide a certain level of protection to United Nations forces, depending on the degree of involvement and the nature of the conflict.[30]

The norms regulating the conduct of combatants in times of conflict are not only of ancient origin but they are also found in diverse cultures on many continents.[31] This is important when considering the notion of "customary" legal norms in international law, and the concept of "universal jurisdiction" over certain violations of humanitarian law. After the piecemeal development of humanitarian law at the end of the nineteenth century and the start of the twentieth century,[32] the experience of the Second World War made the shortcomings in the legal regulation of this field all too apparent. This realisation lead to the adoption in 1949 of four conventions

---

status of United Nations peacekeeping forces and their effective protection, 1(3) INT'L PEACEKEEPING 82 (1994).

[30] This is outlined by Greenwood, *supra* note 17, pp. 30–31; also see Roberts & Guelff, *supra* note 8, p. 623. Article 8(2)(d)(iii) of the Statute of the International Criminal Court also prohibits attacks on peacekeepers "so long as they are entitled to the protection given to civilians or civilian objects under the international law of armed conflict". See COMMENTARY ON THE ROME STATUE OF THE INTERNATIONAL CRIMINAL COURT 277 (Otto Triffterer, ed., 1999); and the reference document of the International Committee of the Red Cross to assist the Preparatory Commission of the International Criminal Court in its work on the elements of crimes, Droit international humanitaire, 1.3 Cour penale internationale, 1.3.3.4 General points common to the offences under Article 8(2)(e) of the ICC Statute, (1999).

[31] James M. Simpson, Study, *supra* note 10, p. 13. See also Christopher Greenwood, *The Relationship of Ius ad Bellum and Ius in Bello*, 9 REV. INT'L STUDIES, pp. 221–334 (1983); HANS-PETER GASSER, INTERNATIONAL HUMANITARIAN LAW – AN INTRODUCTION (trans. from German by S. Fitzgerald & S. Mutti, Haupt, 1993); S. Nahlik, *A Brief Outline of International Humanitarian Law*, and FRITS KALSHOVEN, CONSTRAINTS ON THE WAGING OF WAR 8 *et seq.* (1987).

[32] In 1899, a treaty was adopted that made the principles of the 1864 treaty applicable to the wounded and shipwrecked at sea. In 1906, the 1864 treaty was revised, and in the following year the 1899 treaty was amended along the same lines. In 1929 a convention on the treatment of prisoners of war was adopted. See Kalshoven, *ibid.*, pp. 9–10.

in which most of Geneva law is now codified.[33] The adoption of the 1949 Conventions, coupled with the well developed body of Hague law, meant that traditional inter-state wars or "armed conflicts" to use the language of the Geneva Conventions, were well-regulated, in theory at least.[34] The phrase "armed conflict" was employed to make it clear that the Conventions applied once a conflict between states employing the use of arms had begun, whether or not there had been a formal declaration of war.[35] The Conventions did not provide for the situation where there might be an armed conflict involving the United Nations and a state, or organised groups within a state.

The United Nations system was designed carefully to make war illegal and unnecessary.[36] Nowhere in the United Nations Charter is the concept of war mentioned. If force is used or threatened against the territorial integrity or political independence of any state contrary to the Charter, then there are two possible military options permitted in response, *i.e.*, self-defence and police or enforcement action.[37] However, self-defence under article 51 is only permitted until such time as the Security Council responds and takes the necessary measures to maintain international peace and security.[38] Either response is likely to lead to full-scale conflagration.

---

[33] *Geneva Convention for the Amelioration of the Condition of the Wounded and Sick in Armed Forces in the Field* (1950) 75 UNTS 31; *Geneva Convention for the Amelioration of the Condition of the Wounded, Sick and Shipwrecked Members of the Armed Forces at Sea*, (1950) 75 UNTS 85; *Geneva Convention Relative to the Treatment of Prisoners of War*, (1950) 75 UNTS 135; *Geneva Convention Relative to the Protection of Civilians*, (1950) 75 UNTS 287.

[34] Article 2 common to all four Geneva Conventions of 1949. THE GENEVA CONVENTIONS OF 12 AUGUST 1949 – COMMENTARY: IV GENEVA CONVENTION 20–21 (1958).

[35] See Greenwood, *supra* note 4, pp. 42–43.

[36] T. Franck & F. Patel, *Agora: The Gulf Crisis in International and Foreign Relations Law: United Nations Police Action in Lieu of War: "The Old Order Changeth"*, 85 AM. J. INT'L L. 63 (1991). See also Christopher Greenwood, *The Concept of War in Modern International Law*, 36 INT'L COMP. L. Q. 387 (1987). For general background on the United Nations and humanitarian law, see Christiane Bourloyannis, *The Security Council of the United Nations and the Implementation of International Humanitarian Law*, 20 DENV. J. INT'L L. & POL'Y 335–355 (1992), and George Abi-Saab, *The United Nations and International Humanitarian Law – Conclusions*, Actes du Colloque International de l'Université de Geneve (1996).

[37] The Charter of the United Nations, art. 2(4), prohibits the threat or use of force, while article 51 provides for individual or collective self-defence. See LELAND L. GOODRICH, EDWARD HAMBRO & ANNE P. SIMONS, CHARTER OF THE UNITED NATIONS 43–55, 342–353 (3rd 1969), and Simma, *supra* note 1, pp. 112–136, 788–806, and 701–716.

[38] Charter of the United Nations, art. 39; Goodrich, Hambro & Simons, *ibid.*, pp. 293–302; Simma, *supra* note 1, pp. 788–806.

The system reflects the reality that the advent of the United Nations did not mean an end to war and international conflict. In particular, the old system of wars of self-defence will remain until the system for global collective action and policing becomes a universal reality. Having rendered the concept of the classical "war" redundant, it might have seemed unduly pessimistic for the United Nations to set about regulating that which no longer existed. It was not surprising then that the International Law Commission of the United Nations declined to do so when it came to considering the codification of humanitarian law in 1949. It was believed that if the Commission at the very beginning of its work were to undertake this study, public opinion might interpret its action as showing lack of confidence in the efficiency of the means at the disposal of the United Nations for maintaining peace.[39] In this way, the responsibility to codify and improve the principles of humanitarian law fell upon the International Committee of the Red Cross (ICRC).

None of the existing Geneva Conventions or Additional Protocols addresses the specific issues of United Nations forces, or forces acting on their authority, in situations of armed conflict. It could be said that this situation leaves military forces acting under the control of the United Nations in somewhat of a limbo. However, the *Institut de droit international* has confirmed that the rules of the "law of armed conflict" apply as of right and they must be complied with in every circumstance by United Nations forces engaged in hostilities.[40] If the United Nations is considered the sum of its parts, then it comprises states. In this way a conflict involving the United Nations must also engage individual states acting for or on its behalf. The United Nations is clear that it is capable of being internationally responsible for an internationally wrongful act.[41] While the obligation to comply with the Conventions could be viewed as falling simply on the states concerned, it does not seem correct to allow the Organisation, under whose control and upon whose authority and behalf the states are acting, to evade responsibility.[42] There should be no doubt that an organisation is responsible for the delictual acts committed by that organisation, but not

---

[39] SYDNEY D. BAILEY, PROHIBITIONS AND RESTRAINTS ON WAR 92 (1972).

[40] II *Annuaire de l'Institut* 54 (1971), 466, and 56 (1975), 541. See also Institute of International Law, *supra* note 11, p. 4; and THE LAWS OF ARMED CONFLICTS 903, 907 (D. Schindler & J. Toman, eds., 1988).

[41] See A HANDBOOK ON INTERNATIONAL ORGANIZATIONS 887 (René-Jean Dupuy, ed., 2nd ed., 1998); and Secretary-General's Report on Administrative and Budgetary Aspects of the Financing of United Nations Peacekeeping Operations, UN Doc. A/51/389, reproduced in 37 INT'L LEGAL MATERIALS 702 (1998), para. 4.

[42] See generally C.F. AMERASINGHE, PRINCIPLES OF THE INSTITUTIONAL LAW OF INTERNATIONAL ORGANIZATION 223–248 (1996).

all acts or conduct can be attributable to the organisation. Unlike a state, it must be kept in mind that an international organisation's capacity to act is functional, not sovereign.[43]

III. INTERNATIONAL AND NON-INTERNATIONAL ARMED CONFLICTS

Although it may be argued that the distinction between international and non-international armed conflict has lost much of its significance,[44] it is submitted that this is an overly optimistic assessment. Determining whether a conflict can be characterised as internal or international can still be critically important.[45] This arises from the fact that the rules applicable during internal conflicts remain rudimentary and skeletal compared to those that apply to international conflicts.[46] If a conflict can be regarded as international in character, then the whole *ius in bello* of the Geneva Conventions (more than 400 provisions) apply. However, the protection afforded under common article 3 and Protocol II governing non-international armed conflicts is much more limited in scope. The International Court of Justice decision in the *Nicaragua case* illustrates how far the evaluation of conflict status has shifted from dependence on the classification by the sovereign state alone towards neutral external measurement by international bodies.[47] Distinguishing between international and non-

[43] See Dupuy, *supra* note 41, p. 888.

[44] See D. Schindler, *Significance of the Geneva Conventions for the Contemporary World*, 836 INT'L REV. OF THE RED CROSS 715–729 (1999).

[45] See Theodor Meron, *War Crimes in Yugoslavia and the Development of International Law*, 88 AM. J. INT'L L. 78, 80 (1994); and Christine Byron, *Armed Conflicts: International or Non-International?*, 6 J. CONFLICT AND SECURITY L. 63–90 (2001).

[46] Christopher Greenwood, *supra* note 17, pp. 3, 9; D. Schindler, *The Different Types of Armed Conflicts According to the Geneva Conventions and Protocols*, 163 RECUEIL DES COURS 116–163 (1979). For an overview of international law applicable to armed conflicts to which non-state entities are parties, see Institute of International Law, *supra* note 11, pp. 3–5.

[47] *Military and Paramilitary Activities (Nicaragua v. United States)*, [1986] ICJ Reports 4, 122, esp. paras. 219 and 220. The ICJ contrasted the conflict between the Contras and the Sandinista Government with that between the United States and Nicaragua. The first, as internal, was governed by common article 3 only; the second, as international, fell under the rules governing international armed conflicts. The Court also affirmed that the fundamental general principles of humanitarian law (common article 3, in the opinion of the Court) belong to the body of general international law, in other words, that they apply in all circumstances for the better protection of the victims, regardless of the legal classification of armed conflicts. See Rosemary Abi-Saab, *Humanitarian Law and Internal Conflicts:*

164   RAY MURPHY

international armed conflict in contemporary situations remains difficult,[48] and this is evidenced by the contradictory decisions of the different chambers of the International Criminal Tribunal for the Former Yugoslavia (ICTY) on the nature of the conflict in the former Yugoslavia.[49]

In the *Tadic case*, the ICTY Appeals Chamber ruled that many principles and rules previously considered applicable only in international armed conflict are now applicable in internal armed conflicts, and serious violations of humanitarian law committed within the context of such internal conflicts constitute war crimes.[50] Secondly, on the issue of jurisdiction in the same case, it stated, *inter alia*, that a non-international armed conflict occurs whenever there is "protracted armed violence between governmental authorities and organised armed groups or between such groups within a state".[51] In this way the Appeals Chamber has encouraged the blurring of the distinction between international and non-international armed conflicts as the traditional focus on state sovereignty has shifted toward a human rights approach to international problems.[52] One potential problem with this aspect of the *Tadic* decision is that it could have been interpreted as creating another category of armed conflict, *i.e.*, where protracted armed violence occurs, and a similar line of reasoning was adopted by a Trial Chamber of the International Criminal Tribunal for Rwanda (ICTR) in the *Akayesu case*.[53] Fortunately, more recent decisions of the ICTY have clarified this potential anomaly.[54]

The Evolution of Legal Concern, in ESSAYS IN HONOUR OF F. KALSHOVEN 209–331 (1991).

[48] See generally MARCO SASSOLI & ANTOINE BOUVIER, HOW DOES LAW PROTECT IN WAR 201–217 (1999), and the ICRC reference on the elements of crimes, *supra* note 30.

[49] See Theodor Meron, *The Humanization of Humanitarian Law*, 94 AM. J. INT'L L. 239–278 (2000).

[50] *Prosecutor v. Tadic* (Case no. IT-94-1-AR72), Decision on the Defence Motion for Interlocutory Appeal on Jurisdiction, 2 October 1995, para 70. See Peter Rowe, *The International Criminal Tribunal for Yugoslavia: The Decision of the Appeals Chamber on the Interlocutory Appeal on Jurisdicition in the Tadic Case*, 45 INT'L COMP. L.Q. 691 (1996), and Christopher Greenwood, *International Humanitarian Law and the Tadic Case*, 7 EUR. J. INT'L. L. 265–283, esp. 276 (1996).

[51] *Ibid.*, para. 70. See also Theodor Meron, *Classification of Armed Conflict in the Former Yugoslavia: Nicaragua's Fallout*, 92 AM. J. INT'L L. 236–242, (1998).

[52] The Statute of the ICC has also tended to blur the distinction, see Meron, *supra* note 49, pp. 262 and 275.

[53] *Prosecutor v. Akayesu*, (Case No. ICTR-96-4-T), Judgment, 2 September 1998, para. 619–621. It is noteworthy that the language of Article 8(2)(f) of the Statute of the ICC is similar to that used in the *Tadic decision* and refers to "protracted armed conflict". See Andreas Zimmerman, in Triffterer, *supra* note 30, pp. 284–286.

[54] For example, *Prosecutor v. Tadic* (Case No. IT-94-1-A), Judgment, 15 July 1999, paras. 68–162, esp. 80–97. See also *Prosecutor v. Blaskic* (Case No. IT-95-14), Judgment, 3

In all of these developments the impact of humanitarian law on United Nations forces does not seem to have been given serious consideration.[55] While the intensity and classification of the conflict are fundamental determiners of the application of humanitarian law where United Nations forces are deployed, they can also be an important determiner of United Nations military involvement in intra-state conflicts in the first place. As Somalia and Lebanon show, such conflicts are often not amenable to simple "quick fix" solutions. United Nations forces can find themselves deployed in complex political situations where the international legal framework within which they must operate is anything but clear. Despite claims to the contrary, this is all the more so when it is considered that humanitarian law does not apply to most kinds of United Nations military activities.[56] Recent United Nations operations have involved authorised and mandated operations mounted in situations of conflict where clashes involving local actors or parties and United Nations soldiers were inevitable. These have left casualties on both sides, and they have involved both combatant and non-combatant alike. Often the parties to such conflicts have undergone a sustained period of bitter and bloody conflict. Many combatants are not soldiers of regular armies but militias or groups of armed civilians with little discipline and an ill-defined command structure.[57] Fighters of this nature do not always fit easily into the matrix of humanitarian law combatant status. There is also the vexed question of responsibility for the actions or omissions of United Nations soldiers in the field, and what to do when confronted with human rights abuses on a large scale. In this way, the matter of the applicability of humanitarian law to United Nations forces is of much more than academic interest. It is directly relevant to states contributing contingents, and to the United Nations itself, even if it is not formally a party to the relevant international treaties.

March 2000, paras. 63–72, 75–123, and *Prosecutor* v. *Aleksovski* (Case No. IT-95-14/1-A), Judgment, 24 March 2000, paras. 120–122.

[55] But it is noteworthy that in the Tadic case, *supra* note 50, the Appeals Chamber referred to the finding of the ICJ decision in *Nicaragua* that article 1 of the four Geneva Conventions, *supra* note 33, "lays down an obligation that is incumbent, not only on states, but also on other international entities including the UN" (para. 93).

[56] Peter Rowe, *Maintaining Discipline in United Nations Peace Support Operations: The Legal Quagmire for Military Contingents*, 5 J. CONFLICT & SECURITY L. 45 (2000).

[57] THE BLUE HELMETS – A REVIEW OF UNITED NATIONS PEACEKEEPING 4 (3rd ed., 1996).

166 RAY MURPHY

IV. THE UNITED NATIONS AND THE MAINTENANCE OF INTERNATIONAL PEACE AND SECURITY

It is useful to summarise the role of the United Nations in the maintenance of international peace and security as this is one of the primary purposes of the Organisation, and it has significance for the application of humanitarian law to United Nations operations. The maintenance of international peace and security is one of the primary purposes of the United Nations. Chapters VI and VII of the Charter of the United Nations are significant in this regard, and Chapter VII permits the Security Council to decide on coercive measures or undertake enforcement action against a state or states in response to breaches of the peace or acts of aggression. The importance attached to the Security Council's power to order military measures did not stem from expectations that it would often be necessary to do so.[58] It was thought that the threat of military action would be sufficient to deter aggression and to induce states to comply with measures deemed appropriate by the Security Council to maintain or restore international peace and security. However, the reality is that although the military agreements envisioned under article 43 of the Charter did not materialise, the United Nations has had a significant involvement in military operations of one kind or another since the first major United Nations-authorised operation during the Korean conflict in 1950.

It is important at the outset to make a distinction between peacekeeping and enforcement action. Nonetheless, this distinction can be somewhat blurred in certain instances. This is complicated by the grey area that exists between peacekeeping and so called "peace enforcement". With the end of the Cold War this distinction has become further blurred. Prior to 1990, the United Nations had authorised two enforcement missions, that against North Korea in 1950 and the Congo in 1960 (ONUC).[59] It has since approved a number of major operations with similar characteristics, in Kuwait, Somalia, the former Yugoslavia, Kosovo, East Timor, Albania,[60] the Central African Republic and Sierra Leone. However, some of these

---

[58] Goodrich, Hambro & Simons, *supra* note 37, p. 291.

[59] ONUC amounted to at least *de facto* enforcement action. See Nigel D. White, *The United Nations Charter and Peacekeeping Forces: Constitutional Issues*, in THE UN, PEACE AND FORCE 43, 53 (Michael Pugh, ed., 1996). See *Certain Expenses of the United Nations*, [1962] ICJ Reports 177, where the ICJ said the "the operation did not involve 'preventative or enforcement measures' against any state under Chapter VII".

[60] Though Albania had elements of traditional peacekeeping and peace enforcement combined in one mandate, see Dino Kritsiotis, *Security Council Resolution 1101 (1997) and the Multi-national Protection Force of Operation Alba in Albania*, 12 LEIDEN J. INT'L L. 511–547 (1999).

WHAT RULES APPLY TO PEACEKEEPERS? 167

are United Nations mandated forces, while others are merely authorised "coalitions of the willing".[61]

In addition, since 1985 there has been a significant increase in the number of peacekeeping missions established, with a corresponding increase in the complexity of the mandates. These are often referred to as "second generation" peacekeeping operations.[62] The resolution of internal or domestic conflict has been a dominant feature of recent operations that involved the establishment of democratic governments culminating in the nation building attempted for a time in Somalia. Any interventions by United Nations forces may, intentionally or otherwise, alter the delicate balance of power between the warring parties. The United Nations may then be perceived as not impartial or even hostile.[63] Maintaining impartiality can present peacekeepers with a dilemma, especially when they confront situations in which civilians are victimised, or when United Nations forces are themselves the subject of attack.[64] The question of consent to a United Nations presence is particularly problematic in those situations, and the blue berets involved must be prepared to resort to force rather than be bystanders to large-scale human rights abuses or even genocide. In this way, the continuum from peacekeeping to peacemaking and enforcement can be difficult to track, but when all else fails and the political will exists, the Security Council may resort to the use of force under Chapter VII of the Charter of the United Nations.

United Nations forces can take on many different forms, but the status and nature of a force is important to evaluating the relevance and applicability of humanitarian law principles. The difference between peacekeeping and enforcement action operations is fundamental, but second generation operations, while not constituting enforcement action as originally envisaged under the Charter, possess certain of the characteristics of both types of operations. There is also the problem of distinguishing between United

---

[61] It is best to view the action by NATO forces in Kosovo during 1999 as *sui generis*. See Bruno Simma, *NATO, the United Nations and the Use of Force: Legal Aspects*, 10 EUR. J. INT'L. L. 1–22 (1999); Kai Ambos, *NATO, the United Nations and the Use of Force: Legal Aspects. A comment on Simma and Cassese*, 2 HUMANITÄRES VÖLKERRECHT, DEUTSCHES ROTES KREUZ 114–115 (1999); Antonio Cassese, *Ex iniuria ius oritur: Are We Moving towards International Legitimation of Forcible Humanitarian Countermeasures in the World Community?*, 10 EUR. J. INT'L. L. 23–30 (1999); and C. Guicherd, *International Law and the War in Kosovo*, 41(2) SURVIVAL 19–34 (1999). See also *The Kosovo crisis and international humanitarian law*, 837 INT'L REV. RED CROSS (2000), which the whole edition is devoted to contributions on the topic.

[62] THE BLUE HELMETS, *supra* note 57, p. 5.

[63] Julianne Peck, *The U.N. and the Laws of War: How Can the World's Peacekeepers be Held Accountable*, 21 SYRACUSE J. INT'L L & COM. 283, 288 (1995).

[64] THE BLUE HELMETS, *supra* note 57, p. 5.

Nations mandated operations and those merely authorised to be carried out by "coalitions of the willing". These issues are important in determining the extent, if any, of the application of humanitarian law to United Nations forces. However, the fundamental question regarding the application of humanitarian law remains the existence of an armed conflict. Ultimately, it is the fact of participation in hostilities, not the existence of authority to do so that is significant.[65]

V. PEACE ENFORCEMENT OPERATIONS

In more recent years, when the United Nations has decided to react to international crises but the resources are not available, the Security Council has authorised groups of states to organise "peace enforcement" operations with specific goals in mind. Again, the United States has been to the forefront of these operations in, *inter alia*, Somalia, Haiti and the former Yugoslavia. The operations in question, while not constituting enforcement action as originally envisaged under the Charter, owed much to the half-way house suggested by Boutros-Boutros Ghali in his original *Agenda for Peace* document.[66] In all cases, the relevant resolutions of the Security Council made specific reference to Chapter VII of the Charter. Furthermore, the military action concerned was conducted by states outside their own national borders and in the territory of a foreign country, while being authorised by the United Nations. In this way it could not be said to constitute aggression or the illegal use of force contrary to international law. The military operations were similar to conventional operations involving coalition forces under a complex but essentially unified operational command structure and intended to be governed by the Geneva Conventions and Additional Protocols, and the international law of armed conflict as a whole.[67]

In addition, as discussed above, it is an accepted principle of humanitarian law that it applies in equal measure to all parties involved, irrespective of any other consideration, including the issue of the legality and objective of the resort to the use of force (*ius ad bellum*). There would seem to be broad agreement that humanitarian law norms do apply to United Nations military operations.[68] This view is supported by the terms of the

---

[65] Greenwood, *supra* note 17, p. 11.

[66] UN Doc. A/47/277 – S/24111.

[67] Interviews, United Nations official and senior military officer seconded to United Nations Department of Peacekeeping Operations (DPKO), New York, 1998.

[68] Hilaire McCoubrey, *International Law and National Contingents in United Nations Forces*, 12 INT'L RELATIONS 46 (1992); Greenwood, *supra* note 17, p. 18; Michael Bothe,

relevant Conventions. There is no doctrine of ends and means in the application of humanitarian principles, and the terms of the Geneva Conventions require that "the High Contracting Parties undertake to respect and ensure respect for the present Convention in all circumstances".[69] Not every armed confrontation triggers the application of humanitarian law, but states involved are obliged to ensure its strict implementation once the threshold of "armed conflict" has been reached.

The most contentious missions, both from a legal and political perspective, will probably be those operations where the peace is most precarious. These missions may take place during international or non-international armed conflicts, but in any event the distinction is not crucial to this discussion. Such operations go well beyond traditional peace-keeping precepts and often they slip from peace to conflict and from Chapter VI to Chapter VII of the Charter, even in the course of a single operation. Nevertheless, classifications are needed and standards must be sought.[70] While it is acknowledged that every deployment of troops outside their own territory is subject to international political and legal ramifications, clarification of what these are is needed, especially when the United Nations troops involved are likely to be engaged in hostilities with local actors.

VI. HUMANITARIAN LAW AND UNITED NATIONS OPERATIONS

Bowett has addressed the issue of the application of the law of armed conflict to operations by United Nations forces by examining two preliminary questions: first, what different types of functions a United Nations

---

Peacekeeping, in Bruno Simma, *supra* note 1, p. 648. See also two resolutions adopted by the Institut de Droit International: Resolution on the Conditions of Application of Humanitarian Rules of Armed Conflict to Hostilities in which United Nations Forces may be engaged, adopted in Zagreb in 1971, 54 (II) ANNUAIRE DE L'INSTITUT DE DROIT INTERNATIONAL 465 (1971); and Resolution on the Conditions of Application of Humanitarian Rules of Armed Conflict to Hostilities in which United Nations Forces may be Engaged, adopted in Wiesbaden in 1975, 56 ANNUARE DE L'INSTITUT DE DROIT INTERNATIONAL 540 (1975).

[69] *Geneva Convention for the Amelioration of the Condition of the Wounded and Sick in Armed Forces in the Field*, *supra* note 33, art. 1, and *Protocol Additional to the 1949 Geneva Conventions of 12 August 1949, and Relating to The Protection of Victims of International Armed Conflicts*, (1979) 1125 UNTS 3, preamble.

[70] Toni Pfanner, *Application of International Humanitarian Law and Military Operations Undertaken under the United Nations Charter*, in SYMPOSIUM ON HUMANITARIAN ACTION, *supra* note 3, p. 50.

force may assume, and, second, the question of the different types of command structure that may be adopted for a United Nations force.[71] An analysis of the different types of functions that may be entrusted to United Nations forces suggests that the application of the laws of armed conflict may be relevant to certain types of functions, but not to others. The most fundamental difference to identify in the first instance is that between enforcement action under Chapter VII of the Charter and traditional peace-keeping, though as previously stated, in recent years the distinction is less clear. It is still worthwhile making this initial distinction and dealing in the first instance with enforcement action. Bowett's two questions are also inextricably linked, as the command structure will largely depend on the function of the force.[72] A further complication arises by virtue of the kind of operations conducted under Chapter VII and intended to be enforcement action in nature, despite the failure to conclude the requisite agreements with the United Nations under article 43 of the Charter.[73] The issue of who commands the force, the United Nations or the states concerned, is especially relevant in operations involving "coalitions of the willing".[74]

More significantly, from the point of view of the applicability of human-itarian law, nowhere in Chapter VII, and in article 42 in particular, is "war" mentioned. The Charter refers to "such action by, sea, air or land forces as may be necessary ... [and] may include demonstrations, blockade, and other operations by air, sea or land forces of members of the UN". The obvious implication is that military action taken by the United Nations is not to be regarded as "war", and this was the commonly accepted view of the United Nations action in Korea.[75] Given the intensity of the hostilities during the conflict, this point may seem somewhat esoteric and academic to the ordinary person on the street, or to the soldier acting under United Nations "command".[76] The tendency to view conflicts of this nature as other than war may also confuse the issues somewhat and have its origins in the old just war theory. The problem with this is that it may justify the

---

[71] DAVID W. BOWETT, UNITED NATIONS FORCES 484–485 (1964).

[72] *Ibid.*, pp. 487–488. Bowett identified thee types of command structures: i) command delegated to a State of group of States by the United Nations; ii) command entrusted to an individual appointed by and responsible to the United Nations, but lacking disciplinary authority; iii) command entrusted to an individual appointed by and responsible to the United Nations and having disciplinary authority.

[73] Goodrich, Hambro & Simons, *supra* note 37, pp. 317–326; Simma, *supra* note 1, pp. 760–763.

[74] See Dupuy, *supra* note 41, p. 891.

[75] Bowett, *supra* note 71, p. 53.

[76] See Ray Murphy, *The Legal Framework of United Nations Peacekeeping Forces and the Issue of Command and Control*, 4 J. ARMED CONFLICT L. 41 (1999).

use of violence on a massive scale, and indirectly undermine humanitarian law principles by failing to view those against whom the military action is being taken as equally deserving of their protection.

Writing in 1964, Bowett stated that "there [was] no known case in which the United Nations Command ever claimed exemption from any of the accepted rules of the laws of war, customary or conventional".[77] In fact, there appears to be no record of the United Nations ever claiming that humanitarian law does not apply to operations authorised by or undertaken on behalf of the Organisation. But the policy of the United Nations with regard to the applicability of humanitarian law to forces under its command or operational control is still ambivalent. The end of the Cold War has not brought the realisation of the early optimism associated with that event, and the ambitions for the United Nations and the Security Council, reflected in the Secretary-General's "Agenda for Peace",[78] did not materialise. A more sobering and reflective sequel to this was published a short time later in which the Secretary-General acknowledged certain limitations. In particular, the limited ability of the Security Council and the office of the Secretary-General to deploy, direct, command and control enforcement action operations in response to threats to the peace, breaches of the peace or acts of aggression was acknowledged.

The consequences of this are well known, but worth restating. International and internal armed conflicts have continued to flare around the globe, and one of the ironies of the end of the Cold War is that local or internal conflicts have increased.[79] With the United Nations's inability to respond effectively to these crises, the Security Council has left the establishment and management of international forces to individual member states, in particular the United States. These operations are outside the formal framework of the organisation, and come under the umbrella of traditional and reciprocal inter-power relations to which humanitarian law naturally applies.[80] In some of these cases, the United Nations has divested itself explicitly of its competence in leading enforcement actions and has instead "authorised" member states to undertake enforcement measures by use of force. The two most well known instances are the Korean and Gulf conflicts of 1950 and 1991 respectively. Some have described the action by the Security Council as a form of abdication of responsi-

---

[77] Bowett, *supra* note 71, p. 56.

[78] UN Doc. A/47/277 – S/24111, June 1992.

[79] See DAN SMITH, THE STATE OF WAR AND PEACE ATLAS (1997).

[80] Paolo Benvenuti, *The Implementation of International Humanitarian Law in the Framework of Peacekeeping Operations*, 1 LAW IN HUMANITARIAN CRISES 83, 88 (1995).

bility, with little or no command and control by the United Nations, and no strategic direction either.[81] Not surprisingly, the matter of enforcing humanitarian law was left to the contributing states. Given the universal nature of the principles, this should not prove problematic, but a lot will depend on the country concerned and the level of importance attached to dissemination and training among the armed forces. Such an arrangement cannot be regarded as satisfactory, and it raises the issue of United Nations responsibility for violations of international law in such instances.

While there can be no doubt that the United Nations is a subject of international law and capable of possessing international rights and duties, an analysis of what the International Court of Justice has said and done reveals that it is not possible to give a categorical answer to the question of the legal consequences of personality for international organisations.[82] The United Nations is, however, a separate legal person from and additional to its member states, and it is not simply an aggregation of those states.[83] Once the existence of international personality and rights is conceded, it is not difficult to infer that this will also entail obligations. In the *WHO Agreement case*, the International Court of Justice specifically referred to the existence of obligations at customary international law for international organisations.[84] There are situations where the United Nations would be responsible under customary international law for acts of persons or armed forces acting under its control.[85] In fact, there have been claims by states against the United Nations arising from violations of international law during the ONUC (Congo) operation that were later settled by negotiation.[86]

The United Nations has generally accepted responsibility for illegal acts that may have been committed by armed forces (belonging to member states) acting under its control.[87] Imputability to the United Nations is possible when national contingents become organs of the United Nations

---

[81] See NIGEL D. WHITE, KEEPING THE PEACE 115–128, esp., 117–118 (2nd ed., 1997).

[82] Amerasinghe, *supra* note 42, pp. 92–93. See also Tittemore, *supra* note 4, esp. pp. 92–95.

[83] Amerasinghe, *supra* note 42, p. 229.

[84] [1980] ICJ Reports 67, 90.

[85] Amerasinghe, *supra* note 42, pp. 240–241.

[86] See UN Doc. A/CN.4/195 and Add.1. The principal claimant was the Belgian government. Despite the nature of the authorisation to use force in the ONUC operation, the International Court of Justice found that it "did not involve 'preventive or enforcement" measures against any State under Chapter VII ..."; *Certain Expenses of the United Nations*, [1962] ICJ Reports 177. See Bowett, *supra* note 71, pp. 175–180.

[87] Amerasinghe, *supra* note 42, p. 242, and Dupuy, *supra* note 41, p. 891. The United Nations has acknowledged liability for activities carried out by both UNEF and ONUC.

by being placed under its authority and control. This does not happen when a country or countries retain control of a military force, as in the Gulf War, even if acting in the execution of a United Nations decision. Where national contingents come together to form "coalitions of the willing" in such cases, but do not become organs of the United Nations, or fall under its command and control, then the Organisation cannot be held responsible for their acts.[88] In such cases, the acts of military forces remain the responsibility of the states concerned. However, definitive statements remain problematic due to the linkage with the complex issues surrounding the command and control of United Nations forces, and a lot will depend on the facts of a case.[89] In the meantime, the control test retains its central role in determining liability, and in some cases may even allow for concurrent responsibility because of a limbo status involving an ill-defined form of dual control.[90]

VII. THE UNITED NATIONS POSITION

In 1994, when Serb troops advanced on the United Nations-declared "safe area" of Bihac, the municipal hospital stood in the middle of their line of advance.[91] The Canadian commander of the United Nations forces was reluctant to intervene. The United Nations forces civil affairs officer, an American, urged that the hospital be protected owing to its special status under the Geneva Conventions and that the United Nations Protection Force (UNPROFOR) had a duty to protect it. He drafted a memorandum to this effect to his superior in Sarajevo who then instructed Bangladeshi troops to take up positions with their armoured personnel carriers around the hospital. The Serbs refrained from attacking the hospital, and by passed Bihac in the process.

Two weeks later, the United Nations Office of Legal Affairs issued a statement to set the record straight and ensure that the "Bihac incident" did not set any precedents. United Nations forces are bound only by their Security Council mandate, and they are not legally obliged to uphold the Geneva Conventions. From a strictly legal point of view, obligations arising under humanitarian law are binding on states. Article 103 of the

---

[88] *Ibid.*, p. 243, and Finn Seyersted, *United Nations Forces: Some Legal Problems*, 37 BRIT. Y.B. INT'L L. 362, 421 (1961).

[89] See R. Murphy, *supra* note 76, pp. 41–73.

[90] See *Nissan v. Attorney General*, [1968] 1 Q.B. 286, and [1969] 1 All E.R. 629; Ian Brownlie, *Decisions of British Courts during 1968 Involving Questions of International Law*, 42 BRIT. Y.B. INT'L L. 217 (1968–1969).

[91] Roy Gutman, *The United Nations and the Geneva Conventions*, in CRIMES OF WAR 361 (Roy Gutman & David Reif, eds., 1999).

United Nations Charter may also be relied upon to support the argument that the obligations arising under the Charter of the United Nations upon member states (including those arising from Security Council resolutions) take precedence over other international treaties, including the Geneva Conventions and Additional Protocols.[92] The role of the United Nations is to carry out the will of the international community as expressed by the Security Council.[93] When states assign troops to peacekeeping duties, they are under the command or operational control of the Security Council.

This may be the theory, but even a superficial knowledge of United Nations peacekeeping indicates that the reality is much more complex. Few states ever relinquish full operational control to the United Nations.[94] The "Bihac incident" illustrates the ambivalent attitude of the United Nations to humanitarian law. Not surprisingly, it has been a source of tension between the International Committee of the Red Cross and the United Nations. The United Nations has declared its commitment to the application of humanitarian law to peacekeeping operations, but it has consistently taken the position that United Nations forces act on behalf of the international community, and therefore they cannot be considered a "party" to the conflict, nor a "Power" within the meaning of the Geneva Conventions. The mere presence of United Nations peacekeeping soldiers in an area of conflict or a theatre of war, while performing a humanitarian or diplomatic mission, does not necessarily mean that humanitarian law binds these troops.[95]

In addition, the United Nations is not in a position to become a party to the Conventions or Additional Protocols as this would entail binding the Organisation to detailed provisions that are aimed at states, and do not fit the role and function of an international organisation.[96] Notwithstanding its international legal personality, the United Nations is not itself a state and thus, it does not possess the juridical or administrative powers to discharge many of the obligations laid down in the Conventions.[97] However, this

---

[92] See Simma, *supra* note 1, pp. 1302–1314; and Goodrich, Hambro & Simons, *supra* note 37, pp. 614–617. See also Tittemore, *supra* note 4, esp. 101–108.

[93] Statement to this effect attributed to Stephen Katz, Office of Legal Affairs official, cited in Gutman, *supra* note 91, p. 361.

[94] See Murphy, *supra* note 76, pp. 41–73.

[95] This position has not altered with the Secretary-General's Bulletin on Observance by United Nations forces of international humanitarian law, *supra* note 5. See Section 1(1) discussed *infra*.

[96] On the question of treaty making powers, see Amerasinghe, *supra* note 42, pp. 102–103.

[97] *Reparation for Injuries Suffered in the Service of the United Nations*, [1949] ICJ Reports 174, and SYMPOSIUM ON HUMANITARIAN ACTION, *supra* note 3, p. 43.

does not mean that the conduct of hostilities by United Nations forces will be free from humanitarian constraint or that humanitarian law considerations do not apply.[98] While a relevant factor in determining how United Nations forces will implement humanitarian law, it is not a reason for concluding that it cannot be applicable to them.[99]

The International Committee of the Red Cross has been instrumental in obtaining agreement from the United Nations that international forces acting under United Nations authority would do so in accordance with the "principles and spirit" of relevant law.[100] But once a provision to this effect was incorporated in the regulations of the force and in the agreements with troop contributing states, it did not entail the direct responsibility of the United Nations to ensure respect for humanitarian law by members of its forces. In this regard the relatively recent United Nations Model Agreement with troop-contributing states and the model status of force agreements between the United Nations and host states now include an express provision to this effect.[101] Under that provision, the United Nations undertakes that the operations of the force in question will be conducted with full respect for the principles and spirit of the general international conventions applicable to the conduct of military personnel.

While these developments are welcome, they fail to address the fundamental questions, and more importantly, seem to suggest that the United Nations does not have a duty to monitor the behaviour of third parties. The "Bihac incident" already referred to confirms this policy.[102] This is crucial, as the military culture requires that such duties be spelled out in clear terms. There is, however, a lack of consistency in this regard, as

---

[98] Roberts & Guelff, *supra* note 8, pp. 721.

[99] Greenwood, *supra* note 17, p. 15.

[100] Umesh Palwankar, *Applicability of International Humanitarian Law to United Nations Peacekeeping Forces*, 80 INT'L REV. RED CROSS 227, 229–233 (1993). A provision to this effect was incorporated into the UNEF, ONUC and UNFICYP Force Regulations. As no Regulations were adopted in respect of UNIFIL, no such provision exists for that force.

[101] Shraga & Zacklin, *supra* note 19, p. 44. The Model Agreement with troop contributors contains the following provision: "[The United Nations peacekeeping operation] shall observe and respect the principles and spirit of the general international conventions applicable to the conduct of military personnel. The international conventions referred to above include the four Geneva Conventions of 12 August 1949 and their Additional Protocols of 8 June 1977 and the UNESCO Convention of 14 May 1954 on the Protection of Cultural Property in the event of armed conflict. [The Participating State] shall therefore ensure that the members of its national contingent serving . . . be fully acquainted with the principles and spirit of the conventions".

[102] Roy Gutman, *supra* note 91, pp. 361–364. There were also claims that United Nations forces in Bosnia and Herzegovina ignored evidence of human rights abuses elsewhere.

UNIFIL did monitor the behaviour of Israeli forces in Lebanon after the 1982 invasion.[103]

The recent Bulletin of the Secretary-General on the observance by United Nations forces of humanitarian law does go some way towards addressing these problems.[104] It adds significant weight to the position of the International Committee of the Red Cross and it is import ant in terms of legal certainty by giving obligations substance. Bulletins of this nature are intended to be legally binding on United Nations personnel, in this case United Nations forces.[105] Section 1 of the Bulletin states:

> The fundamental principles and rules of international humanitarian law set out in the present Bulletin are applicable to United Nations forces when in situations of armed conflict they are actively engaged therein as combatants, to the extent and for the duration of their engagement. They are accordingly applicable in enforcement actions, or in peacekeeping operations when the use of force is permitted in self-defence.

The categorisation of United Nations troops as combatants in certain instances may seem unusual, especially to troop-contributing states. However, this Bulletin must be judged in the context of the 1994 Convention on the Safety of United Nations and Associated Personnel, and there is a problematic overlap in the respective regimes covered. Both are incompatible because they are based on fundamentally different principles. The objective of the Convention being to protect United Nations personnel and ensure immunity from attack for other than those engaged in enforcement operations under Chapter VII involving combat against organised armed forces, while the remit of humanitarian law is much broader and respects the combatant's privilege to attack enemy forces once the general rules of international law are followed, and is based on the cardinal principle that combat forces are treated equally.[106]

The Bulletin appears to say that humanitarian law will apply whenever United Nations forces, for whatever reason, are required to resort to the use of force in armed conflict situations. What degree, intensity and duration of

---

[103] Interview, Timor Goksel, UNIFIL spokesman, Naqoura, Lebanon, 1998 and personal experience of writer.

[104] Secretary-General's Bullet in on Observance by United Nations forces of international humanitarian law, *supra* note 5. See Marten Zwanenburg, *The Secretary-General's Bulletin on Observance by United Nations Forces of International Humanitarian Law: Some Preliminary Observations*, 5 INT'L PEACEKEEPING 133 (1999), and Rowe, *supra* note 56, p. 52.

[105] Interview, Official, United Nations Legal Division, New York, December 2000. Bulletins were described as part of the United Nations "internal law, binding within the Organisation's own legal system".

[106] See Roberts & Guelff, *supra* note 8, pp. 623–626. On combatants generally, see Knut Ipsen, *Combatants and Non-Combatants*, in Fleck, *supra* note 2, pp. 65–104.

force are required is unclear, but some threshold must exist and be crossed before triggering the application of humanitarian law. Commanders and soldiers will still find themselves in a kind of legal no man's land trying to determine in the first instance if the situation can be classified as one of armed conflict, and then whether or not the use of force was sufficient to change their status from that of peacekeeper or peace enforcer, to that of combatant. No pocket book of humanitarian law of the kind usually supplied to military personnel will supply easy answers to these questions. At least paragraph 9(4) should provide an answer to those who would see the United Nations stand by in situations that arose in Bihac. Under these provisions, the United Nations shall in all circumstances respect and protect medical personnel and wounded.[107] This places a clear onus on peacekeepers to intervene and actively accept responsibility for the protection of these categories of persons.

The Bulletin also commits the United Nations to ensuring that members of military personnel are fully acquainted with the rules of humanitarian law. It accepts co-responsibility with the contributing states for this whether or not there is a status of forces agreement. What liability the United Nations may be subject to for breach of this duty is unclear. Most important, however, is section 4, to the effect that it is the responsibility of the national courts to prosecute military personnel for violations of humanitarian law. This means that the United Nations will not be required to establish a special tribunal to consider violations of humanitarian law by United Nations troops, and the *status quo ante* remains.[108]

What practical effect this Bulletin will have with United Nations forces on the ground, and the policy of contributing states, remains to be seen. Does it impose a wider duty on United Nations forces to intervene to prevent violations of humanitarian law by third parties in the absence of a specific provision to this effect in the mandate? Common article 1 of

---

[107] Paragraph 9(4) states: "The United Nations shall in all circumstances respect and protect medical personnel exclusively engaged in the search for, transport or treatment of the wounded or sick, as well as religious personnel." Paragraph 9(5) states: "The United Nations shall respect and protect transports of wounded and sick or medical equipment in the same way mobile medical units."

[108] Article 1(2) of the Statute of the Special Court for Sierra Leone, which was established in January 2002, states: "2. Any transgressions by peacekeepers and related personnel present in Sierra Leone pursuant to the Status of Mission Agreement in force between the United Nations and the Government of Sierra Leone or agreements between Sierra Leone and other Governments or regional organizations, or, in the absence of such agreement, provided that the peacekeeping operations were undertaken with the consent of the Government of Sierra Leone, shall be within the primary jurisdiction of the sending State." The Statute was adopted by agreement between the Government of Sierra Leone and the United Nations.

the Conventions provides that "the High Contracting Parties undertake to respect and to ensure respect for the present Convention in all circumstances".[109] It can be argued that this, and a similar provision in Protocol I, places a duty on United Nations forces to take action to prevent such violations.[110] Although this may not have been the original intention of the drafters of the Convention[111] and Protocol, is such an interpretation supported by the agreement to respect and observe the "spirit and principles" of humanitarian law and the recent Secretary-General's Bulletin? It would seem that the United Nations remains reluctant to acknowledge a duty to intervene in such circumstances,[112] and that the Bulletin acknowledges such a duty in very limited circumstances. In this way, as the law currently stands, a United Nations force is not under a general legal duty to intervene on behalf of victims of violations of applicable law in its area of operations, unless the mandate of the force provides otherwise.

The real problem for the United Nations is that acknowledging a duty to intervene then creates an onus to give the force(s) the means and capacity to do so without exposure to unnecessary risk.[113] If a force cannot intervene directly without exposing troops to significant danger, then the duty of a commander must first be to the safety of his or her personnel. Most lightly-armed peacekeepers will not be in a position to prevent large-scale abuses by a party to the conflict. This was the predicament of the Dutch contingent at Srebrenica.[114] But this will not relieve them of responsibility to take some action, as protests on the ground and later through higher channels can have effect. This is the kernel of the dilemma. Will commanders hide behind the cloak of preserving force security to excuse

---

[109] See JEAN S. PICTET, COMMENTARY – GENEVA CONVENTION IV RELATIVE TO THE PROTECTION OF CIVILIAN PERSONS IN TIME OF WAR 16 (1958).

[110] See Greenwood, *supra* note 17, pp. 32–33.

[111] Adam Roberts, *The Laws of War: Problems of Implementation*, 1 LAW IN HUMANITARIAN CRISES 13, 31–32 (1995).

[112] For a discussion of this issue, see Robert Weiner & Fionnuala Ni Aolain, BEYOND THE LAWS OF WAR: PEACEKEEPING IN SEARCH OF A LEGAL FRAMEWORK, 27 COLUM. HUM. RTS. L. REV. 293, 312–320 (1996).

[113] The Report of the Panel on United Nations Peacekeeping Operations, UN Doc. A/55/305 – S/2000/809, 21 August 2000 (the "Brahimi Report"), available at <http.www.un.org.>), recommended that United Nations peacekeepers – troops or police – be authorised to stop violence against civilians, within their means, in support of basic United Nations principles. At present this has no legal status, but it is a significant acknowledgement of the duty to intervene. See generally Reinhard Marx, *A Non-Governmental Human Rights Strategy for Peacekeeping*, 14 NETHERLANDS Q. HUM. RTS. 125–145 (1996).

[114] See Robert Siekmann, *The Legal Position of Ductchbat vis-a-vis Srebrenica*, 1 Y.B. INT'L HUMANITARIAN L. 301–312 (1998).

a failure to protect? It can also be argued that intervention in such circumstances will compromise the impartiality of the force. But if the policy adopted by the United Nations is applied in a consistent and impartial manner, this argument may be rebutted. Acknowledging that such a duty exists by expressly providing so in the mandate of the force may make the mission more difficult, but it cannot be right to allow a United Nations force stand idly by in circumstances where breaches of humanitarian law are taking place in their area of operations.[115]

VIII. THE ICRC POSITION

Having rendered the concept of the classical "war" redundant, the United Nations considered that it could not now set about regulating its conduct, and the responsibility to codify and improve the principles of humanitarian law fell upon the International Committee of the Red Cross. The question of the applicability of humanitarian law to United Nations forces was raised for the first time during the Korean conflict. This highlighted a fundamental problem for the United Nations in regard to ensuring compliance with the principles involved. Having been requested to apply *de facto* the humanitarian law principles protecting war victims and especially common article 3 of the Geneva Conventions, the United Nations commander replied that his instructions were to abide by the humanitarian principles of the 1949 Geneva Conventions, particularly common article 3, and by the detailed provisions of the Prisoners of War Convention.[116] The importance of the latter convention may have arisen from the need to ensure that all prisoners were treated equally, whereas in the case of common article 3, the principles concerned represent a compulsory minimum to be applied irrespective of the nature of the conflict or the issue of reciprocity.[117] However, as the United Nations Commander, he claimed that he did not have the authority to accept, or the means to ensure the accomplishment of responsibilities incumbent upon sovereign

---

[115] See generally Oliver Ulich, *Peacekeeping and Human Rights: Is there a Duty to Protect*, International Human Rights Advocacy (Spring 1996).

[116] Shraga & Zacklin, *supra* note 19, p. 39.

[117] Common article 3, referred to as the mini convention, is contained in all four Geneva Conventions. It applies to armed conflict "not of an international character". See Pictet, *supra* note 109, pp. 25–44. The International Court of Justice has deemed that "certain general and well recognised principles", including those contained in common article 3, reflect "elementary considerations of humanity"; see *Corfu Channel (Merits) (U.K. v. Albania)*, [1949] ICJ Reports 4, 22; and *Military and Paramilitary Activities (Nicaragua v. United States)*, [1986] ICJ Reports 4, 114.

nations under the detailed provisions of the other Geneva Conventions. Since then the ICRC has drawn the attention of the Secretary-General to the application of humanitarian law to the forces at his disposal, and to the desirability that these forces be provided by their contributing governments with adequate instruction in this area.[118]

The essence of the ICRC position is that humanitarian law principles, recognised as part of customary international law, are binding upon all states and upon all armed forces present in situations of conflict.[119] If these rules are binding on all states, then they must be binding on an international organisation that resorts to the use of force on their behalf. This is especially so when this organisation is an independent subject of international law and was established by states bound by the principles in the first place. In this context, the status of the parties or the legality of the use of force is not an issue that will determine the applicability of humanitarian law. Recognising that the United Nations is not a party to the Conventions, and given the nature of the Organisation, it is accepted that the applicability of humanitarian law principles to the Organisation would have to be *mutates-mutandis*.[120]

When member states are authorised by the Security Council to intervene in an internal conflict, such as Somalia, the basic character of the conflict remains internal.[121] However, the forces of the participating members states are carrying out an international mission on the basis of the United Nations resolution. In the relations between the "UN forces" and the parties to the conflict, the rules applicable to international armed conflict must be applied. It is acknowledged that the application of the rules of humanitarian law in their entirety is problematic as this was intended for conflict between states.[122] Nevertheless, it would be a denial of the clear international dimension of such missions if humanitarian law were to be restricted to common article 3 or to Protocol II to the Geneva Conventions.

It is apparent that the adoption of military measures under Chapter VI or VII of the Charter is likely to call for the application of humanitarian law under various profiles. Action against the illegal use of force

---

[118] Both the ICRC and the International Conference of the Red Cross and Red Crescent on many occasions expressed their opinion on the applicability of international humanitarian law to peacekeeping forces, see Palwankar, *supra* note 100, pp. 230–231.

[119] Shraga & Zacklin, *supra* note 19, p. 43.

[120] Thus rules pertaining to prisoners of war and penal sanctions could not apply, whereas rules pertaining to methods and means of combat, categories of protected persons and respect for recognised rights would be fully applicable. Statement by the ICRC at the 47th Session of the General Assembly on 13 November 1992.

[121] Pfanner, *supra* note 70, pp. 49, 55.

[122] *Ibid.*

in the past has involved the use of force by the United Nations or states acting on its behalf. Action of this nature *contra bellum* operates in situations where humanitarian law calls for the application of its *ius in bello* rules.[123] In regard to peacekeeping operations, it is commonly accepted that deployment in situations endangering peace or constituting a threat to international peace and security may also call for preventive measures involving the use of force. If and when conflict does break out and humanitarian law is applicable, it makes little sense to argue that United Nations forces on the ground in such a situation are not bound by these same principles.[124] Adherence to these principles will also assist in facilitating a restoration of the peace, a matter that is ultimately the goal of all United Nations forces.

IX. THE 1994 CONVENTION ON THE SAFETY OF UNITED NATIONS AND ASSOCIATED PERSONNEL

In an effort to address some of the issues surrounding the protection of, and regulations governing United Nations forces, the 1994 Convention on the Safety of United Nations and Associated Personnel (the Convention) was adopted. The declared purpose of the Convention is to protect United Nations and associated personnel from becoming the object of attack by purporting to criminalise attacks by other armed forces on peacekeeping troops. The new Convention clarifies the protective duties of the receiving or host state, and this is a welcome initiative, but in the context of United Nations enforcement measures and humanitarian law, the Convention raises some interesting issues. The outcome, in terms of what has been achieved may in some ways be described as the proverbial camel created by a committee established to design a horse.[125]

Taking into account the preamble, it is evident that the Convention was drafted owing to the concerns of contracting states and contributors to United Nations peacekeeping operations over the scale and frequency of attacks on peacekeeping forces. It acknowledges the contribution of United Nations personnel in the fields of preventive diplomacy, peace-making,

---

[123] Benvenuti, *supra* note 80, p. 85.

[124] Both the ICRC and the International Conference of the Red Cross and Red Crescent on many occasions expressed their opinion on the applicability of international humanitarian law to peacekeeping forces, see Palwankar, *supra* note 100, pp. 230–231.

[125] See Sharp, *supra* note 28, pp. 93–183. Sharp is very critical of the Convention, and he suggested the adoption of a Geneva Protocol III instead. Christopher Greenwood replied to Sharp's article in *Protection of Peacekeepers: The Legal Regime*, 7 DUKE J. COMP. & INT'L L. 185 (1996).

peacekeeping, peace building and humanitarian and other operations. It is noteworthy that there is no specific mention of "peace enforcement" operations. The importance of the fundamental features and traditional characteristics of peacekeeping operations is also emphasised. Also of importance in this context is the non-use of force except in self-defence and the policy of impartiality.[126] The Convention contains a number of "savings clauses" to the effect, *inter alia*, that nothing shall affect the applicability of humanitarian law and universally recognised standards of human rights to United Nations operations and personnel, or their responsibility to respect humanitarian law and standards.[127] One of the interesting features of this provision is that it merely states that the law is applicable, but fails to outline the circumstances when and where this is so. Given the complexity of the issue, and the haste with which the Convention was drafted, this is not surprising.[128] It is unfortunate that an opportunity to clarify and even expand on this area was not availed of.

The Convention provides that United Nations personnel, including those involved in maintaining peace and security, or providing emergency humanitarian assistance, are protected from attack.[129] The negotiators realised that it was necessary to have a clear separation between the situation where the Convention would apply and that where humanitarian law is applicable, so that United Nations and associated personnel and those who attack them would be covered by one regime or the other, but not both.[130]

---

[126] Article 6 of the Convention calls on United Nations personnel to respect the laws of the host state and to refrain from any action or activity incompatible with the impartial and international nature of its duties. Article 20 and the preamble emphasise the issue of consent, while article 21 refers to the right to use force in self-defence.

[127] Article 20(a) of the Convention.

[128] It would seem that the Convention was adopted with undue haste. The Sixth Committee adopted draft resolution A/C.6/49/L.9 by consensus on 16 November 1994. Resolution 49/59 adopting the Convention and declaring it open for signature and ratification was adopted by the General Assembly by consensus on 9 December 1994. See generally Philippe Kirsch, *The Convention on the Safety of United Nations and Associated Personnel*, 2 (5) INT'L PEACEKEEPING 102 (1995).

[129] Evan Bloom, *Protecting Peacekeepers: The Convention on the Safety of United Nations and Associated Personnel*, 89 AM. J. INT'L L. 621, 623–624 (1995). In essence, it covers two types of personnel who carry out activities in support of the fulfilment of the mandate of a United Nations operation. In the first category are those directly engaged as part of a United Nations mandated operation whether in a military, police or civilian capacity. The second category covers "associated personnel", *i.e.*, persons assigned by the Secretary-General or an intergovernmental organisation with the agreement of a competent organ of the United Nations. For example, NATO forces asked to assist UNPROFOR in Bosnia-Herzegovina, and United States assistance under UNITAF in Somalia would fall within this element of the definition.

[130] *Ibid.*, p. 625. However, Article 20(a) of the Convention, a "savings clause", indicates that the special protective status given to non-combatant United Nations forces neither

An important reason for this was not to undermine the Geneva Conventions, which rely in part for their effectiveness on all forces being treated equally. If it became a crime to engage in combat with United Nations forces acting as combatants, this could have a dramatic impact on other parties willingness to adhere to accepted principles of humanitarian law.

Article 1 of the Convention is central to its applicability and scope. The text provides for a two-fold definition. The operation must be established by the competent organ of the United Nations in accordance with the Charter and under United Nations authority and control. In addition, one of two further conditions must be met; *i.e.*, the operations must be for the purpose of maintaining or restoring international peace and security; or where the Security Council or General Assembly has decided for the purposes of the Convention, that there exists an exceptional risk to the safety of the personnel participating in the operation. This means that operations authorised, as opposed to mandated, by the Security Council, but carried out under the command and control of one or more states, are outside the scope of the Convention. The Convention also provides further evidence to substantiate the view already advanced that enforcement measures by the United Nations are subject to humanitarian law. In particular, article 2(2) of the Convention is entirely consistent with the aforementioned view and in defining the scope and application, establishes that it "shall not apply to a United Nations operation *authorised by the Security Council as an enforcement action under Chapter VII* of the Charter of the United Nations in which any of the personnel are *engaged as combatants against organised armed forces* and to which the law of international armed conflict applies".[131]

Having reached agreement on the principles involved, states, with the advice of the ICRC, had to adopt criteria to determine which operations would be covered by the Conventions, and those that would not. Chapter VII operations are thus excluded from the scope of the Convention upon the fulfilment of this cumulative list of conditions.[132] Even if only part of the operation fulfils these conditions, then all of the United Nations elements participating in that operation will be excluded from its protection.

Initially the ICRC and some states had concerns regarding the reference to international armed conflict, but the wording of article 2(2) proved acceptable in the end because it was generally agreed that it was impossible

---

derogates from those provisions of humanitarian law that would protect such forces, nor removes the responsibility of non-combatant United Nations forces to respect the law.

[131] Italics added. This should be read in conjunction with article 1 (definitions) of the Convention.

[132] M. Christiane Bourloyannis-Vrailas, *The Convention on the Safety of United Nations and Associated Personnel*, 44 INT'L COMP. L.Q. 560, 5671995.

for the United Nations to be involved in internal armed conflict. Once United Nations or associated personnel intervened or became engaged in a conflict with a local force (as opposed to acting merely in self-defence), the conflict became by definition "international" in character.[133] Identifying if any of the personnel are engaged as combatants against organised armed forces and whether the operation is one to which humanitarian law applies is problematic. The formulation was designed to be consistent with common article 2 of the Geneva Conventions, and thus the point of analysis is whether the operation involves combat during an international armed conflict, which would trigger the application of article 2 while excluding the application of the United Nations Convention.[134] This provision will prove difficult to interpret in practice, and the fact that there is no agreement on which provisions of humanitarian law apply to United Nations personnel and in what circumstances will only add to the confusion. It can also be predicted that the United Nations and troop-contributing states will be reluctant to recognise that the Convention has ceased to apply, and this may inflate the level of conflict required before it is acknowledged that "armed conflict" is taking place.[135]

Another interpretation is that humanitarian law would continue to apply to United Nations personnel when, in the conduct of a Chapter VII mandated operation, they are actively engaged in a combat mission, regardless of whether the armed conflict is international or internal in character. Humanitarian law would also be applicable in peacekeeping operations which, however peaceful and consensual they may be in theory, can in practice give rise to situations where United Nations personnel can resort to the use of force in self-defence or to resist attempts to prevent them carrying out their mandate.[136] However, in most traditional peacekeeping operations, situations where force is used in self-defence are short and could not be described as involving sustained periods of fighting. Incidents of this nature do not by themselves remove the protection offered by the Convention because the United Nations troops involved are not necessarily engaged as combatants.[137]

Under the Convention traditional peacekeeping forces enjoy a protected status similar to that of non-combatants. However, it does not purport to protect armed forces acting as combatants on behalf of the United

---

[133] Kirsch, *supra* note 128, p. 105.

[134] Bloom, *supra* note 129, p. 625.

[135] See Greenwood, *supra* note 125, p. 200.

[136] Shraga & Zacklin, *supra* note 19, pp. 46–47. See Ray Murphy, United Nations *Peacekeeping in Lebanon and the Use of Force*, 6(2) INT'L PEACEKEEPING 38 (1999).

[137] Bloom, *supra* note 129, p. 625.

Nations. Article 2(2) applies to troops acting under Chapter VII, in particular article 43 of the Charter, in furtherance of United Nations collective security provisions. It is submitted that what is also being referred to in this provision are enforcement operations conducted by third states, such as occurred in the Gulf conflict. These operations are authorised by the Security Council under the umbrella of Chapter VII, and they arise as a direct result of the failure of member states to conclude the necessary agreements for military forces under article 43 of the Charter. The element of consent, which has hitherto been an important factor in distinguishing peacekeeping from enforcement operations, is absent. But the criterion of consent should be applied with some caution. Even in the case of UNIFIL, when deployed in 1978 with the consent of the Lebanese government, the authority of the government barely extended beyond west Beirut. Likewise, in the more recent case of Albania, the government there consented to the deployment of a "coalition of the willing" under a Chapter VII enforcement mandate.[138] However, peace support operations, whether of the traditional peacekeeping or peace enforcement kind, can be distinguished from enforcement action as envisaged under the collective security provisions of the United Nations Charter. When a situation is deemed to pose a threat to the peace, breach of the peace, or act of aggression, the legal groundwork is then laid for military and other action to compel a recalcitrant state to succumb to the will of the international community. This may ultimately lead to combat by United Nations authorised forces against the armed forces of a non-complying party or parties. In this way, article 1(2) of the Convention provides additional evidence of the applicability of humanitarian law to United Nations enforcement operations of this nature.

The Convention effectively repeals the combatant's privilege: soldiers in the field who attack United Nations military personnel pursuant to the orders of their commanders are deemed to be committing a crime for which individual criminal responsibility is established.[139] It has been argued that in effect the Convention purports to change humanitarian law by criminalising attacks on United Nations forces and modifying the combatant's privilege as it applies to such attacks, without a concomitant recognition that the United Nations is governed in such situations by specific norms of the same body of law.[140] This conclusion is flawed. Under humanitarian law, where only non-combatants are protected from attack, United Nations

---

[138] See Kritsiotis, *supra* note 60, p. 511.

[139] Article 9 of the Convention.

[140] Richard Glick, *Lip Service to the Laws of War: Humanitarian Law and United Nations Armed Forces*, 17 MICH. J. OF INT'L L. 53, 81 (1995).

personnel acting as combatants, are both bound to apply these rules and to invoke their protection when appropriate. In this way the Convention and humanitarian law are mutually exclusive, the former regime applying to non-conflict situations, and the latter applying to any situation of sufficient degree of conflict.[141]

The exact scope and nature of United Nations operations covered by the Convention is a matter on which there is a divergence of opinion. Originally the Convention was to be limited to operations "established pursuant to a mandate approved by a resolution of the Security Council".[142] A broader material scope of application of the Convention was eventually agreed.[143] The view that the Convention applies to most kinds of United Nations operations falling short of enforcement action itself is the dominant opinion, although the protection provided for thereunder might not extend to all stages and components of the military operation.[144] The confusion arises primarily from the different perspectives among countries as to the purpose of the Convention in the first place. Many were critical of the scope and expansion of the Security Council's activities in recent years, but were powerless to prevent it. They saw the approval of a Convention covering traditional peacekeepers as a means to curtail these activities. But arguing that it should apply to traditional peacekeeping operations only missed the point somewhat. It was precisely because of the Somalia type operations that pressure was brought to bear to deal with the legal deficiencies that existed in the international regime.[145]

The end result is still unsatisfactory in that the difficulty of distinguishing between peacekeeping and enforcement operations, while making provision for hybrid operations involving both, has not been properly taken into account. This crucial issue, like the question relating to the applicability of humanitarian law to United Nations operations, has been left unresolved by the Convention. It now seems generally accepted that the Convention applies to peace enforcement operations such as

---

[141] Shraga & Zacklin, *supra* note 19, p. 46.

[142] UN Doc. A/AC.242/L.2, proposal by New Zealand and Ukraine, article 1(2). Civilian United Nations personnel were also unhappy with the original proposals (interview, Ambassador P. Kirsch, former chairman of the negotiations on the Convention, Galway, August 2000).

[143] For background see Antoine Bouvier, *Convention on the Safety of United Nations and Associated Personnel*, 309 INT'L REV. RED CROSS 638 (1995).

[144] Shraga & Zacklin, *supra* note 19, p. 46. Steven Lepper, *War Crimes and the Protection of Peacekeeping Forces*, 28 AKRON L. REV. 411, 415 (1995).

[145] Interview, Kirsch, *supra* note 142. There was also concern among some states to avoid condoning the possible future presence of NGO's on their territory, and the issue of consent to the presence of United Nations forces in the first instance.

that established in Somalia. The problem is when and who determines that a confrontation between United Nations troops and others reaches the threshold that the participants may be regarded as combatants under article 2(2) of the Convention. For example, did Aidid's forces in Somalia constitute "organised forces" for the purposes of the Convention? These are not straightforward questions. Why is the Convention so replete with references to the characteristics of traditional peacekeeping duties, *i.e.*, impartiality, host state consent, and non-use of force except in self-defence?[146] The answer can only be that the Convention is a poorly drafted and ill-thought out document that was heavily influenced by political factors. As a compromise document, troop-contributing governments may take some solace from the fact that forces serving with missions in Kosovo and Bosnia and Herzegovina are protected by the terms of the Convention. But how this will work in practice is anyone's guess, and it presents a potential nightmare for a prosecutor seeking to invoke the terms of the Convention.

There is also the issue of European and Western neo-colonialism under the cloak of United Nations activity.[147] How will the Convention operate in a situation like Somalia when a major contributor to the United Nations force decides to target a clan or militia leader, and sometimes operates outside the United Nations command structure? The problem with accepting that peace enforcement operations come within its remit is that is it seeks to criminalise action by military forces against United Nations mandated or authorised peace enforcement operations. What happens when these operations are outside the formal framework of the organisation, and come under the umbrella of traditional and reciprocal inter power relations to which humanitarian law of armed conflict naturally applies? During wartime combat operations, or hostile acts engaged in during an armed conflict, combatants do not commit crimes by killing or wounding the "enemy" if this is carried out in a manner that does not conflict with the rules of humanitarian law.[148] It cannot be correct that military action at the

---

[146] Benvenuti, *supra* note 80, p. 92.

[147] Some states have reviewed their positions and expressed reservations about the Security Council's use of Chapter VII. See J. Ciechanski, *Enforcement Measures under Chapter VII of the United Nations Charter: United Nations Practice after the Cold War*, in Pugh, *supra* note 59, pp. 82–104, at p. 97, and D. Daniel and B. Hayes, *Securing Observance of United Nations Mandates Through the Employment of Military Force*, in Pugh, *supra* note 59, pp. 105–125, at p. 106.

[148] Under the article 85 of the *Geneva Convention Relative to the Treatment of Prisoners of War*, *supra* note 83, prisoners of war, that is, captured enemy combatants, prosecuted under the laws of the Detaining Power for acts committed prior to capture, retain the benefits of the Convention.

behest of political or others leaders, which is otherwise in accordance with humanitarian law, could render the combatants concerned liable to prosecution under the Convention. Such a scenario would place these forces in an invidious position which. it is submitted, is neither the intention nor the effect of the Convention.

Doubts have been expressed about the Convention's usefulness and the question was raised whether it did not belong to *ius ad bellum* – as it contains the prohibition to wage war at the United Nations – rather than to *ius in bello*.[149] The Convention does address what was a significant gap in international law. While humanitarian law governs the conduct of combatants, no international instrument prohibited or provided legal remedies for attacks upon traditional peacekeeping forces acting in that role.[150] This is no longer the case, and the new regime is welcome. However, the Convention does not have a significant impact on the humanitarian law implications of United Nations operations and its adoption marked a lost opportunity to clarify rather than obfuscate the question further. Nor is it clear from the Convention whether humanitarian law may be applicable when the Convention itself applies. It also avoids the thorny issue of the consequences if the procedure and/or the adoption of United Nations resolutions authorising or mandating certain kinds of peace enforcement operations are themselves in accordance the Charter of the United Nations and international law. It bears all the scars of the behind-the-scenes battles regarding the separate, but linked issue of the expanded powers of the Security Council.

X. CONCLUSION

It is undisputed that the United Nations has international legal personality and that it is a subject of international law.[151]

While the principles and basic rules of humanitarian law may be considered to represent fundamental values that have received almost universal acceptance, peacetime efforts to implement them at the national level are nonetheless insufficient.[152] In fact, it is often a marginal item in

---

[149] See comments to this effect in M. Meijer, *supra* note 3, p. 137.

[150] For the limited protection available under the Geneva Conventions and Additional Protocols, see Greenwood, *supra* note 17, pp. 30–31.

[151] *Reparation for Injuries Suffered in the Service of the United Nations*, [1949] ICJ Reports 174. See also Michael Bothe, *Peacekeeping and International Humanitarian Law: Friends or Foes?*, 3 INT'L PEACEKEEPING 91, 94 (1996).

[152] Louis Geiger, *Armed Forces and Respect for International Humanitarian Law: Major Issues*, in SYMPOSIUM ON HUMANITARIAN ACTION, *supra* note 3, p. 60.

military training programmes.[153] Consequently, these rules of law are not as well known or understood as they should be by those who must apply them, especially members of the armed forces. However, the conduct of Canadian and other contingents part of UNOSOM II highlighted the need for training in this area.[154]

After the capture of a United States helicopter pilot shot down over Mogadishu, it was said that the United States recognised too late that there was no international law to protect him.[155] A gap was deemed to exist in international law as no international armed conflict was taking place and the Geneva Convention protecting prisoners did not apply. But to rely upon humanitarian principles in a conflict, both parties must be prepared to demonstrate willingness to respect those principles. Reciprocity, while not a legal requirement, is a practical necessity. A primary consideration in developing principles of humanitarian law was the self-interest of the most protected class of person under the original rules, the combatant. States, and in particular the United States, sought to fill a perceived gap in international law by way of the Convention to Protect United Nations Personnel. This Convention is far from perfect, and may not alter the risk to which United Nations personnel will be exposed. Categorising those who oppose or threaten United Nations personnel as criminals or outlaws carries certain dangers, and if not implemented with caution and skill, it could be associated with a new kind of colonial mentality.[156]

With regard to the initial question posed as to the relevant applicable law to situations where United Nations forces are deployed, this will depend largely on the nature and extent of the conflict. Nevertheless, there appears to be little doubt but that the provisions of humanitarian law that have customary status do apply to United Nations forces. Such provisions bind all states, and may reasonably be suggested to apply to the United Nations itself.[157] The most difficult question arises in respect of those

---

[153] See generally David Lloyd-Roberts, *Training the armed forces to respect international humanitarian law-The perspective of the ICRC Delegate to the Armed and Security Forces of South Asia*, 319 INT'L REV. RED CROSS 433 (1997); F. de Mulinen, The Law of War and the Armed Forces, Series *Ius in Bello*, No. 1 (1992); and Yves Sandoz, *Respect for the Law of Armed Conflict: the ICRC's observations and experiences*, International Seminar on International Humanitarian Law in a New Strategic Environment: Training of Armed Forces, Stockholm, 17–18 June 1996.

[154] Though this need was recognised much earlier by some, see Leslie C. Green, *Humanitarian Law and the Man in the Field*, 14 MIL. LAW & LAW OF WAR REV. 96 (1976).

[155] Lepper, *supra* note 144, p. 415.

[156] ADAM ROBERTS, HUMANITARIAN ACTION IN WAR 70 (1996).

[157] McCoubrey, *supra* note 68, p. 46.

rules that have not yet attained customary status. There seems little sense in a system where combatants engaged in conflict are subject to humanitarian law when they are acting as members of national armed forces, whereas members of armed forces in the same armed conflict acting as peacekeepers are exempted from the obligations to respect the rights of protected persons. This is all the more absurd when these United Nations soldiers represent the Organisation charged with upholding and promoting the fundamental human right that humanitarian law seeks to protect.[158] The application of humanitarian law to United Nations forces will not compromise the mission to promote peace. Moreover, as the declared aim of such operations is the restoration of international peace and security, it is surely not the case that it can be based on action in violation of existing principles of law.

What can or should a United Nations force do when it becomes aware that parties in the country where it is deployed are violating applicable international law. Unless the mandate of a force states otherwise, as the law stands at present, there is no legal duty to protect victims of such violations. However, international military and civilian field personnel cannot be silent witnesses to gross violations of humanitarian law.[159] And nor do they wish to be. The legal obligations of peacekeeping and other United Nations military forces should reflect the notion that they will affirmatively seek to prevent abuses. The *Brahimi Report* suggests a more assertive and interventionist approach in such cases. If a force cannot intervene directly without exposing troops to significant danger, then the duty of a commander must first be to the safety of his or her personnel. Most lightly-armed peacekeepers will not be in a position to prevent Large-scale abuses by a party to the conflict. The Brahimi recommendations are a welcome initiative, but presuppose that United Nations personnel will be given the means and capacity to act in this way when appropriate, a presumption that past experience shows may not be taken for granted. This is the kernel of the dilemma, and some commanders may hide behind the cloak of preserving force security to excuse a failure to act.

Enforcement of humanitarian law is especially problematic in respect of United Nations forces. Relying on the contributing states to use their disciplinary regimes to enforce municipal law is one solution, but this

---

[158] See article 1 of the Charter of the United Nations.

[159] See comment to this effect in Robert Siekmann, *Notes on the Singapore Conference on Humanitarian Action and Peacekeeping Operations*, 4 INT'L PEACEKEEPING 19, 21 (1997). More recently, there were reports that United Nations troops deliberately avoided confronting militias in East Timor, and that French troops belonging to KFOR failed to protect ethnic Albanians in Kosovo (see *The Irish Times*, 30 August 2000, p. 1, and 10 February 2000, p. 14.

requires the cooperation of those states concerned and the existence of an appropriate legal structure to deal with such offences. The *Brocklebank, Rockwood* and similar trials make it clear that there is significant confusion regarding the applicability of international law to the different kinds of United Nations military operations. The use of the courts martial or its equivalent within contributing states still remains the most likely system for dealing with disciplinary matters arising. While the independence of municipal legal regimes and disciplinary procedures must be respected, the current confusion is militating against a uniform and agreed formula for determining the applicability of international law to such operations.

The establishment of the International Criminal Court is the most significant recent development in this regard. Once a state has ratified the Statute, then all nationals of that state will be subject to its provisions.[160] Concern about implementing humanitarian law was one of the driving forces behind proposals for its establishment.[161] The United States was most concerned about the impact this might have on participation in multinational and peacekeeping operations.[162] However, the Court to be established is not a serious alternative for the present system of criminal jurisdiction over peacekeepers.[163] The Preamble to the Statute states that the Court shall be complementary to national criminal jurisdictions.[164] In stark contrast with the Statutes of the *ad hoc* tribunals for the former Yugoslavia and Rwanda, this acknowledges the primacy of national authorities unless they are unable or unwilling to adequately investigate and prosecute alleged offences. Once a state has ratified the Statute, all nationals of that state are subject to its provisions. But fundamental problems remain, as states that refuse to ratify will not be subject to the jurisdiction of the ICC unless an offence is committed by a national of that State on the territory of another state party to the Statute. In addi-

---

[160] See generally William J. Fenrick, Michael Cottier and Andreas Zimmrrmann in Triffterer, *supra* note 30, pp. 180–288; WILLIAM A. SCHABAS, INTRODUCTION TO THE INTERNATIONAL CRIMINAL COURT 1–20 (2001); M. CHERIF BASSIOUNI, THE STATUTE OF THE INTERNATIONAL CRIMINAL COURT – A DOCUMENTARY HISTORY (1998); THE INTERNATIONAL CRIMINAL COURT – THE MAKING OF THE ROME STATUTE 79–126 (Roy Lee, ed., 1999); L. Caflisch, *Toward the Establishment of a Permanent International Criminal Jurisdiction*, 4(5) INT'L PEACEKEEPING 110–115 (1998) (available at http://www.igc.org/icc/>).

[161] Roberts, *supra* note 156, p. 50.

[162] Marten Zwanenburg, *The Statute for an International Criminal Court and the United States: Peacekeepers under Fire?*, 10 EUR. J. INT'L. L. 124, 126 (1999).

[163] *Ibid.*, p. 125.

[164] *Rome Statute of the International Criminal Court*, preamble, para. 10 and articles 1, 12–15, 17–19. see Morten Bergsmo, p. 15, and Otto Triffterer, pp. 59–61 in Triffterer, *supra* note 30.

tion, article 8, which deals with war crimes, is also linked to the notion of armed conflict (international and internal), and is dependent on a minimum threshold of conflict being reached before the relevant provisions can apply.[165] The Statute emphasises the prosecution of war crimes on a large scale, whereas the crimes committed by peacekeepers have been isolated and are not part of a plan or policy sanctioned by higher authorities. Despite this, the possibility of a prosecution for a single act constituting a war crime still exists, and contrasts with the threshold level of gravity for a crime against humanity under the Statute.[166]

In order to ensure humanitarian law is applied and enforced in the course of all relevant United Nations activities, it must first be clarified. This is not as simple a task as it may first appear. In the case of IFOR and SFOR in Bosnia and Herzegovina, and KFOR in Kosovo, Protocol I Additional to the Geneva Conventions was applicable to the Canadian and German contingents, but not to the United States and France. This problem is mitigated somewhat by the fact that many of the relevant norms are part of customary international law which binds all states. Making it mandatory for all United Nations personnel to be educated and trained in this area is essential. Such instruction is a legal obligation on states party to the Geneva Conventions and Additional Protocols.[167] In addition, the United Nations and the ICRC should agree on the rules applicable to military operations conducted on behalf of or by the United Nations. There is an urgent need for codification of the law as "ambiguity is always a fault in legal norms and in international humanitarian law it is potentially a source of disaster".[168] Several commentators have called for the formation of an independent body to police the application of humanitarian law and to recommend revisions where necessary.[169] One means of clarifying the

---

[165] See William J. Fenrick, Michael Cottier and Andreas Zimmrrmann in Triffterer, *supra* note 30, pp. 180–288, esp. pp. 264–278; Schabas, *supra* note 160, pp. 40–52; and Georg Witschel and Wiebke Rûckert in Lee, *supra* note 160, pp. 103–126. Rûckert notes that the Statute contains a substantially lower threshold for internal armed conflict than that laid down in Protocol II.

[166] M. Arsanjani, *The Rome Statute of an International Criminal Court*, 93 AM. J. INT'L L. 33 (1999). Article 7(1) of the Statute provides that particular acts must have been committed as part of a "widespread or systematic attack directed against any civilian population" (Rodney Dixon in Triffterer, *supra* note 30, pp. 126-127).

[167] McCoubrey, *supra* note 68, p. 43.

[168] HILAIRE MCCOUBREY, INTERNATIONAL HUMANITARIAN LAW 17–18 (1999). Although McCoubrey was addressing the confusion surrounding internal and international armed conflicts, the basic logic applies to all issues concerning humanitarian law.

[169] Howard Levie, *When Battle Rages: How Can Law Protect?*, in WORKING PAPERS AND PROCEEDINGS OF THE FOURTEENTH HAMMARSKJÖLD FORUM 6 (John Carey, ed., 1971), RICHARD MILLER, THE LAW OF WAR, 275 (1975). Tittemore recommended the

issues raised would be for both organisations to identify precisely which rules have achieved the status of customary law. Despite the universality of the Geneva Conventions, not all the details of their provisions have simply become declaratory of customary law.[170] The situation is even more uncertain in regard to Protocol I; moreover, not all customary rules may be applicable to operations carried out by United Nations forces.

It is an unavoidable flaw that in relation to the purposes and functions of the United Nations, humanitarian law only plays a secondary role. Furthermore, states perceive criminal jurisdiction over their nationals as part of their jealously guarded sovereignty, and considerable national sensitivities are associated with participation in United Nations military operations.[171] The creation of a special tribunal or court to deal with such matters is one potential solution, but the fact that few if any countries actually place their forces under the full command of the United Nations could be problematic. The matter would be complicated in respect of those countries with dualist legal regimes that do not automatically incorporate international law provisions into their domestic legal systems. Certainly the recent Secretary-General's Bulletin regarding the field of application of humanitarian to United Nations forces and the number of references to it in Security Council resolutions as a "body of law" to be applied "in all circumstances", it may be argued that humanitarian law is part of *ius cogens*.[172]

In most instances the task of applying theoretical principles of international law to specific cases becomes the responsibility of armed forces on the ground. There are a number of measures that contributing states could take to improve the current situation. Up until recently, United States policy was linked to the notion of armed conflict. In accordance with international law, United States military were obliged to comply with humanitarian law in conducting military operations in times of armed conflict.[173] However, military regulations are silent on when an engagement reaches the level of armed conflict, or what demarcates the point at which the laws of armed conflict apply. These distinctions are crucial to peacekeeping operations, and neither the recent Secretary-General's

---

adoption of a further Protocol to the Geneva Conventions permitting the United Nations to ratify the agreements, or the adoption of a report by the Security Council, Tittemore, *supra* note 4, p. 114.

[170] Pfanner, *supra* note 70, p. 49.

[171] Hilaire McCoubrey, *International Humanitarian Law and United Nations Military Action in the "New World Order"*, 1 INTERNATIONAL LAW AND ARMED CONFLICT: COMMENTARY 36, 45 (1994).

[172] See comments to this effect in M. Meijer, *supra* note 3, p. 137.

[173] Turley, *supra* note 7, p. 148.

Bulletin nor the Convention on the Protection of United Nations Personnel shed much light on this area. In 1996 the United States Chairman of the Joint Chiefs of Staff issued an instruction that extended the application of "the law of war principles during all operations that are characterised as Military Operations Other Than War".[174] This effectively covers every conceivable military operation. Most significantly, there is no triggering event wedded to the notion of armed conflict, which is a prerequisite for the application of these principles under international law. This is a welcome initiative, but from a legal perspective, it too has deficiencies in that the instruction refers to principles of war, but gives no indication of what these might be.

Humanitarian law represents fundamental principles of humanity imposed on all of us, including the Security Council and agents of the United Nations. It must be respected in all circumstances, regardless of the existence or nature of the armed conflict. A solution would be for an acknowledgement and declaration that humanitarian law binds United Nations personnel, and that United Nations military and other personnel will be educated, trained and monitored in this regard. Ensuring the universality of the treaties on humanitarian law, including the Statute of the ICC, would serve as an additional guarantee of compliance. After one hundred years of law making, the primary objective must not be a new law, but ensuring compliance with and effective implementation of the laws already in existence.[175] It is the responsibility of the United Nations and all countries contributing troops to United Nations operations to ensure that all personnel undergo systematic training in humanitarian law, and that standing operating procedures be drawn up to deal with violations when they occur.

---

[174] *United States of America: International and Operational Law Note: When Does the Law of War Apply: Analysis of Department of Defence Policy on Application of the Laws of War*, reprinted from The Army Law (1998), in 1 Y.B. INT'L HUMANITARIAN L. 617–619 (1998).

[175] Christopher Greenwood, *International Humanitarian Law and the Laws of War*, Preliminary Report for the Centennial Commemoration of the First Hague Peace Conference 1899 (May 1999), p. 3 (para. 1.6), quoting Sir Franklin Berman.

[10]

The Secretary-General's
Bulletin on Observance by
United Nations Forces of
International Humanitarian
Law: Some Preliminary
Observations

Marten Zwanenburg

1. Introduction

At first glance, international humanitarian law (or humanitarian law) and United Nations (UN) forces[1] appear wholly unrelated. Humanitarian law is concerned with armed conflict and peacekeeping is concerned with peace. Looking beyond appearances, however, it becomes clear that the two are not as unrelated after all. First, UN peacekeepers may be deployed in an area where there is still fighting going on. Secondly, peacekeepers may become involved in conflict-like situations. This may range from an incidental exchange of fire to large-scale operations involving tanks and fighter planes.

In this context, peacekeepers have sometimes been accused of violating norms of international humanitarian law. Such accusations naturally presuppose that international humanitarian law is the proper standard to be applied to peacekeepers. Whether that is indeed the case has been subject of debate for a long time, particularly between the International Committee of the Red Cross (ICRC) and the United Nations.

The promulgation of a Bulletin by the UN Secretary-General entitled 'Observance by United Nations forces of international humanitarian law'[2] on 6 August 1999 constituted an important step forward in this debate. This article first discusses the main points of contention regarding the application of international humanitarian law to UN forces. It then presents the Secretary-General's Bulletin and provides a brief analysis of a number of its most interesting aspects and their impact on the application debate. These are only some preliminary observations: an in-depth analysis of all the Bulletin's provisions is outside the scope of this article.

2. The Debate Concerning the Applicability of Humanitarian Law to Peace-keeping

2.1 ICRC and UN Statements and Practice

The question whether humanitarian law applies to United Nations peacekeeping has been debated since the 1950s. The ICRC in particular has consistently maintained that humanitarian law applies to peacekeeping operations.[3] The United Nations, on the other hand, has held that humanitarian law as such does not apply to United Nations peacekeeping. Rather, it has undertaken to respect the 'principles and spirit of the general international Conventions applicable to the conduct of military personnel'.[4] The international Conventions referred to above include the four Geneva Conventions of 12 August 1949 and their Additional Protocols of 8 June 1977 and the UNESCO Convention of 14 May 1954 on the Protection of Cultural Property in the event of armed conflict.[5] This undertaking has been included in agreements with states in the territory of which peacekeeping operations are deployed,[6] entailing direct responsibility for the UN toward third states.

Members of UN peacekeeping operations remain subject to the exclusive jurisdiction of their respective national states in respect of any criminal offences that may be committed by them.[7] Presumably criminal offences would include violations of the principles and spirit of humanitarian law. It is clear that being bound by the 'principles and spirit' is something else than being bound by humanitarian law as such, the position advocated by the ICRC. The debate between the UN and – principally – the ICRC has focused on the following arguments.

134   *International Peacekeeping   July 1999–October 1999*

Articles

2.2 *Discrimination*

The UN has held that peacekeeping operations act on behalf of the international community at large. They could not be a 'party to an armed conflict' in the sense of humanitarian law because impartiality is one of the basic principles of peacekeeping. Humanitarian law in principle only applies to parties to an armed conflict.

In essence, the UN has claimed that the rules that apply between equal states cannot apply between states and an international organization that may bind states against their will, and is empowered to determine whether the use of force is authorized or not.[8] As a result, the UN should be able to discriminate with regard to the application of humanitarian law.[9]

The objection has been made that this reasoning confuses the issues of *jus ad bellum* and *jus in bello*. The UN has been given the exclusive right to determine whether the use of force is legal. As such it has a privileged position in the field of the *jus ad bellum*. From this the *jus in bello* – the law that regulates the actual use of force whether it is legally resorted to or not must be clearly distinguished. The equality of the parties is a fundamental principle of the *jus in bello*. This is reaffirmed in the preamble to Additional Protocol I to the Geneva Conventions[10] and was also the conclusion of the Institut de Droit International, which stated in 1971 that:

'[t]he humanitarian rules of the law of armed conflict apply to the United Nations as of right, and they must be complied with in all circumstances by United Nations Forces which are engaged in hostilities.'[11]

2.3 *The United Nations is not a party to treaties of humanitarian law*

The United Nations also relies on the fact that it is not a party to any treaty of international humanitarian law, particularly the 1949 Geneva Conventions and their Additional Protocols. These treaties do not explicitly provide for the accession of international organizations, and it is questioned whether such an accession is possible. The Conventions only refer to the possibility of accession by 'Powers', arguably meaning only states. A suggestion by the ICRC to include a provision to allow international organizations to accede in Additional Protocol I was not adopted.[12]

It is objected that this does not preclude the applicability of international customary law. The UN is a subject of international law bound and capable of having rights and duties like states.[13] Large parts of the Geneva Conventions and the Additional Protocols are considered to have customary status.

2.4 *The United Nations cannot apply certain parts of humanitarian law*

The UN maintains that it is unable to apply certain parts of humanitarian law.[14]

Many provisions of humanitarian law are designed to be applied by states. The United Nations does not have the administrative or juridical capacities of a state, such as courts and broad legislating powers. Consequently, it could not apply provisions on grave breaches, for example. To this it can be objected that if the UN cannot strictly apply certain parts of humanitarian law, it can at least apply them *mutatis mutandis*. The use of national resources for exercising criminal jurisdiction is one example of this, although it has serious shortcomings. More generally, it is argued that where states give the UN powers and functions which bring the organization into a situation where certain rules apply, they must also give the organization the necessary means to comply with these rules.[15]

2.5 *The threshold question*

Humanitarian law applies in situations of armed conflict. It has been argued that action undertaken by peacekeeping operations does not reach this threshold. One of the basic principles of peacekeeping is the non-use of force except in self-defense, closely linked to the principle of host-state consent. In principle, the mandates of peacekeeping operations are weighted against the use of force, and thus against situations in which humanitarian law provides guidance.[16]

Nevertheless, situations may arise in which peacekeepers resort to the use of force, such as self-defense. The UN has broadly interpreted the concept of self-defense to include everything from resistance to forceful attempts to prevent the peacekeepers from carrying out their mandate. The doctrine of so-called 'wider peacekeeping' goes even further in not ruling out the use of force for selective purposes other than self-defense. It could be argued that the UN Protection Force (UNPROFOR) was an example of wider peacekeeping.[17] The UN operation in Somalia (UNOSOM I and II) may provide another example. Many states have disagreed with the UN's narrow interpretation of 'armed conflict', considering that judgments delivered by international tribunals support a broad interpretation. Thus, the Appeals Chamber of the International Criminal Tribunal for the former Yugoslavia (ICTY) gave the following definition:

'An armed conflict exists whenever there is a resort to armed force between States or protracted armed violence between governmental authorities and organized armed groups or between such groups within a State.'[18]

Without going as far as saying that humanitarian law applies from the first shot, this statement suggests a broad definition of armed conflict.

3. The Secretary-General's Bulletin

3.1 *History of the Bulletin*

Since the earliest peacekeeping efforts by the UN, the ICRC has consistently called attention to the application of humanitarian law by UN forces.[19] Particularly after the end of the Cold War, sensitivity for this issue also grew

International Peacekeeping July 1999–October 1999 135

Articles

within the UN. UN forces increasingly became involved in situations occasioning the use of force. At the same time, allegations were leveled against UN forces of violations of humanitarian law. In 1995, the UN's Special Committee for Peacekeeping Operations requested the Secretary-General to 'complete the elaboration of a code of conduct for United Nations peacekeeping personnel, consistent with applicable international humanitarian law'.[20] The ICRC took the lead in attempts to draft such a code defining the 'principles and spirit' of humanitarian law. To this end it organized two meetings of experts from military and academic circles in March and October 1995. After one of these meetings a UN expert suggested that the ICRC draft a pamphlet containing the appropriate rules.[21]

This ICRC draft was reviewed jointly by the ICRC and the UN Secretariat, in particular the Department of Peacekeeping Operations. On 10 May 1996, the 'Guidelines for UN forces regarding respect for international humanitarian law' were presented to the Secretary-General.[22]

The term 'Guidelines' was later replaced with 'Directives'. After these Directives were finalized by the Secretariat, they were finally issued in the form of a Secretary-General's Bulletin on 6 August 1999.

3.2 The Form: the Characteristics of a Secretary-General's Bulletin

In the past it has been proposed that the UN bind itself to humanitarian rules by a formal accession to humanitarian law conventions or a formal declaration to respect those conventions. These procedures are different than the promulgation of a Secretary-General's Bulletin. A Secretary-General's Bulletin is an administrative issuance of the Secretary-General.[23]

It is a subsidiary instrument elaborating the Staff Rules issued by the Secretary-General as the highest

administrative authority of the organization.[24] Staff Rules are provided by the Secretary-General to give substance to the Staff Regulations. Staff Regulations embody the fundamental conditions of service and the basic rights, duties and obligations of the UN Secretariat.[25] They represent the broad principles of personnel policy for the staffing and administration of the Secretariat, whereas Staff Rules are more specific. The Secretary-General's Bulletin is part of the internal law of the UN and its addressees are staff members of the UN. The addressees of the particular Bulletin under discussion are the members of United Nations forces, including enforcement actions and peacekeeping operations when the use of force is permitted in self-defence. The Bulletin's field of application is discussed further on.

The Bulletin as part of the internal law of the UN creates obligations for UN forces *vis-à-vis* the UN and not outside this framework. This has potentially important consequences for addressing violations of the Bulletin. In principle, violations of administrative law are addressed by the appropriate administrative procedures within the UN. The Staff Regulations of the UN specify that the Secretary-General may impose disciplinary measures on staff members whose conduct is unsatisfactory.[26] This Regulation is further elaborated in Chapter X of the UN Staff Rules. A question that arises is whether members of national contingents are to be considered as members of the UN secretariat. They are in a different position inasmuch as they retain a certain connection with their troop contributing state. That state is responsible for their pay, for example. It is also responsible for punishing violations of humanitarian law. In this regard, Article 4 of the Bulletin provides that violations of international humanitarian law are subject to prosecution in the national courts of the members of a UN force. It follows from this that UN administrative measures are not contemplated. This is in conformity with UN practice regarding its forces. Rather, national

prosecution is used to implement the service obligations of the members to the UN and not to the troop contributing state. The Bulletin's provisions reflect a part of these service obligations. As such, they can be invoked by national courts in the prosecution of members of UN forces and have a role outside the UN administrative system.

3.3 The Substance: the Bulletin's Provisions

For a clear understanding of the Bulletin's provisions, it is important to recognize its relationship to other relevant legal texts.

First, these are the instruments of humanitarian law, principally the four Geneva Conventions and their two Additional Protocols. The Bulletin's provisions are inspired by and based on provisions in these instruments. It must be noted, however, that the Bulletin comprises only 34 articles and the Conventions and their Protocols together hundreds. Thus, many of the more detailed provisions of these instruments are not reflected in the Bulletin.

Second, the Bulletin must be seen in relation to the 1994 Convention on the Safety of United Nations and Associated Personnel (Safety Convention).[27] This convention[28] establishes a protective regime for UN personnel involved in UN operations by criminalizing a number of enumerated crimes, including attacks on UN personnel. This is a fundamentally different approach than humanitarian law, under which it is fully legal to attack combatants. The Bulletin comprises a preamble and 10 'sections' subdivided in 34 different articles. Sections 1 and 2 deal with the Bulletin's field of application and its relation to certain other instruments and sources of law. Sections 3 and 4 deal with Status of Forces Agreements and jurisdiction over personnel of a UN force. Sections 5–9 are concerned with different groups of provisions of substantive humanitarian law. These groups conform to groups traditionally

136   *International Peacekeeping   July 1999–October 1999*

Articles

distinguished in humanitarian law instruments, including protection of the civilian population, means and methods of combat and protection of the wounded, the sick and medical and relief personnel. Section 10 sets the date of entry into force of the Bulletin at 12 August 1999, exactly fifty years after the adoption of the four Geneva Conventions.

In the following paragraph, a number of the specific provisions of the Bulletin are analyzed. It is outside the scope of this article to discuss all the provisions. Instead, a number provisions, that are particularly relevant in the light of UN forces' practice or provisions that deviate from treaty norms of humanitarian law, are analyzed.

3.4   Field of Application and Relation to Other Instruments and Sources of Law

The preamble to the Bulletin declares that it is promulgated 'for the purpose of setting out the fundamental principles and rules of international humanitarian law applicable to United Nations forces conducting operations under United Nations command and control'. The difference between the term principles and rules, and the term principles and spirit traditionally used by the UN is immediately apparent. It underlines the fact that this is the first time the UN has issued specific rules of humanitarian law for its forces in contrast to the very general undertaking to respect the principles and spirit of humanitarian law. Until now, it was unclear what that undertaking really comprised. The Bulletin is extremely important from the perspective of legal certainty by giving that obligation substance. Section 2 adds that the Bulletin's provisions do not prejudice the application of other principles and rules of humanitarian law. This provision suggests that in addition to the rules included in the Bulletin, the UN may be bound also by rules of customary law. Until the promulgation of the Bulletin, it was frequently

submitted that customary law bound the UN to humanitarian rules.[29]

The Bulletin only applies to forces under UN command and control. Consequently, forces authorized but not commanded by the UN such as SFOR and KFOR are not concerned. Article 1 (1) declares the Bulletin applicable to UN forces in situations of armed conflict where they are actively engaged as combatants, to the extent and for the duration of their engagement. Article 1 (2) adds that the Bulletin does not affect the protected status of UN personnel under the Safety Convention as long as members of UN forces are entitled to the protection given to civilians under the international law of armed conflict. Combatant status excludes the status as a civilian and in this respect the two regimes are mutually exclusive. The Safety Convention, however, states that it applies to:

'1. (c) 'United Nations operation' means an operation established by the competent organ of the United Nations in accordance with the Charter of the United Nations and conducted under United Nations authority and control.

2. (1) This Convention applies in respect of [...] United Nations operations, as defined in article 1. (2) This Convention shall not apply to a United Nations operation authorized by the Security Council as an enforcement action under Chapter VII of the Charter of the United Nations in which any of the personnel are engaged as combatants against organized armed forces and to which the law of international armed conflict applies.'

Consequently, the regimes of the Safety Convention and the Bulletin overlap in the case of operations that meet the criteria stipulated in Article 1 (1) of the Bulletin but not those of Article 2 (2) of the Safety Convention. This category notably includes 'traditional' peacekeeping operations that are not established under Chapter VII

but may nevertheless become involved in protracted hostilities with organized armed forces, to which humanitarian law would otherwise apply. This overlap of regimes is very problematic. The Safety Convention criminalizes attacks on UN personnel while under humanitarian law it is fully legal to attack them as long as they are combatants. It is precisely this fundamental difference that inspired the wish of the drafters of the Safety Convention to clearly delineate between mutually exclusive regimes of humanitarian law and the Convention, a wish they did not succeed in fulfilling. The provisions of the Bulletin reproduce this overlap creating possible confusion concerning which regime applies in a particular situation.

The Bulletin in Article 1 (1) refers to situations of armed conflict without reference to the different regimes applicable to international and non-international armed conflicts respectively. The draft Directives[30] did include such a reference, stating that they were applicable to international and non-international armed conflicts as might be relevant. This represented a departure from the view of most commen-tators, who maintain that UN involvement by definition internationalizes a non-international armed conflict and that therefore only the humanitarian law regime applicable to international conflicts can apply to UN forces.[31] This was also the position of the drafters of the Safety Convention.[32] The provisions of the Bulletin are more supportive of this position than the draft Directives. This is also reflected in Article 5 (1) of the Bulletin that states the principle of distinction between combatants and civilians. The draft Directives used the expression 'persons directly participating in hostilities' instead of 'combatants' in this provision, the latter term only being appropriate for the regime applicable to international armed conflicts. The use of this term in the Bulletin suggests that the regime for non-international conflicts is not deemed applicable to UN forces.

Articles

4. Substantive Rules

Sections 5–9 of the Bulletin contain substantive norms arranged in categories familiar to students of humanitarian law. These norms are principally derived from the 1949 Geneva Conventions and Additional Protocol I with certain modifications. It is outside the scope of this article to discuss all provisions. Only some provisions that are particularly relevant in the light of UN forces' practice or provisions that deviate from treaty norms of humanitarian law are analyzed.

4.1 The Principle of Distinction

Article 5 (1) of the Bulletin states the fundamental principle of distinction between civilians and combatants and between civilian objects and military objectives. Article 5 (2) faithfully reproduces Article 51 (3) of Additional Protocol I in providing that civilians lose this protection for such time as they take a direct part in hostilities. Up to this point the Bulletin is in conformity with Protocol I provisions. Article 5 (4) states that the UN forces shall avoid, to the extent feasible, locating military objectives within or near densely populated areas. Military installations and equipment of peacekeeping operations, as such, shall not be considered military objectives. Article 58 (b–c) of Protocol I does not include this exception for UN installations and equipment. When UN forces become combatants in the sense of Article 1 (1) of the Bulletin, the UN is a party to the conflict. Accordingly, its installations and equipment are military objectives if they fulfil the criteria of Article 52 (2) Protocol I. According to the rules of Protocol I, the UN must consequently, without exception refrain from locating those objectives near densely populated areas and that there should be no exception in this regard.[33] The Bulletin takes another point of view in this regard.

4.2 Treatment of Civilians and Persons hors de combat

Section 7 of the Bulletin regulating the treatment of civilians and persons *hors de combat* brings together rules from all four Geneva Conventions as well as Protocol I, particularly its Article 75. Protected persons shall in all circumstances be treated humanely and without any adverse distinction based on race, sex, religious convictions or any other ground. This enumeration of grounds is broader than that of Article 75 Protocol I, which refers to distinction based upon race, colour, sex, language, religion or belief, political or other opinion, national or social origin, wealth, birth or other status, or any other similar criterion. Although this is a longer list, the Bulletin's or any other ground includes the Protocol's enumeration as well as other grounds that are not necessarily similar to those in the list.

This broad protection in the Bulletin is also found in Article 7 (2) listing acts that are prohibited at any time and in any place against protected persons. Prohibited acts included in this article but not in Article 75 Protocol I are enslavement, pillage, and rape. Article 27 of Geneva Convention IV and Article 76 of Protocol I state expressly that civilian women shall be protected against rape. The more general prohibition in the Bulletin is not restricted to women only and also applies to persons *hors de combat*. The prohibition may reflect the sensitivity of the Bulletin's drafters to incidents involving UN forces. UN forces in Mozambique and Bosnia, among others, have been accused of rape. Ground-breaking jurisprudence by the ad hoc International Tribunals for the former Yugoslavia and Rwanda concerning rape may also have inspired this provision as well as Article 7 (3). This latter article specifically provides that women shall be protected against any attack, in particular against rape, enforced prostitution or any other form of indecent assault.

In another respect the Bulletin is less far-reaching. The draft Directives provided in Article 23 that unless specifically mandated by the Security Council, the UN force shall not detain civilians and that civilians lawfully detained shall unless otherwise provided for not be deprived of their right under internationally recognized standards of human rights. This provision regrettably does not return in the Bulletin. Adequate rules regarding the detention of civilians are needed. The gravest incidents in UN forces have involved the detention of civilians, for instance, concerning the Canadian contingent in Somalia. Human rights law offers an appropriate framework for the treatment of civilians that is better developed than the humanitarian law regime.[34]

4.3 Treatment of Detained Persons

Article 8 (1) of the Bulletin provides that detained persons, without prejudice to their legal status, shall be treated in accordance with the relevant provisions of the Third Geneva Convention of 1949, as may be applicable to them *mutatis mutandis*. The provision is careful not to accord prisoner of war status to detained persons. Doing so would open up the *a contrario* argument that captured UN forces are also prisoners of war. This is very problematical for the UN, because it implies that the UN is a party to the conflict. Article 4 (A) (1) of the Third Geneva Convention states that prisoners of war are, *inter alia*: 'Members of the armed forces of a Party to the conflict as well as members of militias or volunteer corps forming part of such armed forces.' To consider the UN as a party to the conflict calls into question the fundamental principle of impartiality of UN forces. Possibly for this reason no prisoner of war status was claimed on behalf of UN forces captured in Bosnia, even though it could be argued that they were in a position closely analogous with the category set out in

138   International Peacekeeping   July 1999–October 1999

Articles

Article 4 (A) (1) of the Third Geneva Convention.

In Section 2.4, one argument for not applying humanitarian law to UN forces was described as the UN not being able to apply certain parts of the law. This argument is strongest concerning the rules relating to the treatment of detained persons. The UN cannot apply penal and disciplinary sanctions, for instance, because it has no criminal legal system. The UN is also not able to legislate in the sense of Article 82 of the Third Geneva Convention. These shortcomings are addressed by Article 8 of the Bulletin that provides for the application *mutatis mutandis* of the rules of the Third Geneva Convention. The advantage of application *mutatis mutandis* is that it gives some flexibility in looking for pragmatic solutions to vexing questions. For example, it makes it possible to apply certain articles that the UN cannot perform itself to troop contributing states.[35]

The disadvantage of application *mutatis mutandis* is that it opens up the possibility of invoking all sorts of logistical or practical considerations for not complying with the rules on the treatment of detainees. This argument is a dangerous sliding scale. It has the potential of wholly undermining the protection of detained persons.

4.4 Protection of the Wounded and the Sick

Article 9 (1) of the Bulletin states *inter alia* that persons in the power of the UN force who are wounded or sick shall receive the medical care and attention required by their condition. Only urgent medical reasons will authorize priority in the order of treatment to be administered. This provision is based on Article 10 (2) of Protocol I. However, it does not include Article 10 (2)'s clause that medical care and attention shall be given 'to the fullest extent practicable and with the

least possible delay'. The Bulletin's unconditional duty is noteworthy because frequently UN forces have limited mandates and limited means at their disposal. The reason that the Bulletin does not include a restrictive clause may be that the drafters were sensitive to criticism of Dutch UNPROFOR troops in Srebrenica who were allegedly ordered not to treat Muslim civilians wounded during Srebrenica's fall.[36]

5. Supervision

It was pointed out in Section 3.2 that violations of humanitarian law are subject to prosecution in their national courts. Further, discipline within national contingents is primarily exercised by the national commanders of those contingents. Supervision of respect for humanitarian law is thus largely left to national authorities. These authorities have not always exercised that responsibility diligently. The UN Secretariat has started tracking individual cases of misconduct and inquiring about follow-up actions at the national level with member states in recognition of this fact.

The Bulletin presented a unique opportunity to strengthen the system of supervision. It could have strengthened the tracking system, for instance. Also, a humanitarian law ombudsman could have been created, as Amnesty International proposed several years ago.[37] The Bulletin does not contain provisions on supervision, however. An important opportunity was missed in this respect.

6. Conclusion

Allegations of violations by UN forces of international humanitarian law have galvanized attention for the application of that law to the UN. Increasingly, the UN and troop contributing states recognize that the UN must be bound by some rules of humanitarian law. The promulgation

of the Secretary-General's Bulletin on Observance by United Nations forces of international humanitarian law is evidence of this recognition. The Bulletin represents a pragmatic approach to applying the fundamental rules of humanitarian law to forces that were not envisaged by the drafters of the Geneva Conventions and not considered by the drafters of the Additional Protocols. The Bulletin adapts these rules to the particularities of UN forces. The step from binding principles and spirit to principles and rules of humanitarian law is a very important one providing a measure of legal certainty for UN forces as well as protected persons.

That being said, the Bulletin presents a number of problems. The most fundamental problem is that the UN still discriminates with regard to the application of humanitarian law. The Bulletin represents a very rudimentary protection in comparison with the detailed provisions of the Geneva Conventions and the Additional Protocols. It is far from a formal engagement by the UN to respect all conventions on humanitarian law, as has been proposed in the past.

Another problem is that the field of application of the Bulletin is not clear. In particular, the regime appears to overlap with the regime of the Convention on the Safety of UN and Associated Personnel. The two regimes are incompatible because they are based on fundamentally different principles. The overlap may contribute to a subtle raising of the threshold for the application of the law of international armed conflict, a danger that has been pointed out by Professor Greenwood.

Thirdly, the substantive provisions of the Bulletin in certain regards provide a lower level of protection than the rules in the Geneva Conventions and Additional Protocols. Examples are the definition of military

Articles

objectives and the protection of detained persons.

Finally, the Bulletin does not address the problem of supervision. Experience shows that increased supervision is needed for the rules to be adhered to and violations punished.

In sum, the Secretary-General's Bulletin represents a step forward in reconciling the laws applicable to UN forces and humanitarian law. However, there is still a long way to go.

*Marten Zwanenburg**

*Research Associate at the E.M. Meijers Institute of Legal Studies, Leiden University.

Notes

1. In this article, UN forces are defined in the sense of the Secretary-General's Bulletin on Observance by United Nations forces of international humanitarian law of 6 August 1999, UN Doc. ST/SGB/1999/13. They are considered enforcement actions or peacekeeping operations when the use of force is permitted in self-defence conducting operations under United Nations command and control.
2. Secretary-General's Bulletin, Observance by United Nations forces of international humanitarian law of 6 August 1999, UN Doc. ST/SGB/1999/13.
3. *See*, e.g., U. Palwankar, 'Applicability of International Humanitarian Law to United Nations Peace-keeping Forces', *International Review of the Red Cross* No. 294, at p. 227 (1993).
4. *See*, e.g., *Model Agreement between the United Nations and Member States contributing Personnel and Equipment to United Nations Peace-keeping Operations of 23 May 1991*, UN Doc. A/46/185, para. 28 (emphasis added).
5. D. Shraga, 'The United Nations as an Actor Bound by International Humanitarian Law', *International Peacekeeping* 64 (1998), at p. 68.
6. *See*, e.g., 'Exchange of Letters Constituting an Agreement between the United Nations and the Government of the Republic of Cyprus Concerning the Status of the United Nations Peace-Keeping Force in Cyprus of 31 March 1964', *UNTS* Vol. 492, at p. 58, para. 11.
7. *See also*, K. Boustany, Brocklebank: 'A Questionable Decision of the Court Martial Appeal Court of Canada', 1 *Yearbook of International Humanitarian Law* 317 (1998).
8. *See*, e.g., Committee on Study of Legal Problems of the UN, 'Should the Laws of War Apply to United Nations Enforcement Action?', 46 *ASIL* Proc. 216 (1952).
9. 1977 Geneva Protocol I Additional to the Geneva Conventions of 12 August 1949, and Relating to the Protection of Victims of International Armed Conflicts, 16 ILM 1391 (1977). The preamble states: 'Reaffirming further that the provisions of the Geneva Conventions [...] and of this Protocol must be fully applied [...] without any adverse distinction based on the nature or origin of the armed conflict or on the causes espoused by or attributed to the Parties to the conflict.'
10. 'Conditions of Application of Humanitarian Rules of Armed Conflict to Hostilities in which United Nations Forces May be Engaged', 54 *Annuaire de l'Institut de Droit International* 465 (1971), at p. 466.
11. D. Schindler, 'United Nations Forces and International Humanitarian Law', in Chr. Swinarski (ed.), *Etudes et Essais sur le Droit International Humanitaire et sur les Principes de la Croix-Rouge en l'Honneur de Jean Pictet* 521 (1984), at p. 525.
12. *See* 'Reparations for Injuries Suffered in the Service of the United Nations', Advisory Opinion of 11 April 1949, *ICJ* Rep. 1949, at p. 174.
13. *UN Juridical Yearbook* 1972, at p. 153.
14. *See* M. Bothe, 'Peacekeeping and International Humanitarian Law: Friends or Foes?', 3 *International Peacekeeping* 91 (1996), at p. 94.
15. *See* G.-J.F. van Hegelsom, 'The Law of Armed Conflict and UN Peace-keeping and Peace-enforcing Operations', 6 *Hague Yearbook of International Law* 45 (1993), at p. 54.
16. *See* M. Rose, *Fighting for Peace: Bosnia 1994*, at p. 248 (1998).
17. *Prosecutor* v. *Dua o Tadi a.k.a 'Dule'*, Decision on the Defence Motion for Interlocutory Appeal on Jurisdiction, Case No. It-94-1AR72, 2 October 1995, 105 ILR 419 at p. 453, para. 70.
18. *See* U. Palwankar, *supra* note, at 229–231, referring *inter alia* to a memorandum by the ICRC addressed to the states parties to the Geneva Conventions and members of the UN and a letter of 10 April 1978 from the President of the ICRC to the UN Secretary.
19. UN Doc. A/50/230, para. 73.
20. Report on the work of the meeting of experts on the applicability of international humanitarian law to United Nations forces, Geneva, 60 (1995) (Meeting of Experts Report).
21. ICRC Press Release, 15 May 1996.
22. *See Secretary-General's Bulletin*, Procedures for the Promulgation of Administrative Issuances of 28 May 1997, ST/SGB/1997/1.
23. *See* C.F. Amerasinghe, *The Law of the International Civil Service: As Applied by International Administrative Tribunals*, Vol. I, at p. 146 (1988).
24. *Id.*, at 1 (Scope and purpose of Staff Regulations of the United Nations).
25. UN Staff Regulation 10 (2), reproduced in Secretary-General's Bulletin, Staff Rules: Staff Regulations of the United Nations and Staff Rules 100.1 to 112.8 of 26 February 1990, UN Doc. ST/SGB/Staff Rules/1/Rev.7.
26. For the text of the Convention, *see* Annex to General Assembly Resolution 49/59 of 9 December 1994, UN Doc. A/RES/49/59/ Ann. The Convention entered into force on 15 January 1999.
27. For an analysis of the Safety Convention, *see* P. Kirsch, 'The Convention on the Safety of United Nations and Associated Personnel', 2 *International Peacekeeping* 102 (1995), at p. 105.
28. *See*, e.g., H. McCoubrey, 'International Humanitarian Law and United Nations Military Action in the "New World Order"', in: University of Nottingham, *International Law and Armed Conflict: Commentary*, Vol. I, 36 (1994), at p. 42.
29. Draft Directives for UN Forces Regarding Respect for International Humanitarian Law, on file with the author, Art. 4.
30. *See*, e.g., R. Glick, 'Lip Service to the Laws of War: Humanitarian Law and United Nations Armed Forces', 17 *Michigan Journal of International Law* 53 (1995), at p. 81; Shraga, *supra* note, at p. 73.
31. Kirsch, *supra* note, at p. 105.
32. *Cf.* Meeting of Experts Report, *supra* note, at p. 45.
33. *See* Amnesty International, Peace-keeping and Human Rights 23 (1993).
34. *Cf.* Meeting of Experts Report, *supra* note, at p. 45.
35. *See* J. Chao, Dutch Military's Bosnia Role Probed, AP, 11 August 1998.
36. Amnesty International, *supra* note, at p. 38.
37. *See* D. Schindler, 'UN Forces and International Humanitarian Law', in Chr. Swinarski (ed.), *Etudes et Essais sur le Droit International Humanitaire et sur les Principes de la Croix-Rouge en l'Honneur de Jean Pictet* 521 (1984), at p. 528.
38. C. Greenwood, 'Protection of Peacekeepers: The Legal Regime', 7 *Duke Journal of Comparative & International Law* 185 (1996), at p. 202.

[11]

MAINTAINING DISCIPLINE IN UNITED NATIONS PEACE SUPPORT OPERATIONS: THE LEGAL QUAGMIRE FOR MILITARY CONTINGENTS

Peter Rowe*

1 INTRODUCTION

To the question, 'what are armies for?' the answer used to be, 'to fight the armed forces of an enemy state and, possibly, to assist law enforcement agencies within national territory under certain circumstances'. This is now, of course, too simplistic an approach. Contingents of the armed forces of many states are now, in this post Cold War era, to be found serving as part of humanitarian or peacekeeping or peace enforcing operations[1] outside their own territories. The law has not been able to move quite so quickly. There is no ready-made body of international law, unlike that which applies once an 'armed conflict between two or more' states takes place. In peacekeeping/enforcement operations there may be a mix of 'ordinary' criminal law (of the sending and of the receiving states), military law (of the different contingent states) and international law (to govern the relationship between the sending and receiving states and the protection of those not taking any part in

---

* Professor of Law and Head of the Department of Law, University of Lancaster. The author is grateful to Col. Charles Garraway, UK Army Legal Services, and to David Travers, Department of Politics and International Relations, University of Lancaster for their comments on an earlier draft. Views expressed are those of the author.

1 For ease of reference, styled as peace support operations, a term adopted by the Select Committee on Defence, First Report, 1997/98, HC 403. Traditionally, peacekeeping is based under chapter VI of the UN Charter and peace enforcement under chapter VII. For discussion of these concepts and for their distinctions see Bowett, *United Nations Forces* (1964) chapter 15; Hampson, *Non-Governmental Organisations in Situations of Conflict*, in Schmitt and Green (eds.) *The Law of Armed Conflict Into the Next Millennium* (Vol. 71) 233, 256; and for 'operations having a hybrid character,' see Roberts, 'UN Peacekeeping', (1994) 36(3) *Survival*, 93, 102, 110. Different legal consequences may flow from each, see Greenwood, 'International Humanitarian Law and United Nations Operations', in (1998) *Yearbook of International Humanitarian Law(YIHL)*, 3, 11; Harper, Legal Adviser, Department of State, 'On Legal Authority for UN Peace Operations', (1994) 33 *ILM* 821, 828; 'The United States: Administration Policy on Reforming Multilateral Peace Operations', (1994) 33 *ILM*, 795, 803. See also art.2(2) of the Convention on the Safety of UN and Associated Personnel 1994 (1995) 34 *ILM* 484 for the significance of the operation being derived under chap.VII. Operations may start within one concept (such as peace keeping or enforcement) and be converted into another, see Shraga, 'The United Nations as an Actor Bound by International Humanitarian Law', (1998) 5 *International Peacekeeping* 64, 66. Humanitarian assistance may occur alongside peacekeeping (as in Bosnia) or it may be separate (as in the case of a natural disaster). Note art.8.2(e)(iii) of the Rome Statute of the International Criminal Court 1998 which refers only to 'humanitarian assistance or peacekeeping mission.'

46   *Peter Rowe*

hostilities).[2] Add to this confused picture the fact that a national contingent may be placed under the command of a force commander from a different national contingent and the legal uncertainties grow.[3]

In this paper I wish to concentrate on disciplinary issues relating to the purported carrying out of the mandate, but in doing so, I will inevitably refer to other legal issues.[4]

2 DISCIPLINE ISSUES IN PEACE SUPPORT OPERATIONS

These types of operations may be considered by fighting[5] units of an army to be 'useful' and 'easy.' 'Useful' in the sense of giving the unit concerned a sense of purpose, rather than what might appear to be an endless round of training exercises and 'easy' in the sense that the normal risks and prolonged stresses of combat are unlikely to be encountered. This view disguises the real nature and difficulties of peace support operations. As a result, there is a danger of inadequate preparation prior to deployment.[6] Some of the key issues are explored below.

---

[2] It has been argued that, in addition, 'UN law' applies, Siekmann, 'The Fall of Srebrenica and the Attitude of Dutchbat from an International Legal Perspective', (1998) *YIHL* 301, 308. In reality, Siekmann is dealing with the legal status of an order from a UN commander to a national contingent (Dutchbat).

[3] See Roberts, *loc. cit.*, 103 on the political difficulties of placing the contingents of some States under UN control; Bowett, *op.cit.* 487–488; Siekmann, *ibid.*

[4] These are well discussed in an unpublished paper by Col. Paphiti (UK Army Legal Services) and Lt.Col. Blomfield, dated 21 October 1997. For policy issues, see Whaley, 'Improving UN Developmental Co-Ordination within Peace Missions', (1996) *International Peacekeeping* 107. Where soldiers commit crimes unrelated to the carrying out of their mission they will be subject to their own military discipline code, see *Experiences with regard to the United Nations Peacekeeping Forces in Mozambique, Redd Barna Report*, 20 November 1995, detailing alleged sexual exploitation by UN soldiers of Mozambiquan children while serving with ONUMOZ. See also Findlay, *Cambodia: the Legacy and Lessons of UNTAC* (1995) 139 discussing the discipline problems of the Bulgarian contingent to UNTAC, *Allegations of Criminality in Peacekeeping Missions*, (1997) 36(3) *UN Chronicle*, 39. The Code of Conduct is set out in diagramatic form at 40. It was issued on 6 January 1997 under the title, 'Guidance to Commanders of United Nations Military Operations. Standards of Conduct and Performance Criteria'.

[5] As distinguished from specialist military personnel, such as engineers or medical personnel. See the letter of 17 November 1992 from the Secretary-General of the UN to the Italian prime minister requesting the deployment of an engineer battalion to 'carry out de-mining and road and bridge construction', in *The United Nations and Mozambique, 1992–1995* (UN, 1995) 147.

[6] See *R v Brocklebank* (1996) 134 DLR (4th) 377, 384, Decary, Young and Molina, 'IHL and Peace Operations', (1998) *YIHL* 362, 367; Roberts, *loc.cit.*, 116; *Report of the Commission of Inquiry established pursuant to resolution 885 (1993) to investigate armed attacks on UNOSOM II personnel*, UN doc. S/1994/653, 1 June 1994, para.224, '[t]he transition from a fighting posture to peace-keeping is indeed a very difficult one for any professional soldier' *The United Nations and Somalia 1992–1996* (1996) 368; Redd Barna Report, 20 November 1995, *op.cit.*, 9.

2.1 The Mission

In the disciplinary codes of most states a soldier will commit a military offence if he fails to discharge his *duty*,[7] or fails to obey a *lawful* command[8] or imperils the success of any *action or operation*[9] or *who assists*[10] *the enemy.*[11] It is therefore essential to be clear as to what the soldier's duty is, the parameters of lawful commands, who the 'enemy' is and the requirements of military discipline.[12] The starting point will be the mandate. This is likely to be expressed in rather general terms, telling states where the pitch is, who the players are and the objective of the operation, but providing no clear rules to when a yellow or red card should be shown to the players.[13]

In missions involving some enforcement, it is common to express the obligation to use 'all measures necessary' to achieve the objective. This cannot, of course, be taken literally. The fears of one writer[14] that such a form of words is 'not unlike a declaration of martial law, only more severe . . . [since] an "anything goes" atmosphere operates where people can be killed without resort to enquiry; where arbitrary arrests can be made without trial, *habeas corpus* is thrown to the winds; and property can be grabbed or destroyed without compensation' is clearly too alarmist. It is for the separate teams to draw up their own rules, under the guiding principle

---

7   See, for example, ss.24, 29, 29A, 31, 54 of the Army Act 1955 (UK); art.99(8) Uniform Code of Military Justice (US); s.19 Armed Forces Act 1968 (Kenya); s.17(a) Armed Forces Act 1962 (Ghana); s.124 National Defence Act 1985 (Canada). In *R v Brocklebank* (1996) 134 DLR (4th) 377 the accused was charged with the negligent performance of a duty imposed on him, in not preventing a subordinate from assaulting a Somali youth.

8   Ss.34, 36, Army Act 1955 (UK); art. 92 of the Uniform Code of Military Justice (US); ss.28 and 30 Armed Forces Act 1968 (Kenya); s.22 Armed Forces Act 1962 (Ghana).

9   S.26 Army Act 1955 (UK); art.99 Uniform Code of Military Justice (US); s.14(1) Armed Forces Act 1968 (Kenya); s.15 Armed Forces Act 1962 (Ghana).

10   See, for example, s.25 Army Act 1955 (UK); s.14 Armed Forces Act 1968 (Kenya); s.16 Armed Forces Act 1962 (Ghana).

11   The term, 'enemy' is defined in s.225 Army Act 1955 as 'includes all persons engaged in armed operations against any of Her Majesty's forces or any forces co-operating therewith, and also includes all armed mutineers, armed rebels, armed rioters and pirates'. A similar provision is to be found in s.2 Armed Forces Act 1968 (Kenya) and in s.98 Armed Forces Act 1962 (Ghana).

12   It is common in some armed forces to provide a separate offence to deal with acts or omissions to the prejudice of good order and military discipline, see for example, s.69 Army Act 1955; s.68 Armed Forces Act 1968 (Kenya); s.54 Armed Forces Act 1962 (Ghana); s.134 Uniform Code of Military Justice (US).

13   See SC Res. 770 (1992), 776 (1992), 824 (1993) all relating to Bosnia referred to *all measures necessary*. The position was similar with respect to Somalia, see SC Res.794 (1992) 'to establish as soon as possible a secure environment for humanitarian relief operations in Somalia,' and Res.837 (1993) 'against those responsible for the armed attacks [against personnel of UN Operations in Somalia II on 5 June 1993].' See also SC Res.1244 (1999) relating to Kosovo, para.7. The Military technical agreement of 9 June 1999 between the International security Force (KFOR) and the Governments of the Federal Republic of Yugoslavia and the Republic of Serbia authorized 'the use of necessary force to ensure compliance.'

14   Drysdale, *Whatever Happened to Somalia?* (1994), 85.

of the mandate and their obligations under national and international law.[15] It is the *implementation* of this mandate into the military structures of a participating state that will be crucial. This will, in other words, determine what the soldier's *duty* is. It will be wider in nature than the rules of engagement (ROE), discussed below, since it will include all orders given by a soldier's superior officers, whether to act or not to act, and it will provide the context in which the soldier's military law applies.[16] Unless the *limits* of this implemented mandate are made clear to soldiers, uncertainty over the extent of their duty is likely to create disciplinary problems. Is the soldier, for instance, required to carry out what might appear to be the aims and objectives of political leaders? Is this within the parameters of his 'duty'? Decary JA, in *R v Brocklebank*[17] was prepared to hold that a 'rule emanating from the government' would create an obligation upon the soldier and thereby impose a duty upon him. This is, with respect, likely to cause confusion and in any event, a soldier is only obliged to comply with the orders of those within the military chain of command or national or international law. Capt. Lawrence Rockwood of the United States Army was faced with uncertainty over the extent of his duty. He had been a member of the US contingent to the multinational task force in Haiti in 1994[18] and had become aware, through intelligence reports, of the conditions prevailing in the penitentiary in Port au Prince. He believed that his commander should do something about this, but this course of action was rejected. Capt. Rockwood set about this himself and attempted to visit the penitentiary, thereby failing to comply with his specific military orders. Rockwood stated at his court-martial that he had watched the President's televized address and recalled the President saying that one of the reasons for US involvement was 'to stop the brutal atrocities' occurring in Haiti.[19] The US Army Court of Criminal Appeals had little sympathy for this argument, holding that a soldier must obey the implementing orders passed down the

---

[15] It is common in operations under UN command that authority is given to the Force commander to define the rules of engagement (ROE), see para.88 of the *Report of the Secretary-General re Somalia*, UN doc. S/25354, 3 March 1993. It is also likely that the individual contingents will draw up, within these guidelines, their own ROEs.

[16] In *R v Brocklebank*, *supra*, Decary JA, with whom Strayer CJ agreed, concluded that 'a military duty ... will not arise absent an obligation which is created either by statute, regulation, order from a superior, or rule emanating from the government or chief of defence staff,' at p.397. The Court-Martial Appeal Court of Canada was concerned with the interpretation of S.124 of the National Defence Act 1985, which has important differences from the comparable position under S.29A of the Army Act 1955 (UK).

[17] *Ibid.* Decary JA seemed to distinguish statute and regulation from a 'rule emanating from the government.' The latter phrase could be omitted since it is otiose. The instructions of the government are communicated to the armed forces and passed down through the military chain of command.

[18] See generally, Morris, 'Force and Democracy: UN/US Intervention in Haiti', (1995) 2 *International Peacekeeping* 391.

[19] *United States v Captain Lawrence P. Rockwood II,* (1998) 48 MJ 501, 513. In relation to Bosnia the Minister of State for the Armed Forces (UK) explained that the role of British troops was to get 'humanitarian food convoys through', Fourth Report From the Defence Committee, Session 1992–93, United Kingdom Peacekeeping and Intervention Forces, HC 188, 369.

Maintaining Discipline in United Nations Peace Support Operations 49

chain of command from the President to the operational commander.[20] Rockwood's *duty* was therefore constrained by his military orders. He could not 'be allowed to walk on the grass to prevent a rape'.[21]

The case of Capt. Rockwood is, perhaps, a fairly straightforward one in this regard. His request to investigate the conditions in the penitentiary had been expressly rejected by his superior officers. He may have been unsure what the mission of the US forces in Haiti was but he was able to approach his military superiors with his concerns. Other soldiers may not have the same opportunities before acting or not acting, or they may witness serious war crimes being committed against civilians taking no part in the conflict. There is a difference in the legal systems of many countries between being provided with a legal justification for acting and failing to act at all.[22] It is therefore important to define clearly a soldier's duty in a peace support operation, since it is quite unlike his duty when he is engaged in an international armed conflict, where he may use proportionate force against enemy combatants and military objectives. Is he required, as part of his duty, to intervene to prevent serious breaches of international humanitarian law? If so, under what circumstances and at what risk to himself and others?[23]

The nature of the mission will also determine what weapons (if any) are to be carried by soldiers, which, in turn, will set the parameters for the limits of the mission and the consequences of any breach of discipline.[24]

---

[20] *Ibid.*, 506. A soldier had opportunities to seek clarification from his commanders but had no right to 'take action on his own without command authorization.' Further appeal to the United States Court of Appeals for the Armed Forces was dismissed, judgment of 30 September 1999. Cox CJ stated that '[I]t is the commander not the subordinate, who must assess . . . competing concerns and develop command priorities.'

[21] Report of the trial by Francis X.Clinks, 'American Officer's Mission for Haitian Rights Backfires', 2, <http://www.english.upenn.edu/-afilreis/Holocaust/haitian.html> To be fair to the military authorities their priority at the time had been to protect the lives of military personnel following a grenade attack near the Haitian Presidential Palace. See also *The Times*, 27 November (1995).

[22] The Canadian rules of engagement in Somalia permitted force to be used to protect 'noncombatant civilians' but only if the threat to them was 'immediate,' see *R v Mathieu*, below. See also Siekmann, *loc.cit.*, 301, esp. 310, where the German law concept of 'Unterlassene Hilfeleistung [failed relief]' is discussed; Rose, 'Crafting the Rules of Engagement for Haiti', in *The Law of Military Operations* (US Naval War College, Vol.72, 1998) Chapter XI, 231.

[23] See discussion of the rules of engagement, below; Siekmann, *loc.cit.*, who discusses the alleged failure by Dutchbat (the Dutch battalion under the command of UNPROFOR). His conclusion that, 'possible wrongful behaviour of Dutchbat during the fall of Srebrenica cannot legally be attributed to the Netherlands,' at 303 cannot mean that the Dutch soldiers would not be liable individually for any breaches of their military disciplinary code.

[24] Commanders will also have to consider whether soft-skin vehicles are adequate to prevent casualties, see *Report of the Commission of Inquiry established pursuant to resolution 885 (1993) to investigate armed attacks on UNOSOM II personnel*', UN doc. S/1994/653, 1 June 1994, at para.217.

50 *Peter Rowe*

2.2 What Law Applies?

It is assumed that the peace support operation is not being carried out in the territory of the state concerned. A status of forces agreement (between the sending and receiving states) will normally be concluded before deployment.[25] The NATO Status of Forces Agreement 1951[26] (and the PfP version[27]) may not be a suitable precedent since the sending state may wish to secure *exclusive* jurisdiction over members of the force and any civilian component for any acts or omissions contrary to the criminal laws of both states.[28] If this is secured, the soldier will be liable, in terms of national law, only to the criminal and disciplinary law of his own state.

Where there is no status of forces agreement in place prior to deployment peacekeeping forces may face unacceptable legal difficulties in carrying out their mission. These will range from difficulties over freedom of movement in the territory of the receiving state, to uncertainties over the liability of the force to pay local taxes,[29] to procedures for claims against the visiting force and to confusion over civil and criminal jurisdiction. The potential liability of members of the peacekeeping force to the criminal jurisdiction of the state, not only when they are present on the territory but also after they have left it in respect of crimes committed against the local law while present, is the most significant risk. It may be that if the receiving state is unable to act effectively in its territory so as to enter into a status of forces agreement, members of the contingents of peace operations forces will run little risk of local criminal jurisdiction when carrying out their operations, but the risk may change dramatically once an effective government establishes control and seeks the extradition of former peacekeepers as alleged criminals.[30]

[25] This may not be possible if the UN Security Council takes action under chapter VII of the UN Charter and the action is considered as peace enforcement, or where there is no effective governmental authority.

[26] 199 UNTS 67; Cmnd. 9363 (as amended).

[27] Cmnd. 3237 (1996).

[28] As in, for example, the Agreement Between the Republic of Croatia and the North Atlantic Treaty organization (NATO) Concerning the Status of NATO and Its Personnel, (1995) 35 *ILM* 104, art.7; see also the status of forces agreements in respect of UNEF, ONUC, UNFICYP, all of which gave exclusive jurisdiction to the national States, Siekmann, *Basic Documents on United Nations and Related Peacekeeping* (1985). See also the Status of Forces Agreement Between the United States of America and the Republic of Korea, 1966, art.XX11(11) where a primary right of jurisdiction granted to US forces in certain circumstances is transformed into exclusive jurisdiction upon the event of hostilities in the region. See generally, Bowett, *op. cit.* 432.

[29] The UN Secretary-General drew attention to the fact that 'the approved budget of the mission does not include allowance for customs duties, excise taxes, levies, fees. . .which the Government, its agents and local authorities are charging the ONUMOZ,' *Report of the Secretary-General on ONUMOZ*, UN doc. S/25518, 2 April 1993, para.49. Similar problems were faced over freedom of movement which imposed 'restrictions on the effectiveness of the mission,' *ibid.* at para.10. A status of forces agreement was signed by the government of Mozambique and the UN on 14 May 1993, Report of the Secretary-General on ONOMOZ, UN doc. S/26034, 30 June 1993, para.9.

[30] Simpson, *Law Applicable to Canadian Forces in Somalia 1992/93* (a study prepared for the Commission of Inquiry into the Deployment of Canadian Forces to Somalia, Ministry of

Maintaining Discipline in United Nations Peace Support Operations 51

Any argument of the sending state that under customary international law members of a visiting force are immune from the jurisdiction of the receiving state[31] is likely, itself, to be problematic. Even if customary international law did support this proposition it only applied where the consent of the territorial state existed.[32] In the instances where no status of forces agreement is concluded two serious consequences, in terms of criminal jurisdiction,[33] would seem to follow. First, members of national contingents may be liable to be charged before the courts of the receiving state (whether during the peace operations or afterwards) for crimes against the local law. Secondly, the rules of engagement, drawn up by national contingents, are unlikely to take account of the local law and will not therefore protect the soldier, if he complies with them, from this law where there is a difference between the two. The existence or non-existence of a status of forces agreement may therefore have a profound effect on the consequences of non-compliance with the rules of engagement.

Is the soldier liable also to comply with international law? In a peace operation international humanitarian law *may or may not* apply. This will depend, to a large extent, on whether an armed conflict[34] is taking place. This is, of course, much more likely to be the case in a peace enforcing as contrasted with a peacekeeping operation. Even where an armed conflict is taking place it is not clear that national contingents would be 'parties to the conflict.' Greenwood draws attention to the Convention on the Safety of United Nations and Associated Personnel 1994[35] and

Public Works and Government Services, Canada, 1997), concludes that members of the Canadian forces in Somalia 'were *probably* (sic) subject to the criminal law of Somalia, notwithstanding that the Somali criminal justice system was not then functioning,' at 47 and he discusses the possible trial of members of such forces by a Somali court in the future, at 43–46. It is, perhaps, of some significance that the Somali penal code 1962, in art.434 imposes the death penalty for murder, *ibid.*, 2.

[31] See *The Schooner Exchange v McFaddon* (1812) 7 Cr.116; US Reports (L.Ed) 488; King, 'Jurisdiction over Friendly Foreign Armed Forces', (1942) 36 *AJIL* 539, where many of the older cases are cited. Compare the views of Wijewardane, (1965–66) XLI *BYIL* 122 at 143, who supports such a view providing the offence arises out of official duty, whereas Barton, 'Foreign Armed Forces: Immunity from Criminal Jurisdiction', (1950) 27 *BYIL* 186 is not so sure after considering all the authorities. See also Woodliffe, *The Peacetime Use of Foreign Military Installations under Modern International Law* (1992) 170 *et seq.*

[32] This was the reasoning of Marshall CJ in *The Schooner Exchange v McFaddon*, above. The consent of the sovereign to waive jurisdiction could, however, be implied since the Chief Justice referred to national ships of war entering ports open for their reception. See also Simpson, *op. cit.*, 5–7, who also draws attention to the limits of any rule of customary international law.

[33] Other detrimental consequences are discussed above.

[34] Common art.2 to the Geneva Conventions 1949; art.1(3) Additional Protocol I, 1977. For a working definition of the term, 'armed conflict', see *The Prosecutor v Tadic, Decision on the Defence Motion for Interlocutory Appeal on Jurisdiction* (1995) Para.70, Cassese, P. This includes '*protracted* [emphasis supplied] armed violence between governmental authorities and organized armed groups or between such groups within a State.' It does not apply to 'isolated and sporadic acts of violence and other acts of a similar nature, as not being armed conflicts,' art.1, Additional Protocol II to the Geneva Conventions 1949. See also art.8.2(f) of the Rome Statute of the International Criminal Court 1998.

[35] (1995) 34 *ILM* 484. The Convention entered into force on 15 January 1999. The UK is a Party to it.

52 *Peter Rowe*

argues, correctly, that the personnel envisaged by this Convention are protected only if they are not 'engaged as combatants against organized armed forces and to which the law of international armed conflict applies'.[36] It is hardly likely that participating states will wish to accept that they are engaged in an armed conflict and thereby lose the protection of the 1994 Convention, even where their national contingents come under intense fire and a number are killed or wounded.[37] The 1994 Convention prohibits making UN and associated personnel, their equipment and property the object of attack. Should such personnel be combatants in an international armed conflict they could, of course, be attacked within the limits set by the international law of armed conflict.

The UN Secretary-General's Bulletin of 6 August 1999[38] suggests that UN forces would be combatants in its attempt to apply international humanitarian law to such forces. The Bulletin applies 'the fundamental principles and rules of international humanitarian law to UN forces when in situations of armed conflict they are actively engaged therein as combatants'.[39] This formulation appears to overlook the requirement in art. 43(2) of Additional Protocol I that the definition of 'combatant' is drawn from art. 43(1) which refers to 'the armed forces of a Party *to the conflict*'.[40] According to the Bulletin, the 1994 Convention will only come into operation where the UN forces are 'entitled to the protection given to civilians under the international law of armed conflict'.[41] This, however, will only be the case if a civilian takes no direct part in the hostilities.[42] This is to weaken the impact of the 1994 Convention, since once UN forces do take a direct part in hostilities, the Convention ceases to apply. They then become combatants (on this reasoning) and the principles and rules of international humanitarian law will apply.

The Bulletin goes on to add that the 'present provisions do not ... replace the national laws by which military personnel remain bound throughout the

---

[36] Art.2(2); Greenwood, *loc.cit.*, 25. Presumably, the term 'international armed conflict' refers to a situation covered by common art. 2(1) of the Geneva Conventions 1949, since it refers also to UN forces engaged as combatants, and not to a situation envisaged by common art.3 to the 1949 Conventions or, indeed, art.1 of Additional Protocol II of 1977. See also Shraga, *loc.cit.*, 74.

[37] See, for example, SC Res. 837, 6 June 1993, following the attack on Pakistani troops serving in UNISOM II (which Resolution referred to an earlier statement by the President of the Security Council on the safety of United Nations forces and personnel as the basis of their protection rather than international humanitarian law); Statement by the President of the Security Council concerning an attack on United Nations peace-keepers and the killing of seven Indian soldiers near Baidoa on 22 August 1994, *The United Nations in Somalia 1992–96* (UN, 1996), 430. For an account of the casualties suffered by the US Rangers, on 3 October 1993, in attempting to arrest persons suspected of involvement in the 5 June killings of Pakistani soldiers, see *Further Report of the Secretary-General submitted in pursuance of paragraph 19 of resolution 814 (1993)*, UN doc. S/26738, 12 November 1993, para.70.

[38] ST/SGB/1999/13.

[39] S.1 goes on to say that these principles and rules are 'applicable in enforcement actions, or in peacekeeping operations when the use of force is permitted in self-defence.'

[40] Emphasis supplied.

[41] S.1.2.

[42] Art.51(3) Additional Protocol I.

Maintaining Discipline in United Nations Peace Support Operations 53

operation'.[43] The effect of this is that the actions of a soldier taking part in a peace support operation are governed by national law and in those countries where international law has to be incorporated directly into national law, the Bulletin will therefore create no binding obligations, by itself, upon the soldier.

A further example suffices to illustrate the issue. Although Security Council resolution 837 of 6 June 1993 was passed before the 1994 Convention was available for signature the effect of it, 'to authorize all necessary measures against those responsible for the 5 June 1993 attack on Pakistani troops serving in UNOSOM II' placed UN forces on the offensive. The Report of the Commission of Inquiry about this incident draws attention to the fact that '[t]anks, attack planes, attack helicopters and armoured personnel carriers had to be brought in[44] to facilitate offensives against the SNA [under General Aidid, Chairman, of the Somali National Alliance]'. The author goes on to comment that '[I]t is arguable whether resolution 837 really envisaged bombing of houses, garages, radio stations and meetings. Presumably the war [sic] when it started, followed its own dynamics.'[45]

Had the 1994 Convention been in force at the time of the passing of Security Council resolution 837 what would have been the status of the UN forces who implemented it in the ways described above? They would not have been 'engaged as combatants ... to which the law of international armed conflict applies'[46] and thus the Convention would not be prevented from applying. If this is so, there would have been a duty upon the Somali fighters not to attack UN personnel, their equipment or premises so as to prevent them carrying out their mandate.[47] The difficulty with this approach is that by the use of attack helicopters and other forms of aerial bombing the UN forces involved in this operation *looked like* combatants and, therefore 'parties to the conflict', but their adversaries had no legal right to engage them.[48] The answer would seem to be that the protection of the 1994

---

[43] S.2.

[44] The provision of such equipment was urged upon member states by para.8 of resolution 837.

[45] *Report of the Commission of Inquiry established pursuant to resolution 885 (1993) to investigate armed attacks on UNOSOM II personnel*, UN doc. S/1994/653, 1 June 1994, paras 230 and 231.

[46] Art.2(2) of the 1994 Convention.

[47] Paragraph 5 of the resolution is ambiguous. Did it mean that UN forces could 'take all measures necessary against those responsible' for the unprovoked attacks on them on 5 June 1993 *and* 'establish the effective authority of the Operation throughout Somalia' *and* 'secure the investigation of their actions and their arrest and detention'? Or did it mean that the Force could take all measures necessary merely to achieve the other requirements in the paragraph? The first interpretation would enable much greater latitude in using force, as well as restrict further casualties among UN personnel.

[48] There was the added complication that the US forces involved in the 3 October 1993 attempt to arrest those suspected of the 5 June incident were 'deployed in support of the UNOSOM II mandate, but were not under United Nations command or authority', *Further Report of the Secretary-General submitted in pursuance of paragraph 19 of resolution 814 (1993)*, UN doc. S/26738, 12 November 1993, para.71. *Quaere* whether they were UN forces; If they were *not* UN forces they would not be entitled to protection as such; their actions would be governed by the international law relating to non-international armed conflict.

54 *Peter Rowe*

Convention would continue to apply to UN and associated personnel as long as they are not engaged in an *international* armed conflict as a Party to the conflict. Thus, even if they are, technically, parties to a *non-international* armed conflict the protection of the 1994 Convention would apply.[49] The Secretary-General's Bulletin, however, produces a different result. It leads to the conclusion that all combatants, in whatever type of armed conflict, are equal in the eyes of international humanitarian law and that those who attack UN forces have a 'right' to do so[50] providing they also comply with the fundamental principles and rules of that law.

The argument advanced above concerning the applicability of the 1994 Convention would not, however, prevent the rules of international humanitarian law applying as between, or among, the actual parties to the conflict, whether the armed conflict is of an international or of a non-international character. It is for this reason that the UN, states and NGOs urge the application of international humanitarian law, not least to force upon the fighters the point that they may be individually liable under international law for their actions.

In the absence of an armed conflict the provisions of the Geneva Conventions 1949 and the Additional Protocols of 1977 will not come into operation unless it could be argued that the peace operations forces *occupy* the territory of a High Contracting Party. Is it realistic to designate the presence of peace operations forces, mandated by a Security Council resolution as such, on the territory of another state as being in occupation of that territory even where the government concerned is ineffectual or non-existent and where there is, therefore, no status of forces agreement?[51]

The term, 'occupation of the territory of a High Contracting Party' in common article 2 to the Geneva Conventions must involve factual and legal conditions. The factual condition would require the actual authority of the occupier to be placed upon the territory, wholly or partially.[52] A relevant legal condition requires the factual occupation to be carried out by the 'hostile army'.[53] Gasser refers to occupation

---

[49] It is recognized that this distinction, itself, creates uncertainty, see *The Prosecutor v Tadic* (1995), above. Should there be an international armed conflict in existence UN forces (or those operating under its authority) may, at one moment be combatants and in another, non-combatants, *e.g.* NATO airstrikes on Bosnian Serb positions in 1994.

[50] Assuming the UN forces have at some time in the armed conflict taken a direct part in hostilities (if only by defending themselves in a peacekeeping operation).

[51] In Somalia, 'National and regional Somali institutions and civil administration have virtually ceased to exist . . . the non-existence of a government in Somalia is one of the main reasons for the now more robust role of the organization in the country,' Further *Report of the Secretary-General submitted in pursuance of paragraphs 18 and 19 of resolution 794 (1992)*, UN doc. S/25354, 3 March 1993, paras 27 and 41; 'there is still no disciplined armed force . . . no organised civilian police or judiciary,' Further Report of the Secretary-General submitted in pursuance of paragraph 19 of resolution 814 (1993), Un doc. S/26738, 12 November 1993, para. 82.

[52] See art. 42 of the Regulations Annexed to the Hague Convention IV, 1907. Examples of such authority being established over the territory are given in *Manual of Military Law, Part III* (HMSO, 1958), paras 501–509; Gasser in Fleck, *The Handbook of Humanitarian Law in Armed Conflicts* (1995) paras 525–528.

[53] Art.42, *ibid.*

of territory as a 'form of foreign domination' which 'is applicable only in international armed conflicts'.[54] On the other hand, Bowett[55] takes the view that 'a United Nations Force may be in actual "belligerent occupation" of territory',[56] while Simpson[57] argues that Canadian Forces may have been in occupation of territory in Somalia and, in consequence, have brought common article 2 of Geneva Convention IV into force.

The term 'belligerent' occupation would seem to be quite inappropriate to describe the situation, such as Somalia in 1993, where there was no government nor any governmental activities in existence. UNOSOM was not engaged at any time in fighting the armed forces of the state of Somalia. It did find itself having to organize what would normally be considered to be governmental activities simply because there was no alternative. It assumed, *de facto*, many of the powers that a belligerent occupant would, such as taking 'all the measures ... to restore, and ensure, as far as possible, public order and safety'.[58] But that did not make it an 'occupying Power,' let alone a belligerent occupier within the meaning of the Geneva Conventions 1949.[59] The whole of Geneva Convention IV envisages that the inhabitants of occupied territory will require *protection from* the occupying Power and, for instance, it grants them rights to 'make application to the Protecting Power ... as well as any organisation that might assist them'.[60] Moreover, to accept that, for example, Canadian forces were, as part of UNOSOM, in occupation of Somalia within the meaning of Article 2(2) of Geneva Convention IV, would not only cause that Convention to apply, but all other Geneva Conventions of 1949 and Additional Protocol I, thus making those who attack UN forces lawful combatants. It would be strange indeed if, when a UN force has some control of territory where there is no effective government, it is denied the benefits of the 1994 Convention on the Safety of UN and Associated Personnel, when it has been argued above that that Convention, rather than the law of international armed conflict applies to such forces. Occupation of territory, within the meaning of Hague and Geneva law, is therefore restricted to a factual occupation of the whole or part of the territory of a

---

[54] Gasser in Fleck, *op.cit.*, para. 524.6. See also *Manual of Military Law, Part III, op.cit.*, para. 503 where a 'test of occupation' is proposed. This requires that 'the legitimate government should, *by the act of the invader*, be rendered incapable of publicly exercising its authority within the occupied territory' [emphasis supplied]; Oppenheim, *International Law, Vol. 2* (1952) 438, 'the inhabitants are now under his martial law.'

[55] *Op.cit.*, 490–1. See also Roberts, *What is Military Occupation?* (1984) LV *BYIL* 249, 289–91.

[56] Bowett considers that this *'may arise'* if the UN force is established on the territory as a result of enforcement action under chapter VII, similar action under art. 39 of the Charter or by way of the Uniting for Peace Resolution.

[57] *Op.cit*, chapter 2.

[58] Art. 43 of the Regulations Annexed to the Hague Convention IV, 1907. See, for example, *Further report of the Secretary-General submitted in pursuance of paragraph 19 of resolution 814 (1993)*, UN doc. S/26738, 12 November 1993, 3–43.

[59] It is assumed that UN forces would be subject to international humanitarian law and, thus, would assume the same obligations as a state or a peoples within art. 1(3) and (4) of Additional Protocol I, 1977 should they occupy territory.

[60] Art. 30.

56 *Peter Rowe*

state, whose government must be hostile[61] to the occupation. Once this is the case the occupation may continue after the government has ceased to exist[62] or, even when it continues to exist.[63]

If there is no occupation within article 2(2) of Geneva Convention IV does the presence of 'military operations' within another state cause that Convention to apply? Weiler J.A., dissenting on this issue, in *R v Brocklebank*[64] thought so. She concluded that 'a peacekeeping mission is a military operation carried out by armed forces with the aim of preventing hostilities and therefore within the Geneva Convention as enlarged by the 1977 protocols'. The reasoning appeared to be that since Brocklebank was involved in 'military operations' Geneva Convention IV applied; he was ordered to comply with the Geneva Conventions, therefore it was within his duty to do so. Merely to take part in 'military operations' will not cause Geneva Convention IV (as supplemented by Protocol I) to apply.[65] Were it to do so, the same disadvantages, as discussed above, would apply.

For the reasons discussed above, it is difficult to see why States should argue that the Geneva Conventions 1949 and their Additional Protocols should apply to their national contingents. It may, however, take the view that it does not do any harm to remind soldiers of the obligations set out in these treaties.

A sending state may order its soldiers to comply with this body of international humanitarian law, especially in its treatment of those detained by it, or in respect of those not taking part in military-type operations. The Canadian Chief of Defence had issued a Unit Guide to the Geneva Conventions and in *R v Brocklebank*[66] the

---

[61] The Somali Prime Minister requested the Secretary-General of the UN to include the situation in Somalia on the agenda of the Security Council, letter of 15 December 1991, referred to in *The United Nations in Somalia 1992–1996* (UN, 1996) 113.

[62] For other types of occupation see Roberts, *op.cit., BYIL.*

[63] As in the case of the 'safe havens' in Iraq. Iraq 'while opposing the steps taken by United States forces and the foreign forces cooperating with them . . . has not hindered these operations because it is not opposed to the provision of humanitarian assistance to Iraqi citizens who are in need of it'; see the letter dated 21 April 1991 from the Minister for Foreign Affairs of Iraq addressed to the UN Secretary-General and the Memorandum of Understanding, 18 April 1991, between the government of the Republic of Iraq and the United Nations, annexed to UN doc. S/22513, 22 April 1991, set out in *The United Nations and the Iraq-Kuwait Conflict 1990–1996* (United Nations Blue Book Series Vol.IX) 209; Foreign Affairs Committee, 1990–91, Aid to Iraqi Refugees, H.C. 528; Rodley, Freedman and Boren, '"Safe Havens" for Kurds in Post-War Iraq', in Rodley (ed.), *To Loose the Bonds of Wickedness* (1992) 53–62. The position of Kosovo is quite different. SC Res.1244 (1999) noted the acceptance by the Federal Republic of Yugoslavia (FRY) of the establishment of an 'interim administration for Kosovo as part of the international civilian presence under which the people of Kosovo can enjoy substantial autonomy within the FRY,' annex 2, para.5.

[64] (1996) 134 DLR (4th) 377, 410. Compare Decary J.A. and Strayer C.J. at 402.

[65] Art. 51(1) of Additional Protocol I, which provides that the 'civilian population and individual civilians shall enjoy protection against the dangers arising from military operations'. It is clear from art. 48 that military operations must mean acts 'related to hostilities that are undertaken by armed forces', see *Commentary on the Additional Protocols of 8 June 1977* (I.C.R.C., 1987) 600. See also art. 57(4).

[66] (1996) 134 DLR (4th) 377.

Maintaining Discipline in United Nations Peace Support Operations 57

majority concluded that this Guide had no relevance in assessing the duty imposed upon Brocklebank, simply because the particular Geneva Convention 1949 relied upon, Convention IV, had not come into operation.

For states to argue that in UN peace support operations the Geneva Conventions and Additional Protocol I come into operation may be considered to be bad practice[67] since it adds little to the obligations of the soldier under his own criminal law (where, for instance, the ill-treatment of detainees, or members of the civilian population would be a criminal or military offence)[68] and it contributes only further confusion to an otherwise legally confused picture. It is preferable that further detailed instructions are issued to soldiers as to the proper treatment of detainees. These may be broadly in line with Geneva Convention III of 1949 but will reflect the actual conditions and the law of the detaining state.[69] They can then be enforced through a soldier's military law.

It may also be argued that soldiers are not well served by their military or political leaders who argue that the Geneva Conventions apply. Apart from the disadvantages discussed above, five further serious consequences would flow from acceptance of this position. First, a grave breach of the Geneva Conventions or Additional Protocol I would give all states jurisdiction to try an alleged offender and a pre-existing status of forces agreement between the sending and receiving states would be of no legal consequence. The unlawful confinement of a protected person, for example, is a grave breach of Geneva Convention IV. It is certainly arguable that the confinement of Shidane Arone before he was killed by a Canadian soldier in Somalia in March 1993 was unlawful. The maximum penalty for committing a grave breach of the Geneva Conventions which does not involve killing is 14 years imprisonment under Canadian law and under the law of a number of other states.[70] It is not uncommon for UN peace support forces to detain those whom it suspects of various offences. It is preferable that the 'unlawful' element of the

---

[67] Although the reasons for arguing that international humanitarian law applies are laudable. See MacInnis, 'Peacekeeping and International Humanitarian Law', (1996) 3 *International Peacekeeping* 92. The position would be different if the UN forces were acting as combatants in an international armed conflict.

[68] And, in some states, a breach of common art. 3 to the Geneva Conventions 1949 would amount to a criminal offence. See, for example, s.2 of the Expanded War Crimes Act 1997 (USA).

[69] *Quaere* whether such detainees would be entitled to Convention rights under the Human Rights Act 1998 if detained by UK forces abroad. I am grateful to Professor Hampson for this point. In the absence of a derogation from articles 5 and 6 of the European Convention on Human Rights 1950 the issue would revolve around whether such persons are 'within . . . jurisdiction' of the UK, a term that may be wide enough to cover this point, see *Loizidou v Turkey* (1998) 108 ILR. A related issue is the status of a member of a peace operations force captured by dissidents. See art. 8 of the Convention on the Safety of United Nations and Associated Personnel 1994, (1995) 34 ILM 484, detained personnel to be treated until release in accordance with the '*principles and spirit* of the Geneva Conventions 1949.' They are not therefore prisoners of war.

[70] S.3(1)(b) of the Geneva Conventions Act 1990; s.7(4)(b) Geneva Conventions Act 1957 (Australia); s.3(1)(b) Geneva Conventions Act 1970 (Botswana); s.3(1)(ii) Geneva Conventions Act 1968 (Kenya).

58 Peter Rowe

confinement be judged by the national law of the detaining state, rather than leaving it in the air and trusting that no other state will allege a grave breach of the Convention by the soldiers concerned. Secondly, it seems clear that should the Geneva Conventions 1949 and Additional Protocol I apply, the national law of the state in which the alleged offence is committed will not[71] and soldiers will not be liable for their own acts of 'lawful combat.'[72] Thirdly, should the UN force be a party to an armed conflict, its soldiers would come within the jurisdiction of the International Criminal Court.[73] Fourthly, the case of *Brocklebank*[74] illustrates the uncertainty created in defining the duty of a soldier under national military law when the Geneva Conventions are issued to soldiers in peace support operations. Fifthly, there may be considerable practical difficulty in deciding whether the Geneva Conventions have come into effect, which would be difficult for a national court to determine in the circumstances of peace support operations.[75]

The issue of international law may also arise where a soldier contends that an order given to him is contrary to international law, or where he interprets his obligations under international law as requiring him to fulfil that obligation rather than his military orders.[76] A military order requiring the soldier to carry out an act illegal under international law would be an illegal order in itself and could not be used as any justification for the resultant criminal act under national law.[77] In the type of operations under consideration this is not a likely scenario since international law may well be silent as to *specific* obligations imposed on *individuals to act*. It follows that there are unlikely to be many situations where international law would *require* a soldier to act, and where his superior officers have ordered him not to do so.[78]

---

[71] *Public Prosecutor v Koi* [1968] 1 All ER 419, 427. Compare the advice of Lord Guest and Sir Garfield Barwick at 429.

[72] See *R v Page* [1953] 2 All ER 1355, 1359; *R v Howe* [1987] AC 417, 429.

[73] Discussed below.

[74] (1996) 134 DLR (4th) 377.

[75] The legislation of many states provides that in proceedings for a grave breach of the Geneva Conventions the issue of whether common art. 2 to the Conventions applies, the issue *shall be determined* by a foreign minister (or equivalent); see s.1(4) Geneva Conventions Act 1957, as amended by the Geneva Conventions (Amendment) Act 1985 (UK); s.3(4) Geneva Conventions Act 1968 (Kenya); s.4 Geneva Conventions Amendment Act 1987 (New Zealand); s.5 Geneva Conventions Act 1962 (Ireland); s.3(4) Geneva Conventions Act 1985 (Seychelles); s.3 Geneva Conventions Act 1973 (Singapore). Decary J.A.and Strayer C.J concluded that there 'is no evidence that there was a declared war or an armed conflict in Somalia . . . no certificate [by the Minister of External Affairs] having been filed this court is simply not at liberty to assume the existence of a state of war or of an armed conflict in Somalia,' *R v Brocklebank* (1996) 134 DLR 377, 401. See also the difficulties faced by the Italian Fact-Finding Commission, instituted by the Italian Government on 16 June 1997 to investigate alleged incidents of illegal conduct by Italian soldiers in Somalia, Lupi, 'Report by the Enquiry Commission on the Behaviour of Italian Peace-Keeping Troops in Somalia', in (1998) *YIHL* 375.

[76] As Capt. Rockwood had argued.

[77] See, however, art. 33 of the Rome Statute of the International Criminal Court 1998.

[78] *Any obligation to act* would have to be inserted in the *national* ROE and take effect as to bring such a requirement within a soldier's *duty*, in the absence of a specific criminal offence of failing to act to prevent a crime. For the issue of whether US forces in Haiti in

Maintaining Discipline in United Nations Peace Support Operations 59

2.3 Rules of Engagement (ROE)

It is axiomatic that the ROE should be drawn up clearly and that all soldiers taking part in the operation should be trained effectively in their implementation, prior to deployment. Their primary purpose will be keeping the soldier within the law.[79] In the light of the discussion above this will be primarily the criminal law of the sending state, generally enforceable by the military legal system of that state. Their status in law is no greater than that of a superior order. Just as compliance with a military order will not, of itself, relieve a soldier of his liability under national or international law, neither will compliance with an ROE. On the positive side, failure to comply with an ROE obligation will be evidence of a failure or neglect to perform a soldier's duty and thereby render him liable to an appropriate charge under the disciplinary code. The status of a ROE is well summarized by Lord Lowry, CJ, in *R v MacNaughton* (1975)[80] who stated that:

> There was, of course, at the same time in existence what is called the yellow card [a ROE]; something the contents of which, it seems are largely dictated by policy and are intended to lay down guidelines for the security forces but which do not define the legal rights and obligations of members of the forces under statute or common law.

The experiences of the Canadian Airborne Battle Group in Somalia in 1993[81] illustrate the problems in setting out clearly the ROE. There can be no doubt that the torture and killing of the Somali youth, Shidane Arone, on 16 March 1993 by Private Brown and others was unlawful under Canadian law. There was an earlier incident, on 4 March 1993 when two fleeing Somalis were shot at, one of whom, Mr

1994 could use deadly force to protect Haitian civilians from serious criminal offences committed by other Haitians, see the discussion of the US rules of engagement in Rose, *loc.cit.*, 231–233. See also the Sub-Commission on Prevention of Discrimination and Protection of Minorities, *Respect for humanitarian and human rights law provisions in United Nations peacekeeping operations*, Sub-Commission resolution 1997/34, art. 2.

[79] See Rowe, 'The United Nations Rules of Engagement and the British Soldier in Bosnia', (1994) 43 *ICLQ* 946. There may be other purposes, explored by Rose, *loc.cit.* These include a means of 'forcing senior commanders . . . to come to closure regarding their policy for the use of force,' to provide 'commanders with a well-equipped ROE tool kit, inside a flexible framework,' and to 'provide useful sound bites for the inevitable media grillings,' 234, 237.

[80] [1975] N.I .203, 206.

[81] For further discussion of the events in Somalia see Farrell, 'Sliding into War: The Somalia Imbroglio and US Army Peace Operations Doctrine', (1995) *International Peacekeeping* 194. One hundred Nigerian soldiers, part of ECOMOG in Sierra Leone, 'have been arrested after allegations of summary executions,' *The Times*, 18 February 1999. Further examples can be found in Bratt, 'Peace over Justice: Developing a Framework for United Nations Peacekeeping Operations in Internal Conflicts', (1999) 5 *Global Governance*, 63,72. See also the Memorandum from the Minister of Defence to the Speaker of the Lower and Upper Houses of the States-General, 20 January 1997 on *Srebrenica*, <http://www.mindef.nl/nieuws/brief/200197e.htm>

60   *Peter Rowe*

Ahmed Aruush, was killed. Three conclusions may be drawn from these events. First, that the law of the sending state may be unclear as to whether deadly force may be justified in order to protect supplies and equipment (which may include the only real source of food or medical supplies available) and thus whether soldiers would be breaching their own criminal law by complying with an ROE which permitted such force in these circumstances.[82] Secondly, since the status of an ROE is no more than that of a superior order, a superior officer may purport to expand on it by means of oral orders and, thereby, lead himself and his subordinates into a breach of their criminal law.[83] Thirdly, ROEs are likely to vary amongst all the national contingents making it more difficult to engage in combined operations.

These points can be illustrated by *R v Mathieu*.[84] A Lieutenant Colonel, who commanded the Canadian Airborne Brigade in Somalia, was charged with negligently performing his military duty in issuing an order to his subordinates to fire on looters/thieves of equipment fleeing Canadian camps and thereby failing to comply with the ROE. These ROE provided that 'the use of deadly force is to be regarded as a measure of last resort'[85] and the Court concluded that a new trial should be ordered due to a misdirection at his trial over the meaning of negligence in the performance of a duty imposed upon him. By giving the order he did Col. Mathieu had led his subordinates, who killed the Somali on 4 March 1993 into breaking the criminal law of Canada.[86]

The ROEs may need to be changed as the nature of the operation changes and the perceived risks to the force or to those whom it has a duty to protect or assist increase or decrease.[87] It is usually the case that the application of minimum force

---

[82] See for example, the ROE for Canadian Forces in Somalia, set out in *R v Mathieu* (1995) Unrep. Westlaw transcript, 6 November 1995 and for discussion of the ROE in Haiti, see Rose, *loc.cit.*

[83] The Canadian ROE, *ibid.* provided that only the Chief of Defence Staff (CDS) could approve any changes to it. A soldier ordered by his commanding officer to act in a way that is, in fact, contrary to the ROE would not necessarily know (a) whether the ROE had been changed by the CDS, (b) whether his commanding officer was merely interpreting the existing ROE and consistent with them, or (c) whether he was ordering them to breach the ROE. For a detailed analysis of the background to the killing of Mr Aruush on 4 March 1993, see Chapter 38 of the *Commission of Inquiry into the Deployment of Canadian Forces to Somalia* (1997).

[84] *Ibid.* He was charged under the same section of the National Defence Act 1985 as Brocklebank, above.

[85] An extract of the rules of engagement are set out in the judgment of Hugessen J.A. The full version is contained in Simpson, *loc.cit.*, appendix. Unlike the 'yellow card' or the ROE applicable in Northern Ireland, the Canadian ROE is not a restricted document.

[86] This having extra-territorial effect as a result of the National Defence Act 1958.

[87] On 5 June 1993 some 24 Pakistani members of UNOSOM II were killed and a number were injured. SCRes.837 (1993) 'resulted in a virtual war situation between UNOSOM II and [one of the rival Somali groups],'see *Report of the Commission of Inquiry Established Pursuant to Security Council Resolution 885 (1993) to Investigate Armed Attacks on UNOSOM II Personnel Which Led to Casualties Amongst Them*, UN doc. S/1994/653, 1 June 1994, para.125. Further attacks against UNOSOM II forces took place.

Maintaining Discipline in United Nations Peace Support Operations 61

is essential for the protection of the members of the force themselves since they need to keep in mind the potential difficulties of withdrawing from the territory in due course.[88]

The importance and status of ROEs as a means of enforcing discipline amongst peace operations forces cannot be over-emphasized. *R v Mathieu* is a landmark case, since it was concerned with the duty of a soldier under his military law to comply with an ROE drawn up for application outside the territory of the state concerned. He was judged by a court-martial, comprised of military officers who would have specialist knowledge of the circumstances under which an accused acted. A charge of neglect of duty or other military offence is clearly preferable to a charge against the criminal law of the sending state, except where the circumstances justify it.[89]

Whatever the mandate might provide or home governments wish, the soldier taking part in a peace operation must be subject to *some* legal controls over his actions, especially where the relevant Security Council resolution urges 'all necessary means'. He will be so subject, in the unlikely situation, where he is engaged as a member of a force party to an international, or even a non-international, armed conflict. Then he will be bound by international humanitarian law and will be individually answerable at least for serious breaches. For the reasons set out above, it is unrealistic to assert that a soldier taking part in a peace operation is a party to an armed conflict or that his armed forces occupy the territory concerned. So, we must look to national law to provide the answer.

It has been shown that where a status of forces agreement is in place, which grants exclusive jurisdiction to the sending state, the ROEs can reflect the law of that state only. Even then it will not necessarily be easy to apply that law to the circumstances facing a soldier in a foreign land, where the presence of civil disorder, sufficiently severe to justify a peace operation force, may render the application of his home law difficult. To put it another way, were such conditions to be reflected in the soldier's home state it is possible that some form of emergency legislation would have been introduced. If the example of Northern Ireland is taken,[90] it can be seen that extra powers were given to order detention without trial, to enable police constables to detain for a number of days individuals suspected of offences, and to stop and search vehicles, individuals and premises. Members of the armed forces on duty were also given the same powers. Any use of firearms was, however, left to be decided by the ordinary law, albeit in a judge-only court.[91] A few soldiers were convicted of excessive force and were sentenced

---

[88] The withdrawal from Somalia was completed on 2 March 1995. It is described in the *Report of the Secretary-General*, UN doc. S/1995/231, 28 March 1995, paras 52–61.

[89] Such as Brocklebank, who was charged also with committing torture.

[90] See, in relation to the civil disorder that existed in Northern Ireland, the Civil Authorities (Special Powers) Act 1922, the Northern Ireland (Emergency Provisions) Act 1973 (as amended) and the Prevention of Terrorism (Temporary Provisions) Act 1974 (as amended).

[91] The so-called 'Diplock courts', Northern Ireland (Emergency Provisions) Act 1973, s.2.

to terms of imprisonment.[92] Yet, without any of this emergency legislation, a soldier on a peace support operation is required to protect, at least, the lives of members of the force and perform the mission given to him, in circumstances often more difficult than those prevailing in Northern Ireland at the height of the disorder there.

3 LIABILITY OF PEACEKEEPERS/ENFORCERS TO BE TRIED BY THE INTERNATIONAL CRIMINAL COURT

The International Criminal Court was adopted by the United Nations Diplomatic Conference on 17 July 1998,[93] the Statute for which will come into force upon receipt of the 60th instrument of ratification, acceptance or accession.

Peace support operations forces may be operating within a territory where an armed conflict not of an international character is taking place. Acts similar to those committed by several Canadian soldiers in Somalia against Shidane Arone on 16 March 1993 (referred to above) would not, however, come within the jurisdiction of the International Criminal Court.[94] The reason for this is that, as discussed above, UN peace support forces would not be a 'Party to the conflict' as required by common article 3 to the Geneva Conventions 1949 and their actions would not therefore fall within article 8(2)(c) of the Statute of the Court. Neither would they fall within article 8(2)(e) since paragraph (f) limits the jurisdiction to a 'protracted armed conflict between governmental authorities and organized armed groups or between such groups'.

4 CONCLUSION

The legal basis under which soldiers carry out peace support operations is often uncertain. They can reasonably expect their superiors to give them orders that will withstand basic legal challenge. It seems clear that much greater attention should be paid to the legal obligations, particularly under their military code of discipline, of individual soldiers entrusted with the responsibility of implementing a UN peace support resolution as a means of enforcing discipline. The legal risks to the soldiers cannot be ignored where the, sometimes, fine line between an acceptable and a criminal (as defined by national law) or military punishable degree of force may be difficult to draw.

[92]   See *R v Thain* [1985] N.I 457; *R v Clegg* [1995] 1 A.C. 482 (and cases cited therein). A number were acquitted. For statistics, see H.C. Deb. Vol. 253, Col 992, 1 February 1995, and for the details of the rules of engagement (the 'yellow card', a classified document) see Cols. 1000, 1001. See also *Manual of Military Law, Part II*, (HMSO, 1989), ch.5, 'Legal Background to the Employment of Troops in Situations Falling Short of Armed Conflict'. To give some impression of the scale of 'the troubles', 'more than 640 soldiers have been killed and more than 5,500 have been wounded,' H.C.Deb., Vol. 253, Col.1010, 1 February 1995.

[93]   A/Conf.183/9.

[94]   Art. 8.2(c) and (e)(xi). The effect of art. 8.1 does not limit jurisdiction only to war crimes committed as 'part of a plan or policy or as part of a large-scale commission of such crimes.'

[12]

THE FALL OF SREBRENICA AND THE ATTITUDE OF DUTCHBAT FROM AN INTERNATIONAL LEGAL PERSPECTIVE[*]

Robert C.R. Siekmann[**]

1.   INTRODUCTION

In the introduction to their book *Srebrenica: Record of a War Crime,* political scientists Jan Willem Honig and Norbert Both write: '"Srebrenica" has become synonymous with such an extraordinarily horrific crime that exceptional explanations have been proposed. Stories of conspiracy and betrayal abound. The most popular theory is that Srebrenica fell as the result of a plot involving senior UN personnel, the French government and the Serbian government. Others place the blame firmly on the Dutch UN soldiers, whom they accuse of cowardice during the Serb offensive against the safe area. We reject these explanations. Conspiracy theories tend to be neatly constructed so that every decision, or failure to decide, seems to stem from sinister ulterior motives. They leave no room for the dilemmas of real life, nor for miscommunication or outright failure. As such, they rarely bring us closer to the truth, and more often create a fertile breeding ground for dangerous stab-in-the-back myths'.[1] Honig and Both claim that final culpability should, without a doubt, be attributed to the highest Serb officials and officers who organised the crime and gave the orders for its perpetration. The systematic manner in which the crime was committed, the evidence that detailed plans had been drawn up and that procedures established earlier had been painstakingly carried out – all this points to the direct responsibility of the Bosnian Serb leadership in Pale. Moreover, the Serbian leadership in Belgrade had given, if not the order, then still its tacit consent. Honig and Both are of the opinion that a moral dilemma lay at the root of the problem: how could ethnic cleansing be effectively resisted and the establishment of safe areas be promoted while at

---

*   © R.C.R. Siekmann, 1998.

** Head of Research of the T.M.C. Asser Institute for International Law in The Hague.

1. J.W. Honig and N. Both, *Srebrenica: Record of a War Crime* (Penguin Books, 1996) pp. IX-XX.

the same time there was no willingness to endanger the lives of blue helmets in protecting the safe areas?

Professor Van Staden, Director of the Netherlands Institute for International Relations Clingendael, has examined whether the Dutch soldiers completely discharged themselves of their human duties in the hour of need:
'Admittedly, the circumstances were exceptionally hard and the Dutch soldiers had made obvious efforts to alleviate the population's fate. But why did they not give their all to show the Serbs that Dutchbat would only leave the enclave when *all* Muslims were granted unopposed withdrawal? Should they not have at least more strongly protested the separating of men from women? And the deportation without proper supervision of able and not so able men from the UN compound?'[2]

These questions, Van Staden feels, will probably never entirely fade from the discussion, not least because they pre-eminently concern dilemmas which are morally highly charged. They do not lend themselves to objective answers, free from personal moral standards. Some critics have, after the fact, demanded acts of the Dutchbat soldiers which would, in reality, have amounted to far-reaching self-sacrifice or even martyrdom. Others defend the lack of heroic resistance on the Dutch part by pointing to the suspected futility of such behaviour.

The question I wish to discuss here — and which seems to have been overly neglected, as if the Srebrenica tragedy took place in a legal vacuum — is how the behaviour of Dutchbat may be qualified from a legal perspective. The first question concerns the relationship between the sending state, the Netherlands, and the UN peacekeeping force UNPROFOR, that is, the responsibility of the Dutch government for the acts of Dutchbat in Srebrenica. The second question concerns whether Dutchbat acted in accordance with its mandate: were the powers based on the mandate used or were the obligations arising from it met? In this, two phases may be distinguished: the attack on Srebrenica and the evacuation of its Muslim population. Both questions concern UN law on peacekeeping operations. The third and last question pertains to the witnessing of violations of international humanitarian law by Dutch UN soldiers during the evacuation of the Muslims: does Dutchbat's failure to intervene constitute a punishable act? I have attempted to select the 'facts' which seem most relevant to providing an answer to the legal questions mentioned. The author is fully aware that such a selection is, up to a certain point, inevitably arbitrary. To this it may be added that the developments surrounding the fall of Srebrenica were many and complex.

---

2. A. Van Staden, *De fuik van Srebrenica — een bijdrage aan nadere oordeelsvorming* [The Srebrenica trap — a contribution to the further formation of judgment] (Nederlands Instituut voor Internationale Betrekkingen 'Clingendael', March 1997) pp. 26-27.

On the other hand, it is not entirely clear which law applies to the 'facts' or in which way the law, if available, should be applied in order to come up with conclusions about the legitimacy of Dutchbat's behaviour in Srebrenica. The following is, in any event, an attempt to provide a legal evaluation. Perhaps the conclusion should be that Dutchbat did, in fact, act wholly or partly inside a legal vacuum.

As far as the descriptions of fact are concerned, they have been based on the very well-documented and, by now, in the Netherlands, authoritative books of Honig/Both and Westerman/Rijs[3] and the parliamentary papers concerning Srebrenica.[4] I have purposely omitted the names of Dutch and UN officials so as to depersonalise the rendition of the facts.

2.   UN COMMAND AND INVOLVEMENT OF THE NETHERLANDS

First of all, it needs to be established that Dutchbat was under the operational command of UNPROFOR, which, like all modern UN peacekeeping forces, enjoyed the status of subsidiary organ to the Security Council. This means that the Dutch Government was not entitled to give orders to Dutchbat. The soldiers in UN peacekeeping forces are not endowed with a 'double loyalty' *vis-à-vis* the UN and their own sending state. Dutchbat was not a representative of the Netherlands but instead directly represented the United Nations. If the Netherlands obeyed this fundamental rule, possible wrongful behaviour of Dutchbat during the fall of Srebrenica cannot be legally attributed to the Netherlands.

With regard to contact made by the Netherlands during the crisis in Srebrenica, the Dutch Minister of Defence at the time declared that, in three urgent cases, direct contact had been established with officials who were part of the UN command structure in order to convey the Dutch point of view. In each of these three cases, the UN command structure remained intact. No operational commands were given to the Dutchbat commander from the Netherlands.

The first case concerned the Dutch view that, given the scale of the Bosnian Serb offensive, a battle between Dutchbat and the forces invading the enclave would result in a pointless bloodbath and be coupled with great risk to the civilian population and the UN soldiers involved. The second case entailed a request by the Dutch Minister of Defence to the Special Representative of the UN Secretary-General in the former Yugoslavia to persuade NATO to call off a new air strike

---

3. *Supra* n. 1 and *infra* n. 5, respectively.
4. Bijl. Hand. II (Annexes to Parliamentary Proceedings) No. 22 181, Nos. 1-181 concerning 'The situation in (former) Yugoslavia'.

304   *R.C.R. Siekmann*

at Srebrenica. In the third instance, UN authorities were informed of the Dutch opinion that Dutchbat should in no way cooperate in separating the Srebrenica men from the other refugees during the evacuation.

As a result of a passage in the 1997 book entitled *Srebrenica: het zwartste scenario* [Srebrenica: the bleakest picture] by journalists Frank Westerman and Bart Rijs,[5] doubts had arisen in the Dutch Parliament as to whether the Ministry of Defence had interfered with the UN chain of command during the evacuation of Dutchbat itself. These doubts involved a fax, written in Dutch, containing guidelines for negotiation with the Bosnian Serb general, Ratko Mladić. This fax had been drawn up in the absence of the UNPROFOR commander by the Chief of Staff and his closest associate, two Dutch UN officers at UNPROFOR headquarters in Sarajevo. This explained why the guidelines to the Srebrenica Dutchbat commander had been drawn up in the Dutch language, so the Minister of Defence declared in parliament. The impression had possibly been created that these were national guidelines. The Dutchbat Commander had, however, never received orders from the Netherlands. The UN command structure had at all times been left intact. Written instructions to UN troops were generally given in English. However, communication in one's own language was not at all uncommon within the UN. Dutch UN officers were no exception to this state of affairs. In the hectic circumstances of those days, speedy and efficient communication was of greatest importance. Formally speaking, the text should have been translated into English. In the rush, this had been omitted by those involved.

It was also asked why the Deputy of the absent UNPROFOR Commander had not drawn up the instructions. The answer was that the instructions to Dutchbat had been discussed within the UNPROFOR staff in the presence of the Deputy Commander. It had, at that time, been decided that the (Dutch) UNPROFOR Chief of Staff would formulate the guidelines, after which they would be transmitted by his (Dutch) military assistant to the Dutchbat commander. The instructions to the Dutchbat commander said that, if negotiations came to a halt, immediate referral back to the Chief of Staff at UNPROFOR headquarters in Sarajevo (who was called the 'mandated negotiator on behalf of the Dutch Government and UNPROFOR') should be effected. Parliament asked how this appointment as mandated negotiator on behalf of the Dutch Government related to his international staff function in the UNPROFOR chain of command. The Government replied that there had been no official appointment on behalf of the Dutch government. The Dutch Chief of Staff had, however, been informed by

5. F. Westerman and B. Rijs, *Srebrenica: Het zwartste scenario* [Srebrenica: the bleakest picture] (Amsterdam/Antwerpen, Uitgeverij Atlas 1997) pp. 182-183.

the Government that he could also negotiate on its behalf on the evacuation of Dutchbat. As a UN Commander, he was in a better position to judge the situation on the spot and could more rapidly react to new developments. The UN command structure was thus left intact, according to the Minister of Defence.

This explanation can only be understood if one realises that logistics, personnel and equipment are national responsibilities in the UN context, and that the guidelines for negotiating with General Mladić on the evacuation of Dutchbat — which had been drawn up by the Chief of Staff (in his joint capacity as 'negotiator on behalf of the Dutch Government') for the benefit of the Dutchbat Commander — did, in fact, regard these matters.

Another possible explanation is that evacuation of Dutchbat from Srebrenica implied withdrawal from UNPROFOR. This also meant that the highest authority over the Dutch force would be reallocated to the Dutch government because this would end the participation in UNPROFOR. The UN chain of command had, however, remained intact as it was denied that it had been interfered with by the Netherlands. The evacuation of Dutchbat was, therefore, a 'UN evacuation' and not a Dutch matter, because it was not based on a Dutch decision to withdraw.

In view of the above, the Netherlands cannot be held legally responsible for the acts of Dutchbat in relation to the attack on Srebrenica, nor for the evacuation of the Muslim refugees or that of Dutchbat itself, as a contingent of the UN peacekeeping force UNPROFOR in Srebrenica (which topic is closely related to the other two, although it is, strictly speaking, outside the scope of this contribution). The UN cannot recoup its own responsibility in the matter on the Netherlands, as operational command lay with the UN and it has not been established that the Netherlands issued orders in contravention of it.

3. VIOLATION OF THE UN MANDATE BY DUTCHBAT?

3.1 The Bosnian Serb attack on Srebrenica

According to UN Security Council Resolution 819 of 16 April 1993, the town of Srebrenica and its surroundings formed a 'safe area', which indicated that the area should be free from any armed attack or any other hostile acts. In paragraph 5 of Resolution 836 of 4 June 1993, UN troops were ordered to deter attacks against the safe areas; to monitor the ceasefire; to promote the withdrawal of military and paramilitary units other than those of the government of the Republic of Bosnia and Herzegovina; and to occupy some key points on the ground, in addition to participating in the delivery of humanitarian relief to the population. According to this paragraph, UN troops were only ordered to 'deter' and not to engage in battle. Paragraph 9, however, seemed to go further. This paragraph

306   *R.C.R. Siekmann*

authorised UNPROFOR, in carrying out the mandate defined in paragraph 5,
acting in self-defence, to take the necessary measures, including the use of force,
in reply to bombardments against the safe areas by any of the parties or to armed
incursion into them, or, in the event of any deliberate obstruction in or around
those areas, to the freedom of movement of UNPROFOR or of protected
humanitarian convoys. Except for deterring attacks, the UN troops were, thus,
also entitled to defend themselves against attack. As a rule, self-defence in UN
peacekeeping operations implies that UN troops may use force in return when
they are forcefully prevented from carrying out their mandate. Attacks on
Srebrenica meant the obstruction of Dutchbat's duties. Therefore, Dutchbat was
entitled to react. Moreover, 'in and around the safe areas', the use of air power
was permitted.[6] Dutchbat could, if necessary, request air support from NATO.
A confidential UNPROFOR Directive[7] provided, however, that 'the execution
of the mandate is secondary to the security of UN personnel', and that force
could only be used as a last resort. In addition, the military means to ward off
an attack were extremely limited. At the moment of the Bosnian Serb attack on
Srebrenica at the beginning of July 1995, only 429 Dutch soldiers were still
present in the enclave. Only half of them were infantry; the remainder were
support and medical troops. Even though they disposed of about 30 YPR
armoured infantry battle vehicles, several anti-tank rocket systems and half a
dozen 81 mm mortars, they had very little fuel and munitions.

The Bosnian Serb attack on the 'safe area' Srebrenica commenced on 6 July
1995. The Dutchbat commander was faced with an acute dilemma: should fire
be answered in a legitimate attempt at self-defence, should he request air support
or should he try to allay the crisis through diplomacy? He chose the latter option:
the Bosnian Serbs were asked for an explanation. They, in turn, demanded that
the Dutch request be entered in writing. On 9 July, Dutchbat received the order
to assume 'blocking positions' with all means available to prevent a further break-
through into and march on Srebrenica by Serbian units of the highest echelons.
To support the 'blocking positions', the UNPF (United Nations Peacekeeing
Force, of which UNPROFOR was a part) Commander and the Special Representative of the UN Secretary-General in the former Yugoslavia sent the Serbs
an ultimatum. If the 'blocking positions' were attacked, use would be made of
NATO 'close air support'. In such a case, according to another UNPROFOR
Directive[8], UNPROFOR first had to lodge a request with UN Sector North-East
in Tuzla. From there, the request had to be sent on to the next link in the chain

---

6. Para. 10 of Resolution 836.
7. Directive Confidential Commander HQ UNPROFOR Directive 2/95 of 29 May 1995.
8. UNPROFOR Directive OPO 14/94.

of command, UNPROFOR in Sarajevo. If consent was received from there, the request would be transmitted to the highest headquarters of the UN peacekeeping force in the former Yugoslavia in Zagreb. The UNPF Commander would then consult the Special Representative. If they consented, the request would be lodged with NATO (the 'dual-key' formula). On 10 July, the Dutchbat Deputy Commander requested air support when the Bosnian Serbian attack was still in full swing. The UNPF Commander and the Special Representative of the Secretary-General in the end only agreed that, *if* the Dutch were attacked, air strikes could be carried out on actively attacking Serbian forces or 'smoking guns' (firing tanks, mortars and artillery). Dutchbat, however, expected air support to be deployed at the first opportunity that presented itself. UNPF and UNPROFOR, on the other hand, were, in fact, waiting for Dutchbat to contact them as soon as a new Bosnian Serb attack occurred, as was the usual practice regarding air support. After two air strikes had taken place, the Bosnian Serbs sent an ultimatum: if the air strikes would not cease immediately, they would kill the Dutch soldiers who had been taken hostage and open fire on both Dutchbat and the refugees. Thereupon, the air strikes were called off by the Special Representative and the UNPROFOR Commander in Sarajevo.

Did Dutchbat, as part of the UN peacekeeping force in the former Yugoslavia, disregard its obligations under the operation's mandate, i.e., did Dutchbat, in contravention of the law, fail to employ its powers during the Bosnian Serb attack on Srebrenica? Or, more specifically, did Dutchbat disobey or insufficiently obey orders of higher Commanders? After all, it may be that the mandate of a UN peacekeeping force is not binding and it may be that an actual duty to use force to carry out that mandate does not exist (UNPROFOR was merely 'authorized' to use force), but military orders for the implementation of a mandate (in this case, to assume blocking positions) should, of course, be carried out. Still, one cannot reasonably arrive at the conclusion that Dutchbat violated UN law, also considering the fact that the safety of the blue helmets had to prevail over the UNPROFOR mandate (Dutch soldiers were, moreover, being held hostage by the Bosnian Serbs). In addition, one should consider the important fact that due to circumstances, real air support had not been given.

3.2 The evacuation of the Muslims from Srebrenica

On 11 July 1995, Srebrenica fell. The Dutchbat Commander was summoned to Bratunac by General Mladić, as it emerged later from his testimony before the International Criminal Tribunal for the Former Yugoslavia in The Hague. This meant that a Lieutenant-Colonel was to negotiate with a General. His superiors in Sarajevo would have sent the UNPROFOR Chief of Staff with the rank of General by helicopter, but Mladić did not consent to this flight over the territory of the *Republika Srpska*. He wished to do business with Dutchbat directly. To still maintain some control over the course of the meeting, UN command transmitted from its Sarajevo headquarters orders for defence of Dutchbat and protection of refugees in Srebrenica, among which were: 'Enter into local negotiations with BSA [Bosnian Serb Army] forces for immediate ceasefire', 'Take all reasonable measures to protect refugees and civilians in your care' and, 'Continue with all possible means to defend your forces and installations from attack. This is to include the use of close air support if necessary'. In his report of 12 July on the meeting with Mladić, which was, *inter alia*, addressed to the UNPF commander, the Dutchbat commander wrote that he was not able to defend the Muslims nor his own battalion.

On 17 July 1995, a meeting was held in Srebrenica between the new Bosnian Serb 'authorities' of Srebrenica and the UNPROFOR representative, the Dutchbat Deputy Commander. The meeting was also attended by three representatives of the Muslim refugees, who had also been present at meetings with General Mladić on 11 and 12 July. Among other items, the Dutchbat departure from the Dutch compound in Potocari featured on the agenda. At the end of the meeting, the Bosnian Serbs unannouncedly asked the three representatives of the Muslim refugees to sign a 'declaration'. The declaration consisted of two parts. The largest part dealt with what had allegedly been discussed at the meeting of 12 July in Bratunac between the same representatives and General Mladić. At this meeting, the Dutchbat commander had also been present. According to the declaration, it had, at that time, been agreed that the Muslim population would be evacuated 'voluntarily' and under UN military escort.

The declaration did not refer to any differentiation as to groups of refugees. The second part of the text, the actual declaration, established that the evacuation of the refugees had been carried out in a correct manner and in accordance with what had been agreed on 12 July and with due regard to the Geneva Conventions and international humanitarian law. The declaration was signed by one of the representatives of the Muslim refugees, who did not object to its contents, and by the representative of the Bosnian Serbs. The Deputy Commander of Dutchbat was, hereupon, as a representative of UNPROFOR, requested to co-sign the declaration. The declaration, which, at his request, had first been translated into English, could, in his opinion, only refer to convoys which had in reality been escorted by Dutch UN soldiers. He therefore refused to accept the declaration for those convoys which Dutchbat had not or insufficiently been able to supervise; this explains his handwritten (restricting) addition to the text.

Did Dutchbat violate UN law during the evacuation of the Muslims from Srebrenica? The superior orders stipulated the taking of 'all reasonable measures' to protect refugees and civilians after the fall of Srebrenica. This specifically concerned the thousands of people who had fled to Potocari. The guidelines, which prescribed that the safety of Dutch soldiers was to prevail over the mandate, was also in force during this phase. What, given the circumstances, was 'reasonable' in the talks between the Dutchbat commander and Mladić and during the evacuation itself? It was the Dutchbat Commander who had to decide what was 'reasonable', and there are no criteria available to afterwards test his line of action. In any event, reasonableness is a different criterion from moral or ethical ones. From a legal/normative perspective (in the UN context), it cannot be concluded that Dutchbat acted unlawfully during the evacuation of Srebrenica.

4. DUTCHBAT AS A WITNESS OF WAR CRIMES

In the above, I have limited myself to an attempt to apply UN law to the (un)lawfulness of Dutchbat action concerning the fall of Srebrenica and the evacuation of Muslims from that town. The question remains whether, perhaps, other rules of public international law may be held to be applicable in this case. In 1995, Dr. Heike Spieker of the Institute for International Law of Peace and Armed Conflicts of the University of Bochum posed the interesting question whether members of Dutchbat who had witnessed war crimes were not themselves also guilty of war crimes through their passive behaviour:

> The execution of Muslims and the firing at Muslim refugees are in principle to be qualified as serious violations of the Fourth Geneva Convention of 1949 concerning the protection of civilians in times of war and, therefore, as a war crime pursuant to article 147 of the Convention in case the Muslims found themselves in occupied territory. Pursuant to article 146 paragraphs 1 and 2 of the Convention, only the person who commits this serious crime or orders its perpetration is criminally responsible according to public international law. The Dutch soldiers have never been accused of the perpetration of such a crime on their own initiative or the giving out of orders as to its perpetration. The First Additional Protocol of 1977 to the Geneva Conventions does, in fact, in article 85 paragraph 3 contain serious breaches *vis-à-vis* all civilians, but on the condition of a deliberate attack as intended by article 51 of Protocol I in the sense of active doings, so as to preclude public international law responsibility on the part of the Dutch soldiers in that respect as well.

The Statute of the *ad hoc* Tribunal for the former Yugoslavia has extended criminal responsibility based on humanitarian law. It extends to the events mentioned as serious violations of the Geneva Conventions in Article 2 and as genocide in Article 4. Those responsible are persons who, according to these provisions, have committed these acts either in person (Arts. 2 and 4) or who have given orders thereto (Art. 2). Individual responsibility before the Tribunal has been broadened in Article 7 paragraph 1 of the Statute to include the

310   *R.C.R. Siekmann*

individual responsibility of a person who plans one of the punishable acts mentioned, incites others to their commitment or otherwise facilitates the commitment thereof during the stages of planning, preparation or perpetration of the acts. The Dutch soldiers have, however, not been accused of personally planning or inciting the commitment of the acts mentioned. This leaves the question whether, through aiding and abetting, international legal responsibility has been incurred for the commitment of the acts. Seeing that, up to this time, it does not appear from the coverage in the media that the soldiers in any way through active doings took part in the crimes, only that criminal responsibility remains which springs from not having prevented war crimes, of which omission they may be accused.

In German criminal law, this fits the description of the so-called *'psychische Beihilfe'* [mental assistance], the *'Beihilfe durch Unterlassen'* [assistance by negligence] or the so-called *'Unterlassene Hilfeleistung)* [failed relief]. *'Unterlassene Hilfeleistung'* is described in Article 323(c) of the Criminal Code and concerns the criminal liability of a person who does not render assistance to victims of accidents, even though assistance is obviously necessary and may be demanded of him given the circumstances. It involves a separate punishable act which is used to include certain borderline cases between individual acts and participation in the acts of others.

Neither treaty law nor customary international criminal law nor the Statute of the Tribunal, however, contain a similar provision. The two legal concepts of *'psychische Beihilfe'* and *'Beihilfe durch Unterlassen'* were developed in German case law through interpretation of Article 27 of the Criminal Code, according to which he shall be punished who has assisted another in his act. At the same time, criteria have been elaborated for these constructions which motivate and limit the criminal liability. In principle, Article 7 paragraph 1 of the Statute would also be open to a wider interpretation. For the time being, however, these limiting criteria are not (yet) known in present international criminal law and consequently, these legal concepts are definitely not applicable to the negligence of which the Dutch soldiers may possibly be accused. According to the present state of public international law, the Dutch soldiers have not committed a punishable act.[9]

As far as the question of applicability of international humanitarian law to UN peacekeeping forces is concerned, the UN has always taken the position that it is bound by 'the principles and spirit of the general international Conventions

---

9. In a BoFax of 31 October 1995 (BoFaxes are analyses of the Institut für Friedenssicherungsrecht und Humanitäres Völkerrecht of the Ruhr-Universität of Bochum and are published by the T.M.C. Asser Institute in the Dutch translation).

applicable to the conduct of military personnel'. In May 1994, Guidelines (later termed Directives) for UN forces regarding respect for international humanitarian law were drawn up in cooperation between the International Committee of the Red Cross and the UN Secretariat. Although these have not yet been formally accepted by the UN, they contain a number of generally accepted points of departure and may, as such, be regarded as a codification of applicable law.

Firstly, they specify the principles and rules of international humanitarian law applicable to UN forces when in situations of armed conflict they are actively engaged as combatants. Secondly, the Directives are applicable to UN forces conducting operations under UN command and control. Thirdly, they are applicable to both peacekeeping and enforcement operations, where the use of force is authorised either in self-defence or in pursuance of a mandate of the Security Council. Fourthly, they are applicable to international and non-international armed conflicts as may be relevant.[10]

Did international humanitarian law apply to Dutchbat? Dutchbat was part of UNPROFOR and UNPROFOR stood under UN command and control. UNPROFOR was, in any case, at least a peacekeeping operation (use of force in self-defence), if not a so-called peace-enforcement operation. The conflict in Bosnia was, in any case, 'at least' a non-international armed conflict in the sense of Article 3 of the Geneva Conventions and Additional Protocol II to these Conventions. Dutchbat itself was not, however, during the evacuation of the Muslim population of Srebrenica, involved in a situation of armed conflict as a combatant. International humanitarian law was, therefore, not applicable to Dutchbat. A '*Beihilfe*' or similar rule as a rule of international criminal law does not (yet) exist. From a UN law perspective, an order had merely been given to take all 'reasonable' measures for the protection of refugees and civilians. I have concluded that the behaviour of Dutchbat during the evacuation of the Muslims may not be qualified as unreasonable and, therefore, unlawful. The same goes for the behaviour in witnessing war crimes committed by the Bosnian Serb forces.

Apart from UN law and the possible applicability of international humanitarian and criminal law, members of UN peacekeeping forces remain subject to the criminal jurisdiction of their respective national states in accordance with the laws and regulations of those states.

Dutch criminal law is applicable to military personnel who are guilty of a criminal offence outside the Netherlands.[11] One of the offences in the Dutch Criminal Code is very similar to the German '*unterlassene Hilfeleistung*': the

---

10. For a fuller discussion of the international law applicable to UN forces, see Greenwood, *supra* p. 3.
11. Art. 4 of the Military Criminal Code.

312   *R.C.R. Siekmann*

violation concerning those in need, i.e., omitting, while being a witness to the immediate life-threatening situation in which the other finds himself, to grant such assistance as can, without reasonable fear of danger to himself or others, be granted, if such person in need does, in fact, die. However, if Dutch soldiers had acted to prevent war crimes, they would undoubtedly have exposed themselves to danger without, moreover, having been able to accomplish much against the Bosnian Serb military dominance.

Generally speaking, one cannot blame, under Dutch criminal law, members of Dutchbat, as witnesses of war crimes, for the death of Muslims during their evacuation from Srebrenica.

5.   CONCLUSIONS

• The Dutch government cannot be held responsible for the acts of Dutchbat in respect of the fall of Srebrenica and the evacuation of the Muslims. If Dutchbat's actions were unlawful, then such a legal disqualification is attributable to the UN. It has, in fact, not been established that the Netherlands acted in contravention of the UNPROFOR chain of command.

• Dutchbat did not violate the UNPROFOR mandate or superior orders during the attack on Srebrenica nor during the evacuation of its Muslim population.

• No criminal responsibility of Dutchbat can be established with regard to the witnessing of and not intervening in the commission of war crimes by the Serbs during the evacuation of the Muslim population.

In short, the behaviour of Dutchbat surrounding the fall of Srebrenica can, notwithstanding moral and ethical considerations, stand the test of legal criticism.

Human Rights

[13]

The creation and control of places of protection during United Nations peace operations

by
Bruce M. Oswald

One means of providing protection to civilians who are being deliberately targeted during armed conflict[1] is to create and control places of protection[2] either with, or without, the consent of some or all the parties to the conflict.[3] In recent years the Security Council has, without the consent of some or all the belligerents, authorized the creation of places of protection to safeguard civilians from the ravages of armed conflict (for example, safe areas in the former Yugoslavia,[4] and the humanitarian protected zone in Rwanda[5]), and to varying extents has mandated United Nations peace operations[6] to control them. It is in this context that the *Report of the Panel for United Nations Peace Operations* (the Brahimi Report)[7] states:

> "The Security Council has ... established, in its resolution 1296 (2000), that the targeting of civilians in armed conflict and the

MAJOR BRUCE M. OSWALD CSC is Deputy Director of International Law, Defence Legal Office, Canberra, Australia. He has also worked with the ICRC as Delegate to the Armed and Security Forces. This article was written while the author was a Visiting Scholar at the Lauterpacht Research Centre for International Law, Cambridge (UK). The author gratefully acknowledges the helpful guidance of, amongst others, Daniel Bethlehem, A.P.V. Rogers OBE, Tim McCormack, Michael Kelly and Liz Saltnes. The views expressed in this article do not necessarily reflect those of the Government of Australia.

denial of humanitarian access to civilian populations afflicted by war may themselves constitute threats to international peace and security and thus be triggers for Security Council action.

1 An armed conflict exists "wherever there is a resort to armed force between States or protracted armed violence between governmental authorities and organised armed groups or between such groups within a State". *The Prosecutor* v. *Dusko Tadic*, Decision of the Appeals Chamber, 2 October 1999, 105 *International Law Reports*, p. 488, para. 70.

2 In the context of this paper a "place of protection" is any area that affords protection to civilians who are being deliberately targeted during armed conflict.

3 This paper will not consider places of protection created and controlled with consent and pursuant to international humanitarian law. See e.g. Geneva Convention for the Amelioration of the Condition of the Wounded and Sick in Armed Conflicts in the Field, 12 August 1949, Art. 23; Geneva Convention relative to the Protection of Civilian Persons in Time of War, 12 August 1949, Arts 14 and 15; and Protocol Additional to the Geneva Conventions of 12 August 1949, and relating to the Protection of Victims of International Armed Conflicts, 8 June 1977 (Protocol I), Arts 59 and 60, which provide for, *inter alia*, hospital zones and localities, neutralized zones and the immunity from attack of non-defended localities. For further discussion of these places see ICRC, *Hospital Localities and Safety Zones*, ICRC, Geneva, 1952; ICRC, *Report concerning Hospital and Safety Localities and Zones*, ICRC, Geneva, 1946, Series IV, No. 1; J. Pictet (ed.), *The Geneva Conventions of 12 August 1949: Commentary, vol. I, Geneva Convention for the Amelioration of the Condition of the Wounded and Sick in Armed Forces in the Field*, ICRC, Geneva, 1952, pp. 206-216 (dealing with Art. 23) and vol. IV, *Geneva Convention relative to the Protection of Civilian Persons in Time of War*, ICRC, Geneva,

1958, pp. 118-132 (dealing with Arts 14 and 15); Y. Sandoz, C. Swinarski, B. Zimmermann (eds), *Commentary on the Additional Protocols of 8 June 1977 to the Geneva Conventions of 12 August 1949*, ICRC/Martinus Nijhoff Publishers, Geneva, 1987, pp. 699-713 (dealing with Arts 59 and 60 of Protocol I). Nor will this paper address the creation of "open towns", "undefended places" and "demilitarized zones", as these are discussed in R. Y. Jennings, "Open Towns", *British Yearbook of International Law*, vol. 22, Oxford, 1945, pp 258-263; H. W. Elliott, "Open Cities and (Un)defended Places", The Army Lawyer, April 1995, pp. 39-45; and S. D. Bailey, "Non-military areas in UN Practice", *AJIL*, vol. 74, 1980, pp. 499-524.

4 Safe areas were created in the former Yugoslavia pursuant to S/RES/819(1993), 16 April 1993; S/RES/824(1993-), 6 May 1993; and S/RES/836(1993), 4 June 1993.

5 A humanitarian protected zone was created in the south-east of Rwanda pursuant to S/RES/929(1994), 22 June 1994.

6 "UN peace operations" refers to military operations that are authorized by the United Nations. These operations are a means by which the UN fulfils its stated purposes, *inter alia*, maintaining international peace and security, strengthening universal peace, the peaceful settlement of disputes and the promotion of social, economic and humanitarian welfare. See UN Charter, preamble and Art. 1.

7 On 7 March 2000, the Secretary-General convened a high-level Panel, chaired by Lakhdar Brahimi, to undertake a review of UN peace and security activities. The Panel's report to the Secretary-General is attached to "The identical letters dated 21 August 2000 from the Secretary-General to the President of the General Assembly and the President of the Security Council", UN Doc. A/55/305–S/2000/809, 21 August 2000.

If a United Nations peace operation is already on the ground, carrying out those actions may become its responsibility, and it should be prepared."[8]

In order for UN Forces[9] to carry out their responsibilities in relation to the creation and control of places of protection they will want to know, *inter alia*, whether such places must be created explicitly by the Security Council; whether armed force may be used to defend the place of protection; and whether the UN Force may administer[10] the place of protection.

The aim of this paper is to explore the UN's competence during armed conflict to create and control, without the consent of belligerents, places of protection for humanitarian reasons,[11] including the protection of civilians who are being deliberately targeted by belligerents. Understanding the way international law applies to the creation and control of places of protection will help UN Forces to be better prepared to defend and assist civilians during armed conflict.

Creation of places of protection

Recently, in Resolution 1296(2000) on the protection of victims of armed conflict, the Security Council stated that it would:
"consider the appropriateness and feasibility of temporary security zones and safe corridors for the protection of civilians and the delivery of assistance in situations characterized by the threat of genocide, crimes against humanity and war crimes against the civilian population".[12]

Resolution 1296 indicates the Security Council's willingness to create places of protection without the consent of the belligerents and an intention that UN Forces may be mandated by the

8 *Ibid.*, para. 50.

9 "UN Forces" are military forces authorized by the UN to conduct peace operations. These Forces, depending on the type of operation, may be under UN, coalition or national command and control.

10 "Administer" refers to the functions that would normally be conducted by the local authorities of a State, such as the maintenance of law and order; maintenance of the local infrastructure, and the provision of health care and humanitarian assistance.

11 These reasons may include denial to humanitarian access, mass displacements of population and gross violations of human rights.

12 S/RES/1296(2000), 19 April 2000, para. 15.

Council to use armed force to protect those who have taken sanctuary in such places of protection. In these circumstances, the Security Council's competence to create places of protection without the belligerents' consent stems primarily from its enforcement powers pursuant to Chapter VII of the UN Charter. However, before looking at these provisions it is necessary to say a few words about the Security Council's powers to authorize the creation of places of protection under Chapter VI of the Charter.

Chapter VI has two key legal features of relevance when considering the creation of places of protection. First, the Chapter provides for the "pacific settlement of disputes" and, secondly, it limits the Security Council to making recommendations to, rather than imposing binding decisions upon, the parties to a dispute. In relation to the pacific settlement of disputes, Member States are encouraged to seek peaceful settlements to their disputes,[13] and where this cannot be achieved, they are to refer their dispute to the Security Council.[14] Upon referral, or in circumstances where it "deems that the continuance of the dispute is in fact likely to endanger the maintenance of international peace and security",[15] the Security Council may recommend terms of settlement that it considers appropriate. These provisions raise the possibility of the UN creating places of protection in situations where the belligerents ·request the Security Council, or agree to a suggestion by the Council, to create a place of protection.

In practice it is usual for the belligerents to agree to the creation of a place of protection and for the Security Council to mandate UN Forces to control that place. For example, this was the case when the Armistice Demarcation Line and the demilitarized zones were created as a part of the Armistice Agreements between Israel and Syria and Israel and Egypt in 1949.[16] Chapter VI therefore limits the Security Council to creating places of protection with the consent of

---

13 Art. 33, UN Charter.
14 Art. 37(1), UN Charter.
15 Art. 37(2), UN Charter.
16 See Armistice Agreement signed between Israel and Syria and Armistice Agreement signed between Israel and Egypt, reprinted in R. Higgins *United Nations Peacekeeping 1946-1967: Documents and Commentary, The Middle East*, vol. 1, Oxford University Press, London, 1969, pp. 38-42 and 43-48 respectively.

RICR Décembre IRRC December 2001 Vol. 83 N° 844 **1017**

the belligerents. Should the Security Council wish to create a place of protection without the consent of the parties it will need to do so pursuant to Chapter VII of the Charter.

Creation of places of protection pursuant to authorization by Chapter VII

The competence of the Security Council to authorize the creation of places of protection without the belligerents' consent is based primarily on Chapter VII of the Charter. Chapter VII is concerned with "action with respect to threats to the peace, breaches of the peace, and acts of aggression", and lays down the specific powers of the Security Council in relation to the maintenance of international peace and security.[17] Article 39, the first provision of the Chapter, states:

> "The Security Council shall determine the existence of any threat to the peace, breach of the peace, or act of aggression and shall make recommendations, or decide what measures shall be taken in accordance with Articles 41 and 42, to maintain or restore international peace and security."[18]

The Charter is silent on what constitutes threats to or breaches of the peace and consequently, the Security Council "is not bound by any rigid definition of the acts ... calling for measures of enforcement".[19] It is clear that the threat, or use, of armed force between States would come within the scope of the phrase "threats or

---

[17] The Security Council's responsibility for the maintenance of international peace and security also stems from Art. 24(1) of the UN Charter which states: "In order to ensure prompt and effective action by the United Nations, its Members confer on the Security Council primary responsibility for the maintenance of international peace and security, and agree that in carrying out its duties under this responsibility the Security Council acts on their behalf."

[18] In practice the Security Council often "acts under Chapter VII without discussing the question of jurisdiction under Article 39".

D. J. Harris, *Cases and Materials on International Law*, 5th ed., Sweet and Maxwell, London, 1998, p. 942.

[19] L. Oppenheim, *International Law – A Treatise: Disputes, War and Neutrality*, Vol. II, 7th ed., Longmans, Green and Co, London, 1952, p. 163. See also M. Akehurst, *A Modern Introduction to International Law*, 6th ed., Harper Collins, London, 1991, p. 219: "a threat to the peace is whatever the Security Council says is a threat to the peace"; and Y. Dinstein, *War, Aggression and Self-Defence*, Grotius Publications, Cambridge, 1988, pp. 257-258.

breaches to the peace".[20] The question must, however, be asked whether situations involving gross humanitarian violations, such as the deliberate targeting of civilians, may be considered to breach the peace? Rosalyn Higgins has argued that "[t]he only way in which ... military sanctions for human-rights purposes could lawfully be mounted under the Charter is by the legal fiction that human-rights violations are causing a threat to international peace".[21] She has acknowledged, however, that "there may be an increasing tendency for the Security Council to characterize humanitarian concerns as threats to international peace — and thus bring them within the potential reach of Chapter VII of the Charter".[22] It may therefore be concluded that if the Security Council acts in accordance with the principles and purposes of the UN Charter its actions are likely to be *intra vires*.[23] It should also be noted that a Chapter VII determination by the Security Council has the effect of overriding the constraints placed by Article 2(7)[24] of the Charter that restricts the UN from interfering in the internal affairs of another State.

20 L. Goodrich, E. Hambro and A. Simons, *Charter of the United Nations: Commentary and Documents*, 3rd ed., Columbia University Press, New York, 1969, p. 297.

21 R. Higgins, *Problems and Processes: International Law and How We Use It*, Clarendon Press, Oxford, 1994, p. 255.

22 *Ibid.*, pp. 256-257.

23 The principles and purposes of the UN are found mainly in the preamble and Arts 1 and 2 of the UN Charter, and include maintenance of international peace and security, international cooperation and human rights. See Goodrich *et al.*, *op. cit.* (note 21), pp. 23-72. Brierly has argued that except for the Security Council's general obligation to "act in accordance with 'the Purposes and Principles of the United Nations', there is nothing to ensure that the measures which it decides shall be taken shall either respect the legal rights of states affected or be just in themselves". J. L. Brierly, *The Law of Nations: An Introduction to the International Law of Peace*, 5th ed., Oxford University Press,

Oxford, 1956, p. 302. Alston adds: "it is up to the Council itself to determine what matters it will treat as falling within its competence. In doing so, the Council must act in good faith and in conformity with the overall objectives of the Charter (...) [O]nce the Council has agreed to concern itself with a particular situation, it will not exclude human rights concerns from the purview of United Nations action taken in that regard." P. Alston, "The Security Council and human rights: Lessons to be learned from the Iraq-Kuwait crisis and its aftermath", *Australian Year Book of International Law*, vol. 13, 1982, pp. 107-176, 139.

24 Art. 2(7) of the UN Charter states: "Nothing contained in the present Charter shall authorize the United Nations to intervene in matters which are essentially within the domestic jurisdiction of any state or shall require the Members to submit such matters to settlement under the present Charter; but this principle shall not prejudice the application of enforcement measures under Chapter VII."

RICR Décembre IRRC December 2001 Vol. 83 N° 844 1019

The Security Council has, in at least two cases, authorized the creation of places of protection based on humanitarian concerns. In Bosnia and Herzegovina the Security Council authorized the creation of a safe area in Srebrenica because it was "[d]eeply concerned … [about] the continued and deliberate armed attacks and shelling of the innocent civilian population by Bosnian Serb paramilitary".[25] In relation to Rwanda the Security Council determined "that the magnitude of the humanitarian crisis … constitutes a threat to peace and security in the region"[26] and therefore authorized the creation of a place of protection in the south-west of Rwanda.

The Security Council, having determined the existence of a threat to the peace, a breach of the peace, or an act of aggression in accordance with Article 39 of the Charter, may take such action as it thinks necessary, including authorizing the creation of places of protection. Such enforcement action by the Security Council will be legally binding upon all UN member States,[27] and applicable to "States that are not members of the United Nations and to bodies not recognized as States".[28]

The practice of the Security Council in authorizing the creation of places of protection without the consent of the parties affirms the role that Chapter VII has to play. In Bosnia and Herzegovina, for example, the Security Council, acting pursuant to Chapter VII of the UN Charter, demanded that "all the parties and others concerned treat Srebrenica and its surroundings as a safe area which should be free from any armed attack or any other hostile act".[29] In May 1993 the Security Council, again acting under Chapter VII, extended the concept of safe areas to apply to "Sarajevo, and other such threatened areas, in particular the towns of Tuzla, Zepa, Gorazde,

25 S/RES/819(1993), 16 April 1993, preamble.

26 S/RES/929(1994), 22 June 1994, preamble.

27 Article 25 of the UN Charter states: "The Members of the United Nations agree to accept and carry out the decisions of the Security Council in accordance with the present Charter."

28 Oppenheim, *op. cit.* (note 19), p. 166.

29 S/RES/819(1993), 16 April 1993, para. 1. Note that S/RES/770(1992) formally recognized, pursuant to Article 39 of the UN Charter, that "the situation in the Bosnia and Herzegovina constitutes a threat to international peace and security…".

[and] Bihac ...".[30] Similarly, in 1994 French-led troops conducted *Operation Turquoise* which involved the creation of a place of protection to protect Rwandan civilians and combatants. The Security Council authorized the French-led troops, pursuant to Chapter VII, to create a "...humanitarian protected zone in the Cyangugu-Kibuye-Gikongoro triangle in south-western Rwanda".[31]

The Security Council decisions authorizing the establishment of safe areas in Bosnia and Herzegovina and the humanitarian protected zone in Rwanda were made without the consent of the belligerents, and the terms under which they were created were binding on all belligerents. Serb forces were against the creation of the safe areas, as evidenced, for example, by the fact that the Serb paramilitary forces continued to threaten and attack Srebrenica even after the Security Council adopted Resolution 819.[32] In Rwanda, the Rwanda Patriotic Front, having recently taken control of most of the country from the previous regime, expressed its strong opposition to the French establishing the zone but did not use armed force to oppose the French-led forces.[33]

From the above brief examination of Chapter VII and Security Council practice it may be concluded that the Security Council may explicitly mandate UN Forces to create places of protection without the consent of the belligerents. However, the Security Council may not always explicitly mandate the establishment of a

30 S/RES/824(1993), 6 May 1993, para. 3. For a detailed account of the developments in relation to the safe areas in Bosnia and Herzegovina see M. Weller, "Peace-keeping and peace-enforcement in the Republic of Bosnia and Herzegovina", *Heidelberg Journal of International Law*, 1996, pp. 69-177, and Y. Akashi, "The use of force in a United Nations peace-keeping operation: Lessons learnt for the safe areas mandate", *Fordham Interna-tional Law Journal*, vol. 19, 1995, pp. 312-323.

31 *The Blue Helmets: A Review of United Nations Peace-keeping*, 3rd ed., UN Department of Public Information, New York, 1996, p. 352.

32 Report of the Secretary-General pursuant to Security Council Resolution 819 (1993), para. 24, S/25700(1993), reprinted in D. Bethlehem and M. Weller (eds), *The 'Yugoslav Crisis in International Law: General Issues*, Part I, Cambridge University Press, Cambridge, 1997, pp. 612-619.

33 Report of the Secretary-General on the situation in Rwanda, S/1994/924 (1994), reprinted in *The United Nations and Rwanda 1993-1996*, UN Department of Public Information, New York, 1996, p. 326.

RICR Décembre IRRC December 2001 Vol. 83 N° 844 1021

place of protection, and the question consequently needs to be asked whether such authorization might be implied by the mandate to the UN Force? The answer is likely to be yes, if the Security Council has determined to take enforcement action pursuant to Chapter VII of the Charter. For example, a Chapter VII enforcement operation that mandates a UN Force to "provide security and protection to civilians at risk" implies that the Force may take necessary and reasonable steps, such as the creation of a place of protection, to discharge that mandate.

Creation of places of protection without Chapter VII authorization

A more legally controversial situation arises when the Security Council has not made a Chapter VII determination and a UN Force witnesses gross violations of human rights being committed by the belligerents. As discussed above, in such a case the Force will be acting under Chapter VI and will not have a mandate to create places of protection without the belligerents' consent. Consequently, it is arguable that without a Chapter VII determination the Force is legally hamstrung, unable to create a place of protection to protect civilians from gross violations of human rights because of the limitation placed on intervention by Article 2(7) of the Charter. A Force that finds itself in this predicament should immediately seek a mandate from the Security Council, pursuant to Chapter VII of the Charter, permitting that Force to undertake military enforcement action to create a place of protection without the parties' consent. However, this course of action may not be open to the Force where the humanitarian emergency urgently requires people to be protected. In such a situation, instead of standing by and watching violations of international law, the Force may create a place of protection without the consent of the belligerents, on the grounds that such a place was required for its own protection and that of the people who were being targeted. The legal justification for this act of survival may be based on the exercise of the right of individual and collective self-defence.[34] The Force would be

34 The right of UN Forces to use force in individual and collective self-defence has been recognized since early peace-keeping operations. See for example Report of the

acting out of necessity and its actions would need to be limited to what was necessary and proportional at the time.

It is also contended here that in humanitarian emergencies, a further source of legal justification for the Force to create such places may derive from treaty law or general principles of international law. For example, if the attack was serious enough to qualify as an act of genocide,[35] then the creation of a place of protection by a UN Force may be justified under Article 1 of the Convention on the Prevention and Punishment of the Crime of Genocide.[36] The creation thereof may also be justified under customary international law principles that prohibit targeting or attacking civilians deliberately.[37] For example, it may be argued that there is a general right for UN Forces to protect persons in such places because "[a]cting for the protection of man...in time of armed conflict, accords with the aims of the United Nations no less than does the maintenance of international

United Nations Secretary-General, *United Nations Emergency Force: Summary Study of the Experience Derived from the Establishment and Operation of the Force*, UN Doc. A/3943, 9 October 1958, paras 178 and 179. It has been argued that the right of UN forces to use force in self-defence is similar to the defence of self-defence in municipal law. See P. Rowe, "The United Nations rules of engagement and the British soldier in Bosnia", *International Comparative Law Quarterly*, vol. 43, October 1994, p. 954. See also D. W. Bowett, *United Nations Forces: A Legal Study of United Nations Practice*, Stevens and Sons, London, 1964, pp. 486-487.

35 Art. 2 of the 1948 Convention on the Prevention and Punishment of the Crime of Genocide states: "...genocide means any of the following acts committed with intent to destroy, in whole or in part, a national, ethnical, racial or religious group, as such:

(a) Killing members of the group;

(b) Causing serious bodily or metal harm to members of the group;

(c) Deliberately inflicting on the group conditions of life calculated to bring about its physical destruction in whole or in part;

(d) Imposing measures intended to prevent births within the group;

(e) Forcibly transferring children of the group to another group."

36 Art. 1 of the Genocide Convention states: "The Contracting Parties confirm that genocide, whether committed in time of peace or in time of war, is a crime under international law which they undertake to prevent and to punish." *Contra*: Y. Dinstein, "The Thirteenth Waldemar A. Solf Lecture in International Law", *Military Law Review*, vol. 166, 2000, pp. 100-101. Dinstein argues that it is not sufficient to read Art. 1 in isolation. He maintains that the Genocide Convention does not permit States to use force unilaterally to prevent genocide. Prevention or termination of genocide by States must occur either through the Security Council (Art. 8, Genocide Convention) or the International Court of Justice (Art. 9).

37 A.P.V. Rogers, *Law on the Battlefield*, Manchester University Press, Manchester, 1996, p. 14. See Arts 51(6), 52(1), 53(c), 54(4), and 56(4) of Protocol I.

RICR Décembre **IRRC** December 2001 Vol. 83 N° 844   **1023**

peace and security". [38] The Force should ensure that its actions in creating a place of protection are necessary and proportional to protect the civilians who are being deliberately targeted.

It is relevant to this discussion to note that the proposition of creating places of protection in the absence of an explicit Chapter VII authorization has been supported by the practice of some States with regard to the creation of safe havens in northern Iraq to protect the Kurds at the end of the Gulf War in 1991. The repression of Kurds by Iraqi authorities led the Security Council to insist that Iraq allow "immediate access by international humanitarian organizations to all those in need of assistance in all parts of Iraq and to make available all necessary facilities for their operations". [39] However, the Iraqi repression of the Kurds reached a level which prompted British Prime Minister John Major to propose, pursuant to Security Council Resolution 688(1991), "the establishment of a safe haven in northern Iraq under United Nations control where refugees, particularly Kurds ... would be safe from attack and able to receive relief supplies in a regular and ordered way". [40]

Control of places of protection
Control of places of protection with Chapter VII authorization

It is accepted that where the Security Council, acting in accordance with its powers under Chapter VII, has determined that there is a threat to international peace and security in accordance with Article 39 of the Charter, it "may take such action by air, sea or land forces as may be necessary to maintain or restore international peace and security". [41] The Security Council may therefore authorize UN Forces to use all necessary measures, including recourse to armed force, to defend and administer such places. The use of force in such

---

38 Sandoz *et al.*, *op. cit.* (note 3), para. 3596.
39 S/RES/688(1991), 5 April 1991, para. 3.

40 M. Weller (ed.), *Iraq and Kuwait: The Hostilities and their Aftermath*, Grotius Publications, Cambridge, 1993, pp. 714-715.
41 Art. 42, UN Charter.

circumstances must be "confined to what is necessary and proportionate to the achievement of the goals set out by the Security Council".[42]

In the case of the safe areas created in Bosnia and Herzegovina, the Security Council mandated the United Nations Protection Force (UNPROFOR) to:

> "deter attacks against the safe areas, to monitor the cease-fire, to promote the withdrawal of military or paramilitary units other than those of the Government of Bosnia and Herzegovina and to occupy some key points on the ground, in addition to participating in the delivery of humanitarian relief to the population".[43]

The Security Council added that UNPROFOR was authorized:

> "in carrying out...[its] mandate...acting in self-defence, to take the necessary measures, including the use of force, in reply to bombardments against the safe areas by any of the parties or to armed incursions into them or in the event of any deliberate obstruction in or around those areas to the freedom of movement of the Force or of protected humanitarian convoys." [44]

Weller suggests that there are three possible interpretations of this authorization by the Security Council to use force to protect the safe areas. First, UNPROFOR was limited to using force to protect itself alone; second, UNPROFOR could use force in reply to bombardments against and armed incursions into the safe areas;[45] and third, UNPROFOR was authorized to use force to carry out the mandate. In practice UNPROFOR adopted the second interpretation,[46] as the first and third interpretations were seen as too narrow and too broad respectively.[47] However, had UNPROFOR chosen to

---

42 C. Greenwood, *International Humanitarian Law (Laws of War): Revised Report for the Centennial Commemoration of the First Hague Peace Conference 1899*, pursuant to A/RES/52/154 and A/RES/53/99, p. 19. Judith Gardam also argues that the limitations of necessity and proportionality apply to unauthorized Chapter VII operations as well. J. Gardam, "Proportionality and force in international law", AJIL, vol. 87, p. 392.

43 S/RES/836(1993), 4 June 1993, para. 5.

44 *Ibid.*, para. 9.

45 Weller, *op. cit.* (note 30), pp. 108-109.

46 S/1994/555, 9 May 1994, Report of the Secretary-General pursuant to Resolution 844 (1993), para. 4.

47 Weller, *op. cit.* (note 30), pp. 108-109.

RICR Décembre IRRC December 2001 Vol. 83 N° 844   **1025**

adopt the third interpretation, that is, the use of armed force to defend the mandate, it would not have acted beyond the authority given to it by the Security Council.[48] Perhaps the fact that the use of force to defend the mandate was expressed in terms of "self-defence" caused some confusion and consequently led the Force to adopt the second interpretation.

Resolution 836(1993) also authorized Member States (acting nationally or through regional organizations), in coordination with the Secretary-General and UNPROFOR, to take "...all necessary measures, through the use of air power, in and around the safe areas...to support [UNPROFOR]...in the performance of its mandate". [49] The North Atlantic Treaty Organization (NATO) accepted this task and stated:

> "if any Bosnian Serb attacks involving heavy weapons are carried out on the United Nations-designated safe areas of Gorazde, Bihac, Srebrenica, Tuzla and Zepa, these weapons and other Bosnian Serb military assets as well as their direct and essential military support facilities, including but not limited to fuel installations and munitions sites, will be subject to NATO air strikes." [50]

This interpretation as to when force could be used to protect the safe areas appears to have reflected the UNPROFOR interpretation.

In the case of Rwanda, the French-led troops were authorized to use "all necessary means to achieve humanitarian objectives set out in paragraphs 4(a) and (b)[51] of Resolution 925(1994)",[52] thus permitting them to resort to the use of armed force to protect the

48 *Ibid.*, pp. 172-173.

49 S/RES/836(1993), 4 June 1993, para. 10.

50 S/1994/498, 22 April 1994, para. 9(a), reprinted in Bethlehem/Weller, *op. cit.* (note 32), p. 697.

51 Paras. 4(a) and (b) of S/RES/925(1994), 8 June 1994, stated:

"Reaffirms that UNAMIR [United Nations Assistance Mission in Rwanda], in addition to continuing to act as an intermediary between the parties in an attempt to secure their

agreement to a cease-fire, will:

Contribute to the security and protection of displaced persons, refugees and civilians at risk in Rwanda, including through the establishment and maintenance, where feasible, of secure humanitarian areas; and provide security and support for the distribution of relief supplies and humanitarian relief operations."

52 S/RES/929(1994), 22 June 1994, para. 3.

area. Consequently, it was lawful for the French-led troops to prohibit all military activity and "oppose the entry of all armed persons, no matter what their origin, into the humanitarian safe area".[53]

The mandate may also explicitly state who may be defended in the place of protection. It may, for example, authorize the UN Force to protect all civilians, paramilitary and military forces of one of the belligerents. Such a step may be considered necessary to maintain or restore international peace and security and therefore within the power granted to the Security Council under Chapter VII. In the case of Srebrenica, this is what occurred when the Security Council extended the protection afforded by the area to civilians so as to include the military and paramilitary units of the Government of Bosnia and Herzegovina.[54]

As evidenced by the resolutions relating to the places of protection in Bosnia and Herzegovina and Rwanda, the Security Council's authorization of the use of armed force was broad and unspecific, with no guidance as to how much force could be used and what principles of law applied to the use thereof. It is clear that where a UN Force is a belligerent it is required, as a matter of law, to comply with the relevant principles of international humanitarian law which applies during armed conflict. In circumstances where the UN Force is not a belligerent, it is generally accepted that the Force is required to apply the principles and spirit of international humanitarian law when using force.[55]

---

53 Letter dated 2 July from the Secretary-General to the President of the Security Council, UN Doc. S/1994/798, 6 July 1994, reprinted in *op. cit.* (note 33), p. 311.

54 S/RES/836(1993), 4 June 1993, para. 5 stated that UNPROFOR's mandate was to "promote the withdrawal of military or paramilitary units other than those of the Government of the Republic of Bosnia and Herzegovina".

55 The Secretary-General's Bulletin: Observance by United Nations Forces of International Humanitarian Law, UN Doc. ST/SGB/1999/13, 6 August 1999, supports

this approach. For a detailed discussion of the application of international humanitarian law to UN Forces see D. Bowett, *United Nations Forces: A Legal Study of United Nations Practice*, Stevens and Sons, London, 1964; C. Greenwood, "International humanitarian law and the United Nations military operations", *Yearbook of International Humanitarian Law*, vol. 1, T.M.C. Asser Press, The Hague, 1998, pp. 3-34; and P. Rowe, "Maintaining discipline in United Nations peace support operations: The legal quagmire for military contingents", *Journal of Conflict and Security Law*, No. 1, 2000, pp. 45-62.

RICR Décembre IRRC December 2001 Vol. 83 N° 844   **1027**

Do UN Forces have a duty to protect places of protection? Unless the Security Council states otherwise, it is difficult to find the legal source of such a duty.[56] A military commander must be able to judge whether the use of force is appropriate in the circumstances. For example, a commander may have a reasonable belief that because his or her troops are heavily outnumbered, it is better to refrain from the use of force in order not to further jeopardize the lives of those in the place of protection.

In concluding this brief exploration of the use of armed force to defend a place of protection, a few words need to be said about the perceived impartiality of a UN Force should it defend a place to the detriment of the interests of one or more of the belligerents. In the context of the safe areas in Bosnia and Herzegovina, it has been argued that UNPROFOR's existence in the safe areas "appeared to thwart only one army in the conflict, thus jeopardizing ... [its] impartiality".[57] However, as Weller correctly emphasizes, failing to defend places of protection on the basis that to do so would adversely affect the Force's impartiality in the conflict "reveals a profound confusion" as to the role of a Force in circumstances where a belligerent profits militarily from the atrocities that it commits and acts in violation of Security Council determinations.[58] There can be little argument that a place of protection created without the consent of the parties is likely to require a credible military force to defend the place from attacks by one or more belligerents.

Article 2(7) of the UN Charter limits a UN Force from interfering in the domestic jurisdiction of a Member State unless the Force has the consent of that State or the Security Council has authorized enforcement action pursuant to Chapter VII of the Charter. Consequently, should the Security Council wish to authorize the UN Force to undertake activities such as maintaining law and order, restricting the freedom of movement of people, and disarming people

---

56 Greenwood, *op. cit.* (note 55), p. 32.

57 UN Doc. S/1994/555, 9 May 1994, para. 15, reprinted in Bethlehem/Weller, *op. cit.*, (note 32), p. 700.

58 Weller, *op. cit.* (note 30), p. 143.

in the place of protection, then the Force will need either the consent of the belligerents or due authorization to take enforcement action.

If the mandate does not explicitly authorize a Force to administer a place of protection, may the Force infer that it has such a power? The answer is likely to be "yes" if the Force has the consent of the local authorities or is in belligerent occupation. If the Force has the parties' consent it may administer the place within the limits stipulated by the agreement between the belligerents and the Force. In situations where a military force is a belligerent in occupation, international humanitarian law requires it to administer the place of protection in accordance with the laws of occupation.[59] It is possible that a UN Force could "find itself in belligerent occupation of territory, and that most or all of customary and conventional laws of war would apply to them".[60] In this context, Christopher Greenwood has argued:

> "It is perfectly possible that the United Nations itself or a State or States acting under its authority could occupy part or all of the territory of an adversary in the course of an international armed conflict. In such a case, the law of belligerent occupation could apply but only unless and until the Security Council used its Chapter VII powers to impose a different regime as a part of the measures which it considered necessary for the restoration of peace and security."[61]

If the UN Force does not have the consent of the local authority, is not in belligerent occupation, and the Security Council's mandate does not expressly authorize the Force to administer the place of protection, it may be *ultra vires* for the Force to conclude that it has such powers. Much depends on what aspects of life in the place of protection the Force wishes to administer. For example, facilitating humanitarian assistance and restoring and/or maintaining the

---

59 The law in relation to belligerent occupation is found principally in sections III and IV of the Fourth Geneva Convention. The law of occupation covers the following issues with regard to administration in the area under occupation: inviolability of rights; deportations, transfers and evacuations;

hygiene and public health; and penal legislation and treatment of detainees.

60 A. Roberts, "What is military occupation", *British Yearbook of International Law*, vol. 50, 1984, p. 291.

61 Greenwood, *op. cit.* (note 55), p. 28.

RICR Décembre IRRC December 2001 Vol. 83 N° 844 1029

infrastructure are unlikely to prove controversial in the circumstances of a humanitarian emergency. However, a UN Force taking on the role of carrying out legislative and/or executive governmental functions, without the consent of the local authorities or explicit Security Council authorization, may well find that it is acting *ultra vires*.

Danesh Sarooshi argues that the Security Council must delegate the power of internal governance in express terms and that one cannot assume such authorization by implication.[62] He examines the case of the UN's involvement in Somalia and concludes that the competence of the Secretary-General's Special Representative to promulgate a law that had the effect of being legally binding within Somalia was questionable. Sarooshi argues that the "reference of the consolidation and maintenance of a secure environment throughout Somalia cannot justify the exercise of what is in fact a legislative power: the promulgation of a legal code".[63]

It is contended here that, in situations where the belligerents are unable to administer a place of protection, a UN Force may be legally justified in administering it until the Security Council is able to give its express authorization or until the local authorities are able to resume governance. It is difficult to see why a UN Force, with a Chapter VII mandate to "use all necessary means" cannot assume that it may, in very limited circumstances, administer the place of protection. Clearly, the extent of administration that the Force would be justified in undertaking would be limited to what was reasonable and necessary in the circumstances and would not go beyond the time it takes the local authorities to resume responsibility for the area.

It has also been argued that a Force may not be in belligerent occupation but may nonetheless find itself "organizing some kind of 'occupation by consent'".[64] Adam Roberts suggests that the law of occupation may apply in situations where:

" (i) There is a military force whose presence in a territory is not sanctioned or regulated by a valid agreement, or whose

62 D. Sarooshi, *The United Nations and the Development of Collective Security: The Delegation by the UN Security Council of its Chapter VII Powers*, Clarendon Press, Oxford, 1999, p. 63.
63 *Ibid.*
64 *Op. cit.* (note 60), p. 291.

activities there involve an extensive range of contacts with the host society not adequately covered by the original agreement under which it intervened; (ii) the military force has either displaced the territory's ordinary system of public order and government, replacing it with its own command structure, or else has shown the clear physical ability to displace it; (iii) there is a difference of nationality and interest between the inhabitants on the one hand and the forces intervening and exercising power over them on the other, with the former not owing allegiance to the latter; (iv) within an overall framework of a breach of important parts of the national or international legal order, administration and the life of society have to continue on some legal basis, and there is a practical need for an emergency set of rules to reduce the dangers which can result from clashes between the military force and the inhabitants."[65]

Michael Kelly adds that the extent of the application of the Fourth Geneva Convention:

"will depend on the instruments a State is party to and the circumstances of the case. Such situations can be summarised as those where there is no consent to the intervention from a recognisable sovereign apparatus, regardless of whether an armed conflict is in existence either between the intervening force and the State or local armed elements."[66]

Without entering into a debate as to whether the law of belligerent occupation applies in situations short of armed conflict, there can be little objection in international law to using the framework of the 1949 Fourth Geneva Convention[67] to ensure that the rights and obligations of both the UN Force and the people in the place of protection are maintained. For example, the UN Force may

---

65 *Ibid.*, pp. 300-301.

66 M. Kelly, *Restoring and Maintaining Order in Complex Peace Operations: The Search for a Legal Framework*, Kluwer Law International, The Hague, 1999, p. 227.

67 The Convention may be used to provide military forces with a framework for dealing with such issues as restoring public order,

general treatment of the population, minimum standards to be applied to any legal process taken by the Force, basic humanitarian standards to be applied to detainees, and preventative security measures that may be taken against the population in the place of protection.

find it appropriate to use the provisions of this Convention to provide an interim justice system that strikes a balance between the military imperative of achieving the mandate and the rights of the people in the place of protection to natural justice and due process.

In the case of the safe areas in Bosnia and Herzegovina and that of the humanitarian protection zone in Rwanda, there was no explicit Security Council authorization mandating the UN Forces to administer them. In relation to safe areas created in Bosnia and Herzegovina, UNPROFOR was mandated to: (1) deter attacks against the safe areas; (2) monitor the cease-fire; (3) promote the withdrawal of military or paramilitary units other than those of the Government of Bosnia and Herzegovina; (4) occupy some key points on the ground; and (5) participate in the delivery of humanitarian relief to the population.[68] Use of the words "deter", "monitor", "promote" and "participate" by the Security Council suggests that it was consciously limiting UNPROFOR's mission to administering the safe areas. There was no suggestion by UNPROFOR that it exercised any administration powers without the consent of the belligerents, this notwithstanding the Secretary-General's report to the Security Council that the infrastructure had collapsed and that there were serious law and order problems in Srebrenica.[69] UNPROFOR's contact with the local population in the safe areas appeared to have been limited and consequently there did not appear to have been any issue as to whether the Force could have taken on activities that may have been considered as interfering with the authority of the Bosnian authorities. In Srebrenica, for example, the Dutch Battalion's closest contact with the locals came through its medical unit, mine-awareness classes and the rebuilding of schools.[70]

In the humanitarian protection zone in Rwanda the task of the French-led troops was to contribute "... in an impartial way to the security and protection of displaced persons, refugees and civilians at risk in Rwanda...".[71] The French-led troops also undertook the

---

68 S/RES/836(1993), 4 June 1993, para. 5.

69 UN Doc. S/1994/291, 11 March 1994, para. 17.

70 J. W. Honig and N. Bothe, *Srebrenica:*

Record of a War Crime, Penguin Books, London, 1996, p. 132.

71 S/RES/918(1994), 17 May 1994, para. 3.

distribution of humanitarian aid in the zone[72] and emphasized to the UN that they were seeking to maintain a presence "... pending the arrival of an expanded UNAMIR [United Nations Assistance Mission in Rwanda]".[73] The French led troops do not appear to have considered that the law of occupation applied to them, nor do they appear to have administered the territory that they controlled. However, Kelly submits that the Fourth Convention "applied to south-western Rwanda in Operation Turquoise where the French had no permission from any Rwandan entity in the confused aftermath of the civil war"[74] and that consequently, they should have applied the law of occupation.

Control of places of protection without Chapter VII authorization

Defending a place of protection in circumstances where the UN Force has not been given Chapter VII enforcement powers is likely to be more controversial. In such a case the Force may have to rely upon the right of individual and collective self-defence, and/or defence of the mandate, and/or general principles of international law. For example, during the conflict in the former Yugoslavia the UN accepted that "... the use of force in self-defence is an inherent right of United Nations Forces exercised to preserve a collective and individual defence".[75] Thus, the UN Force could lawfully use armed force to protect itself and others in the place of protection. The right to use force in defence of the mandate was also recognized during the conflict in the former Yugoslavia by the Secretary-General stating that

---

72 Letter dated 2 July from the Secretary-General to the President of the Security Council, UN Doc. S/1994/798, 6 July 1994, reprinted in *op. cit.* (note 33), p. 311.

73 Letter dated 20 June from the Permanent Representative of France to the United Nations addressed to the Secretary-General, UN Doc. S/1994/734, 21 June 1994, *ibid.*, p. 307.

74 *Op. cit.*, (note 66), pp. 155-156.

75 Letter in reply to the Special Representative of the Secretary-General in the former Yugoslavia from a UN Legal Counsel, 19 July 1993, quoted in B. de Rossanet, *Peacemaking and Peacekeeping in Yugoslavia*, Kluwer Law International, The Hague, 1996, p. 91. This opinion is consistent with the traditional UN approach to the use of force in self-defence. See e.g. United Nations Emergency Force: Summary study of the experience derived from the establishment of the operation of the Force, UN Doc. A/3943, 9 October 1958, para. 165.

RICR DÉCEMBRE IRRC DECEMBER 2001 VOL. 83 N° 844 1033

UNPROFOR was authorized to use force in "situations in which armed persons attempt by force to prevent United Nations troops from carrying out their mandate".[76] Consequently, if the Force was mandated to "provide protection and security to displaced persons, refugees and civilians at risk" it would be lawful for it to defend a place of protection as a means of achieving that mandate. Finally, the use of force to defend a place of protection may be justified on general principles of international law, such as preventing genocide.

The authority of UN Forces to administer places of protection without the consent of the parties or without a Chapter VII mandate is also likely to be controversial. For example, in a place of protection where the local authorities are no longer functioning the UN Force may, in order to maintain its own security, find it necessary to administer certain aspects of life, such as law and order. In this situation, the UN Force should first seek the consent of the local authorities to administer the place until those authorities are in a position to resume their responsibilities. If this course is not possible, then the Force may have to administer the place of protection until then on the basis of necessity. The UN has accepted that, in some circumstances, the Force may have to carry out functions that are not specifically mandated by the Security Council but are nonetheless necessary for the efficient functioning of the Force. For example, in 1958 the Secretary-General acknowledged:

> "[a] right of detention which normally would be exercised only by local authorities is extended to UNEF [United Nations Emergency Force] units. However, this is so only within a limited area where the local authorities abstain from exercising similar rights, whether alone or in collaboration with the United Nations".[77]

---

76 UN Doc. S/24540, 10 September 1992, para. 9. This view is consistent with the traditional UN approach that force may be used to defend the mandate. See e.g. S/11052/Rev.1, 27 October 1973, para. 4(d) concerning the use of force by UN Emergency Force II to resist attempts to prevent it from discharging its mandate.

77 A/3943, 9 October 1958, para. 165.

Conclusion

It is uncontroversial that the Security Council may authorize a UN Force to create a place of protection with the consent of the belligerents. It is also uncontroversial that in situations where there is no consent, the Security Council is competent to explicitly mandate a UN Force pursuant to Chapter VII of the United Nations Charter to create a place of protection. It is suggested here that if a UN Force has not been explicitly authorized to create a place of protection it may infer such an authority if it has a Chapter VII mandate. It is also suggested that in situations where the UN Force does not have a Chapter VII mandate it may, on the basis of self-defence and/or wider principles of international law, be legally justified in creating a place of protection to protect civilians at risk. In such situations the UN Force should seek, and the Security Council should give, approval for the place of protection as soon as possible. The UN Force's decision to create such a place without Security Council authorization would be based on what is necessary and proportional at the time.

It is also clear that the Security Council may authorize UN Forces to control places of protection pursuant to Chapter VII of the Charter. If there is no explicit authority to defend the place of protection, the UN Force may infer such authority as being implicit in its Chapter VII mandate. If there is no Chapter VII mandate, the Force may justify its defence of a place of protection as being based on self-defence and/or general principles of international law. A UN Force in belligerent occupation of a place of protection is required to apply the law of belligerent occupation at least until such time as the Security Council directs otherwise. Where the UN Force does not have the consent of the belligerents, is not a belligerent occupier, and there is no explicit mandate given to the Force, the administration of the place of protection will need to be justified on the basis of necessity and proportionality.

RICR Décembre IRRC December 2001 Vol. 83 N° 844   **1035**

Résumé

La création et le contrôle de zones protégées lors des opérations de paix des Nations Unies
par Bruce M. Oswald

La création de zones protégées est un moyen de mettre la population civile à l'abri des hostilités. Cet article examine le régime juridique de la création et du contrôle de zones protégées lors des opérations de paix des Nations Unies. L'auteur se penche sur le droit international et la pratique des États dans les cas où les forces des Nations Unies ont, en application du Chapitre VII de la Charte, établi et contrôlé des zones protégées, sans le consentement de certaines ou de l'ensemble des parties au conflit. Il étudie en outre les éléments juridiques, sur lesquels se fondent les forces des Nations Unies pour créer et contrôler des zones protégées, alors qu'aucun mandat ne leur a été explicitement donné. L'auteur conclut que les casques bleus peuvent, dans certaines circonstances, être juridiquement fondés à agir de la sorte même s'ils n'ont pas un mandat explicite du Conseil de sécurité.

International Criminal Law

[14]

Responsibilities of States Participating in Multilateral Operations with Respect to Persons Indicted for War Crimes

Diane F. Orentlicher[*]

Introduction

The creation of two international criminal tribunals in recent years has presented a raft of novel issues relating to the interaction of national and international legal authority. Among these, surely none has greater practical importance than questions bearing on responsibility for apprehending indicted suspects.

When the United Nations Security Council established the Yugoslavia and Rwanda Tribunals, it was contemplated that responsibility for apprehending indicted suspects would fall to state authorities.[2] In the case of the Yugoslavia Tribunal, it soon became clear that reliance solely on national authorities would hobble the Tribunal's operation, as those in a position to arrest most of the indicted suspects were determined to shield them from prosecution.

Thus, attention naturally turned to the possibility of arrest authority being conferred upon an international entity. This possibility was realized through the Dayton Peace Agreement, concluded in late 1995, which authorizes but does not require the NATO force deployed in Bosnia—originally the Implementation Force (IFOR) and now the Stabilization Force (SFOR)— to arrest suspects indicted by the International Criminal

[*] Professor of Law and Director of the War Crimes Research Office, American University, Washington, D.C. I am grateful to Graham T. Blewitt, Robert K. Goldman, Christopher Keith Hall, W. Hays Parks, Yves Sandoz and Bruno Zimmermann for comments on earlier drafts of this paper, and to Amjad Atallah and Ewen Allison for research assistance.

2. Article 29 of the Statute of the International Criminal Tribunal for the former Yugoslavia and Article 28 of the Statute of the International Criminal Tribunal for Rwanda require "States" to "comply without undue delay with any request for assistance or an order issued by a Trial Chamber," including requests and orders relating to the "arrest or detention of persons" and to the "surrender or the transfer of the accused" to the Tribunal.

194   *14 Nouvelles Études Pénales 1998*

Tribunal for the former Yugoslavia (ICTY).[3] While the North Atlantic Council (NAC) could act on that authorization by encouraging SFOR to search for and arrest suspects indicted by the ICTY, it has instead made clear that arrests are to be made only if SFOR troops encounter indicted suspects without searching for them and the circumstances make it prudent to effect an arrest. It took 19 months before NATO commanders deemed it appropriate to make such an arrest, and SFOR has to date attempted to arrest only two suspects.

Public debate concerning NATO's controversial stance has focused principally on policy concerns. While this is scarcely surprising, it is incorrect to assume that NATO's position on apprehension is solely a matter of policy: this question is also governed by law. Several sources of international law require SFOR to search for and, where reasonably possible, to arrest suspects indicted by the ICTY.

Obligations Relating to Grave Breaches of the Geneva Conventions and Protocol 1

One source of a duty to search for and arrest indicted suspects is the Geneva Conventions of 1949 and Additional Protocol I of 1977.[4] Each of

---

3.   After elaborating specific powers of IFOR, Annex 1-A of the Dayton Peace Agreement provides, in Article VI:

> 4. The Parties understand and agree that further directives from the [North Atlantic Council] may establish additional duties and responsibilities for the IFOR in implementing this Annex.

Since Annex 1-A also requires parties to the agreement to cooperate fully with the ICTY, *see* art. X, Article VI(4) enables the North Atlantic Council to vest IFOR with authority to assist in implementing these obligations. A resolution adopted by the U.N. Security Council following conclusion of the Dayton accord recognizes that the parties thereto are required to cooperate fully with the ICTY and have authorized IFOR "to take such actions as required, including the use of necessary force, to ensure compliance with Annex 1-A of the Peace Agreement." S.C. Res. 1031, para. 5 (1995).

4.   Geneva Convention for the Amelioration of the Condition of the Wounded and Sick in Armed Forces in the Field, Aug. 12, 1949, 6 U.S.T. 3217, T.I.A.S. No. 3362, 75 U.N.T.S. 31; Geneva Convention for the Amelioration of the Condition of Wounded, Sick and Shipwrecked Members of Armed Forces at Sea, Aug. 12, 1949, 6 U.S.T. 3217, T.I.A.S. No. 3363, 75 U.N.T.S. 85; Geneva Convention Relative to the Treatment of Prisoners of War, Aug. 12, 1949, 6 U.S.T. 3316, T.I.A.S. No. 3364, 75 U.N.T.S. 135; Geneva Convention Relative to the Protection of Civilian Persons in Time of War, Aug. 12, 1949,

these conventions, which establish rules governing armed conflicts between states,[5] identifies certain violations as "grave breaches." For example, the Fourth Geneva Convention of 1949 identifies the following as "grave breaches" when committed against protected persons: "wilful killing, torture or inhuman treatment . . ., wilfully causing great suffering or serious injury to body or health, unlawful deportation or transfer or unlawful confinement of a protected person . . ., taking of hostages and extensive destruction and appropriation of property, not justified by military necessity and carried out unlawfully and wantonly."[6]

Although parties to these conventions are required to suppress *all* violations,[7] they have special enforcement duties in respect of grave breaches. The conventions provide in clarion terms: "Each High Contracting Party shall be under the obligation to search for persons alleged to have committed, or to have ordered to be committed, such grave breaches, and shall bring such persons, regardless of their nationality, before its own courts" or hand such persons over for trial to another High Contracting Party.[8]

---

6 U.S.T. 3516, 75 U.N.T.S. 287 [hereinafter Fourth Geneva Convention][hereinafter collectively Geneva Conventions of 1949]; Protocol Additional to the Geneva Conventions of 1949 and Relating to the Protection of Victims of International Armed Conflicts, *opened for signature* Dec. 12, 1977, 1125 U.N.T.S. 3, 16 I.L.M. 1391 (1977) [hereinafter Protocol I]

5.   Although Article 3 common to the four Geneva Conventions of 1949 establishes obligations that apply in situations of non-international armed conflict, the conventions generally apply "to all cases of declared war or of any other armed conflict which may arise between two or more of the High Contracting Parties, even if the state of war is not recognized by one of them," and to "all cases of partial or total occupation of the territory of a High Contracting Party, even if the said occupation meets with no armed resistance." Geneva Conventions of 1949, *supra* note 4, common art. 2.

6.   Fourth Geneva Convention, *supra* note 4, art. 147.

7.   *See* Geneva Conventions of 1949, *supra* note 4, arts. 49/50/129/146; Protocol I, *supra* note 4, art. 86(1).

8.   Geneva Conventions of 1949, *supra* note 4, arts. 49/50/129/146; *see* Protocol I, *supra* note 4, art. 85. Although these provisions contemplate prosecution by national courts, the drafting history of the 1949 conventions makes clear that the language establishing a duty to prosecute grave breaches "does not exclude handing over the accused to an international criminal court whose competence has been recognized by the Contracting Parties." INTERNATIONAL COMMITTEE OF THE RED CROSS, IV COMMENTARY ON THE GENEVA CONVENTIONS OF 12 AUGUST 1949: GENEVA CONVENTION RELATIVE TO THE PROTECTION OF CIVILIAN PERSONS IN TIME OF WAR 593 (Jean S. Pictet, general ed. 1958) [hereinafter

There can be no doubt that "persons alleged to have committed, or to have ordered to be committed," grave breaches are at large in Bosnia. Virtually all of the suspects who have been publicly indicted by the Tribunal have been charged with committing or ordering grave breaches.[9] The issue is whether the duty to search for and arrest these men applies to SFOR.

Extraterritorial Application of Geneva Conventions

Military lawyers in the U.S. government, which commands SFOR, as well as NATO legal advisors have argued that SFOR is not bound by this obligation. These lawyers have put forth two principal arguments in support of their position. First, the Pentagon's General Counsel asserts that the duty of High Contracting Parties to search for and arrest persons alleged to have ordered or committed grave breaches does not apply extraterritorially. In her view, the United States is obligated to search for and arrest suspects in its own territory, even when the alleged grave breaches were committed in Bosnia—but this duty stops at the borders of the United States.[10]

While U.S. officials have not elaborated the grounds for this position, one possible basis may be that treaties generally have territorial application.[11] But this is a general, and not exclusive, rule. That the Geneva Conventions and Protocol I are exceptions to the general rule is plain. These conventions, which establish rules principally governing the conduct

COMMENTARY ON FOURTH GENEVA CONVENTION]. *See also* INTERNATIONAL COMMITTEE OF THE RED CROSS, COMMENTARY ON THE ADDITIONAL PROTOCOLS OF 8 JUNE 1977 TO THE GENEVA CONVENTIONS OF 12 AUGUST 1949 at 975 n. 10 (Yves Sandoz et al. eds. 1987) [hereinafter COMMENTARY ON ADDITIONAL PROTOCOLS].

9.   Articles 2-5 of the Statute of the ICTY establish the Tribunal's subject-matter jurisdiction over four categories, of which the first, set forth in Article 2, is "Grave breaches of the Geneva Conventions of 1949." Of 78 suspects publicly indicted by the ICTY, at least 72 have been charged under Article 2, typically in conjunction with other charges.

10.   *See An Interview with Defense Department General Counsel Judith A. Miller*, NAT'L SECURITY L. REP. 1, 2 (Summer 1996). *See also* Col. John T. Burton, *"War Crimes" During Operations Other than War: Military Doctrine and Law 50 Years After Nuremberg and Beyond*, 149 MIL. L. REV. 199, 203 (1995).

11.   *Cf.* Vienna Convention on the Law of Treaties, art. 29, May 23, 1969, U.N. Doc. A/CONF. 39/27 (*entered into force* Jan. 27, 1990) ("Unless a different intention appears from the treaty or is otherwise established, a treaty is binding upon each party in respect of its entire territory.").

of interstate armed conflict,[12] would be meaningless if their provisions applied only within the territory of Contracting Parties.

A second possible and interrelated claim in support of the U.S. position is that, whatever the general territorial scope of the Geneva Conventions, the provisions establishing a duty to search for and arrest suspected war criminals should be interpreted as applying on a territorial basis in view of the fact that, under international law, states generally can exercise police powers only within their own territory.[13]

But there are well-established exceptions to this general rule. For example combatants have long been liable to arrest on war crimes charges in the theatre of war,[14] and occupying forces have broad police and judicial authority in occupied territories.[15] Most importantly for present purposes, states may exercise police powers outside their own territory with the consent of the host state.[16] The Bosnian government has consented to NATO's exercise of police powers (and, indeed, has repeatedly urged it to arrest war crimes suspects). By letter dated 21 December 1995, the Bosnian Minister of Foreign Affairs, Muhamed Sacirbey, agreed as follows:

> With regard to the arrest warrant of the International war crimes Tribunal in the Hague concerning the citizens of the Republic of Bosnia and Herzegovina we agree that these tasks be performed, along with our police force, also by members of the IFOR.

---

12. *See supra* note 5.

13. *See* IAN BROWNLIE, PRINCIPLES OF PUBLIC INTERNATIONAL LAW 307 (4th ed. 1990).

14. *See* Ex Parte Quirin, 317 U.S. 1, 28-29 (1942) ("An important incident to the conduct of war is the adoption of measures by the military command not only to repel and defeat the enemy, but to seize and subject to disciplinary measures those enemies who in their attempt to thwart or impede our military effort have violated the law of war."); *see also* In re Yamashita, 327 U.S. 1, 11-13 (1946); Johnson v. Eisentrager, 339 U.S. 763 (1950).

15. For provisions relating to the enforcement of penal law by an Occupying Power, see Fourth Geneva Convention, *supra* note 4, arts. 64-77. On various forms of military jurisdiction, see generally Robinson O. Everett & Scott L. Silliman, *Forums for Punishing Offenses Against the Law of Nations*, 29 WAKE FOREST L. REV. 509 (1994); Elbridge Colby, *Occupation Under the Laws of War*, 25 COLUM. L. REV. 904 (1925).

16. *See* BROWNLIE, *supra* note 13, at 307.

We also agree that those persons arrested in connection with the warrants of the tribunal be handed over by the IFOR to the International Tribunal for war crimes.[17]

The legal advisor to NATO's Supreme Headquarters Allied Powers Europe (SHAPE) has conceded that, "[w]ith that authorization," his office's "concerns about a possible affront to [the Bosnian government's] sovereignty and, more importantly, actual authority for IFOR personnel to do what the NAC allowed, evaporated."[18]

Further, both the Dayton Peace Agreement and various U.N. Security Council resolutions make clear that NATO forces may lawfully exercise police powers in Bosnia.[19] Pursuant to this authority and based on consultations between NATO and ICTY officials, Tribunal judges amended the ICTY's Rules of Procedure and Evidence to make clear that NATO forces are authorized to arrest indicted suspects.[20]

The drafting history of the Geneva Conventions and Protocol I provides scant insight into the scope of the duty to search for and arrest persons allegedly responsible for grave breaches, but an authoritative commentary published by the International Committee of the Red Cross (ICRC) suggests that the drafters anticipated at least some extraterritorial applications of the duty. It was, to be sure, contemplated that a principal venue for fulfilling this obligation would be the territory of High

---

17. *Quoted in* Remarks of M.S. Johnson, Jr., Legal Advisor, Supreme Headquarters Allied Powers Europe, "NATO's Detention Policy Concerning Persons Indicted for War Crimes by the International Criminal Tribunal for the Former Yugoslavia," at 5, presented at "Partnership for Peace Status of Forces Agreement Implementation, International Humanitarian Law/Law of War and War Crimes" conference, Garmisch-Partenkirchen, Germany, 10-13 September 1996 [hereinafter *Johnson Remarks*].

18. *Johnson Remarks, supra* note 17, at 5.

19. *See supra* note 3 and accompanying text.

20. Rule 59 *bis*(A) of the Tribunal's Rules of Procedure and Evidence, adopted in January 1996, authorizes the transmission to "an appropriate authority or international body or the Prosecutor" of an arrest warrant, "together with an order for his prompt transfer to the Tribunal in the event that he be taken into custody by that authority or international body or the Prosecutor." This rule was adopted "to provide for the transmission of arrest warrants to, *inter alia*, the NATO-led International Implementation Force (IFOR), deployed in Bosnia and Herzegovina under the Dayton Accord." THE PRACTICE OF THE INTERNATIONAL CRIMINAL TRIBUNAL FOR THE FORMER YUGOSLAVIA AND THE INTERNATIONAL CRIMINAL TRIBUNAL FOR RWANDA 134 (John R.W.D. Jones ed., 3d edition, June 1997).

Contracting Parties.[21] But the Commentary on Protocol I published by the ICRC implicitly recognizes that this duty was also intended to apply extraterritorially when possible and appropriate. Writing of the duty established by the four conventions of 1949 and Protocol I to search for, arrest and ensure prosecution of someone alleged to have ordered or committed a grave breach, the commentary explains:

> The possibility of handing over the accused to be tried by another Contracting Party willing to prosecute him is an option open to the Contracting Party *in whose territory the accused is or in whose hands he has fallen.*[22]

In larger perspective, the object and purpose of the grave breaches provisions is best served if the duty to search for and arrest persons alleged to have ordered or committed grave breaches applies wherever High Contracting Parties lawfully exercise arrest authority with respect to such persons. The core aim of the grave breaches provisions, which establish mandatory universal jurisdiction, is to foreclose impunity for such breaches.[23] This aim would be ill served if Contracting Parties' obligations

---

21. One passage in the Commentary to the 1949 Geneva Conventions published by the ICRC seems to reflect this assumption. Concerning the grave breaches provisions, the commentary notes: "As soon as a Contracting Party realizes that there is *on its territory* a person who has committed a grave breach, its duty is to ensure that the person concerned is arrested and prosecuted with all speed." COMMENTARY ON FOURTH GENEVA CONVENTION, *supra* note 8, at 593 (emphasis added). But the principal thrust of this observation was to emphasize the "active" nature of the duty to arrest persons accused of ordering or committing a grave breach. *Id.* Moreover, as noted *infra* note 22 and accompanying text, the Commentary on Protocol I published by the ICRC contemplates extraterritorial application of the grave breaches obligations of the 1949 conventions.

22. COMMENTARY ON ADDITIONAL PROTOCOLS, *supra* note 8, at 1026 (emphasis added). The commentary further asserts: "As long as the penal repression of grave breaches is ensured, the right of each Contracting Party to choose between prosecuting a person *in its power* or to hand him over to another Party interested in prosecuting him therefore remains absolute . . . ." *Id.* at 1029 (emphasis added).

23. *Cf.* COMMENTARY ON FOURTH GENEVA CONVENTION, *supra* note 8, at 587 (noting that the "universality of jurisdiction" provided for in the grave breaches provisions "is some basis for the hope that they will not remain unpunished . . . "). Providing further indication of the breadth of the grave breaches duty, the Diplomatic Conference that drafted the 1949 conventions rejected an Italian proposal to limit these obligations to states that were parties to the armed conflict in which the grave breaches occurred. In response to this proposal, the

were inapplicable in territories where those states exercise lawful power to arrest persons allegedly responsible for grave breaches.[24]

A variation on the claim that the duty to search for and arrest persons alleged to have ordered or committed grave breaches does not apply to the NATO force in Bosnia is the observation, which has been put forth by NATO and U.S. military lawyers, that IFOR/SFOR "is not an army of occupation."[25] But the fact that IFOR/SFOR is not an occupying army does not negate its authority pursuant to the Dayton Peace Agreement, various Security Council resolutions, and the Bosnian government's consent to arrest suspects indicted by the ICTY.

Application of Geneva Conventions to Multilateral Operations

The second principal argument offered in support of the U.S./NATO position is that neither NATO nor SFOR is a party to the Geneva

---

Dutch delegate asserted that "each Contracting Party should be under this obligation, even if neutral in a conflict," and the President of the conference expressed the opinion that "a neutral State did not violate its neutrality by trying or handing over an accused, under an international obligation." Final Record of the Diplomatic Conference of Geneva of 1949, Vol. II, Section B, para. 5, 116. *See also* COMMENTARY ON ADDITIONAL PROTOCOLS, *supra* note 8, at 975 n. 8 (observing that the "Contracting Parties" referred to in the grave breaches provisions of the 1949 conventions include "neutral States or States not Parties to the conflict").

24. This does not necessarily preclude recognizing that some states—notably the host state—may have priority vis-a-vis other states with respect to the exercise of arrest power. Nor does it preclude making distinctions between the respective mandates of various forces participating in a multilateral operation. That SFOR as a whole is authorized to arrest persons indicted by the ICTY does not, for example, preclude SFOR commanders from designating and training special units to execute arrests. But these distinctions should not be made in a manner that defeats the grave breaches provisions by ensuring impunity or by causing undue delay in the capture and prosecution of persons alleged to have ordered or committed grave breaches.

25. *See, e.g., Johnson Remarks, supra* note 17, at 6. Mr. Johnson continues: "[N]o single document or collection of documents have vested IFOR with plenary police powers to deal with alleged war criminals." *Id. See also* Colonel F.M. Lorenz U.S. Marine Corps, *War Criminals—Testing the Limits of Military Force,* JOINT FORCES Q. 59, 61 (Summer 1997).

Siracusa Impunity Conference 201

Conventions and Protocols; only states are parties. This position has been urged by, *inter alia*, NATO legal advisor Max S. Johnson, Jr.[26]

But this misses the point: the issue is not whether NATO or SFOR themselves are bound by the conventions (although some legal experts believe they are).[27] The core question is whether parties to the conventions, such as the United States, may evade their commitments by joining a multinational force. This question fairly answers itself: by Mr. Johnson's logic, any state could violate the Geneva Conventions with impunity merely by joining other countries in a military alliance.

The ICRC has consistently taken the position that each state remains individually responsible for applying these treaties when it contributes contingents to multilateral peacekeeping forces.[28] It has also taken the position that breaches of the conventions must be repressed by the national authorities of the contingent concerned,[29] making clear its view that states'

---

26. Letter from Max S. Johnson, Jr., Legal Advisor to the Supreme Allied Commander Europe (SACEUR), to Amnesty International, March 12, 1996.

27. Debate over the question whether multilateral operations are subject to the Geneva Conventions has focused on U.N. peacekeeping operations. The International Committee of the Red Cross has consistently taken the position that such operations are bound to comply with international humanitarian law whenever they become engaged in armed conflict, *see, e.g.*, Final Declaration, International Conference for the Protection of War Victims (Geneva, 30 August-1 September 1993), while the United Nations has generally opposed this position. The U.N.'s reasons include the fact that humanitarian law treaties make no provision for non-state parties; the impossibility of classifying the United Nations as a "party to a conflict"; and the difficulty, if not impossibility, for a non-state body to implement certain provisions, including those requiring prosecution and punishment of certain offenses. The U.N. has, however, declared that its forces should observe the principles and spirit of humanitarian law conventions. A clause to this effect now appears in the U.N.'s model Status of Forces agreement for peacekeeping operations. *See* Antoine Bouvier, *"Convention on the Safety of United Nations and Associated Personnel": Presentation and analysis*, 35 INT'L REV. RED CROSS 638, 651-652 (1995; Umesh Palwankar, *Applicability of international humanitarian law to United Nations peace-keeping forces*, 33 INT'L REV. RED CROSS 227, 231-232 (1993). Moreover the Convention on the Safety of United Nations and Associated Personnel, adopted in 1994, implicitly recognizes the direct application of international humanitarian law to U.N. forces in some circumstances. G.A. Res. 49/59, Annex, art. 2(2) (1994).

28. *See* Palwankar, *supra* note 27, at 230, *citing* 1961 ICRC Memorandum entitled "Application and dissemination of the Geneva Conventions."

29. *See id.*

obligations as High Contracting Parties do not vaporize when they participate in multilateral operations.

The United States and other states that have contributed forces to multilateral operations have repeatedly acted in accordance with the ICRC's position. In fact, the U.S. and other states have insisted that their contingents remain subject to national authority, notwithstanding a unified command structure governing multinational operations, for such purposes as disciplining troops who commit war crimes.[30]

In the wake of recent revelations about abuses committed by Italian contingents participating in a U.S.-led operation in Somalia, for example, U.S. officers stated that, although they were aware of the abuses, they believed they "had no power of jurisdiction to investigate or punish."[31] A U.S. officer who commanded the Somalia operation told a reporter,

> When the first incidents took place we sat down with our judge advocate and asked ourselves, 'what is the U.S. responsibility as the lead element with operational control?' We decided that although we have tactical control and combatant command, we don't have discretionary authority [over discipline]. That rests with the national forces.[32]

---

30. *Cf.* Kenneth S. Freeman, *Recent Developments: Punishing Attacks on United Nations Peacekeepers: A Case Study of Somalia*, 8 EMORY INT'L L. REV. 845, 847 (members of U.N. military contingents "remain subject to the laws and jurisdiction of their member state at all times"), *citing* INTERNATIONAL PEACE ACADEMY, PEACEKEEPERS HANDBOOK 365 (3d ed. 1984).

31. Ben Barber, *U.S. officers concede knowing of atrocities*, WASH. TIMES, July 27, 1997.

32. *Id.* (bracketed text in original article). This approach seems essentially consistent with a policy adopted by the Chairman of the Joint Chiefs of Staff (CJCS) last year. An Instruction promulgated by the CJCS in August 1996 sets forth the policy of the Department of Defense that U.S. Armed Forces will observe the law of war during the conduct of military operations in armed conflict, as well as during "all operations that are characterized as Military Operations Other Than War"; U.S. obligations under the law of war will be enforced by the U.S. Armed Forces; and violations of the law of war "alleged to have been committed by . . . allied military or civilian personnel will be reported through appropriate command channels for ultimate transmission to appropriate agencies of allied governments." CJCSI 5810.01, August 12, 1996.

Accordingly, when U.S. officials received word of possible abuses by non-U.S. troops participating in the operation, they turned the information over for investigation by the relevant national authority.[33]

Alleged abuses by troops participating in this and other multinational operations in Somalia[34] have in fact been investigated by their own national authorities. Reports of possible abuses by U.S. soldiers participating in the U.S.-led Somalia operation were investigated and, in one case, prosecuted by U.S. military authorities.[35] Alleged abuses by Italian, Canadian and Belgian soldiers who participated in multilateral operations in Somalia have also been investigated and in some cases prosecuted by their respective national authorities.[36]

The United Nations likewise takes the position that responsibility for disciplining abusive soldiers who participate in U.N. peacekeeping operations remains with national authorities. In the wake of recent reports of abuses by troops participating in a U.N. operation in Somalia, a U.N. spokesman explained that "ultimately, when something goes wrong, the UN, under its arrangement with troop-contributing countries, does not have the authority to discipline troops." While the U.N. could investigate reports, if it found cause to believe violations had occurred it would ask the state contributing the forces to discipline those responsible for the abuses.[37]

States' insistence on retaining national control over discipline of their soldiers who participate in multilateral operations is difficult to reconcile

---

33. Ben Barber, *supra* note 31.

34. There were three separate multinational operations in Somalia between 1992 and 1995. The first, UNOSOM I, was a U.N. peacekeeping operation. The second, the United Task Force (UNITAF), was a multinational coalition authorized by the U.N. Security Council but commanded by the U.S. military. The third, UNOSOM II, was a U.N. operation in which the United States participated by, *inter alia*, providing the deputy commander and other senior officers and contributing a 1,300-man Quick Reaction Force that operated under the operational control of a U.S. general.

35. Ben Barber, *supra* note 31.

36. *See* Jenny Kuper, *How to stop the massacre of innocents*, THE INDEPENDENT (London), July 15, 1997; Vera Haller, *Italy to Probe Army Torture Allegations*, WASH. POST, June 18, 1997; *Somalia welcomes Italian decision to reopen torture probe*, AFP, Aug. 26, 1997; Jennifer Gould, *UN Soldiers Acquitted: New Photos Emerge*, VILLAGE VOICE, July 15, 1997; DISHONORED LEGACY, THE LESSONS OF THE SOMALIA AFFAIR: REPORT OF THE SOMALIA COMMISSION OF INQUIRY, July 1997 (Canadian Government).

37. *More torture allegations investigated by UN*, JANE'S DEFENSE WEEKLY, July 9, 1997.

with the view, implicit in the argument that the grave breaches obligations of the Geneva Conventions of 1949 do not apply to SFOR or NATO because neither is a party to the conventions, that contributing states in effect cease to operate as national forces when they participate in multilateral operations.

The Duty to Comply with Arrest Orders and Requests for Assistance

Even if states contributing to SFOR were not parties to the Geneva Conventions, they would be bound to arrest at least some of the suspects indicted by the ICTY. The Security Council resolution establishing the Tribunal, S.C. Resolution 827, requires states to comply with arrest orders and requests for assistance pursuant to Article 29 of the ICTY Statute.[38] Article 29(2) of the Statute provides that "States shall comply without undue delay with any request for assistance or an order issued by a Trial Chamber, including, but not limited to . . . the arrest or detention of persons . . ."

As a decision of the Security Council, the duty imposed by S.C. Resolution 827 is legally binding on U.N. Member States.[39] Thus any Member State that the Tribunal either orders or requests to arrest suspects is legally bound to comply.

Generally the Tribunal directs arrest warrants to the governmental authorities in the area where indicted suspects are believed to be located. But the Tribunal also can issue international arrest warrants, and these are directed to all states.

The Tribunal has issued such international warrants in respect of several of the suspects whom the Prosecutor has indicted. In the cases of Radovan Karadzic and Ratko Mladic, a Trial Chamber directed "the authorities and officers and agents of all States to act promptly with all due diligence to secure the arrest, detention and transfer to the Tribunal" of the suspects. In light of this directive, it would be untenable for countries contributing to SFOR to claim that they have no duty to arrest these men

---

38. S.C. Res. 827, para. 4 (1993).

39. Article 25 of the U.N. Charter provides: "The Members of the United Nations agree to accept and carry out the decisions of the Security Council in accordance with the present Charter."

when they have both the authority and opportunity to do so. In the case of Milan Martic, a Trial Chamber specifically "directed" IFOR (as well as "the authorities and all officers and agents of all States") "to act promptly with all due diligence to secure the arrest, detention and transfer to the Tribunal" of Martic. By virtue of S.C. Resolution 1088 (1996), which establishes SFOR as the legal successor to IFOR, this directive now applies with continuing effect to SFOR.

As for indicted suspects who are not the subject of international arrest warrants, it appears that the ICTY's indictments and arrest warrants—at least those that are public—have been made available to NATO pursuant to arrangements between ICTY and NATO concerning IFOR/SFOR's detention of persons indicted by the Tribunal.[40]

Far from disputing IFOR/SFOR's general duty to comply with U.N. Security Council resolutions regarding cooperation with the ICTY, NATO lawyers have recognized this obligation. Before the Security Council adopted Resolution 1031, which established IFOR's legal authority, the Legal Advisor to NATO's Internal Staff concluded that, in view of the operational control that NATO would have over IFOR, it had an obligation under S.C. Resolution 827 to cooperate with the ICTY and that this duty should be made clear in S.C. Resolution 1031.[41]

---

40. *See Johnson Remarks, supra* note 17, at 4 (noting that, pursuant to an agreement reached between NATO and the ICTY shortly after the Dayton accord was concluded, Tribunal Judge Jorda by special order made 52 indictments and arrest warrants available to the Supreme Headquarters Allied Powers Europe).

41. This opinion is summarized in *Johnson Remarks, supra* note 17, at 3. In the view of Mr. Johnson, a Security Council resolution was not a *sine qua non* for IFOR's detention policy. *See id.* at 3-4. This view seemingly implies that, in Mr. Johnson's view, IFOR's authority to detain war criminals was or could be established on the basis of other authority, including the consent of the Bosnian government. *Cf.* Col. John T. Burton, *supra* note 10, at 203-205 (expressing the opinion that the ICTY has authority to issue orders that are binding on Member States, including those participating in the NATO operation in Bosnia, but that implementation by soldiers requires a directive from the NAC, and also expressing the view that if the then-anticipated peace accord were to require parties to comply with orders of the ICTY, a military implementation force might, by virtue of its mandate to enforce the peace agreement, have authority to arrest indicted war criminals).

The Genocide Convention

Finally, the Convention on the Prevention and Punishment of the Crime of Genocide,[42] which the United States has ratified, requires parties to "prevent and punish" genocide.[43] When a state that has the power to arrest persons whom the ICTY has charged with genocide[44] stands aside and allows the suspects to evade arrest, it dishonors this solemn undertaking.

Significantly, in a decision on jurisdiction in a suit brought against the Federal Republic of Yugoslavia by Bosnia, the International Court of Justice rejected Yugoslavia's claim that its duties under the Genocide Convention stopped at its territorial borders. Instead, the Court ruled, states parties' duties to prevent and punish genocide are not territorially limited.[45]

Conclusion

While Western countries have rejected calls for NATO forces in Bosnia to seek to arrest suspects indicted by the Hague Tribunal on the ground that SFOR has no mandate do so, their response is largely beside the point. States that have legal authority to arrest suspected war criminals also have defined obligations—both moral and legal—to bring these men to the bar of justice.

---

42. 78 U.N.T.S. 277, *entered into force* Jan. 12, 1951.

43. *Id.*, art. I.

44. At least seven suspects indicted by the ICTY have been charged with genocide. Both of the suspects whom SFOR attempted to arrest in July 1997 had been charged with genocide. One, Simo Drljaca, was shot dead by SFOR soldiers when he resisted arrest. The other, Milan Kovacevic, was arrested by SFOR and transferred to The Hague to stand trial.

45. Although U.S. legislation enables American courts to *prosecute* genocide only when the crime was committed in U.S. territory or by a U.S. national, 18 U.S.C. § 1091(d), this limitation does not apply to the United States' exercise of its authority to *arrest* persons indicted for genocide in Bosnia.

[15]

The Ambiguities of Security Council Resolution 1422 (2002)

Carsten Stahn*

Abstract

SC Resolution 1422 (2002) is one of the most controversial resolutions of the Security Council. In order to surmount the United States' threat to block future UN peacekeeping missions, the members of the Council voted in favour of a resolution that requests the ICC to defer potential prosecutions of peacekeepers from non-state parties to the Statute for a 12-month period. What has been praised as a 'pragmatic solution' to the US demands is in fact a highly questionable legal compromise challenging not only the framework of the Rome Statute, but also the role and powers of the Security Council. This article discusses both the interplay between the Council's request and the Rome Statute, and the possible implications of the resolution for the ICC and its member states.

1 Introduction

On 12 July 2002, the United Nations Security Council adopted Resolution 1422 (2002), requesting the International Criminal Court (ICC) to refrain from initiating investigations or proceedings related to peacekeepers of non-states parties to the Statute, while reaffirming its intention to 'renew the request ... under the same conditions each 1 July for further 12-month periods ...'.[1] This compromise has dissolved the threat of a US veto against future United Nations peacekeeping operations. Furthermore, it represents a significant retreat from the initial US demand for permanent immunity of US military personnel within the framework of peacekeeping operations. But many critical questions remain. The resolution sends

---

* LL.M (Köln-Paris), Fellow of the Max Planck Society for the Advancement of Science, currently NYU, School of Law.
1 See SC Res. 1422 (2002) of 12 July 2002, UN. Doc. S/RES/1422 (2002), available at http://www.un.org. See on this issue also MacPherson, 'Authority of the Security Council to Exempt Peacekeepers from International Criminal Court Proceedings', *ASIL Insight*, July 2002, available at http://www.asil.org/insights.htm.

86   *EJIL* 14 (2003), 85–104

the message that peacekeepers from non-state parties to the Statute are more equal before the law than peacekeepers from state parties, because they benefit from a 12-month exemption from war crimes and other charges under the Statute. Such an exception breaks with the non-discriminatory character of international criminal law and is certainly not in keeping with the treaty regime of the ICC, which has jurisdiction over nationals of third states.[2] Every state may prosecute the crimes committed by foreign nationals on its territory, irrespective of their nationality. It is difficult to see why a different rule should apply to the ICC, which exercises its powers on the basis of the delegated territorial jurisdiction of its member states.[3]

Security Council members argue that the deal reached on 12 July 2002 was necessary in order to counter the US threats to block the collective security system of the Charter. While that threat was indeed troubling,[4] the disturbing precedent set by SC Resolution 1422 (2002) is no less troubling. The application of this resolution leaves many uncertainties, which make it unlikely that the compromise of 12 July 2002 will, in fact, mark the final say in the dispute over the immunity of US servicemen from the jurisdiction of the ICC.

2 The Link to Chapter VII

Resolution 1422 (2002) was approved unanimously by the Council and was based on Chapter VII of the Charter. However, it is doubtful how the exemption of peacekeepers from the jurisdiction of the ICC may be linked to a threat to the peace within the meaning of Article 39 of the Charter, which is a pre-requisite for the application of Chapter VII. It is well known that the Council has adopted a very broad interpretation of the notion of threat to the peace.[5] Nevertheless, the establishment of immunities on the basis of Article 39 of the Charter marks a novelty in the practice of the Council. Immunities and privileges of peacekeepers have so far been defined by Status-of-Mission Agreements concluded between the territorial state and the United Nations, but not directly under Chapter VII of the Charter.[6] Although the Council did not go so

---

[2] For a full analysis, see Paust, 'The Reach of ICC Jurisdiction over Non-signatory Nationals', 33 *Vanderbilt Journal of Transnational Law* (2000), at 1 *et seq.*; Scharf, 'The ICC's Jurisdiction over the Nationals of Non-Party States', in S. B. Sewall and C. Kaysen (eds), *The United States and the International Criminal Court* (2002), at 213 *et seq.*; Stahn, 'Gute Nachbarschaft um jeden Preis', 60 *ZaöRV* (2000) 631, at 642 *et seq.* But see Wedgwood, 'The International Criminal Court: An American View', 10 *EJIL* (1999) 93, at 99.

[3] See Article 12(2)(a) of the ICC Statute.

[4] Due to the lack of support for its proposal to obtain immunity for peacekeepers, the US vetoed the renewal of the Bosnian mandate on 30 June 2002 and suggested that it would cease paying its 25% share of the UN peacekeeping operations budget.

[5] One of the most far-reaching precedents is SC Res. 748 (1992), in which the Council determined that 'the failure by the Libyan Government to demonstrate by concrete actions its renunciation of terrorism and in particular its continued failure to respond fully and effectively to the requests in resolution 731 (1992) constitute a threat to international peace and security.' See para. 7 of the preamble of SC Res. 748 (1992) of 31 March 1992, UN. Doc. S/RES/748 (1992). For a survey of the practice of the Council, see Frowein, 'On Article 39', in B. Simma (ed.), *Charter of the United Nations* (1994), at 610.

[6] See Bothe and Dörschel, 'The UN Peacekeeping Experience', in D. Fleck (ed.), *The Law of Visiting Forces* (2001) 487, at 491–492.

far as to qualify the potential prosecution of peacekeepers by the ICC as such as a threat to the peace, its determinations in paragraphs 6 and 7 of the preamble of Resolution 1422 (2002) come close to such a finding. Only a very general link to Article 39 of the Charter may be derived from paragraph 6 of the preamble to the resolution, where the Council points out that peacekeeping operations are usually 'deployed to maintain or restore international peace and security'. Far more significant is the Council's reference to 'the interests of international peace and security to facilitate Member States' ability to contribute to operations established or authorized by the United Nations Security Council' in paragraph 7 of the preamble, which illustrates the curiosity of the argument: the threat to the peace seems to be based less on the existence of a specific conflict situation than on the potential inability of the United Nations to address future threats without US military personnel. Such an assumption raises serious concerns, because it ultimately implies that the non-contribution of troops to United Nations peacekeeping operations is in itself a threat to the peace. Any generalization of this principle would render Article 39 borderless.[7]

The only plausible argument which might be employed to justify the invocation of Chapter VII is that the adoption of Resolution 1422 (2002) was closely linked to the extension of the mandate of the UN military presence in Bosnia,[8] and that it does not make a difference in substance, whether its content is drafted once and for all in general terms or incorporated individually in every resolution establishing or authorizing a United Nations peacekeeping operation. Nevertheless, this argument does not provide a satisfying answer to the more far-reaching question as to what extent the exemption of peacekeeping personnel from criminal jurisdiction lies in the interests of the maintenance of peace and security in a given conflict situation.

Finally, US forces were not even exposed to a concrete 'threat of prosecution' by the ICC at the time of adoption of the resolution. The UN statistics on troop-contributions to peacekeeping missions reveal that the ICC lacked jurisdiction over US military personnel involved in peacekeeping operations deployed in July 2002 because US troops were either stationed in states not parties to the ICC Statute or subject to the primary jurisdiction of the ICTY.[9]

---

[7] It does not come as a surprise that such an understanding of the notion of threat to the peace has encountered criticism by several states in a public hearing of 10 July on a draft of Resolution 1422 (2002). See the statements of New Zealand, Canada and Mexico at the 4568th meeting of the Security Council on 10 July 2002, UN. Doc. SC/7445/Rev.1. The full wording of the statements is available at http://www.iccnow.org.

[8] See SC Res. 1423 (2002) of 12 July 2002, UN. Doc. S/RES/1423 (2002), available at http://www.un.org.

[9] See the Chart of the Coalition for an International Criminal Court of July 2002, illustrating the non-exposure of US peacekeepers to the jurisdiction of the ICC, at http://www.iccnow.org/html/press.html.

88   *EJIL* 14 (2003), 85–104

3 The Interplay between the Council's Request and the Rome Statute

Even more controversial is the relationship between the operative part of SC Resolution 1422 (2002) and the Rome Statute. The legal construction of the resolution reveals some of the difficulties that its drafters encountered in the negotiating process. Although the resolution was based on Chapter VII, its para. 1 was not drafted in the form of a binding 'decision', but as a 'request' to the ICC.[10] This approach may be explained by two factors: first, the fact that the Court enjoys its own, independent legal personality under Article 4 of the Rome Statute[11] and is therefore not directly bound by resolutions of the Council addressed to United Nations Member States;[12] second, the obvious intention of the members of the Council to bring the text of the resolution into compliance with the wording of Article 16 of the Statute, which expressly speaks of a 'request' in a resolution adopted under Chapter VII. This construction suggests that the legal obligations of the Court do not arise from the determinations of the Council but from the legal framework of the Statute, which imposes a deferral of investigations or prosecutions in the case of a Security Council request under Article 16 of the Statute.

The troublesome development is that the interpretation of Article 16 in SC Resolution 1422 (2002) is not identical with that reflected in the Rome Statute. The wording of the resolution itself is based on the understanding that the compromise adopted on 12 July 2002 meets the requirements of the Statute. This follows clearly from paragraph 1 of SC Resolution 1422 (2002), which makes reference to a request 'consistent with the provisions of Article 16 of the Rome Statute'. This clause can only be interpreted in the sense that the Council considers its resolution to be consistent with the Statute. But the interpretation of the Council is not necessarily an authoritative interpretation of the Statute. On the contrary, a closer look at the history and context of Article 16 reveals that it is highly questionable whether the reading of the provision in Resolution 1422 (2002) reflects its meaning under the Statute.

A *SC Resolution 1422 (2002) versus Article 16 of the Statute*

1 *The* ex ante *Deferral of Proceedings*

Paragraph 1 of Resolution 1422 (2002) is based on the assumption that a request under Article 16 of the Rome Statute may be made in generic terms, even in the absence of a specific conflict between the diverging interests of justice and the maintenance of peace and security in a concrete situation. Such an interpretation may be compatible with the wording of Article 16, which simply states that no investigation or prosecution may be commenced or proceeded with after a deferral

---

[10] See para. 1 of SC Res. 1422 (2002).

[11] See on the international legal personality of the ICC, Lüder, 'The Legal Nature of the International Criminal Court and the Emergence of Supranational Elements in International Criminal Justice', *International Review of the Red Cross*, No. 845, 79.

[12] For further discussion, see Section 4B.

request, without spelling out when such a request may be made. But it is hard to reconcile with the purpose of the provision and its systematic position in the Statute. The drafting history of Article 16 makes it quite clear that the founding fathers of the Statute intended to limit the use of the deferral possibility to case-by-case interventions by the Council.[13]

The current version of Article 16 has its origin in Article 23 of the International Law Commission's Draft Statute of an International Criminal Court, which provides that '[n]o prosecution may be commenced under this Statute arising from a situation which is being dealt with by the Security Council as a threat to or breach of the peace or an act of aggression under Chapter VII of the Charter, unless the Security Council otherwise decides.'[14] But, in particular, the flabby expression 'being dealt with' has come under criticism in the Preparatory Committee, because it seemed to imply the Council could bar the exercise of jurisdiction of the ICC by merely putting a given situation on its agenda.[15] It was therefore replaced by a proposal submitted by Singapore, which was guided by the intention to limit the suspension of the jurisdiction of the ICC to cases in which the Council requests the Court not to initiate or continue specific proceedings.[16] The Singapore text read: '[n]o investigation or prosecution may be commenced or proceeded with under this Statute where the Security Council has, acting under Chapter VII of the Charter of the United Nations, given direction to that effect.'[17] This proposal was later amended by a proposal of Costa Rica, which required a 'formal and specific decision' of the Security Council,[18] and a British proposal, which replaced the word 'direction' by 'request'[19] and became the basis of the current Article 16 of the Statute. The purpose of this provision is quite clear. It was negotiated to enable the Council to delay the exercise of jurisdiction by the ICC in situations in which the resolution of a specific conflict warrants a deferral of prosecution. Perhaps the most classical example is the suspension or omission of

---

[13] See also the statements of New Zealand and Canada at the hearing of 10 July 2002. Furthermore, The Permanent Representative of Germany at the United Nations noted: 'It is the strong belief of Germany that — beyond the case-by-case possibilities clearly contained in Article 16 of the ICC Statute — the Security Council would do itself and world community a disservice if it passed a resolution under Chapter VII of the UN Charter, to, in effect, amend an important treaty ratified by 76 states.'

[14] See ILC, Draft Statute for an International Criminal Court, Report of the International Law Commission on the work of its forty-sixth Session, 1 September 1994, UN Doc. A/49/355 of 21 February 1997, available at: http://www.npwj.org/iccrome/statute.html.

[15] See Bergsmo and Pejic, 'On Article 16', in O. Triffterer and C. Rosbaud (eds), *The Rome Statute of the International Criminal Court* (2000), at 377, para. 9.

[16] See Zimmermann, 'The Creation of a Permanent International Criminal Court', *Max Planck Yearbook of United Nations Law*, Vol. 2 (1998) 169, at 218.

[17] Reprinted in Bergsmo and Pejic, *supra* note 15, at 375, para. 4.

[18] The proposal of Costa Rica read: 'No investigation or prosecution may be commenced or proceeded with under this Statute, where the Security Council has, acting under Chapter VII of the Charter of the United Nations, taken a formal and specific decision, and limited for a certain period of time, to that effect.' See *ibid.*, at 376, n. 21.

[19] The British proposal read: 'No investigation or prosecution may be commenced or proceeded with under this Statute [for a period of twelve months] after the Security Council [, acting under Chapter VII of the Charter of the United Nations,] has requested the Court to that effect; that request may be renewed by the Council under the same conditions.' See *ibid.*, at 376, para. 5.

90   *EJIL* 14 (2003), 85–104

proceedings that might destabilize peace negotiations. But Article 16 was certainly not meant to provide a basis for the immunity of a whole group of actors in advance and irrespective of any concrete risk of indictment or prosecution.

Furthermore, a systematic interpretation of the provision under the Statute lends support to the view that it was merely supposed to serve as a basis for a case-by-case deferral by the Council. In particular, the specific position of Article 16 in the Statute indicates that the Council may only bar the exercise of jurisdiction by the Court once a concrete 'investigation' or 'prosecution' is taking place. Articles 13, 14 and 15 of the Statute determine that investigations may be initiated by the Prosecutor upon the referral of a situation either by a state party to the Statute or the Security Council, or by a *proprio motu* action of the Prosecutor. The fact that Article 16 was inserted after, and not before Articles 14 and 15, illustrates that the deferral request was not conceived as an instrument of preventive action for the Council, but requires instead the initiation of specific ICC proceedings. Any action of the Prosecutor presupposes, at least, the existence of a situation, which may give rise to investigations or prosecutions. The logical sequence underlying the functioning of the Court under Articles 13 to 16 of the Statute is that such a situation must exist before the Council may make a request under Article 16.

The authority of the Council under Article 16 to bar even the '*commencement*' of 'investigations' does not provide a more extensive basis for preventive action. The initiation of investigations is not the first stage of proceedings conducted under the auspices of the Prosecutor. On the contrary, it may be inferred from Article 15(6) that the Statute formally distinguishes the stage of investigations from 'preliminary examinations'[20] undertaken by the Prosecutor in the period before the Pre-Trial Chamber's authorization under Article 15(4).[21] The powers of the Council to block the commencement of 'investigations' under Article 16 can therefore only be interpreted in the sense that the Council may defer investigations conducted by the Prosecutor after the Pre-Trial Chamber's authorization under Article 15(4), but shall not intervene in the activities of the Court before that stage.[22]

---

[20]   Art. 15(6) states: 'If, after the *preliminiary examination* referred to in paragraphs 1 and 2, the Prosecutor concludes that the information provided does not constitute a reasonable basis for an investigation, he or she shall inform those who provided the information' (emphasis added). The stage of preliminary examinations is further described in Art. 15(2) of the Statute, which provides that the Prosecutor 'may seek additional information from States, organs of the United Nations, intergovernmental or non-governmental organizations, or other reliable sources that he or she deems appropriate, and may receive written or oral testimony at the Seat of the Court.'

[21]   The expression '[n]o investigation ... may be commenced' in Art. 16 is visibly linked to Art. 15(4), which provides: 'If the Pre-Trial Chamber, upon examination of the request and the supporting material, considers that there is a reasonable basis to proceed with an investigation, and that the case appears to fall within the jurisdiction of the Court, it shall authorize the *commencement of the investigation*, without prejudice to subsequent determinations by the Court with regard to the jurisdiction and admissibility of a case' (emphasis added).

[22]   See Bergsmo and Pejic, *supra* note 15, at 379, para. 15. 'It may not be concluded, however, that by referring to both "investigation" and "'prosecution", article 16 extends the Security Council's deferral power to the totality of activities of the Prosecutor ... Among the steps which the Prosecutor can take before an investigation starts are seeking "information from States, organs of the United Nations,

SC Resolution 1422 (2002) seeks to avoid a conflict between its own terms and the case-by-case approach enshrined in the Statute by noting that no investigation or prosecution shall be commenced or proceeded with '*if a case arises* involving current or former officials or personnel from a contributing State not a Party to the Rome Statute.'[23] But this compromise does not solve the problem because it does not address the main concern, which is that the request itself is made *ex ante* and only linked to a hypothetical case.

B *The Quasi-permanent Nature of the Deferral*

Further ambiguities arise from para. 2 of SC Resolution 1422 (2002), in which the Council '[e]xpresses the intention to renew the request in paragraph 1 under the same conditions each 1 July for further 12-month periods for as long as may be necessary'. The 'intent clause' conflicts with the general conception of Article 16 as a temporary bar to the activity of the Court after a deferral request of the Council. Article 16 of the Statute states that a request is limited to a 12-month period, but renewable under the same conditions. The Statute does not determine how many times the request may be repeated. The Council could therefore formally uphold its request indefinitely. However, the 12-month limitation as such makes it clear that the creation of a permanent exception to the exercise of jurisdiction by the Court on the basis of Article 16 was not envisaged by the drafters of the Statute, even though the number of renewals was not specifically limited.[24] The original proposal made by the US in the preliminary stages of the drafting of SC Resolution 1422 (2002) directly contravened this intention by providing for an automatic renewal of the immunity exception contained in the resolution.[25] But this solution was openly rejected by the vast

---

intergovernmental or non-governmental organizations, or other reliable sources that he or she deems appropriate", receiving "written or oral testimony at the Seat of the Court", as well as analysing the information received. The Security Council cannot prevent the Prosecutor from taking these steps on the basis of article 16.'

[23] See para. 1 of SC Res. 1422 (2002) (emphasis added).

[24] To avoid an unlimited deferral by the Council was precisely the object and purpose of the widely supported Singapore proposal. On the background, see Arsanjani, 'The Rome Statute of the International Criminal Court', 93 *AJIL* (1999) 22, at 26–27.

[25] The US Draft Resolution of 19 June 2002 operated on the principle that immunity was the rule, which could only be lifted by a waiver of either the contributing state or the Security Council. The proposal read as follows: 'The Security Council ... [a]cting under Chapter VII of the Charter, 1. Decides that Member States contributing personnel participating in operations established or authorized by the UN Security Council to promote the pacific settlement of disputes or to maintain or restore international peace and security shall have the responsibility to investigate crimes with respect to which they have jurisdiction and, as appropriate, prosecute offenses alleged to have been committed by their nationals in connection with the operation; 2. Decides that persons of or from contributing states acting in connection with such operations shall enjoy in the territory of all Member States other than the contributing State immunity from arrest, detention, and prosecution with respect to all acts arising out of the operation and that this immunity shall continue after termination of their participation in the operation for all such acts; 3. Decides that the contributing state may waive such immunity whenever and to the extent that, in its judgment, the interests of justice will be served; 4. Decides further that in the absence of a waiver by the

92 *EJIL* 14 (2003), 85–104

majority of states.[26] The search for a compromise addressing the concerns of both sides has led to the adoption of the formula contained in paragraph 2 of SC Resolution 1422 (2002), which requires an annual renewal of the request by an affirmative vote of at least nine of the 15 Security Council members, including all permanent members, but highlights at the same time the Council's expressed intention to do so 'each 1 July . . . for as long as may be necessary'.

This approach is formally in line with Article 16 of the Statute because the granting of immunity depends on a new request each year. However, it does not need much wisdom to tell where its shortcomings lie. Both the obligation of the Council to put the issue on its agenda and the factual pressure on its members to renew the deal make it rather obvious that the solution enshrined in paragraph 2 of SC Council Resolution 1422 (2002) entails *de facto* much more than a provisional limitation on the powers of the ICC.[27] Furthermore, the concrete legal significance of the 'intention clause' itself is ambiguous. The clause appears to be unprecedented in the practice of the Council. It goes beyond the usual finding of the Council to 'remain seized of the matter'.[28] But

---

contributing state, the Security Council shall have the exclusive authority to waive the immunity in the interests of justice . . . .' See US Draft Resolution of 19 June 2002, in CICC, *ICC Update*, Assembly of States Parties Special Edition, Sept. 2002, at 4. A later draft circulated by the US on 3 July 2002 provided that 'the request not to commence or proceed with investigations or prosecutions as set forth in paragraph 1 shall be renewed and extended during successive twelve-month periods thereafter unless the Security Council decides otherwise.' The proposal read in full: 'The Security Council, Acting under Chapter VII of the Charter, 1. Requests, consistent with the provisions of Article 16 of the Rome Statute, that the ICC for a twelve-month period shall not commence or proceed with any investigations or prosecutions involving current or former officials or personnel from a contributing State not a Party to the Rome Statute for acts or omissions relating to UN established or authorized operations; 2. Decides by this resolution, acting consistent with Article 16 of the Rome Statute, that on July 1 of each successive year, the request not to commence or proceed with investigations or prosecutions as set forth in paragraph 1 shall be renewed and extends during successive twelve-month periods thereafter unless the Security Council decides otherwise and directs the Secretary-General to communicate these annual requests of the Security Council to the ICC; 3. Decides that Member States shall take no actions, such as arrest or surrender, inconsistent with the requests set forth in paragraphs 1 and 2.'

[26] On 3 July 2002, the UN Preparatory Commission for the ICC convened a meeting to discuss the US draft. Most delegations opposed the proposals, arguing that they amended or misused Art. 16 of the Rome Statute. For a survey of Government and UN responses concerning the US Draft Proposal, see the statements collected at: http://www.iccnow.org. Furthermore, the UN Secretary-General addressed a Letter to US Secretary of State Colin Powell, which states: 'The United States has put forward a proposal invoking the procedure laid down in Article 16 of the Rome Statute of the ICC. This provision means that the Security Council can intervene to prevent the Prosecutor of the ICC to proceed with a particular case. The article, which is meant for a completely different situation, is now proposed to be used by the Security Council for a blanket resolution, preventing the Prosecutor from pursuing cases against personnel in peacekeeping missions. Contrary to the wording of Article 16, which prescribes that such resolutions by the Council can be adopted for a period of 12 months, which period is renewable, it is proposed that the resolution is automatically prolonged, unless the prohibition is lifted.' See Letter from UN Secretary-General Kofi Annan to US Secretary of State Colin Powell of 3 July 2002, at http://www.iccnow.org/html/press.html.

[27] See also the Letter signed by the Ambassadors of New Zealand, South Africa, Brazil and Canada of 12 July 2002: 'Further, the request to the Court in the draft resolution would be renewable on an annual basis which, for all intents and purposes, would amount to creating a perpetual obstacle to Court action.'

[28] This finding is contained in para. 4 of SC Res. 1422 (2002).

what does it mean in legal terms? The expressed intention to renew the request certainly imposes an obligation on all Council members to seriously consider the matter on an annual basis. Moreover, the anticipated declaration of intent by the Council may entail special responsibilities for the permanent members not to exercise their veto powers on purely political grounds. But what about future non-permanent members? Are their voting rights in the Council equally curtailed in advance by paragraph 2 of SC Resolution 1422 (2002)?

Finally, the greatest paradox of the 'intent clause' is that it seems to invite state parties to the Statute, which are at the same time members of the Council, to regularly reapprove a legal instrument that runs counter to the objectives of the Rome Statute.

C SC Resolution 1422 (2002) and Other Provisions of the Statute

The proposed exemption of peacekeepers from proceedings before the ICC conflicts not only with Article 16 but also with several other provisions of the Statute.

1 Article 12(2) of the Statute

The envisaged creation of a permanent immunity for peacekeepers on the basis of paragraph 1 of SC Resolution 1422 (2002) establishes a distinction between individuals from state parties and third states that is not provided for under the jurisdictional regime of the ICC. Article 12(2) of the Statute, which was at the heart of discussions until the very last hours of the Rome Conference, stipulates that the Court operates on the basis of two alternative bases of jurisdiction: the jurisdictional nexus of the nationality of the accused and territorial jurisdiction. The request under paragraph 1 of SC Resolution 1422 (2002) severely limits the territorial jurisdiction of the Court for a specific group of persons, namely peacekeepers from non-state parties to the Statute, if it is practised on a permanent rather than on a provisional basis by the Council. Although such a limitation does not have a severe impact on the functioning of the Court in terms of numbers, it is nevertheless troubling, because it calls into question the jurisdictional reach of the Court. The territorial jurisdiction of states over foreign nationals may be limited in the field of peacekeeping[29] because peacekeepers usually enjoy privileges and immunities through two types of agree-

[29] Art. 4 of the Bulletin on the Observance by United Nations Forces of Humanitarian Law of 6 August 1999 provides that '[i]n case of violations of international humanitarian law, members of the military personnel of a United Nations force are subject to prosecution in their national courts.' See United Nations, Secretary-General's Bulletin, ST/SGB/1999/13 of 6 August 1999, in 38 ILM (1999), at 1656. Thus, the United Nations position appears to be that contributing states are the only authorities able to prosecute their own peacekeepers in cases of war crimes. This position is questionable because the agreements usually concluded within the framework of peacekeeping missions are only binding upon its parties, namely the United Nations, the host state, and the troop-contributing states. A state that is neither a party to the SOFA nor to the Contribution Agreement cannot be bound by them. It is therefore difficult to see how Art. 4 of the Bulletin on the Observance by United Nations Forces of Humanitarian Law could prevail over the universal jurisdiction of third states. The only justification may be found in Art. 105(2) of the Charter. But it is doubtful whether this provision grants peacekeeping forces immunity for war crimes.

94   *EJIL* 14 (2003), 85–104

ments concluded by the United Nations for each peacekeeping mission: a Status-of-Forces Agreement (SOFA) with the host country, which accords exclusive criminal jurisdiction to the troop-contributing state in the case of military personnel[30] and a Troop Contribution Agreement between the UN and the sending state, which specifies that peacekeeping personnel shall enjoy the privileges and immunities accorded in the SOFA[31] and be tried for criminal offences by the sending state.[32] But this practice does not per se limit the jurisdiction of the ICC. The approach reflected in the Statute is clearly that the ICC has jurisdiction over peacekeepers committing crimes under the Statute on the territory of a contracting party. The Statute treats the problem of the immunity of peacekeepers under the heading of cooperation and surrender of persons to the Court (Art. 98),[33] but not as an issue of jurisdiction.[34] The introduction of an additional, quasi-permanent bar to the exercise of jurisdiction over peacekeepers on the basis of Art. 16 is therefore a critical step, which does not fit within the overall structure of the Statute. Perhaps the only comfort lies in the fact that by pushing for the adoption of Resolution 1422 (2002) the US has incidentally recognized that the jurisdiction of the ICC extends to nationals of third states.

2 Article 27 of the Statute

The exemption of peacekeepers from proceedings before the ICC is also difficult to reconcile with Article 27 of the Statute which rules out immunities based on official capacity.[35] It is quite clear that peacekeepers do not enjoy immunity from crimes

---

[30] The United Nations usually concludes a Status-of-Mission Agreement (SOMA) with the host country, currently based on a 1990 model SOFA. Para. 47(b) of the SOMA accords exclusive jurisdiction to the military personnel of the sending state. It provides: 'Military members of the military component of the United Nations peace-keeping operation shall be subject to the exclusive jurisdiction of their respective participating States in respect of any criminal offences which may be committed by them in [host country/territory].' See Model Status-of-Forces Agreement for Peacekeeping Operations, UN. Doc. A/45/594 of 9 October 1990, reprinted in Fleck, *supra* note 6, at 603 *et seq.*

[31] See para. 5 of the Model Agreement between the United Nations and Member States Contributing Personnel and Equipment to United Nations Peace-Keeping Operations, UN Doc. A/46/185 of 23 May 1991, reprinted in Fleck, *supra* note 6, at 615: 'Accordingly, the military and/or civilian personnel provided by [the Participating State] shall enjoy the privileges and immunities, rights and facilities and comply with the obligations provided for in the status agreement.'

[32] See para. 25 of the Model Contribution Agreement: '[The Participating State] agrees to exercise jurisdiction with respect to crimes or offences which may be committed by its military personnel serving with [the United Nations peacekeeping operation]. [The Participating State] shall keep the Head of Mission informed regarding the outcome of such exercise of jurisdiction.'

[33] See Prost and Schlunck, 'On Article 98', in Triffterer, *supra* note 15, at 1131, para. 1: 'The article recognizes protections flowing from international obligations relating to diplomatic or state immunity and those arising from an agreement such as Status of Forces Agreements.'

[34] See on the general distinction between the issues of jurisdiction and cooperation within the context of peacekeeping also Kaul and Kreß, 'Jurisdiction and Cooperation in the Statute of the International Criminal Court: Principles and Compromises', *Yearbook of International Humanitarian Law*, Vol. 1 (1999), at 143 *et seq.*

[35] See also *Human Rights Watch*, U.S. Proposals to Undermine the International Criminal Court Through a U.N. Security Council Resolution, Statement of 25 June 2002, available at http://www.hrw.org/campaigns/icc/usproposal.htm.

within the jurisdiction of the Court under the rules of the Rome Statute.[36] The basic rule is that if peacekeepers operate on the territory of a contracting party, they may generally be prosecuted by the ICC.[37] This may be derived from the drafting history of the Statute and Article 27.

The issue, whether peacekeepers are immune from the jurisdiction of the ICC, has been discussed in the negotiations before the Rome Conference. France had originally proposed the inclusion of a provision in the Statute, which exempted peacekeepers from international criminal responsibility. The proposal was contained in Article 26(2) of the Draft Report of the Intersessional Meeting of 19–30 January 1998 in Zutphen, the Netherlands. It provided that '[p]ersons who have carried out acts ordered by the Security Council or in accordance with a mandate issued by it shall not be criminally responsible before the Court'.[38] However, an accompanying footnote stated that there were 'widespread doubts about the contents and the placement of this paragraph'.[39] It therefore does not come as a surprise that the provision was neither included in the Report of the Preparatory Committee on the Establishment of an International Criminal Court,[40] nor in the Statute itself.

Furthermore, Article 27 of the Statute makes it quite clear that peacekeepers are not above the law by virtue of their position. The provision reads:

> 1. This Statute shall apply equally to all persons without any distinction based on official capacity. In particular, official capacity as a Head of State or Government, a member of a

---

[36] The traditional thinking was that international humanitarian law did not even apply to United Nations peacekeepers because they were not deemed parties to a conflict. But the prevailing view today is that international humanitarian law applies to United Nations operations when they are engaged in hostilities. The original position of the United Nations was to encourage peacekeepers to observe the 'principles and spirit' of international law, but to deny that they were bound by such standards. However, as peacekeepers became more involved in using force within the framework of United Nations missions, the ICRC and others began to advocate that international humanitarian law applied to peacekeepers when they used force and became a party to the conflict, and to identify which rules applied to peacekeepers. In 1999, Secretary-General Annan issued guidelines that helped clarify the UN position on the question of the applicability of international humanitarian law to peacekeepers. These guidelines establish that the 'fundamental principles and rules of international humanitarian law ... are applicable to United Nations forces when in situations of armed conflict they are actively engaged therein as combatants.' See Art. 2 of the Bulletin on the Observance by United Nations Forces of Humanitarian Law, *supra* note 29. See generally on these guidelines Shraga, 'UN Peacekeeping Operations: Applicability of International Humanitarian Law and Responsibility for Operations Related Damage', 94 *AJIL* (2000), at 406 *et seq.*

[37] Military forces operating on the territory of a foreign state usually enjoy immunity for acts committed in their official capacity. But these immunities do not extend to the core crimes of the Statute. The special status attached to foreign forces acting abroad does therefore not affect their prosecution by the ICC. See Wirth, 'Immunities, Related Problems, and Article 98 of the Rome Statute', 12 *Criminal Law Forum* (2001) 429, at 450.

[38] See M. C. Bassiouni, *International Criminal Court Compilation of United Nations Documents and Draft ICC Statute before the Diplomatic Conference* (1998) 143, at 183.

[39] *Ibid.*

[40] See Report of the Preparatory Committee on the Establishment of an International Criminal Court, Draft Statute & Draft Final Act, UN. Doc. A/Conf.183/2/Add.1, 1998, reprinted in Bassiouni, *supra* note 38, at 7.

96   *EJIL* 14 (2003), 85–104

> Government or parliament, an elected representative or a government official shall in no case exempt a person from criminal responsibility under this Statute, nor shall it, in and of itself, constitute a ground for reduction of sentence.
>
> 2. Immunities or special procedural rules which may attach to the official capacity of a person, whether under national or international law, shall not bar the Court from exercising its jurisdiction over such a person.

Although peacekeepers are not formally listed as persons with 'official capacity' in Article 27(1) sentence 2, they obviously fall under this category. The general rule enunciated in Article 27(1) sentence 1 is that *all* persons with 'official capacity' shall be treated equally in the sense that the nature of their capacity does not exempt them from their individual criminal responsibility under international law. Furthermore, the term 'official capacity' refers to activities which are carried out by the organs of a state, or at least attributable to a state.[41] These features are clearly met by military personnel. Moreover, the fact that peacekeeping forces may enjoy immunity under SOFA agreements with the host state is irrelevant because Article 27(2) reaffirms that such international agreements do not bar the jurisdiction of the Court. On the contrary, the general system of the Statute is again that bi- or multi-lateral agreements providing for immunity may prevent the ICC from ordering a request for surrender of persons under Article 98, but that they do not categorically exclude their individual criminal responsibility under the Statute.[42]

One might be tempted to argue that paragraph 1 of the Security Council Resolution does not call into question the principles enshrined in the Statute because it leaves states the power to try peacekeepers on the basis of their national jurisdiction. Some indications in this direction may be found in paragraph 5 of the preamble of the resolution, in which the Council notes 'that States not Party to the Rome Statute will continue to fulfil their responsibilities in their national jurisdictions in relation to international crimes.' But the reference to domestic mechanisms of prosecution is only of limited value under the Statute. The exclusive reliance on the jurisdiction of the troop-contributing state within the framework of United Nations peacekeeping operations has so far been justified by the fact that there was no independent international institution to deal effectively with these abuses.[43] The object and purpose of the Statute is to close this gap through the establishment of a novel and independent law enforcement mechanism with jurisdiction over peacekeepers.[44] Although the Court does not replace domestic jurisdictions, it nevertheless modifies

---

[41]   See Triffterer, 'On Article 27', in Triffterer, *supra* note 15, at 509, para. 13.

[42]   See Triffterer, *supra* note 41, at 513, paras 24 and 514, para. 26; Prost and Schlunck, *supra* note 33, at 1132, para. 2 ('It is important to note that [Article 98] does not accord an immunity from prosecution to individuals, which the Court may seek to prosecute. Art. 27 makes it clear that no such immunity is available').

[43]   See Zwanenburg, 'Compromise or Commitment: Human Rights and International Humanitarian Law Obligations for UN Peace Forces', 11 *Leiden Journal of International Law* (1998) 229, at 243.

[44]   See Zwanenburg, 'The Statute of the International Criminal Court and the United States: Peacekeepers under Fire?', 10 *EJIL* (1999) 124, at 129.

the traditional system of prosecution of peacekeepers by establishing a complementary jurisdiction for cases in which states prove to be unable or unwilling to prosecute peacekeepers.[45] The re-introduction of the exclusive jurisdiction of states under SC Resolution 1422 (2002), on the contrary, marks a severe setback, because it deprives the Statute of its intended complementary effect.

4 The Effect of SC Resolution 1422 (2002)

The multiple inconsistencies between SC Resolution 1422 (2002) and the Rome Statute raise the questions about whether and to what extent the determinations of the Security Council prevail over the provisions of the Statute. The answer to this question mainly depends on two factors: (1) the authority of the Council to adopt a resolution that runs counter to provisions of the Statute, and (2) its binding effect on the Court.

A *The Legality of Security Council Resolution 1422 (2002)*

The Council is not bound by the provisions of the Rome Statute. Its authority to adopt SC Resolution 1422 (2002) must therefore be assessed on the basis of its Chapter VII powers under the Charter.

1 *SC Resolution 1422 (2002) and the Chapter VII Powers of the Council*

Although the Council enjoys broad freedom of judgement concerning action under Chapter VII, it is not above the law. In discharging its functions, the Council is expressly bound by the restrictions laid down in Articles 1(1) and 24 of the Charter, namely the duty to act in accordance with the 'purposes and principles of the Organization'.[46] Furthermore, a strong case can be made that a decision of the Council taken in violation of the Charter is not binding upon UN member states, because Members of the United Nations have only agreed 'to accept and carry out ... decisions of the Security Council in accordance with the ... Charter' (Article 25 of the Charter).[47] This position finds support, in particular, in the Advisory Opinion of the ICJ in the *Admissions* case, where the Court held that '[t]he political character of an organ cannot release it from the observance of treaty provisions established by the Charter, when they constitute limitations on its powers or criteria for its judgment.'[48]

---

[45] See Art. 17 of the Statute.
[46] See Delbrück, 'On Article 24', in Simma, *supra* note 4, at 404, at para. 11. For a full analysis, see Gill, 'Legal and Some Political Limitations on the Power of the UN Security Council to Exercise its Enforcement Powers under Chapter VII of The Charter', 26 *Netherlands Yearbook of International Law* (1995) 33, at 72 *et seq.*
[47] See Bowett, 'The Impact of Security Council Decisions on Dispute Settlement Procedures', 5 *EJIL* (1994) 89, at 95; Doehring, 'Unlawful Resolutions of the Security Council and their Legal Consequences', 1 *Max Planck Yearbook of United Nations Law*, (1997) 98 ('The position that the whole peacekeeping system of the United Nations would collapse if states would be free to judge themselves about the legality of resolutions and to deny binding effect to an autonomous judgment, may be conclusive but not coherent and, in the end not convincing. This position would result in an obligation to do wrong').
[48] See ICJ, *Conditions of Admission to the United Nations*, Advisory Opinion, ICJ Reports (1948), at 64.

98   *EJIL* 14 (2003), 85–104

But it is questionable whether the Council did in fact overstep such limits when adopting SC Resolution 1422 (2002). Some states have taken this view at the open Council meeting convened on 10 July 2002. The Representative of Jordan stated that the Council would 'edge itself toward acting *ultra vires* — that is, beyond its authority under the UN Charter' if it considered 'the adoption of a draft resolution on the ICC falling under Chapter VII'.[49] Moreover, the Permanent Representative of Canada emphasized at the same meeting that the 'adoption of the resolutions currently circulating could place Canada and, we expect, others in the unprecedented position of having to examine the legality of a Security Council resolution.'[50]

However, this *ultra vires* claim is difficult to justify in legal terms. The Council's wide interpretation of Article 39 of the Charter would hardly suffice to establish that SC Resolution 1422 (2002) has no basis in the Charter. While it is critical to invoke Chapter VII in a situation in which the threat to peace stems primarily from the declared intent of a Council member not to support future UN peacekeeping operations, the determination of a given situation as a threat to the peace remains in substance a political decision which lies at the heart of the Council's discretion and should not be subject to review by individual UN Member States.[51]

Furthermore, SC Resolution 1422 (2002) does not appear to violate *jus cogens* or the purposes and principles of the United Nations, to which the Council is bound by virtue of Article 24 of the Charter. A valid *ultra vires* argument could be made if peacekeepers from non-state parties to the ICC had been exempted from individual criminal responsibility (and not only from the jurisdiction of the Court) because such a decision would have entailed a flagrant violation of the principle of equality.[52] But this is obviously not the case because para. 1 of the resolution refers only to proceedings before the ICC, leaving the whole system of national prosecution of peacekeepers for core crimes under the Statute unaffected.[53] Moreover, there is no rule of customary international law which would require that peacekeepers be brought before an international jurisdiction.[54]

Some states have challenged the lawfulness of SC Resolution 1422 (2002) arguing that the Council was not vested with treaty-making and treaty-reviewing powers and could not alter the content or the meaning of international agreements, such as the Rome Statute, freely entered into by states.[55] But this argument is not persuasive.

---

[49]   See the Statement of the Representative of Jordan to the United Nations at the meeting of 10 July 2002, at http://www.iccnow.org.

[50]   See the Statement of the Representative of Canada to the United Nations at the meeting of 10 July 2002, at http://www.iccnow.org.

[51]   See Bowett, *supra* note 47, at 94.

[52]   See Gowlland-Debbas, 'The Relationship between the Security Council and the Projected International Criminal Court', 1 *Journal of Armed Conflict Law* (1996) S. 97 (114).

[53]   See also para. 5 of the preamble to Resolution 1422 (2002). 'Noting that States not Party to the Rome Statute will continue to fulfil their responsibilities in their national jurisdictions in relation to international crimes.'

[54]   See also MacPherson, *supra* note 1.

[55]   See the Statement of the Representative of Brazil to the United Nations at the meeting of 10 July 2002, at http://www.iccnow.org.

Article 2(7) second sentence of the Charter contains an express limitation of the *domaine réservé* of states in relation to measures under Chapter VII of the Charter. One may therefore hardly claim that the Council exceeded its powers by interfering in the exclusive rights of states to conclude or amend treaties. Furthermore, it follows from Articles 25 and 103 of the Charter that the Council may override specific rights and obligations of states under an existing treaty regime by using its authority under Chapter VII. In fact, Article 103 of the Charter does not directly state that a Chapter VII decision of the Council prevails over any other inconsistent treaty provision. But the obligation of UN Member States under Article 25 of the Charter to 'accept and carry out decisions of the Security Council' is an 'obligation under the Charter' within the meaning of Article 103. UN Member States are therefore bound by Article 103 to give obligations arising from binding Chapter VII resolutions of the Council priority over any other commitments.[56] This view has been taken by the Security Council in its Resolution 670 (1990), in which the Council expressly recalled the 'provisions of Article 103 of the Charter', and then went on to decide

> that all States, *notwithstanding the existence of any rights or obligations conferred or imposed by any international agreement* or any contract entered into or any license or permit granted before the date of the present resolution, shall deny permission to any aircraft to take off from their territory if the aircraft would carry any cargo to or from Iraq or Kuwait other than food in humanitarian circumstances.[57]

The same reasoning underlies the practice of the Council in the *Lockerbie* case, in which the Council decided that Libya must surrender the persons charged with the terrorist action against PanAm flight 103 to the United Kingdom and the United States, despite the applicability of the Montreal Convention for the Suppression of Unlawful Acts against the Safety of Civil Aviation of 23 September 1971, which is based on the principle *aut dedere aut judicare*.[58] The ICJ accepted this view in its two Orders of 14 April 1992,[59] in which the Court noted:

> Whereas both Libya and the United Kingdom, as Members of the United Nations, are obliged to accept and carry out the decisions of the Security Council in accordance with Article 25 of the Charter; whereas the Court, which is at the stage of proceedings on provisional measures, considers that prima facie this obligation extends to the decision contained in resolution 748 (1992); and whereas, in accordance with Article 103 of the Charter, the obligations of the Parties in that respect prevail over the obligations under any other international agreement, Including the Montreal Convention....[60]

---

[56] See Bernhardt, 'On Article 103', in Simma, *supra* note 5, at 1120, para. 10.
[57] See the preamble and para. 3 of SC Resolution 670 (1990) of 25 September 1990, UN Doc. S/RES/670 (1990) (emphasis added).
[58] See para. 1 of SC Resolution 748 (1992) of 31 March 1992, UN. Doc. S/RES/748 (1992).
[59] See also Mosler, 'On Article 92', in Simma, *supra* note 5, at 991, para. 87.
[60] See ICJ, *Case Concerning Questions of Interpretation and Application of the 1971 Montreal Convention arising from the Aerial Incident at Lockerbie* (Libya v. United Kingdom), ICJ Reports (1992), at 16, at para. 39.

100   *EJIL* 14 (2003), 85–104

The question is therefore not so much whether the Council violated its obligations under the Charter when adopting Resolution 1422 (2002), but rather whether states that are both Council members and parties to the Rome Statute violated their obligations under the Statute, when voting in favour of the resolution in the Council.

2 SC Resolution 1422 (2002) and the Obligations of Council Members under the Statute

Permanent members like France or the United Kingdom face a difficult conflict in the Council when they adopt decisions related to the ICC. They are, on the one hand, part of the Council as an organ of the United Nations and, on the other hand, bound by the provisions of the Rome Statute.[61] The conflict between the exercise of voting rights in the Council and the obligation to act in accordance with the provisions of an existing treaty regime has been directly addressed in the context of the Common Foreign and Security Policy (CFSP) of the European Union. Article 19(2) of the European Union Treaty[62] states:

> Member States which are also members of the United Nations Security Council will concert and keep the other Member States fully informed. Member States which are permanent members of the Security Council will, in the execution of their functions, ensure the defence of the positions and the interests of the Union, without prejudice to their responsibilities under the provisions of the United Nations Charter.

This provision makes it clear that France and the United Kingdom remain bound by the general principles of the CFSP, when acting in the Council. But the disclaimer clause ('without prejudice to their responsibilities under the provisions of the United Nations Charter') clarifies that they continue to enjoy political discretion in their decision-making process in the Council.[63] They are, in particular, not obliged to veto any Security Council resolution, which runs counter to the goals of the CFSP.[64] The Rome Statute, however, does not contain a similar disclaimer. Does this mean that its contracting parties may not act contrary to the terms of the Statute when they adopt decisions in their capacity as members of the Council?

The answer is yes, if one takes the position that the provisions of the Statute contain an accurate and conclusive reflection of the powers of the Council under the

---

[61]   See Art. 26 of the Vienna Convention on the Law of Treaties.

[62]   See on the ambiguities of this clause, Frowein, 'Auf dem Weg zu einer Gemeinsamen Außen- und Sicherheitspolitik', 36 *Berichte der Deutschen Gesellschaft für Völkerrecht* (1997) 11, at 16–17; Fink-Hoijer, 'The Common Foreign and Security Policy of the European Union', 5 *EJIL* (1994) 173, at 188.

[63]   See Winkelmann, 'Europäische und mitgliedstaatliche Interessenvertretung in den Vereinten Nationen', 60 *ZaöRV* (2000) 413, at 416.

[64]   See Cremer, 'On Article 19', in C. Calliese and M. Ruffert (eds), *Kommentar zu EU-Vertrag und EG-Vertrag* (1999), at 166, para. 3.

Charter.[65] Any more far-reaching limitation of the powers of the ICC through a decision of the Security Council would then be a violation of the state's duties under the Statute because the primacy of the Charter over other international agreements under Article 103 is limited to 'obligations' of UN Members under the Charter and does not extend to the exercise of their rights, such as voting rights in the Council.[66]

Nevertheless, even if one accepts this view, it remains questionable whether such a violation occurred in the case of the adoption of SC Resolution 1422 (2002) because the resolution itself contains many ambiguous passages, which leave its impact on the Statute and its contracting parties unclear.

B *The Binding Force of SC Resolution 1422 (2002)*

1 *SC Resolution 1422 (2002) and the ICC*

The compromise formula adopted by the Council on 12 July 2002 leaves some doubts as to whether the resolution binds the ICC. The current framing of the resolution would suggest that it does not. The US had originally proposed a Chapter VII decision of the Council, stating

> that persons of or from contributing states ... shall enjoy in the territory of all Member States other than the contributing State immunity from arrest, detention, and prosecution with respect to all acts arising out of the operation and that this immunity shall continue after termination of their participation in the operation for all such acts.[67]

This approach did not meet the approval of the state parties to the Statute, which preferred a solution in accordance with Article 16 of the Statute. The Council finally refrained from issuing a binding 'decision' under Chapter VII, addressing instead a 'request' to the Court.[68] This 'request' represents more than a mere 'recommendation' under Article 39 of the Charter.[69] Nevertheless, the very nature of a request is that it has no binding force on the ICC per se, even if it has been pronounced under the

---

[65] See in this sense P. Arnold, *Der UNO-Sicherheitsrat und die Verfolgung von Individuen* (1999), at 176, who argues that the 12-month deferral under Art. 16 of the Statute is consistent with Art. 103 of the Charter because it reflects the position of the broad majority of states as to when a deferral of ICC procceedings by the Council is proportional under Chapter VII of the Charter. See also Zimmermann, *supra* note 16, at 236 ('It is worth noting that the powers of the Security Council to act under Chapter VII of the Charter have thereby for the first time been limited in an international instrument, since the Security Council would eventually by virtue of article 16 of the Statute of the ICC be forced to renew any such request for deferral but could not provide for a deferral *sine die*').

[66] The duty to act in accordance with the Statute does not collide with an *obligation* under the Charter, because Security Council members enjoy wide discretion in their decision-making process in the Council.

[67] See the first US proposal of 19 June 2002 ('Acting under Chapter VII of the Charter ... Decides that'), *supra* note 25.

[68] See para. 1 of SC Resolution 1422 (2002).

[69] See generally on recommendations of the Security Council under Art. 39, Frowein, *supra* note 5, at 614, paras 29 *et seq.*

102 *EJIL* 14 (2003), 85–104

heading of Chapter VII. Article 25 of the Charter establishes only a duty to carry out 'decisions' of the Council. The obligation to implement the request follows therefore not from the Charter itself,[70] but from Article 16 of the Statute,[71] which states that 'no investigation or prosecution may be commenced or proceeded with under this Statute for a period of 12 months' after a Security Council request in a resolution adopted under Chapter VII. The fact that the Council noted that the ICC 'shall ... not commence or proceed with investigation or prosecution', does not lead to a different result because the legal impact of this formulation is again expressly linked to the terms of the Statute.[72]

The interpretation that SC Resolution 1422 (2002) does not directly bind the Court is further reinforced by the current construction of the Charter as an instrument which creates legal duties for its members, but does not impose obligations on other international organizations or entities themselves.[73] Article 48(2) of the Charter posits the principle that Council decisions are carried out through the intermediate action of UN member states in 'the appropriate international agencies of which they are members'. This rule applies equally to the ICC which enjoys its own international legal personality under Article 4 of the Statute. Even Article 103 of the Charter cannot be invoked in support of the claim that the ICC is directly bound by binding secondary law of the Security Council because Article 103 merely binds states, but not the Court.[74]

Accordingly, the main question is whether the ICC may dismiss a deferral request of the Security Council under the rules of its own Statute. Some doubts as to the existence of such a power arise from the wording of Article 16 ('[n]o investigation or prosecution may be commenced or proceeded with ... after the Security Council ... has requested the Court to that effect'), which does not appear to grant the Prosecutor any discretion in its decision over the suspension or continuation of proceedings before the Court after a Chapter VII request. But the Court is the final arbiter over the interpretation of the Statute. One may therefore infer that it is vested with the authority to refuse to implement a Council request that exceeds the limits of Article 16 of the Statute.

---

[70] But see Bergsmo and Pejic, *supra* note 15, at 381, para. 23 ('Obliging the Council to issue a Chapter VII resolution serves two other purposes as well. First, it ensures that the deferral of an investigation or prosecution is undertaken on the basis of a legally binding Security Council decision, thereby establishing a legal duty on the Court to comply with the request').

[71] Para. 1 of the resolution speaks of requests, 'consistent with the provisions of Article 16 of the Rome Statute'.

[72] *Ibid.* But see MacPherson, *supra* note 1, sub. II. D. who notes that the Council's intent was to bind the Court 'shown by the Council's express reliance on Chapter VII of the Charter and its use in the operative part of the resolution of the words "shall ... not commence or proceed".

[73] See Bryde, 'On Article 48', in Simma, *supra* note 5, at 653, para. 10.

[74] See Hoffmeister and Knoke, 'Das Vorermittlungsverfahren vor dem Internationalen Strafgerichtshof — Prüfstein für die Effektivität der neuen Gerichtsbarkeit im Völkerstrafrecht', 59 *ZaöRV* (1999) 785, at 805.

2 SC Resolution 1422 (2002) and the Obligations of State Parties to the Rome Statute

The sole fact that the ICC may possibly disregard paragraph 1 of SC Resolution 1422 (2002) does, of course, not significantly enhance the risk of prosecution of peacekeepers from third states because the ICC's trial system lays dormant if states are pre-empted from surrendering suspects to the Court. The introductory part of paragraph 3 of SC Resolution 1422 (2002) seems to establish a prohibition of states to cooperate with the Court in cases involving peacekeeping personnel from third states. The relevant passage states that the Security Council '[d]ecides that Member States shall take no action inconsistent with paragraph 1 ...'. Being drafted as a binding decision under Chapter VII, this obligation would override the obligations of UN Members under the Rome Statute by virtue of Article 103 of the Charter. But it is controversial whether such a far-reaching obligation was in fact envisaged by the resolution. Paragraph 3 declares that Member States shall take no action inconsistent with paragraph 1, but continues '... and with their international obligations'. This last passage can be read as a reference to Article 103 of the Charter, clarifying that state parties to the Statute must comply with their obligations under the UN Charter. However, the language chosen by the drafters of the resolution deviates from that used in Article 103. Paragraph 3 does not speak of action 'not consistent with obligations under the Charter', but uses the much broader notion of 'international obligations'. A case can be made that these 'international obligations' include obligations under the Rome Statute. The impact of the resolution on state parties to the Statute would then be much more limited, leaving their rights and obligations under the Statute virtually unaffected. One may therefore conclude that the effect of the compromise formula embodied in paragraph 3 of the resolution on parties to the Statute depends largely on its interpretation.

5 The Scope of Application of Resolution 1422 (2002)

Further interpretational difficulties arise from the proposed scope of application of the resolution. The resolution applies to any 'United Nations established or authorized operation'. There may be different understandings of what constitutes a 'UN authorized' operation. The wording of paragraph 1 of the resolution suggests that the deferral request extends to all operations that have been explicitly authorized by the Security Council. But what about cases for which Security Council authorization is less evident? It is well known that cases of doubt have arisen in the practice of the Council. The most recent example is the (non-)authorization of Operation Enduring Freedom by the Security Council.[75] Paragraph 2(b) of SC Resolution 1373 (2001) contains a clause which states that 'all States shall ... [t]ake the necessary steps to prevent the commission of terrorist acts'. This phrase has been interpreted as an

---

[75] For further discussion, see Stahn, 'Security Council Resolutions 1368 and 1373: What They Say and What They Do Not Say', at http://www.ejil.org/forum-WTC.

104   *EJIL* 14 (2003), 85–104

'almost unlimited mandate to use force', providing 'the U.S. with an at least-tenable argument whenever it decides for political reasons, that force is necessary to "prevent the commission of terrorist acts".'[76] The US may, in fact, claim that its counter-terrorist operations are 'UN authorized'. However, such an interpretation would, most likely, conflict with the view of other states according to which the deferral applies only to operations explicitly authorized by the Council.

Finally, one may note that the current wording of the resolution will most likely have at least one unattended, but highly welcome, side-effect. The risk of divergent interpretations of SC Resolution 1422 (2002) may, in fact, present an incentive for the Council to refrain from issuing ambiguous Chapter VII mandates and authorizations in the future.

6 Conclusion

SC Resolution 1422 (2002) is one of the most controversial resolutions of the Security Council. The Council stretched its Chapter VII powers to its utmost limits when treating the issue of the immunity of peacekeepers as a matter of international peace and security under Article 39 of the Charter. Moreover, the resolution may mark a deplorable setback for the development of international law if it is used as an instrument to permanently bar the exercise of jurisdiction of the ICC over peacekeep-ers of non-state parties. Such a step would not only severely limit the independent prosecutorial powers of the Court, which was one of the major achievements of the Rome Conference, but also call into question the principle of equality before the law. However, it is still uncertain whether international legal practice will finally develop in this direction. The compromise adopted on 12 July 2002 leaves significant room for interpretation. The ICC may find that the request is not binding on it because it exceeds the limits of Article 16 of the Statute. State parties to the Statute may claim that their obligations under the Statute continue to apply. Finally, Council members may simply refuse to renew the request. Therefore, SC Resolution 1422 (2002) certainly sets a dangerous, but not an irreversible, precedent in international law.

---

[76] See Byers, 'Terrorism, the Use of Force and International Law', 51 *ICLQ* (2002) 401, at 402.

Responsibilities and Liabilities of Peacekeeper

[16]

THE INTERNATIONAL RESPONSIBILITY OF THE UNITED NATIONS FOR ACTIVITIES CARRIED OUT BY U.N. PEACE-KEEPING FORCES

By

Judge BORHAN AMRALLAH

THE INTERNATIONAL RESPONSIBILITY OF THE UNITED NATIONS FOR ACTIVITIES CARRIED OUT BY U.N. PEACE-KEEPING FORCES

The Legal Capacity of the U.N. to Bear International Responsibility for the Activities of its Organs:

As a result of the Peace-Keeping activities of the U.N. which are becoming more and more numerous and increasingly important every day, the problem of legal responsibility of the U.N. for the activities concerning the Peace-Keeping operation is acquiring greater importance demanding deeper study. The peace-keeping activities are giving rise to new issues concerning responsibility for damages or injuries that may be caused by the peace-keeping forces. The peace-keeping forces are likely to cause cases of responsibility while these forces (which are composed of contingents drawn from various states owing their allegiance to their national governments) are operating outside the territorial jurisdiction of their parent state under the operational control of the U.N. This character of the U.N. forces consisting of contingents having dual relations and operating in a state outside their own respective territories gives rise to the problem of the determination of the international responsibility of each party involved in the peace-keeping operation, i.e. :

1) The U.N. as a legal entity capable of bearing responsibility,

2) All the member states of the U.N. taken individually,

3) The states providing contingents,

4) And lastly the host state in whose territory the force opera-
tes/or which it assists.

If we proceed on the assumption that the U.N. should bear the
international responsibility for the activities of its forces, we are faced
with another problem i.e. the applicability of the general principles
of international law of responsibility in inter-state relations to the
U.N., as the U.N. has not the same extent of legal capacity as that
of a state and is not organized in the same way as a state, and it
does not perform the same function as does a state, and the procedures developed to fit states do not fit so well the U.N.'s unique character. Therefore the aforesaid general principles are to be applied to
the U.N. responsibility as they are, or they need certain modifications
to fit the unique character of the U.N. and its peace-keeping operations.

To begin with I propose to discuss the principle of the legal
capacity of the U.N. to bear international responsibility for activities
carried out by its organs. If it is established that the U.N. can bear
such a responsibility, we shall try to answer the question if the U.N.
bears the total responsibility for the activities of the U.N. peace-keeping forces while there are several parties, enumerated above, involved
in such operations. Finally we shall discuss to which extent the general rules of international responsibility (in inter-state relations) could
be applied to the U.N.

On the Legal Capacity of the U.N. to Bear International Responsibi-lity for Activities Carried Out by its Organs :

In the past International law was centered only on states. States
were the only international entities who had the international personality, legal capacity and could engage the international responsibility as
well. The development of international law gave rise to other international persons which are not states. These developments also gave
rise to a new legal problem concerning these new international subjects, inter alia, the recognition of their international personality, their
legal capacity especially relating to international responsibility.

International personality is attributed to every entity which has
the eligibility to possess international rights or obligations, or, even
one of these rights (1). This personality is separate from and inde-

---

(1) Badr Kasme, La capacité de l'organisation des Nations Unies de con-
clure des traités, Paris, 1960, pp. 25, 31.

pendent of those persons who created it or who are part of it (2).

It is necessary to point out that the international personality is different from the international legal capacity. The latest is like a sheaf of international rights and duties that the international person can assume. As 'the international persons are not identical (in their nature, functions, aims and they are not party to the same legal arrangements which add to or subtract from their rights and duties), then they have not the same extent of legal capacity i.e. they do not possess identical rights and duties.

The actual international law admits different types of international persons which have different extent of rights and duties, and the procedure by which they are claimed or enforced may likewise vary in each situation. The application of the international law of responsibility would therefore be different for each such person (3).

As for the U.N., we must determine such preliminary elements before dealing with its international responsibility, the subject of the present study i.e. Does the U.N. have an international personality? And if it has, is her legal capacity identical with state's capacity? In other words, can the U.N. be legally responsible for activities carried out by its organs ? And if so, is its responsibility of the same nature and extent as that of the state? At present no one denies the international personality to the U.N. specially after the advisory opinion of the ICJ on reparations case 1949. The U.N. has also international legal capacity to assume rights and duties under international law. But this capacity is not identical with that of a state. « To say that the United Nations is an international person, said the ICJ, does not mean that it has the same rights and duties as state, nor that it is a 'super-state', whatever that expression may mean »... « What it does mean is that it is a subject of international law, and capable of possessing international rights and duties ». Which « depend upon its purposes and functions as specified or implied in its constituent documents and developed in practice » (4).

Is the U.N. capable of assuming international responsibility for

---

(2) Clyde Eagleton, International Organization and the Law of Responsibility, R.C.A.H., 1950, I, p. 327.
(3) Eagleton, op. cit., p. 343.
(4) I.C.J. Reports, 1949, pp. 179-180.

activities carried out by its Organs? We will try here to demonstrate
the principle of the U.N. capacity to assume international responsibility for the aforesaid activities. This discussion will depend upon sur-
veying the ICJ theory, U.N. provisions, practice and follow up by a
short legal argument.

In its advisory opinion on reparations case, the ICJ defined international subject, as an entity which has legal capacity on international
plane, i.e. which is capable of possessing international rights and duties (5). It continued, that the international persons are not identical
in the extent of their legal capacity (6). Afterwards, the Court came
to the conclusion that the U.N. « was intended to exercise and enjoy,
and is in fact exercising and enjoying, functions and rights which can
only be explained on the basis of the possession of a large measure of
international personality » (7).

When we examine the terms used by the Court concerning the
international personality of the U.N., we can easily find out that the
Court, after enumerating the rights and duties which the U.N. possesses came to the conclusion that : Having large measure of legal capacity, the U.N. has international personality separate from and independent of its member states. Moreover, such personality is of an
objective nature which legally exists regarding other international entities even those which had not recognized the Organization. Accordingly, the U.N. has the capacity to maintain its rights by bringing
international claims, against the respondent state even if the latest
was not one of its members. The Court stated « that the fifty state,
representing the vast majority of the members of the international
community, has the power, in conformity with international law, to
bring into being an entity possessing objective international personality — and not merely personality recognized by them alone — together with capacity to bring international claims »(8).

Although the Court did not give an answer to the question of
the capacity of the U.N. to bear the responsibility for its unlawful
acts or omissions, the recognition of such capacity — according to the
dominant doctrine — is educed from the internal logic of the Court's

_____

(5) I.C.J., op. cit., p. 179.
(6) Badr Kasme, op. cit., p. 16.
(7) I.C.J. Reports, 1949, p. 179.
(8) I.C.J. Reports, 1949, p. 185.

advisory opinion (9). The rights and duties of a legal person are indissociable. Where there are rights, there are also duties; and we must assume that the U.N., as a legal person, has duties as well as rights, and for failure to perform these duties it may be possible to claim reparation from the U.N. (10).

As a matter of principle the extent of the U.N. legal capacity depends upon the provisions of its constituent documents beside the implied powers as developed in practice. But the capacity of the U.N. to make reparation for the damages caused by its activities does not depend upon whether this reparation is necessary for the purposes of the organization. The legal capacity of the U.N. to honour its obligation is absolute because the legal obligation must be honoured » (11). This argument was also put forward by the Permanent Court of International Justice : « It is principle of international law, and even a general conception of law, that any breach of an engagement involves an obligation to make reparation » (12).

Keeping in view the advisory opinion of the ICJ on the reparations case of 1949, we cannot see how the U.N. as an organization established to implement principles of justice, can bring international claim of responsibility against others but cannot be held responsible for its own acts or omissions (13).

The ICJ gave two more advisory opinions supporting its theory. On the Effect of Awards of Compensation Made by the U.N. Administrative Tribunal of 1954, the ICJ rejected the view that the power of the Assembly General to approve the Organization's expenditure will override the power of compensation Awards given by U.N.A.T. The Court declared that « the function of approving the budget does not mean that the General Assembly has an absolute power to approve or disapprove the expenditure which arises out of obligations already incurred by the organization, and to this extent the General Assembly has no alternative but to honour these engagements » (14).

---

(9) De Visscher, Paul, Le Fondement du Principe de la Responsabilité de l'ONU, Annales de Droit et de Sciences Politiques, XXIII, 1963, pp. 134-135.
(10) Eagleton, op. cit., p. 385.
(11) Jean-Pierre Ritter, La protection diplomatique à l'égard d'une Organisation · Internationale, Annuaire Français de Droit International (AFDI), 1962, p. 430.
(12) Chorzow Factory Case (1928), P.C.I.J. Ser. A, No. 17, p. 29.
(13) De Visscher, op. cit., p. 135.
(14) I.C.J. Reports, 1954, p. 59.

In its advisory opinion on certain expenses of U.N. 1962, The ICJ recognized the U.N. responsibility for the action of its agent even if such action was « Ultra vires » (15). The Court also declared that « Financial obligations which, in accordance with the clear and reiterated authority of both the Security Council and General Assembly, the Secretary General incurred on behalf the United Nations, Constitute obligations of the organization... » (16).

According to Art. 104 of the U.N. Charter, the U.N. enjoys in the territory of each of its members such legal capacity as may be necessary for the exercise of its functions and fulfilment of its purposes. The legal capacity of bearing responsibility for unlawful acts carried out by U.N. Peace-Keeping forces is also necessary for the exercise of U.N. functions and fulfilment of its purposes relating peace-keeping operations. If the U.N. avoids its responsibility for the unlawful activities carried out by its forces, the states which provide their contingents may depend upon the U.N. denial of responsibility as a plea to interfere in the functions and purposes of the U.N. peacekeeping operation and also to contest the authority of the U.N. Secretary General and his representatives in the field as well. Such interference may badly affect even the nature of peace-keeping operation. Instead of being one U.N. operation it becomes a multinational operation. Consequently, the U.N. cannot perform its functions and fulfil its purposes relating to peace-keeping operations without possessing the complete and exclusive operational control over the forces. It cannot also deny its responsibility for unlawful acts committed by these forces because authority and responsibility are indissociable concepts. Also if the U.N. denies its responsibility, the member states may refuse to participate with their contingents in any U.N. peacekeeping operation. They will not be willing to bear the international responsibility for the unlawful acts of their contingents, so long as these contingents will be operating not under their control but under the exclusive operational control of the U.N.

The convention on the privileges and immunities of the U.N., February 13, 1946, recognizes that the U.N. has juridical personality and, inter alia, capable to contract and institute legal proceedings. Section 29 states that U.N. shall make provisions for :

(15) .C.J. Report, 1962. The Advisory Opinion on certain Expenses of the U.N., p. 168 and p. 219 where Judge Krylov referred expressly to the position of the U.N. as a defendant. See also, Ibid., p. 270.
(16) I.C.J. Reports, 1962, p. 177.

A) Appropriate modes of settlement of disputes arising out or contracts or other claims of private law character to which the U.N. is a party, and

B) Disputes involving any official of the U.N. who by reason of his official position enjoys immunity (17).

In conformity with these provisions the U.N. concluded several agreements with other states concerning, **inter alia,** the settlement of claims of responsibility against the U.N. for unlawful acts committed by its forces (18). In addition to this, the U.N .Secretary General enacted regulations to be applied to the U.N. peace-keeping force. All such provisions are giving a very strong foundation to the principle of the U.N. responsibility for activities carried out by its peace-keeping forces.

Up till now the U.N. does not contect the principle of such responsibility when it is legally engaged (19). The U.N. Secretary-General declared that the organization was not and also will not escape from its responsibility when it is legally engaged (20).

The U.N. was paying compensations for activities carried out by UNEF as ONUC. In some cases it also paid reparation for such claims arising out of the shooting of a person by one member of the force where no official function or superior order required that member to shoot, even though the person was prosecuted in his home country for having shoot the person in question (21).

---

(17) Convention on the Privileges and Immunities of the U.N., adopted by General Assembly on Feb. 13, 1946. (U.N.T.S., 1946-1947, pp. 16-26.

(18) Such as : Status agreements of UNEF, 8-2-1957 (A/3526, General Assembly Official Records, 11th Session. Annexes, agenda item, 66, p. 52, ONUC of 27-11-1961, U.N.T.S., Vol. 414, p. 231 and UNFICYP 31-3-1964, U.N.T.S., Vol. 555, p. 261 ; and (Knok-For-Knok) agreement between U.N. and U.A.R. concerning the settlement of claims arising out of traffic accidents (U.N.T.S., Vol. 388, p. 143). Also, Reparation agreement between U.N. and Belgium of Feb. 20, 1965, concerning, **inter alia,** settlement of reclamations of compensation presented by Belgian subjects in Congo. (Spaak and U-Thant agreement, U.N. Security Council, (6597).

(16) De Visscher, op. cit., p. 135. See also D.W. Bowett, United Nations Forces, London, 1964, p. 242.

(20) U-Thant, letter dated July 5, 1965 to the Belgian Minister of Foreign Affairs. Quoted by J.A. Salmon, AFDI, 1965, p. 479. Also ibid, The Secretary-General's answer dated 6.8.75, to Morozov, the Representative of U.S.S.R.

(21) Fin Seyersted, United Nations Forces. Some Legal Problems, B.Y.I.L., 1961, 37, p. 430.

II. THE U.N. INTERNATIONAL RESPONSIBLITY
IN RELATION TO THE OTHER PARTIES INVOLVED

Who is responsible ?

The U.N. peace-keeping force is a subsidiary organ of the U.N., established under the provisions of the charter (Art. 22 or 29) (22), and consists of the commander and all personnel placed under his command by member states. Although the members of the force remain in their national service during the period of their assignment to the force, they are international personnel under the authority of U.N. and subject to the instructions of the commander through the chain of command. The U.N. Secretary-General has repeatedly stated that the U.N. force is necessarily under exclusive command of the U.N. (23) Appointed by and acting under the orders of the U.N., the commander of the force has full and direct command authority over the force. He is operationally responsible for the performance of all functions assigned to the force by the U.N., and for deployment and assignment of the troops placed at the disposal of the force. Also he has general responsibility for the good order and discipline of the force (24). The functions of the U.N. force are exclusively international, and the members of it have to discharge these functions and regulate their conduct with the interest of the U.N. only in view (25). The status agreements concerning UNEF, ONUC, UNFICYP envisages the member of those forces as an agent of the U.N. (Para. 30, 25, respectively).

Keeping in view the aforesaid character of the U.N. peace-keep-

---

(22) UNEF status agreement, op. cit., par. 23 ; UNFICYP agreement par. 23 ; Secretary General's Regulations issued to UNEF, regulations, 6, 7 (ST/SGB/UNEF/1, 20.2.1957) and to UNFICYP, Regulations, 6, 10, (ST/SGB/UNFICYP/1, 25.4.1964) ; see also, Dudly H. Chapman, 5, Ed. Legal Status of UNEF, Michigan Law Review, 57 ; 1958, p. 72.

(23) Secretary General's first report on the implementation of the Security Council resolution S/4387 of 14.7.1960 (doc. S/4389, p. 18) ; his aide-mémoire concerning certain questions pertaining to the role and functioning of UNFICYP, par. 4, (doc. S/5653, p. 2). See also, F. Seyersted, op. cit., pp. 406-412.

(24) Status agreements of UNEF has UNFICYP, par. 1 ; UNEF regulations 4,5 (a), 11, 12, 13, 16, 19 and UNFICYP regulations, 4, 5 (a), 11, 12, 13, 17,20.

(25) UNEF Regulations, 6 and UNFICYP Regulation 6.

ing force we come to the conclusion that the U.N. would be the proper respondent in a case of claims arising out of the official duties of the member of the Force (26), and also sometimes in cases of unlawful acts of the members outside their official duties (27). In the 3rd report on state's responsibility to the 23 Session, 1971, of the International Law commission Prof. Ago stated that a state would be responsible for unlawful acts or omissions committed by agents who were put under its disposal by another subject of international law, as long as those acts or omissions were committed in the exercise of a function of the state and under its exclusive authority (28).

Accordingly, the U.N. would be responsible for the unlawful activities carried out by the armed contingents put under its disposal by participating states as long as those activities are committed in the exercise of U.N. functions and under its real and exclusive operational control. As we have already seen, the U.N. in practice was always recognizing its responsibility — when it its legally engaged — and was paying reparations for damages caused by peace-keeping forces (29).

If it is established that the U.N. is responsible for the unlawful activities committed by its forces, one could ask : What is the legal position of other parties to the peace-keeping operation ? That is, if all the member states of the U.N., The States providing contingents and the host state can be held responsible?

As far as all THE MEMBER STATES (taken individually) of the U.N. are concerned, they cannot be held responsible for the activities carried out by U.N. force, since the U.N. has an objective legal personality of its own which is distinct from that of its individual member states. The force is operating under the full and exclusive command of the organization and not under the individual member states (30). The U.N. is internationally responsible — and not its individual member states — even vis-à-vis the non-member states which have not recognized it.

« Seidl-Hohenveldern in a study on international responsibility

---

(26) D.W. Bowett, op. cit., p. 245.
(27) See below, pp. 30-31.
(28) Year Book of International Law Commission, 1971, p. 248/S. (doc. A/CN/246/addendum 3).
(29) J. Salmon, op. cit., p. 429 S. ; Paul Reuter, Droit International Public Paris, 1973, 4e 6d., p. 175 ; Spaak-U-Thant agreement mentioned above, note 18, S.
(30) F. Seyersted, op. cit., p. 405,

vis-à-vis non-member states for the acts of international organizations, supports the view that intergovernmental organizations have no international personality in relation to non-member states which have not recognized them, and submits, as a logical consequence, that the international responsibility vis-à-vis these states vests in the several member states or in those member states which the non-member state concerned holds responsible for the act » But he reserves the position of the U.N. whose objective international personality has been recognized on special grounds, such as its duty to maintain international peace and security etc... (31).

Besides, if a non-member state brings a responsibility claim against the U.N. it is not feasible that the latest will evade its responsibility by pretending that it has no legal personality vis-à-vis the claimant state. Moreover, it is unimaginable that the claimant state will raise the point of U.N. such legal capacity because a claim of responsibility against the U.N. implies the recognition for it as an international subject having legal capacity to bear international responsibility for its acts.

The responsibility of a state in international law is measured by the actual degree of control which it may exercise within or out of its territory. That degree of control varies with every state as with every legal person. A state, or any international legal person, may be held responsible only to the extent that it has rights and duties which it is free to exercise (32).

The « amount of operational control or authority » which is exercised over the U.N. force can be a useful criterion to determine the responsibility of the various parties involved in the peace-keeping operation other than the U.N. such as the participating state and the host state.

A quick review of the precedents relating to the U.N. force leads to the idea that the U.N. international responsibility for activities carried out by these forces differs from one operation to another, according to the degree of operational control which was exercised by U.N. For example, the U.N. force in Korea was operating entirely under the United States command and not under that of the Organization

---

(31) F. Seyersted, Objective Internationl Personality of Intergovernmental Organizations, Copenhagen, 1963, p. 62.
(32) Eagleton, op. cit., p. 386.

or the participating states (33). Accordingly, the claims for illegal acts of warfare were made to the United States by the Soviet Union and the People's Republic of China, and the U.S. paid the reparations whereas the U.N. never accepted any responsibility (34).

We have already seen that the U.N. forces of UNEF, ONUC and UNFICIF were operating under the exclusive control and authority of the U.N. (35). In all these operations the participating states had no operational control over their contingents as they had placed them under the direct command of the U.N. and its exclusive orders, even though the sanctions for disobedience of U.N. orders can be applied only by the authorities of the respective participating state under its own national law (36).

It is difficult to agree with the views of Judge Koretsky in his dissident opinion in the case of certain expenses of the U.N. (37) or of Ross (38), which consider that the several contingents put under U.N. disposal should continue to be national armed forces of the participating states and should not be considered as U.N. forces. Such a literal interpretation of Art. 42, para. 2, of the charter, leads to unacceptable legal conclusions concerning responsibility. That is the participating states — and not the U.N. — bear international responsibility for unlawful activities carried out by their contingents, so long as these states do not exercise any kind of operational control over its contingents. Moreover, this view is contrary to the legal nature of the U.N. peace-keeping forces as subsidiary organ of the U.N. (39).

It is also difficult to agree with M.P. DE VISSCHER who considers both the U.N. and the participating state concurrently responsible for the unlawful acts of the U.N. force :

« dans l'état présent de la situation, le degré d'internationalisation des forces d'urgence des Nations Unies n'est pas tel que l'on

---

(33) F. Seyersted, op. cit., B.Y.I.L., 1961, p. 370.
(34) A. Di Blase, Evolution of U.N. System for Maintenance of Peace and Security. Cyclostyled report to the Center for Studies and Research of Hague Academy of International Law, 1975. Also F. Seyersted. op. cit., B.Y.I.L., 1961, p. 431 S.
(35) S. Seyersted, op. cit., B.Y.I.L., pp. 406-411 . Also, above, pp. 15-16.
(36) F. Seyersted, op. cit., 1961, p. 410.
(37) I.C.J. Reports, 1962, p. 257.
(38) F. Seyersted, op. cit., B.Y.I.L., 1961, p. 409.
(39) See above, pp. 15-17.

puisse dire que la personnalité de l'O.N.U. ait entièrement absorbé celle des Etats qui participent à la mise en oeuvre des mesures de sécurité collective. Aussi longtemps que les forces de l'O.N.U. seront formées de contingents 'nationaux' placés 'volontairement à la disposition du Secrétaire Général par des Etats Souverains et ne constitueront pas une véritable force supranationale, il faudra admettre la possibilité de mettre en cause la responsabilité propre de ces Etats concurremment avec celle de l'Organisation » (40)

Indeed, that the U.N. force is consisting of several national contingents provided by member states and the participating states are applying national sanctions over their contingents. But, as we have already illustrated above, these contingents are fully put under the U.N.'s exclusive 'substantive' (legislative and administrative) jurisdiction concerning operational matters. The participating state could be held responsible concurrently with the U.N. if the state was sharing with the U.N. the command or the control over its contingents in operational matters, and in that case the extent of such responsibility could be measured by the amount of its participation.

Also the non-member state which has not recognized the U.N. cannot free the U.N. from its responsibility for unlawful acts, and direct its reparation claim to the participating state whose contingent caused the unlawful damage. In such a case the non-member state cannot base its claim, against the aforesaid participating state, upon the general principle of law that « a creditor is not obliged to accept a new debtor in lieu of the old one (41). Because, when the U.N. bears responsibility for unlawful acts committed by a member of its force, this does not mean that the U.N. is a new debtor to replace the participating state whose contingent committed the unlawful act. As the national contingents were placed under the exclusive substantive jurisdiction of the U.N. in operational matters, these contingents became an organ of the U.N. and their unlawful acts are imputable to it. Consequently, the U.N. continue to be both the old debtor and the new one (42).

As FOR THE HOST STATE, its international responsibility is

(40) Paul De Visscher, op. cit., p. 136.
(41) F. Seyersted, Objective International Personality, op. cit., p. 62 S.
(42) F. Seyersted, U.N. Forces, op. cit., B.Y.I.L., 1961, p. 410.

determined and measured by the degree of operational control exercised over the peace-keeping force (43). The host state cannot be held responsible for the unlawful act committed by the U.N. force operating in its territory, so long as it does not possess any jurisdiction over this force in operational matters. The members of the force are immune from the criminal jurisdiction of the host state and also from its civil jurisdiction in matters related to their official duties (44).

Nevertheless, the host state may bear international responsibility — in addition to the U.N. responsibility — for unlawful acts of the U.N. force if it commits an act of complicity in the aforesaid unlawful act, i.e., to instigate or facilitate its commital. In such a case the host state will have its own responsibility separate and distinct from that of the U.N. i.e. The host state will become responsible for its own action, and it cannot seek protection of the umbrella of U.N. responsibility (45).

Besides, the non-member state which has not recognized the U.N. cannot held the host state responsible on the plea that « no new debtor may be imposed without the consent of the creditor ». As the host state cannot be held responsible for all the acts performed on its territory, but only for such acts which its organs ought to and could have prevented (46).

As a result of the above cited discussions we come to the conclusion that international responsibility for unlawful acts of the U.N. peace-keeping force rests exclusively with the United Nations, in the same manner as for other organs of the Organization (47).

---

(43) We should keep in mind the special character of the U.N. operation in Korea, and also the position of the host state in that case as its armed forces were brought under the United States Command at an early stage. F. Seyersted, op. cit., B.Y.I.L., 1961, pp. 362-370, 430 S.

(44) This is clearly reflected in the Status Agreements and Secretary General's Regulations concerning, UNEF, ONUC, ONUC, UNFICYP ; as well as in Secretary General's Reports to the General Assembly (doc. A/3302, 6.11.1956) and to the Security Council (doc. S/4389, 18.7.1960) ; U.N. Charter (Art. 103-105) ; and the Convention on the Privileges and Immunities. See also, F. Seyersted, op. cit., B.Y.I.L., p. 428.

(45) Jean-Pierre Ritter, op. cit., pp. 444-445 ; F. Seyersted, Objective International Personality, op. cit., p. 69.

(46) F. Seyersted, Objective International Personality, op. cit., pp. 67, 70, 73.

(47) F. Seyersted, U.N. Forces, B.Y.I.L., op. cit., p. 429.

After we have discussed the principle of the U.N. responsibility and its position vis-à-vis all the other parties involved in responsibility claim, we shall procede to discuss to what extent the principles' of international law of responsibility regarding inter-state relations could be applied to the U.N. peace-keeping operations.

III. THE APPLICABILITY OF THE GENERAL RULES OF INTERNATIONAL LAW OF RESPONSIBILITY TO THE U.N. FOR ACTIVITIES CARRIED OUT BY ITS FORCES

Whenever a duty established by any rule of international law has been breached by an act or an omission, a new legal relationship automatically comes into existence. This relationship is established between the subject to which the act is imputable, who must « respond » by making adequate reparation, and the subject who has a claim to reparation because of the breach of duty (48).

The general rules of international law of responsibility are supposed to be applied to responsibility claims in inter-state relations. Such rules deal with international entities which can possess a full legal capacity under international law.

The international responsibility is derived from, and is limited to the extent of the legal capacity of the international person. Recognized as international person, the U.N. is not a super state or even a state. Then the extent of its legal capacity must be different from that of states in such a way that influences its field of responsibility. Moreover, the U.N. has a different structure and procedures which require the settlement of claims against it in a fashion different from that to which states are accustomed. The U.N. is not organized in the same way as is a state, it does not perform the same functions as does a state, and procedures developed to fit states do not fit so well its unique character (49).

Accordingly, there is a general presumption that the principles concerning international responsibility in inter-state relations apply 'mutatis mutandi', though certain adjustments are necessary because of the inherent character of the U.N. (50).

---

(48) Max Sorensen, Manual of Public International Law, London, 1968, p. 533 ; P.C.I.J., Ser. A, 1928, No. 17, p. 29 ; I.C.J. Reports, 1949, pp. 23-24.
(49) Eableton, op. cit., pp. 401-403.
(50) Max Sorenson, op. cit., p. 595.

We proceed now to discuss the constituent elements of U.N. international responsibility, and the system of settlement of claims against the U.N. for activities carried out by its forces.

A) THE CONSTITUENT ELEMENTS OF U.N. INTERNATIONAL RESPONSIBILITY

The elements essential to the establishment of International Responsibility are : 1) Unlawful act or omission. 2) Imputability. 3) Damage. But we are going to handle the first two elements because of their special importance in relation to the present study. Afterwards, it will be necessary to discuss the applicability of the rule of exhaustion of local remedies to the U.N. responsibility claims.

1) UNLAWFUL ACT OR OMISSION :

The breach of any international obligation established by a rule of international law may engage the U.N. responsibility. This essential element of the U.N. responsibility is to be seen in an objective sense, i.e., without the requirement of the fault or guilt of the individual whose conduct is ascribed to the U.N. (51). The U.N. may be held responsible for the unlawful acts of the member of its force even if such acts were « bona fide » (52) or were « ultra vires » (53).

As the U.N. peace-keeping operation involves military issues, the force has to respect the principles and spirit of the general international conventions applicable to the conduct of military personnel (54). In the view of « La Commission d'étude instituée par la Ligue Belge pour la Défense des Droits de l'Homme » the U.N. is subject to all humanitarian rules of the Laws and Customs of war and must respect human rights as well as the general principles of the Law recognized by civilized nations (55). Any violation of the aforesaid obligations may involve the U.N. responsibility (56). The principle, established by Art. 3 of the 4th convention of The Hague, 1907 relating to the rules of land war, of the absolute responsibility of the state for all the unlawful acts of its forces is also applicable to the

---

(51) Sorenson, op. cit., p. 535 S. ; See also : Stefan Glaser, Infraction International, Paris, 1957, p. 114, Note 10.
(52) Sorenson, op. cit., pp. 535-536.
(53) I.C.J. Reports, 1962, p. 168.
(54) Regulations of UNEF, ONUC and UNFICYP, Art. 44, 43, 40 respectively.
(55) Paul De Visscher, op. cit., pp. 137-138.
(56) Bowett, op. cit., p. 247.

U.N. to the extent of its operational control or authority over its force. The U.N. may be held responsible for the unlawful acts of a member of the force even if such acts were committed outside of the course of his official duties (57). We have already mentioned the instance when the U.N. compensated for an unlawful act of shooting committed by a member of its force where no official function or superior order required him to shoot (58).

The U.N. will not bear responsibility for damages caused by its lawful military operations or arising from military necessity (59). On the other hand, the U.N. accepted its responsibility for all damages which were not justified by any military necessity such as : destructions without necessity, pillage, murder, executing persons without trial, imprisonments, arbitrary expulsions and irregular requisitions etc... (60). In his letter dated 20-2-1965 adressed to the Belgian minister M.P.H. Spaak, U-Thant, the Secretary General of the U.N., declared that : « It has stated that it would not evade responsibility where it was established that the United Nations agents had in fact caused unjustifiable damage to innocent parties » (61).

With the same spirit of the classic international law of responsibility, the U.N. excluded the case of legitimate defence from the ambit of its responsibility (62).

U-Thant also summarized the general principles which determine the scope of the U.N. responsibility for activities carried out by U.N. peace-keeping force as follows :

> « It has always been the policy of the United Nations, acting through the Secretary-General, to compensate individuals who have suffered damages for which the Organization was legally liable. This policy is in keeping with generally recognized legal

---

(57) Jean-Pierre Queneudec, La Responsabilité Internationale de l'Etat pour les Fautes Personnelles de ses Agents, Paris, 1966, pp. 34-35, 187.

(58) Seyersted, U.N. Forces, B.Y.I.L., op. cit., p. 420.

(59) Bowett, op. cit., p. 247 ; Spaak and U-Thant agreement of 20.2.1965, op. cit. Also see letter addressed to Morosov the Representative of U.S.S.R. to the U.N. from the Secretary General on 6.8.1975, quoted by R. Simmonds, Legal Problems arising from the U.N. Military Operations in the Congo. The Hague, 1968, pp. 240-241. Also see J. Salmon, op. cit., p. 480 and for the determination of « military necessity », Stefan Glaser, op. cit., pp. 86-88.

(60) Salmon, op. cit., p. 481.

(61) U.N. Security Council Doc. S/6597.

(62) Salmon, op. cit., p. 482.

principles and with the convention on Privileges and Immunities of the United Nations. In addition, in regard to the United Nations activities in the Congo, it is reinforced by the principles set forth in the international conventions concerning the protection of the life and property of civilian population during hostilities as well as by considerations of equity and humanity which the United Nations cannot ignore » (63).

Accordingly, the U.N. responsibility could sometimes be based upon the considerations of equity and humanity where no unlawful act could be imputed to it. In special circumstances the principles of equity and humanity may serve as a base for the U.N. obligation to pay reparation to the injured parties.

During a fight which took place in Elizabethville on December 1961, three members of Red Cross International Committee were later found killed. The appointed enquiry Commission established that the bullet which had killed the three victims were not of the type used by the Katangese Forces at the time, but the commission itself studiously refrained from passing upon the question of who was responsible. In spite of this, the U.N., without accepting any legal or financial obligation, made a lump some payment to the International Committee of the Red Cross (64).

2) THE IMPUTABILITY OF THE UNLAWFUL ACT TO THE U.N. :

The international responsibility of the U.N. may be involved only if the unlawful act, which caused the damage, is imputable to the Organization. To determine whether an unlawful act is imputable to the U.N., the fundamental rule of international law of responsibility in inter-state relations should be applied i.e. the international responsibility should be borne by state whose organ or agent had committed the unlawful act (65). The U.N. may be held responsible for the unlawful act committed by a member of its force as long as this

---

(63) Simmonds, op. cit., p. 240.
(64) Simmonds, op. cit., p. 190. See also U-Thant's letter to Belgian Minister of Foreign Affaires dated 5.7.1965, quoted by Salmon, op. cit., p. 479. « L'Organisation ne saurait se soustraire et ne soustraira pas-à sa responsabilité morale s'il est établi que ces agents de l'O.N.U. ont effectivement fait subir un préjudice à des innocents ».
(65) Ritter, op. cit., p. 441.

member could be considered acting as an organ or agent of the U.N., i.e., when the involved person is acting upon the U.N. instructions and placed under its control (66).

According F. SEYERSTED, the national contingents become an organ of the U.N. « If and to the extent the states providing them have placed them under the authority of the Organization (or under a commander appointed by and taking his orders from it) and have thereby ceded their organic jurisdiction over them » (67).   The U.N. should not be held responsible for activities carried out by a member state using its own organs and under its full organic jurisdiction and control, even if those activities were in application of a decision took by the U.N., as was the case in Korea for instance (68).   The U.N. has accepted responsibility only in respect of actions under its authority. Accordingly, it assumed no responsibility in respect of aircraft employed by states providing contingents for the purpose of transporting supplementary national supplies to their contingents in Congo (69). Also, the U.N. excluded from the scope of its responsibility unlawful acts of persons who were not members of its force in Congo such as the acts of Katangese mercenaries, the troops of national army of Congo and the Balubese (70).

To sum up, if the U.N. Force is operating under its operational command or authority, in such a case the unlawful act committed by a member of the force may be imputable to the U.N. and it should be held responsible for such acts to the same extent and conditions as in the case of a state which has to own responsibility for activities carried out by one of its organs or agents (71).

3 THE RULE OF EXHAUSTION OF LOCAL REMEDIES :

This rule is only relevant to the claim made by states in the exercise of their right of diplomatic protection of their nationals and in respect of an injury to one of them.   It cannot be applied when the claim is made in respect of direct injury to the state itself because states are not subject to the jurisdiction of Foreign Courts.

---

(66) Eagleton, op. cit., p. 390.
(67) Quoted by Ritter, op. cit., p. 442, Note 27. See also, Ibid., p. 444.
(68) See above, p. 20 and Note 43.
(69) Seyrested, U.N. Forces, op. cit., p. 421.
(70) Salmon, op. cit., p. 482.
(71) Ritter, op. cit., p. 441. See also, Paul Reuter, op. cit., p. 184.

The function of the rule is to give the respondent state the opportunity to redress the committed violation by its own means, within
the framework of its own domestic legal system. The foundation
of this rule lies in the fact that the sovereignty and jurisdiction competent to deal with the question through its local courts must be
respected. If an unlawful act occurs within a state, the injured individual will have to resort to the local remedies available and he would
be expected to have exhausted them, before his state would be allowed
to intervene in his behalf. The rule of exhaustion of local remedies
cannot be applied if there are actually no local remedies to exhaust
or when the existing remedies are « obviously futile » or « manifestly
ineffective » (72).

As far as the U.N. responsibility is involved, Clyd Eagleton is
of the view that it is difficult to apply the requirement of the exhaustion of local remedies since the U.N. « has no courts and none of
the usual administrative procedures which states have for the protection of aliens; and it has so little need for such agencies that it does
not seem worthwhile to establish them for the limited number of
claims which might be advanced » (73). He came to the conclusion
that « any claim made against the U.N. would necessarily have to
by-pass the rule of local redress and be presented as a direct diplomatic claim » (74).

Nevertheless, such a view does not prevent the applicability of
the rule of exhaustion of local remedies so far as the U.N. have
established available procedures through which the claimant individual
may make his claims against the U.N. (75). The U.N. may establish
judicial, administrative or arbitral procedures for the settlement of
claims made by individuals against it. The question to be discussed

in this connection is whether such procedures could be considered as
local remedies in inter-state relations.

In conformity with section 29 of the Convention on the Privileges
and Immunities of the U.N., the United Nations makes provisions for
appropriate mode of settlement of disputes envisaged in this section.
Though the agreements, concluded between the U.N. on the one
hand and the participating and host states on the other hand, concern-

---

(72) Sorenson, op. cit., pp. 582 S.
(73) Eagleton, op. cit., p. 394 S and pp. 402-406.
(74) Eagleton, op. cit., p. 412.
(75) Ritter, op. cit., pp. 454-455 ; Bowett, op. cit., pp. 247-248.

ing U.N. peace-keeping operations UNEF, ONUC, UNFICYP, and
the relevant Secretary-General's regulations, the U.N. established
such procedures through which the responsibility claims should be
settled. Accordingly, the procedures established by the U.N. in this
regard should be considered as local remedies which must be exhausted before the individual's state could be allowed to interpose a claim
in his behalf. Indeed, such remedies are not identical to those local
procedures available within a state, because the U.N. is not a state
but only an international organization. The U.N.'s unique character,
therefore, gives a special form to its local remedies. Apart from this
adjustment of the shape of the internal procedures as local redress,
the rule of the exhaustion of local remedies is applied to the U.N. to
the same extent (and with the same exceptions) as in inter-state
relations. The U.N. as an organization, representing worldwide interests, has a dignity that must be respected by giving it the opportunity
to make reparations through its own available procedures, before
bringing international claim against it.

.. B) THE SYSTEM OF SETTLEMENT OF DISPUTES AGAINST THE U.N. FOR ACTIVITIES CARRIED OUT BY ITS FORCES

The U.N. enjoys in the territory of each of its members such
privileges and immunities as are necessary for fulfilment of its purposes (Art. 105 of the Charter). In conformity with section 29 of the
Convention of the Privileges and Immunities of 13-2-1946 the U.N.
is entitled to make provisions for the appropriate modes of settlement
of disputes of private law character which may arise against it, and
also other disputes involving one of its officials who by reason of his
official position enjoys immunity. The U.N. peace-keeping force,
as subsidiary organ of the U.N., will be subject to the aforesaid principles. The modes of settlement of claims arising out of activities
carried out by such a force will be made by the U.N. itself. Consequently, the U.N. made several provisions for the modes of settlement of disputes concerning each of its peace-keeping operations (76).
Those modes of settlement were enlisted in the respective status
agreements with the host state, agreements with states providing contingents to the force and in the regulations issued by the Secretary
General for each of the U.N. Force.

---

(76) UNEF, ONUC and UNFICYP status agreement, op. cit., par. 38-40, 10,
11, 46, 38-40 respectively.

« B. Amrallah — The International Responsibility » 77

From a quick review of the abovesaid provisions we come across certain interesting facts :   First, the modes of settlement of disputes made by the U.N. are not quite identical in all the U.N. peace-keeping operations.   We observe some difference in this connection whose source may be traced to the way of financing the respective peace-keeping operation.   For example, since the U.N. was heavily committed to the financial support of the Congo, there was no need of making provisions in the status agreement of ONUC for the modes of settlement of disputes of private law character between the U.N. and the Congo.   There was no need to establish lengthy procedures for the settlement of such disputes which would finally mean nothing more than a book-keeping exercise with the figures showing what financial assistance had been provided to the Congo (77). On the other hand, when the UNFICYP was not financed under the regular budget of the U.N. but partly by the participating states, we were faced by such provision in paragraph 16 of the UNFICYP Regulations providing that... « within the limits of available voluntary contributions he (The Secretary-General) shall make provisions for the settlement of any claims arising with respect to the force that are not settled by the Governments providing contingents or the Government of Cyprus » (78). Also, as far as U.N. force in Korea was concerned, we have already seen that it was the U.S. and not the United Nations, who paid the preparations for unlawful acts committed by the force (79) Secondly : We may observe that the provision made by the U.N for settlement of disputes involving the members of the force are made having regard to the special functions of the force and the interests of the U.N. and not keeping in view the personal benefit of those members (80).   Accordingly, the members of the force are not entitled to forego the arrangements envisaged in the respective provisions or to accept other jurisdiction not made by the U.N.

We shall proceed on presenting the modes of settlement of disputes which arise out of the peace-keeping activities.   I propose to deal with them under two heads : Claims of private law character and those of criminal law.

---

(77) Bowett, op. cit., p. 243 ; and in the same sense, Simmonds, op. cit., p. 232.
(78) ST/SGB/UNFICYP/6, op. cit.
(79) See above, p. 20.
(80) UNEF, ONUC, UNFICYP status agreements, op. cit., par. 10, 11, 12 respectively.

1) CLAIMS OF PRIVATE LAW

a) Claims between the U.N. and the Host State :

The host state may bring claims against the U.N. for unlawful acts which caused a direct damage to it in order to obtain reparations from the U.N. As we have already mentioned that in ONUC status agreement there were no provisions dealing with such sort of claim (81). Such claims are to be settled in conformity with section 29 of the Convention on the Privileges and Immunities of the U.N.

As for the modes established by the UNEF and UNFICYP, we observe that these modes were identical in both the status agreements. In conformity with para. 38 of the two aforesaid agreements, the claims of private law character made by the host state against the U.N. Force or one of its members, should be settled by a claim Commission. This commission is composed of two members and a chairman. One member is appointed by the Secretary-General, the other by the host state and the chairman jointly by the Secretary-General and the Government of the host state. If the Secretary-General and the host state fail to agree on the appointment of a chairman, the President of the ICJ shall be asked by either to make the appointment. An award made by the claims commission against the force or a member thereof, shall be notified to the Commander to make satisfaction (82).

We should keep in mind the reservation above cited relating to regulation 16 of the UNFICYP (83). Such reservation is only relevant to the UNFICYP and it must be seen in the light of the way of financing this Force. According to par. 6 of the Security Council resolution of March 4, 1964 (S/5575) the Council recommended that all costs pertaining to the Force are to be met, in a manner agreed upon by them, by the Governments providing contingents and by the Government of Cyprus. The Secretary-General may also accept voluntary contributions for this purpose. Accordingly, the obligation of the commander of UNFICYP to make satisfaction as provided for in par. 38 (b) of the status agreements is limited to the extent that funds are available to him for this purpose. The participating states and

---

(81) See above, pp. 41-42.
(82) Par. 38 (b) of each UNEF and UNFICYP status agreements, op. cit., see also Secretary General's Regulations to UNEF and UNFICYP, op. cit., regulation 34 (d) and 29 (d) respectively.
(83) See above, pp. 41-42.

the host state are therefore asked to get in agreement upon the funds to be fixed to cover the reparations decided by the Claims Commission.

All differences between the U.N. and the Government of the host state arising out of the interpretation or application of the respective status agreement, which involve a question of principle, concerning the Convention on the Privileges and Immunities of the U.N. shall be referred to the ICJ in accordance with section 30 of that Convention, unless it is agreed upon by the parties to have recourse to another mode of settlement (84).

All other disputes between the U.N. and the Government of the host state concerning the interpretation or application of these arrangements which are not settled by negotiation or other agreed mode of settlement shall be referred for final settlement to a tribunal of three arbitrators, one to be named by the Secretary-General of the United Nations, one by the Government of the host state and an umpire to be chosen jointly by the Secretary-General and the said Government. If the two parties fail to agree on the appointment of the umpire within one month of the proposal of arbitration by one of the parties, the President of the International Court of Justice shall be asked by either party to appoint the umpire. Should a vacancy occur for any reason, the vacancy shall be filled within thirty days by the same method laid down for the original appointment. The Tribunal shall come into existence upon the appointment of the umpire and at least one of the other members of the tribunal. Two members of the tribunal shall constitute a quorum for the performance of its functions, and for all deliberations and decisions of the tribunal a favourable vote of two members shall be sufficient (85).

b) **Claims between the U.N. and individuals :**

The U.N. force is not subject to the jurisdiction of the local courts. In conformity with section 29 of the Convention on the Privileges and Immunities, the U.N. is entitled to make provisions for the appropriate mode of settlement of disputes or claims, of a private

---

(84) Par. 39 of each UNEF and UNFICYP status agreements, op. cit., also section 30 of the Convention on the Privileges and Immunities of the U.N., op. cit.

(85) UNEF, ONUC and UNFICYP status agreements, op. cit., par, 40, 46, 40 respectively.

law character, to which it is a party, other than those covered in the
respective status agreements (86).   Also, a member of the force may
commit an unlawful act or omission which may result in a damage
to an individual.   The status agreements between the U.N. and the
host state determined the modes of settlement of claims arising out
of such cases.   The way of settlement of such claims is determined
by the manner in which the act of the member of the force was
related to his official duties.   We are more concerned with the claims
based upon an act of the member of the force relating to his official
duties, because only such acts are imputable to the U.N. and may
engage its responsibility.

Unlike ONUC agreement, the UNEF and UNFICYP agreements
in par. 38 (b) (i), mention the citizen of the host state (and not its
resident) as a claimant against a member of the force (87).   I am of
the view that the procedures envisaged in these agreements for the
host state's citizen are applicable to the residents of that state as
well. The aforesaid provisions are related to settlement of disputes
which arise out of acts committed on the territory of the host state.
Such procedures, established by both U.N. and the host state in status
agreement, are applicable to all individuals residing in the host state
in conformity with the general rule of territoriality of the law of procedures.

(i)   **Claims for official acts :**

As far as the ONUC was concerned, the U.N. was supposed to
settle the dispute by negotiation or any other method agreed upon
between the parties.   If it was not found possible to arrive at an
agreement in this manner, the matter would be submitted to arbitration at the request of either party (88).   The special representative
of the Secretary-General would arrange for any arbitral procedure
necessary for the hearing and deciding such disputes under the provisions of par. 10, of the agreement (89).

As for UNEF and UNFICYP, the claims for official acts were
settled by the claim commission in the same ways as the claims between the host state and the U.N. were settled (90).

---

(86) Par. 38 (a) of each UNEF and UNFICYP status agreements.
(87) Ibid., par. 12 (a).
(88) ONUC status agreement, op. cit., par. 10 (b).
(89) Ibid., par. 11.
(90) See above, pp. 43-46.

It is essential to determine whether or not the act of the member of the force was related to his official duties. As far as UNEF and UNFICYP is concerned, the commander of the force was entitled to certify on that point (91). In case of difference of opinion concerning the nature of the committed act and how far it was related to the member's official duties, the issue should be decided on the basis of the interpretation of the term « official duties » mentioned in the respective status agreement and should be in accordance with the procedure laid down therein (92).

(ii) **Claims for non-official acts :**

The ONUC agreement determined the way of settlement of such claims in its par. 10 (c) which reads :

> « If evidence is submitted of the existence of an obligation at civil law binding upon or in favour of a member of the force or an official serving under the United Nations in the Congo or a dependant of such member of the force or official, and arising out of his presence in the Congo but not related to his official duties, the United Nations shall use its good offices to assist the parties in arriving at a settlement. If the dispute cannot be settled in this manner or by any other agreed mode of settlement, it shall be submitted to arbitration at the request of either Party ».

Also, par. 11 of the agreement was to be applied as we have already mentioned above (93).

As far as the UNEF and UNFICYP were concerned, the members of those forces were subjected to the civil jurisdiction concerning their non-official acts of private Law character (94). Nevertheless, the claimant had the choice to have his claim dealt with the claims commission in accordance with par. 38 (b) of the aforesaid agree-

---

(91) UNEF and UNFICYP status agreements, par. 13 of each.
We must keep in mind that no akin provision was needed in ONUC agreement because the members of that force were not subjected to the jurisdiction of local Courts of the host state, without making distinction between official and non-official acts.

(92) See above, pp. 45-46.

(93) See above, pp. 48-49.

(94) UNEF and UNFICYP status agreements, par. 12 (b) of each.

ments (95). Where a claim was adjudicated or an award was made in favour of the claimant, by a court of the host state or by the claims commission under par. 38 (b), was not satisfied, the Government of the host state could seek the good offices of the Secretary-General to obtain satisfaction (96).

2) CLAIMS OF CRIMINAL LAW

As regards the the criminal offences which might be committed by members of the force in the host state, it may be useful to remember that such members were subject to the exclusive jurisdiction of their respective national states (97).

---

(95) Ibid., par. 12 (c).
(96) Ibid.
(97) UNEF, ONUC and UNFICYP status agreements, par. 11, 9, 11, respectively.

[17]

UN PEACEKEEPING OPERATIONS: APPLICABILITY OF INTERNATIONAL HUMANITARIAN LAW AND RESPONSIBILITY FOR OPERATIONS-RELATED DAMAGE

DAPHNA SHRAGA

In the five decades that followed the Korea operation, where for the first time the United Nations commander agreed, at the request of the International Committee of the Red Cross (ICRC), to abide by the humanitarian provisions of the Geneva Conventions, few UN operations lent themselves to the applicability of international humanitarian law.

By the mid-1990s, however, when fatalities sustained by UN forces dramatically increased, and the international community was devising means to enhance the safety and security of UN and associated personnel, the United Nations Organization was confronting its own responsibility for both combat-related and ordinary operational activities of UN forces. The excesses committed by members of UN operations in situations of armed conflict,[1] and the extent of property damage and personal injury caused by them in their ordinary operational activities, prompted the United Nations to reaffirm the applicability of international humanitarian law to UN forces and redefine the international responsibility of the Organization and its third-party liability for operations-related damage.

An internal review of the scope of UN responsibility for peacekeeping activities resulted in the promulgation of the Secretary-General's Bulletin on the Observance by United Nations Forces of International Humanitarian Law,[2] and the establishment of principles of third-party liability of the Organization within a range of temporal and financial limitations. Unrelated as these two initiatives may have been in practice, together they represent the UN doctrine of the Organization's international responsibility for activities of UN forces under international humanitarian law and the general principles of the laws of tort.

I. RESPONSIBILITY FOR COMBAT-RELATED ACTIVITIES

Applicability of International Humanitarian Law to UN Forces

For nearly half a century, the United Nations was disinclined to recognize the applicability of international humanitarian law to UN forces or to abide formally by its provisions.[3] For the

---

[1] On violations of human rights and international humanitarian law committed by members of UN forces in the Congo and Somalia, see R. SIMMONDS, LEGAL PROBLEMS ARISING FROM THE UNITED NATIONS MILITARY OPERATIONS IN THE CONGO 188–91 (1968); FINN SEYERSTED, UNITED NATIONS FORCES IN THE LAW OF PEACE AND WAR 189–97 (1966); Robert Fox & Agence France-Presse, *Belgian UN troops admit to "roasting" Somali boy*, DAILY TELEGRAPH (London), June 24, 1997, at 15; Alex de Waal, *A Brutal Peace*, GUARDIAN, Oct. 30, 1997, at 21; Mark Huband, *UN Forces Deny Somali Detainees Legal Rights*, GUARDIAN, Sept. 25, 1993, at 14; Keith B. Richburg, *Somalis' Imprisonment Poses Questions about U.N. Role*, WASH. POST, Nov. 7, 1993, at A45; Report of the Commission of Inquiry established pursuant to Security Council resolution 885 (1993) to investigate armed attacks on UNOSOM II personnel which led to casualties among them, UN Doc. S/1994/653, paras. 231, 236, 237; Report of the expert of the Secretary-General, Ms. Graça Machel, submitted pursuant to General Assembly resolution 48/157, UN Doc. A/51/306, para. 98 (1996).

[2] Bulletin on the Observance by United Nations Forces of International Humanitarian Law, UN Doc. ST/SGB/1999/13 (1999), *reprinted in* 38 ILM 1656 (1999) [hereinafter Bulletin].

[3] On the applicability of international humanitarian law to UN forces, see SEYERSTED, *supra* note 1, at 178–220; SIMMONDS, *supra* note 1, at 168–96; Paul De Visscher, *Les Conditions d'application des lois de la guerre aux opérations militaires des Nations Unies*, [1971] 1 ANNUAIRE DE L'INSTITUT DE DROIT INTERNATIONAL 1; Resolution I, Conditions of Application of Humanitarian Rules of Armed Conflict to Hostilities in Which United Nations Forces May Be Engaged, *in id.* at 465; Yves Sandoz, *L'Application du droit humanitaire par les forces armées de l'Organisation des Nations Unies*, INT'L REV. RED CROSS, NO. 206, Sept.–Oct. 1978, at 274; Dietrich Schindler, *United Nations Forces and International*

first time, in 1993, it undertook in the Agreement on the Status of the United Nations Assistance Mission for Rwanda to ensure that UN forces would conduct their operations there with full respect for the *principles and spirit* of the general conventions applicable to the conduct of military personnel, including the four Geneva Conventions of 1949, their two Additional Protocols of 1977, and the Hague Convention on the Protection of Cultural Property in the Event of Armed Conflict of 1954.[4] The United Nations further undertook to ensure that members of UN operations would be fully acquainted with the principles and spirit of the above-mentioned international instruments.[5]

No sooner had it been introduced in the status of forces agreements than the "principles and spirit" clause proved inadequate and too abstract to guide members of peacekeeping operations on questions of practical application. In the operations of the United Nations Protection Force and the United Nations Operation in Somalia, questions concerning the legal status of UN forces taken hostage, that of combatants or other detainees held by UN peacekeepers, the use of certain types of weapons, and the feigning of the UN distinctive emblem and military insignia demanded clear answers. The need to concretize the broad formula of "principles and spirit" had thus become acute.

Against this background, in 1995 the ICRC initiated a series of meetings of experts to discuss the applicability of international humanitarian law to UN forces with the aim of drawing up a list of core rules of international humanitarian law applicable to peacekeeping operations and enforcement actions, to be taught in training programs for state-contributed troops. The text elaborated by the group of experts was subsequently submitted by the ICRC to the Office of Legal Affairs of the UN Secretariat, and formed the basis of what was later to become the above-mentioned Secretary-General's Bulletin.

Bulletin on the Observance by United Nations Forces of International Humanitarian Law

The main provisions. In compliance with his obligation under the status of forces agreements concluded after 1993 to acquaint members of UN operations with the principles and rules of international humanitarian law, on August 6, 1999, the Secretary-General promulgated the

---

Humanitarian Law, in STUDIES AND ESSAYS ON INTERNATIONAL HUMANITARIAN LAW AND RED CROSS PRINCIPLES IN HONOUR OF JEAN PICTET 521 (Christophe Swinarski ed., 1984); Umesh Palwankar, *Applicability of International Humanitarian Law to United Nations Peacekeeping Forces,* INT'L REV. RED CROSS, NO. 294, May–June 1993, at 227; CLAUDE EMANUELLI, LES ACTIONS MILITAIRES DE L'ONU ET LE DROIT INTERNATIONAL HUMANITAIRE (1995); Richard D. Glick, *Lip Service to the Laws of War: Humanitarian Law and United Nations Armed Forces,* 17 MICH. J. INT'L L. 53 (1995); Christopher Greenwood, *Protection of Peacekeepers: The Legal Regime,* 7 DUKE J. COMP. & INT'L L. 185 (1996); Daphna Shraga, *The United Nations as an Actor Bound by International Humanitarian Law, in* THE UNITED NATIONS AND INTERNATIONAL HUMANITARIAN LAW 11 (Actes du Colloque International de l'Université de Genève, 1996); HILAIRE MCCOUBREY & NIGEL D. WHITE, THE BLUE HELMETS: LEGAL REGULATION OF UNITED NATIONS MILITARY OPERATIONS (1996); Brian D. Tittemore, *Belligerents in Blue Helmets: Applying International Humanitarian Law to United Nations Peace Operations,* 33 STAN. J. INT'L L. 61 (1997).

[4] Convention for the Amelioration of the Condition of the Wounded and Sick in Armed Forces in the Field, Aug. 12, 1949, 6 UST 3114, 75 UNTS 31; Convention for the Amelioration of the Condition of the Wounded, Sick, and Shipwrecked Members of Armed Forces at Sea, Aug. 12, 1949, 6 UST 3217, 75 UNTS 85; Convention Relative to the Treatment of Prisoners of War, Aug. 12, 1949, 6 UST 3316, 75 UNTS 135 [hereinafter Third Geneva Convention]; Convention Relative to the Protection of Civilian Persons in Time of War, Aug. 12, 1949, 6 UST 3516, 75 UNTS 287; Protocol Additional to the Geneva Conventions of 12 August 1949, and Relating to the Protection of Victims of International Armed Conflicts, *opened for signature* Dec. 12, 1977, 1125 UNTS 3 [hereinafter Protocol I]; Protocol Additional to the Geneva Conventions of 12 August 1949, and Relating to the Protection of Victims of Non-International Armed Conflicts, *opened for signature* Dec. 12, 1977, 1125 UNTS 609; Convention for the Protection of Cultural Property in the Event of Armed Conflict, May 14, 1954, 249 UNTS 240.

[5] Agreement on the Status of the United Nations Assistance Mission for Rwanda, Nov. 5, 1993, UN-Rwanda, Art. 7, 1748 UNTS (forthcoming). An identical provision was subsequently inserted in the following agreements: Agreement on the Status of the United Nations Mission in Haiti, Mar. 15, 1995, UN-Haiti, Art. 7, 1861 UNTS 249; Agreement on the Status of the United Nations Peacekeeping Operation in Angola, May 3, 1995, UN-Angola, 1864 UNTS (forthcoming); Agreement between the United Nations and the Government of the Republic of Croatia, May 15, 1995, *id.*; Agreement on the Status of the United Nations Interim Force in Lebanon, Dec. 15, 1995, UN-Leb., 1901 UNTS (forthcoming); Agreement concerning the Status of the United Nations Mission in Western Sahara, Feb. 11, 1999, UN-Morocco (similar agreements were concluded with Algeria and Mauritania on Nov. 3 and 20, 1998, respectively).

Bulletin on the Observance by United Nations Forces of International Humanitarian Law. It was to enter into force on August 12, 1999, fifty years to the day after the conclusion of the four Geneva Conventions.

Designed to be the core regulations for UN forces in situations of armed conflict, the instructions in the Bulletin reflect the quintessential and most fundamental principles of the laws and customs of war, those embodied in the Geneva Conventions and their Additional Protocols and the 1954 Convention on the Protection of Cultural Property. In a short, succinct, and simplified document of nine sections in all, the Secretary-General's Bulletin sets out the principles and rules governing protection of the civilian population in the UN area of operation and in the area controlled by the other party;[6] means and methods of combat;[7] treatment of civilians and persons *hors de combat,* and women[8] and children, in particular;[9] treatment of detained members of the armed forces and other persons taking no part in hostilities, in accordance with the relevant provisions of the Third Geneva Convention and without prejudice to their status as prisoners of war;[10] treatment of the wounded and sick; protection of medical and relief personnel; and collection and identification of the dead left on the battlefield.[11]

In concretizing the "principles and spirit" of the Geneva Conventions and their Additional Protocols, the Secretary-General did not consider himself necessarily constrained by the customary international law provisions of the Conventions and Protocols as the lowest common denominator by which all national contingents would otherwise be bound.[12] Provisions such as the prohibitions on using methods of warfare intended to cause widespread, long-term, and severe damage to the natural environment,[13] rendering useless objects indispensable to the survival of the civilian population,[14] and causing the release of dangerous forces with consequent severe losses among the civilian population[15] were thus included in the Bulletin regardless of their conventional international law nature.[16] Given their importance and the devastating effect that violating them could wreak on the natural environment and the civilian population at large, their inclusion amounted above all to an undertaking to abide by the highest standard of conduct within the general consensus of states.

Scope of application and legally binding effect. The instructions for UN forces are applicable to UN operations conducted under UN command and control. They are not, as such, applicable to UN-authorized operations conducted under national or regional command and control; the responsibility "to respect and ensure the respect" for international humanitarian law in the latter case rests with the states or regional organizations conducting the operation.

---

[6] Bulletin, *supra* note 2, §5. On the basis of the distinctions between civilians and combatants, and civilian objects and military objectives, the UN force is instructed to take all feasible precautions to avoid or minimize incidental loss of life and property, and, in its area of operation, to refrain from locating military objectives within or near densely populated areas. In recognition of the "peaceful nature" of military installations and equipment used in peacekeeping operations, section 5.4 provides: "Military installations and equipment of peacekeeping operations, as such, shall not be considered military objectives."

[7] *Id.,* §6. The following types of weapons are prohibited: asphyxiating, poisonous, or other gases and biological methods of warfare; bullets that explode, expand, or flatten easily in the human body; and certain explosive projectiles, nondetectable fragments, antipersonnel mines, booby traps, and incendiary weapons. Also prohibited are methods of warfare that cause superfluous injury or unnecessary suffering, destroying objects indispensable to the survival of the civilian population, and installations that contain dangerous forces whose release would cause severe losses among the civilian population.

[8] *Id.,* §§7.2, 7.3.

[9] *Id.,* §7.4.

[10] *Id.,* §8. For the Third Geneva Convention, see *supra* note 4.

[11] Bulletin, *supra* note 2, §9.

[12] On the customary international law nature of the Geneva Conventions as a whole, see Theodor Meron, *The Geneva Conventions as Customary Law,* 81 AJIL 348 (1987); Report of the Secretary-General pursuant to paragraph 2 of Security Council resolution 808 (1993), UN Doc. S/25704, para. 35 (1993), *reprinted in* 32 ILM 1159 (1993).

[13] Additional Protocol I, *supra* note 4, Art. 55; Bulletin, *supra* note 2, §6.3.

[14] Additional Protocol I, *supra* note 4, Art. 45(2); Bulletin, *supra* note 2, §6.7.

[15] Additional Protocol I, *supra* note 4, Art. 56; Bulletin, *supra* note 2, §6.8.

[16] These provisions were considered innovative at the time of their adoption, and though no longer innovative, they are still, two decades later, considered conventional international law provisions. *See* Christopher Greenwood, *Customary Law Status of the 1977 Geneva Protocols, in* HUMANITARIAN LAW OF ARMED CONFLICT: CHALLENGES AHEAD 93, 101, 104, 110 (Astrid J. M. Delissen & Gerard J. Tanja eds., 1991); Georges Abi-Saab, *The 1977 Additional Protocols and General International Law: Some Preliminary Reflexions, id.* at 115, 121–22.

The instructions apply to members of UN forces when they are actively engaged in situations of armed conflict as combatants, to the extent and for the duration of their engagement. They accordingly take effect in enforcement actions when the use of force is authorized in pursuance of a Chapter VII mandate, and in peacekeeping operations when it is permitted in self-defense. While the 1994 Convention on the Safety of United Nations and Associated Personnel[17] implicitly recognized the applicability of international humanitarian law in peacekeeping operations, the fine line between the applicability of the protective regime of the Convention—under which an attack against peacekeepers is an international crime—and that of international humanitarian law remained undefined. When in 1998 the Rome Statute of the International Criminal Court defined war crimes to include attacks against peacekeepers "as long as they are entitled to the protection given to civilians or civilian objects" under the international law of armed conflict, the line between the protected status of peacekeepers "as civilians" and their status otherwise as combatants was finally drawn.[18]

The Secretary-General's Bulletin is binding on members of UN forces in the same way as are all other instructions issued by the Secretary-General in his capacity as "commander in chief" of UN operations. A Secretary-General's Bulletin was also the form in which the regulations were issued for the United Nations Emergency Force,[19] the United Nations Force in the Congo,[20] and the United Nations Force in Cyprus.[21] The source of the legal obligation, however, lies in the international humanitarian law provisions incorporated in the respective national laws, by which members of the force remain bound throughout their service with the UN operation, or in the customary international law provisions that are independently binding on them.

II. RESPONSIBILITY FOR DAMAGE IN ORDINARY OPERATIONAL ACTIVITIES

In compliance with its obligation under section 29 of the 1946 Convention on the Privileges and Immunities of the United Nations,[22] the United Nations has undertaken, in the status of forces agreements with host states, to settle claims of a private-law character to which the UN peacekeeping operation or any of its members is a party, by means of a standing claims commission.[23] Although for various reasons the standing claims commission envisaged under these agreements has never been created, UN-based claims review boards were established, instead, in almost every peacekeeping operation to settle third-party claims for personal injury, property loss, or damage attributable to activities of members of the force in the performance of their official duties.

For four decades the number and value of third-party claims remained relatively low, the administrative and financial burden of settling them was shouldered by the Organization with relative ease, and the procedure for settlement of disputes functioned to the satisfaction of both the Organization and third-party claimants. As peacekeeping operations have expanded in size, territorial scope, and diversity of tasks, the scope of interaction between the UN force

---

[17] Convention on the Safety of United Nations and Associated Personnel, Dec. 9, 1994, Art. 20, 34 ILM 482 (1995).

[18] Rome Statute of the International Criminal Court, July 17, 1998, Art. 8(2)(b)(iii) & (e)(iii), UN Doc. A/CONF.183/9*, *reprinted in* 37 ILM 999 (1998). The Bulletin, *supra* note 2, §1.2, provides in that respect as follows:

> The promulgation of this bulletin does not affect the protected status of members of peacekeeping operations under the 1994 Convention on the Safety of United Nations and Associated Personnel or their status as non-combatants, as long as they are entitled to the protection given to civilians under the international law of armed conflict.

[19] UN Doc. ST/SGB/UNEF/1 (1957), 271 UNTS 135.

[20] UN Doc. ST/SGB/ONUC/1 (1963), *reprinted in* BASIC DOCUMENTS ON UNITED NATIONS AND RELATED PEACE-KEEPING FORCES 89 (Robert C. R. Siekmann ed., 1985).

[21] UN Doc. ST/SGB/UNFICYP/1 (1964), 555 UNTS 119.

[22] Feb. 13, 1946, 21 UST 1418, 1 UNTS 16. Under Article 29 of the Convention, the United Nations is obliged to provide for appropriate modes of settlement of disputes of a private-law character, to which the United Nations is a party, or which involve any of its officials who by reason of his official duties is immune from legal process.

[23] Exchange of Letters Constituting an Agreement concerning the Status of the United Nations Emergency Force in Egypt, Feb. 9, 1957, UN-Egypt, Art. 38, 260 UNTS 61. A standard clause to that effect is inserted in paragraph 51 of the model status of forces agreement, UN Doc. A/45/594 (1990).

and the civilian population has correspondingly grown, and with it the risk of damage to the person or property of third-party individuals. The correlative increase in the number, amount, and complexity of third-party claims, from individuals and governments alike, at a time when the United Nations was overstretched and underfunded, its financial and human resources scarce, prompted the General Assembly to call upon the Secretary-General to devise means for limiting the third-party liability of the Organization.[24]

At the General Assembly's request, the Secretary-General presented a two-stage report in which the principles and scope of UN liability for both combat-related and ordinary operational activities of UN forces were established,[25] and criteria and guidelines for implementing the temporal and financial limitations on UN liability were elaborated.[26] The General Assembly adopted the Secretary-General's recommendations in these reports in its Resolution 52/247 of June 22, 1998.[27]

The Principle of Limited Liability

The financial limitation on the third-party liability of the Organization was a policy decision mandated by the General Assembly whose implementation was left to the Secretary-General. Designed to allocate the risks of peacekeeping operations between the United Nations and the states in whose territories UN operations are deployed, it was predicated on the assumption that, in consenting to a peacekeeping operation in its territory for its own benefit, the host country is consenting to bear, at least in part, the financial consequences of that presence.

In developing specific measures, criteria, and guidelines for limiting the Organization's third-party liability, the Secretary-General had to ensure that, while derogating from the general principles of liability in tort, the proposed financial and temporal limitations would be consistent with the practice in other fields of international law, where limited liability is recognized. In doing so, he also had to see to it that a balance was struck between considerations of justice and fairness to potential claimants, and the interests of the Organization.

Accordingly, financial limitations are not applicable to damage caused by gross negligence or willful misconduct; in those cases, the Organization assumes its responsibility vis-à-vis the third party and bears its liability for compensation in full, while retaining the right to seek reimbursement from the member of the force or his troop-contributing state.[28] Those limitations are equally inapplicable, though for different reasons, in cases of "operational necessity," where the United Nations incurs no liability for damage caused "from the necessary actions taken by a peacekeeping force in the course of carrying out its operations in pursuance of its mandate." Developed in the practice of peacekeeping operations by analogy to "military necessity," "operational necessity," in the ordinary activities of the force, functions as an exception to the rule of tortious liability. Like its twin concept in combat situations, it legitimizes what would otherwise be unlawful.

[24] GA Res. 50/235, UN GAOR, 50th Sess., Supp. No. 49, Vol. 2, at 33, UN Doc. A/50/49 (1996); GA Res. 51/13, UN GAOR, 51st Sess., Supp. No. 49, Vol. 1, at 282, UN Doc. A/51/49 (1996). What triggered the call to limit UN liability was an undocumented joint claim submitted by Bosnia and Herzegovina against the United Nations in the amount of $70 million, of which $64 million was for damage caused in the normal use of roads, bridges, and parking places by UN vehicles. In receiving notice of the claim, the Advisory Committee on Administrative and Budgetary Questions noted: "This sort of information is, in the view of the Committee, compelling evidence of the need for the United Nations to develop, as quickly as possible, effective measures which could limit its liability." Report of the Advisory Committee on Administrative and Budgetary Questions, Administrative and budgetary aspects of the financing of the United Nations peacekeeping operations: financing of the United Nations peacekeeping operations, UN Doc. A/51/491 & annex (1996).

[25] Report of the Secretary-General, Administrative and budgetary aspects of the financing of the United Nations peacekeeping operations: financing of the United Nations peacekeeping operations, UN Doc. A/51/389 (1996).

[26] Report of the Secretary-General, Administrative and budgetary aspects of the financing of the United Nations peacekeeping operations: financing of the United Nations peacekeeping operations, UN Doc. A/51/903 (1997).

[27] Third-party liability: temporal and financial limitations, GA Res. 52/247 (June 22, 1998).

[28] *See* Model Contribution Agreement between the United Nations and [Participating State] Contributing Resources to [the United Nations Peace-keeping Operation], Art. 9, *in* Note by the Secretary-General, Reform of the procedures for determining reimbursement to Member States for contingent-owned equipment, UN Doc. A/50/995, annex (1996).

In discharging the Organization from the liability it would otherwise entail, "operational necessity" must meet four cumulative conditions: the force commander, who holds the discretionary power to decide on the operational necessity of any given measure, must be convinced that an operational necessity exists; that the measure itself is strictly necessary and not just a matter of mere convenience or expediency; that it is part of an overarching operational plan and not the result of a rash individual action; and that the damage inflicted will be proportional to what is strictly necessary to achieve the operational goal.

The limitations on the Organization's tortious liability for damage caused in the ordinary operational activities of the force apply to those types of damage most commonly encountered in the practice of UN operations: namely, nonconsensual use and occupancy of premises; personal injury; and property loss and damage as a result of negligence, not otherwise warranted or justified by "operational necessity."

Temporal and Financial Limitations

The temporal limitation for the submission of claims against the United Nations was established as six months from the time of the damage, or from when it was known or could have been known to the claimant, and in any case not later than one year after the mandate of the operation has terminated. In view of the relatively short duration of most peacekeeping operations, the six-month period within which claims against the Organization may be received was considered both reasonable and fair. It enables the Organization to investigate the claim while still in the area of operation, and allows claimants a sufficient amount of time to prepare their claims. When the period of limitation expires, all claims of whatever nature are barred.

Establishing financial limitations for personal injury, and property damage or loss, was by far more difficult than choosing a single temporal limitation for the submission of claims of all kinds. Given the diversity of potential damage, the Secretary-General proposed a range of financial limitations by reference to categories of injury or loss, maximum ceiling amounts, or relevant criteria.

Accordingly, compensation for personal injury, illness, or death was limited to economic loss (i.e., medical expenses, loss of earnings, and financial support), measured by local standards of compensation not to exceed a ceiling of U.S. $50,000. Noneconomic loss such as pain and suffering was excluded. Compensation for property loss or damage was limited by reference to relevant criteria: for nonconsensual use or damage to premises, an adequate compensable amount was determined on the basis of fair rental value or repair costs; and for personal property, it was set at reasonable costs of repair or replacement of the personal property damaged.[29]

The proposed financial limitations on the liability of the Organization for peacekeeping activities were designed to be applicable wherever UN peacekeeping operations are deployed, and to both states and individual claimants over which, obviously, the United Nations has no legislative authority.

To ensure that the financial and temporal limitations are legally binding in the relationship between the United Nations and the host country, and between the United Nations and third-party claimants, they were incorporated in a General Assembly resolution, a liability clause in the status of forces agreement, and the terms of reference of the claims review boards. A General Assembly resolution on the limited liability of the United Nations, while recommendatory for member states, is mandatory for the Organization and binds the Secretary-General to compensate claimants within the temporal and financial limitations prescribed; when incorporated by reference in a status of forces agreement, it also constitutes the legal basis for the parties' consent to abide by the limitations.[30] If, as is expected, UN claims review boards continue to settle private-law claims between the Organization and third-party claimants, the

---

[29] Report of the Secretary-General, *supra* note 26, paras. 30–36.

[30] For the liability clause proposed by the Secretary-General to be included in future status of forces agreements, see *id.*, para. 40.

incorporation of the financial and temporal limitations in their terms of reference will constitute the applicable law by which third-party claims will be decided.

III. CONCLUSION

In taking stock of the experience accumulated in the peacekeeping operations of the early 1990s and redefining the UN responsibility for the activities of UN operations, the Secretary-General has in most cases codified existing practice. As regards both combat-related and ordinary operational activities, UN responsibility was implicitly assumed and practically implemented long before its formal recognition, and its scope, within established limitations, was made legally binding.

Paradoxically, however, by the time the lessons of the peacekeeping operations of the early 1990s were learned and were about to be implemented, the realities of the second half of the decade dramatically changed and the nature of peacekeeping shifted again. "Peacekeeping fatigue," and the realization of the full scale of the setback to UN operations in the former Yugoslavia, Somalia, and Rwanda, produced a call for a return to traditional, truly consensual, so-called Chapter VI peacekeeping operations. By the mid to late 1990s, in Bosnia and Herzegovina, Georgia, Liberia, Sierra Leone, and the Central African Republic, regional peacekeeping operations gradually replaced multilateral enforcement actions, while UN operations became increasingly civilian and multidimensional in nature, involving civilian police, political, humanitarian, human rights, and electoral components. "Post-conflict, peace-building" operations, a term coined by former Secretary-General Boutros Boutros-Ghali in his Agenda for Peace,[31] has become the distinctive feature of the current generation of peacekeeping operations.

Although the likelihood of the use of force in the present generation of peace-building operations is slight, the need for the instructions to UN forces on the observance of international humanitarian law—though perhaps less acute—is not for all that obviated. Disseminated in times of peace, the instructions for UN forces will diminish the risk of violations in times of war, and will remain a challenge for UN forces as they constantly adapt to the needs and exigencies of each successive peacekeeping generation.

DAPHNA SHRAGA[*]

Protection of Peacekeeping Forces

[18]

Protection of Personnel in Peace Operations[1]

Ola Engdahl

1   Introduction

Violence and threats directed towards personnel engaged in peace operations could have serious effects upon the success of such operations as a whole. For example, the attack on the UN headquarters in Baghdad in 2003 is clear evidence of this. There appears to exist, however, a firm commitment on the part of the international community to strengthen the levels of protection of such personnel and to punish those responsible for attacks. This is evidenced, *inter alia*, in resolutions of the Security Council and the continuing work on an additional protocol extending the scope of application of the 1994 Convention on the Safety of UN and Associated Personnel (Safety Convention).[2]

This article examines from a broad perspective the protection of personnel in peace operations under international law. Legal norms establishing a protection are found in such areas as human rights and international humanitarian law, privileges and immunities accorded representatives of states and international governmental

---

1   This article is based upon, and includes parts of, the dissertation "Protection of Personnel in Peace Operations: The Role of the Safety Convention against the Background of General International Law," defended at Stockholm University in April 2005.

2   Convention on the Safety of United Nations and Associated Personnel, 9 Dec. 1994, 2051 UNTS 361 (78 parties 2005-01-01 according to the UN Treaty Section http://untreaty.un.org/English/treaty.asp). On the work on extending the scope of application of the convention, see Report of the Ad Hoc Committee on the Scope of Legal Protection under the Convention on the Safety of United Nations and Associated Personnel, UN GAOR 57th Sess., Supp. No. 52, UN Doc. A/57/52 (2002), Report of the Ad Hoc Committee on the Scope of Legal Protection under the Convention on the Safety of United Nations and Associated Personnel, UN GAOR 58th Sess., Supp. No. 52, UN Doc. A/58/52 (2003), and Report of the Ad Hoc Committee on the Scope of Legal Protection under the Convention on the Safety of United Nations and Associated Personnel, UN GAOR 59th Sess., Supp. No. 52, UN Doc. A/59/52 (2004).

1

Bruce Oswald, Sarah Finnin (Eds.),

International Peacekeeping: The Yearbook of International Peace Operations, Volume 10, 2005, pp. 1-17.

© *Koninklijke Brill N.V. Printed in the Netherlands*

organisations and international criminal law. A systematisation of these norms in relation to the protection of personnel in peace operations is presented. Special attention is given to the Safety Convention, since this is a multilateral instrument that deals exclusively with the protection of personnel in peace operations.

The Safety Convention is first and foremost a criminal law instrument and should be viewed against the background of the increasingly volatile environment in which peace operation personnel were required to operate at the beginning of the 1990s.[3] In relation to other instruments protecting personnel in peace operations, it is mainly one of enforcement. Its purpose is to prevent and punish deliberate attacks on protected personnel. States parties are under a duty to ensure the safety and security of UN and associated personnel. The Safety Convention defines a number of criminal acts and obligates parties to the convention to criminalise such acts in their national legislation.[4] Furthermore, it states that the personnel concerned shall not be the object "of any action that prevents them from discharging their mandate."[5] It is clearly a duty imposed upon states parties not to interfere, and to prevent others from interfering, with personnel in the execution of their official duties.

However, the drafters of the Safety Convention also aimed at other objectives. It therefore includes references to other legal areas concerned with the legal status of such personnel. The Safety Convention, however, has received criticism and was the subject of a review for the purpose of strengthening and enhancing its protective regime, and its development in this respect is of particular interest. At the time of writing the review was still in progress.

2   Terminology

2.1   *Protection*

The term "protection" can be divided into two parts. These are procedural and substantive rules. In this work the former concerns the right of states and organisations to protect their interests when one of its citizens or agents has been maltreated; while the latter refers to rules that pertain to the legal status of the individual and

---

3   See, for example, UN Secretary-General, *Supplement to An Agenda for Peace: Position paper of the Secretary-General on the occasion of the Fiftieth Anniversary of the United Nations*, paragraphs 15-16, UN Doc. A/50/60-S/1995/1 (1995).

4   Criminal acts under the Safety Convention are "murder, kidnapping or other attack upon the person or liberty of any United Nations or associated personnel" and "violent attack upon the official premises, the private accommodation or the means of transportation of any United Nations or associated personnel likely to endanger his or her person or liberty". Article 9 includes, *inter alia*, threats and attempts to commit such crimes.

5   Safety Convention, Article 7(1).

the responsibilities of states (and belligerent groups) to ensure the protection of that status. The right of states to preserve their own interests when one of their nationals has been harmed in another state is commonly referred to as diplomatic protection and could be described as procedural rules. It is now beyond doubt that the UN possesses the right to bring an international claim against a state found to be responsible for injuries suffered by one of its agents.[6] Presumably this right also exists for other intergovernmental organisations enjoying international capacity.

The right of a state and/or organisation to claim reparation for an internationally wrongful act is not specific to the topic examined in this article. Although an integral part of ensuring respect for the legal status of personnel, this article will instead deal primarily with the substantive rules. In this respect the term protection, for the purpose of this analysis, could be defined as *the duty of states to prevent and punish wrongful acts against personnel in peace operations corresponding to their legal status*. While this duty falls primarily upon the state hosting a peace operation, it has largely, through the Safety Convention, become elevated from a national to a universal level.

A state that fails to protect personnel present within its territory might well be in breach of an international obligation, either of a treaty-based or of a customary law character. The very nature of peace operations, however, means that the personnel concerned will be deployed in areas characterised by human suffering, violence, possible armed conflicts and chaos. It is therefore not uncommon to find such a host state not in control of certain areas of its territory. It may even be that no governmental authority at all exists to exercise territorial control. The obligations of the host state concerned must thus be judged against those things that are practically possible in relation to the requirements of the situation at hand. This fact does not alter the legal status of the personnel in question but it may affect their legal protection. It is possible that a state may not be in breach of its international obligations if it shows due diligence in its efforts to ensure the legal status of personnel.[7]

---

6   Reparation for injuries suffered in the service of the United Nations (Advisory Opinion) ICJ Rep 74 (1949). Cf. Applicability of Article VI, Section 22, of the Convention on the Privileges and Immunities of the United Nations (Advisory Opinion) 1989, ICJ Rep 194 and Difference Relating to Immunity from Legal Process of a Special Rapporteur of the Commission on Human Rights (Advisory Opinion) 1999, ICJ Rep 62. These latter cases are of great concern for personnel representing the UN.

7   In the Home Missionary Society Claim the Tribunal stated, "It is a well-established principle of international law that no government can be held responsible for the act of rebellious bodies of men committed in violation of its authority, where it is itself guilty of no breach of good faith, or of no negligence in suppressing insurrection." Home Missionary Society Claim (United States of America v Great Britain) (1920) 6 Rep Intl Arbitral Awards 42. However, it should be noted that the standard of responsibility depends on the content of the primary obligation in question. There is, for example, no general rule in this respect in the ILC's Draft Articles on State Responsibility

Another important aspect in this regard is the way personnel in peace operations are perceived by the local population. An effective protection is probably dependent on the fact that the legal status of the personnel in question appears as legitimate by the population within the host state. This could be a particularly important issue in relation to immunity from criminal jurisdiction of the host state. Another area of concern lies in the applicability of international humanitarian law in situations where force is used between a peace operation's military personnel and local opposition. Even if theoretically sound, it is of importance for the materialisation of the protection that it is also perceived as such. The behaviour of the protected personnel concerned is therefore of the utmost importance. Any abuse of their status could prove to be detrimental in relation to the respect shown towards the operation as a whole.

2.2   *Peace Operations*

The term "peace operation" is here used as an overall term denoting the wide range of activities in support of the maintenance of international peace and security. It includes operations ranging from traditional peacekeeping to peace enforcement operations, based upon a UN mandate but not necessarily under UN command and control. In many respects the term peace operation, as applied here, is similar to the term "United Nations operation" in the Safety Convention.[8] It is wider, however, since it does not exclude operations conducted by other international organisations or states. It is also narrower since the term "peace operation" in this work is primarily focused on operations involving a military component. The terminology in this area, however, is vast, but it is possible to distinguish some categories of peace operation.[9]

According to the Report of the Panel on United Nations Peace Operations (Brahimi Report), peace operations include "conflict prevention and peacemaking;

---

of 2001. See James Crawford, *The International Law Commission's Articles on State Responsibility. Introduction, Text and Commentaries*, 82 (2002).

8   "United Nations operation" means an operation established by the competent organ of the United Nations in accordance with the Charter of the United Nations and conducted under United Nations authority and control: (i) Where the operation is for the purpose of maintaining or restoring international peace and security; or (ii) Where the Security Council or the General Assembly has declared, for the purposes of this Convention, that there exists an exceptional risk to the safety of the personnel participating in the operation (Article 1).

9   Durch, for example, refers to four categories of peace operations: "traditional peacekeeping, multidimensional peace operations, humanitarian intervention, and peace enforcement". William J. Durch, "Keeping the Peace: Politics and Lessons of the 1990s", in *UN Peacekeeping, American Politics, and the Uncivil Wars of the 1990s*, 1, 3-10 (William J. Durch, ed., 1996).

peacekeeping; and peace-building."[10] Bothe states that the Secretary-General's report *An Agenda for Peace*[11] including its supplement[12] and the Brahimi Report on the evaluation of peacekeeping "reflect a practice of operations, in the new terminology 'peace operations', of a much more complex character than the initial peacekeeping operations."[13] As this article is primarily limited to those operations that include a military component, peacekeeping operations (as the term is used within the UN system) are central to it. Peace operations also include those operations mandated with enforcement powers under Chapter VII of the UN Charter. This study, however, stops short of cases where operations involve personnel as a party to an armed conflict.

3   The System of Protection

It is a well-established principle of international law that a state has the responsibility of ensuring the protection of individuals within its jurisdiction. According to the Secretary-General, the host government assumes the primary responsibility for UN and related personnel, and "this responsibility flows from every Government's normal and inherent functioning of maintaining order and protecting persons and property within its jurisdiction."[14]

A categorisation in this article has been made between general and special protection. A *general* protection encompasses all personnel, irrespective of positions in the operation, and is provided, for example, by human rights law and international humanitarian law.[15] By representing states and/or international governmental

---

10   Report of the Panel on United Nations Peace Operations, para. 10, UN Doc. A/55/305-S/2000/809 (2000).

11   UN Secretary-General, *An Agenda for Peace: Preventive Diplomacy, Peacemaking and Peace-keeping*, UN Doc. A/47/277-S/24111 (1992).

12   UN Secretary-General, *Supplement to An Agenda for Peace: Position paper of the Secretary-General on the occasion of the Fiftieth Anniversary of the United Nations*, UN Doc. A/50/60-S/1995/1 (1995).

13   Michael Bothe, "Peacekeeping," *The Charter of the United Nations. A Commentary*, Vol. 1, 648, 663 (Bruno Simma et al. eds., 2nd ed., 2002). The conclusions of the reports have as a matter of principle been endorsed by the Security Council. Ibid.

14   UN Secretary-General, *Security of United Nations operations*, para. 4, UN Doc. A/48/349-S/26358 (1993).

15   The general protection is based upon an examination of three areas of international law: (1) The law on diplomatic protection of aliens and more specifically the international minimum standard; (2) international human rights law; and (3) international humanitarian law of armed conflict. The fact that most current armed conflicts are of a non-international character, and that protection under human rights law may be derogated from in situations of emergency, has led to the necessity of identifying fundamental standards protecting individuals applicable in all situations, irrespective of how a particular conflict becomes classified. A process of identifying *fundamental standards of*

organisations personnel may also enjoy a *special* protection. Such protection goes beyond a general protection and is afforded some personnel based upon their position in the operation concerned. Diplomatic and international privileges and immunities are areas of international law included in this category.[16] The practice of concluding bilateral agreements with a state hosting a peace operation is of particular importance in this respect. A Status of Forces Agreement (SOFA) is a bilateral agreement concluded between the entity (international organisation or state) leading the operation and the host state. A UN Model SOFA was issued in 1990 to function as the model for future agreements.[17] A SOFA is of principal importance to members of military contingents who are generally not covered by multilateral treaties providing privileges and immunities to personnel representing international organisations. The legal norms stipulated in SOFAs draw primarily on the law on visiting forces and international privileges and immunities, as well as on diplomatic privileges and immunities.[18]

The emerging *legal regime against impunity* in relation to the commission of crimes committed against personnel in peace operations has in this work been referred to as a third category of protection. The Safety Convention has been an important tool in the development of this regime. It is modelled upon so-called "terrorist-conventions" and includes a prosecute-or-extradite mechanism (*aut dedere aut judicare*). Crimes committed against UN and associated personnel were, for example, included, as one out of five categories of crime, in the Draft Code of Crimes against Peace and Security of Mankind.[19] Attacks on personnel in peacekeeping operations and humanitarian assistance enterprises are, moreover, listed as

---

humanity was at the time of writing taking place within the framework of the UN Commission on Human Rights. See, for example, Fundamental standards of humanity. Report of the Secretary-General submitted pursuant to Commission Resolution 2000/69, para. 4, UN Doc. E/CN.4/2001/91 (2001).

16 Privileges and immunities accorded agents of international governmental organisations are often referred to as international privileges and immunities. See, for example, D.B. Michaels, International Privileges and Immunities: a Case for a Universal Statute, (1971), C. Wilfred Jenks, International Immunities (1961), C.F. Amerasinghe, *Principles of the Institutional Law of International Organizations*, (1996).

17 Report of the Secretary-General, *Model status-of-forces agreement for peacekeeping operations*, UN Doc A/45/594 (1990).

18 Dieter Fleck, Introduction, in *The Handbook of The Law of Visiting Forces*, 6 (Dieter Fleck, et al. eds. 2001) and Derek, W. Bowett, *United Nations Forces. A Legal Study of United Nations Practice*, 434 (1964).

19 Draft Code of Crimes against Peace and Security of Mankind, Report of the International Law Commission on the work of its forty-eighth session, UN GAOR, 51st Sess., Supp. No. 10, paras. 45 and 50, UN Doc. A/51/10 (1996). See in this respect the article by M.-Christiane Bourloyannis-Vrailas on Crimes Against United Nations and Associated Personnel, in *Substantive and Procedural Aspects of International Criminal Law. The Experience of International and National Courts, Vol. I Commentary*, 337 (Gabrielle Kirk McDonald and Olivia Swaak-Goldman eds. 2000).

a particular war crime under the statute of the International Criminal Court (ICC).[20] This category of protection must be viewed against other instruments providing personnel with a certain legal status. If general and special protections are to be regarded as shields for protected personnel, then the symbol for this regime against impunity is the sword.[21]

4   The Safety Convention in International Law

The Safety Convention was concluded in 1994 and came into force in 1999. It seeks to protect personnel deployed in operations under UN authority and control that are established for the purpose of maintaining or restoring international peace and security. Personnel in UN operations of another character are not automatically protected. It requires a declaration from the Security Council or the General Assembly that, for the purposes of the Safety Convention, there exists an exceptional risk to their safety. Such a condition carries with it sensitive political considerations and to date no such declaration has been made. The protected categories of personnel are either *UN personnel*, that is, those forming part of the military, the police, or the civilian component of an operation, and other UN officials (for example, staff members of the UN secretariat) present in an official capacity in the area of a UN operation, or *associated personnel*, that is, those connected with the operation through a formal agreement with the competent organ of the UN (for example, personnel of humanitarian NGOs and military forces assisting a UN operation). Associated personnel also need to carry out activities in support of the fulfilment of the mandate of a UN operation.[22]

The Safety Convention's scope of application, which turned out to be the most problematic provision to draft, also concerns the relationship between the convention

---

20 Statute of the International Criminal Court, UN Doc. A/CONF.183/9, 17 July 1998, 37 ILM 999.

21 Bassiouni states that since international criminal law (ICL) incorporates human rights law protection, "it can be said that where human rights law is the shield, ICL is the sword". M. Cherif Bassiouni, "The Sources and Content of International Criminal Law: A Theoretical Framework," in *International Criminal Law* Vol. I, *Crimes*, 3, 46 (M. Cherif Bassiouni, ed., 2nd ed., 1999).

22 In terms of *protection* afforded by the convention, there is no difference between "United Nations Personnel" and "Associated personnel". Both categories enjoy the same protection under the convention. To be able to fall under the category of "Associated personnel" it is necessary to have a link with the UN. That link may be established in three different ways. A government, or an intergovernmental organisation, may assign the persons in question, by *agreement* with the UN; they may be *engaged* by the UN; or be *deployed* by a humanitarian NGO or agency under an *agreement* with the UN. The UN may act through a competent organ. The connection to the UN, however, is not enough to qualify as associated personnel. A special link to a UN *operation* is also required.

and international humanitarian law. Peace operation personnel deployed in the area of an armed conflict generally enjoy the protection entitled to civilians under international humanitarian law. If *military* personnel in the operation concerned become engaged in the armed conflict, as combatants, they would lose their protected status as civilians, under international humanitarian law, and become a legitimate military target. To criminalise attacks against military personnel, engaged as combatants in an armed conflict, would be contradictory to their status under international humanitarian law. The drafters of the Safety Convention were aware of this dilemma and inserted an exclusion clause. The result, however, begs a few questions. According to the convention it does not apply to UN enforcement operations "in which any of the personnel are engaged as combatants against organized armed forces and to which the law of international armed conflict applies". The clause makes the Safety Convention non-operative in relation to *all* personnel, although it could have continued to apply in relation to the non-military personnel of an operation. The reference to the law of international armed conflict creates an overlap between the Safety Convention and the law of non-international armed conflict. The Safety Convention applies simultaneously as international humanitarian law in non-international armed conflicts. The experiences of US forces in Somalia were essential to the creation of this overlap, which aimed to strengthen the level of protection of personnel in non-international armed conflicts. The US delegation, up to this point in the negotiations very conscious of the importance of separating the regimes, argued for an "overlap" with regard to non-international armed conflicts. Its position was influenced by the tragic events enacted in Somalia and the captured helicopter pilot Durant. The US delegation regarded this overlapping "as a necessary exception to that general rule".[23]

The Secretary-General noted in his report, of 2000, that the "combatant-exception" in the convention "gives rise to the suggestion that enforcement actions carried out in situations of internal armed conflict (UNOSOM II type of operations), are included within the scope of the Convention and subject to its protective regime."[24] He states in this regard that the distinction between the two mutually exclusive regimes will eventually be settled in practice. The Secretary-General concluded,

---

23 Steven J., Lepper, "The Legal Status of Military Personnel in United Nations Peace Operations: One Delegate's Analysis," 18 *Houston Journal of International Law*, 359, 395 (1996). In non-international armed conflicts, the Geneva Convention on the treatment of prisoners of war does not apply and if UN military personnel are engaged as combatants in an armed conflict (without the current "overlap") neither would the Safety Convention. In such situations only Common Article 3 to the four Geneva Conventions applies or possibly Additional Protocol II.

24 Report of the Secretary-General, Scope of legal protection under the Convention on the Safety of United Nations and Associated Personnel, 9 note 3, UN Doc. A/55/637 (2000).

however, that it was not the nature or character of the conflict that should determine whether the convention or the international humanitarian law applied but rather "in any type of conflict, members of United Nations peacekeeping operations are actively engaged therein as combatants, or are otherwise entitled to the protection given to civilians under the international law of armed conflict".[25] His report clearly supported an interpretation that the regime of the Safety Convention and that of international humanitarian law are mutually exclusive. However, this presumption is only partly true. With civilians, the regime of the Safety Convention hardly contradicts the protection provided to them under international humanitarian law. The regime of the Safety Convention and that of international humanitarian law cannot in this regard be regarded as being mutually exclusive. It should also be noted that the Secretary-General appears to add a condition of being "actively" engaged as a combatant for the international humanitarian law to be applicable.[26]

It should be noted, however, that individuals taking part in a non-international armed conflict may be prosecuted under *national* law for acts which, had they been committed in the context of an international armed conflict, would have been considered a legitimate act of war. Criminalisation of attacks on military personnel engaged in a peace operation and taking part in a non-international armed conflict may thus, by analogy, be an expression of *lex lata*.

However, one needs to take into consideration the internationalisation of modern armed conflicts and the perception of parties to such conflicts. Although the criminalisation of attacks on the military personnel of a peace operation taking part in a non-international armed conflict may have a sound theoretical basis, the protection afforded may in the long run be eroded if it is *perceived* that immunity from attack, even in situations where such personnel take an active part in hostilities, contravenes international humanitarian law. In this respect, the words of Sir Hersch Lauterpacht should perhaps be considered: "[i]t is impossible to visualize the conduct of hostilities in which one side would be bound by rules of warfare without benefiting from them and the other side would benefit from them without being bound by them".[27]

The Safety Convention's provisions on criminal law and jurisdiction, however, are rather straightforward. It follows a tested formula where state parties are obligated to criminalise certain acts and to either prosecute or extradite (*aut dedere aut judicare*) suspected perpetrators of such crimes. The Convention on the Prevention

---

25 *Ibid.*

26 It is not a condition for being a combatant to have to take an active part in hostilities. However, it should be noted the protection afforded civilians under Additional Protocol I (AP I) is based upon the condition that they do not "take a direct part in hostilities." Article 51(3) of AP I.

27 Hersch Lauterpacht, "The Limits of the Operation of the Law of War," 30 *BYIL*, 206, 212 (1953).

and Punishment of Crimes against Internationally Protected Personnel including Diplomatic Agents of 1973[28] has largely functioned as a model for these provisions. The different nature of the Safety Convention is evidenced by the fact that participation in an attack by "organising or ordering others" is a criminal act under that convention. The Safety Convention thus takes into account the role that military and political superiors might play as possible instigators of attacks in a military context.[29]

The condition that the protection of operations not established for the purpose of maintaining or restoring international peace and security is dependent on a declaration of exceptional risk, by the Security Council or the General Assembly, has been much criticised. The purpose of an additional protocol would be to expand the scope of application of the Safety Convention by disposing of such a requirement. The Safety Convention would then be automatically applicable to a broader category of operations. No agreement has yet been reached on the scope of application of such a protocol. Two main positions, however, have crystallised through the deliberations. Some states favour a scope of application that is as broad as possible. They find that the guiding principle should be the *purpose* of the operation. They have suggested that in addition to operations already protected by the convention, the protocol should also automatically protect those operations whose purpose is the delivering of humanitarian, political or development assistance. The other position instead favours a risk-criterion. Those states advocating this position argue that only such operations that are inherently risky should benefit from the protective regime of the Safety Convention through an additional protocol.

What appears to be the most contentious issue in this respect is Article 8 of the Safety Convention and its relationship to non-governmental organisations (NGOs) and locally employed personnel. It states that "if United Nations or associated personnel are captured or detained in the course of the performance of their duties and their identification has been established, they shall not be subjected to interrogation and they shall be promptly released and returned to United Nations or other appropriate authorities".[30] This has commonly been interpreted, both by states arguing for a broad scope of application as well as by those supporting a more restrictive approach, as providing such personnel with immunity from the criminal jurisdiction of the host state in question. This interpretation is contested in this article.

---

28 Convention on the Prevention and Punishment of Crimes against Internationally Protected Personnel including Diplomatic Agents, 14 December 1973, 1035 UNTS 167.

29 Evan T., Bloom, "Protecting peacekeepers: The Convention on the Safety of United Nations and Associated Personnel," 89 *AJIL* 621, 626 (1995).

30 Article 8 of the Safety Convention. The rest of the article goes as follows: "Pending their release such personnel shall be treated in accordance with universally recognized standards of human rights and the principles and spirit of the Geneva Conventions of 1949."

Article 8 was inserted against the background of the difficulties surrounding the status of military personnel captured by opposing forces in the peace operations in Somalia and the former Yugoslavia.[31] In relation to host state authorities, which have *consented* to the operation, it should only be regarded as a bar against interference with the official duties of personnel.[32] Article 8, together with a number of other articles, has been identified as a key provision of the Safety Convention. Apart from any symbolic value, the purpose of identifying key provisions is that they should, if possible, be included in bilateral status of forces agreements (SOFAs) with host nations and thereby be applicable even where the host nation concerned is not a party to the Safety Convention.[33]

---

31 According to Bloom, part of the US delegation during the negotiations on the convention, Article 8 ensures that personnel captured or detained shall be released immediately, in contrast to the proposition of being returned at the end of hostilities – a stipulation applicable to prisoners of war. The provision therefore limits the risk of a situation developing whereby a claim that soldiers should be treated in accordance with international humanitarian law standards is answered by the argument that soldiers should be regarded as being prisoners of war and would accordingly be released at the end of hostilities. Bloom, 629.

32 The first version of Article 8, proposed by the US delegation, read: "States shall not detain United Nations personnel for acts taken in performance of an enforcement or a peacekeeping mission. If United Nations personnel engaged in such a mission are captured or detained, they shall be immediately released . . ." UN General Assembly, *Report of the Ad Hoc Committee on the Work Carried out During the Period from 28 March to 8 April 1994*, para. 73, UN Doc. A/AC.242/2 (1994). In the end, the reference "for acts taken in performance of/for acts carried out in the course of" was rejected for the current phrase "captured or detained in the course of the performance of their duties". The apparent difference is that a phrase indicating that the Safety Convention provides functional immunity for the personnel concerned was discarded for a phrase moving away from such an interpretation.

33 In his 2004 report on the Scope of Legal Protection under the Convention on the Safety Convention of United Nations and Associated Personnel, the Secretary-General reported, *inter alia*, on the practice of including key provisions of the Safety Convention into SOFAs and SOMAs. According to the Report, such provisions had been included in the agreement "between the United Nations and Member States, including the agreement with the Government of Lebanon regarding the status of military observers of the United Nations Truce Supervision Organization (UNTSO) of 2 July 2003; the agreement with the Government of Liberia concerning the status of the United Nations Mission in Liberia (UNMIL) of 13 October 2003; the agreements with the Government of Côte d'Ivoire on the status of the mission in Côte d'Ivoire (MINUCI) of 18 September 2003 and on the status of the United Nations Operation in Côte d'Ivoire of 29 June 2004 (UNOCI); the agreement with the Government of Haiti concerning the status of the United Nations Operation in Haiti (MINUSTAH) of 9 July 2004, and most recently, the agreement with the Government of Sudan concerning the activities of the United Nations Mission in Sudan of 5 August 2004". Report of the Secretary-General, *Scope of legal Protection under the Convention on the Safety Convention of United Nations and Associated Personnel*, para. 4, UN Doc. A/59/226 (2004).

5   Challenges to an effective protection

Current peace operations often include a regional dimension and are frequently under the command of organisations other than the UN. The multifunctional character of peace operations requires a wide range of personnel, from military forces to civilian contractors. They are often based upon Chapter VII of the UN Charter and charged with enforcement capabilities. Recent operations have also included a direct mandate to protect civilians under imminent threat of violence. The Safety Convention, and the protection of peace operation personnel as a whole, must be able to respond effectively to these trends.

5.1   *Broadening the Scope of Application of the Safety Convention*

During the drafting of the Safety Convention it was a matter of major concern for several delegations that operations that were protected should stay within control of the UN. The peculiar criterion "under UN authority and control" is evidence of the compromise that was finally reached.[34] The text of the Safety Convention, however, has proved to be adaptable to new realities. The peace operations in Bosnia-Herzegovina, Kosovo, and Afghanistan are three examples where military forces, acting upon a mandate from the Security Council, have assisted a UN non-military operation. If the Safety Convention protects these UN operations then there are good reasons to also include the personnel of the NATO and EU-led military operations. They are definitely assigned by a government or an international governmental organisation with the agreement of the competent organ (the Security Council) of the UN and they carry out activities in support of the fulfilment of the mandate of a UN operation. An additional protocol would extend the automatic application of the Safety Convention to new categories of operation. This would also mean that larger numbers of military forces assisting UN operations would be protected. It is surprising, however, that this has not yet been an issue for debate in the Ad Hoc Committee.

From the perspective of combating the notion of impunity there is no compelling reason why the protective regime of the Safety Convention should be restricted to operations conducted under UN authority and control. It is here suggested that an additional protocol should emphasise the criminal law character of the protection and aim for a broad scope of application. Current challenges for the Safety

---

34 According to Kirsch, chairman of the Ad Hoc Committee and its working groups, as well as the working groups established within the framework of the Sixth Committee, this was a "heavily negotiated compromise language falling somewhere between UN command and control, on the one hand, and UN authority, on the other". Philippe Kirsch, "Convention on the Safety of United Nations and Associated Personnel," *Canadian Council on International Law*, Proceedings 182, 186 (1994).

Convention appear not to relate to its penal law character (a more refined criminal law instrument would probably have made the Safety Convention more effective). The wider scope of application here suggested would necessitate a common under-standing that Article 8 only concerns a bar on interfering in the performance of the official duties of personnel. It was never the intention to create an instrument accord-ing immunity for protected personnel. The disputed article has not been treated as an immunity provision in those cases where it has been inserted in SOFAs.[35] An approach embracing the Safety Convention as being primarily a penal law instru-ment, excluding rules of immunity, would be conducive to the ongoing negotia-tions, and any expansion of its scope of application should be less controversial.

5.2 *Conformity of SOFA norms*

While the fact that more peace operations are being conducted under the command of organisations other than the UN creates special challenges with regard to the application of the Safety Convention to such operations, the trend also entails a diverse practice with regard to SOFAs. The inclusion of broad categories of per-sonnel in SOFAs is in many respects positive, as complex peace operations rely upon an increasing number of personnel exercising a wide range of functions. However, there are examples of SOFAs, in operations not under UN command, where the definition of personnel is particularly vague.[36] The SOFA applicable to the International Security Assistance Force (ISAF) in Afghanistan, provided privi-leges and immunities to "ISAF and supporting personnel, including associated liai-son personnel."[37] There was no definition of "supporting personnel, including associated liaison personnel" in the SOFA. The protections set out in the agreement applied not only to ISAF and all its personnel, but also "to forces in support of the ISAF and all their personnel."[38] The application of unclear definitions has probably been a means of extending the protection available under the SOFA to more or less everyone supporting the peace process. But in the end, this might have the oppo-site effect. The fact that *military* personnel cannot be tried before local courts is bal-anced by the fact that sending states exercise exclusive criminal jurisdiction over their military forces. Immunity from local jurisdiction for other personnel under a SOFA may not so readily be balanced by a duty of their national states to exercise

35 Agreement between the Democratic Republic of East Timor and the United Nations Concerning the Status of the United Nations Mission of Support in East Timor (2002) 2185 UNTS 367 (UNMISET SOFA), paragraph 49.
36 41 ILM 1032 (2002) (ISAF SOFA).
37 ISAF SOFA, Article 1.
38 *Ibid.*, Article 18.

jurisdiction. The trend initiated by the EU to provide military officers with a status equivalent to that of diplomatic agents may have the effect of blurring the distinction between military officers and diplomatic agents.[39] As their functions are fundamentally different, it is important to uphold the separation between these two categories of personnel. The use of the UN Model SOFA, as a basis for specific SOFAs in operations led by other organisations, would contribute to the formation of common norms applicable to *all* peace operations from the very beginning.

5.3   *Responsibility and Accountability*

Complex peace operations assuming traditional state functions have prompted questions on the whole subject of responsibility and accountability of organisations and individuals enjoying a special protection under international law. These issues, for instance, have been outlined in a report by the Ombudsperson in Kosovo.[40] From the standpoint of sending states it is naturally of the greatest importance that their citizens be entitled to the best protection possible when performing functions for international organisations abroad. However, if such personnel are perceived by the local population to be above the law, then respect for their protected status will deteriorate. The main problem of protection is, in fact, largely connected to a lack of respect of applicable rules. Positive perception alone may go a long way for the materialisation of the protection that personnel could expect. In this respect it is imperative that a privileged status is combined with a supervising and enforcement mechanism enabling appropriate authorities to effectively deal with criminal acts committed by protected personnel. The argument that some states lack jurisdiction for what their citizens do abroad during peace operations should be met by demanding that all sending states adjust their national laws in order to effectively close this loophole of jurisdiction, about which the former UN Secretary-General Dag Hammarskjöld warned.[41] While his warning primarily related to military personnel,

---

39   Agreement between the European Union and the Former Yugoslav Republic of Macedonia on the status of the European Union-led Forces (EUF) in the Former Yugoslav Republic of Macedonia.

40   Ombudsperson Institution in Kosovo. Special Report No. 1 on the compatibility with recognized international standards of UNMIK Regulation No. 2000/47 on the Status, Privileges and Immunities of KFOR and UNMIK and Their Personnel in Kosovo (18 August 2000) and on the implementation of Regulation No. 2000/47 On the Status, Privileges and Immunities of KFOR and UNMIK and their Personnel in Kosovo (UNMIK/REG/2000/47), 18 August 2000. http://www.ombudspersonkosovo.org/

41   According to the Secretary-General, the important system of exclusive criminal jurisdiction of sending states over their military personnel "should not result in jurisdictional vacuum, in which a given offence might be subject to prosecution by neither the host State nor the participating State". *Report of the Secretary-General: Summary study of the experiences derived from the establishment and operation of the Force*, para. 136, UN Doc. A/3943 (1958).

it is today relevant for all personnel participating in peace operations who enjoy immunity from local jurisdiction. If the question of accountability is not properly dealt with, the materialisation of the required protection of personnel in peace operations will be at risk. Drafters of future SOFAs need to move away from the use of very loose definitions of personnel associated with peace operations.

5.4 *Combating Impunity Effectively*

Under the principle of universal jurisdiction, states have a *right* to prosecute any criminal on the sole basis of physical presence. It has, however, been suggested that some crimes subject to a treaty-based *duty* to prosecute or extradite are of such a nature and character that all states maintain the *right* to exercise jurisdiction without any special connection to the criminal act itself.[42] Of all crimes subject to a treaty-based duty to prosecute or extradite alleged offenders, which is not yet beyond doubt crimes under customary international law, crimes committed against UN and associated personnel stand out as representing one of the most serious types of criminality.[43] International concern over crimes committed against UN and associated personnel supports an interpretation that all states have a *right* – but not necessarily a duty – to prosecute an alleged perpetrator of such crimes on the sole basis of the accused being present in the state in question.

Creation of mechanisms enforcing individual criminal responsibility is perhaps one of the most important trends in international law today. An advanced system of international criminal law will possibly have a deterring effect on potential attackers launching assaults on protected persons. States are under a customary law duty to prevent and punish criminal acts *within* their jurisdictions. The Safety Convention, however, has provided international leverage to this duty and established an inter-state obligation of penal cooperation. From the perspective of combating impunity,

---

42 See Kenneth C., Randall, Universal Jurisdiction Under International Law, 66 *Texas Law Review* 785, 825-827 (1988), M. Cherif Bassiouni, and Edward M., Wise, *Aut Dedere Aut Judicare: The Duty to Extradite or Prosecute in International Law*, 24 (1995).

43 See, for example, the reason put forward by the ILC for including such crimes as one out of five categories of in the Draft Code of Crimes against the Peace and Security of Mankind. Attacks against United Nations and associated personnel constitute violent crimes of exceptionally serious gravity which have serious consequences not only for the victims, but also for the international community. These crimes are of concern to the international community as a whole because they are committed against persons who represent the international community and risk their lives to protect its fundamental interest in maintaining the international peace and security of mankind. [. . .] Attacks against such personnel are in effect directed against the international community and strike at the very heart of the international legal system established for the purpose of maintaining international peace and security by means of collective security measures taken to prevent and remove threats to the peace. Draft Code of Crimes against Peace and Security of Mankind, Report of the ILC, 105-106.

which is the main purpose of the Safety Convention, the inclusion of key provisions in SOFAs is of limited importance. A host state is already obligated to prevent illegal acts being committed against personnel and to prosecute alleged offenders. The "right" states are those with no special connection to any criminal act committed against UN and associated personnel. The seriousness of the crime has already been accounted for, and the idea that it entails universal jurisdiction. Combating this 'culture of impunity' effectively requires, however, universal adherence to the Safety Convention. The duty to prosecute or extradite is probably not yet a principle of customary international law.

5.5   *International Humanitarian Law and Peace Operations*

As current peace operations are often decided under Chapter VII of the UN Charter, and personnel are given rather wide powers to defend themselves and the operation, as well as the local population, the impact of international humanitarian law is bound to be a relevant issue in the future. The solution chosen by the drafters of the Safety Convention would probably guide a local court, in cases of doubt, whether an attack on UN forces constituted either an act of war or a criminal act, to rule in favour of the latter. However, the simple solution by the ICC statute recognises, in contrast to the Safety Convention, that it is still a war crime to attack *civilian* members of a peace operation even though its forces act as combatants. A similar solution of the Safety Convention would recognise that it continues to apply in relation to the operation's civilian personnel irrespective of any engagement of its military forces in armed conflict.

To decide at what point peace operation forces become combatants in an armed conflict will not be an easy task. It is indeed a matter of great disagreement in the literature and it has even been asserted that they should never assume that status and that it should always be a crime to attack them.[44] The differences of opinion among legal scholars, the incongruous definitions of the ICC statute and the Safety

---

44   See, for example, Walter Gary Sharp, Sr., *Jus Paciarii, Emergent Legal Paradigms for U.N. Peace Operations in the 21st Century*, 86 (1999), Daphna Shraga, The Applicability of International Humanitarian Law to United Nations Operations, in Blue Helmets: Policemen or Combatants?, 17, (Claude Emanuelli, ed., 1997), Brian D. Tittemore, Belligerents in Blue Helmets: Applying International Humanitarian Law to United Nations Peace Operations, 33 *Stanford Journal of International Law*, 61, (1997), Francoise Hampson, States' military operations authorized by the United Nations and international humanitarian law, in *The United Nations and International Humanitarian Law*, 371, (Luigi Condorelli et al. eds., 1996). Richard D. Glick, Lip Service to the Laws of War: Humanitarian Law and United Nations Armed Forces, 17 *Michigan Journal of International Law*, 53, (1995) Gert-Jan F. van Hegelsom, The Law of Armed Conflict and UN Peace-Keeping and Peace-Enforcing Operations, 6 *Hague Yearbook of International Law*, 45, (1993), Finn Seyersted, *United Nations Forces. In the Law of Peace and War*, 210, (1966).

Convention, and the criticised Secretary-General's Bulletin on the observance by UN forces of international humanitarian law,[45] is evidence of the complexity of the problem. In the end, effective levels of protection require a theoretically sound underpinning compatible with the system of international law as a whole. By overreaching, good intentions might cause a loss of respect for such protection and this could adversely affect the chances of success for the operation in question.

6 Conclusions

The Safety Convention became the tool for the creation of an effective system of interstate penal law co-operation for crimes against UN and associated personnel. States parties are obliged to co-operate in order to effectively prosecute offenders in relation to stipulated crimes. Such crimes, through this convention, have been elevated from the purely local or national level to a universal level. It thus represents a means of confronting and repressing this 'culture of impunity' in relation to serious crimes committed against UN and associated personnel. As such it reflects a common determination of will on the part of the international community. There is not as yet a universal adherence to the Safety Convention but its normative character has influenced other instruments. The protection afforded by the convention may therefore be characterised as that of a major step forward towards an effective legal regime against impunity shown by offenders responsible for criminal acts against personnel in peace operations. The system is not yet faultless. It will require universal adherence to the Safety Convention, or development of the *aut dedere aut judicare* mechanism for such crimes at a level of customary law. If all states had a similar duty to that of host states, to punish perpetrators of such crimes, protection for personnel might, from that perspective, be of a universal nature. There would then be a universal duty to punish offenders, wherever such crimes were committed. The protected status of personnel might consequently be legally enforced through national courts throughout the international community. Such a duty could be characterised as a *universal protection*. A truly effective system, however, ultimately requires a genuine will on the part of states to take seriously the fight against impunity. The problems encountered during the work on an additional protocol to the Safety Convention are perhaps evidence of the challenges ahead to such a system.

---

45 Secretary-General's Bulletin, *Observance by United Nations Forces of International Humanitarian Law*, 6 August 1999, UN Doc. ST/SGB/1999/13.

Part V
International Administrations

[19]

FROM DANZIG TO EAST TIMOR AND BEYOND:
THE ROLE OF INTERNATIONAL TERRITORIAL ADMINISTRATION

RALPH WILDE

The United Nations is currently engaged in one of its most ambitious roles ever: the administration of two territories—Kosovo and East Timor. Attention has focused on the challenges raised by the performance of this role, such as international officials' need for new skills and experience.[1] It has also focused on the problems caused by the context of administration, in which local governmental institutions must be constructed or reconstructed before they can be administered.[2] However, a more profound question needs to be asked as well: why is the United Nations there at all? This piece analyzes the official reasons put forward to explain the deployment of international organizations in the administration of territory. It challenges the popular idea that the Kosovo and East Timor projects are unique. Actually, the involvement of international organizations in varying degrees of territorial administration has a long history, stretching back to the start of the League of Nations. Moreover, it includes at least three further current examples: the administration of camps housing refugees and internally displaced persons by the UN High Commissioner for Refugees (UNHCR); the operation of material assistance programs by international organizations in various territories; and the conduct of governmental activities by the Office of the High Representative of the International Community (OHR) in Bosnia and Herzegovina. I argue that the current projects are the latest manifestations of a policy institution that is used to serve two purposes rooted in certain ideas of international law. Valuable lessons for current and future projects can be learned from the way this institution has served these purposes in the past.

The piece begins by briefly establishing how the international administration projects operate. Drawing on historical precedents, I then analyze the official justifications put forward for the projects, establishing what purposes the projects are supposedly set up to serve. I argue that these projects are framed in terms of a response to two problems, each related to administration in the territory concerned. In the first place, they attempt to address a perceived "sovereignty problem" regarding the identity of those local actors exercising administrative control. In the second place, they attempt to address a perceived "governance problem" regarding the conduct of governance by local actors. After a detailed analysis of the different circumstances in which these purposes have been invoked in relation to the institution, the relationship between the institution and three other international policy institutions is explained. This study focuses on international organizations, as such actors are understood in international law. As regards the administration of post-1945 Germany and Austria, I include the Allies within this definition, since the conventional view is that, although in certain respects control was divided between the individual members of the

---

[1] *E.g.*, Report of the Panel on United Nations Peace Operations, UN Doc. A/55/305–S/2000/809, para. 77, *reprinted in* 39 ILM 1432 (2000) [hereinafter Brahimi Report]. I discuss this issue in *The Complex Role of the Legal Adviser When International Organizations Administer Territory*, 95 ASIL PROC. 251, 252 n.7 (forthcoming 2001).

[2] *E.g.*, Brahimi Report, *supra* note 1, para. 77; Hansjörg Strohmeyer, *Collapse and Reconstruction of a Judicial System: The United Nations Missions in Kosovo and East Timor*, 95 AJIL 46 (2001).

584   THE AMERICAN JOURNAL OF INTERNATIONAL LAW   [Vol. 95:583

alliance, administration was conducted on behalf of the Allies as a whole.[3] I also include OHR and the EU Administration of Mostar (the EUAM) on the grounds that these two institutions enjoy distinct legal personality under their administration mandates.[4]

I. THE ACTIVITY OF INTERNATIONAL TERRITORIAL ADMINISTRATION

To understand the official purposes of granting administrative control over territory to international organizations, one must appreciate how such control operates. In certain circumstances, states hand over responsibility for running camps housing refugees and/or internally displaced persons (refugee camps) to UNHCR.[5] One example is the Dadaab camps of Kenya.[6] These camps resemble small cities where education, medical services, and basic infrastructure are provided by a network of international agencies under the control of UNHCR. More generally, UN agencies, notably the World Food Programme, implement programs of material assistance in a variety of places. For example, the UN Inter-Agency Humanitarian Programme has been exclusively responsible for distributing "humanitarian supplies" (e.g., medicine, foodstuffs) in three of the northern governorates of Iraq since 1996.[7] In Bosnia and Herzegovina, OHR, created by the 1995 Dayton Agreement, has interpreted its vague powers in that Agreement to encompass various governmental acts, including the passing of laws and the dismissal of elected officials.[8] Other international organizations appoint foreign nationals as members of certain key governmental institutions (e.g., the Constitutional Court).[9] In the Brcko District, an OHR "Supervisor" was given certain administrative prerogatives in 1997 by the arbitral tribunal charged with determining the

---

[3] M. E. BATHURST & J. L. SIMPSON, GERMANY AND THE NORTH ATLANTIC COMMUNITY: A LEGAL SURVEY 41–45 (1956); JAMES CRAWFORD, THE CREATION OF STATES IN INTERNATIONAL LAW 274 (1975); F. A. MANN, STUDIES IN INTERNATIONAL LAW 646 (1973); Robert Y. Jennings, *Government in Commission*, 1946 BRIT. Y.B. INT'L L. 112, 141.

[4] For OHR's legal rights and duties, see General Framework Agreement for Peace in Bosnia and Herzegovina with Annexes, Dec. 14, 1995, Bosn. & Herz.–Croat.–Fed. Rep. Yugo. [FRY], Annex 10, 35 ILM 75 (1996) [hereinafter Dayton Agreement]; SC Res. 1031 (Dec. 15, 1995), *reprinted in* 35 ILM 235 (1996). For the EUAM's legal rights and duties, see Memorandum of Understanding on Mostar, July 5, 1994, Member States of the European Union, Member States of the Western European Union, Republic of Bosnia and Herzegovina, Federation of Bosnia and Herzegovina, Local Administration of Mostar East, Local Administration of Mostar West, Bosnian Croats (unpublished) (on file with AJIL) [hereinafter Mostar MOU].

[5] The term "refugee camps" is used hereinafter since it is the most common. The word "refugee," however, is misleading, since internally displaced persons are by definition not (legal) refugees. *See, e.g.*, Convention Relating to the Status of Refugees, July 28, 1951, Art. 1, 189 UNTS 150.

[6] This information is drawn from RALPH WILDE, BEYOND THE YOKE: WOMEN'S RIGHTS IN THE DADAAB REFUGEE CAMPS OF KENYA (1997) (on file at UK House of Commons Library); Ralph Wilde, *Quis Custodiet Ipsos Custodes? Why and How UNHCR Governance of 'Development' Refugee Camps Should Be Subject to International Human Rights Law*, 1 YALE HUM. RTS. DEV. L.J. 5 (1998) [hereinafter Wilde, *UNHCR*].

[7] The governorates involved are Arbil, Dihouk, and Suleimaniyeh. *See* SC Res. 986, para. 8(b) (Apr. 14, 1995); Memorandum of Understanding on the Implementation of Security Council Resolution 986 (1995), May 20, 1996, UN-Iraq, UN Doc. S/1996/356 §§II, VI, & Annex I (1996). For background information, see the Web site of the UN Office for the Iraq Program, <http://www.un.org/Depts/oip/index.html> [hereinafter UN Iraq Web site].

[8] *See* Dayton Agreement, *supra* note 4, Annex 10; *OHR Info* (June 6, 2000), *at* <http://www.ohr.int/info/info.htm>; *Decisions by the High Representative*. OHR decisions are available online at <http://www.ohr.int/decisions.htm>.

[9] International appointments are set out in the Dayton Agreement, *supra* note 4. The president of the European Court of Human Rights makes certain appointments to the Constitutional Court (Annex 4, Art. VI(1)) and the Commission for Displaced Persons (CDP) (Annex 7, Art. IX). The Committee of Ministers of the Council of Europe makes certain appointments to the Human Rights Chamber (Annex 6, Arts. VII(2), X(2)). The director-general of the United Nations Educational, Social and Cultural Organization makes certain appointments to the Commission to Preserve National Monuments (CPNM) (Annex 8). The president of the European Bank for Reconstruction and Development makes certain appointments to the Commission on Public Corporations (CPC) (Annex 9, Art. I). The International Monetary Fund appointed the first governor of the Central Bank (Annex 4, Art. VII). The chairman-in-office of the Organization for Security and Co-operation in Europe (OSCE) appoints the human rights ombudsperson (Annex 6, Art. IV). On all but the CDP, CPNM, and CPC, international appointees cannot be nationals of Bosnia and Herzegovina or a neighboring state; in practice, this restriction has been adopted for all the international appointments. Telephone interviews between the author and local officials (July 20 & 23, 2001). For all institutions but the CPC, the Dayton Agreement allows for the presence of international appointees to end at certain dates from 2001 onwards; at the time of writing, no arrangements in this regard could be formally confirmed.

district's future status.[10] In June 1999, the United Nations Mission in Kosovo (UNMIK) was created to provide an "interim administration" in that territory.[11] In the same year, the United Nations Mission in East Timor (UNAMET) conducted a popular consultation on East Timor's future status, and the United Nations Transitional Authority in East Timor (UNTAET) was later created to administer the territory until independence.[12]

Each project involves a claim made by an international organization relating to territorial administration. Here, "territorial administration" refers to a formally constituted, locally based management structure operating with respect to a particular territorial unit; it can be limited (e.g., a territorial program concerned with certain matters) or plenary (e.g., a territorial government) in scope. The international organization asserts the right either to supervise and control the operation of this structure by local actors, or to operate the structure directly. The right is exercised from within the territory, and can pertain to the structure as a whole, or certain parts of it (e.g., the legislature). This activity should be contrasted with merely monitoring and/or assisting local actors in operating such a structure, although the distinction is sometimes difficult to make in practice, particularly in the case of conduct and assistance. The spatial identity of the international organization and its officials—as "international"—is distinct from and opposed to the "local" identity of the territorial unit and population affected, even if the organization's activities are limited to that territory and some of the "internationals" are actually local nationals. This divergence between the two spatial identities marks the projects off from the European Communities. There, the EC institutions share the same spatial identity as the legal order in respect of which they perform administrative functions (even if this legal order cuts across the distinct legal orders of member states). Similarly, although the enjoyment of privileges and immunities in state territory gives international organizations near-exclusive administrative competence by default, such competence usually covers only the property and personnel of the organization (the provision of consular protection is similarly limited). As demonstrated below, the description in this paragraph reflects the salient features of the activity in terms of the official purposes served by the projects. I propose to characterize this activity as "international territorial administration" (ITA).

Because of the plenary administrative powers seemingly asserted in the Kosovo and East Timor projects, and the involvement of the United Nations, the two projects are often regarded as groundbreaking.[15] An extreme view holds that the East Timor undertaking is

---

[10] See text at note 63 infra.

[11] See Agreement on the Principles (Peace Plan) to Move Towards a Resolution of the Kosovo Crisis Presented to the Leadership of the Federal Republic of Yugoslavia by the President of Finland, Martti Ahtisaari, representing the European Union, and Viktor Chernomyrdin, Special Representative of the President of the Russian Federation, June 3, 1999, UN Doc. S/1999/649 [hereinafter Kosovo Peace Plan]; SC Res. 1244 (June 10, 1999), reprinted in 38 ILM 1451 (1999). On this mandate, see, for example, Michael J. Matheson, United Nations Governance of Postconflict Societies, 95 AJIL 76, 78–81 (2001); Ralph Wilde, From Bosnia to Kosovo and East Timor: The Changing Role of the United Nations in the Administration of Territory, 6 ILSA J. INT'L & COMP. L. 467 (2000).

[12] For the consultation and UNAMET, see Agreement Regarding the Modalities for the Popular Consultation of the East Timorese Through a Direct Ballot, May 5, 1999, Indon.–Port.–UN Sec'y-Gen., at <http://www.un.org/peace/etimor99/agreement/agreeFrame_Eng03.html>; Agreement on Security, May 5, 1999, Indon.–Port.–UN Sec'y-Gen., at <http://www.un.org/peace/etimor99/agreement/agreeFrame_Eng04.html>; Agreement on the Question of East Timor, May 5, 1999, Indon.–Port., at <http://www.un.org/peace/etimor99/agreement/agreeFrame_Eng01.html>, and Appendix, A Constitutional Framework for a Special Autonomy for East Timor, at <http://www.un.org/peace/etimor99/agreement/agreeFrame_Eng02.html> [hereinafter Indonesia-Portugal Agreement]; SC Res. 1246 (June 11, 1999); UN Secretary-General, Letter to the President of the Security Council Regarding the Result of the Popular Consultation, UN Doc. S/1999/944 (1999). For UNTAET, see SC Res. 1272, Arts. 1, 2(a), (b), 3(a), 6 (Oct. 25, 1999), reprinted in 39 ILM 240 (2000); Indonesia-Portugal Agreement, supra; see also Matheson, supra note 11, at 81–83; Wilde, supra note 11.

[15] As for seemingly asserting plenary authority, see, for example, UNMIK Regulation 1999/1 (as amended), contained in Regulation 2000/54, §1.1 (Sept. 27, 2000), at <http://www.un.org/peace/kosovo/pages/regulations/regs.html>; SC Res. 1272, supra note 12, pmbl., para. 1; UNTAET Regulation 1999/1, §1.1 (Nov. 27, 1999), at <http://www.un.org/peace/etimor>. The Brahimi Report places two post–Cold War missions (that can only be UNMIK and UNTAET) in a class of their own as responding to "extreme" situations: "United Nations operations were given executive law enforcement and administrative authority where local authority did not exist

586   THE AMERICAN JOURNAL OF INTERNATIONAL LAW   [Vol. 95:583

unprecedented, since nowhere else has UN administration been used to bring a new state into existence.[14] No doubt, these projects are unusual and in some respects unique. However, if we are asking why the United Nations is engaged in these missions, such exceptionalist approaches probably do not offer a meaningful basis for classification. In the next section, I argue that ITA—irrespective of the international organization concerned, and despite different degrees of administrative involvement—has been used since the inception of the League as a device for certain policy ends. To understand how likely the current projects are to succeed, we need to consider them in this historical perspective.

II. WHY ITA AMOUNTS TO A POLICY INSTITUTION: ITS TWIN PURPOSES

International organizations first exercised territorial administration in the Free City of Danzig, where the League of Nations enjoyed certain governmental prerogatives from 1920 to 1939. In addition, the League administered the German Saar Basin (the Saar) between 1920 and 1935, and the Colombian town and district of Leticia (Leticia) from 1933 to 1934. It also appointed the president of the Upper Silesia Mixed Commission in 1922 and the chair of the Memel Harbor board in Lithuania in 1924. Immediately after the Second World War, Germany and Austria were administered by the Allies. With the creation of the United Nations, the new international organization was authorized in 1947 to exercise certain governmental powers in what would have become the Free Territory of Trieste, but the free territory plan was never realized.

The United Nations first exercised territorial administration in the 1960s, asserting various administrative prerogatives in the Congo between 1960 and 1964, and administering West Irian for seven months between 1962 and 1963. In 1967, the UN Council for what was then South West Africa (later Namibia) was established to administer the territory, but South Africa prevented the council from taking up this role. Over twenty years later, in 1991 the United Nations was authorized to perform administrative functions in Western Sahara and Cambodia; although these functions were exercised in Cambodia from 1991 to 1992, they are yet to be fully performed in Western Sahara. From 1994 to 1996, a different institution—the EUAM—administered the city of Mostar in Bosnia and Herzegovina. Then, as part of the Dayton process, the territory of Eastern Slavonia, Baranja, and Western Sirmium (Eastern Slavonia) in Croatia was placed under UN administration from 1996 to 1998. In some of the aforementioned missions, and in others as well, the mandates of international organizations have called for the performance of two particular administrative functions: controlling or conducting some form of territory-wide popular consultation and/or "community building" through the creation of local institutions. In addition to the authorized projects, other ITA projects were proposed but never agreed upon for Fiume in Dalmatia (in 1919), Memel (between 1921 and 1923), Alexandretta in Syria (in 1937), Jerusalem (since 1947), and Sarajevo (in 1994).[15]

---

or was not able to function." Brahimi Report, *supra* note 1, para. 19. Matheson, *supra* note 11, at 83, describes "[t]he novel . . . undertakings in Kosovo and East Timor." For Strohmeyer, *supra* note 2, at 46, "[t]he scope of the challenges and responsibilities deriving from these mandates [UNMIK and UNTAET] was unprecedented in United Nations peacekeeping operations."

As for working on the territory's legal and judicial system, Strohmeyer, *id.* at 60, states that "[n]owhere other than Kosovo and East Timor [where such a task was part of a UN mandate] . . . did this task require the establishment of a coherent judicial and legal system for an entire territory virtually from scratch." On the exceptional character of the two missions, see also Michèle Griffin & Bruce Jones, *Building Peace Through Transitional Authority: New Directions, Major Challenges*, INT'L PEACEKEEPING, Winter 2001, at 75.

[14] *E.g.*, Jarat Chopra, *The UN's Kingdom of East Timor*, 42 SURVIVAL 27, 27 (2000); *see also* James Traub, *Inventing East Timor*, FOREIGN AFF., July/Aug. 2000, at 74, 75 (East Timor mission exceptional because of the broad mandate and lack of preexisting institutions).

[15] For Fiume, see MEIR YDIT, INTERNATIONALISED TERRITORIES 51–59 (1961); for Memel, see *id.* at 48; for Alexandretta, see STEVEN R. RATNER, THE NEW UN PEACEKEEPING: BUILDING PEACE IN LANDS OF CONFLICT AFTER THE COLD WAR 97 (1995); for Sarajevo, see DAVID OWEN, BALKAN ODYSSEY 199, 210, 212, 215, 235–36, 238–40,

This brief survey demonstrates, then, that the activity of ITA is nothing new. However, the historical examples constitute more than precedents for the existence of this activity. They illustrate how it is used as a means of serving two related purposes, each reflecting certain international legal ideas. The following discussion of these official purposes is confined to those projects that were actually authorized.

In appreciating why it is used, ITA is best understood in a negative way, in terms of what it is not. It is seen as a substitute for territorial administration as it is "normally" practiced: by actors whose spatial identity, as local, corresponds to that of the territorial unit and its population. ITA has been and is being used as a device to replace local actors in the activity of administration, either partially or fully, because of two perceived problems with the "normal" model. In the first place, ITA is used to respond to a perceived sovereignty problem with the presence of local actors exercising control over the territory. In the second place, ITA is used to respond to a perceived governance problem with the conduct of governance by local actors. The first problem concerns the identity of the local actors being excluded from administration; the second problem concerns the quality of governance being exercised in the territory.

The First Purpose: Responding to a Sovereignty Problem

In Leticia, West Irian, Eastern Slavonia, the Saar, and Mostar, ITA was used or proposed to solve what might be called a "sovereignty problem" caused by the identity of certain local actors who enjoyed or might enjoy administrative control. The key to understanding the role of ITA here is the link between administrative control and sovereignty. The question of who exercises administrative control—a fortiori administrative control as the governmental authority—is often regarded as determinative of who is legally sovereign.[16] ITA actively interferes in the sovereignty process by displacing or calibrating the level of administrative control by certain local actors. It is introduced because, in the light of their respective spatial identities, the international organization is seen as "neutral" when compared with the local actors to whom the sovereignty problem relates. In responding to a sovereignty problem, ITA can operate in different ways. In Leticia, West Irian, and Eastern Slavonia, it responded to a concern stemming from a wider question about the status of the territory. In the Saar and Mostar, ITA was the response to the status question itself.

ITA was first used to respond to a concern associated with a wider sovereignty question in 1933, when Peruvian irregulars invaded and occupied the Colombian town and district of Leticia and Peru then pledged to defend them if Colombia attempted to drive them out.[17] Plenary administration by a League commission, accompanied by the withdrawal of the Peruvian irregulars, was introduced for a maximum one-year period.[18] The League

---

242–43, 263 (1995); for Jerusalem, see, for example, MOSHE HIRSCH, DEBORAH HOUSEN-COURIEL, & RUTH LAPIDOTH, WHITHER JERUSALEM? PROPOSALS AND PETITIONS CONCERNING THE FUTURE STATUS OF JERUSALEM (1995); YDIT, *supra*, at 273–314, bibliography at 315; Report of the UN Trusteeship Council, Annex II, Statute for the City of Jerusalem, UN GAOR, 5th Sess., Supp. No. 9, at 1, 19, UN Doc. A/1286 (1950).

[16] In international law, this issue is relevant to both statehood and territorial title. Regarding statehood, see, for example, CRAWFORD, *supra* note 3, at 42–47; regarding territorial title, see, for example, IAN BROWNLIE, PRINCIPLES OF PUBLIC INTERNATIONAL LAW 105–67 (5th ed. 1998).

[17] For background, see, for example, F. P. WALTERS, A HISTORY OF THE LEAGUE OF NATIONS 525–26, 536–40 (1952); YDIT, *supra* note 15, at 59–62; L. H. Woolsey, *The Leticia Dispute Between Colombia and Peru*, 27 AJIL 317 (1933); L. H. Woolsey, *The Leticia Dispute Between Colombia and Peru*, 29 AJIL 94 (1935) [hereinafter Woolsey 1935]; John V. Czerapowicz, International Territorial Authority: Leticia and West New Guinea 6–94 (1972) (unpublished Ph.D. dissertation, Indiana University).

[18] Agreement Relating to the Procedure for Putting into Effect the Recommendations Proposed by the Council of the League of Nations, May 25, 1933, Peru-Colom., 138 LNTS 253 [hereinafter Geneva Agreement]. On the League administration, see 14 LEAGUE OF NATIONS O.J. 944–45 (1933); WALTERS, *supra* note 17, at 538–40; YDIT, *supra* note 15, at 59–62; Woolsey 1935, *supra* note 17, at 95–99; Czerapowicz, *supra* note 17, at 9–76.

administered Leticia "in the name of the Government of Colombia," and Colombia was responsible for the commission's expenses and the cost of administration;[19] the Colombian flag flew alongside the League flag and Colombia provided troops for the commission.[20] These features of the mission reflected the common acceptance that Leticia was part of Colombia.[21] So why did League administration, rather than Colombian control, replace control by the Peruvian irregulars? For Colombia, it was a staging post in between control by the Peruvian irregulars and control by Colombian authorities.[22] For Peru, however, it ensured that the territory would not be transferred to Colombia until the wider border dispute between the two countries was resolved.[23] Given this disagreement and the silence of the administration mandate as to whom the League would transfer control, ITA by the League cannot, at its conception, be viewed as having necessarily been aimed at effecting a transfer of territory from Peru to Colombia. Rather, ITA was intended to "insulate the territory from further conflict while the disputants conducted comprehensive negotiations on all outstanding issues," by removing the possibility of administrative control by either disputant.[24] Only on the resolution of these outstanding issues, which came before the end of the commission's term in the form of a border agreement, could control be transferred to Colombia.[25]

In addition to removing a sovereignty-related obstacle to the settlement of a territorial dispute, ITA has also been used to remove this type of obstacle to the implementation of a settlement once reached. The territory of West Irian had remained under Dutch administration on the gaining of independence by the rest of the Dutch East Indies as Indonesia. The Netherlands and Indonesia disagreed about the future status of the territory,[26] the Netherlands arguing that its administration had treated what had become Indonesia separately from West Irian, and that each territory was entitled to external self-determination. Indonesia disputed this contention, claiming that the entire Dutch East Indies was a single self-determination unit and that West Irian should be assimilated automatically into Indonesian territory. The compromise reached involved the transfer of territorial control from the Netherlands to Indonesia, followed by a UN-monitored popular consultation asking whether the people wished to "remain with" or "sever their ties with Indonesia."[27] The administrative role of the United Nations—exercised by the United Nations Temporary Executive Authority (UNTEA)—was to facilitate the transfer by administering the territory for seven months (October 1962 to May 1963), providing a buffer between Dutch and Indonesian control.[28]

---

[19] Geneva Agreement, *supra* note 18, Arts. 2, 7, respectively.

[20] Czerapowicz, *supra* note 17, at 27–29 (the flag); Woolsey 1935, *supra* note 17, at 96; YDIT, *supra* note 15, at 61 (the troops).

[21] Czerapowicz, *supra* note 17, at 16.

[22] This was also the view taken by the League commission. Czerapowicz, *supra* note 17, at 88–91.

[23] *Id.* at 83–84, 89–90.

[24] *Id.* at 226; *see also id.* at 9.

[25] Protocol of Friendship and Co-operation, May 24, 1934, Colom.-Peru, 164 LNTS 21.

[26] On this period in West Irian's history, see, for example, D. W. BOWETT, UNITED NATIONS FORCES 255–56 (1964); CRAWFORD, *supra* note 3, at 332–33, 382 n.132 (and sources cited therein); THOMAS M. FRANCK, NATION AGAINST NATION 76–82 (1985); 2 ROSALYN HIGGINS, UNITED NATIONS PEACEKEEPING 93–100 (1970); William J. Durch, *UN Temporary Executive Authority, in* THE EVOLUTION OF UN PEACEKEEPING 285, 285–87 (William J. Durch ed., 1994) (and sources cited therein); Michla Pomerance, *Methods of Self-Determination and the Argument of 'Primitiveness,'* 1974 CAN. Y.B. INT'L L. 38.

[27] Agreement Concerning West New Guinea (West Irian), Aug. 15, 1962, Indon.-Neth., Art. XVIII(c), 437 UNTS 273 [hereinafter Indonesia-Netherlands Agreement]; Exchange of Letters (with Annexed Memorandum of Understanding) on Cessation of Hostilities, Aug. 15, 1962, Indon. & Neth.-UN, 437 UNTS 294.

[28] For the powers of UNTEA, see Indonesia-Netherlands Agreement, *supra* note 27, Arts. II–III, XIII–XV; Annual Report of the Secretary-General on the Work of the Organization, June 16, 1962–June 15, 1963, UN GAOR, 18th Sess., Supp. No. 1, at 35, UN Doc. A/5501 (1963).

This use of ITA resurfaced thirty years later in Eastern Slavonia, which by 1995 was occupied by local Serb forces loyal to the Federal Republic of Yugoslavia (FRY).[29] Croatia and "local Croatian Serb authorities" signed an agreement introducing a transitional period, which ran from 1995 to 1998, during which the territory was administered by the United Nations Transitional Administration for Eastern Slavonia (UNTAES).[30] After this period, administrative control would be handed over to Croatia.[31] In West Irian and Eastern Slavonia, ITA was used as a bridge between Dutch and local Serb control, on the one hand, and Indonesian and Croatian control, on the other. Although agreements had been reached involving the transfer of territorial control from one party to another, the actual implementation of these agreements proved difficult. A general history of dispute marked the relations between the parties; and a party that had previously objected to territorial control by the other would now have to facilitate such control through its own action. The United Nations, as a neutral actor, offered a face-saving alternative.

In these examples, the border agreement between Colombia and Peru and the transfers of control to Indonesia and Croatia constituted the response to the wider sovereignty question. ITA merely allowed this response to emerge, or helped to realize it once agreed. However, in the Saar and Mostar, ITA was proposed or actualized in a more radical way—as itself the device for either preventing or solving a sovereignty question.

One objective of the Versailles Treaty at the end of the First World War was to allow France to obtain reparations from Germany by exploiting mines in the Saar for fifteen years.[32] Because French administrative control of the Saar was objectionable in view of that country's ambitions to annex the territory, League administration was introduced for the duration of the exploitation period.[33] The League was seen as neutral with respect to sovereignty claims, enabling the formal preservation of German sovereignty. In addition to preventing a sovereignty question from arising, ITA was proposed or actualized, again in the Saar and also in Mostar, to resolve such a question once it had arisen. After the fifteen-year exploitation period, the population of the Saar was given the choice between "union with Germany" and "union with France," to be expressed in a plebiscite and "taken into account" by the League in its disposal of the territory.[34] The Versailles Treaty anticipated the problem if neither option was favored by providing a third option—the continuance of the "régime established" in the territory.[35] Accordingly, ITA served as part of the solution to this problem by allowing control to be given to neither Germany nor France. In fact, the problem never

---

[29] RICHARD C. HOLBROOKE, TO END A WAR 236–39 (1998); LAURA SILBER & ALLAN LITTLE, THE DEATH OF YUGO-SLAVIA 370–71 (2d ed. 1996).

[30] Basic Agreement on the Region of Eastern Slavonia, Baranja and Western Sirmium, Nov. 12, 1995, 35 ILM 184 (1996), Annex to Letter from the Permanent Representative of Croatia to the United Nations Addressed to the UN Secretary-General, UN Doc. A/50/757–S/1995/951 (quotation from text of the letter); *see also* SC Res. 1037 (Jan. 15, 1996), *reprinted in* 35 ILM at 189; SC Res. 1079 (Nov. 15, 1996); SC Res. 1120 (July 14, 1997); Report of the Secretary-General, UN Doc. S/1996/705. On these arrangements, see, for example, SILBER & LITTLE, *supra* note 29, at 370–71; Michael Bothe, *The Peace Process in Eastern Slavonia*, INT'L PEACEKEEPING, Dec. 1995–Jan. 1996, at 6; *The New UN Mission in Eastern Slavonia, id.* at 11; *UNTAES Chronology* (Jan. 15, 1998), *at* <http://www.un.org/Depts/DPKO/Missions/untaes_e.htm>.

[31] SC Res. 1023 pmbl., paras. 1–2 (Nov. 22, 1995), *reprinted in* 35 ILM 188 (1996); Bothe, *supra* note 30, at 6.

[32] On the background to, and operation of, the League administration in the Saar, see, for example, W. R. BISSCHOP, THE SAAR CONTROVERSY (1924); WALTERS, *supra* note 17, at 89–90, 239–43, 337–38, 416, 586–98; YDIT, *supra* note 15, at 44–48. On the reason for French exploitation of the mines, see Treaty of Peace, June 28, 1919, Art. 45, 2 Bevans 43 [hereinafter Versailles Treaty]; WALTERS, *supra*, at 89.

[33] On France's powers to exploit the mines, see Versailles Treaty, *supra* note 32, Arts. 45, 46, 50, & Annex to pt. III, §IV (after Art. 50), ch. I, and the commentary by BISSCHOP, *supra* note 32, at 20–22, 52–56. On the League administration, see Versailles Treaty, *supra*, Arts. 46, 49, & Annex to pt. III, §IV (after Art. 50), Arts. 16–33; BISSCHOP, *supra*, at 22–31, 38–52, 87–133.

[34] Versailles Treaty, *supra* note 32, Arts. 47, 49, & Annex to pt. III, §IV (after Art. 50), Arts. 34–40 (the first two quotations come from the Annex, *supra*, Art. 34, and the third from *id.*, Art. 35).

[35] Versailles Treaty, *supra* note 32, Annex to pt. III, §IV (after Art. 50), Art. 34.

arose because the outcome of the plebiscite (honored by the League) supported union with Germany.[36]

In 1993 this use of ITA resurfaced in the city of Mostar in Bosnia and Herzegovina. Mostar was politically and militarily split into West and East, the two halves controlled, respectively, by the Bosnian Croats and the Bosniacs.[37] To address the apparent inability of local actors to agree on governing the city as a unified entity, the EUAM was introduced from 1994 to 1996 to administer the city as a whole pending local agreement on unification.[38]

Using ITA to solve a sovereignty problem reflects and constitutes the sovereignty matters at stake. In Eastern Slavonia and Mostar, ITA solved what was presented as an exclusively "internal" problem. In Eastern Slavonia, it enabled the transfer of territory not from one state to another, but from separatist local forces to the state governmental authority. In Mostar, it was presented as a response to a dispute between two factions concerning city government within the state of Bosnia and Herzegovina. Presenting sovereignty problems as exclusively internal necessarily eliminates the idea that they are "external." In the case of Eastern Slavonia, the local Serb forces favored unification with the FRY as part of a "Greater Serbia." The agreement was brokered by the United States in a secret pact between FRY President Milošević and Croatian President Tuđman to remove the final obstacle to the normalization of relations between the two countries.[39] This pact was transformed into the agreement once President Milošević obtained the support of the local Serbs.[40] The transfer, effected through ITA, enabled the FRY to abandon the separatist cause of the local Serbs to promote the broader interests of its relations with Croatia. Similarly, presenting the dispute in Mostar as exclusively internal denied the aspirations of the Bosnian Croats to make West Mostar part either of a new state of Herzeg-Bosna (constituting the Croatian areas of Bosnia and Herzegovina) or of Croatia proper. In self-determination terms, the people in each territory—the Serbs in Croatia, the Croats in Mostar—were to enjoy "internal" but not "external" self-determination. The territories concerned, Eastern Slavonia and West Mostar, were therefore not self-determination units or parts of such units, and could not unite with a Greater Serbia or Croatia/Herzeg-Bosna, respectively. In Mostar, imposing a "united" administration in a city emblematic of the Bosniac/Croat divisions in the country generally symbolized the international commitment to a united state of Bosnia and Herzegovina.

In contrast to ITA's use in Mostar and Eastern Slavonia, the proposal or actualization of ITA in the Saar, Leticia, and West Irian presented the sovereignty problem as external—the territory's international status was in question. However, the options in this case were narrow: control by one or both of two specified states—Germany and France in the Saar; Colombia and Peru in Leticia; and the Netherlands and Indonesia in West Irian. Control by any other state, or the people of the territory within the framework of independent statehood, was necessarily excluded. Moreover, only in the Saar did the people of the territory play any direct role in the decision. Consequently, the plebiscite options there, taking place as they did in the League era, can perhaps be regarded as reflecting an emergent form of the right to external self-determination.

---

[36] WALTERS, *supra* note 17, at 587–98; YDIT, *supra* note 15, at 45 n.1.

[37] On the divisions in Mostar, see, for example, MISHA GLENNY, THE FALL OF YUGOSLAVIA 246 (3d ed. 1996); OWEN, *supra* note 15, at 239; International Crisis Group, *Reunifying Mostar: Opportunities for Progress* (Apr. 19, 2000), at <http://www.intl-crisis-group.org>.

[38] See generally Mostar MOU, *supra* note 4, in particular Article 2. On the background to the EUAM, see, for example, OWEN, *supra* note 15, at 212, 238–40, 257.

[39] HOLBROOKE, *supra* note 29, at 264–65; SILBER & LITTLE, *supra* note 29, at 370–71.

[40] HOLBROOKE, *supra* note 29, at 264–65; SILBER & LITTLE, *supra* note 29, at 370–71.

The West Irian project, however, took place when external self-determination was accepted as the basis for establishing the international status of colonial territories.[41] Nevertheless, the external sovereignty issue was, as with the League-era projects, narrowly conceived—control by one state or another—and decided by the two disputant states. Thus, the transfer of control from the Netherlands to Indonesia treated West Irian as if its population did not enjoy the right to external self-determination. At the same time, the Netherlands-Indonesia agreement treated the population as if it did enjoy the right to some form of external self-determination by providing for the consultation on whether to remain part of or separate from Indonesia. The transfer and the consultation, therefore, were based on opposing ideas, corresponding to the positions of Indonesia and the Netherlands. Moreover, the handover transformed the situation on the ground, affecting the subsequent consultation. Indonesia could manipulate the circumstances of the consultation to ensure the outcome it desired.[42] Despite the endorsement of the UN monitors, the consultation was widely criticized as a sham, involving only a small number of the local elite, and many local people have engaged in a self-determination struggle ever since.[43] By facilitating the solution to the narrow sovereignty question—the territorial transfer—ITA served not only to deny the existence of the wider sovereignty question but also partially to determine its eventual outcome. As such, it was partially constitutive of the denial of the form of self-determination that had been granted by the consultation agreement.

Using ITA to solve a sovereignty question represents a failure of what might be called the "normal" sovereignty model. The character of this model depends on whether the sovereignty question at issue is considered internal or external. When ITA solves an internal sovereignty question, as in Mostar, failure lies in not realizing the normal model of internal sovereignty: unified governmental structures. Equally, when ITA used for this purpose is later discontinued, as happened in Mostar in 1996, the normal model of internal sovereignty is considered to have been restored: Mostar was supposedly reunified.[44] When ITA is used to solve an external sovereignty question, failure lies in not realizing the normal model of external sovereignty: making the territory a state or part of a state. Here, ITA alone does not suffice, as it cannot resolve the status question by itself. In the Saar plebiscite, the third option, representing the alternative to union with Germany and union with France, involved not only continued League administration, but also Germany's making "such renunciation of her sovereignty in favour of the League of Nations as the latter shall deem necessary."[45] This option potentially suggested an additional device—what might be called "international territorial sovereignty"—that would make the Saar League territory.

Despite replacing local actors, using ITA to respond to a sovereignty problem reinforces the notion that local territorial administration, and locally identified "state" sovereignty, although unobtainable, are both the ideal. When addressing a concern related to a wider sovereignty question, ITA envisages some form of local territorial administration as the outcome to that wider question. Even when it is proposed as the answer to the sovereignty question, ITA is the solution of last resort. Agreement cannot be reached on how local actors should enjoy control, so ITA is used because it involves no control by any local actor.

---

[41] See Western Sahara, Advisory Opinion, 1975 ICJ REP. 12 (Oct. 16); Legal Consequences for States of the Continued Presence of South Africa in Namibia (South West Africa) Notwithstanding Security Council Resolution 276 (1970), Advisory Opinion, 1971 ICJ REP. 16 (June 21) [hereinafter Namibia Opinion]; GA Res. 2625 (XXV) (Oct. 24, 1970); GA Res. 1541 (XV) (Dec. 15, 1960); GA Res. 1514 (XV) (Dec. 14, 1960).

[42] On the consultation, see, for example, CRAWFORD, supra note 3, at 382 n.132 and sources cited therein; FRANCK, supra note 26, at 81–82; MICHLA POMERANCE, SELF-DETERMINATION IN LAW AND PRACTICE 32–35 (1982); Durch, supra note 26, at 295–96 (on UNTEA); Pomerance, supra note 26, at 48–62.

[43] For such criticism, see the citations of FRANCK, supra note 26, POMERANCE, supra note 42, and Pomerance, supra note 26, in note 42 supra.

[44] In the case of Mostar, this conclusion is misleading. See text at note 82 infra.

[45] Versailles Treaty, supra note 32, Annex to pt. III, §IV (after Art. 50), Art. 35.

Thus, the spatial identity of international organizations has been exploited through ITA as a means of solving sovereignty problems. This is only half of the picture, however, since ITA is also used to solve governance problems within the territories concerned.

The Second Purpose: Responding to a Governance Problem

ITA can be used as a response to a perceived governance problem regarding local territorial administration. The problem is not the identity of those local actors acting in the role of the government authority but, rather, the conduct of governance by such actors. It can have two related features. Local actors may be considered practically incapable of conducting any governance at all. The problem therefore amounts to a lack of governance. Alternatively, there may be a perceived risk that local actors will exercise their governmental powers in a manner that conflicts with certain policy objectives. Here, the problem is the absence of "good governance."

Problems of the first type, where local actors are incapable of exercising administrative authority, are exemplified by UNHCR-run refugee camps, most of which are in poor countries lacking the means to administer camps themselves.[46] Similarly, international organizations usually run material assistance programs when local authorities cannot provide social support. After the defeat of Germany at the end of the Second World War, the Allies filled the governmental vacuum in Germany and Austria by administering both territories for a time.[47] The first UN mission to fill a governmental vacuum was the United Nations Operation in the Congo (ONUC) between 1960 and 1964.[48] ONUC interpreted a mandate to provide technical assistance flexibly, performing governmental functions directly—sometimes against the wishes of the local government.[49] Initially, the assumption of these functions was deemed necessary because Belgium, the former colonial state, had failed to train local people prior to its departure; later, government collapsed because of the ensuing conflict, disputes between different government factions, outside interference by Belgium, and the attempt at secession by Katanga province.[50] In 1967 when the United Nations set up the UN Council for South West Africa/Namibia, ITA was used to respond to a different administrative vacuum.[51] The council was to administer Namibia, filling a vacuum created not by ongoing threats to the existing government, but by the anticipated withdrawal of South Africa following the termination of its mandatory power and the General Assembly's assumption of direct responsibility for the territory.[52] However, the council was denied entry to Namibia by South Africa; it used its de jure administrative authority, inter alia, to issue travel documents and pass a Decree on Natural Resources.[53]

---

[46] Wilde, *UNHCR, supra* note 6, paras. 4–7.

[47] *See* Declaration Regarding the Defeat of Germany, June 5, 1945, TIAS No. 1520, 68 UNTS 189; BATHURST & SIMPSON, *supra* note 3; CRAWFORD, *supra* note 3, at 273–79 (and sources cited therein at 273 n.10, 311 n.70); NORMAN HILL, INTERNATIONAL ORGANIZATION 511 (1952); MANN, *supra* note 3, at 634–705; Jennings, *supra* note 3.

[48] For the constitutive and other contemporary documents relating to ONUC, see 3 HIGGINS, *supra* note 26 (1980). On ONUC, see, for example, RATNER, *supra* note 15, at 102–09; William J. Durch, *The UN Operation in the Congo: 1960–1964, in* THE EVOLUTION OF PEACEKEEPING, *supra* note 26, at 315.

[49] SC Res. 143 (July 14, 1960); *see* RATNER, *supra* note 15, at 105–09.

[50] RATNER, *supra* note 15, at 105–09.

[51] GA Res. 2248 (S-V) (May 19, 1967); *see also* GA Res. 2372 (XXII) (June 12, 1968). On South West Africa/Namibia generally, see, for example, JOHN DUGARD, THE SOUTH WEST AFRICA/NAMIBIA DISPUTE 409–13, 436–46 (1974); LAURENT C. W. KAELA, THE QUESTION OF NAMIBIA (1996) (and sources cited therein at 205–11); Lawrence L. Herman, *The Legal Status of Namibia and of the United Nations Council for Namibia,* 1975 CAN. Y.B. INT'L L. 306.

[52] For the termination, see Namibia Opinion, *supra* note 41; GA Res. 2145 (XXI) (Oct. 27, 1966); *see also* SC Res. 264 (Mar. 20, 1969).

[53] On South Africa's refusal, see, for example, DUGARD, *supra* note 51, at 436, 440. On the council's activities, see United Nations Council for Namibia, Decree No. 1 on Natural Resources of Namibia, UN Doc. A/C.131/33, *in* Report of the Council for Namibia, Addendum, UN GAOR, 29th Sess., Supp. No. 24A, at 27, UN Doc. A/9624/Add.1 (1974); GA Res. 2372 (XXII), *supra* note 51, para. 4; GA Res. 2325 (XXII) (Dec. 16, 1967); J. F. Engers, *The United Nations Travel and Identity Document for Namibians,* 65 AJIL 571 (1971); Herman, *supra* note 51,

When South Africa finally agreed to Namibian independence in 1988, the administrative role exercised by the United Nations Transitional Assistance Group (UNTAG) was limited to supervising and controlling the elections.[54]

Over thirty years after the Council for Namibia was created, UNMIK and then UNTAET realized the council's role in Kosovo and East Timor. In June 1999, ITA filled the vacuum caused by the departure of the FRY governmental presence in Kosovo, following the NATO bombing campaign and the human rights abuses and mass displacement of the local Albanian population perpetrated by FRY forces. Since the population of Kosovo was to enjoy "substantial autonomy," UNMIK provided administration pending the establishment of institutions through which self-government could be exercised.[55] Later that year, ITA was introduced in East Timor after the Australian-led military force INTERFET restored order in the wake of a rampage of killing and property destruction by pro-Indonesian militias.[56] The militias' actions followed the outcome of the UNAMET-run popular consultation, which overwhelmingly favored separation from Indonesia. After restoring order, INTERFET and a few UNAMET personnel attempted to fill the administrative vacuum created by the departure of Indonesian officials and exacerbated by the destruction.[57] UNTAET was created in part to take over this activity.

In addition to filling a vacuum in local territorial governance, ITA has been used in other situations for a broader and less well defined purpose. The problem is not with the existence of governance, but the quality of governance being performed. ITA has addressed three main policy objectives for governance: the attainment of a certain status for the territorial unit concerned, the continued operation of governmental institutions, and furtherance of democratic practices.

The first administrative policy enabled by ITA is the promotion of a certain status for the territory concerned. Like the use of ITA in response to a sovereignty problem, this use supports the determination of a sovereignty question; however, the threat comes not from the presence of certain local actors in the role of the governmental authority, but from the way governance is practiced. ITA is used to facilitate the future adoption of a certain territorial agenda; to bring a territorial settlement into being; or to support the continuance of a territorial settlement once adopted.

ITA was first employed to promote the adoption of a certain territorial agenda in the Saar. As an alternative to both French and German administration, League control prevented either country from altering the Versailles plan for determining the territory's status. When the General Assembly terminated South Africa's mandate and introduced council administration, it aimed at replacing one administration that opposed the future realization of a particular form of external self-determination—independence—with another that supported it. This use of ITA resurfaced in the 1990s, with the dissolution of the former Yugoslavia. As discussed previously, the EUAM administered Mostar from 1994 to 1996 so as to temporarily solve the sovereignty problem caused by the failure of local factions to agree on governing the city jointly. It also responded to a governance problem by replacing governments in West and East Mostar opposed to unification with a (single) government supporting unification. By promoting unification, it would try to solve the sovereignty problem permanently, removing the need for its presence as the temporary solution to that problem.

---

at 320. A member of the commissioner's office remarked in 1971 that the council operated "as a kind of UNTEA *in partibus* or as the second World War governments-in-exile." Engers, *supra*, at 574.

[54] SC Res. 632 (Feb. 16, 1989); SC Res. 435 (Sept. 29, 1978); LIONEL CLIFFE, THE TRANSITION TO INDEPENDENCE IN NAMIBIA 65–77, *passim* (1994); KAELA, *supra* note 51, at 96–125; Virginia Page Fortna, *United Nations Transition Assistance Group in Namibia, in* THE EVOLUTION OF UN PEACEKEEPING, *supra* note 26, at 353.

[55] Kosovo Peace Plan, *supra* note 11, para. 5; SC Res. 1244, *supra* note 11, paras. 10, 11.

[56] Progress Report of the Secretary-General on the Question of East Timor, UN Doc. A/54/654, paras. 32–37 (1999) [hereinafter Secretary-General Report]; SC Res. 1264, para. 3 (Sept. 15, 1999).

[57] Secretary-General Report, *supra* note 56, paras. 36, 37.

The same objective lay behind the introduction of the OHR supervisor in the Brcko District. At the end of 1995, the city of Brcko, formerly a multiethnic community, was divided, together with its surrounding area, between the two constitutive entities of Bosnia and Herzegovina—the Bosniac-Croat Federation (the Federation) and Republika Srpksa (the RS)—with each side claiming exclusive title over the whole district.[58] As in many areas of the country, population movements, whether voluntary or forcible, in conjunction with killing, had "cleansed" each part of the district of members of the opposing ethnic group(s).[59] On the one hand, the Dayton Agreement accepted the ethnic division of Bosnia and Herzegovina between the two entities according to the Inter-Entity Boundary Line.[60] On the other hand, it promoted the return of migrants to their former homes, attempting to reverse the migratory aspect of ethnic cleansing and to foster a unified, multiethnic politics cutting across that boundary.[61] Since agreement on the Brcko section of the boundary was not reached at Dayton, the determination of this section was placed before an arbitral tribunal.[62] In 1997 the tribunal considered that the RS had failed to implement its "return" and free movement obligations, and granted an OHR supervisor certain administrative powers—including the power to legislate—to promote the objectives of return and democratization.[63] These objectives can be explained as means of promoting conditions for a unified, multiethnic politics in the district, enabling the tribunal eventually to establish a unified Brcko as the solution to the boundary dispute.[64] Whereas in Mostar obstructions to a unified city were addressed as both a sovereignty and a governance problem, in Brkco the tribunal preferred not to replace divided structures immediately with an internationally run unified structure.[65] Rather, it enabled the supervisor to exercise governance within the divided structures to enhance the possibility that a unified structure would be supported in the future.

In Kosovo, the territory's future status has been placed open to question, and UNMIK is charged with "[f]acilitating a political process" to determine this status.[66] It replaces the Serb and FRY governments, which in 1999 opposed any alteration in Kosovo's status. Like the Saar project before it, the Kosovo undertaking is distinctive within this group of projects. Whereas ITA promotes a future change in territorial status, the form this status will take is unclear. UNMIK must therefore promote the idea of a possible change in status, rather than the definite adoption of a certain status (e.g., statehood in Namibia). In the Saar, the status question was to be determined according to a pre-set formula on a predetermined date; in Kosovo, however, UNMIK is also partially responsible for the very resolution of this question.

Besides promoting the future adoption of a particular territorial agenda, ITA has been used to effect the immediate enactment of such an agenda. This result can be accomplished in two ways—either by performing positive administrative acts, or by transferring administrative control to certain local actors. In Mostar in 1994, and Brcko in 2000, positive admin-

---

[58] Brcko is at the intersection between both the two parts of RS and the main part of the Federation and additional Federation territory. See the map in GLENNY, *supra* note 37, at xii. For the situation in Brcko by 1995, see, for example, Dispute over Inter-Entity Boundary in Brcko Area (Rep. Srpska v. Fed. of Bosn. & Herz.) (arb. Feb. 14, 1997), UN Doc. S/1997/126, paras. 42–57, *reprinted in* 36 ILM 396 (1997) [hereinafter Brcko Award 1997]. By the end of 1997, the RS controlled 48% and the Federation 52% of the territory, *id.*, para. 52. On Brcko generally, see, for example, International Crisis Group, *supra* note 37.

[59] Brcko Award 1997, *supra* note 58, paras. 50, 53.

[60] For the boundary, and the Constitution of Bosnia and Herzegovina, see Annexes 2 and 4, respectively, Dayton Agreement, *supra* note 4.

[61] Dayton Agreement, *supra* note 4, Annex 7.

[62] *Id.*, Annex 2, Art. V. Tribunal decisions are obtainable online at <http://www.ohr.int/brcko.htm> [hereinafter OHR Brcko site] (visited Aug. 6, 2001).

[63] *See* Brcko Award 1997, *supra* note 58, paras. 54, 104.

[64] In its final award. *See* note 67 and corresponding text *infra*.

[65] On the tribunal's consideration of this option, see, for example, Brcko Award 1997, *supra* note 58, para. 68.

[66] SC Res. 1244, *supra* note 11, para. 11, & Annex 1, para. 6; Kosovo Peace Plan, *supra* note 11, para. 8 (quotation from SC Res. 1244, para. 11).

istrative acts by the EUAM and the OHR supervisor, respectively, brought the model of unified city government into existence. In Mostar, it was achieved through the creation of the EUAM itself. In Brcko, a new territorial settlement crafted by the arbitral tribunal in 1999 established the district as a condominium between the two entities, run locally by a unified multiethnic government.[67] This new settlement was implemented through certain administrative acts by the OHR supervisor. In the immediate sense, these acts included imposing a new Statute for District Government (enacted in 2000); scheduling new elections; determining when the Inter-Ethnic Boundary Line no longer had any effect in the district; and creating an interim regime (including an Interim District Assembly) pending the outcome of the elections.[68] Given that Kosovo is to enjoy "substantial autonomy" within the FRY, the plenary (rather than "substantial") administrative powers apparently asserted by UNMIK can be explained as a mechanism for ensuring that the local population can practice autonomous government without having to rely on the Serb and Yugoslav authorities.[69] UNMIK has assumed what is effectively (though not in name) the federal-type role of the Serb and FRY authorities, because these authorities failed to perform that role in the past. On the anticipated resolution of Kosovo's future status, UNMIK is also mandated to bring this status into being by effecting the transfer of authority from those institutions under the "substantial autonomy" arrangements to those institutions under the final settlement.[70]

ITA was conceived to implement a territorial settlement in the second way—through giving up its administrative powers to certain local actors—in the Saar, Namibia, Mostar, and Kosovo. In the Saar, placing the League, rather than France or Germany, in administrative control in 1935 ensured that control would be transferred to whoever prevailed following the 1935 plebiscite. In Namibia, a corollary to the reason for introducing ITA—to replace one government opposed to independence with another that supported it—was the UN intention eventually to give up administrative control to local actors, enabling a declaration of independence to be made. This perhaps explains the lack of a council-type role for the United Nations in 1988: contrary to its behavior in 1967, the existing administrative actor (the South African government) had agreed to enable independence by relinquishing its authority to the people of Namibia. In Mostar in 1996, an externally imposed settlement for unified government run by local actors was implemented through ITA. It was effected both by the creation of new local structures, as in Brcko in 2000, and by the transfer by EUAM of its plenary authority to these structures. In Kosovo, insofar as the future arrangements do not involve an administrative role for the United Nations, UNMIK will transfer its authority to the appropriate locally run institutions.

Using ITA, either positively or negatively, to implement a particular territorial agenda distinguishes all these projects from the East Timor project, since in East Timor ITA was not used to replace an existing authority opposed to independence. Although Indonesia had originally been opposed, UNTAET was conceived subsequent to, and quite apart from, Indonesia's belated acceptance and consequent withdrawal.[71] At the same time, UNTAET cannot continue its administration indefinitely, since it is implicitly mandated to administer itself out of existence by transferring authority to local actors in the future.

[67] Dispute over Inter-Entity Boundary in Brcko Area, paras. 11, 34, 36 (Final Award, Mar. 5, 1999), at <http://www.ohr.int/docu/d990305c.htm> [hereinafter Brcko Award 1999].

[68] See Statute of the Brcko District of Bosnia and Herzegovina, Dec. 7, 1999, 39 ILM 879 (2000); Supervisor of Brcko, Supervisory Order on the Establishment of the Brcko District of Bosnia and Herzegovina (Mar. 8, 2000), at <http://www.ohr.int/docu/d20000308c.htm>; Brcko Award 1999, supra note 67, paras. 36, 38, 39, 40, 41. The supervisor performed further acts to implement the district settlement, including establishing the interim regime. See the orders of the supervisor from March 8, 2000, onwards, at OHR Brcko site, supra note 62.

[69] On asserting plenary authority, see note 13 supra.

[70] SC Res. 1244, supra note 11, para. 11.

[71] See Indonesia-Portugal Agreement, supra note 12, Art. 6; Secretary-General Report, supra note 56, para. 39.

In Danzig, Trieste, Bosnia and Herzegovina, Mostar, and Kosovo, ITA was conceived to promote the continuance of a territorial agenda once adopted. In Danzig at the end of the First World War and Trieste at the end of the second, ITA formed part of the response to a territorial dispute between certain states (Germany and Poland over Danzig; the victorious Allies, Italy, and Yugoslavia over Trieste).[72] The solution was to reconstitute, on a permanent basis, Danzig as a "free city" and Trieste as a "free territory." Each territory would be self-administered, with certain administrative powers given to the League or the United Nations to ensure that governance by others supported the new "free" status.[73] In Trieste, this settlement, although authorized, was never enacted because of continuing disagreements.[74] Danzig was a "free city" from 1920 to 1939.[75]

In Danzig, administrative powers were granted primarily to the free city authorities; Poland enjoyed certain domestic authority and responsibility for the conduct of foreign policy.[76] The territory was placed under the "protection" of the League, which was to play two roles: first, to settle disputes between the free city and Poland, and second, to exercise certain administrative powers to ensure that administration by others did not compromise Danzig's free city status.[77] The League drafted the constitution in conjunction with representatives of the free city and then guaranteed it by retaining a veto over future amendments.[78] It could veto certain militaristic plans, as well as the conclusion of any treaty by Poland on behalf of Danzig if it was inconsistent with either Poland's rights over the free city or the status of the free city.[79] This settlement remained an uneasy compromise; the failure of the League to "protect" Danzig from Nazi occupation on September 1, 1939, formed part of the wider collapse of the League system and the resumption of war in Europe.[80]

OHR has gradually begun to assert administrative authority to ensure the continuation of Bosnia and Herzegovina as a state. For example, on March 7, 2001, OHR dismissed Ante Jelavić as the elected Croat representative of the state presidency, and banned him from holding public and party offices in the future, because of Jelavić's declaration of independence on the part of Herzeg-Bosna.[81] Since Herzeg-Bosna is the Croatian component of the Federation entity, OHR exercised governance in an effort to prevent the Federation from unraveling. Similarly, some of the international appointees were introduced to ensure that the institutions involved supported the existing territorial settlement in their decisions. In Mostar, the unified settlement imposed in 1996 was not supported locally, and full agree-

[72] On the background to the Danzig dispute, see, for example, JOHN BROWN MASON, THE DANZIG DILEMMA 3–76 (1946); YDIT, supra note 15, at 186–90, 227; John Kuhn Bleimaier, The Legal Status of the Free City of Danzig 1920–1939: Lessons to Be Derived from the Experience of a Non-State Entity in the International Community, 1989 HAGUE Y.B. INT'L L. 69, 70–81. On the background to the Trieste dispute, see, for example, CRAWFORD, supra note 3, at 161–62; YDIT, supra note 15, at 231–71 and sources cited therein at 272.

[73] For the Free City of Danzig, see Versailles Treaty, supra note 32, Arts. 100–08. For the Free Territory of Trieste, see Peace Treaty with Italy, Feb. 10, 1947, pt. II, §III, Arts. 21–22, & Annexes VI–VIII, 49 UNTS 126.

[74] YDIT, supra note 15, at 268–71.

[75] On the Free City of Danzig, see CRAWFORD, supra note 3, at 164–66 and sources cited at 163 n.118, 165 n.126; MASON, supra note 72, and sources in the bibliography, id. at 308–22; WALTERS, supra note 17, at 82, 90, 131, 140, 301, 453–55, 615–21, 793–97; YDIT, supra note 15, at 185–228 and sources in the bibliography, id. at 229–30; Bleimaier, supra note 72, and bibliography, id. at 93; Malcolm Lewis, The Free City of Danzig, 1924 BRIT. Y.B. INT'L L. 89.

[76] See CONST. (Danzig), LEAGUE OF NATIONS O.J. Spec. Supp. 7, at 1 (1922), as amended, 11 LEAGUE OF NATIONS O.J. 1794 (1930) [hereinafter DANZIG CONST. 1930]; Treaty of Paris, Nov. 9, 1920, Pol.-Danzig, 6 LNTS 189; Versailles Treaty, supra note 32, Art. 104; MASON, supra note 72, at 61–66, 89–227; YDIT, supra note 15, at 191–211.

[77] Versailles Treaty, supra note 32, Arts. 102, 103 (quotation from Art. 102); see also Treaty of Paris, supra note 76, Arts. 7, 8, 18, 20, 22, 25, 26, 39; MASON, supra note 72, at 77–88; WALTERS, supra note 17, at 301, 454–55; YDIT, supra note 15, at 194–97, 211–23.

[78] DANZIG CONST. 1930, Art. 49; Versailles Treaty, supra note 32, Art. 103.

[79] DANZIG CONST. 1930, Art. 5; Treaty of Paris, supra note 76, Art. 6.

[80] WALTERS, supra note 17, at 453–54, 615–21, 793–97; YDIT, supra note 15, at 218–21, 227.

[81] OHR, Decision Removing Ante Jelavic from his Position as the Croat Member of the BiH Presidency and Further Banning Jelavic from Holding Public and Party Offices (Mar. 7, 2001); see supra note 8.

ment on unified governance remains elusive.[82] As a result, OHR has asserted certain governmental powers within Mostar to promote the operation of the unified structures.[83] In Kosovo, not only is UNMIK administration bringing "substantial autonomy" into being; it is ensuring the continuance of this arrangement pending the final realization of the territory's future status.

Thus, the first administrative policy enabled by ITA is the promotion of a certain territorial status, whether free city/territory status (Danzig and Trieste), unified city/district status (Mostar and Brcko), statehood (Namibia and Bosnia and Herzegovina), substate autonomy (Kosovo), or an undetermined future status (the Saar and Kosovo). ITA promotes the future adoption of territorial status, brings territorial status into being (either positively or negatively), and supports the continuance of an existing status. In this respect, the Kosovo mission is the most complex use of ITA so far, since it performs all three functions.

As for the second administrative policy promoted by ITA, the institution enabled the operation of governmental institutions in Danzig, Upper Silesia, and Bosnia and Herzegovina. Under the free city settlement in Danzig, the League was to appoint the president of the Port and Waterways Board if the free city and Poland failed to do so.[84] In 1921 the Allies partitioned Upper Silesia between Germany and Poland after the local population divided 60:30 in a plebiscite on the question.[85] Germany and Poland introduced a fifteen-year "special regime" in the region as a whole, implemented by a Mixed Commission comprising German and Polish appointees and a president appointed by the League.[86] In Bosnia and Herzegovina, the international appointees to statewide institutions (other than the human rights ombudsperson) hold office alongside individuals appointed by the two entities. In these three different places, international appointments were used to avoid deadlock caused by either the inability of others to agree on the appointment or the adoption of opposing positions by other appointees. Introducing "neutral" members enables the institution to function.

The third main trigger for ITA concerning the quality of governance is a situation where governance is, in some sense, "undemocratic." The use of ITA to ensure a particular feature of democratic politics—free and fair popular consultations (also called "elections," "plebiscites," and "referendums")—has a long history. International organizations have either exercised control and supervision over the conduct of popular consultations by local actors or taken over such conduct themselves.[87] The consultations involved can be divided into two types, the first involving the determination of territorial status. This type characterized the 1935 League-run plebiscite in the Saar and the 1999 UN-run consultation in East Timor, as well as various consultations in trust and non-self-governing territories that were either administered or supervised by the United Nations.[88] Consultations of this type were also authorized, but not implemented, in Jammu and Kashmir (the UN Military Observer Group in India and Pakistan [UNMOGIP], created in 1948) and Western Sahara (the UN

---

[82] International Crisis Group, *supra* note 37, esp. at 12.

[83] *E.g.*, OHR, Decision Adding the Fundamental Interest Clause and the Position of Deputy Head of Municipality to the Mostar City Municipalities Statutes (July 6, 1999); *see supra* note 8.

[84] Treaty of Paris, *supra* note 76, Art. 19.

[85] For the plebiscite, see *infra* note 114. For the partition, see YDIT, *supra* note 15, at 46.

[86] For the special regime, see YDIT, *supra* note 15, at 46–47.

[87] The United Nations classifies its electoral operations into eight types. The first two (A and B)—conduct and supervision/control—fall within the scope of this study. The other categories cover monitoring (including verification), observation, and assistance, and have taken place in various trust and non-self-governing territories, as well as Angola, El Salvador, Eritrea, Ethiopia, Haiti, Liberia, Mexico, Malawi, Mozambique, Nicaragua, and South Africa. *See* Report of the Secretary-General, UN Doc. A/49/675, Annex III (1994); Report of the Secretary-General on Enhancing the Effectiveness of the Principle of Periodic and Genuine Elections, UN Doc. A/46/609 (1991) [hereinafter Secretary-General Report 1991]; UN Dep't Pol. Aff., *Member States' Requests for Electoral Assistance to the United Nations System Since 1989* (as of June 1999), at <http://www.un.org/Depts/dpa> (visited Aug. 2, 2001).

[88] For consultations in trust and non-self-governing territories, see Secretary-General Report 1991, *supra* note 87, paras. 6, 7, 12, & Annex.

Mission for the Referendum in the Western Sahara [MINURSO], created in 1991.[89] The second type of consultation elects local actors to governmental positions. International involvement began in various trust and non-self-governing territories and has since spread to states and parts of states.[90] International organizations either exercise supervision and control over local actors (UNTAG in Namibia), or operate the consultation directly (e.g., the UN Transitional Authority in Cambodia [UNTAC] in 1992, the OSCE in Bosnia and Herzegovina from 1996, the EUAM in Mostar in 1996, UNTAES in Eastern Slavonia in 1997, and UNMIK [delegated to the OSCE] in Kosovo from 1999).[91] In most cases, international control or conduct is deployed because of a fear that, if left to other actors, the process would either not take place or fail to be free or fair. Where the consultation in question is an "act of self-determination," it reflects an international commitment to the realization of some form of self-determination for the population involved.

The international conduct or control of popular consultations is sometimes accompanied by more general ITA to furnish governmental support for the consultation process. In Western Sahara, MINURSO was authorized to exercise all necessary administrative measures, including changing laws and maintaining law and order, to ensure that the consultation operated properly and was free and fair.[92] In Cambodia, the 1991 Paris peace agreements facilitated the election of a new government in the UNTAC-run consultation.[93] In the transitional period before this government took office, the Supreme National Council—comprising the four Cambodian factions—enjoyed governmental authority; UNTAC was granted certain powers of supervision and control over governmental institutions to ensure that the exercise of governance would not compromise the elections.[94]

Since the mission in Cambodia, the scope of democratic politics promoted by ITA has extended beyond popular consultations. However, in its application to the protection of minorities, this broader agenda echoes some of the League-era projects. In the Saar, League administration protected the German population from persecution under the alternative of French administration. In Upper Silesia, the League's appointment of the president of the Mixed Commission was to guarantee that the policy of minority protection in each part

---

[89] For UNMOGIP, see SC Res. 47 (Apr. 21, 1948); UNITED NATIONS, THE BLUE HELMETS: A REVIEW OF UNITED NATIONS PEACEKEEPING 133–43, UN Sales No. E.96.I.14 (3d ed. 1996). For MINURSO, see SC Res. 690 (Apr. 29, 1991); Report of the Secretary-General, UN Doc. S/22464 (1991); Report of the Secretary-General, UN Doc. S/21360 (1990); William J. Durch, *United Nations Mission for the Referendum in Western Sahara, in* THE EVOLUTION OF UN PEACEKEEPING, *supra* note 26, at 406. For the latest situation, see, for example, Report of the Secretary-General on the Situation Concerning Western Sahara, UN Doc. S/2001/613 (2001). On the Sahrawis' right to external self-determination, see Western Sahara, *supra* note 41.

[90] For consultations held in trust and non-self-governing territories, see note 88 *supra*.

[91] For UNTAC, see Cambodia Settlement, *infra* note 93, Arts. 2, 12–14, & Annex 1, §D, Annex 3; SC Res. 745 paras. 1, 2 (Feb. 28, 1992); Report of the Secretary-General on Cambodia, UN Doc. S/23613 & Add.1 (1992); *see also* TREVOR FINDLAY, CAMBODIA: THE LEGACY AND LESSONS OF UNTAC 33–74, 101–07, 213–22 (1995); JANET E. HEININGER, PEACEKEEPING IN TRANSITION: THE UNITED NATIONS IN CAMBODIA (1994); UNITED NATIONS, THE UNITED NATIONS AND CAMBODIA 1991–1995, at 15–37, *passim*, UN Sales No. E.95.I.9 (1995); Steven R. Ratner, *The Cambodian Settlement Agreements*, 87 AJIL 1, 9–18, 20–22 (1993). For the OSCE in Bosnia and Herzegovina, see Dayton Agreement, *supra* note 4, Annex 3. For the EUAM in Mostar, see Mostar MOU, *supra* note 4, Art. 2; International Crisis Group, *supra* note 37, at 12. For UNTAES in Eastern Slavonia, see Report of the Secretary-General, UN Doc. S/1997/487, paras. 2, 3. For UNMIK (delegated to the OSCE) in Kosovo, see SC Res. 1244, *supra* note 11, para. 11(c); OSCE, Permanent Council [P.C.], Decision No. 305, Agenda item 2, para. 3, & Doc. PC.JOUR/237/ Corr, OSCE P.C.J., No. 237, 1999.

[92] See the sources cited in note 89 *supra*.

[93] This was part of a wider settlement to end the 20-year-old conflict in the country. Final Act of the Paris Conference on Cambodia, Oct. 23, 1991, Agreement on a Comprehensive Political Settlement of the Cambodia Conflict, Oct. 23, 1991 [Cambodia Settlement], Agreement Concerning the Sovereignty, Independence, Territorial Integrity and Inviolability, Neutrality and National Unity of Cambodia, Oct. 31, 1991, and Declaration on the Rehabilitation and Reconstruction of Cambodia, UN Doc. A/46/608–S/23177 (1991), *reprinted in* 31 ILM 174 (1992). On the settlement, see, for example, FINDLAY, *supra* note 91, at 1–20; HEININGER, *supra* note 91, at 9–30; UNITED NATIONS, *supra* note 91, at 5–9; Ratner, *supra* note 91, at 2–8 and sources cited at 2 n.2, 3 n.7.

[94] Cambodia Settlement, *supra* note 93, Arts. 1, 3, 5, Annex 1, §§A, B. On the elections, see FINDLAY, *supra* note 91, at 75–100; HEININGER, *supra* note 91, at 100–16; UNITED NATIONS, *supra* note 91, at 38–53.

of the territory would be implemented by the commission.[95] These early precedents were followed in Eastern Slavonia, where the three-year duration of ITA was designed to reassure the local Serbs who feared the immediate resumption of Croatian control.[96] They also find an echo in the current UN program of distributing "humanitarian supplies" in three of the northern Iraqi governorates. This distribution forms part of the wider UN "oil-for-food" program, which uses Iraqi oil revenues to pay for, inter alia, "humanitarian supplies" for the whole country.[97] As in the U.S.-UK-imposed no-fly zone above the 36th parallel, UN distribution in the three northern governorates (rather than Iraqi distribution, as in the rest of the country) is explained with reference to the Iraqi government's persecution of the local Kurds. The United Nations administers assistance because of the perceived unwillingness, rather than inability (as in most other international assistance programs), of the local government to do so.

In both Bosnia and Herzegovina generally, and Mostar and Brcko in particular, ITA has been used to promote a multiethnic social and political culture—the other side of the coin from the territorial agenda mentioned earlier. Hence OHR's imposition of a new countrywide license plate bearing no indication of the district in which the car is registered.[98] To the same effect, measures were taken to promote return; for example, in Brcko, the OHR supervisor was charged with establishing a return program, and in the country generally OHR introduced legislation creating the legal basis for the reoccupation of property.[99] In Kosovo, ITA was introduced to ensure that governance would no longer perpetrate human rights abuses against the Kosovar Albanians. An administration that drove about eight hundred thousand Kosovar Albanians from Kosovo and forcibly displaced a further five hundred thousand within the territory was replaced with another regime mandated to enable these people to return.[100] A related use of ITA in societies perceived to be divided involves international organizations in ensuring governmental impartiality. For example, the Council of Europe appoints the human rights ombudsperson in Bosnia and Herzegovina, who investigates complaints against the state and entity authorities.[101]

The "democratic" use for ITA is triggered when local actors are deemed to be either actively opposed to a particular political agenda or unable to govern satisfactorily because they are insufficiently rooted in a "democratic" tradition. UNMIK's initial exercise of full administrative powers, despite being charged with effecting "substantial autonomy," was undertaken not only because institutions of self-government had not yet been created, but also because local people were not "ready" to handle administrative authority. Equally, the continuation of UNTAET's administration after the filling of the administrative vacuum can be understood partially on the grounds that local people were seen as unable to take over immediately. In Bosnia and Herzegovina, the international appointments—such as that of the governor of the Central Bank by the IMF—introduced individuals with democratic experience alongside local appointees perceived as lacking in such experience.

The use of ITA to ensure that governance conforms to certain policy objectives can lie behind its use to fill an administrative vacuum. In Namibia and Kosovo, the refusal of the

---

[95] This policy was one of the central planks of the special regime. See YDIT, supra note 15, at 46–47.

[96] Bothe, supra note 30, at 6.

[97] For the constitutive documents of the "oil-for-food" program, see the UN Iraq Web site, supra note 7.

[98] OHR, Decision on the Deadlines for the Implementation of the New Uniform License Plate System (May 20, 1998); see supra note 8.

[99] On the return agenda generally, see note 61 supra and corresponding text; for the supervisor's return program mandate, see Brcko Award 1997, supra note 58, paras. 54, 104. On property legislation, see the section "Decisions in the Field of Property Laws, Return of Displaced Persons and Refugees and Reconciliation" of the list Decisions by the High Representative, supra note 8.

[100] See SC Res. 1244, supra note 11, para. 11(k). The figures come from Report of the Secretary-General on the United Nations Interim Administration Mission in Kosovo, UN Doc. S/1999/779, paras. 8–9, quoted by Matheson, supra note 11, at 78 n.22.

[101] For this appointment, see note 9 supra.

600   THE AMERICAN JOURNAL OF INTERNATIONAL LAW   [Vol. 95:583

South African authorities to allow future independence, and the refusal of the FRY and Serb authorities to allow autonomy (and some future status) for Kosovo and to desist from human rights violations, led to the displacement of these local authorities by the United Nations, so that government policy would change. ITA thus filled a governmental vacuum created by its own displacement of the existing authorities. In East Timor, by contrast, ITA was introduced not to displace local actors, but to fill the void created by Indonesia's abandonment and the militias' destruction. Nevertheless, once certain basic institutions had been restored and local leaders presented themselves, ITA was continued, partly because these leaders were deemed "not ready" for the challenge of democratic responsibility—meaning that ITA was now, as in Kosovo from the start, filling a void of its own making. Only in the cases of the Congo mission and UN-run refugee camps has the official reason for ITA remained the preexisting incapacity of local actors.

In addition to the three main policies outlined above, ITA has been involved in promoting further administrative policies. One reason for ITA in the Saar was that a fifteen-year regime of French exploitation in the context of German administrative control was viewed as unrealistic: Germany might at some future point prevent the continuance of this regime.[102] ITA introduced an administrative authority that would support the regime throughout the period. In Upper Silesia, a further objective of the "special regime," to mitigate the problems the partition might cause for the integrated economy of the region, was to be achieved by enabling the free movement of people and certain goods across the new frontier, and the operation of joint transportation services.[103] As with the earlier policy of minority guarantees, making the president of the Mixed Commission a League appointee sought to ensure that the commission could implement this policy effectively. In Memel, the League's appointment of the chair of the Harbor Board guaranteed that the policy of maintaining the port as an open waterway and trade center would be implemented.[104]

When ITA responds to a governance problem, it operates in two ways—"reactive" or "proactive." In reactive projects, it is grafted onto an existing governance structure operated by local actors, and power is exercised in an ad hoc fashion—when governance by local actors threatens certain policy objectives or, as in the Congo, simply does not exist. Thus, the exercise of powers by the League in Danzig, the United Nations in Cambodia (other than conducting elections), and the supervisor in Brcko between 1997 and 2000—whether negative (e.g., vetoes) or positive (e.g., appointments, passing legislation)—was aimed at stepping in to correct "mistakes." If mistakes were not made, the powers would not be exercised. Thus, as regards the return policy in Brcko, the supervisor would act only if local actors failed to implement this policy. In the Congo and Bosnia and Herzegovina (both generally and with respect to Mostar after 1996), the very existence of governmental powers only became clear when they were used for the first time; in the case of Bosnia and Herzegovina, the scope of these powers is ever increasing. Again, regardless of whether a power is positive or negative, it is exercised reactively when local governance has fallen or will fall short. For example, OHR imposes specific legislative measures when the legislature is deemed unwilling or incapable of passing such legislation itself.

In proactive projects, by contrast, the need for ITA is assumed from the beginning. This occurs when plenary administrative control is asserted, as in UN-run refugee camps, Eastern Slavonia, Mostar (the EUAM), Kosovo, and East Timor; or when particular administrative acts are performed because local actors are assumed to be permanently unable or unsuitable to perform them (e.g., conducting popular consultations). Here, ITA does not operate alongside the existing governmental authority so as to correct its deficiencies when nec-

---

[102] See the sources cited in note 32 *supra.*

[103] For the special regime, see note 86 *supra.*

[104] *See* Convention Concerning the Territory of Memel, May 8, 1924, Lith.–Principal & Allied Powers, Annex II, Port of Memel, Art. 5, 29 LNTS 87; *see also* YDIT, *supra* note 15, at 48–49.

essary. Instead, it permanently takes over from an existing authority entirely or in part. Instead of reacting to or anticipating instances of "bad governance," ITA initiates "good governance" at the outset.

A notable feature of using ITA to address either type of governance problem is that the character of the problem can change over time. One set of problems creates a need for ITA—such as the persecution of the Kosovar Albanians by the Serb-dominated FRY government—and then another set of problems arises once ITA is under way. The persecution of the Serbs by the Albanians in Kosovo not only represented a direct reversal of the original problems, but also was made possible in part by the ITA-effected solution to those original problems. A related feature of ITA is that, once an original set of objectives places an international organization in a position to exercise territorial administration, this organization sometimes chooses to adopt additional objectives. For example, in Germany the emergence of East-West splits led the "Allies" to use "its" administrative authority—originally in play to fill a vacuum—to support the particular territorial agenda of carving up Germany into two separate entities, the German Democratic Republic and the Federal Republic of Germany, and dividing Berlin into West and East.[105] In Bosnia and Herzegovina, OHR has chosen to promote a particular democratic agenda that it fears would be undermined if governance were left to local actors. ITA is exercised in an effort to ensure a market economy (e.g., by legislating to allow privatization) and free media (e.g., by appointing the Board of Governors of the Republika Srpska's public broadcasting service).[106] Whereas this agenda can be explained in terms of the original objectives, alternatively it suggests a model of ITA in which objectives are constantly supplemented as the mission proceeds.

In addressing a governance problem, ITA can take two approaches. As discussed above, the first directly substitutes international organizations for local actors. Some of the projects are limited to this short-term approach, which is not designed to prevent the problems from arising in the first place. Thus, in the Saar the risks associated with French and German administration during the exploitation period were accepted as a given. Similarly, UNHCR administration of refugee camps can be seen as a semipermanent means of "burden sharing" between the poor host states and the rich states that fund the agency. This approach necessarily assumes the long-term incapacity of host states, transferring responsibility elsewhere rather than enhancing local capabilities. In most projects, however, ITA adopts a second approach in tandem with the first: changing the structural features of local governance to remove the problem that led to the need for ITA. International organizations perform what is usually called a "state-building" role, though perhaps "community building" might be more appropriate, not least because of the formal status of some of the territorial units involved. ITA is used to construct or reconstruct institutions, broadly defined, including material infrastructure, public bodies, commercial enterprises, media and telecommunications, and civil-society organizations. When governance itself has failed, these initiatives are designed to enhance the possibility that governance can be conducted by local actors. When good governance has failed, they seek to enhance the possibility that local actors will govern in conformity with certain policy objectives. Thus, ITA adopts a dual-track approach, both palliative and remedial. The second UN operation in Somalia (UNOSOM II), however, through a broad interpretation of its mandate to "assist" (cf. the Congo), attempted unsuccessfully to create government institutions in 1993 without also trying to fill the more general administrative vacuum in the meantime.[107]

[105] See, e.g., CRAWFORD, supra note 3, at 275–77.

[106] On privatization legislation, see, for example, OHR, Decision Imposing the Framework Law on Privatisation of Enterprises and Banks in BiH (July 22, 1998). On the appointments, see OHR, Decision on the Appointment of the Board of Governors of Radio-Television of the RS (July 27, 2000), at <http://www.ohr.int/mediares/d20000727.htm>.

[107] See SC Res. 814, para. 4 (Mar. 26, 1993); JARAT CHOPRA, PEACE MAINTENANCE: THE EVOLUTION OF INTERNATIONAL POLITICAL AUTHORITY 49, 158 (1999).

Using ITA to respond to a governance problem represents the failure in realizing the "normal" model of local territorial governance. When ITA steps in to fill a vacuum that it did not create, governance itself has "failed." When ITA actively displaces governance by local actors, these actors have failed to govern in a preferred manner. As with the use of ITA to respond to a sovereignty problem, using ITA in response to a governance problem supports the notion that local territorial governance is the "ideal." In reactive projects this notion is supported by the assumption that local territorial governance is the norm and is to be corrected only when necessary. In some of these projects, and in all the proactive ones, the notion is also supported by the designation of the projects as temporary; control is to be transferred to local actors at some future date, or, in the case of refugee camps, occupants will supposedly be offered a durable solution involving repatriation or resettlement. Finally, in both types of project, the notion is supported by community-building initiatives aimed at positively altering the conditions for governance by local actors.

III. ITA AND THREE RELATED POLICY INSTITUTIONS

ITA cannot be fully understood without appreciating its relationship to three other international policy institutions: (1) "protectorates," (2) the old experiments in territorial administration by bodies composed of representatives from different states ("representative bodies"), and (3) foreign state administration under the mandates and trusteeship systems. In these institutions, the administering actor is either a collective of state representatives (acting in a representative capacity) or a foreign state. Nonetheless, the official purposes they have served suggest that they relate to ITA as precursors or, in the case of the mandates and trusteeships institution, an alternative.

As James Crawford remarks, the protectorate institution "is one of the oldest features of international relations."[108] It involves the exercise of some form of administrative control by one or more states over a separate territorial entity, without formal incorporation; plenary administration was the hallmark of the primarily African "colonial protectorate" that emerged in the nineteenth century.[109] Powerful European states used protection to ensure access to markets and prevent territorial control by rivals; in the colonial context, it was also associated with the "white man's burden" of redeeming "primitive" people. Thus, it responded to a sovereignty problem by removing the possibility of control by rivals, and to a governance problem by enabling the realization of particular policies—alliance and preferential trade with the protecting state or states; "civilizing" the "natives"—within the territories concerned.

ITA is protection—and colonialism—in a new guise, ostensibly serving objectives set by the member states of international organizations collectively, rather than by European states individually. It enables the same underlying process without attracting the opprobrium that the foreign state administration model, especially in the colonial context, came to attract in the twentieth century. Ironically, in Namibia, Western Sahara, and East Timor, the process that enabled colonization was later utilized as an instrument of decolonization.

Territorial administration by representative bodies was used from the early nineteenth century to respond to some of the same problems that ITA would address later; these projects fall into four broad categories. In the first—including projects in Cracow (1815–1846), Shanghai (1854–1943), Crete (1897–1909), Tangier (1923–1957), and Albania (1913–1914) —certain powerful states vied with each other and, sometimes, local actors for control over

---

[108] CRAWFORD, *supra* note 3, at 187. On protectorates generally, see, for example, *id.* at 187–208.

[109] *Id.* at 199. On the colonial protectorate, see, for example, Antony Anghie, *Finding the Peripheries: Sovereignty and Colonialism in Nineteenth-Century International Law*, 40 HARV. INT'L L.J. 1, 54–57 (1999).

the territories concerned.[110] The attempted solution established various representative bodies to exercise either plenary administration or certain administrative prerogatives in those territories.[111] This addressed a sovereignty problem by denying the possibility for any individual state to enjoy control, and/or a governance problem by ensuring that territorial governance supported a particular status for the territory (e.g., condominium status). The second category comprises the various waterway commissions (e.g., the Central Rhine Commission begun in 1804, and the International Danube Commission begun in 1856).[112] These commissions exercised various administrative powers over their respective waterways, responding to a governance problem that, without joint administration, individual riparian states might hinder free navigation through active restriction or neglect.[113] The third category covers the international commissions created by the Treaty of Versailles to hold plebiscites in certain territories, including the 1921 plebiscite in Upper Silesia.[114] These commissions ensured that the plebiscites would actually take place and be conducted fairly. Finally, mixed commissions were created to implement particular policies in certain territories. These included the Upper Silesia Mixed Commission discussed above, and the 1923 commission created to implement the exchange of Turkish and Greek individuals between Greece and Turkey, which enjoyed certain powers to alter property rights in each territory.[115] These four groups of experiments were also precursors to the ITA institution. Not only did they enable the same underlying process (as protectorates); they also involved bodies with a similar spatial identity to international organizations. The role of international organizations in territorial administration in the twentieth and twenty-first centuries can thus be traced to the era before such institutions existed in their present form.

Foreign state administration of certain territories under the mandates and trusteeships systems, by contrast, operated in conjunction with, respectively, the League of Nations and the United Nations, and existed alongside territorial administration by these organizations in other places. The League mandates system covered certain territories of the defeated powers after the First World War.[116] The UN trusteeship system covered the mandated territories, together with territories detached from Germany and Italy in the Second World War.[117] It was available for use in other territories (though not those with UN membership) voluntarily placed under the system, but no such territories were so placed.[118] In both systems, each territory was administered by an individual state "on trust" for humanity, and administration was supervised by the relevant international organization. The League Covenant divided the mandates into three classes—A, B, and C—corresponding to the perceived level of development in the territory; an explicit commitment to future independence was made only for A-class mandates.[119] Trust territories, on the other hand, were

---

[110] YDIT, *supra* note 15, at 32, 95–108 (Cracow), 23–24, 127–53 (Shanghai), 28–29, 109–26 (Crete), 27–28, 154–84 (Tangier), 29–33 (Albania). According to Ydit, proposals were made, but never realized, for similar experiments in Istanbul (1821 and 1896), Mount Athos (1913), and Spitzbergen (1914). *Id.* at 32–33 (Istanbul), 33–34 (Mount Athos), 34–39 (Spitzbergen).

[111] See citations in note 110 *supra.*

[112] On the waterway commissions, see, for example, HILL, *supra* note 47, at 507–10. For the proposed International Congo River Commission in 1885, see YDIT, *supra* note 15, at 25–27.

[113] *See* HILL, *supra* note 47, at 507–10.

[114] For the plebiscite commissions generally, see *id.* at 505–06; SARAH WAMBAUGH, PLEBISCITES SINCE THE WORLD WAR (2 vols. 1933). For the Upper Silesia plebiscite, see Versailles Treaty, *supra* note 32, Art. 88 & Annex to pt. III, §VIII (after Art. 82); WAMBAUGH, *supra*, at 206–70; YDIT, *supra* note 15, at 45–46.

[115] On the 1923 Commission, see, for example, HILL, *supra* note 47, at 505.

[116] LEAGUE OF NATIONS COVENANT Art. 22 [hereinafter LEAGUE COVENANT]. On the mandates system, see, for example, 1 OPPENHEIM'S INTERNATIONAL LAW §86 & sources cited at 295 (Robert Jennings & Arthur Watts eds., 9th ed. 1992) [hereinafter OPPENHEIM]; QUINCY WRIGHT, MANDATES UNDER THE LEAGUE OF NATIONS (1930).

[117] *See* UN CHARTER, ch. XII, esp. Art. 77. On the trusteeship system, see, for example, OPPENHEIM, *supra* note 116, §§89–95 & sources cited at 308.

[118] UN CHARTER Art. 77(1)(c) (open to further territories), Art. 78 (not open to UN members); CRAWFORD, *supra* note 3, at 335 n.6 (no new trusteeships created).

[119] LEAGUE COVENANT Art. 22.

to be administered with a view to enabling the "progressive development towards self-government or independence" of the local population.[120] In both cases, international legal doctrine subsequently considered the population in the territories concerned to enjoy the right of external self-determination.[121]

The mandates and trusteeship institution clearly served some of the purposes addressed by ITA. It responded to the perceived sovereignty problem of the defeated states' continued possession of certain territories. Insofar as some form of eventual self-determination was envisaged for the local population, it also responded to the perceived governance problem that local people were incapable, in the short term, of self-administration: they were "not yet able to stand by themselves under the strenuous conditions of the modern world."[122] In addition to filling an administrative vacuum, then, the "advanced nation" was to engage in community building—a system of "tutelage" designed to remove the need for permanent foreign administration.[123]

Given this overlap, it might be asked why ITA was used in certain situations, and state administration under the mandates and trusteeship systems in others. Here, the background to the mandates system is illuminating. Originally, direct League administration was considered; it was rejected partly on the grounds of practicalities (a concern that did not prevent plenary League administration in the Saar and Leticia), but mainly because some of the victorious powers wanted to annex the territories in question as their own.[124] As a compromise, the victorious powers were allowed to administer the territories they had captured, but the concept of "trust" and some form of eventual self-administration was introduced.[125] At the end of the Second World War, the same sovereignty and governance problems prevailed, and the mandates approach was adopted as the basis for the trusteeship system on the grounds that it had worked well.[126] Although this system envisaged the administering actor as being either "one or more states or the Organization [the United Nations] itself," in practice the League state model was continued.[127] The only deviation was when one mandatory power, South Africa, refused to begin the process of self-determination in South West Africa, and the United Nations terminated South Africa's mandate and adopted direct responsibility for the territory itself.[128]

The mandates and trusteeship institution therefore dealt with a subset of situations that could have been addressed under the wider ITA institution. ITA was not used because of the need to allow the occupying powers to conduct administration after the First World War, and the adoption of the League precedent after the Second World War. When the new situations of Kosovo and East Timor arose, which were deemed to require plenary administration by external actors, and self-government or independence was set as the agenda for the territories, not only was UN rather than foreign state administration introduced, but the territories were not even placed under the trusteeship system. Whereas the unequivocal right of the population in trust territories to external self-determination might have posed a problem in Kosovo, there was no such problem in East Timor.[129] Consequently, at least for

---

[120] UN CHARTER Art. 76(b).

[121] See Western Sahara, Namibia Opinion, GA Res. 1514, all *supra* note 41.

[122] LEAGUE COVENANT Art. 22(1).

[123] LEAGUE COVENANT Art. 22(2); UN CHARTER Art. 76(b) (quotation taken from the former).

[124] WRIGHT, *supra* note 116, at 26–34.

[125] *Id.*

[126] OPPENHEIM, *supra* note 116, §89, at 308.

[127] UN CHARTER Art. 81.

[128] *See supra* note 52 and corresponding text.

[129] In the case of Kosovo, there is also the possibility of a barrier because of the nonapplicability of the trusteeship system to "territories which have become Members of the United Nations" under Article 78 of the UN Charter. However, whereas the FRY government was claiming to represent the Socialist Federal Republic of Yugoslavia (SFRY)—an existing UN member—at the time when ITA was introduced in Kosovo, the Security Council

now, the institution of foreign state administration under the trusteeship system seems not to be considered appropriate. At the start of the twenty-first century, the institution of ITA has become the device of choice when it is decided that problems relating to territorial administration are to be addressed through administration by foreign actors.

IV. CONCLUSION

The exceptionalist appraisal of the Kosovo and East Timor projects ignores the place of these two projects as the latest manifestations of a historical policy institution, which I have termed "international territorial administration." Given ITA's recent resurgence, and its apparent preeminence in relation to foreign state administration under the trusteeship system, the institution might be used again.[130] In understanding ITA's future potential, we cannot examine the current projects exclusively, since these projects address only a governance problem. The alternative use of ITA to address a sovereignty problem—recently in play in Mostar and Eastern Slavonia—would be ignored. Equally, focusing exclusively on situations of plenary administration and/or those where the international organization involved is the United Nations arbitrarily excludes other projects that have served the same purposes in the same manner. Furthermore, my purposive analysis suggests that three labels popularly used to characterize the projects holistically are unhelpful. To label ITA as necessarily "temporary," "interim," "transitional," and so forth, ignores those projects in which ITA's temporal duration is conceived as permanent (e.g., Danzig) or left open (e.g., Bosnia and Herzegovina). To label the projects as "state building" or "nation building" is to adopt one mechanism through which ITA addresses a governance problem—creating institutions—as ITA's defining characteristic. Apart from mischaracterizing projects where no such enterprise is in play at all—e.g., those, like Leticia, addressing a sovereignty problem exclusively—this occludes the complementary mechanism often used alongside community-building administration: providing administration until institutions are up and running. Finally, presenting ITA as a "postconflict" phenomenon is misleading. Whereas ITA has been used after conflict in many cases (though not all; cf. West Irian), it does not follow that all the problems addressed by the institution are necessarily understood in terms of conflict (cf. the legacy of totalitarian governance in Bosnia and Herzegovina and Kosovo).

Now that it is clearer why, on their own terms, these projects take place, we can begin to examine whether international organizations should engage in this kind of activity at all.[131] For example, using ITA to ensure local "democracy" raises the question whether international organizations can and should be in the business of promoting democracy, both generally and through the conduct of territorial administration. Understanding ITA's different official objectives enables us to ask whether these objectives are achievable—for example, how might they be undermined, as well as supported, by ITA? It may also help us to appreciate the full range of ITA's potential effects (whether intended or not); for example, when ITA is ostensibly used to address a governance problem exclusively but through its very presence ends up affecting or creating a sovereignty problem (cf. Kosovo

---

had determined that the SFRY no longer existed, and recommended to the General Assembly that the FRY apply for UN membership. SC Res. 777 (Sept. 19, 1992). After the fall of the Milošević government in 2000, the FRY joined the United Nations. *See* GA Res. 55/12 (Nov. 10, 2000); SC Res. 1326 (Oct. 31, 2000); UN Doc. A/55/528–S/2000/1043.

[130] The Brahimi Report, *supra* note 1, para. 78, remarks:

> Although the Security Council may not again direct the United Nations to do transitional civil administration, no one expected it to do so with respect to Kosovo or East Timor either. Intra-State conflicts continue and future instability is hard to predict, so that . . . other such missions may indeed be established in the future
> . . . .

[131] This question is raised, but not addressed, in *id.*

and Iraqi Kurdistan). Moreover, we can question why ITA is deployed selectively, and ask how such selectivity affects the institution's realization of its own objectives. Finally, appreciating mainstream understandings of ITA allows us to investigate the alternative objectives that may lie behind its use and condition its effects.[132]

RALPH WILDE*

[20]

THE UNITED NATIONS ADMINISTRATION OF EAST TIMOR

Boris Kondoch*

ABSTRACT

In October 1999, the Security Council adopted Resolution 1272 (1999) which established under chapter VII of the UN Charter the United Nations Transitional Administration in East Timor (UNTAET). Together with the United Nations Interim Administration in Kosovo (UNMIK) UNTAET is unprecedented in the history of UN peacekeeping operations with respect to the scope of the responsibilities and the range of the mandate granted to the mission. Resolution 1272 empowered UNTAET to take over all branches of government on East Timor, namely to exercise all legislative and executive authority, including the administration of justice. The purpose of this article is to examine the practice of the UN's administration of East Timor and to discuss the various legal issues arising from it. After providing an overview of the development of international peace-keeping, the article turns to the relationship between East Timor and the United Nations. The next sections deal with the mandate and structure of UNTAET and its predecessors. Then the author discusses the legal basis of the establishment of such administrations and the legal constraints on the power of the Security Council, such as human rights law and international humanitarian law. Finally, the article concludes with remarks on the UN administration of East Timor.

1 INTRODUCTION

For most of their history, United Nations peacekeeping operations[1] have been deployed in situations of international conflict with a mandate to monitor cease-fire agreements and buffer zones. These operations have been referred to as the first generation of UN peacekeeping missions.[2] The operations were based on the

---

* Research Fellow, Institute of Public Law, Johann Wolfgang Goethe University, Frankfurt am Main. The article is a revised and updated version of a paper delivered at the Conference 'Nationbuilding in East Timor' organized by the Centro Português de Estudos do Sudeste Asiático (CEPESA) and the London School of Oriental and African Studies (SOAS), Lisbon (Portugal), 21–23 June 2001. The author is grateful to Rita Silek (Ministry of Foreign Affairs/ Hungary) and Cedric de Coning (Civil Affairs Officer with UNTAET) for critical comments.

[1] For general information on UN peacekeeping operations see for example, M. Bothe, 'Peace-Keeping', in B. Simma (ed.), *The Charter of the United Nations* (1996) 565–603; O. Ramsbotham/ T. Woodhouse, *Encyclopedia of International Peacekeeping* (1999), United Nations (ed.), *The Blue Helmets, A Review of United Nations Peacekeeping* (3rd ed., 1996).

[2] The UN Charter does not explicitly authorize peacekeeping operations and does not even mention peacekeeping. However, it is generally accepted that the legal basis for peacekeeping operations falls between chapter VI and chapter VII. Under chapter VI the Security Council can adopt various techniques in pursuit of peaceful settlement of disputes (mediation, negotiation, etc.). Under chapter VII the Security Council may take enforcement measures to maintain or restore international peace and security.

246 *Boris Kondoch*

principle that the consent of the parties was required and they did not constitute enforcement measures under chapter VII of the UN Charter. That meant the use of force was only allowed in self-defence.

This traditional concept of international peacekeeping has changed to a great extent. Since the end of the cold war most of the conflicts the UN has to face are domestic rather than international. Increasingly, the UN has become engaged in more complex missions; providing civilian administrators and policemen, as well as soldiers, to oversee the implementation of peace plans negotiated by parties in conflict that have agreed to resolve their disputes at the ballot box. Examples of these operations, known as the 'second generation' of peacekeeping operations, were the missions in Cambodia (UNTAC), Namibia (UNTAG) and Mozambique (ONUMOZ).[3] Common to all of these missions was the fact that they were still based on the consent of the parties.

Another development in the field of peacekeeping was the deployment of peacekeeping troops authorized to enforce actions taken pursuant to chapter VII of the UN Charter. The consent of the parties to the conflict is not needed for chapter VII operations. Examples include the missions UNPROFOR implemented in the former Yugoslavia and UNOSOM II in Somalia. In recent years the Security Council has also granted particular states or groups of states, such as NATO or INTERFET, a mandate to undertake specific enforcement actions. In some cases these enforcement operations were supplemented by a UN peacekeeping presence, as with UNMIK and KFOR in Kosovo, for example.

A further new mechanism is represented by the United Nations governance in East Timor and Kosovo.[4] On 10 June 1999, the Security Council established the United Nations Interim Administration in Kosovo (UNMIK) by Resolution 1244 and on 25 October 1999 the United Nations Transitional Administration in East Timor (UNTAET) by Resolution 1272. The UN was authorized to exercise all legislative and executive powers over both territories including the administration of justice.[5] The scope of the responsibilities and the range of the mandate in these cases were unprecedented in the history of UN peacekeeping operations. Missions of this type, which also acquire a broad legal dimension, have been called 'new trusteeships' or the fourth generation of peacekeeping.[6]

---

[3] F.E. Hufnagel, *UN Friedensoperationen der zweiten Generation* (1996).
[4] On the administration of Kosovo see R. Büllesbach, 'Aufgaben öffentlicher Sicherheit für KFOR Soldaten im Kosovo' (2001) 14 *Humanitäres Völkerrecht-Informationsschriften* 83; P. Dreist, 'Rechtliche Aspekte des KFOR Einsatzes' (2001) 43 *Neue Zeitschrift für Wehrrecht* 1; M. Matheson, 'United Nations Governance of Postconflict Societies' (2001) 95 *AJIL* 78–81; M. Ruffert; 'The Administration of Kosovo and East Timor by the International Community' (2000) 50 *ICLQ* 613; C. Stahn, 'International Territorial Administration in the former Yugoslavia: Origins, Developments and Challenges Ahead' (2001) *Zeitschrift für ausländisches öffentliches Recht und Völkerrecht* 108; M. Wagner, 'Das erste Jahr der UNMIK' (2000) 47 *Vereinte Nationen* 132.
[5] In the case of UNMIK see UNMIK/REG/1999/1.
[6] W. Kühne, 'Zukunft der UN – Friedenseinsätze Lehren aus dem Brahimi Report' (2000) *Blätter für deutsche und internationale Politik* 1355.

The United Nations Administration of East Timor 247

The following article describes the law and practice related to the administration of East Timor, and discusses various problems flowing from it, such as the legal basis for the Security Council to set up such interim administrations.

2 THE RELATIONSHIP BETWEEN THE UNITED NATIONS AND EAST TIMOR

East Timor's struggle for independence has been on the agenda of the United Nations for a long time.[7] East Timor became a Portuguese colony in the 18th century while West Timor was under Dutch control at that time. West Timor became a part of Indonesia when the country gained independence in 1949. In 1960, the General Assembly decided that Timor and Dependencies were a non-self-governing territory[8] according to chapter IX of the UN Charter[9] and to which the General Assembly Resolution on the Granting of Independence to Colonial Countries and Peoples[10] applied. East Timor remained under Portuguese administration till 1975. After Portugal's withdrawal Indonesia occupied East Timor by military force and integrated it as its 27th province. The General Assembly passed several resolutions from 1975 to 1982, calling upon Indonesia to withdraw from the territory. The Security Council reacted in the same manner with Resolutions 384[11] and 389,[12] demanding that Indonesia withdraw its troops from East Timor, but neither condemned the invasion as an act of aggression nor as a breach of article 2 (4) of the UN Charter prohibiting the use of force. Although Indonesia did not comply, no further steps were taken by the Council.

Since the eighties, the United Nations tried to resolve the issue together with Indonesia and Portugal. In June 1998, Habibie, the new President of Indonesia, proposed a special status for East Timor which, at that time, excluded full independence. The talks continued and finally a set of agreements was reached between Indonesia and Portugal on 5 May 1999,[13] entrusting the United Nations to organize a 'popular consultation', giving the citizens of East Timor the choice to

---

[7] For a very detailed overview see D.C. Turack, 'Towards Freedom: Human Rights and Self-Determination in East Timor' (2000) 2 *Asia Pacific Journal on Human Rights and the Law* 55 and additionally R.S. Clark, 'East Timor Indonesia and the International Community' (2000) 14 *Temple ICLJ* 75; C. Schreuer, 'The United Nations and East Timor' (2000) 2 *International Law Forum du droit international* 18; The United Nations and East Timor: A Chronology, http:www.un.org/peace/etimor99/chrono/body.html.

[8] T.D. Grant, 'East Timor, the U.N. System, and Enforcing Non-Recognition in International Law' (2000) 3 *Vanderbilt Journal of Transnational Law* 273.

[9] GA Res. 1542.

[10] GA Res. 1514, 15 UN GAOR, Supp. (No.16), UN Doc. A/4686 (1960) 66.

[11] SC Res. 384 (1975).

[12] SC Res. 385 (1976).

[13] Agreement between Indonesia and Portugal (5 May 1999); with an Appendix Regarding a Constitutional Framework for a Special Autonomy for East Timor, Agreement Regarding the Modalities for the Popular Consultation of the East Timorese through a Direct Ballot, reprinted in(1999) 5(4–5) *International Peacekeeping* (Kluwer Law International) 149–155.

248   *Boris Kondoch*

decide either to become an autonomous province of Indonesia or an independent state.[14]

In July 1999, the Security Council established by Resolution 1246 the United Nations Missions in East Timor (UNAMET)[15], the task of which was to organize and conduct the popular consultation.[16] The referendum was held on 30 August 1999 where 78.5 per cent of the votes were cast in favour of independence. As a result the Indonesian military and pro-Indonesian militias started terrorizing the people of East Timor by looting, killing and expelling the Timorese from their homes. More than 500,000 people were displaced. As the situation escalated most of UNAMET's personnel had to be evacuated.

Relatively quickly by United Nations standards the Security Council acted by adopting Resolution 1264 on 15 September 1999,[17] determining that the situation in East Timor constituted a threat to peace and security and authorizing under chapter VII the establishment of a multinational force until replaced by a UN peacekeeping mission. The Australian led coalition, called INTERFET[18] was authorized 'to take all necessary measures' to fulfil its mandate, namely to restore peace and security, protect and support UNAMET, and facilitate humanitarian assistance operations. Due to INTERFET's presence UNAMET's personnel could return. A few weeks after INTERFET's arrival only less than half of the East Timorese population returned to their homes and the situation remained critical without a functioning administration and with the imminent collapse of essential services.

On 25 October 1999, shortly after formal recognition by the Indonesian People's Consultative Assembly of the outcome of the consultation, the Security Council established by Resolution 1272[19] the United Nations Transitional Administration in East Timor (UNTAET). Its task is to administer the territory until it is strong and stable enough to become fully independent. On 28 February 2000, the handover of command of military operations from INTERFET to UNTAET was completed. By Security Council Resolution 1338 of 31 January 2001,[20] the mandate of UNTAET

---

[14] A.J.J. de Hoogh, 'Some Random Remarks on Complaints Regarding the East Timor Popular Consultation' (2000) 13 *LJIL* 997.

[15] SC Res. 1246 (1999) reprinted in (1999) 5 *International Peacekeeping* (Kluwer Law International) 113.

[16] For an analysis on UNAMET see J. Toole, 'A False Sense of Security: Lessons Learned from the United Nations Organization and Conduct Mission in East Timor' (2000) 16 *American University ILR* 199.

[17] SC Res. 1264 (1999) reprinted in (1999) 5 *International Peacekeeping* (Kluwer Law International) 147.

[18] For more information on INTERFET and the legal issues involved in particular from the Australian perspective see M.J. Kelly, T.L. McCormack, P. Muggleton, B.M. Oswald, 'Legal Aspects of Australia's Involvement in the International Force for East Timor' (2001) 83 *ICRC Review* 101; for a comment on collective action in regard to East Timor see L. H. Miller, 'East Timor, Collective Action, and Global Order' (2000) 14 *Temple ICLJ* 89.

[19] SC Res. 1272 (1999) reprinted in (1999) 5 *International Peacekeeping* (Kluwer Law International) 148.

[20] SC Res. 1338 (2001).

has been extended until January 2002, bearing in mind the possible need for adjustments related to the independence timetable.

3 THE MANDATE AND STRUCTURE OF UNTAET

UNTAET's mandate consists of the following elements:

- to provide security and maintain law and order throughout the territory of East Timor,

- to establish an effective administration,

- to assist in the development of civil and social services,

- to ensure the co-ordination and delivery of humanitarian assistance, rehabilitation and development,

- to support capacity-building for self government,

- to assist in the establishment of conditions for sustainable development.[21]

UNTAET is headed by the Transitional Administrator, who is currently the Special Representative of the Secretary General, Sergio Vieira Del Mello, from Brazil. As of 31 July 2001 the operation has an authorized strength of 7,969 military, 1,428 civilian police and 123 military observers, which are supported by 1,033 civilian personnel and 1,933 local civilian staff.[22]

Where necessary UNTAET issues legislative acts[23] in the form of regulations.[24] It has to the present day promulgated 51 regulations (4 in 1999, 36 in 2000 and 22 in 2001). At the beginning the problem of the applicable law, defining the law enforcement functions of UNTAET, arose from a conflict with the local law. According to the very first regulation the Dutch based Indonesian law applicable to East Timor remains in force unless it conflicts with UN human rights standards or with the UNTAET mandate.[25] In practice the UN regulations and the municipal law complement each other. Certain Indonesian laws, such as the 'Law on Subversion', are explicitly excluded from application by UNTAET Regulation 1999/1. The way the United Nations set up a legal framework for East Timor is certainly one of the weak points of the administration. Up to now there is no central record or archive of the laws applicable to East Timor by UNTAET. There is a lack of review of the

---

[21] SC Res. 1338 (2001).

[22] http://www.un.org/peace/etimor/Untaet.htm.

[23] For a closer examination of legislative acts by UN administrations see J. Frowein, 'Die Notstandsverwaltung von Gebieten durch die Vereinten Nationen' in Arndt/Knemeyer/Kugelmann/Meng/Schweitzer (eds.), *Völkerrecht und Deutsches Recht* (2001) 43.

[24] UNTAET/REG/1999/1.

[25] UNTAET/REG/1999/1.

remaining Indonesian law and its compatibility with international law. This proved to be very problematic in respect to Indonesian Criminal Law and the Indonesian Criminal Procedure Code. An example is the case of Takeshi Kashigawa. The Japanese national was arrested for criticizing Xanana Gusmao, the leader of the independence movement. He was released after 18 days in detention. The Transitional Administrator reacted by issuing an executive order stating that defamation was not a criminal offence and should never be the basis for criminal charges. [26]

Progress has been made by the establishment of a Legislation Committee in autumn 2000 which includes representatives from the Cabinet, the Office of the Principal Legal advisor, the Judicial Affairs Department, the Human Rights Unit and the Gender Affairs Department of the National Planning Department. The committee reviews draft regulation and advises the Cabinet on necessary changes.

At the beginning of its work UNTAET failed to consult and involve the people of East Timor in the decision-making process although Security Resolution 1242 stressed '. . . the need for UNTAET to consult and cooperate closely with the East Timorese people in order to carry out its mandate effectively with a view to the development of local democratic institutions . . .'. The growing criticism of the policy not to consult the East Timorese led UNTAET to set up the National Consultative Council composed of a third of UN-representatives and two thirds East Timorese. The Council provided the East Timorese with the possibility to express their opinion in the legislative process, although the Transitional Administrator could ignore its advice.[27] The National Consultative Council was later replaced by the National Council which consists of 36 members coming from local parties and social groups.[28] The Council can also initiate or modify regulations but the final decision is made by the Transitional Administrator. Furthermore, a cabinet was established which acts as a quasi-government and is led by the Transitional Administrator. A very important task will be performed by the Constituent Assembly,[29] which is the first democratically elected body in the history of East Timor. Its primary task is to draft a constitution for an independent and democratic East Timor. It can also consider draft regulations as may be referred by the National Administrator. The Constituent Assembly will become the legislature in an independent East Timor.

The widespread violence which destroyed most private homes and governmental buildings, and the fact that most civil servants, being faithful to the Indonesian government and fearing repression, left East Timor, led to the collapse of the entire administrative and judicial system.[30] That made it necessary for

---

[26] S. Linton, 'Rising from the Ashes: The Creation of a Viable Criminal Justice System in East Timor' (2001) 25 *Melbourne University Law Review*, http://www.austlii.edu.au/au/journals/MULR/2001/5.html, Amnesty International, East Timor: Justice past, present and future, ASA 57/001/2001.

[27] UNTAET/REG/1999/2.

[28] UNTAET/REG/2000/24, UNTAET/REG/2000/33.

[29] UNTAET/REG/2001/2.

[30] H. Strohmeyer, 'Building a New Judiciary for East Timor: Challenges of a Fledgling Nation' (2000) 11 *Criminal Law Forum* 259; H. Strohmeyer, 'Collapse and Reconstruction of A Judicial System: The United Nations Missions in Kosovo and East Timor' (2001) 95 *AJIL* 46.

UNTAET to establish by its regulations a judicial system, a fiscal authority, a tax regime, a civil service, and a currency. Another important regulation created a panel of judges with exclusive jurisdiction to deal with serious criminal offences (see 5.2.5).[31] Except in the case of the Serious Crimes Panel the composition of the judiciary is to be wholly East Timorese. An important decision in the peace-building process was the approval by the National Council on 20 June 2001 of the UNTAET regulation establishing a Commission for Reception, Truth and Reconciliation[32] in East Timor. The Commission has a threefold task; providing a truth-telling mechanism, facilitating community reconciliation and recommending further action to the government. An interesting aspect is that the Commission will inquire into human rights violations committed during the entire East Timor conflict from 1974 to 1999.[33] Amnesties may be provided for minor offences such as theft or minor assault if the offender agrees to perform within a time limit an act of reconciliation, which may include community service, reparation, public apology and /or other acts of contrition. The Commission is expected to start work in the final quarter of 2001.

4 PREDECESSORS TO THE UNITED NATIONS ADMINISTRATIONS IN KOSOVO AND EAST TIMOR

There are various examples in history where a single state, a group of states, an international organization or an individual state mandated by an international organization as a foreign power, exercised certain administrative functions on a territory.[34] The Saar territory[35] was administered by the League of Nations in 1920–1935, and, after a plebiscite in 1935, was reunited with Germany. Another example is the occupation of Germany after the second world war when Germany was divided by the Allied Powers into four occupation zones. In this case the Control Council acted on behalf of Germany, for example by concluding legal arrangements. The United Nations itself had very little experience in the administration of territories until the end of the cold war. Only a supervisory function was given to the United Nations under the trusteeship system of the United Nations.[36] According to article 77 of the United Nations Charter the system applied to territories previously placed under the mandate system of the League of Nations, detached from enemy states as a result of the second world war or voluntarily

---

[31] UNTAET/REG/2000/15.

[32] UNTAET/REG/2001/10.

[33] Fact Sheet by UNTAET Press Office, Reconciliation Commission, 7 July 2001.

[34] A comprehensive overview is provided by C. Stahn, *op. cit.*, 121–137.

[35] F. Münch, 'Saar Territory', in R. Bernhardt (ed.), *Encyclopedia of Public International Law*, Vol. IV (2000) 334.

[36] In all, eleven territories have been placed under the Trusteeship System. Ten former Mandates of the League of Nations have been transmuted (British and French Cameroons, British and French Togoland, Tanganyika, Rwanda-Urundi, Samoa, New Guinea, Nauru, the Pacific Islands) and the former Italian colony, Somaliland, as the only territory detached from an enemy state had been transmuted.

committed to the system by states responsible for their administration. However, the actual governance was carried out by the state that granted the trusteeship and acted on behalf of the United Nations. The idea of bringing back the various forms of trusteeship has been raised in recent years in respect of failed states and self-determination disputes.[37] But in fact, the United Nations never used the trusteeship system again. The legal reason for not using it was that article 78 of the UN Charter precludes the application of the trusteeship administration in the case of member states. From a political point of view the application could be criticized as an act of neo-colonialism because it used to be common practice that the former colonial powers administered the trust territory.

The first precedent for a non-trusteeship United Nations administration of a territory was the United Nations Temporary Executive Authority (UNTEA), which governed West New Guinea from 1962–1963.[38] After a long dispute over the terri-tory, Indonesia and the Netherlands concluded a treaty transferring the adminis-tration to the UN in the form of UNTEA[39] and the General Assembly then authorized the Secretary General to carry out the tasks entrusted to him in the Agreement. According to the agreement UNTEA was empowered to legislate, to appoint government officials and to guarantee law and order in West New Guinea. Furthermore, UNTEA established a court system and regional councils. During the operation which helped the transfer from Dutch to Indonesian rule, Dutch officials were replaced by UN officials. UNTEA must be distinguished from the later experi-ences of the United Nations to administer a territory, such as UNTAET in the case of East Timor. UNTEA was established as a response to the dispute between the Netherlands and Indonesia concerning the status of West New Guinea. The main purpose of the mission was the peaceful handing over from one country to another and not to building a state machinery for an independent West New Guinea. The establishment of an administration was therefore a necessary side effect but not the main objective of UNTEA.[40]

The very first occasion when the United Nations had been entrusted to take over key aspects of the administration of a member state was the United Nations Transitional Authority (UNTAC) in Cambodia.[41] The unprecedented role of UNTAC was laid down in the 1991 Agreement on a Comprehensive Political Settlement of the Conflict in Cambodia.[42] UNTAC's tasks were to directly control 'all administrative agencies, bodies and offices acting in the field of foreign affairs, national defence, finance, public security and information' and to supervise other

---

[37] R.E. Gordon, 'Some Legal Problems with Trusteeship' (1995) 28 *Cornell ILJ* 301; E. Franckx, A. Pauwels & S. Smis, 'An International Trusteeship for Kosovo: Attempt to find a Solution to the Conflict' (1999) 52 *Studia Diplomatica* 155.

[38] See N. Schrijver, 'Some Aspects of UN involvement with Indonesia, West Irian and East Timor' (2000) 2 *International Law FORUM du droit international* 26.

[39] Agreement between the Republic of Indonesia and the Kingdom of the Netherlands concerning West New Guinea (West Irian), 15 August 1962, 437 UNTS, 273.

[40] F-E. Hufnagel, *op. cit.*, 31–33.

[41] S.R. Ratner, 'The Cambodia Settlement Agreements' (1994) 87 *AJIL* 1.

[42] Reprinted in (1993) 31 ILM 180.

agencies that could influence the outcome of the elections. Furthermore, UNTAC had to repatriate the refugees, disarm the Cambodian factions, monitor and enforce human rights, train the police, as well as prepare and oversee the elections.

Another recent example is the UN Transitional Administration for Eastern Slavonia (UNTAES) established by Security Council Resolution 1037[43] under chapter VII of the UN Charter on 15 January 1996. The UN Transitional Administrator, Jaques Paul Klein, had comprehensive control over civil affairs and the multi-national military component. The military component had to oversee the demilitarization of Eastern Slavonia, the return of refugees and internally displaced persons as well as to facilitate the maintenance of stability. The civilian component was mandated, *inter alia*, to set up a temporary police force, to supervise the judicial system, to facilitate a functioning civil administration and to assist in the supervision and organization of the election. The mandate ended after two years on 15 January 1998 when the administration achieved its goal, which was the peaceful transition of the territory from Serb to Croatian administrative rule.[44]

If one compares the UN administration in East Timor and Kosovo with the old trusteeship system, it becomes apparent that both concepts serve similar purposes. According to article 76 of the UN Charter one of the main objectives of the trusteeship system was 'to promote ... (the) progressive development towards self-government or independence'. Security Council Resolution 1244 established the international civilian presence in Kosovo 'in order to provide an interim administration ... under which the people of Kosovo can enjoy substantial autonomy within the Federal Republic of Yugoslavia while establishing and overseeing the development of self governing institutions ...'. Security Council Resolution 1272 laid down that UNTAET 'was endowed with overall responsibility for the administration of East Timor ... and to support capacity building for self government.' Both concepts also share objectives to further international peace and security and to promote the well being of the inhabitants in the respective territories.

However, the United Nations administrations in East Timor and Kosovo are different from earlier experiences of the organization in governing a territory. On the one hand, they are based on chapter VII of the United Nations Charter and not on the consent of the parties involved, on the other hand, Security Council Resolutions 1244 and 1272 vested the United Nations with mandates unprecedented in scope and complexity and empowered it to exercise all legislative and executive authorities including the administration of justice. For the first time, the United Nations functions as the direct administrator of a territory, taking over all governmental branches. The latter aspect distinguishes the administrations in Kosovo and East Timor from all previous peacekeeping missions. This concept of conflict management has been characterized by some commentators as a 'trusteeship administration'.[45] The

---

[43] SC Res. 1037 (1996), reprinted in M. Bothe/T. Dörschel (eds.), *UN Peacekeeping – A Documentary Introduction* (1999) 219.

[44] See in detail Ramsbotham & Woodhouse (eds.), *op. cit.*, 61–68.

[45] M. Bothe/T. Marauhn, 'The United Nations in Kosovo and East Timor – Problems of a Trusteeship Administration' (2000) 6 (4–6) *International Peacekeeping*, 26.

254 *Boris Kondoch*

United Nations has not used this terminology but has chosen to use the terms interim and transitional administrations.

5 THE LEGAL BASIS OF INTERIM UN ADMINISTRATIONS

Jarat Chopra, the former head of UNTAET's office of district administration described the administration as the UN's 'Kingdom of East Timor'. According to him, 'the organisational and juridicial status of the UN in East Timor is comparable of a pre-constitutional monarch in a sovereign kingdom'.[46] Does this mean there are no legal constraints to this type of UN administration? Are there legal limitations on the Security Council when it decides to establish such mechanisms? This will be discussed in the next paragraph.

5.1 Chapter VII as the Legal Basis for the UN Administration

When establishing the UN administrations in Kosovo and East Timor, the Security Council has based the decision on its chapter VII powers. Chapter VII provides the framework under which the Security Council may act to maintain or restore international peace.

It may be questioned whether chapter VII can serve in this case as a legal basis. Hans Kelsen wrote in 'The Law of Nations',[47] although without elaboration, that 'the organisation is not authorised by the Charter to exercise sovereignty over a territory which has not the legal status of trust territory'. His argument would be correct if the UN Charter allows only UN governance under the trusteeship system regulated in chapters XII and XIII of the UN Charter. Article 78 of the UN Charter only precludes the application of the trusteeship system to Members of the United Nations but does not prohibit the establishment of another mechanism allowing UN governance.

Could the principle of non-intervention bar the Security Council from establishing a UN administration under chapter VII? Article 2 (7) states the principle of non-intervention, meaning that states should refrain from intervening in matters which international law recognizes as solely within domestic jurisdiction. However, article 2 (7) cannot bar action under chapter VII as the article makes an express exception to the general prohibition allowing intervention for 'enforcement measures under Chapter VII'.

Therefore the creation of the UN administration in East Timor would be legitimate if it complied with the conditions under chapter VII.

---

[46] J. Chopra, 'The UN's Kingdom of East Timor' (2000) 42 *Survival* 27.
[47] H. Kelsen, *The Law of Nations* (1951) 651.

5.1.1 Article 39 of the UN Charter

Before adopting measures under chapter VII, two preconditions have to be fulfilled. Firstly the Security Council must have determined in accordance with article 39 of the UN Charter 'the existence of a threat to peace or breach of peace or an act of aggression', and secondly the measures to be taken should serve 'to maintain or restore international peace and security'. The Charter provides no restrictions on the Security Council's discretion to determine the existence of a threat to the peace, breach of the peace, or act of aggression.

The humanitarian catastrophe and not the infringement of the right of self-determination in East Timor appears to be the decisive element in the Council's decision to determine the existence of a threat to peace. In Resolution 1272, according to which UNTAET was established, the Security Council expressed its deep concern '. . . at reports indicating that systematic, widespread and flagrant violations of international humanitarian and human rights law have been committed . . .'. The very same wording had been used in Resolution 1264 authorizing the deployment of INTERFET.

It was the third time in the history of the United Nations that the Security Council characterized grave human rights abuses and humanitarian emergencies in an internal conflict as the sole reason to determine the existence of a threat to peace. In all other cases, the transnational consequences of the internal human rights violations, for example the flow of the Kurdish refugees towards the border caused by the Iraqi repression, must be regarded as the decisive element why the Security Council considered these situations as threats to peace.[48] Only the resolutions passed in response to the conflicts in Rwanda and Somalia[49] can be cited as further examples where the Security Council viewed massive but purely internal human rights violations, without transboundary effect, as a threat to the peace. Nevertheless, one may conclude from recent practice that the Council is currently more inclined to find that gross violations of human rights and humanitarian emergencies constitute threats to peace.

As the Security Council possesses very broad discretion to determine what constitutes a threat to international peace, the determination that the circumstances in East Timor constituted a threat to peace must be considered as a proper exercise of its article 39 powers.

---

[48] SC Res. 688 of 5 April 1991. Another example is SC Res. 1199 of 23 September 1998 in regard to the Kosovo crisis, stating on the one hand deep concern for the rapid deterioration in the humanitarian situation throughout Kosovo and on the other hand deep concern regarding the flow of refugees into northern Albania, . . . and other European countries.

[49] SC Res. 734 of 3 December 1992 concerning the situation in Somalia; SC Res. 918 of 17 May 1994 concerning the situation in Rwanda.

256 *Boris Kondoch*

5.1.2 Articles 41 and 42 of the UN Charter

Resolution 1272 did not specify which article of the Charter authorized the Security Council to establish UNTAET. Under chapter VII the Security Council has two forms of enforcement action available to it. According to article 41, action not involving the use of armed force and according to article 42 military action by air, sea and land forces. Article 42 serves as the legal basis for the military component of UNTAET but a closer analyses is required to see whether article 41 is the precise legal basis concerning the civilian component of UNTAET.

Article 41 provides:

> The Security Council may decide what measures not involving the use of armed force are to be employed to give effect to its decision, and it may call upon the members of the United Nations to apply such measures. These may include complete or partial interruption of economic relations and of rail, sea, air, postal, telegraphic, radio and other means of communication, and the severance of diplomatic relations.

The list of possible measures and actions is illustrative and not exhaustive. Therefore, the Council can take other measures and actions than those found in article 41. This interpretation has also been confirmed by the Appeals Chamber of the International Tribunal for the Former Yugoslavia in the *Tadic Case*[50] and reaffirmed by the practice of the Security Council in the last decade when it imposed a variety of new mechanisms under chapter VII. Examples are certain subsidiary organs created pursuant to Security Council Resolution 687,[51] which Iraq had to accept to end the second Gulf War. The UN Boundary Commission was the first organ in the history of the United Nations to demarcate the border between two member states. The United Nations Special Commission (UNSCOM) deals with the destruction of Iraq's weapons of mass destruction and the United Nations Compensation Commission addresses the compensation of victims of Iraqi aggression. Another innovative step was the establishment of the International Criminal Tribunal for the Former Yugoslavia by Resolution 827[52] and the International Tribunal for Rwanda by Resolution 955.[53] Both tribunals are responsible for the prosecution of persons who have committed serious violations of international humanitarian law in these territories. The creation of international criminal tribunals with primacy over national jurisdiction strongly indicates that the Security Council has the power to override structures of national and local government.

Therefore one can conclude that the Security Council can take, under article 41

---

[50] *Prosecutor v Tadic*, Appeal on Jurisdiction, No. IT-94-AR72, paras 32–38 (2 Oct. 1995), reprinted in (1996) 35 ILM 32.
[51] SC Res. 687 reprinted in (1991) 29 ILM 847.
[52] SC Res. 827 reprinted in (1993) 32 ILM 1203.
[53] SC Res. 955 reprinted in (1994) 33 ILM 1602.

of the UN Charter, non-military measures such as the UN administrations for Kosovo and East Timor.

5.2 Legal Limitations on the Security Council to Establish Interim UN Administrations under Chapter VII

The next question to be considered is whether, under international law, there are any substantive limits of the Security Council's power to set up an interim administration.

Some might argue that the Security Council can act above international law and therefore no legal limits exist to the Council's measures which are adopted within the framework of chapter VII. This interpretation is based on the wording of articles 103 and 25 of the UN Charter. Article 103 of the UN Charter states that 'in the event of a conflict between the obligation of the Members of the United Nations under the present Charter and their obligation under any other international agreement, their obligation under the present Charter shall prevail'. Under article 25 of the UN Charter the Members of the United Nations 'agree to accept and carry out the decisions of the Security Council in accordance with the Charter.' However, this interpretation cannot be accepted on the following grounds:

(i)   According to article 24(1) read together with articles 1 and 2 of the UN Charter the Council's decisions must be in accordance with the purposes and principles of the United Nations. Promoting and encouraging respect for human rights and fundamental freedoms are among these purposes, therefore the Council always has to take them into account when acting under chapter VII. Since, as argued by some legal commentators,[54] humanitarian law can be perceived as 'human rights in armed conflicts', the Council is also bound by rules of international humanitarian law.

(ii)   Another limitation is imposed by legal norms which are considered to be *jus cogens*. The doctrine of *jus cogens* was developed in the late 1960s and can be found in article 53 of the Vienna Convention 1969. The effect of norms regarded as *jus cogens* is that states cannot derogate from them and it is commonly accepted that these standards also apply to Security Council enforcement measures taken under chapter VII of the UN Charter.[55] As the hard core of human rights and international humanitarian law do amount to *jus cogens*, these limits also apply to measures imposed by the Security Council under chapter VII.

[54] L. Doswald-Beck, S. Vite, 'International Humanitarian Law and Human Rights Law' (1993) No.293 *ICRC Review* 94.
[55] T.D. Gill, 'Legal and Some Political Limitations on the Power of the UN Security Council to Exercise Its Enforcement Powers under Chapter VII of the Charter' (1995) 26 *NYIL* 33, 79.

(iii)   This view is also supported by Justice Weeramantry of the International Court of Justice stating that, 'the history of the United Nations . . . corroborates the view that a limitation on the plenitude of the Security Council's power is that those powers must be exercised in accordance with the well-established principles of international law.'[56]

(iv)   The role of the Security Council, as laid down in articles 24–26 of the UN Charter is to bear responsibility for the maintenance of international peace and security. It would be clearly contrary to its role if the Council disregarded the rule of law[57] because a peaceful world order can only be based and maintained on the rule of law.[58]

5.2.1   *The Duty to Respect Human Rights Law*

Since the UN Charter contains only vague references to Charter principles and rights it is necessary to define more specifically the Council's power in the present context, firstly by addressing human rights.

   Like the trusteeship system which was aimed at encouraging respect for human rights in the trust territory (see article 76(c) of the United Nations Charter), the UN administrators have to guarantee the human rights of the inhabitants of East Timor.[59] This duty has been reaffirmed by the first UNTAET regulation, which stated that 'everybody undertaking public duties or holding public office in East Timor shall recognize international human rights standards'.

   It must be noted in the present context that all major human rights instruments allow derogation of certain rights in times of public emergency. However, some rights, including the right of life, the right to be free from torture or cruel, inhuman or degrading treatment cannot be derogated from and therefore must be respected at all times.[60]

---

[56] *Order with regard to request for the Indication of Provisional Measures in the Case Concerning Questions of Interpretations and Application of the 1971 Montreal Convention Arising from Aerial Incident at Lockerbie* (*Libya v United States*), ICJ (1992); (1992) 31 ILM 694–696.

[57] Other authors have also suggested that the principle of good faith constitutes a limit to the enforcement powers of the Security Council, see V. Gowlland-Debbas, 'Security Council Enforcement Action and Issues of State Responsibility' (1994) 43 *ICLQ* 93–94.

[58] H-P. Gasser, 'Collective Economic Sanctions and International Humanitarian Law-An Enforcement Measure under the United Nations Charter and the Right of Civilians to Immunity: An Unavoidable Clash of Policy Goals' (1996) 56 *Zeitschrift für ausländisches öffentliches Recht und Völkerrecht* 880–881.

[59] See section 2 of UNTAET/REG/1991/1.

[60] To the author's knowledge the United Nations has not derogated from human rights in East Timor.

5.2.2 The Duty to Respect International Humanitarian Law

The next issue to be addressed is whether international humanitarian law imposes any limitation on the UN administration in East Timor. International humanitarian law can be defined as 'those international rules, established by treaty or custom, which are specifically intended to solve humanitarian problems directly arising from international and non-international armed conflicts and which for humanitarian reasons, limit the right of the parties to a conflict to use methods and means of warfare of their choice or protect persons and property that are or may be affected by the conflict'.[61]

For a long time there has been a debate regarding the extent to which peacekeeping forces are bound by international humanitarian law.[62] According to the Secretary-General's Bulletin on Observance by United Nations Forces of International Humanitarian Law[63] of 1999, not the whole set but the fundamental principles and rules of international humanitarian law are to be applied by the United Nations forces. As for the application of international humanitarian law it appears that with the latest arrival of UNTAET there was no armed conflict in East Timor, thus heralding an end to the ordinary application of the laws of war.

However, common article 2 to the Geneva Conventions does not limit its application to an armed conflict – it extends to 'all cases of partial or total occupation . . . even if said occupation meets without armed resistance'. From a theoretical point of view one might therefore argue that there are analogies between traditional occupation and the UN administration in East Timor, as both exercise authority on a foreign territory and therefore, UNTAET should be subject at least to the principles derived from the law of belligerent occupation, as laid down in the Regulations annexed to the 1907 Hague Convention No. IV on the Laws and Customs of War on Land, and that of the 1949 Geneva Convention No. IV. For example, the Australian Defence Force, which was the leading contingent of INTERFET and was deployed before the establishment of UNTAET, applied the law of military occupation only by way of guidelines. The legal application of the law of armed conflict was rejected on the following grounds. Firstly there was no armed conflict between INTERFET and Indonesia, secondly there was no armed conflict between UNTAET and the militia and thirdly no armed conflict between UNTAET and the people of East Timor.[64]

---

[61] H-P. Gasser, *International Humanitarian Law* (1993) 16.

[62] On the application of international humanitarian law to United Nations Peacekeeping Forces see for example M. Bothe, 'Peacekeeping and International Humanitarian Law: Friends or Foes' (1996) 3(4–6) *International Peacekeeping* (Kluwer Law International) 91; C. Greenwood, 'International Humanitarian Law and the United Nations Military Operations' (1998) 1 *Yearbook of International Humanitarian Law* 3; D. Shraga, 'UN Peacekeeping Operations: Applicability of International Humanitarian Law and Responsibility for Operations-related Damage' (2000) 94 *AJIL* 406; M. Zwanenburg, 'The Secretary-General's Bulletin on Observance by United Nations Forces of International Humanitarian Law: Some Preliminary Observations' (1999) 5(4–5) *International Peacekeeping* (Kluwer Law International) 133.

[63] ST/SGB/1999/13 of 6 August 1999, reprinted in (1999) 5(4–5) *International Peacekeeping* 160.

[64] Kelly, McCormack, Muggleton, Oswald, *loc. cit.*, 113–115.

260 *Boris Kondoch*

In respect to UNTAET international humanitarian law is also not applicable from a legal point of view as UNTAET and the people of East Timor are not belligerent parties. Too many nations would also deny the application of international humanitarian law *de facto* in times of peace as a matter of customary international law on the ground of national sovereignty. Another fundamental difference is that under the law of belligerent occupation the authority of the occupying authority is a *de facto* authority while UNTAET's authority is based on a chapter VII mandate, therefore on a *de jure* authority. That means if peacekeepers on East Timor get involved in situations which cannot be regarded as an armed conflict but might involve the use of force, they have to observe internationally recognized human rights standards and not international humanitarian law.

5.2.3 *The Duty to Respect the Right of Self-Determination*

Another limitation flows from the right of self-determination, which is one of the founding principles of the UN Charter and is well recognized as a legal right under international law. Its precise scope and application was and is still under debate. It is almost undisputed, that it does not entail the right of groups to secede from the state to which they belong[65] or the right of third parties to implement the principle.[66] It may suffice to say in the present context that the principle of self-determination postulates the right of a people to determine its own political status in a democratic way.[67]

In respect of UN administrations[68] it means that the United Nations cannot impose a particular form of government upon the population of a territory or a state by means of invoking the enforcement provisions of the UN Charter against the will of the people concerned.[69] In the present case, the United Nations has not violated the right of self-determination of the East Timorese when it organized the referendum. By organizing the popular consultation it has left the decision to become independent or to become an autonomous province to the people of East Timor. Furthermore, the subsequent establishment of UNTAET must be seen in the light of the atrocities and human rights violations committed after the ballot as helping to end the conflict and providing peaceful living conditions by creating a functioning administration.

If we regard self-determination as the right of people to determine their own political system freely without any kind of external domination in the political decision making process,[70] one may argue that the way the East Timorese can participate in the legislature, for example by leaving the Transitional Administrator

---

65 D. Thürer, 'Self-Determination', in R. Bernhardt, *Encyclopaedia of Public International Law*, Volume 8 (1985) 474.
66 P. Malanczuk, 'The Kurdish Crisis and Allied Intervention in the Aftermath of the Second Gulf War' (1991) 2 *EJIL* 124.
67 T.M. Frank, 'The Emerging Right to Democratic Governance' (1992) 86 *AJIL* 52.
68 H.R. Richardson, 'A Critical Thought on Self Determination for East Timor and Kosovo' (2000) 14 *Temple ICLJ* 101.
69 T.D. Gill, *loc. cit.*, 74–79.
70 R.E. Gordon, *loc. cit.*, 320–321.

a veto right in the legislative process, is an infringment of the East Timorese right to self-determination.

5.2.4 *Time Limitation*

Another important issue to be addressed is for how long can UNTAET undertake governmental functions over the people of East Timor?

The question 'How long can the Security Council uphold enforcement measures adopted under Chapter VII' is frequently asked. In particular, the issue has arisen concerning the durability of the sanctions regime imposed on Iraq. The answer has always been the same: as long as a threat to peace and security exists, the Council can keep the enforcement measures in force. Neither in Kosovo nor in East Timor did the United Nations want to install a permanent presence. Both administrations are only interim as in the case of UNMIK or transitional as in the case of UNTAET. Like all peacekeeping missions their mandate is only limited for a period of time. If the United Nations wants to continue their mission on East Timor the mandate has to be prolonged.

5.2.5 *The Duty to Prosecute Serious International Crimes*

One may raise the question whether there is a duty upon the United Nations to prosecute persons who have been accused of crimes against humanity and other serious crimes[71] committed in the aftermath of the referendum in East Timor. Under international law a duty to extradite or prosecute exists, for example in respect of genocide and torture, based on the Genocide Convention of 1948 and the Torture Convention of 1984. Although the United Nations is not a party to the above mentioned conventions it is undisputed that the United Nations has legal personality,[72] which implies that the United Nations can be bound *mutatis mutandis* by customary international law. In the present case the United Nations is also bound by the *aut dedere aut judicare* obligation laid down in the Genocide and Torture Conventions, as the conventions constitute customary international law and the United Nations takes over the functions of a state.[73] However, it is

---

[71] The crimes committed on East Timor are well documented, see the report of the International Commission of Inquiry on East Timor UN Doc. A/54/726, S/2000/59 of 31 January 2000; the report of the Indonesian Commission of Investigation into Human Rights Violations in East Timor (KPP-HAM), http://www.jsmp.minihub.org/ Reports/KPP%20Ham.htm. and the report of the UN Special Rapporteur James Dunn, Crimes Against Humanity in East Timor, January to October 1999: Their Nature and Causes of 14 February 2001, http://www.etan.org/ news/2001a/dunn1.htm.

[72] See the advisory opinion of the ICJ in *Reparations for Injuries Suffered in the Service of the United Nations*, ICJ-Reports, 1949, 174.

[73] *Reservation to the Convention on Genocide*, 1951, ICJ 23 (advisory opinion); *Prosecutor v Anto Furundzija*, Judgment (IT-95-17/1-T) para.156 et seq.

262 *Boris Kondoch*

questionable whether such a duty exists in respect of crimes against humanity and in particular of war crimes in an internal conflict.[74] In respect of crimes against humanity there is no treaty imposing a duty to prosecute. In the absence of such a treaty, the universal jurisdiction of crimes against humanity is generally regarded as permissive but not mandatory.[75] The same arguments apply to war crimes committed in an internal conflict. Irrespective of the existence of such a legal duty, the United Nations recognized its special obligation to see justice done for East Timor, as UNTAET established a 'Serious Crimes Investigation Unit', investigating primarily in ten priority cases[76] and the 'Serious Crimes Panel' within the District Court of Dili with exclusive jurisdiction over serious criminal offences[77] exercising jurisdiction over international crimes such as genocide, war crimes, crimes against humanity, torture as well as murder and sexual offences as they are defined in the Indonesian Criminal Code.[78] The panel consists of one East Timorese and two international judges. The temporal jurisdiction of the panels is limited to offences committed in the period between 1 January and 25 October 1999. Despite the indictment of approximately 50 persons and the first judgments[79] the Serious Crimes Investigation Unit has been criticized for the slow pace of its investigations. According to NGO reports the Crimes Unit lacks financial and material resources, educated and experienced personnel as well as a clear strategy to bring perpetrators to justice.[80] Another obstacle to justice is the lack of co-operation by Indonesia, although the United Nations and Indonesia had signed a Memorandum of Understanding[81] on 6 April 2000 according to which the parties would assist each other in investigations and court proceedings. The transfer of suspects to East

---

[74] In more detail see K. Ambos, *'Völkerrechtliche Bestrafungspflichten bei schweren Menschenrechtsverletzungen?'* (1999) 37 *Archiv des Völkerrechts* 318; B. Kondoch/R. Silek, 'Special Court for Sierra Leone' (2001) 1 *Conflict Trends* 28; A.J.M. McDonald, 'Sierra Leone's Uneasy Peace: The Amnesties Granted in the Lome Peace Agreement and the United Nations' (2000) 13 *Humanitäres Völkerrecht-Informationsschriften* 18.

[75] M.P. Scharf, 'The Amnesty Exception to the Jurisdiction of the International Criminal Court' (1999) *Cornell ILJ* 519.

[76] UNTAET Press Office, Justice and Serious Crimes, 6 July 2001.

[77] UNTAET/REG/2000/15.

[78] In more detail see B.C. Alexander, 'East Timor: Will There be Justice?' (2000) 1 *Human Rights Brief* 5; B. Kondoch, 'Neueste Entwicklungen im Völkerstrafrecht aufgezeigt am Beispiel Sierra Leone, Kambodscha und Ost-Timor' (2001) 19 *Vierteljahresschrift für Sicherheit und Frieden* to be published; S. Linton, 'Rising from the Ashes: The Creation of a Viable Criminal Justice System in East Timor' (2001) 25 *Melbourne University Law Review*, http://www.austlii.edu.au/au/journals/MULR/2001/5.html.

[79] For further information on the cases see Judicial System Monitoring Programme, http://www.jsmp.minihub.org/. Worth mentioning is a lawsuit brought against the Indonesian General Lumintang, on 28 March 2000 in a District of Columbia federal court, see Indonesia Generals on Trial in US Courts, http://etan.org/news/2000a/11suit.htm.

[80] Amnesty International, East Timor: Justice past, present and future, ASA 57/001/2001.

[81] Memorandum of Understanding Between the Republic of Indonesia and the United Nations Transitional Administration in East Timor Regarding Co-operation on Legal, Judicial and Human Rights Related Matters, http://etan.org/et2000c/december/10-16/14mou.htm.

Timor is one of the major problems for UNTAET since most of the military leaders and members of the militias are currently in Indonesia.

Indonesia, on the other hand, has started its own investigations. In January 2001, the Attorney General presented a list with 22 suspects, but none of the people accused of crimes has yet stood for trial. In April 2001, former President Wahid decided to set up a Human Rights Court for East Timor by a presidential decree (Keppres 53/2001). However, the court's jurisdiction was limited to post ballot crimes. This would have meant that crimes committed before the referendum, such as the massacre at the Liquica Church where more than 50 people had been killed, would have gone unpunished. In summer 2001, his successor, Megawati Sukarnoputri, corrected the decision by extending the court's jurisdiction to crimes committed in April and September but not to the entire period between April and September 1999. The proceedings are expected to start in October 2001.[82] The court will have jurisdiction over serious human rights violations including genocide and crimes against humanity.[83]

However, the failure of Indonesia to deliver justice and the slow pace of the investigations by the Serious Crimes Unit has led to the call upon the international community to set up an international tribunal.[84] The Security Council has already established two ad hoc tribunals, the ICTY and the ICTR. As explained above such powers are granted to the Security Council by article 41 under chapter VII. In order to establish such an international tribunal for East Timor, the Security Council has to determine 'the existence of a threat to peace or breach of peace or an act of aggression'. However, it appears to be doubtful that under the present circumstances any of the required conditions is met. On the one hand, a threat to the peace occurred in East Timor two years ago, and this has been determined by the Security Council in several resolutions.[85] Finally, the presence of INTERFET and UNTAET brought an end to the gross violations of human rights and humanitarian law. Therefore, the current situation cannot be regarded as a threat to peace anymore. On the other hand, one may point out that even after two years the situation is still inherently unstable because of the continuing lack of accountability for these serious crimes, which breeds instability for East Timor and the region. Such a precarious situation might be regarded as a threat to peace.

Since UNTAET has already been granted full authority over the territory, including the administration of justice, the question is whether UNTAET could establish an international tribunal. This possibility must be rejected as UNTAET's mandate only extends to East Timor and not to Indonesia.

---

[82] 'Ad hoc tribunal starts in October?', *The Jakarta Post*, 9 August 2001.
[83] Law on Human Rights Courts (Law No. 26/2000); Amnesty International, Amnesty International's Comments on the Law on Human Rights Courts (Law No. 26/2000), ASA 21/005/2001; Amnesty International, Indonesia: Comments on the draft law on Human Rights Tribunals, ASA 21/025/2000; International Crisis Group, Indonesia: Impunity versus Accountability for Gross Human Rights Violations, ICG Asia Reports No. 12.
[84] See NGOs' statement on justice for East Timor, http://etan.org/et2001b/june/10-16/13justce.htm; UN Official Calls For War Crimes Tribunal for East Timor, *Associated Press* of 13 July 2001, http://www.pcug.org.au/~wildwood/01julun.htm.
[85] SC Res.1264, 15 Sep.1999; SC Res. 1272, 22 Oct.1999.

5.2.6 The Duty to Respect the Right to Good or Democratic Governance

One of the issues at the heart of the current agenda of the United Nations is the issue of global governance. The commitment to global governance has been, for example, reflected in the Agenda for Peace,[86] in which the former Secretary General of the United Nations, Boutros Boutros Ghali, pointed out 'there is an obvious connection between the democratic practices – such as the rule of law and transparency in decision making and the achievement of true peace and security in any new and stable political order. These elements of good governance need to be promoted at all levels of international and national political communities.'

His successor, Secretary General Kofi Annan, has stated:

> UN Programs now target virtually all the key elements of good governance, safeguarding the rule of law, verifying elections, training police, monitoring human rights, fostering investments; and promoting accountable administration. Good governance is also a component of our work for peace. It has a strong preventive aspect; it gives societies sound structures for economic and social development. In post conflict settings, good governance can promote reconciliation and offer a path for consolidating peace.[87]

It is questionable whether there is an obligation under international law that the United Nations or states must practise good governance. The issue has increasingly been debated by legal scholars.[88] Thomas M. Frank has argued for example that there is an emerging right to democratic governance[89] but he did not come to the conclusion that such a right already exists.[90] It is true that neither the UN Charter nor conventional law deal with good governance or provide a precise definition of it. However, certain components which could be part of the right to good governance, such as the right of self-determination, are well established under international law. Article 25 of the International Covenant on Civil and Political Rights provides that every citizen has the right to take part in the conduct of public affairs, directly or through freely chosen representatives. Similar provisions can be found in the European Convention on Human Rights and the American Convention on Human Rights. Certain principles are also mentioned in the Charter of Paris of the CSCE of 1990, such as the commitment to the rule of law and human rights. On the

---

[86] 'An Agenda for Peace', reprinted in M. Bothe/T. Dörschel (eds.), *UN Peacekeeping – A Documentary Introduction* (1999) 19.

[87] K. Annan, 'The Quiet Revolution' (1998) 4 *Global Governance* 123.

[88] For example, B. Bauer, *Der völkerrechtliche Anspruch auf Demokratie* (1998); J. Crawford, 'Democracy and International Law' (1993) 64 *BYIL* 113; G.H. Fox/ B.R. Roth (eds.), *Democratic Governance and International Law* (2000).

[89] T.M. Franck, 'The Emerging Right to Democratic Governance' (1992) 86 *AJIL* 45.

[90] A. Cassese argues in a very similiar way by stating that 'it may be argued that a general norm is currently in process of coming into being which grants a right to democracy' but it '. . . has not yet taken root either as a human right . . . or as a legal entitlement accruing to any state . . .' see A. Cassese, *International Law* (2001) 371.

other hand, customary international law has not yet developed to the point that there is a constant and uniform usage of states, which they consider as a legally binding minimum standard of good governance.

In any case, the United Nations is well advised to take the concept of good governance as a moral imperative by developing structures of self-governance, organizing free and fair elections, taking into account the political aspirations of the people of East Timor and assisting them in the development of political institutions.

6 CONCLUDING REMARKS

For the very first time in United Nations history the organization attempted to build and manage an entire state. The main achievement of UNTAET is that it created a stable and secure environment for a nation which has not lived in peace for decades. The Constituent Assembly was the first elected body in the history of East Timor. After independence the United Nations will not leave behind a completely effective administration[91] but a structure which enables the East Timorese to organize their state on their own. To the present day many problems are unresolved. One may mention the weak infrastructure, the problems of the educational system, approximately 80,000 refugees remaining in camps and the above mentioned problems of the judicial system. Many mistakes made by UNTAET appear to be excusable because of a lack of experience and the chaotic situation UNTAET met upon arrival.

The East Timor Model could also be applied to other scenarios, for example, at the request of governments and parties to a conflict. The take-over of all governmental functions *in toto* by the United Nations could increase the chance of bringing to an end certain conflicts by re-establishing a functioning state machinery based on the rule of law. However, several lessons must be learnt from UNTAET's experience. The local population should be consulted from the beginning. The capabilities of the United Nations in building a transitional system, in particular a criminal justice system have to be increased.[92] Less power should be vested in the hands of a transitional administrator and a more sophisticated system of checks and balances must be installed. Whether such enterprises could be financed and whether parties to a conflict would be willing to hand over the entire administration of a territory or state is another matter.[93]

---

[91] S.V. de Mello, 'Here is a Big Day for East Timor', *International Herald Tribune*, http://www.iht.com/articles/30693.htm.

[92] The problem has also been identified by the Report of the Panel on United Nations Peace Operations (The Brahimi Report), UN doc. A/55/305, S/2000/809, 21 August, paras 76–83.

[93] For an assessment of UNTAET's work see Reports of the Secretary General on the United Nations Transitional Administration in East Timor: S/2001/436 (2001); S/2001/142 (2001), S/2000/738 (2000); J. Chopra, *loc. cit.*, 27; C. de Coning, 'The UN Transitional Administration in East Timor (UNTAET): Lessons Learned from the First Hundred Days' (2000) 6 *International Peacekeeping* 83; K. Ishizuka, 'UNTAET: Some Current Issues' (2000) 29(5–6) *Peacekeeping and International Relations* 5; L. Richards, 'UNTAET: Cooperation and Community Policing in East Timor' (2000) 62(2) *Gazette* 14; J. Traub, *Inventing East Timor* (2000) 75.

[21]

Institution-Building and Human Rights Protection in Kosovo in the Light of UNMIK Legislation

MARCUS G. BRAND
University of Vienna

Abstract. By analyzing specific legislative and institutional aspects of UNMIK's administration of Kosovo, this article attempts to highlight the discrepancy between the nature of
an international security presence and civilian administration (under Security Council peacekeeping mandate), and effective human rights remedies, as well as principles of democratic
governance such as accountability, lawfulness and constitutionality. The 'constitutional' aspects of the current system of governance in Kosovo are described and difficulties of creating
an international administration, which seeks to gain a certain level of acceptance by the subjected population, are pointed out.[1] The article explains how UNMIK went about establishing
a Joint Interim Administrative Structure while dismantling parallel, illegitimate power structures. It further addresses the Constitutional Framework for Provisional Self-Governance and
evaluates briefly its human rights-related aspects. Legislative issues and questions concerning
the rule of law are discussed in another section, which deals with UNMIK's formal commitments to adhere to the highest level of internationally recognized human rights standards.
Several important Regulations issued by the Special Representative of the Secretary General
(SRSG) are analyzed. Consequently, the most significant structures and mechanisms for the
protection, promotion and monitoring of human rights are shortly presented and put in context.
The article raises several crucial questions concerning the access to effective remedy and the
effectiveness of human rights institutions in an environment of legal uncertainty, the absence
of the rule of law and the supremacy of international authority, which is beyond the reach of
judicial control or review. It concludes that if effective human rights protection shall be the
outcome of structures dedicated to human rights, these structures have to be constructed to
offer real remedies, proper judicial procedures and legal clarity. The present nature of international peace missions (military and civilian) is not compatible with the requirements of a
law-based administration according to the *Rechtsstaat*-model, which is arguably a prerequisite
for effective human rights protection.

1. Introduction

The international community has justified both armed intervention and costly
reconstruction efforts *inter alia* with the need to improve Kosovo's human

---

[1] The situation described will change by the transfer of certain responsibilities to elected
institutions of provisional self-government following the elections on 17 November 2001. The
envisaged new structures are referred to only selectively in this paper, while the focus is on
the period preceding the general elections.

rights situation. After the UN took over administrative authority, including legislative and executive powers, there has been neither a shortage of political nor legislative commitments to 'human rights'. UNMIK has incorporated 'human rights' both in its mandate and structure while at the same time international and local human rights advocates continue to pay much attention to human rights in Kosovo. The Constitutional Framework for Provisional Self-Government includes a catalogue of human rights commitments and provides for certain protection mechanisms and safeguards.[2] Yet, the human rights situation is far from satisfying, not least according to UNMIK's and the OSCE's own assessments. Who then is responsible for the shortcomings? Can human rights be seen completely disconnected from any link to state authorities? Can interethnic violence and discrimination be singled out as human rights violations, while effective remedies and redress remains unavailable for the people of Kosovo at large? How can human rights be entrenched in an administration and a society, if the only legitimate authorities, UNMIK and KFOR, are protected by immunities and privileges, and can operate above the law? How can human rights be effectively protected if the rules on the applicable law are marred by lack of clarity and leave much room for misunderstandings? While these questions can only partially be answered here, this paper examines critically UNMIK's commitments to human rights and protection mechanisms. It concludes that there is an inherent contradiction between the rule of law and democratic governance, preconditions for effective human rights protection, and the nature of an international administration by the UN (and KFOR).

2. Mandate and Structure of UNMIK

With Resolution 1244 the UN Security Council laid down its objective to create 'substantial autonomy and meaningful self-administration for Kosovo'.[3] It set up the UN Interim Administration Mission in Kosovo (UNMIK)

> in order to provide an interim administration for Kosovo under which the people of Kosovo can enjoy substantial autonomy within the Federal Republic of Yugoslavia, and which will provide transitional administration while establishing and overseeing the development of provisional demo-

---

[2] Regulation 9/2001, signed on 15 May 2001. The Constitutional Framework obliges the future provisional institutions of self-government to observe human rights standards, and makes a set of international documents directly applicable in Kosovo, but only in regard to the newly created institutions.

[3] UN Security Council Resolution 1244, of 10 June 1999.

cratic self-governing institutions to ensure conditions for a peaceful and normal life for all inhabitants of Kosovo.[4]

Resolution 1244 is not explicit as to whether it transfers the exercise of state sovereignty over the territory of Kosovo in its entirety to UNMIK.[5] However, it is the most plausible interpretation of the Resolution, which lists a series of 'main responsibilities', but does not restrict the powers of Special Representative of the Secretary General (SRSG) the as the sole legislative and executive authority in Kosovo. In any case, the SRSG has interpreted UNMIK's mandate to that extent in subsequently issued legislative acts, especially his Regulations on the Authority in Kosovo and the Applicable Law. 'Basic civilian administrative functions' hence came to mean that *all* administrative functions, as basic as they may be under the circumstances, are exercised by UNMIK alone. UNMIK is therefore the only legitimate authority in Kosovo.[6] The Federal Republic of Yugoslavia (FRY) and Russian Federation have occasionally protested against this practice, reminding of the Resolution's apparent confirmation of the FRY's sovereignty over Kosovo. Nevertheless, the understanding that UNMIK has no obligations or vertical connections to the FRY, and can therefore exercise immediate authority normally attributed to a holder of sovereignty, seems to have been accepted in international law.[7] Recent contacts between UNMIK and the FRY with regard to the Constitutional Framework or questions concerning taxation, customs regulations or the central elections have confirmed this relationship, as UNMIK insisted on labelling the dialogue 'an exchange of information' as opposed to 'negotiations'.

The FRY has forfeited its ability to exercise sovereign jurisdiction over Kosovo through Resolution 1244, and in combination with Regulations later adopted by UNMIK, supports the newly established practice. This situation, where UNMIK and KFOR exercise authority normally attributed to the sov-

[4] Ibid.

[5] A discussion of UNMIK's exercise of powers normally attributed to sovereign power as well as a comparison with other internationalized territories can, for instance, be found in Julie Ringelholm, "The Legal Status of Kosovo", in *Kosovo, 1999–2000, The Intractable Peace*, Report of the Balkans Working Group, European University Institute, published at www.iue.it.

[6] Report of the Secretary General on the United Nations Interim Administration of Kosovo, UN Doc. 2/1999/1259 of 23 December 1999, para. 35.

[7] The question of what this means for the fiction of FRY sovereignty over Kosovo, although formally confirmed by UNSCR 1244, has been raised already during the last period of negotiations before the eventual NATO intervention: 'What does it mean to say that borders have not been changed when the "state" that is supposedly defined by them has no governmental authority within what is putatively its own sovereign territory?', asks Robert M. Hayden, "The State as Legal Fiction", *East European Constitutional Review*, Fall 1998, pp. 45–50.

ereign, leads to the question of who is responsible for what is happening in Kosovo in the context of state responsibility.[8] In particular KFOR's responsibility and accountability has been subject to much debate within the Kosovo legal and human rights community.[9]

Entrusted with the civil administration of Kosovo, UNMIK constituted itself in a structure of 'four pillars', each reporting to the SRSG: Pillar I (Humanitarian Affairs) in the responsibility of the UNHCR, mainly in charge of preparing for the enormous 'winterization' programme; Pillar II (Civil Administration), run by the UN itself, in charge of the actual day-to-day administrative management of public affairs; Pillar III (Democratization and Institution Building) under the OSCE Mission in Kosovo; and Pillar IV (Economic Reconstruction)[10] for which the European Union was put in charge. Each 'Pillar's' head is at the same time a Deputy of the SRSG within the UNMIK structure. In the meantime, UNHCR has left this structure in June 2000, although it still maintains a presence in Kosovo. Until recently, UNMIK, therefore, had only three pillars. Following the adoption of the Constitutional Framework in May 2001, a 'new Pillar I' under the direct supervision of the SRSG was created. It is responsible for 'Law Enforcement and Justice' and has taken over functions normally attributed to Ministries of Justice and the Interior/Home Affairs.[11]

Resolution 1244 also establishes an international security presence in Kosovo (KFOR), which coordinates extensively with but remains outside of UNMIK itself and does, therefore, not operate under the authority the SRSG. In practice, KFOR has constituted itself in five Multinational Brigades (MNBs), each one assigned to an MNB commander.[12] On a central level, an overall Commander of KFOR, rotating among NATO countries on a six-

---

[8] See also EUI Report.

[9] See, for instance, John Cerone, "Outlining KFOR Accountability in Post-Conflict Kosovo", www.asil.org/insights, October 2000.

[10] The EU's own reconstruction efforts, however, are channelled through the European Agency for Reconstruction, which is based in Pristina, but not formally integrated or connected to UNMIK.

[11] It is important to note that, with the establishment of the Joint Interim Administrative Structure (JIAS), as described below, UNMIK and the pillar structure have not ceased to exist, and have not been replaced by the JIAS. However, the bulk of the civilian-administrative work of the UN and the EU are henceforth conducted in the framework of JIAS. The concept of the 'pillars' continues to exist in parallel to the joint administration run jointly with Kosovo representatives. Thereby, major policies continue to be conceived and elaborated without Kosovar participation.

[12] The five MNBs are under British, American, German, French and Italian command respectively.

month basis, fulfils the coordinating role with the SRSG and exercises supreme authority related to security matters in Kosovo.[13]

3. UNMIK's Commitments to Human Rights

Human rights have become an integral component of every UN field mission, in particular UN peacekeeping operations. This inclusion of human rights concerns is anchored in several UN documents, and has been reiterated by recent strategic documents, such as the Brahimi report.[14] The legal and political necessity for the UN and its operations to adhere to international human rights standards is obvious. While general commitments have become the norm, the development of effective mechanisms of human rights protection under a UN peacekeeping arrangement or an interim administration, is much less advanced.

With human rights high on the international agenda during the 1998–1999 Kosovo crisis, human rights naturally found consideration in the planning of the international administration of Kosovo. Early on, international human rights groups gave specific recommendations on giving high priority to human rights issues, but few went into the details of how exactly the structures and mechanisms of a *de facto* protectorate can best provide effective human rights protection.[15] Commitments to human rights have been associated with high moral standards and motivations, while not so much conceptual thought has been invested toward precisely how and which human rights should be protected, who should protect, and from which perpetrators should protection be provided.

Resolution 1244 explicitly mandated UNMIK to protect and promote human rights in Kosovo. It did not specify, however, how this objective should be pursued in practice. According to the Resolution,

> [the] main responsibilities of the international civil presence will include: (i) Maintaining civil law and order, including establishing local police forces and meanwhile through the deployment of international

[13] The Commanders of KFOR have so far come from the UK, Germany, Spain, Italy and Norway respectively. The current commander of KFOR, Marcel Valentin, is a French national.

[14] Report of the Panel on United Nations Peace Operations, UN Doc. A/55/305-S/2000/809, www.un.org.

[15] See, for instance, "Amnesty International's Recommendations for the Protection of Human Rights in Post-Conflict Peace Building and Reconstruction in Kosovo", AI-index EUR 70/091/1999, 1 June 1999, Amnesty International On-line, http://www.amnesty.org; see also, "Amnesty International, Kosovo: Human Rights Must Be Central in the Implementation of the UN Peace Plan", AI INDEX: EUR 70/93/99, 10 June 1999, Amnesty International On-line, http://www.amnesty.org.

466   MARCUS G. BRAND

police personnel to serve in Kosovo; ... (j) Protecting and promoting human [rights;].

As one of the few concrete suggestions, Amnesty International's 15-point Program for Implementing Human Rights in International Peace-keeping Operations[16] demands that,

> [a] mechanism should be established with powers to investigate allegations of human rights violations by peace-keeping personnel. States contributing troops to the peace-keeping operation should promptly conduct independent and impartial investigations into reports of violations of human rights and humanitarian law by their nationals and bring to justice those responsible. Those suspected of such violations should be suspended from duty pending the outcome of investigations.

As it became clear that KFOR had to undertake policing functions until UNMIK's own civilian police would be deployed, observers warned that human rights standards must in any case be upheld.[17]

From the outset of UNMIK's existence, international human rights groups have cast a watchful eye on Kosovo. Several made recommendations on the human rights policy of the SRSG, which has been incorporated into UNMIK's structures and operations. Many reports have been prepared, but few succeed in nailing down the structural legal and organizational obstacles for effective human rights protection in practice. Many reports limit themselves in lamenting the deplorable situation of certain groups of individuals in Kosovo (the Serbs, the Roma, trafficked women, etc.). The human rights discourse in Kosovo has been characterized by condemning crime, in particular interethnic violence. The general perception is that Kosovo Serbs and other minorities are persecuted by the Kosovo Albanian majority population, and that the structures of the international presence, UNMIK and KFOR, do their best to physically protect these groups from assaults, mainly by segregation. This focus in the human rights debate has somehow failed to shed light on other, more structural issues, such as procedural guarantees, which require state authorities to take very specific institutional precautions in exercising administrative authority.[18]

The Permanent Council of the OSCE determined that the OSCE Mission in Kosovo constitutes a distinct component within the overall framework of

---

[16] AI Index: IOR 40/01/94.

[17] "Clarification into Police Functions Undertaken by KFOR Crucial", News Service 135/99, AI INDEX: EUR 70/103/99, 16 July 1999, Amnesty International On-line, http://www.amnesty.org.

[18] See, for instance, Articles 5 and 6, but also 13 of the ECHR.

UNMIK. Within this overall framework, the OSCE Mission in Kosovo was mandated to take the lead role in matters relating to institution and democracy building and human rights, and therefore concentrate its work in a number of enumerated areas, among which 'monitoring, protection and promotion of human rights, including, *inter alia*, the establishment of an Ombudsman institution'.[19] Thus, within the UNMIK pillar structure, it was the OSCE that took over the main responsibility for the monitoring, protection and promotion of human rights. Also the UNHCR has taken a considerably active role in human rights monitoring and continues to cooperate with the OSCE on the elaboration and publication of their joint periodical reports on the situation of ethnic minorities in Kosovo.

The Office of the High Commissioner for Human Rights also maintains a certain presence in Kosovo and regularly reports on the human rights situation. However, it is not formally integrated into the UNMIK structure. In practice, the presence of the OHCHR is completely overshadowed by the OSCE and can therefore not be seen as a significant factor. The SRSG's Office has also set up a Human Rights Advisor's Office, which was originally staffed with a high profile international human rights expert.[20]

4. The Development of Statehood in Kosovo

Resolution 1244 also outlines the future development of state authority in Kosovo. In an initial phase the main tasks of UNMIK are to perform basic civilian administrative functions and maintain civil law and order. Next, UN-MIK is to organize provisional institutions for democratic and autonomous self-government through elections, gradually establishing substantial autonomy[21] and self-government in Kosovo. As these provisional local institutions are established and consolidated, UNMIK will gradually transfer its administrative responsibilities.[22] In the meantime, UNMIK is also tasked with fa-

[19] OSCE Permanent Council Decision No. 305, 237th Plenary Meeting, PC Journal No. 237.

[20] Bill O'Neill left UNMIK in January 2000. After his departure, the Office's prominence was drastically reduced.

[21] It probably has to be understood, that the drafters of the Resolution, as well as the brokers for the end of hostilities in June 1999, meant 'autonomy within the FRY' as opposed to within Serbia. This contradicts the Yugoslav–Serbian constitutional set-up, which only foresees the status of an autonomous province within Serbia, while the FRY constitution does not even mention Kosovo as a federal unit. This is in contrast to the earlier Yugoslav Federation (SFRY) in which Kosovo was one of the eight federal units and was represented in all federal organs, while at the same time enjoying autonomy within the Socialist Republic of Serbia.

[22] However, no criteria or a timetable for the transfer of authority was indicated by the Resolution. In practice, UNMIK intends to transfer authority to Kosovo institutions only after it

cilitating a political process designed to determine Kosovo's future status, to be determined in a political settlement. In a final stage, it will oversee the transfer of authority from Kosovo's provisional institutions to the institutions established under the political settlement. It should be noted that whatever institutions (laws and institutional structures) are being established in the meantime, have interim character and can, theoretically, be undone at any moment by the SRSG, or by the permanent institutions after the (complete and irrevocable) transfer of authority.

An SRSG-brokered agreement between the three eminent Kosovo political leaders of 15 December 1999 foresaw the establishment of joint institutions with which the SRSG was to share 'provisional administrative management' with representatives from Kosovo, while retaining the full legislative and executive authority. In return for the inclusion in the structures administering Kosovo, in particular a seat in the Interim Administrative Council (IAC), the Kosovar leaders had to give up their earlier titles and claims, and dissolve all 'parallel structures' by a deadline of 31 January 2000.[23] From the outset, the objective of participation of Kosovo Serbs was an integral element of the JIAS agreement, which stipulated that Kosovo Serb representatives would be included at all levels of the joint administration. However, the Kosovo Serbs[24] were not ready to accede to the agreement and dismissed it as a violation of Resolution 1244. Instead, they demanded self-government for the remaining Serbs in Kosovo. Although a small part of the Kosovo Serb community has participated in certain JIAS structures as 'observers' since, Kosovo Serbs have never formally acceded to the JIAS agreement.

When the two eminent Kosovar leaders, Ibrahim Rugova and Hashim Thaçi decided to join the agreement and to participate in JIAS, their positions were *de jure* reduced to mere advisors of the SRSG, Bernard Kouchner. The decision of the SRSG of 12 December 1999 to give in to pressure from Albanian judges and declare the 1989 Kosovo law the applicable law in Kosovo was certainly an important factor in the political dynamics of the time. Whatever political horse-trading might have paved the way for the signing of the agreement, it seems that it was the only possible way to ascertain UN-

will have determined that Kosovo political forces are sufficiently 'mature' for being entrusted with such authority.

[23] This concerned in particular Hashim Thaçi as the 'Prime Minister of the Provisional Government of Kosova', Ibrahim Rugova, as the 'President of the Republic of Kosova', as well as the 'Parliament of the Republic of Kosova' controlled by Rugova's LDK.

[24] The Kosovo Serbs have been represented by a variety of institutions. The chosen one of the time was the Serb National Council of Gracanica under the leadership of Bishop Artemje Radosavljevic.

MIK's authority in Kosovo. The agreement was eventually transformed into a Regulation by the SRSG and thereby became applicable law in Kosovo.[25]

While the JIAS agreement provided a basis for the mechanism of the central institutions of the administrative structure, it would be mistaken to describe it as a constitution. The competences and inter-relations of the created institutions are kept largely vague, and underscore the political, rather than legal nature of the agreement and the JIAS as a whole. Importantly, what the agreement on JIAS omitted was to give Kosovo the status of legal subjectivity (i.e. legal personality as an entity of Kosovo law), which would normally represent the 'state' in a legal order. Kosovo under JIAS, therefore, can rather be described as a territory with a mixed UN and local administration, but not as a state, neither in the sense of international law, nor in the sense of constitutional law and legal theory. With the introduction of the Constitutional Framework in May 2001, however, Kosovo's legal subjectivity was explicitly recognized.[26]

5. The Applicable Law in Kosovo

Resolution 1244 empowers the SRSG 'to change, repeal or suspend existing laws to the extent necessary for the carrying out of his functions, or where existing laws are incompatible with the mandate, aims and purposes of the interim civil administration' and 'to issue legislative acts in the forms or regulations'[27] to remain in force until repealed by the SRSG or suspended by rules issued by the institutions established under a political settlement (i.e., the Kosovo authority of self-government once it is established).[28]

[25] Regulation 1/2000 of 14 January 2000 (originally promulgated as Regulation 2000/28). Subsequently, each of the 20 Administrative Departments, was established by Regulation in the course of 2000.

[26] See Chapter 1, paragraphs 1.1 to 1.3 (General Provisions) of Regulation 9/2001. Before the long-awaited clarification by the CFPSG, Kosovo had an international administration, but no legal personality. Before 1989, Kosovo was one of the eight federal units of the later disintegrated SFRY, and enjoyed autonomy both within the Socialist Republic of Serbia and within the federal state. It had its own constitution and state institutions, such as a judicial system including a constitutional court, police, legislative assembly, executive government and representatives in federal organs. The CFPSG acknowledged this tradition of statehood by reference to Kosovo's 'historical, legal and constitutional development' and by setting out Kosovo as an 'undivided territory', with a 'people' and democratic self-government on the municipal and central level.

[27] Report of the Secretary General to the Security Council of 12 June 1999, UN Document 1999/779, paras. 39 and 41.

[28] UNMIK Regulation 1/1999, Section 4. A literal interpretation of this provision would mean that the Assembly elected on 17 November 2001 is not entitled to repeal UNMIK Regulations.

For the time being, the laws that should be applied in Kosovo are UNMIK Regulations and, wherever a subject has not been regulated yet by UNMIK, the law applicable in Kosovo on 22 March 1989[29] (presumably without its constitutional/institutional arrangements complemented by Yugoslav or Serbian laws) applies, and where there is no other provision in Kosovo law. In practice, there is much confusion about the law, a situation that is not conducive to the entrenchment of democratic practices.[30] With his decision SRSG Bernard Kouchner re-instituted the law applicable in 1989 without explicitly exempting the then applicable constitutional texts. It was, however, generally understood that constitutional-institutional laws were not applicable.[31]

Through the end of October 2001, UNMIK has issued a total of 127 Regulations (27 in 1999, 69 in 2000, 31 until November 2001). Regulations have the force of law as soon as they are signed by the SRSG. At times, the SRSG has also given retroactive force to Regulations. There is no requirement for due publication for Regulations to enter into force. The English version is sufficient and binding. The legislative process of UNMIK has demonstrated significant shortcomings, such as the delay in publishing an Official Gazette.[32] Some laws enforced by UNMIK, embodied in Administrative Directions, Executive Orders (both issued by the SRSG) or Administrative Instructions (issued by JIAS Department Co-Heads), have not been duly promulgated and are still largely inaccessible to the public.

Some Regulations, according to content, resemble constitutional provisions. The Constitutional Framework of May 2001 even explicitly refers to a general legal framework of binding nature for other subsidiary legislation. Yet, no rules tie the supreme legislative and executive authority, i.e. the SRSG, and he is free to amend or repeal any of his previous Regulations at any time and without limits, except Resolution 1244. The absence of a Constitutional Court (or an equivalent body) means that there is no instance in the current system, which could check the legality of legislative or executive acts by

[29] On 23 March 1989, the Kosovo Assembly was forced to agree to changes envisaged in the Constitution of the Socialist Republic of Serbia, which led to a gradual erosion and eventual removal of Kosovo's autonomous status.

[30] See, for instance, various reports of the OSCE on the Rule of Law in Kosovo, published on its website.

[31] This statement is based on conversations by the author with relevant officials from the SRSG's Legal Advisors Office in Pristina throughout 2000.

[32] The first trilingual version of the Official Gazette, containing the first 20 Regulations issued by the SRSG, was released in January 2001. Until October 2001, a total of six volumes has been produced and distributed to courts and prosecutors. Later issues of the Gazette also included Administrative Directions. Administrative Instructions are not included.

UNMIK or JIAS organs.[33] The separation of powers, a classical requirement for allowing a system of checks and balances, and therefore guaranteeing democratic governance, is entirely absent.

With the development of UNMIK law in its Regulations and Administrative Directions, a legislative piecemeal approach to institutional development has been chosen, whereby each sector of governance (the judiciary, the municipalities, each of the central administrative departments) is regulated in a separate Regulation. These Regulations are weak legal documents as they can be revoked with the strike of a pen by the SRSG. In addition, they are largely unknown to the general public, as they are translated and published with great delays. They cannot therefore, provide the stabilizing effect and firm anchorage that a constitution contributes to a legal system. Concerning content, they give only preliminary and temporary roles to the established institutions and their organs, while reserving all 'authority' for the international administration.

Regulation No. 1999/1 of 25 July 1999 on the Authority of the Interim Administration in Kosovo followed two Emergency Decrees issued during the first weeks of UNMIK's presence in Kosovo and was intended to lay down the overall principles of authority of the SRSG and UNMIK where Resolution 1244 remained vague. This Regulation was later amended by a separate Regulation on the Applicable Law, 24/1999. The amendment was effectuated through Regulation 25/1999, itself amended by Regulation 59/2000, and a revised Regulation on the Authority in Kosovo, 54/2000. Regulation No. 1/1999 determines that 'all legislative and executive authority with respect to Kosovo, including the administration of the judiciary, is vested in UNMIK and is exercised by the Special Representative of the Secretary-General'. The Regulation further states that the SRSG 'may appoint any person to perform functions in the civil administration in Kosovo, including the judiciary, or remove such person'.[34]

Section 2 of Regulation 1/1999 provides a general rule for the exercise of civilian authority in Kosovo and thereby confirms the political commitment to human rights standards:

---

[33] Also the Supreme Court Chamber, which, according to the Constitutional Framework, will be in charge of settling inter-institutional disputes concerning the Constitutional Framework in the future, will not have any authority over or be otherwise able to bind UNMIK or KFOR.

[34] With this prescription UNMIK removed any remaining state authority or official function from any previous institution or public office holder in Kosovo. Serbian judges and municipal officials found themselves in a situation that the UN had removed their legitimacy, and invited them and their UÇK-appointed competition to apply for a position within the interim administration.

> In exercising their functions, all persons undertaking public duties or holding public office in Kosovo shall observe internationally recognized human rights standards and shall not discriminate against any person on any ground such as sex, race, color, language religion, political or other opinion, national, ethnic or social origin, association with a national community, property, birth or other status.

This commitment has become part of the standard language used in various legislative acts up to the present and represents the most important limitation for the exercise of international authority in Kosovo, although these commitments have not been matched by actually enforceable rights *vis-à-vis* UNMIK on behalf of the residents of Kosovo.

Although the founding document of UNMIK's authority has been amended with regard to its provisions on the applicable law, it is worthwhile taking a look at the wording of the original version before moving on to the presently valid version. The Regulation determined that the 'laws applicable in the territory of Kosovo prior to 24 March 1999'.[35] Accordingly, the Serbian and Yugoslav laws prior to the adoption of a state of war legislation shall continue to apply in Kosovo insofar as they do not conflict with internationally recognized human rights standards, fulfilment of the mandate given to UNMIK, or Regulations issued by the SRSG. These human rights standards were, however, never defined. Potentially, they could have made the entire body of Serbian–Yugoslav laws inapplicable, as some Kosovar jurists argued because their legal basis was the discriminatory and unlawful abolition of Kosovo's autonomy between 1989 and 1992. With the SRSG's decision to declare the March 1989 body of laws the basis for applicable law, this debate was cut short.

Regulation 1/1999 also specifies the entry into force and promulgation of Regulations issued by UNMIK: 'Regulations shall be approved and signed' by the SRSG and 'shall enter into force upon the date specified therein'. Several important Regulations have retroactively been 'deemed to have entered into force' on 10 June 1999, the date of the adoption of Resolution 1244.

Although the regulation clearly states that 'regulations shall be published in a manner that ensures their wide dissemination by public announcement and publication', UNMIK has not been able to do so because qualified translation services for translation into Albanian and Serbian were not provided for in the Office of the Legal Adviser.[36] Wide dissemination of applicable

---

[35] UNMIK Regulation 1/1999, Section 3.

[36] UNMIK regulations shall be issued in Albanian, Serbian and English. In case of divergence, the English text shall prevail.

law, including regulations, has therefore not been the case in Kosovo under UNMIK administration.[37]

Regulation 2000/54 of 27 September 2000 basically reissued Regulation 1999/1 on the Authority of the Interim Administration in Kosovo as amended by Regulations 1999/24 on the Law Applicable in Kosovo and 1999/25 of 12 December 1999. The Regulations 'shall be deemed to have entered into force as of 10 June 1999'. Other than restating the applicable law, the amendments changed the original Regulation 1999/1 in the section on the administration of property, presumed to be regarding Yugoslav and Serbian state property, now 'socially owned property' is also included. The omission of socially owned property in Regulation 1/1999 led to misunderstandings between the management of several (formerly) socially owned companies and UNMIK in its search of buildings for its interim administration.[38]

6. A Constitutional Framework for Provisional Self-Government

On 15 May 2001, SRSG Hans Haekkerup, signed the Constitutional Framework for Provisional Self-Government (Constitutional Framework), which outlines the establishment and functioning of institutions following elections in November 2001.[39] While the Constitutional Framework eventually goes quite far in undermining FRY sovereignty over Kosovo, it carefully protects UNMIK's own ultimate authority, steering clear of procedural or substantive limits to the exercise of its authority, or even allowing any subordination under its own laws or standards.

While the Constitutional Framework gives wide competencies to the institutions of self-government, the elected Assembly, the President of Kosovo, the Government, etc., it reserves ultimate authority for UNMIK alone. After a long list of 'powers and responsibilities' reserved expressly for the SRSG in Chapter 8 (a to z), Chapter 12 (Authority of the SRSG) provides a general clause under which the SRSG and UNMIK will be able to override practically every decision of the elected institutions:

[37] The most useful guide and reference to the regulations issued so far has been produced by ABA/CEELI, which published a two-volume *Cumulative Index of United Nations Legal Materials and Applied in Kosovo* in October and November 2000. As already mentioned in Chapter I, an Official Gazette has started to be published only in January 2001.

[38] The 'administration' of property is separated from the property title as such: Administration by UNMIK of property shall be without prejudice to the right of any person or entity to assert ownership or other rights in the property in a competent court in Kosovo, or in a judicial mechanism to be established by regulation.

[39] Regulation 9/2001 of 15 May 2001.

The exercise of the responsibilities of the Provisional Institutions of Self-Government under this Constitutional Framework shall not affect or diminish the authority of the SRSG to ensure full implementation of UNSCR 1244(1999), including overseeing the Provisional Institutions of Self-Government, its officials and its agencies, and taking appropriate measures whenever their actions are inconsistent with UNSCR 1244(1999) or this Constitutional Framework.

Chapter 13 (Authority of KFOR) contains an even more far-reaching exemption for the international security presence: 'Nothing in this Constitutional Framework shall affect the authority of the International Security Presence (KFOR) to fulfil all aspects of its mandate under UNSCR 1244 (1999) and the Military Technical Agreement (Kumanovo Agreement)'.

Regulation 2001/19 on the Executive Branch of the Provisional Institutions of Self-Government in Kosovo of 13 September 2001 goes in the same direction. Section 6 of that Regulation reserves for the SRSG the power to 'take such measures as may be required to enhance the effectiveness' of the Government, the Ministries and agencies. He may also 'assign international and other personnel to Ministries and Executive Agencies to perform such functions as he judges appropriate and necessary'. Furthermore, the SRSG can 'instruct the Ministries and Executive Agencies to carry out such functions and duties' as he may require.

Although the ideal of serving the general interest has become the ruling idea of modern public administration, the exercise of UNMIK's administrative authority has not been based on any set of rules normally associated with democratic constitutions: A set of rules for administration normally raises expectations of service, honesty and transparency, and are mainly supported by the idea of equality and fairness. Sajo has described constitutionalism as an institutional reaction to a Murphy's Law of political history: 'Where there can be an abuse of power, there will be an abuse of power'.[40] The method selected by the UN and the SRSG to promote 'democracy' in Kosovo has been to create a 'dictatorship of virtue'.[41] The consent of the elected representatives of the people is not very relevant for decision-making. In the words of Hayden, it is surely an odd democracy in which the un-elected representatives of foreign powers can ignore the elected representatives of the people of the country.[42]

---

[40] Andras Sajo, "Corruption, Clientelism, and the Future of the Constitutional State in Eastern Europe", *East European Constitutional Review*, Spring 1998, pp. 37–46.

[41] The expression has first been used by Robert M. Hayden to describe a similar phenomenon, the authority of the OHR in post-Dayton Bosnia.

[42] Robert Hayden, *Blueprints for a House Divided – The Constitutional Logic of the Yugoslav Conflict*, Michigan University Press, 2000.

7. UNMIK Legislation on Human Rights

In order to provide a general safeguard for the inclusion of human rights in the work of UNMIK, the commitment by UNMIK to adhere to internationally recognized human rights standards was formalized by Regulation 24/1999. It is however important to analyze the provision very carefully and compare it to other texts binding an administration to international human rights, in particular, the constitutions of Bosnia and Herzegovina after the Dayton Agreement, but also the newly established Constitutional Framework. For Kosovo, UNMIK has ruled out any form of discrimination[43] and has in particular determined that:

> [i]n exercising their functions, all persons undertaking public duties or holding public office in Kosovo shall observe internationally recognized human rights standards, as reflected in particular in:
>
> — The Universal Declaration of Human Rights of 10 December 1948;
> — The European Convention for the Protection of Human Rights and Fundamental Freedoms of 4 November 1950 and the Protocols thereto;
> — The International Covenant on Civil and Political Rights of 16 December 1966 and the Protocols thereto;
> — The International Covenant on Economic, Social and Cultural Rights of 16 December 1966;
> — The Convention on the Elimination of All Forms of Racial Discrimination of 21 December 1965;
> — The Convention on Elimination of All Forms of Discrimination against Women of 17 December 1979;
> — The Convention Against Torture and Other Cruel, Inhumane or Degrading Treatment or Punishment of 17 December 1984;
> — The International Convention on the Rights of the Child of 20 December 1989.[44]

The important question in this context is, whether the above-mentioned international declarations and conventions are in fact directly applicable and have direct effect in Kosovo. The wording chosen by the SRSG, 'shall observe internationally recognized human rights standards, as reflected in', does not

---

[43] 'No person undertaking public duties or holding public office in Kosovo shall discriminate against any person on any ground such as sex, race, colour, language, religion, political or other opinion, natural, ethnic or social origin, association with a national community, property, birth or other status'.

[44] Regulation 24/1999.

seem to suggest that the conventions are directly applicable law in Kosovo, or that they even take precedence over statutory laws such as Regulations and the 1989 Kosovo law. If such an effect had been intended, the wording of the Regulation could have made this clear. Also, if the aforementioned texts are to form the basis for administrative conduct in Kosovo, UNMIK would have had to see to a better dissemination of these basic laws across the territory in all relevant languages: English, Albanian and Serbian. As things stand, the catalogue can only be seen as a declaratory political commitment to a high standard of human rights, yet without putting the practice to the test of local judicial remedies or international supervision through international human rights bodies.

In addition to the general, quasi-constitutional texts of Regulations 1/1999 and 24/1999, several other Regulations contain commitments to high standards of human rights adherence. The Municipal Law, for instance, laid down by Regulation 45/2000 on the Self-Government of Municipalities in Kosovo[45] spells out a principle of legality[46] as a basic rule for municipal administration:

> Law and justice shall bind the administration of the municipality, and in particular the human rights and freedoms contained in the European Convention for the Protection of Human Rights and Fundamental Freedoms and the Protocols thereto shall be observed. All administrative actions shall comply with the applicable law.

In addition to this very explicit obligation for the municipal administration to observe the ECHR, the Regulation also provides for an exception to the rule of hierarchical obedience based on a human rights clause: 'All municipal civil servants shall carry out the instructions of their superiors and follow their directives unless the instruction given is contrary to law or counter to human rights and freedoms or the rights of communities'.[47] As an additional safeguard, UNMIK reserves a special supervisory role for the UNMIK Municipal Administrator, who 'shall intervene so as to ensure that fundamental principles of human rights and equal treatment are respected and that the rights and interests of communities are protected'.[48]

The Constitutional Framework, which lays down the legal framework for the functioning of democratically elected institutions, constitutes huge progress in the clarification of applicability of international human rights standards. Once formally established after democratic elections, the provisional institutions of self-government

---

[45] Signed on 11 August 2000.
[46] UNMIK Regulation 45/2000, Section 33.
[47] Ibid., Section 34.4.
[48] Ibid.. Section 48.2.

shall observe and ensure internationally recognized human rights and fundamental freedoms, including those rights and freedoms set forth in:

- The Universal Declaration on Human Rights;
- The European Convention for the Protection of Human Rights and Fundamental Freedoms and Its Protocols;
- The International Covenant on Civil and Political Rights and the Protocols thereto;[49]
- The Convention on the Elimination of All Forms of Racial Discrimination;
- The Convention on the Elimination of All Forms of Discrimination against Women;
- The Convention on the Rights of the Child;
- The European Charter for Regional or Minority Languages; and
- The Council of Europe's Framework Convention for the Protection of National Minorities.

Most significantly, it is now clear that 'The provisions on rights and freedoms set forth in these instruments shall be directly applicable in Kosovo as part of this Constitutional Framework'.[50] While this is a welcome and necessary clarification, it is deplorable that this direct effect of human rights is extended only to the future provisional institutions of self-government, and not to all 'persons undertaking public duties or holding public office in Kosovo', thereby including international officials acting on behalf of UNMIK or KFOR.

8. Privileges and Immunities of UNMIK and KFOR

In trying to place Kosovo's institutions and human rights mechanisms into context, it seems relevant to briefly discuss the rules on privileges and immunities of UNMIK and KFOR. These rules are standard for a peacekeeping operation, but provide limited protection under civilian administration or military organizations in the democratic world during peacetime. Although the rules foresee the possibility for waivers, it is unlikely that UNMIK or KFOR will ever be as respectful of Kosovo laws and institutions, as they are of their own internal rules and regulations. The Ombudsman has declared the

[49] Interestingly, the International Covenant on Economic, Social and Cultural Rights is not mentioned here. So far, according to Applicable Law (Regulation 24/1999), standards contained in that Covenant were explicitly to be observed by public office holders as well.

[50] CFPSG, Article 3.3.

relevant regulation as is incompatible with recognized international human rights standards.[51]

KFOR personnel 'shall respect the laws applicable in the territory of Kosovo and regulations' issued by the SRSG 'insofar as they do not conflict with the fulfilment of the mandate given to KFOR' under UNSCR 1244.[52] For members of UNMIK, the obligation is more concrete: 'UNMIK personnel shall respect the laws applicable in the territory of Kosovo and (*sic*) regulations' issued by the SRSG. 'They shall refrain from any action or activity incompatible therewith'.[53]

KFOR as well as UNMIK, their associated property, funds and assets are immune from any legal process.[54] Even 'locally recruited KFOR personnel shall be immune from legal process' in respect to tasks carried out exclusively related to their services to KFOR. The immunity for international KFOR officers is specified as including immunity 'from jurisdiction before courts in Kosovo in respect of any administrative, civil or criminal act committed by them in the territory of Kosovo', as well as the immunity 'from any form of arrest or detention other than by persons acting on behalf of their respective sending States'.[55]

The SRSG, his five Deputies, the Police Commissioner, 'and other high-ranking officials as may be decided from time to time' by the SRSG, 'shall be immune from local jurisdiction in respect of any civil or criminal act performed or committed by them in the territory of Kosovo'.[56] It would be problematic if this 'time to time' immunity can be extended to whoever the SRSG considers a high-ranking official, in particular, as this formulation opens the possibility to also extend immunity to Kosovars who happen to be represented in high political bodies. Orders issued by the SRSG to UNMIK Police to not take any action against high political figures, such as the members of the IAC, without his prior approval, could fall into this category. The immunity for all other UNMIK personnel, including locally recruited staff, is slightly less far-reaching: They 'shall be immune from legal process in respect of words spoken and all acts performed by them in their official

[51] Special Report No. 1 on the compatibility with recognized international standards of UNMIK Regulation No. 2000/47 on the Status, Privileges and Immunities of KFOR and UNMIK and Their Personnel in Kosovo (18 August 2000) and on the implementation of the above Regulation addressed to Mr. Hans Haekkerup, Special Representative of the Secretary General of the United Nations.

[52] Regulation 47/2000. Section 2.2.

[53] Ibid., Section 3.5.

[54] Ibid., Sections 2.1 and 3.1.

[55] Ibid., Section 2.3.

[56] Ibid., Section 3.2.

capacity'.[57] While legal process is thereby made possible for at least acts outside the official capacity, all UNMIK staff 'shall be immune from any form of arrest or detention'.

The rules on waivers to UNMIK's immunity include important qualifications:[58] The Secretary-General[59] 'shall have the right and the duty to waive the immunity of any UNMIK personnel in any case where, in his opinion, the immunity would impede the course of justice and can be waived without prejudice to the interest of UNMIK'. For members of the OSCE and EU led Pillars of UNMIK, 'any waiver of immunity shall be carried out in consultation with the heads of those components'. The Regulation was issued on 18 August 2000, but the Regulation specified that it 'shall be deemed to have entered into force on 10 June 1999', the day UNSCR 1244 was adopted.

Diplomatic immunity protecting UNMIK officials from prosecution in Kosovo, as well as the *de facto* immunity extended by the SRSG over 'public figures', runs counter to principles of accountability for public servants. Immunities can and have been lifted, and internal audits and investigations have disclosed some of the inappropriate uses of power. Yet, for an administration to be democratic and based on the rule of law, this is hardly sufficient.

9. Human Rights Institutions in Kosovo

Apart from weaving human rights commitments into the founding legal texts forming the basis for UNMIK's interim administration, UNMIK has also created a number of bodies and institutions whose specific role is the protection, promotion and monitoring of human rights in Kosovo. Judging by the wording of its mandate and the expectations raised by its launch, the Ombudsperson Institution is probably the most prominent of these, in particular since it formally enjoys 'independence' within UNMIK and the interim administration. Also, the SRSG's Office itself is equipped with a human rights advisor and while a significant part of the mandate of the OSCE Mission in Kosovo, formally a part of UNMIK, is the 'protection, promotion and monitoring of human rights' in Kosovo.

[57] 57 Ibid., Section 3.3.
[58] Ibid., Section 6.
[59] This is an interesting 'right and duty' for the Secretary-General of the United Nations, who has otherwise no functions in the governance and legal system of Kosovo.

480   MARCUS G. BRAND

10. The Courts[60]

Many international human rights observers admonished that it was crucial
for UNMIK to develop a functioning judiciary quickly in Kosovo if it was to
establish the rule of law and thereby protect human rights.[61] This urgent need
had been recognized early in the planning phase for an international presence
in Kosovo, even before it was clear that it would be organized under the
auspices of the UN. However, the OSCE as the competent component within
UNMIK for questions pertaining to the rule of law, has itself reported several
times that the justice system continues to feature major shortcomings and
fails to provide the institutional gravity that the rule of law needs to spread.[62]
At the same time, the international administration of Kosovo through its self-
binding to *inter alia* the ECHR, has practically committed itself to provide
'effective remedy before a national authority'.[63]

The judiciary in Kosovo is structured along the lines of the previous administration of the Serbian state and the Kosovo autonomous province: There
is a basic three-level structure of Municipal Courts, five District Courts and a
Supreme Court.[64] Not all of these elements of the eventually foreseen structure are operational as of yet. The Supreme Court only consists of an Ad-Hoc
Court of Final Appeal acting as an appeal body in criminal proceedings.[65]
Judges and lay judges have been appointed ad interim by the SRSG, but
whose appointments may be renewed after a period of trial and observation.[66]
During 2000, international judges have been placed first at the Mitrovica District Court,[67] and later all over Kosovo[68] in an attempt to ensure ethnically
unbiased court rulings.[69] For cases of non-commercial property disputes, a
special Housing and Property Claims Commission has been set up.[70] For war
and ethnic crimes, a special Kosovo War and Ethnic Crimes Court (KWECC)
was planned, but has not been established so far. A Commercial Court ex-

[60] The cursory description of the judicial system may appear insufficient to some readers.
Since the OSCE's reports and assessments are publicly available and comprehensively deal
with the matter, a more detailed analysis was considered unnecessary here.

[61] See, for instance, Lawyers Committee for Human Rights, "A Fragile Peace: Laying the
Foundations for Justice in Kosovo", October 1999, www.lchr.org.

[62] See the OSCE Mission in Kosovo's reports on www.osce.org/kosovo. The last comprehensive update on the judicial system was published in April 2001.

[63] Article 13 of the ECHR.

[64] The system also includes Minor Offence Courts.

[65] Regulation 5/1999.

[66] See Regulations 6/1999, 7/1999, and 18/1999 (lay judges).

[67] Regulation 6/2000.

[68] Regulation 34/2000.

[69] See also Regulations 46/2000 (languages at court), 64/2000 (assignments), and 2/2001.

[70] Regulations 23/1999 and 60/2000 (procedure).

ists in Pristina, but it operates with a reduced number of judges and deals with only a fraction of the cases its competency permits under the applicable pre-1989 laws.

11. Administrative Complaints, Redress and Judicial Review

In principle, since no special legislation has been promulgated UNMIK, the 1989 law on administrative procedures continues to be valid and applicable for the civil administration in Kosovo. In principle, this should also hold true for the international (i.e., UNMIK-staffed) positions in the administration in particular, as long as they hold actual administrative authority, and no administrative act can be taken without their approval. This is particularly valid for UNMIK Municipal Administrators who continue to have far-reaching authority over the elected municipal assemblies and the newly created municipal administrations as long as the administrative authority is not transferred from UNMIK to the municipalities. Also, this must apply for UNMIK Regional Administrators, who have wide powers that have not been matched or altered by the Agreement on the Joint Interim Administrative Structure.[71] To adhere to the principle of legality, the central level Administrative Departments should also be applying Kosovo administrative procedure due to the lack of any other source of law. In practice, however, it is unlikely that UNMIK's administrative officials apply or are familiar with Kosovo administrative codes in their day-to-day operations.

With a clear human rights and legality background, the Municipal Law includes a section on complaints and judicial protection.[72] It grants a person the right to 'file a complaint about an administrative decision of a municipality' if she claims that her 'rights have been infringed by the decision'. Complaints must be submitted in writing or in person to the Chief Executive Officer, or to the President of the Municipality within one month. The Chief Executive Officer (the local head of the municipal administration), or the President (the mayor elected by the Municipal Assembly) 'shall re-examine both the legality of the decision and the administrative process by which it was reached'. Within a month the CEO or the President shall give the complainant a reasoned response in writing. If unsatisfied, 'the complainant may refer the matter to the Central Authority, which shall consider the complaint and decide upon the legality of the decision' in writing within another month.[73] Importantly however, 'the rights set out in this Section shall be additional

[71] See Regulation 14/1999.
[72] Regulation 45/2000, Section 35.
[73] The 'Central Authority' in the Municipal Law is 'the SRSG and UNMIK'. However, it is unclear who exactly would take such complaints and decide according to which procedures.

to any rights that the person may have to refer an administrative decision to the Ombudsperson or to a court of law'. The Regulation further states, 'a person may seek relief in a court of law against decisions of a municipality, in accordance with the rules and procedures of the relevant court'.[74] Although this Regulation does not preclude appeal, it does not establish any path for the judicial redress against administrative decisions. No Regulation has, as of yet, addressed the issue of judicial (or independent and impartial tribunal) review of administrative decisions.[75]

12. Ombudsperson Institution

With the arrival of UNMIK and the build-up of the interim administration, human rights protection and promotion was a consistent element of the rhetoric of Kosovo's international administrators. Yet, the establishment of the Ombudsperson Institution by UNMIK Regulation took more than a full year and it took another several months before the new Ombudsman established the office in Pristina.[76] For several months, the UN, the OSCE and KFOR haggled over the precise wording of the Ombudsman's mandate and powers. The outcome was marred by compromise and fell short of the expectations of many. Yet even with the most powerful mandate and far-reaching powers and capacities, an Ombudsman cannot replace a non-existent or fledgling justice system, substitute for true accountability of police and security forces, or serve as the sole provider of effective legal remedies to citizens. It is too early to say what role the Ombudsman may fill over the coming years in Kosovo, or to determine the way his activities will contribute to the human rights situation in Kosovo.

The Ombudsman has been given a general mandate to 'promote and protect the rights and freedoms of individuals and legal entities and ensure that all persons in Kosovo are able to exercise effectively the human rights and fundamental freedoms safeguarded by international human rights stan-

---

[74] Regulation 45/2000, Section 36.

[75] The Constitutional Framework partially addresses these obligations. Its Chapter 9 contains the following provisions: '9.4.2: Each person claiming to have been directly and adversely affected by a decision of the Government or an executive agency under the responsibility of the Government shall have the right to judicial review of the legality of that decision after exhausting all avenues for administrative review'; '9.4.3: Each person shall be entitled to have all issues relating to his rights and obligations and to have any criminal charges laid against him decided within a reasonable time by an independent and impartial court'. While these commitments are laudable, they should have been expressly made much earlier. Also, the practical implementation of these guarantees will create considerable challenges for UNMIK.

[76] The current Ombudsman is the Polish human rights expert Marek Nowicki.

dards',[77] in particular the ECHR and its Protocols and the ICCPR. To that end, the Ombudsman 'shall provide accessible and timely mechanisms for the review and redress of actions constituting an abuse of authority by the interim civil administration or any emerging central or local institution'. It was unfortunately left open, what exactly constitutes 'abuse of authority'.

The Ombudsman was in general conceived as entity to which citizens affected by administrative decisions could direct complaints. The Ombudsman has 'jurisdiction (*sic*) to receive and investigate complaints from any person or entity in Kosovo concerning human rights violations and actions constituting an abuse of authority by the interim civil administration or any emerging central or local institution' whereby actions include 'acts, omissions and decisions'.[78] The possibilities for the Ombudsman to receive and investigate allegations of human rights violations or improper conduct of members of KFOR had been one of the most contested issues during the drafting of the Regulation. After KFOR in Kosovo had in principle agreed to being subjected to scrutiny by the Ombudsman, NATO's headquarters in Brussels decided to exempt KFOR from any such relationship with the Ombudsman. NATO insisted on the following formulation: 'In order to deal with cases involving the international security presence, the Ombudsperson may enter into an agreement with the Commander of the Kosovo Forces (COMKFOR)'.[79] To date, no such agreement exists.[80]

Yet, even with regard to the powers *vis-à-vis* the civilian administration, the Ombudsman's functions and powers are limited to those of a non-judicial, political body rather than legal body: He can 'receive complaints, monitor, investigate, offer good offices, take preventive steps, make recommendations and advise on matters'[81] relating to his functions, and shall 'take all necessary steps and actions to address complaints – including directly intervening with the relevant authorities, which are then required to respond within a reason-

---

[77] UNMIK Regulation 38/2000, of 30 June 2000.

[78] Ibid., Section 3.1.

[79] Ibid., Section 3.4.

[80] Amnesty International had welcomed the early proposal of the UN Secretary General, set forth in his 12 July report on UNMIK to establish a human rights ombudsman in Kosovo, but added that it

> understands that this institution will have the authority to investigate allegations of abuses by KFOR troops. Amnesty International would welcome confirmation that KFOR will fully cooperate with such an institution and will ensure that troop-contributing countries recall from duty any of their personnel against whom the above mechanism has found evidence of human rights violations and that they are brought to justice in accordance with international standards.

[81] UNMIK Regulation 38/2000, Section 4.1.

able time'.[82] The most severe sanction the Ombudsman can impose, in cases where authorities do not take appropriate measures, is to draw the SRSG's attention to the matter and make a public statement about this.[83]

Although the Ombudsperson's independence of action is formally guaranteed by the Regulation, the long arm of authority of the SRSG reaches the Ombudsperson: The SRSG may remove the Ombudsperson from office whenever the SRSG considers that the Ombudsperson has failed 'in the execution of his functions' or 'has been placed, by personal conduct or otherwise, in a position incompatible with the due exercise of his or her functions'.[84] Last but not least, the legal foundation for the financing of the Ombudsperson make this institution appear much less independent and sustainable than the original idea may have suggested: 'For the year 2000, the Ombudsperson institution shall be funded by international donors. In subsequent fiscal years, the Ombudsperson may request funds from international donors and/or the Kosovo Consolidated Budget for the operation of the institution'.[85]

Over the past few months, the Ombudsman has taken a particularly critical position *vis-à-vis* the legal status of UNMIK and KFOR in Kosovo as well as concerning several Regulations in conflict with international human rights standards. Although the Ombudsman himself cannot become effective remedy in the sense of international human rights standards, he has become an important independent and corrective voice inside Kosovo.

13. Administrative Department for Democratic Governance and Civil Society

The OSCE Mission in Kosovo took over responsibility for only one of the 20 Administrative Departments.[86] UNMIK internal controversies delayed the passing of the Regulation for the Department until summer 2000.[87] The Department has been a small unit within the JIAS, and has been given the mandate to provide advice to other Departments and to the IAC on issues concerning democratic governance, equal opportunities and human rights

[82] Ibid., Section 4.5.

[83] Ibid., Section 4.11.

[84] Ibid., Section 8.2.

[85] Ibid., Section 18.

[86] The OSCE developed a concept for the Department of Democratic Governance and Civil Society, nominated its international co-head and provides for the running costs and international staff of the Department. The Kosovo Co-Head has been an independent Kosovo physician, who has gained prominence as a human rights activist over the past decade, Dr Vjosa Dobruna, co-founder of the Centre for Protection of Women and Children.

[87] Regulation No. 2000/40 on the Establishment of the Administrative Department for Democratic Governance and Civil Society of 10 July 2000.

from within the system. It has been raising human rights issues in important political forums such as the 'Council of Ministers', a regular policy meeting of all 40 national and international Co-Heads with the SRSG, as well as discretely working with other Administrative Departments on respective human rights and equality issues within their structures and policies. Its powers and resource capacities, however, have been extremely limited. In the future, it will be transformed into an office attached to the Prime Minister's Office providing internal government advice and recommendations on human rights issues.[88]

14. OSCE Mission in Kosovo

As mentioned above, the OSCE Mission in Kosovo (OMIK) is a distinct part of UNMIK. The exact nature of its relationship with the SRSG and UNMIK, as well as with the UN-led Pillar II responsible for civil administration, has not been entirely clarified and continues to puzzle many involved. For all practical purposes, OMIK is a separate organization, with its own staff, rule and procedures, reporting mechanism, distinct needs for visibility, organizational culture and corporate identity. One of its Departments is in charge of 'Human Rights and Rule of Law' issues where the OSCE has specific experience and competence, in particular in the geographic region. The Mission has until recently been employing some 45 human rights officers, seconded by the OSCE's participating governments, and deployed in more than a dozen field offices and regional centres across Kosovo. Their primary duty is the monitoring and reporting of human rights violations. Although the mandate originally given by the OSCE includes the 'protection' of human rights, OMIK is reluctant to get involved with individual cases. In addition, its monitoring focus is very much directed towards the occurrence of inter-ethnic violence, in particular violence and discrimination against the ethnic minorities in Kosovo.[89] However, inter-ethnic violence and discrimination is rarely committed by state actors similar to the existing authorities in Kosovo, UNMIK and KFOR.

For the most part, human rights violations monitored and reported by the OSCE's human rights division are committed by persons unknown, or by criminal elements of the Kosovo Albanian majority population of Kosovo. In some cases, the OSCE's human rights division has asserted an active involvement of the UÇK, as well as of the Kosovo Protection Corps after the

[88] Regulation No. 2001/19 on the Executive Branch of the Provisional Institutions of Self-Government in Kosovo of 13 September 2001.

[89] At the same time, the OSCE has paid considerably less attention to other forms of human rights violations committed by private actors, such as violence against women.

UÇK had been de-militarized. Also, political groupings with leanings toward 'extremist' solutions, in particular those who had advocated armed struggle against the Serbian regime's forces, have been associated with human rights abuses. Yet, human rights violations are not limited to non-state actors. Together with the OSCE's legal system monitors, the human rights division has detected ethnic biases of the judiciary that is mainly staffed by ethnic Albanian judges. General reports about the OSCE's findings are published on the OSCE's website, and contain detailed descriptions of individual cases.[90]

However detailed this monitoring may be, it must be seen as insufficient for the effective protection of human rights in Kosovo. Hardly any complainant who has shared his or her story with the OSCE's human rights monitors has found remedy. Judging by the OSCE's own assessments, the situation for the ethnic minorities in Kosovo, in particular the Kosovo Serbs in enclaves and the Kosovo Roma, has not improved.[91] The OSCE's focus on inter-ethnic violence within its human rights mandate has not only overshadowed other very important (general) human rights questions, but has also apparently not contributed to relief for the dire situations of ethnic minorities the OSCE so decries.

Whenever the OSCE has not been focussing on inter-ethnic problems, issues of criminal law and criminal procedure have been in the foreground. Here, OMIK has been concerned with questions relating to detention facilities and duration, in particular pre-trial detention. Recently, OMIK has examined means to ensure that pre-trial detention is surrounded by adequate guarantees and does not exceed the periods prescribed by international standards, in particular Article 5 of the ECHR. In this context, OMIK officers have been examining the practice of Kosovo's law enforcement authorities. Findings show that detention is often extended beyond 24 hours due to lack of holding cells in the municipality and security concerns in transporting to and from the regional detention facilities.[92] OMIK's concern for detention matters has been constant from the outset of its operations in Kosovo. The OSCE has also taken the dramatic step of denouncing an UNMIK Regulation as 'unlawful', when its determined that it 'fails to strike a proper balance between the imperative duty to safeguard the right to liberty and the need to detain those charged with serious criminal offences'.[93] Another report identified 26 cases in which criminal defendants have been held in pre-trial detention longer

---

[90] www.osce.org/kosovo.

[91] In cooperation with UNHCR, the OSCE Mission in Kosovo has been publishing regular updates on the situation of ethnic minorities in Kosovo, the latest of which in March 2001.

[92] OSCE Mission in Kosovo, Weekly Report 12/2001, of 21 March 2001.

[93] OSCE Mission in Kosovo, Observations and Recommendations of the OSCE Legal System Monitoring Section: Report No. 6 – Extension of Custody Time Limits and the Rights of Detainees: The Unlawfulness of Regulation 1999/26; 29 April 2000. The Regulation had

than the applicable limit and 'recommended urgent action to address those cases'.[94]

15. International Monitoring Outside UNMIK, Access to International Bodies

This paper cannot explore in detail all international treaty-based or other human rights monitoring and reporting mechanisms, which have been involved in Kosovo since UNMIK took over administrative responsibilities. This area is certainly interesting to analyze, as it raises questions of how Kosovo fits into the international system under the continuation of the FRY's formal sovereignty over the territory, yet without being made responsible for what is happening in that territory, as it has lost its executive authority there. The UN Commission of Human Rights, including the Special Rapporteur of the Commission on Human Rights on the Situation of Human Rights in Bosnia and Herzegovina, the Republic of Croatia and the Federal Republic of Yugoslavia (Jiri Dienstbier), the ICCPR Committee of Human Rights and other committees have been seized with matters relating to Kosovo and have deliberated on Kosovo's human rights situation. Since the objective of this paper is to address questions specific to actual human rights protection in Kosovo, these international monitoring mechanisms can be left aside here.

The possibility of access to international human rights bodies by Kosovo citizens is another open question. So far, no such case is known. When the possibility of local remedy is non-existent, the European Commission and Court of Human Rights should be explored especially if the alleged human rights violations have been committed by officials belonging to countries, that have recognized the competence of the Strasbourg institutions.

16. Conclusion

The absence of statehood has had significant consequences for the governance of Kosovo. To look at a UN peacekeeping mission from the perspective of constitutionalism and lawfulness of governance may be unusual, but is nevertheless necessary. This is particularly true in view of UNMIK's early commitments of protecting and promoting human rights and establishing the

extended the maximum detention period from six to nine months, where proceedings are conducted for a crime carrying a possible prison sentence of more than five years.

[94] OSCE Mission in Kosovo, Observations and Recommendations of the OSCE Legal System Monitoring Section: Report No. 3 – Expiration of Detention Periods for Current Detainees, 8 March 2000 as well as an Update in Report No. 4 of 18 March 2000.

rule of law in Kosovo, as well as its eventual need to transfer authority to a hopefully capable and democratic self-government. Issues classically connected with field work of international agencies, such as diplomatic immunity to local jurisdiction, lacking legal and political accountability, and a general vagueness of the structures created, have all cast considerable doubt on whether the interim UN administration, as it is constructed today in Kosovo, can fulfil the requirements of democratic governance and the rule of law, and in consequence, effective human rights protection. The rule of law can obviously not be established as long as the scope of applicable law is not sufficiently beyond doubt, and as long as the executive authority in place, be it military or civilian, is not firmly bound to it.

The international administration in Kosovo was organized with many good intentions. Respect for the human rights for all people in Kosovo was one of the leading motifs for international efforts over the past three years. Yet, ethnic violence and a climate of lawlessness persist, much to the chagrin of UNMIK and KFOR. International observers in Kosovo and around the world tend not to hold KFOR and UNMIK responsible as the controlling authorities, but rather view the Kosovo Albanians collectively 'responsible' for the situation. At the same time, human rights issues of a less spectacular nature, such as the absence of clear procedural constraints that would bind the executive authority and the lack of effective access to courts and legal remedies, affect the majority of the population and reinforce the climate of lawlessness. Substantive commitments to high standards without corresponding legal remedies, either local or international, is not sufficient to effectively protect human rights. Also, it is not possible to describe the current UNMIK administration, which holds the totality of authority in civilian matters in Kosovo, as a democratic and law-based system of governance. This has implications for the human rights of the subjects of such an administration. Only a state with a balance of powers and system of mutual checks and balances (i.e. adhering to the principles of constitutionalism) can effectively provide a rule of law system that protects human rights, and correspondingly, will hold itself responsible and accountable for shortcomings.

[22]

Minding the Gap: Outlining KFOR Accountability in Post-Conflict Kosovo

John Cerone*

Abstract

Notwithstanding the unique conditions of its deployment, KFOR does not act in a legal vacuum. As an entity deployed under UN auspices and by virtue of its exercise of public authority in Kosovo, it is bound by provisions of international human rights and humanitarian law to the extent of its control over individuals there. There are at least three different modalities through which international human rights law may apply to the conduct of KFOR soldiers in Kosovo: the mandate of Resolution 1244; the human rights obligations of the Federal Republic of Yugoslavia; and the human rights obligations of the governments of the national contingents of KFOR. All of the national governments of the various KFOR contingents are bound by the Geneva Conventions, which form the core of modern humanitarian law. As Kosovo may be considered occupied territory, the humanitarian law of occupation is applicable. Further, the failure of KFOR troops to meet international standards for the treatment of individuals may give rise to individual state accountability. Finally, should KFOR or its participating states choose to declare a derogation, they would remain bound by the minimum standards provided by humanitarian law.

1 Introduction

Protecting individuals from gross violations of human rights was the proclaimed purpose and justification of the March 1999 NATO intervention in Kosovo. In the aftermath of the armed conflict, violence has continued to plague the territory and has required a firm response by the Kosovo Force (KFOR), the NATO-led 'security

* Executive Director, War Crimes Research Office, Washington College of Law (The American University). The views expressed in this article are solely those of the author.

470   *EJIL* 12 (2001), 469–488

presence' deployed under Security Council Resolution 1244.[1] As the international community considers strategies for quelling the violence, it is essential to recall the limitations on those strategies, in particular the constraints on KFOR's treatment of individuals under its control, that are imposed by international law.

A quick glance at the core international human rights and humanitarian law instruments might lead one to conclude that KFOR, owing to the unique conditions of its deployment, is not bound by the provisions of those instruments.

Many of the major human rights instruments, and notably those binding on NATO countries, oblige states to ensure to everyone *within their territory* or *subject to their jurisdiction* the rights contained therein.[2] Kosovo could not be considered part of the national territory of any state but the Federal Republic of Yugoslavia (FRY),[3] and any other state's exercise of jurisdiction in the strict sense (e.g. by applying and enforcing its own domestic laws with respect to the local population) would clearly be illicit.

As for application of the 1949 Geneva Conventions and Additional Protocols thereto,[4] which embody the bulk of modern humanitarian law (i.e. the laws of war designed to protect individuals and to restrict the methods and means of warfare), it would appear that there has been a general cessation of hostilities following the signing of the Military Technical Agreement in June 1999, thus heralding an end to the ordinary application of the laws of war.

If KFOR were not bound by the norms contained in these instruments, a profound gap in legal accountability for human rights abuses would exist, perhaps as serious as

---

[1] Security Council Resolution 1244 (1999).

[2] International Covenant on Civil and Political Rights (ICCPR), Article 2, GA Res. 2200A (XXI), 21 UN GAOR Supp. (No. 16) at 52, UN Doc. A/6316 (1966), 999 UNTS 171, entered into force 23 March 1976 ('to respect and to ensure to all individuals within its territory and subject to its jurisdiction'); European Convention for the Protection of Human Rights and Fundamental Freedoms (ECHR), Article 1, 213 UNTS 222, entered into force 3 September 1953 ('shall secure to everyone within their jurisdiction'); American Convention on Human Rights (ACHR), Article 1, OAS Treaty Series No. 36, 1144 UNTS 123, entered into force 18 July 1978, reprinted in 'Basic Documents Pertaining to Human Rights in the Inter-American System', OEA/Ser.L.V/II.82 Doc.6 Rev.1, at 25 (1992) ('to ensure to all persons subject to their jurisdiction'). While Article 2 of the ICCPR refers to all individuals within a state's territory *and* subject to its jurisdiction, the Human Rights Committee has interpreted these to be independent grounds for application of the Covenant. See, e.g., *Delia Saldias de Lopez v. Uruguay*, Communication No. 52/1979 (29 July 1981), UN Doc. CCPR/C/OP/1, at 88 (1984).

[3] Resolution 1244, *supra* note 1, preamble ('*Reaffirming* the commitment of all Member States to the sovereignty and territorial integrity of the Federal Republic of Yugoslavia ...').

[4] Geneva Convention for the Amelioration of the Condition of Wounded, Sick and Shipwrecked Members of Armed Forces at Sea, entered into force 21 October 1950; Geneva Convention for the Amelioration of the Condition of the Wounded and Sick in Armed Forces in the Field, entered into force 21 October 1950; Geneva Convention Relative to the Treatment of Prisoners of War, entered into force 21 October 1950; Geneva Convention Relative to the Protection of Civilian Persons in Time of War, entered into force 21 October 1950 ('Fourth Geneva Convention'); Protocol Additional to the Geneva Conventions of 12

the Meron gap,[5] in which only non-derogable human rights obligations remain binding.[6]

However, a more thorough examination of the instruments and the meanings of their provisions as established in international jurisprudence reveals that KFOR is in fact bound by both human rights and humanitarian law, or at the very least, provides strong arguments for drawing such a conclusion.

2 The International Presence in Kosovo

In Resolution 1244, the UN Security Council, acting under Chapter VII,[7] authorized the creation of KFOR and UNMIK (the United Nations Interim Administration Mission in Kosovo), the public authorities that would operate in Kosovo on behalf of the international community with the purposes of securing and administering the territory. KFOR, the 'international security presence', was to be established by 'Member States and relevant international organizations',[8] while UNMIK, the 'international civil presence', was to be established by the 'Secretary-General, with the assistance of relevant international organizations'.[9]

KFOR, which is led by and primarily composed of NATO forces, is charged with: '[d]eterring renewed hostilities, maintaining and where necessary enforcing a ceasefire, and ensuring the withdrawal ... of Federal and Republic ... forces ...; [d]emilitarizing the Kosovo Liberation Army (KLA) and other armed Kosovo Albanian groups ...; [e]stablishing a secure environment ...; [e]nsuring public safety and order

---

August 1949, and Relating to the Protection of Victims of International Armed Conflicts ('Protocol I'), entered into force 7 December 1979; Protocol Additional to the Geneva Conventions of 12 August 1949, and Relating to the Protection of Victims of Non-International Armed Conflicts ('Protocol II'), entered into force 7 December 1979.

[5] The Meron gap refers to the situation that arises when a country is in a state of civil unrest that does not rise to the level of internal armed conflict. In such a situation, a country may be able to derogate from most of its obligations under human rights law, while at the same time avoiding application of the norms of humanitarian law applicable in internal armed conflicts. Even within the Meron gap, however, a state's non-derogable human rights obligations would continue to apply. For more on non-derogable rights, see *infra* note 99, and the accompanying text. See also Meron, 'Towards a Humanitarian Declaration on Internal Strife', 78 *AJIL* (1984) 859–868. For the proposition that there are 'no substantive legal gaps in the protection of individuals in situations of internal violence', see 'Fundamental Standards of Humanity'; Report of the Secretary General submitted pursuant to Commission resolution 2000/69, January 2001, E/CN.4/2001/91.

[6] Non-derogable human rights obligations, typically protecting individuals from the most serious abuses, would remain binding in Kosovo in any case through the law of state responsibility. Under the traditional law of state responsibility, a state could be held legally responsible on the international plane for injury to aliens that resulted from acts contrary to international law. The doctrine of diplomatic protection permitted the state of nationality of the victim to espouse the victim's claim. The standard applied to such claims was an international minimum standard, drawn from general principles of law and notions of natural law. Over the past few decades, there has been a degree of convergence between international human rights law and the law of state responsibility, such that acts constituting the most serious human rights violations would also engage state responsibility if committed by state actors abroad.

[7] Resolution 1244, *supra* note 1, final preambular paragraph.

[8] *Ibid.*, at para. 7.

[9] *Ibid.*, at para. 10.

472   *EJIL* 12 (2001), 469–488

until the international civil presence can take responsibility for this task; [s]upporting, as appropriate, and coordinating closely with the work of the international civil presence ...'.[10]

UNMIK, which is composed of four 'pillars' led by the UN, the UNHCR, the OSCE and the EU, is mandated to 'provide an interim administration for Kosovo under which the people of Kosovo can enjoy substantial autonomy within the Federal Republic of Yugoslavia'.[11] It is specifically responsible for, *inter alia*: '[p]romoting the establishment ... of substantial autonomy and self-government in Kosovo ...; [p]erforming basic civilian administrative functions ...; [o]rganizing and overseeing the development of provisional institutions for democratic and autonomous self-government ...; [m]aintaining civil law and order; [p]rotecting and promoting human rights'.[12]

Together, these two entities are effectively authorized and mandated to exercise all public authority in Kosovo.

3 Human Rights Law

There are several different modalities through which international human rights law is in force in Kosovo. First, human rights law is incorporated into the mandate of the actors deployed under UN auspices in Resolution 1244. Secondly, the human rights obligations of the Federal Republic of Yugoslavia remain in force throughout the territory and may be said to be binding by reasoning from established principles of the law of state succession. Thirdly, the human rights obligations of the governments of the various national contingents of KFOR apply to the conduct of their troops abroad.

A *The UN Mandate*

While Resolution 1244 expressly mandates UNMIK to protect and promote human rights, this task is not listed among the responsibilities of KFOR, which has a separate mandate and is outside of UNMIK's command.[13] Nor is any limitation on the means KFOR may use in carrying out its responsibilities expressly stated in the Resolution.

Further, it is unclear whether UNMIK regulations requiring public authorities in Kosovo to comply with international human rights law are applicable to KFOR. UNMIK's chief administrator, the Special Representative of the Secretary-General (SRSG), has signed several regulations requiring the application of international

---

[10] *Ibid.*, at para. 9.
[11] *Ibid.*, at para. 10. See also Report of the Secretary-General on the United Nations Interim Administration Mission in Kosovo ('Report of the Secretary-General'), at para. 35, S/1999/779, 12 July 1999 ('The Security Council, in its Resolution 1244 (1999), has vested in the interim civil administration authority over the territory and people of Kosovo. All legislative and executive powers, including the administration of the judiciary, will, therefore, be vested in UNMIK.').
[12] Resolution 1244, *supra* note 1, at para. 11.
[13] While UNMIK and KFOR are each mandated to 'coordinate closely' with the other (Resolution 1244, *supra* note 1, at paras 6 and 9(f)), responsibility for their establishment is given to separate entities and they are placed under separate chains of command.

human rights standards in Kosovo.[14] UNMIK Regulation 1999/24 stipulates that '[i]n exercising their functions, all persons undertaking public duties or holding public office in Kosovo shall observe internationally recognized human rights standards'.[15] It then provides an impressive list of major international human rights instruments from which these standards are to be drawn.[16]

Despite the considerable range of human rights protection afforded by UNMIK regulations, they may be inapplicable to KFOR. While the SRSG exercises 'all legislative and executive power' in Kosovo, he may only regulate 'within the areas of his responsibilities laid down by the Security Council in its resolution 1244'.[17] He may thus be wholly precluded from regulating the activities of KFOR, which is given a separate area of responsibility under Resolution 1244.[18]

There are, however, at least two arguments for holding that KFOR has been mandated by the UN to act in conformity with human rights law. The first is that as a security presence deployed 'under United Nations auspices',[19] KFOR is bound to comply with the purposes of the United Nations, among which is the promotion of human rights.[20] Secondly, as noted above, Resolution 1244 lists among KFOR's responsibilities supporting, as appropriate, the work of the international civil presence. Further, Resolution 1244 requires 'that both presences operate towards the same goals and in a mutually supportive manner'.[21] As UNMIK is responsible for protecting and promoting human rights, KFOR's obligation to support UNMIK

---

[14]   See, e.g., UNMIK Regulations 1999/1, 1999/23 and 1999/24. See also *Belul Beqaj and Dita v. Temporary Media Commissioner*, Office of the Media Appeals Board, Kosovo, FRY, www.osce.org/kosovo/media/ditavtmc (September 2000).

[15]   UNMIK Regulation 1999/24, section 1.3.

[16]   This list includes: the Universal Declaration on Human Rights of 10 December 1948; the European Convention for the Protection of Human Rights and Fundamental Freedoms of 4 November 1950 and the Protocols thereto; the International Covenant on Civil and Political Rights of 16 December 1966 and the Protocols thereto; the International Covenant on Economic, Social and Cultural Rights of 16 December 1966 (ICESCR); the Convention on the Elimination of All Forms of Racial Discrimination of 21 December 1965 (CERD); the Convention on the Elimination of All Forms of Discrimination Against Women of 17 December 1979 (CEDAW); the Convention Against Torture and Other Cruel, Inhuman or Degrading Treatment or Punishment of 17 December 1984 (CAT); and the International Convention on the Rights of the Child of 20 December 1989 (CRC).

[17]   Report of the Secretary-General, *supra* note 11, at para. 39.

[18]   Given the plain meaning of UNMIK's mandate to protect and promote human rights, it could equally well be argued that regulating KFOR to the extent necessary to protect human rights is 'within the areas of [the SRSG's] responsibilities laid down by the Security Council in its Resolution 1244'. However, UNMIK Regulation 2000/47 provides that 'all KFOR personnel shall respect the laws applicable in the territory of Kosovo and regulations issued by the Special Representative of the Secretary-General *insofar as they do not conflict with the fulfilment of the mandate given to KFOR under Security Council Resolution 1244*'. UNMIK Regulation 2000/47, section 2.2 (emphasis added). While the Regulation purports to apply to the conduct of KFOR troops, it emphasizes that the security mandate overrides the applicable law. The same regulation also deprives the courts of Kosovo of jurisdiction over KFOR or KFOR soldiers. See *infra* note 95.

[19]   Resolution 1244, *supra* note 1, at para. 5.

[20]   Charter of the United Nations, Article 1(3) (1945); see also Article 55(c).

[21]   Resolution 1244, *supra* note 1, at para. 6.

474   *EJIL* 12 (2001), 469–488

requires that it, at the very least, refrain from undermining this objective. This can only be achieved through compliance with international human rights standards.[22]

B *Succession*

The Socialist Federal Republic of Yugoslavia (SFRY), the predecessor to the FRY,[23] was a party to all of the major universal[24] human rights instruments.[25] As the law of state succession provides for automatic succession with respect to human rights obligations,[26] the obligations of the SFRY continue in force in the FRY.[27]

While these human rights obligations technically apply only to the FRY Government, the principle of automatic succession for human rights obligations may imply obligations on the part of any public authorities acting in the place of the FRY Government. If the rationale underlying the principle is that obligations pass with control over territory and that beneficiaries of rights are entitled to maintain them,[28]

---

[22] This proposition is also supported by a 4 July 1999 statement by then Acting SRSG, Sergio Vieira de Mello. While recalling that KFOR was responsible for ensuring public safety and order until such time as UNMIK was capable of doing so, he emphasized that KFOR would be bound by international human rights standards in the performance of these duties. 'Statement on the Right of KFOR to Apprehend and Detain', Office of the Acting SRSG, UNMIK, 4 July 1999.

[23] While the United Nations does not consider the FRY to be *the* successor state to the SFRY for the purpose of taking up the seat of the SFRY in the General Assembly, the FRY is one of the successor states to the SFRY for the purpose of succession to treaty obligations. See *infra* note 26.

[24] In this article, the term 'universal', when used in reference to instruments or institutions, serves to distinguish treaty regimes open to all states from the regional systems.

[25] The SFRY had ratified the ICCPR, the ICESCR, CEDAW, CERD, CAT and the CRC. It was not, however, a party to the ECHR.

[26] *British Yearbook of International Law* (1994) 627 (European Union asserting the position that successors to the former Yugoslavia 'must abide by their obligations deriving from this International Covenant [on Civil and Political Rights]'). See also the Vienna Convention on Succession of States in Respect of Treaties, Article 34(a), 17 ILM (1978) 1488 ('any treaty in force at the date of the succession of States in respect of the entire territory of the predecessor State continues in force in respect of each successor State so formed'). While few states are parties to the Vienna Convention, its provisions have been regarded as declaratory of customary international law. *Case Concerning the Gabcikovo-Nagymaros Project*, No. 92 (25 September 1997); *Digest of United States Practice in International Law* (1980) 1041 n. 43 (State Department Legal Adviser expressing the opinion that the rules of the Convention were 'generally regarded as declarative of existing customary law by the US'); *M v. Federal Department of Justice and Police*, 75 ILR 107, at 110 (Switzerland Federal Tribunal, 1979) ('It can be accepted that this draft codification reflects a considerable level of agreement on the rules of international law governing the matter and that the Federal Tribunal can consider it as an authority.'). Finally, the FRY's continued compliance with the reporting obligations contained in the various human rights treaties to which the SFRY was a party indicates its acceptance of the obligations contained therein.

[27] Note also that, as the legal system of the FRY is monist with respect to the integration of international norms, obligations arising from treaties to which the FRY is a party are a 'constituent part of the internal legal order'. The Constitution of the Federal Republic of Yugoslavia, Article 16 (1998).

[28] As stated by the Human Rights Committee, 'once the people are accorded the protection of the rights under the Covenant, such protection devolves with territory and continues to belong to them, notwithstanding change in government of the State party, including dismemberment in more than one State or State succession or any subsequent action of the State party designed to divest them of the rights guaranteed by the Covenant'. General Comment No. 26, 'Issues Relating to the Continuity of Obligations to the International Covenant on Civil and Political Rights', 8 December 1997.

then it would not be unreasonable to conclude that UNMIK and KFOR are bound by the obligations that ensure protection of those rights.

C Human Rights Obligations of Individual States

The various KFOR contingents may also be bound by the human rights obligations of their sending states. This third approach is particularly significant because, unlike the first two, it can provide for individual state accountability.

The vast majority of states, including almost all NATO countries, are parties to the International Covenant on Civil and Political Rights (ICCPR). In addition, all of the European member states of NATO are parties to the European Convention on Human Rights (ECHR).

As noted above, these instruments limit the scope of their application to persons subject to the jurisdiction of the state party. However, the term 'jurisdiction' as used in this context has been construed broadly by international human rights institutions.

The Human Rights Committee, whose interpretation of states' obligations under the ICCPR is authoritative,[29] has consistently held that the Covenant can have extraterritorial application,[30] and has thus clearly demonstrated its understanding that a state's jurisdiction extends beyond its territorial boundaries. Further, it has found that the expressed scope of Article 2(1) 'does not imply that the State party concerned cannot be held accountable for violations of rights under the Covenant which its agents commit upon the territory of another State, whether with the acquiescence of the Government of that State or in opposition to it'.[31]

In *Delia Saldias de Lopez v. Uruguay*, the Committee held that Uruguay violated its obligations under the Covenant when its security forces abducted and tortured a Uruguayan citizen then living in Argentina. Following the command of Article 5(1) that '[n]othing in the present Covenant may be interpreted as implying . . . any right to engage in any activity . . . aimed at the destruction of any of the rights and freedoms recognized herein', the Committee reasoned that 'it would be unconscionable to so interpret the responsibility under Article 2 of the Covenant as to permit a State party

---

[29] UN Doc. CCPR/C/SR 371, at para. 1; Frank Newman and David Weissbrodt, *International Human Rights: Law, Policy, and Process* (2nd ed., 1996) 94.

[30] See, e.g., Human Rights Committee, Comments on United States of America, at para. 19, UN Doc. CCPR/C/79/Add 50 (1995) ('The Committee does not share the view expressed by the Government that the Covenant lacks extraterritorial reach under all circumstances. Such a view is contrary to the consistent interpretation of the Committee on this subject, that, in special circumstances, persons may fall under the subject matter jurisdiction of a state party even when outside that state's territory.'); Consideration of Reports Submitted by States Parties under Article 40 of the Covenant: Iran (Islamic Republic of), at para. 63, 30 July 1993, CCPR/C/SR.1253 ('The existence and the scale of application of the death penalty — compounded, as in the matter of Salman Rushdie, by extraterritorial persecution — constituted a flagrant violation of the State party's commitment under the Covenant to protect the right to life. Notwithstanding Mr Mehrpour's claim to the contrary, those were certainly issues that rightfully fell within the Committee's sphere of competence.').

[31] *Delia Saldias de Lopez v. Uruguay*, at para. 12.3, Communication No. 52/1979 (29 July 1981), UN Doc. CCPR/C/OP/1, at 88 (1984).

476   *EJIL* 12 (2001), 469–488

to perpetrate violations of the Covenant on the territory of another State, which violations it could not perpetrate on its own territory'.[32]

While one could argue that the ambit of the Committee's holding in *Delia Saldias de Lopez* is strictly limited to extraterritorial violations committed *against a state's own national*, that factor providing a solid basis for finding that the victim was subject to the perpetrating state's jurisdiction, the language of its holding is broad enough[33] to cover cases involving extraterritorial mistreatment of non-nationals. The latter proposition has been carried forward by the regional human rights institutions.[34]

In *Loizidou v. Turkey (Preliminary Objections)*,[35] the European Court of Human Rights faced the issue of whether certain acts committed against individuals by Turkish armed forces deployed in northern Cyprus were capable of falling within Turkish 'jurisdiction' within the meaning of Article 1 of the European Convention. In finding that such acts were capable of falling within the scope of Article 1, the Court tied the application of human rights obligations to the fact of control over the individual alleging a violation. The Court held: 'Bearing in mind the object and purpose of the Convention, the responsibility of a contracting party may also arise when as a consequence of military action — whether lawful or unlawful — it exercises effective control of an area outside its national territory.'[36] It reasoned that '[t]he obligation to secure, in such an area, the rights and freedoms set out in the Convention derives from the fact of such control'.[37] It also stated that it was irrelevant whether such control is 'exercised directly, through [a state party's] armed forces, or through a subordinate local administration'.[38]

In that particular case, the alleged wrongful conduct was the continuous denial by Turkish forces of the applicant's access to her property in northern Cyprus and the ensuing loss of all control over the property. In the merits phase of the case, the Court found that this interference with the applicant's rights 'is a matter which falls within Turkey's "jurisdiction" within the meaning of Article 1 and is thus imputable to Turkey'.[39]

The Inter-American Commission on Human Rights has similarly found states bound by human rights obligations in their extraterritorial treatment of non-

---

[32]   *Ibid.*

[33]   Recognizing the breadth of the holding, one Committee member filed a separate statement attempting to limit its scope, even citing the case of occupied territory as a situation in which the obligations of the ICCPR should not apply. *Delia Saldias de Lopez v. Uruguay*, Communication No. 52/1979 (29 July 1981), UN Doc. CCPR/C/OP/1, at 88 (1984) (individual opinion appended to the Committee's views at the request of Mr Christian Tomuschat). No other Committee members joined in this opinion.

[34]   Given the pervasive phenomenon of cross-fertilization among international fora, particularly among human rights fora, it is not uncommon to cite jurisprudence from regional fora as precedent for universal regimes. Regional practice is also particularly useful since the regional institutions, the combined membership of which comprises a large proportion of UN member states, tend to be more active, and thus have broader bases of experience within their spheres of competence.

[35]   *Loizidou v. Turkey* (Preliminary Objections), ECHR (1995) Series A, No. 310, 23 February 1995.

[36]   *Ibid.*, at para. 62.

[37]   *Ibid.*

[38]   *Ibid.*

[39]   *Loizidou v. Turkey* (Merits), 40/1993/435/514, 18 December 1996, at para. 57.

nationals.[40] Indeed, the reasoning of the *Loizidou* Court was taken a step further in a recent report of the Commission. In *Coard et al. v. United States*,[41] the Commission examined allegations that the military action led by the armed forces of the United States in Grenada in October 1983 violated a series of norms of international human rights and humanitarian law. Specifically, the petitioners alleged that they had been, *inter alia*, detained by United States forces in the first days of the military operation, held incommunicado for many days, and mistreated, all in violation of the United States' obligations under the American Declaration of the Rights and Duties of Man.[42]

Before addressing the question of whether the actions of the US forces violated rights contained in the American Declaration, the Commission had to determine whether the petitioners were subject to US jurisdiction.[43] Citing Theodor Meron's scholarship for the proposition that a state's human rights obligations obtain where its agents exercise power and authority over persons outside national territory,[44] the Commission found that the phrase 'subject to its jurisdiction' 'may, under given circumstances, refer to conduct with an extraterritorial locus where the person concerned is present in the territory of one state, but subject to the control of another state — usually through the acts of the latter's agents abroad'.[45] The Commission further stated that '[i]n principle, the inquiry turns not on the presumed victim's nationality or presence within a particular geographic area, but on whether, under the specific circumstances, the State observed the rights of a person subject to its authority and control'.[46]

Finding that the United States forces were bound by norms of both human rights

---

[40] See, e.g., *Haitian Centre for Human Rights v. United States*, Case 10.675, Report No. 51/96, Inter-AmCHR, OEA/Ser.L/V/II.95 Doc. 7 Rev. at 550 (1997) (finding that the United States, in intercepting Haitian refugees in boats on the high seas and returning them to Haiti, had violated its obligations under the American Declaration of the Rights and Duties of Man); Report 31/93, Case 10.573, United States, published in Annual Report of the IACHR 1993, OEA/Ser.L/V/II.85, Doc. 9 Rev., 11 February 1994, at 312 (admitting case concerning actions of United States forces in Panama).

[41] *Coard et al. v. United States*, Case 10.951, Report No. 109/99, 29 September 1999.

[42] American Declaration of the Rights and Duties of Man ('American Declaration'), OAS Res. XXX, adopted by the Ninth International Conference of American States (1948), reprinted in Basic Documents Pertaining to Human Rights in the Inter-American System, OEA/Ser.L.V/II.82 Doc.6 Rev.1, at 17 (1992). It is well established that the American Declaration 'constitutes a source of international obligation'. *Coard, supra* note 41, at para. 36 (citing Inter-American Court of Human Rights, Advisory Opinion OC-10/89, 14 July 1989, 'Interpretation of the American Declaration of the Rights and Duties of Man Within the Framework of Article 64 of the American Convention on Human Rights', Series A, No. 10, at paras 43–46).

[43] While the Declaration does not contain language expressly narrowing the scope of its application to individuals 'subject to the jurisdiction' of the state party, the Commission read in this requirement. *Coard, supra* note 41, at para. 37 ('Given that individual rights inhere simply by virtue of a person's humanity, each American State is obliged to uphold the protected rights of any person subject to its jurisdiction.').

[44] Meron, 'Extraterritoriality of Human Rights Treaties', 89 *AJIL* (1995) 78, at 81.

[45] *Coard, supra* note 41, at para. 37.

[46] *Ibid.*

478   *EJIL* 12 (2001), 469–488

and humanitarian law[47] during the course of their activities in Grenada, the Commission declared that the deprivation of the petitioners' liberty effectuated by those forces did not comply with the terms of Articles I, XVII and XXV of the American Declaration.

A recent admissibility decision of the European Court of Human Rights illustrates the extent to which this point of law has developed. In response to a claim by Iraqi citizens of violations alleged to have been perpetrated by Turkish armed forces on Iraqi soil in the course of Turkish military operations there, the European Court declared the application admissible without even mentioning the extraterritorial nature of the incident.[48]

Synthesizing the holdings of the cases above, the following rule may be drawn. A state's human rights obligations may apply with respect to its treatment of non-nationals abroad, where such individuals find themselves under its control, whether directly, through that state's armed forces, or through a subordinate local administration. Further, the legality of the state's presence abroad or whether that state is acting alone or with the acquiescence of the state in whose territory the violation occurs is irrelevant.

KFOR would appear to fall within this rule. KFOR is an organ of state control in Kosovo in at least two senses. First, it exercises public authority in Kosovo. Secondly, it consists of sections of the armed forces of participating states.[49] The fact that its presence is lawful, having been authorized by the Security Council acting under Chapter VII, is irrelevant.[50]

---

[47] While the Commission found that the United States was simultaneously bound by both human rights and humanitarian law, it essentially deferred to humanitarian law as *lex specialis* in order to 'help ... define whether the detention of the petitioners was "arbitrary" or not under the terms of Articles I and XXV of the American Declaration' (*Coard, supra* note 41, at para. 42) given the climate in which the alleged violation occurred. While the Commission also pointed out that, where human rights and humanitarian law 'provide levels of protection which are distinct, the Commission is bound by its Charter-based mandate to give effect to the normative standard which best safeguards the rights of the individual', its *renvoi* to humanitarian law to ascertain the standard of 'arbitrariness' may have undermined that mandate. Normally, where a state is unable to afford the full protection of certain rights, it is required to enter a derogation. That would be preferable in this case as well, rather than risking the dilution of human rights standards and the integrity of human rights law as a separate and independently applicable body of public international law.

[48] *Issa, Omer, Ibrahim, Murty Khan, Muran and Omer v. Turkey*, Decision as to the Admissibility of Application No. 31821/96, 30 May 2000.

[49] For the nexus between the sending state and its forces under KFOR command, see *infra* section 5.

[50] While it may be theoretically possible for the Security Council to override a state's human rights obligations (at least those that have not achieved the status of *jus cogens*) by issuing a resolution under Chapter VII, which would be binding on all member states and would be superior to conflicting international obligations (UN Charter, Articles 25 and 103), it would have to do so expressly. This flows from the general principle of interpretation that obligations should be construed, where possible, so as to avoid conflicting obligations. This would be especially true with respect to the abrogation of human rights obligations, given the great importance placed on them by the international community. For the proposition that the Security Council could not override *jus cogens* norms, see *Case Concerning Application of the Convention on the Prevention and Punishment of the Crime of Genocide (Bosnia and Herzegovina v.*

The primary ground for distinction[51] would appear to be the degree of control exercised by the relevant forces. In its *Loizidou* judgment, the European Court referred to the fact that the Turkish army exercised 'effective *overall* control over that part of the island'.[52] While KFOR and UNMIK together exercise overall control in Kosovo, KFOR alone has limited responsibilities.

First, KFOR's mandate is limited to acting as a security force, including some police functions. It is not charged with civilian administration. Secondly, it is composed of troops from several different countries, each sharing a portion of the overall security responsibility. Thirdly, the responsibilities of the various KFOR contingents vary depending upon the region of Kosovo in which they are deployed. For example, in some regions KFOR actively polices, running the prisons and conducting investigations; in others it acts only as back-up to the UNMIK Police. Thus, an individual state's troops in Kosovo stand in a different position from that occupied by Turkish forces in northern Cyprus.

The *Coard* decision, on the other hand, did not require overall control of a particular territory. It only required control *vis-à-vis* the individual alleging a violation of his or her rights. The European Court's decision in *Issa*, where the application was held admissible in the case of an extraterritorial military operation falling short of effective overall control of a territory, appears to employ a similar approach.[53]

Several factors support this progressive development of the law and provide a sound basis for arguing that the reach of a state's human rights obligations is commensurate with its degree of control over individuals in foreign territory.

First, the International Court of Justice has held that, with respect to treaty

---

Yugoslavia (Serbia and Montenegro)) (Separate Opinion of Judge Lauterpacht), ICJ Reports (1993), at 325 ('The concept of *jus cogens* operates as a concept superior to both customary international law and treaty. The relief which Article 103 of the Charter may give the Security Council in case of conflict between one of its decisions and an operative treaty obligation cannot — as a matter of simple hierarchy of norms — extend to a conflict between a Security Council resolution and *jus cogens*.').

51 The fact that the FRY is not a party to the European Convention could not serve as a basis for distinguishing the case of KFOR in Kosovo from the cases above. First, as mentioned above, the FRY is a party to the ICCPR. Secondly, even if the *Loizidou* holding is to be limited to interpretation of the ECHR, neither the fact that the applicant was a national of a state party to the ECHR nor the fact that the violation occurred on the territory of a state party was relied on, or even mentioned, by the Court in its determination of Turkey's responsibility. Finally, the European Court found the application in *Issa* admissible even though Iraq, which is not a party to the ECHR, is both the country of citizenship of the complainants and the state in which the violations are alleged to have occurred.

52 *Loizidou v. Turkey* (Merits), 40/1993/435/514, 18 December 1996, at para. 56.

53 It should also be noted that, in an earlier decision in the *Loizidou* case, the European Commission on Human Rights had used broader language than the Court subsequently used. In ascertaining whether the applicant was subject to Turkey's jurisdiction, the Commission had held 'that nationals of a State, including registered ships and aircraft, are partly within its jurisdiction wherever they may be, and that authorized agents of a State, including diplomatic or consular agents and armed forces, not only remain under its jurisdiction when abroad but *bring any other persons or property "within the jurisdiction" of that State, to the extent that they exercise authority over such persons or property*. Insofar as, by their acts or omissions, they affect such persons or property, the responsibility of the State is engaged.' *Chrysostomos, Papachrysostomou and Loizidou v. Turkey*, Decision as to the Admissibility of Application Nos 00015299/89, 00015300/89 and 00015318/89, Hudoc reference number: REF00002448, 3 April 1991 (emphasis added).

480   *EJIL* 12 (2001), 469–488

interpretation, a contextual approach, rather than a literal approach, should be employed.[54] That being said, it is important to recall that the purpose of human rights law is to protect individual human beings.[55] Further, in promulgating the ICCPR, the state parties 'recogniz[ed] that these rights derive from the inherent dignity of the human person' and recalled their Charter obligation to promote the universal protection of human rights,[56] thus clearly implying an obligation to acknowledge the rights of all human beings. Secondly, human rights instruments in particular are subject to a method of dynamic interpretation, one which can respond to developments in international affairs, as well as to the changing realities of peoples' everyday lives.[57] Related to these is the effectiveness principle, which requires that the provisions of human rights treaties 'be interpreted and applied so as to make [their] safeguards practical and effective'.[58]

In light of these legal principles, the very fact that the various KFOR contingents exercise different powers and discharge different responsibilities supports the notion that their level of obligation should be tied to their fields of operation. At the same time, as the European Court held in *Loizidou* that the legality of the state's presence was irrelevant and that the state's obligation flowed from the fact of its control, it is reasonable to conclude that the state's level of obligation should be tied to the degree of actual control, even where it exceeds the degree of lawful control. This is also supported by the well-established rule that a state's responsibility is engaged even where a state actor is acting *ultra vires*, or beyond the scope of his official capacity.[59] Thus, for example, if a KFOR contingent were to undertake activities outside of its

---

[54] *The Legal Consequences for State of the Continued Presence of South Africa in Namibia (South West Africa) Notwithstanding Security Council 271*, ICJ Reports (1970), at 31, at para. 53. See also Vienna Convention on the Law of Treaties, Article 31(1), 24 April 1970, 8 ILM 679.

[55] *Loizidou v. Turkey* (Preliminary Objections), ECHR (1995) Series A, No. 310, 23 February 1995, at para. 72.

[56] ICCPR, third and fifth preambular paragraphs.

[57] For the proposition that the European Convention is a living instrument which must be interpreted in the light of present-day conditions, see, *inter alia, Tyrer v. United Kingdom*, ECHR (1978) Series A, No. 26, 25 April 1978, at 15–16, at para. 31.

[58] *Loizidou v. Turkey* (Preliminary Objections), ECHR (1995) Series A, No. 310, 23 February 1995, at para. 72. See also *Velásquez-Rodriguez*, Judgment of 29 July 1988, Inter-AmCHR (1988) Series C, No. 4, at para. 167; Human Rights Committee, General Comment No. 16; ICESCR Committee, General Comment No. 5, at para. 11 (1994); *Artico v. Italy*, ECHR (1980) Series A, No. 37, at 16 ('The [European] Convention is intended to guarantee not rights that are theoretical or illusory but rights that are practical and effective.'); *A v. UK*, Application No. 15599/94, Report of 18 September 1997, at para. 48 (European Commission stating that '[i]n order that a State may be held responsible it must in the view of the Commission be shown that the domestic legal system ... fails to provide practical and effective protection of the rights guaranteed').

[59] *Velásquez-Rodriguez, supra* note 58, at paras 169–170 ('Whenever a State organ, official or public entity violates one of [the rights recognized in the Convention], this constitutes a failure of the duty to respect the rights and freedoms set forth in the Convention. This conclusion is independent of whether the organ or official has contravened provisions of internal law or overstepped the limits of his authority: under international law a State is responsible for the acts of its agents undertaken in their official capacity and for their omissions, even when those agents act outside the sphere of their authority or violate internal law.').

legally prescribed mandate, the state's human rights obligations would apply nonetheless.

4 Humanitarian Law

All of the national governments of the various KFOR contingents are bound by the Geneva Conventions,[60] which contain the core of modern humanitarian law. The question then is whether humanitarian law is applicable to the present situation in Kosovo. As shown below, several lines of argument support the proposition that the provisions of humanitarian law apply to the conduct of KFOR operations.

Before advancing to those arguments, however, mention should be made of the UN Secretary-General's Bulletin, 'Observance by United Nations Forces of International Humanitarian Law'.

A *UN Observance of Rules of International Humanitarian Law*

In August 1999, the UN Secretary-General promulgated a code of 'principles and rules of international humanitarian law applicable to United Nations forces conducting operations under United Nations command and control'.[61] It essentially sets forth, in summary fashion, the main provisions of the Geneva Conventions and holds that they are applicable 'to United Nations forces when in situations of armed conflict they are actively engaged therein as combatants, to the extent and for the duration of their engagement'.[62] It further provides that: 'They are accordingly applicable in enforcement actions, or in peacekeeping operations when the use of force is permitted in self-defence.'[63]

While not technically binding on KFOR, which is not, strictly speaking, a United Nations force (i.e. blue berets), nor capable of directly giving rise to state accountability, the promulgation of this code is important for two reasons. First, as KFOR is a 'security presence' deployed 'under United Nations auspices', it should in principle be held to the same standards as UN forces. Secondly, it lends support to the proposition that humanitarian law is applicable in peacekeeping operations.

B *Obligations of States Contributing Forces to KFOR*

Whatever the level of hostilities in Kosovo prior to March 1999, it is clear that from the inception of the NATO air campaign an international armed conflict existed,

---

[60] Almost all countries in the world are parties to the Geneva Conventions. Further, the substantive provisions of the Geneva Conventions are widely regarded as having achieved the status of customary international law, and are thus binding on all states. See, e.g., *Case Concerning Military and Paramilitary Activities In and Against Nicaragua*, ICJ Reports (1986) 14.
[61] 'Observance by United Nations Forces of International Humanitarian Law', ST/SGB/1999/13, 6 August 1999.
[62] *Ibid.*, at section 1.1.
[63] *Ibid.*

482   *EJIL* 12 (2001), 469–488

triggering the application of humanitarian law.[64] The issue examined herein is whether humanitarian law continued to apply following the withdrawal from Kosovo of Yugoslav security forces in June 1999.

In the course of any analysis of the applicability of the Geneva Conventions, it is important to bear in mind that one of the main strengths of the Conventions is that they apply once a given set of factual circumstances arises, regardless of the label applied by the parties[65] or of the legality of the initial resort to armed force.[66]

Even assuming that the FRY's agreement to the principles annexed to Resolution 1244[67] and its signing of the Military-Technical Agreement[68] (MTA) brought an end to armed combat between the parties,[69] this does not necessarily mean that international humanitarian law has ceased to apply.

According to Article 6 of the Fourth Geneva Convention, its provisions apply from 'the outset of any conflict or occupation' until there has been a 'general close of military operations'.[70] In the case of occupied territory, its provisions continue to apply beyond the general close of military operations.[71]

Before determining whether there has been a general close of military operations, it is necessary to consider whether Kosovo can be deemed an occupied territory.

---

[64] According to the ICRC (International Committee of the Red Cross) Commentary to the Fourth Geneva Convention: 'Any difference arising between two States and leading to the intervention of members of the armed forces' is an international armed conflict, regardless of 'how long the conflict lasts, or how much slaughter takes place.' Jean Pictet (ed.), *Commentary: IV Geneva Convention Relative to the Protection of Civilian Persons in Time of War* (1958) (1994 reprinted edition) 20. The International Criminal Tribunal for the Former Yugoslavia (ICTY) has held that: 'an armed conflict exists whenever there is a resort to armed force between States or protracted armed violence between governmental authorities and organized armed groups or between such groups within a State.' *Prosecutor v. Dusko Tadic*, Decision on the Defence Motion for Interlocutory Appeal on Jurisdiction, 2 October 1995, IT-94-1-AR72 (RP D6413–D6491), at para. 70. The NATO bombing campaign clearly meets these standards.

[65] See, e.g., Fourth Geneva Convention, *supra* note 4, Article 2 (the Convention applies even if a state of war is not recognized by one of the parties). See also ICRC Commentary, *supra* note 64, at 21 ('The Convention only provides for the case of one of the Parties denying the existence of a state of war. What would the position be, it may be wondered, if both the Parties to an armed conflict were to deny the existence of a state of war. Even in that event it would not appear that they could, by tacit agreement, prevent the Conventions from applying. It must not be forgotten that the Conventions have been drawn up first and foremost to protect individuals, and not to serve State interests.').

[66] It is a fundamental principle of the laws of war that *jus in bello* is independent of *jus ad bellum*.

[67] Annex 2, S/RES/1244 (1999).

[68] The Military-Technical Agreement, concluded on 9 June 1999 by NATO military authorities and the Federal Republic of Yugoslavia, dealt with the procedures and modalities for the withdrawal from Kosovo of Yugoslav security forces for the purpose of 'establish[ing] a durable cessation of hostilities'. Military-Technical Agreement, at para. 4(a), S/1999/682, 9 June 1999.

[69] Given the continuing violence in Kosovo among members of the local population and between KFOR and members of the local population, it may be possible to argue that active hostilities continue.

[70] Fourth Geneva Convention, *supra* note 4, Article 6. According to the ICTY, the law of armed conflict 'extends beyond the cessation of hostilities until a general conclusion of peace is reached'. *Tadic* Jurisdiction Decision, *supra* note 64, at para. 70. Considering present conditions within Kosovo and the rest of the FRY, it may be difficult to argue that a general conclusion of peace has been reached.

[71] *Ibid.*

(i) The Law of Occupation

As noted above, the provisions of the Geneva Conventions apply from the outset of any conflict or occupation. The definition of occupation as the term is used in the Geneva Conventions is broad. Unlike the definition used in the Regulations annexed to the Fourth Hague Convention of 1907, which requires that the 'territory actually [be] placed under the authority of the hostile army' before it can be considered occupied, the Geneva Conventions apply 'even [to] a patrol which penetrates into enemy territory without any intention of staying there' with respect to 'its dealings with the civilians it meets'.[72] Further, paragraph 2 of Article 2 provides that the Convention applies to all cases of partial or total occupation, 'even if the said occupation meets with no armed resistance'.[73]

The period after which application of the Convention ceases depends upon the nature of the occupation. The Convention contemplates two types of occupation. The first is the case in which occupation is 'carried out under the terms of the instrument which brings hostilities to a close: an armistice, capitulation, etc.'.[74] As the ICRC Commentary explains: '[I]n such cases the Convention will have been in force since the outbreak of hostilities or since the time war was declared.'[75] Thus, the application of the Convention to this type of occupation follows from the first paragraph of Article 2.[76] The second type of occupation is covered by the second paragraph of Article 2, which 'refers to cases where the occupation has taken place without a declaration of war and without hostilities, and makes provision for the entry into force of the Convention in those particular circumstances'.[77]

While application of the Convention to the first type of occupation terminates one year after the general close of military operations,[78] the Convention continues to apply fully to the second type for the duration of the occupation.[79]

---

[72] ICRC Commentary, *supra* note 64, at 60.
[73] Fourth Geneva Convention, *supra* note 4, Article 2.
[74] ICRC Commentary, *supra* note 64, at 63.
[75] *Ibid.*, at 21.
[76] The first paragraph of Article 2 states: 'the present Convention shall apply to all cases of declared war or of any other armed conflict which may arise between two or more of the High Contracting Parties, even if the state of war is not recognized by one of them.' Fourth Geneva Convention, *supra* note 4, Article 2. See ICRC Commentary, *supra* note 64, at 21 ('The application of the Convention to territories which are occupied at a later date, in virtue of an armistice or a capitulation, does not follow from [paragraph 2], but from paragraph 1. An armistice suspends hostilities and a capitulation ends them, but neither ends the state of war, and any occupation carried out in wartime is covered by paragraph 1.').
[77] ICRC Commentary, *supra* note 64, at 21.
[78] Note, however, that certain provisions of the Convention continue to apply after one year has expired in so far as the occupying power continues to exercise governmental functions. Fourth Geneva Convention, *supra* note 4, Article 6. For those states that have ratified Protocol I to the Geneva Conventions, the provisions of that Protocol and the Conventions continue to apply fully for the duration of the occupation. Protocol 1, *supra* note 4, Article 3(b).
[79] ICRC Commentary, *supra* note 64, at 63.

484 *EJIL* 12 (2001), 469–488

(ii) Kosovo as Occupied Territory

The primary criteria for determining whether the presence of foreign troops in a given territory constitutes an occupation would logically be whether the sovereign has been displaced from the exercise of public authority over the territory, and whether that sovereign has consented to the displacement.

As noted above, KFOR and UNMIK exercise public authority in Kosovo to the virtual exclusion of Belgrade authorities from the territory. Recalling the fact that a patrol penetrating into enemy territory without any intention of staying there is sufficient to trigger the law of occupation, this criterion would be clearly satisfied.

As for the second criterion, while the FRY did consent to the KFOR presence in signing the MTA, whether that consent was anything more than formal consent is doubtful. In light of the emphasis of the Geneva Conventions on factual circumstances, as opposed to labels, formal consent would probably be insufficient to overcome the presumption of occupation that arises from the circumstances leading up to the signing of the MTA.

Further, formal consent may itself be lacking in this case. Although the FRY did express its consent in signing an international agreement, that consent may be vitiated if the agreement is found to be invalid. While duress does not usually constitute grounds for holding a treaty invalid, Article 52 of the Vienna Convention on the Law of Treaties provides that: 'A treaty is void if its conclusion has been procured by the threat or use of force in violation of the principles of international law embodied in the Charter of the United Nations.'[80] This essentially means that the validity of the MTA turns on the legality of the initial NATO intervention, which is a question that has not been definitively settled.[81]

The fact that KFOR's presence has been authorized by the Security Council adds little to this analysis. While the presence of KFOR has been rendered legal by virtue of Resolution 1244 and must be accepted by the FRY,[82] this does not directly[83] affect application of the Geneva Conventions, which consciously avoid inquiries into the legality of resort to the use of force. However, the fact that KFOR is given a limited

---

[80] Vienna Convention on the Law of Treaties, *supra* note 54, Article 52; see also Vienna Convention on the Law of Treaties Between States and International Organizations or Between International Organizations, Article 52.

[81] It may be interesting to note here the possible intersection of *jus ad bellum* and *jus in bello*. Application of the law of occupation (*jus in bello*) turns on whether the situation constitutes an occupation, which turns on the existence of FRY consent, which can be inferred from an agreement, the validity of which turns on the legality of the NATO intervention (*jus ad bellum*).

[82] Obligations arising from the exercise of the Security Council's Chapter VII powers are binding on all member states (UN Charter, Article 25), are superior to all other international obligations (*ibid.*, Article 103), and override the non-intervention principle (*ibid.*, Article 2(7)). While the FRY is not a member state of the United Nations, it insists that it is the successor state to the SFRY. Thus, it could be argued that the FRY lacks standing to object to being bound by obligations arising from Security Council resolutions.

[83] The Security Council could theoretically abrogate certain non-fundamental norms of humanitarian law, as with human rights law (see *supra* note 50). Thus, it could be argued that KFOR is not bound by humanitarian law to the extent it receives directly conflicting commands from the Security Council. It should be noted here that the statement in paragraph 7 of Resolution 1244 authorizing member states to establish the international security presence 'with all necessary means to fulfil its responsibilities', read in

mandate under the Resolution, and is thus not itself exercising the full range of public authority in Kosovo, may mean that its obligations apply only to the extent that it exercises control over the areas governed by the relevant provisions of the Geneva Conventions.[84] Thus, where it polices, detains civilians, investigates crimes and runs prisons, it would have to comply with the relevant norms applicable to occupied territories.

It remains to be determined which type of occupation is being carried out in Kosovo. If KFOR is seen as a mere continuation of the NATO force that launched the bombing campaign in March 1999, then it would clearly be engaged in an occupation of the first type (i.e. an occupation by hostile forces during or subsequent to hostilities). If KFOR is viewed as a new, independent entity deployed in Kosovo following the passage of Resolution 1244, then it may constitute an occupation of the second type (i.e. an occupation meeting with no armed resistance). Given the fact that KFOR is largely composed of NATO forces, and that part of its mandate was to ensure the withdrawal of Yugoslav forces, it would seem to constitute an occupation of the first type; as such, the Geneva Conventions would continue to apply for one year following the close of military operations.[85]

Whether there has been a close of military operations is also subject to debate. According to the ICRC Commentary, 'in most cases the general close of military operations will be the final end of all fighting between all those concerned'.[86] While NATO and FRY forces may no longer be in open conflict, hostilities continue to surface in Kosovo and Serbia proper. As some violent acts have been committed against KFOR in an organized fashion, it may be difficult to dismiss these as purely isolated instances of internal violence.

In any event, the law of occupation would have fully applied at least until June 2000.[87] After that, KFOR would still be bound by certain provisions of the Fourth Convention to the extent that it continued to exercise public authority in the fields to which those provisions apply.

5 Piercing the Intergovernmental Veil: State Accountability for Violations

As the vast majority of participating states are parties to the instruments cited above, it is clear that KFOR can be collectively held to the standards contained therein.

---

conjunction with the decision in paragraph 5 to deploy the civil and security presences 'with appropriate equipment and personnel', clearly refers to the provision of adequate resources to the security presence and not to any sort of blanket permission to use whatever method of repression KFOR decides is necessary in carrying out its mandate.

[84] This is supported by the example in the ICRC Commentary of the cross-border patrol that is bound by the provisions on occupied territories of the Fourth Convention to the extent that it has dealings with civilians in the foreign territory. See *supra* note 72, and the accompanying text.

[85] Again, this limitation would not apply to state parties to Protocol I, which provides that the Geneva law continues to apply for the duration of the occupation. See *supra* note 78.

[86] ICRC Commentary, *supra* note 64, at 62.

[87] See *supra* note 85.

486   *EJIL* 12 (2001), 469–488

However, assigning individual state accountability for violations of those standards is a more complex matter.

While alleged violations would have to be assessed on a case-by-case basis, there are a number of factors generally weighing in favour of or against a finding of individual state accountability. The strongest factor weighing against a finding of individual state accountability is that formally each national contingent is an integral part of KFOR and does not purport to be acting in Kosovo on behalf of its sending state. However, notwithstanding this formal affiliation with KFOR,[88] the home governments of the KFOR contingents retain a substantial degree of residual control over their forces. For example, each national contingent follows its own rules of engagement. While KFOR has some common rules of engagement, the interpretations of each contingent vary widely. In addition, orders given by KFOR command are subject to the now famous 'red card' procedure,[89] providing a strong back-link to the home government of the contingent. Each contingent's tie to its home government is made explicit in UNMIK Regulation 2000/47, which provides that KFOR personnel are 'subject to the exclusive jurisdiction of their respective sending States' and are 'immune from any form of arrest or detention other than by persons acting on behalf of their respective sending States',[90] and that '[r]equests to waive jurisdiction over KFOR personnel shall be referred to the respective commander of the national element of such personnel for consideration'.[91] Thus, while the KFOR leadership[92] nominally assumes responsibility for directing the activities of the forces, the national governments of the contingents ultimately retain significant control over their soldiers, bolstering a finding of individual state accountability for the acts of the troops each state has contributed to KFOR.

Further, even if it could be demonstrated that the individual home governments lacked effective control over the troops that they contributed to KFOR, accountability would still arise based upon their freely entering into a multinational operation if human rights violations resulted from that operation.[93]

---

[88]   Recall that KFOR was not created by the UN. Although deployed under UN auspices, its creation was left to 'Member States and relevant international organizations'. Resolution 1244, *supra* note 1, at para. 7.

[89]   The 'red card' procedure was best exemplified by Michael Jackson's refusal to eject the Russian troops from Slattina airport in June 1999.

[90]   UNMIK Regulation 2000/47, section 2.4.

[91]   *Ibid.*, at section 6.2.

[92]   Another possible argument for a finding of individual state accountability could be drawn from corporate law. If one state (or perhaps a small group of states) so clearly dominated the command of KFOR that KFOR could be said to be acting on behalf of that state, then, by 'piercing the corporate veil', that state could be held responsible for the acts of KFOR.

[93]   *Matthews v. United Kingdom* (Judgment), at paras 33–34, Application No. 24833/94, 18 February 1999 ('The United Kingdom, together with all the other parties to the Maastricht Treaty, is responsible *ratione materiae* under Article 1 of the Convention and, in particular, under Article 3 of Protocol No. 1, for the consequences of that Treaty... In particular, the suggestion that the United Kingdom may not have effective control over the state of affairs complained of cannot affect the position, as the United Kingdom's responsibility derives from its having entered into treaty commitments subsequent to the applicability of Article 3 of Protocol No. 1 ...'); see also *Waite and Kennedy v. Germany* (Judgment), Application No. 26083/94, 18 February 1999, at para. 67 ('The Court is of the opinion that where States establish

Another factor weighing in favour of individual state accountability is the effectiveness principle mentioned above.[94] States should not be able to escape accountability for the conduct of their forces by acting through an intergovernmental organization.[95] The practical and effective protection of individual rights requires that there be accountability for violations of those rights. If national governments are not held responsible for the conduct of their troops, no legal subject can be held accountable under international human rights law[96] for violations committed by those troops. The resulting lacuna in accountability would be anathema to the effective protection of individuals that is the very purpose of human rights and humanitarian law.

6 Derogation

All of the major human rights instruments provide for the possibility of derogation in times of public emergency. In such cases, state parties may take measures derogating from their obligations under the respective treaties 'to the extent strictly required by the exigencies of the situation'.[97] In such cases, states must declare their derogation. For example, the ICCPR requires a derogating state party to 'immediately inform the other States Parties to the present Covenant, through the intermediary of the Secretary-General of the United Nations, of the provisions from which it has derogated and of the reasons by which it was actuated'.[98] A small number of rights are non-derogable, meaning that they are never subject to derogation.[99]

---

international organizations in order to pursue or strengthen their cooperation in certain fields of activities, and where they attribute to these organizations certain competences and accord them immunities, there may be implications as to the protection of fundamental rights. It would be incompatible with the purpose and object of the Convention, however, if the Contracting States were thereby absolved from their responsibility under the Convention in relation to the field of activity covered by such attribution. It should be recalled that the Convention is intended to guarantee not theoretical or illusory rights, but rights that are practical and effective.').

[94] See *supra* section 3.

[95] Another significant feature of UNMIK Regulation 2000/47 is that it deprives the Kosovo courts of any type of jurisdiction, civil or criminal, over KFOR itself or over KFOR soldiers. Although remedies may be theoretically available in the courts of the sending state, those courts are physically and financially inaccessible for most residents of Kosovo. Further, the Human Rights Ombudsperson for Kosovo, established by UNMIK Regulation 2000/38, is not authorized to receive complaints of abuses committed by KFOR. Thus, in the absence of individual state accountability, if internal KFOR complaints procedures fail to provide adequate redress, a situation of effective impunity would result and victims would be left without access to a remedy.

[96] Unlike human rights law, the violation of certain norms of humanitarian law may give rise to individual criminal responsibility under international law. See Statute of the ICTY, 25 May 1993.

[97] ICCPR, *supra* note 2, Article 4(1). See also ECHR, *supra* note 2, Article 15(1); and ACHR, *supra* note 2, Article 27(1).

[98] ICCPR, *supra* note 2, Article 4(3). See also ECHR, *supra* note 2, Article 15(3); and ACHR, *supra* note 2, Article 27(3).

[99] See, e.g., ICCPR, *supra* note 2, Article 4(2); ECHR, *supra* note 2, Article 15(2); and ACHR, *supra* note 2, Article 27(2). These non-derogable rights typically include the right to life, freedom from torture and slavery, and freedom from retroactive application of criminal laws. See *supra* note 5 and the accompanying text.

488	*EJIL* 12 (2001), 469–488

No declarations of derogation have been lodged for armed forces deployed in Kosovo. Nor can deployment as a 'security presence' imply an intrinsic derogation since human rights obligations fully apply to a state's armed forces.[100]

Humanitarian law is never subject to collective derogation.[101]

7 Conclusion

Despite the unique situation in which KFOR finds itself, it does not occupy a legal vacuum. As an entity deployed under UN auspices and by virtue of its exercise of public authority in Kosovo, it is bound by provisions of international human rights and humanitarian law to the extent of its control over individuals there.

In addition, the failure of KFOR troops to meet international standards for the treatment of individuals may give rise to individual state accountability, particularly in light of the substantial degree of control retained by the sending states as well as the intolerable situation that would otherwise result.

Finally, should KFOR or its participating states choose to declare a derogation, it is important to remember that they would remain bound by the minimum standards provided by humanitarian law.

---

[100] See *Loizidou v. Turkey* (Preliminary Objections), ECHR (1995) Series A, No. 310, 23 February 1995.

[101] Although Article 5 of the Fourth Geneva Convention provides for a limited degree of derogation with respect to rights of communication of a 'person under definite suspicion of activity hostile to the security of the Occupying Power', there is no provision permitting derogation with respect to the general population.

[23]

Crossing the Boundary from the International to the Domestic Legal Realm: UNMIK Lawmaking and Property Rights in Kosovo

Leopold von Carlowitz

Considering that the resolution of property issues is often pivotal for the success of a peacebuilding process in a postconflict situation, it is surprising that the United Nations Interim Administration Mission in Kosovo (UNMIK) is so far the only UN peace operation that took on the responsibility of regulating them in a comprehensive manner. The comparable governance missions in Cambodia, Eastern Slavonia, and East Timor yielded to the democratically legitimated local authorities in matters relating to property although they were facing a similar property crisis during their administration. The only other international administration that dealt with property issues on a larger scale was the Office of the High Representative under the Dayton Peace Agreement in Bosnia and Herzegovina, which, however—unlike UNMIK—does not possess full legislative and executive powers.[1]

In terms of substantive property-related lawmaking, UNMIK serves as an important precedent for future international territorial administrations that might be established in postconflict situations defined by ethnic conflict and discrimination, a mass refugee crisis, large-scale housing destruction, and an underdeveloped court and property registration system.[2] Of particular interest are UNMIK's regulatory efforts concerning property issues from the date the mission was established, 10 June 1999 to 10 December 2001, the date of the inauguration of Kosovo's first assembly as the cornerstone for the establishment of the provisional institutions of self-government foreseen by Security Council Resolution 1244.

These efforts provide insight into what difficulties an international peace operation with full government functions faces when confronting a complex legal area that not only challenges the mission's enforcement powers, but also questions its legislative capability to ensure compatibility of its regulations with the domestic legal system. UNMIK was in principle required to act (and to legislate) in accordance with the applicable domestic laws unless they conflicted with internationally recognized human rights standards or UNMIK regulations issued in the fulfillment of its mandate.[3] Yet this requirement caused serious difficulties for the international mission staff who lacked, for the most part, sufficient knowledge of the local languages, structures, and legal systems.[4]

By simultaneously performing international peace maintenance and running a territorial administration accountable to the local population,[5] UNMIK is characterized by a functional duality[6] that combines elements of global and domestic governance.[7] In fact, the mission has come close to the old idealist notion of a world government in the sense that a presumably legitimate international organ can perform government functions that have a direct impact on the local population and normally fall within the *domaine réservé* of a sovereign state. In this context, UNMIK's property-related lawmaking is of particular interest, since property issues may be said to lie at the very heart of a domestic legal system.

UNMIK, headed by a special representative of the secretary-general (SRSG), initially comprised the following four pillars: Pillar I, the UN High Commissioner for Refugees (UNHCR), for humanitarian affairs; Pillar II, the UN, for civil administration; Pillar III, the Organization for Security and Cooperation in Europe (OSCE), for institution building; and Pillar IV, the European Union (EU), for reconstruction and development.[8] It also set up a Joint Interim Administrative Structure (JIAS) to integrate the major local political forces in the decisionmaking process. The present case study illustrates how the transitional administration dealt with the various responsibilities of a multifunctional peace operation, entailing not only traditional peacekeeping activities, but also elements of peace enforcement and peacebuilding. It provides insight into how different legislative approaches were used and how the degree of local involvement varied depending on the challenge and interest behind each individual regulatory effort.

Property Crisis and UNMIK's Initial Response

During the initial deployment to Kosovo in June 1999, UNMIK faced numerous problems related to property rights. It urgently needed to address them to avoid a destabilization of the peacebuilding process. Approximately 50 percent of all available housing had been destroyed during the armed conflict in 1998 and 1999.[9] Tens of thousands of people were homeless, a situation that resulted in a rapid increase in illegal housing occupations and that became a general threat to safety and security in the province. Large numbers of refugees returned to Kosovo to find they could not move into their own houses or apartments and were forced to look for alternative shelter.[10]

There was also widespread confusion regarding occupancy and ownership rights as a consequence of discriminatory legislation imposed on Kosovo by the Serb authorities during the preceding decade. In the early 1990s, the Belgrade government introduced a series of laws and administrative measures to consolidate the dominance of the Serb minority over the Albanian majority population in Kosovo. In this context, the government reassigned to Serbs socially owned apartments formerly occupied by Albanians.[11] These measures came in retaliation for Albanian mass strikes in protest against Belgrade's withdrawal of Kosovo's substantial autonomy in March 1989. Moreover, property sales from Serbs to Albanians were prohibited by law and subsequent administrative practice. The vast majority of Kosovars did not accept these measures, which led to multiple property claims and a circumvention of the laws through informal property transactions.[12]

With ethnic tensions rising high and the court system broken down, there was no independent and impartial mechanism to resolve the various disputes in a fair and equitable manner and to generally regularize housing and property rights. Furthermore, the existing property registration system was highly outdated and ineffective, and many records had been destroyed or removed by the withdrawing Serb authorities.[13]

The secretary-general responded to the crisis by requesting that the UN Centre for Human Settlements (Habitat) immediately send an expert team to provide UNMIK with property-related technical and legal assistance. Two months later, in August 1999, the team submitted a comprehensive plan of action on the regularization of housing and property rights.[14] The plan identified three major areas of concern: the first related to the housing shortage and security matters, the second addressed discriminatory legislation and the establishment of an impartial dispute settlement mechanism, and the third concerned a reform of the cadastre and property registration system. UNMIK's civil administration approved the plan, and corresponding programs were developed with Habitat as the implementing agency.

Prevention of Access

At the outset, the mission's administrative capacity was extremely limited. Enforcement of law and order had to be executed by the military presence, Kosovo Force (KFOR), over which the SRSG had no control. At the same time, the Kosovo Liberation Army established "parallel government structures," Kosovo Serbs continued to leave the province in high numbers, and ethnically motivated fighting flared up at strategically important places, such as the main bridge in the ethnically divided city of Mitrovica in northern Kosovo. With a view to addressing the latter problem, UNMIK adopted Regulation No. 1999/2, Prevention of Access by Individuals and Their Removal to Secure Public Peace and Order, on 12 August 1999.[15] The regulation was an emergency measure adopted after only a few days of consultations in the nucleus administration, which had yet to be properly staffed.[16]

The regulation provided a legal basis for several enforcement actions against individuals in case of a threat to the public peace, which could be posed by any act that jeopardized public and private property.[17] What exactly constituted a "threat to public peace" was, however, not further defined and needed to be complemented by the corresponding domestic laws. UNMIK could nevertheless use the regulation to deal with its own property-related concerns, as the administration needed to be accommodated quickly. While UNMIK had the authority to temporarily administer the property owned by the Federal Republic of Yugoslavia,[18] "parallel structures" and the Kosovo Liberation Army had illegally occupied many public properties, such as municipal city halls. Regulation No. 1999/2 offered a useful legal means to gain control over such buildings.[19] With respect to private housing, the lack of further specification of the regulation caused confusion and presented difficulties for the international police forces, who were to apply the provision in practice and who encountered an increasing number of illegal occupations.

Temporary Allocation of Housing

Shortly after the adoption of Regulation No. 1999/2, the Housing and Property Task Force, consisting of representatives from different UNMIK offices, Habitat, KFOR, and some local human rights lawyers, submitted for legal review a draft regulation that addressed housing matters more distinctly. The draft Regulation on Temporary Use of Vacant Residential Property was a rapid response to urgent needs in the housing sector. It was to provide a provisional legal basis for the temporary allocation of abandoned housing and for the anticipated evictions of illegal occupants in refugee return cases.[20] Recognizing the seriousness of the issue, various UNMIK offices at headquarters and in the regions discussed the draft at length but finally rejected it. At a time when the International Crisis Group issued a report entitled "Waiting for UNMIK"[21] and police presence was poor, doubts prevailed regarding the capacity of the newly established mission to effectively and consistently administer and enforce the proposed scheme. Another main argument against the draft concerned the potential liability of the UN in determining property disputes that would normally require court adjudication.

In light of the pressing need to address the deteriorating housing situation, the SRSG authorized UNMIK's twenty-nine municipal administrators in October 1999 to temporarily allocate vacant housing to homeless people on humanitarian grounds. Subsequently, the Council of Europe provided international experts to draft guidelines for the municipalities to carry out this task.[22] By mid-November, other topics dominated the property-related agenda, yet illegal occupations and the lack of rule of law in the housing sector continued. A proposed expert body on property, the Housing and Property Directorate, was supposed to further develop a housing allocation scheme and make decisions on the basis of which evictions could be carried out. Pending its establishment, an international shelter program averted a severe housing catastrophe in the first postwar winter with the general assistance and solidarity of the local population.

Repeal of Discriminatory Legislation

In the early stage of the mission, two other property-related regulations were discussed. The first related to discriminatory legislation in the property sector passed after Kosovo had lost its autonomy in 1989. Following thorough legislative research carried out by a Habitat-led team of local and international lawyers, the Housing and Property Task Force drafted the Regulation on the Repeal of Certain Discriminatory Legislation. It identified two Serb laws that had been promulgated in the early 1990s to stop increasing sales of Serb properties to Albanians and to secure Serb domination over the province of Kosovo. The *Law on Changes and Supplements on the Limitation of Real Estate Transactions*[23] determined that property transactions needed to be approved by the Serb ministry of finance with a view to maintaining Kosovo's ethnic structure. In practice, Albanians were thus excluded from purchasing property from Serbs. According to the *Law on the Conditions, Ways and Procedures of Granting Farming Land to Citizens Who Wish to Work and Live in the Territory of the Autonomous Province of Kosovo and Metohija*,[24] socially owned land in Kosovo could be given to individuals provided that this was in Serb interest. Purchasers were granted particularly favorable conditions for payment through a development fund to prevent Serb emigration and to increase the Serb and Montenegrian population in Kosovo.[25]

As the draft regulation redressed clear cases of ethnic discrimination against the Albanian majority population, the draft enjoyed wide popular acceptance. It also had an unmistakable human rights–based justification and was in line with the limited regulatory precedents of former peace operations. Therefore, international circles and the Joint Advisory Council on Legislative Matters (JAC) approved the draft quickly. UNMIK had established this consultative organ to review and to comment on draft regulations and to propose new legislation where appropriate. The JAC was composed of twenty local and seven international legal experts.[26] The local members had been selected on the basis of their expertise and previous work experience. The JAC did not include any Serb members given the prevailing ethnic tensions and the general lack of cooperation by the Serb authorities with UNMIK at the beginning of the mission.

On 13 October 1999, the SRSG adopted the regulation as UNMIK Regulation No. 1999/10.

Impartial Dispute Settlement and the Housing and Property Directorate and Claims Commission

A further regulation addressed the issue of fair and impartial dispute settlement. In the absence of a functioning court system and with ethnic tensions flaring, Habitat and the civil administration pillar proposed to establish a Housing and Property Directorate and Claims Commission (HPD/CC). This internationally supervised quasi-judicial dispute settlement mechanism was to resolve property disputes in three specific claims categories resulting from the above-mentioned discriminatory legislation and the recent armed conflict. The claims categories concerned residential property claims by (1) persons who had lost property rights after 23 March 1989[27] on discriminatory grounds, (2) persons who voluntarily entered into informal transactions after 23 March 1989 (because discriminatory legislation prevented their court validation), and (3) persons who involuntarily lost property rights after 23 March 1999.[28] In addition, the HPD was to provide orientation and support in various property-related fields, including the allocation of abandoned housing. Its main purposes were to protect the right to adequate housing and to ensure the protection of property rights as stipulated in international human rights instruments; to create the conditions for the return of refugees; and to reestablish civil law and order in property matters—all objectives expressly covered by Security Council Resolution 1244.

When shaping the HPD/CC mandate, UNMIK drew on the experiences of the Commission for Real Property Claims of Displaced Persons and Refugees (CRPC) in Bosnia, which was established by Annex VII of the Dayton Peace Agreement. Operating as a mixed local and international mass claims adjudication body with a jurisdiction to decide on war-related property disputes,[29] this commission served as an important precedent for the HPD/CC. Consequently, former CRPC legal experts drafted the regulation on the HPD/CC with the support of and in close cooperation with all relevant UNMIK pillars and KFOR. However, the JAC delayed its adoption. Although the Albanian members of the council agreed with the objective to eliminate ethnic discrimination, they did not fully consent to excluding the majority of housing and property disputes from the jurisdiction of the local courts. Following a concerted appeal to the SRSG by all pillars, and given the impossibility of the Serbian population to defend their rights, the SRSG nevertheless adopted UNMIK Regulation No. 1999/23, Establishment of the Housing and Property Directorate and the Housing and Property Claims Commission, on 15 November 1999, to guarantee a fair and impartial settlement of property disputes. The fact that the local judicial system had completely broken down and that the restoration of the criminal justice system took priority over the needs and demands of the civil court side supported this reasoning.[30] Furthermore, a timely adoption of the regulation was required to provide sufficient impetus for fundraising efforts at the upcoming main donor conference for the year 2000.

At the beginning of the mission, UNMIK adopted Regulation No. 1999/23, which established the general principle of an internationally supervised special adjudication process; it developed a detailed regulation providing the rules of procedure for the HPD/CC in a more thorough manner once the mission was better staffed and the JIAS had been created. This joint administration was set up in December 1999 to effect participation of the main political parties in the decisionmaking process. Its centerpiece was the Interim Administrative Council (IAC), which operated as a nucleus cabinet charged with proposing policy guidelines to the administrative departments and with making recommendations for amendments to the applicable law and for new UNMIK regulations.[31] The SRSG presided over the eight-member body of which four members were the deputies of the SRSG and the remaining four were the heads of the main local parties, including one Serb. Decisionmaking was aimed at reaching consensus to the extent possible, and in principle

314   *From the International to the Domestic Legal Realm*

the SRSG had to accept a decision by consensus or a three-quarters majority of the members who were present and voted. However, if the council did not make such a decision, the SRSG had to make a decision himself.[32]

From December 1999, international and local consultants under HPD/CC guidance undertook extensive legal and historical research to ensure sustainability of approach and compatibility with the domestic legal system.[33] A previous UNMIK decision complicated the latter by declaring the laws in force on 22 March 1989, the date before the Serb government unilaterally had withdrawn Kosovo's autonomous status, to be generally applicable.[34] As a consequence of a time lapse of a decade, Kosovo's applicable law no longer reflected the realities of 1999/2000, and major uncertainties arose as to the treatment of property transactions based on post-1989 law.

The draft regulation set out the procedure for the HPD/CC in detail and determined the basic principles according to which residential property claims had to be resolved. The main substantive principles of law governing the HPD/CC can be summarized as follows: (1) any property right that was validly acquired according to the law applicable at the time of its acquisition remains valid (unless otherwise determined in the regulation); (2) any person who lost property after 23 March 1989 due to ethnic discrimination has a right to restitution or, in the case of a third party bona fide acquisition, a right to compensation; (3) any transaction after 23 March 1989 that was illegal under discriminatory law but would otherwise have been legal is valid; and (4) any refugee or displaced person who has lost possession has a right to return to the property or to dispose of it in accordance with the law. The regulation also provided legal basis for the eviction of illegal occupants either following a decision by the Claims Commission or, in exceptional situations, after administrative determination by the Directorate.[35]

The question of who should bear the burden of proof for discrimination—that is, the Albanian claimant or the (most likely) Serb respondent—caused much controversy, and an agreement needed to be worked out in the international arena. With a view to impartiality between the ethnicities, UNMIK finally resolved the argument by deciding against a provision that would deviate from the principle that the claimant must prove his or her case with sufficient evidence. In the absence of evidence to the contrary, however, UNMIK encouraged the HPD/CC to introduce a presumption of discrimination in its Internal Judicial Practice or otherwise to set the precedent that a property had been lost due to discrimination, if it found that justice could only be served this way or, in the light of efficiency considerations in mass claims proceedings, if certain incidents of discrimination appeared in large numbers during certain periods of time.

Following (international) legal review, the HPD/CC discussed the proposed regulation intensely in the legal expert council JAC. Its local members made a series of comments, most of which did not concern the substance of the regulation but often only related to issues of definition and language. Some of the comments were included in the draft; other proposals exceeded the mandate of the HPD/CC or were clarified after consultations. Subsequently, the draft was presented to the political consultation organ IAC, and all the represented local parties and ethnic groups approved the regulation with minor changes—all before UNMIK held the first municipal elections at the end of October.[36] On 31 October 2000, the SRSG adopted UNMIK Regulation No. 2000/60, Residential Property Claims and the Rules of Procedure and Evidence of the Housing and Property Directorate and the Housing and Property Claims Commission.

While the Directorate had started accepting claims in June 2000, the regulation provided the necessary legal basis for the beginning of the work of the dispute settlement functions by the HPD/CC. The Claims Commission issued its first decisions on 31 January 2001, and UNMIK and its implementing agency, Habitat, continued with efforts to make the institutions fully operational. Meanwhile, the local civil courts were also becoming more functional and had commenced dealing with their residuary jurisdiction in property matters.[37] Following a request by the Pristina District Court for clarification, the SRSG provided guidance on the relationship between the HPD/CC and the local courts and established a consultation mechanism between the Administrative Department of Justice and the HPD/CC for the resolution of jurisdictional and other issues.[38] Subsequently, his legal adviser issued a clarification sent to all courts throughout Kosovo, and an interpillar working group was established to further address the matter.[39] Moreover, UNMIK, the HPD/CC, and the OSCE organized workshops and training sessions in which jurisdictional and other issues were discussed.

Cadastre Reform and the Kosovo Cadastral Agency

A program for the reestablishment of the land cadastre[40] and property title system paralleled the preceding regulatory efforts. As mentioned, UNMIK had recognized the deficiency of the property registration system at the outset. The initial work in the area was predominantly technical in nature.[41] In March 2000, local cadastral experts and representatives of UNMIK,

Habitat, and interested donor countries jointly developed a project document within a logical framework analysis seminar held in Sweden.[42] During this seminar, the Kosovars led the discussion on the state of affairs of the present cadastre system and formulated the document with support from the seminar organizers. Given the breakdown of the pre-existing Belgrade-centered institutional system in postconflict Kosovo, one of the main concerns was to create one central Pristina-based institution to coordinate all cadastral affairs throughout Kosovo. Another major concern was the need for legal reform of the property title system.

The seminar and the subsequent program document provided the material basis for the cadastre reform, including the adoption of new legislation. In addition, there was a need to embrace the program legally and to create a corresponding institution in the UNMIK framework: the Kosovo Cadastral Agency (KCA). Unlike the earlier establishment of the HPD/CC, the creation of the KCA did not require a regulation. The constitution of the JIAS allowed individual JIAS departments to implement their tasks on the basis of subsidiary administrative directions.[43] Since the main donor had made its pledge dependent on the formation of a central institution, UNMIK decided not to initiate a regulation requiring full consultations but to draft an administrative direction that would not require approval from the two local consultative bodies and UN headquarters.[44] As the cadastre program was the responsibility of the Department of Public Services, Administrative Direction No. 2000/14 Implementing UNMIK Regulation No. 2000/12 on the Establishment of the Administrative Department of Public Services, dated 7 June 2000, established the KCA. Based on the proposals made in the seminar in Sweden, the direction determined that the KCA was the coordinating body for all UNMIK activities relating to the cadastre system and property registration reform in Kosovo.[45]

The Property Rights Register

By developing a new regulatory framework for a modern land administration system, the KCA was to foster the rule of law in the property sector and to create a formal property market. Given the mandate of the EU-led pillar for reconstruction and development, the KCA primarily addressed the technical-legal questions of the property title system, whereas Pillar IV worked on a commercial law reform program dealing with, among other things, privatization issues and mortgage law.[46]

Legal reform began in spring 2001 with sound research on relevant pre- and post-1989 legislation. The KCA was free to use the applicable Yugoslav, Serb, and Kosovar laws that had been prepared and translated into English. The agency carried out a careful analysis with the help of local jurists and formulated a legal policy that took regional precedents into account.[47]

The property registration system in Kosovo had been influenced by various legal systems. Originally, the Ottoman *tapia* system[48] applied, but it was considered outdated by the 1920s. Thereafter, the Yugoslav authorities commenced property reform by introducing a uniform land cadastre and property rights register in the late 1920s. The regime was based on the Austro-Hungarian legal traditions that had been applied in the northern parts of Yugoslavia. Due to the different Ottoman legal heritage and a general lack of emphasis on property rights in the socialist regime, the property rights register was never de facto introduced in Kosovo nor in many other southern parts of the former Yugoslavia. Ongoing reform efforts were interrupted by Kosovo's recent turbulent history. Instead, cadastre entries based on a court certification of relevant legal documents replaced the registration function to some extent. Yet the cadastre did not provide legal title to ownership, and the registration procedure was complicated and opaque.[49] This coincided with a partial tendency in the region to rely on spoken transactions, partially due to financial considerations. For these reasons, the registration procedure was often not adhered to and the cadastral records became largely outdated.[50]

To foster local ownership of the reform efforts, the KCA decided to maintain existing legislation as much as possible but to reform it where needed. To ensure compatibility with the domestic legal system, any new legislation was to conform to the civil law principles prevailing in Kosovo and Yugoslavia.[51] The civil administration pillar and the KCA intended to undertake the reform in a three-step approach. As immediate measures to allow the agency to commence with necessary investments for a modern computerized register, a legal instrument establishing the property rights register was to be drafted implementing the existing applicable law. In a second step, a postelection transformation law was envisaged in which existing possession rights could automatically be transformed into ownership rights. Third, a comprehensive reform of the cadastral information and property registration system was planned for a later stage. With this reform, UNMIK intended to streamline and simplify the existing procedures and institutional responsibilities involved in registering and determining property rights in Kosovo.

In addition, UNMIK considered for the postelection future developing a uniform land code comprising all procedural and substantial provisions concerning property rights and registration.[52] To safeguard a uniform approach in various UNMIK departments and pillars, an interpillar working group had been formed to develop the reform process jointly under the lead of the KCA.[53] The transformation law and the comprehensive reform were supposed to be developed and adopted within the legislative procedure of the provisional institutions of the self-government.

In July 2001, the KCA discussed and further developed the legal policy in a seminar with Kosovar judges and other members of local and international legal communities. Thereafter, the working group drafted an administrative direction establishing a property rights register and presented a first draft at an October 2001 meeting with key members from all levels of the local judiciary, the University of Pristina, and other local legal institutions. In light of the primarily technical nature of the project, all participants generally agreed on the approach. All the participants actively discussed the first draft, proposing changes in drafting and approach. Using written comments, with adequate translation support, the KCA prepared a second draft accompanied by active consensus-seeking, particularly of the local players in informal consultations. In a second meeting of the group, the large majority of the participants approved the draft administrative direction establishing a property rights register, which was subsequently submitted for review to the SRSG's legal adviser.[54]

During legal review, doubts appeared with respect to the appropriate legal instrument for the register. Given the importance of the matter, the form of a regulation was deemed to be more suitable than an administrative direction. Meanwhile, the provincial elections in November 2001 overshadowed the project, and UNMIK preferred that the property rights register be legitimized through the provisional institutions of self-government.[55]

Difficulties in International and Local Cooperation

In general, in-depth legal cooperation between international legal experts and members of the local legal community such as judges, professors or administrative lawyers proved to be extremely challenging. Besides the problematic communication gap, the search for local partners with excellent professional skills and sufficient flexibility was very cumbersome. Most Kosovo Albanians who had been expulsed from public institutions had not practiced their profession since 1989.[56] As a consequence, they had only limited experience with modern administrative structures and a postsocialist legal system, and their technical and managerial standards were often outdated. Potential qualified staff had also been drained out of Kosovo, as an estimated 30 percent of the overall population had left the province, including much of the former Albanian elite, who had fled discrimination by the Serb authorities or emigrated to pursue better career opportunities abroad. After the armed conflict in 1999, the majority of the Kosovo Serbs fled Kosovo to avoid Albanian retaliation, taking their experience and knowledge of the previous administration with them. Moreover, qualified local counterparts were very difficult to attract because of the extremely low salaries offered to local public servants by UNMIK in comparison to the private sector. Based on Kosovo's estimated future domestic revenues and donor grants as well as a comparison with the public salary scales in neighboring countries, the average salary for a local JIAS official was set to be DM 273 per month, while a municipal judge would earn DM 600 per month.[57] Given that young drivers and interpreters were paid as local UNMIK staff according to a higher UN salary scale and that prices were skyrocketing in response to the sizable injection of international money into the local economy, the motivation of highly qualified Kosovars to join the JIAS administration and its regulatory efforts was limited.[58]

Cooperation was also made difficult by factors lying in the international sphere. The Brahimi Report outlined in general the difficulties encountered by the UN in recruiting suitably qualified international staff for its peacekeeping missions.[59] Complication also derived from the double role of the international staff, who were both international civil servants and temporary quasi-government officials. Confusion in approach resulted also from the fact that UN staff was not often trained in governmental activities such as drafting legislative or building state institutions.[60] The dual role also entailed potentially conflicting responsibilities, and UNMIK staff was not given guidance on how to reconcile or prioritize them. The role of the international civil servant is to pay primary attention to international security considerations and to remain neutral in the work with the opposing parties. In contrast, government officials tend to see the world primarily through domestic lenses and to act according to domestic power relations that might contradict established UN policies.[61]

As regards international rule of law programs, most international legal experts possess scant knowledge of local languages, structures, and legal systems, and their tendency to ignore local input and to present "quick successes" instead of sustainable legal reform have been noted as shortcomings of technical legal assistance.[62] In Kosovo, applying domestic laws became particularly difficult following the decision to declare the laws in force on 22 March 1989 applicable. Kosovo's (pre-)1989 laws reflected neither the sociopolitical changes of the past decade nor the postsocialist realities of 1999 and 2000. This discrepancy led to major uncertainties in judging legal relations—for example, concerning property transactions based on post-1989 legislation.

UNMIK's civil administration pillar tried to improve international and local cooperation through the development of the Kosovo Expert Support Programme and through attempts to make more systematic use of Kosovar migrants living in the diaspora.[63] This program was based on the assumption that, in certain cases, migrants would be particularly well suited to international cooperation and development.[64] Migrants speak the local language(s), are familiar with domestic cultures and traditions, and often have a vested interest in the well-being of the administered territory through personal attachment. Having lived in different cultural environments, they tend to possess the cultural competencies required to cope with an international environment, and they also often have received a better education than peers in their country of origin.[65] For UNMIK, the (mostly Albanian) lawyers with an international education were the perfect candidates to cross the boundary from the international to the domestic legal realm. Since suitable candidates often did not fit or qualify as professional international staff, they were employed as UN volunteers, consultants, or National Professional Officers.[66] In the case of the property registration reform, a young Kosovar lawyer of Albanian and Croatian descent who was born and raised in Germany contributed significantly to the legislative preparatory work by safeguarding that fundamental civil law principles were observed and that local partners were properly involved.

Registration of Property Transactions in Specific Geographical Areas

While the preparations for the cadastre and property registration reform were being made, a more political property issue headed UNMIK's agenda. In November 2001, representatives of the Serb National Council, the organ representing Kosovo Serb interests in the JIAS, raised the issue of special protection of Serb properties in Kosovo. The council was participating in the Joint Committee on Returns, which sought to develop and examine strategies for the return process of Kosovo Serbs. The committee also comprised representatives from UNHCR and different UNMIK pillars and offices, but it had no Kosovo Albanian members.

The majority of the committee members voiced concern about reports of involuntary sales of Serb properties; some reports pointed to "organized" Albanian agents who allegedly aimed to change the ethnic balance in Kosovo and frightened property owners into selling below market price.[67] As a countermeasure and to create favorable conditions for return, the Serb National Council proposed a general moratorium on property sales involving Serb properties.[68]

The international community faced a dilemma. On the one hand, it shared the view that measures needed to be taken to keep Serbs in Kosovo, to foster the return process, and to combat criminal activities in the property sector. As a consequence, the SRSG ordered that a corresponding legal instrument be developed. However, despite long inter-pillar consultations at various levels, disagreement prevailed over what measures should be taken and whether a regulation prohibiting or restricting property transactions would be the suitable instrument. The main concerns were that any such measures would conflict with the right to free disposal of property as stipulated by the European Convention on Human Rights (ECHR)[69] and that the roots of the problem lay in a lack of security for the minority communities in Kosovo rather than in weaknesses in legislation. Such measures would further contradict UNMIK's policy of eliminating ethnic discrimination in connection with interethnic property sales by repealing discriminatory Serb legislation. Moreover, it was expected that such measures would not stop the Serb sales but that, like in the previous decade, informal transactions would still be carried out. Alternatively, a proposal was made to tighten the security framework and to increase support to the HPD/CC to strengthen its ability to establish law and order in the property sector.[70]

With the upcoming elections, for which Serbian support was not yet ensured,[71] political pressure prevailed to adopt a regulation that would demonstrate UNMIK's active support for the Serb minority in Kosovo. To avoid a violation of the ECHR, UNMIK did not pursue the general moratorium on interethnic property sales as proposed by the Serb National Council.[72] Instead, the civil administration pillar prepared a draft regulation that provided for the designation of specific geographical areas where all property transactions needed to be registered with the municipal administrator before the civil court could validate the transaction in accordance with the applicable domestic law. Unlike previous intentions to "freeze" the ethnic balance in Kosovo, the regulation was narrowed down to address a systematic buyout of properties in strategically important locations in minority areas. Geographical areas needed to be designated on the basis of a solid justification relating to security and minority rights. The registration requirement was introduced only for monitoring purposes, and each municipal administrator was obliged to register the transaction according to a specific procedure and time frame. Registration could be refused and access temporarily prevented if in the course of the registration process the municipal administrator had reasonable grounds to believe that the transaction was based on intimidation or was part of a scheme of systematic "soft" ethnic cleansing.[73]

Although these concerns had not entirely disappeared and doubts prevailed as to whether the municipal administrators had the capacity to implement the scheme, the SRSG was determined to push the regulation through the lawmaking process. A campaign by the Kosovo Albanian press against the draft, alleging a return to the discriminatory practices of the preceding decade, did not change the SRSG's approach.[74] The JAC also vehemently opposed the planned measures, using the same objections raised by the press and claiming that the draft was in part technically incompatible with the domestic legal system and provided too much administrative flexibility for the municipal administrator.[75] Despite these comments, the SRSG introduced the same draft to the IAC and overruled its Kosovo Albanian members who also strongly rejected the draft. Ironically, the draft also met with objections from a Serb National Council member, who objected that the measures did not go far enough.[76] On 22 August 2001, UNMIK Regulation No. 2001/17, Registration of Contracts for the Sale of Real Property in Specific Geographical Areas of Kosovo, was adopted without changes. For all relevant municipalities, specific geographical areas were designated for registration on 19 October 2001 by virtue of an administrative direction.[77]

Conclusion

It is still too early to fully judge the successes and failures of UNMIK's regulatory efforts in the property sector—much will depend on program implementation and on the political developments in Kosovo. Moreover, there is neither an accepted approach according to which parameters one can measure the success of peacebuilding efforts[78] nor would a detailed analysis of all aspects of UNMIK's property-related lawmaking fit the scope of the present article.

Nevertheless, I have some comments regarding UNMIK's property-related lawmaking. Most certainly, it was disappointing that UNMIK failed to stop the illegal occupations taking place during its administration. This failure was not primarily due to a legislative problem but was rather caused by a lack of enforcement power and insecurities on how to combine an effective eviction scheme with international human rights standards. To date, implementation continues to be the central challenge in UNMIK's property-related program, the HPD/CC. It comes as no surprise that the institution and its parent organizations are struggling to effectively fulfill the HPD/CC's mandate, given its dependence on voluntary contributions at a time of increasing donor fatigue and in light of the organizational and bureaucratic complexity of the UN system. In an ideal world, the international community should have ascertained before intervening with a particular measure that it had the management capabilities and necessary funding for a consistent and sustainable approach. Although the HPD/CC's long-term effect remains to be evaluated, its existence proved to be very useful during the period under review. UNMIK lessened ethnic tensions by sensitively balancing Albanian and Serb property interests through its policy of addressing both past ethnic discrimination and illegal postconflict occupation. The combination of this approach with the principle of international adjudication served as an important first step for ethnic reconciliation. Furthermore, by creating a specialized adjudication mechanism for particularly sensitive matters, UNMIK managed to significantly relieve the burden of the newly created fragile local judiciary, which otherwise would have had jurisdiction.

As for the cadastre and property registration program, UNMIK regulation gave the necessary legal basis for the commencement of major technical investments in the land administration sector and the creation of the corresponding institution. By emphasizing local participation when drafting the legal instrument for the property rights register, UNMIK contributed to local capacity building. It also provided the provisional institutions of self-government with important preparatory work for an ongoing reform project in a legal sector essential for the rule of law and economic recovery. Most importantly, UNMIK resisted the temptation to quickly impose domestic legislation that would be neither locally embraced nor compatible with existing civil law traditions in southeastern Europe.[79]

Finally, regardless of the criticism of its legislative approach, its administrative inefficiency, and its violation of the ECHR, the registration requirement for property transactions in specifically designated minority areas served a significant political purpose shortly before the elections in relation to the international community's objective to uphold a multiethnic Kosovo: Regulation No. 2001/17 not only sought to accommodate Serb fears relating to their personal security, but also sent a strong signal of UNMIK's resistance to organized Albanian attempts to quietly cleanse Kosovo of its minorities.

In addition, some general observations can be made on the basis of the cases discussed with respect to the regulatory activities of an international

324   *From the International to the Domestic Legal Realm*

transitional administration with full executive and legislative powers. Overall, there was a gradual movement from fast-track decree-like regulations to the establishment of new institutions or programs to more invasive legal instruments introducing substantive changes to the domestic legal system. As regards UNMIK lawmaking in general, there appeared to be a similar tendency toward more substantial lawmaking. A survey conducted by the SRSG in May 2001 of all UNMIK regulations that the pillars and departments intended to have adopted before the provincial elections indicated that about half of the envisaged regulations had a strong development component and foresaw either major revisions of existing domestic laws or the introduction of new substantive legislation.[80] That UNMIK did not adopt most of these regulations before the elections was due to a general policy not to preempt the responsibilities of the provisional institutions of self-government.

There was also a general development in UNMIK's regulatory activities toward greater local participation and a recognition of the existing domestic legal system. The establishment of participatory mechanisms and advisory organs like the JAC and IAC supported this process. Furthermore, the international staff's growing knowledge of domestic structures and applicable laws fostered local participation and led to an increased focus on the compatibility of UNMIK lawmaking with the domestic legal system. Once the UNMIK system had been properly established and its basic principles were set, it became easier to include locals in the decisionmaking process and to concentrate on matching legal systems.

Possibly according to the principle "two steps forward, one step back," UNMIK's practice did not always follow such tendencies. Until the establishment of the provisional institutions of self-government, the newly created participatory mechanisms undoubtedly did not diminish the SRSG's sole executive and legislative responsibility and power. Under certain political conditions—for example, those leading to the adoption of Regulation No. 2001/17, Registration of Property Transactions in Specific Geographical Areas—a heavy-handed approach dictated the legislative outcome without much consideration to local acceptance or legal compatibility. It seems that fast-track and nonparticipatory decree ruling was used particularly in the context of peace enforcement in light of pressing security concerns and human rights violations and to ensure UNMIK's maintenance of power (or the image of it). However, involvement of local stakeholders and a sound analysis of the domestic legislation were objectives of UNMIK lawmaking, mainly in connection with peacebuilding efforts to create local institutions and to reform the local legal system. With increasing capacity of the mission, these objectives became more critical and efforts were made to achieve them.[81]

The described regulatory efforts raise important legal and conceptual questions for future peace operations on which further research should be carried out.[82] In terms of legitimacy, it needs to be determined how far international lawmakers may intrude in the domestic legal realm for the purpose of maintaining (international) peace and security. Also, the concentration of legislative and executive powers in the hands of the SRSG stands in some contradiction to the objective of good governance and the participation of the administered population in the decisionmaking process, a relationship that needs to be clarified. Moreover, politically, it is difficult for the transitional administration to decide how best to regulate in light of the known weaknesses of multinational forces and the UN administration in enforcing and implementing their objectives while in the process of being set up.

The international presence should take a cautious approach to its regulatory activities, since its credibility may severely suffer if legislation is adopted that cannot be enforced or implemented subsequently. Restraint should also be applied with respect to lawmaking with a peacebuilding objective to reform the domestic legal system. Legislative cooperation between internationals and locals can be very cumbersome and requires many financial resources and personal energy of the officers involved to make such legislation a high-quality product. Invasive legislative reform supports the cause of peace only if it is compatible with domestic legal traditions and is embraced by the local population. The more the international administration can ensure these elements in its regulatory activities, the more it may engage in them.

Notes

Leopold von Carlowitz is a research fellow at the Peace Research Institute Frankfurt and a doctoral candidate at the Freie Universität Berlin. From 1999 to 2001, he served as head of the Property Verification and Claims Unit and as policy/legal adviser in UNMIK (Civil Administration). He also worked as counsel before international legal proceedings and was previously employed by the International Tribunal for the Law of the Sea and other offices of the United Nations system. The present article was written with the support of the Peace and Governance Programme of United Nations University.

1. OHR's property-related lawmaking centered mainly on refugee return issues and the enforcement of the decisions of the Commission for Real Property Claims of Displaced Persons and Refugees. For an interesting overview of the respective legislative activities, see Lynn Hastings, "Implementation of the

Property Legislation in Bosnia Herzegovina," *Stanford Journal of International Law* 37, no. 2 (2001): 221–254.

2. This article deals with property issues pertaining to the civil administration pillar of UNMIK. Property issues that have arisen in the context of the commercial law reform program run by the European Union pillar for reconstruction and development is addressed only in passing.

3. Report of the Secretary-General on the United Nations Interim Administration Mission in Kosovo, 12 July 1999, UN Doc. S/1999/779, pars. 36, 39.

4. See Report of the Panel on UN Peace Operations (Brahimi-Report), 21 August 2000, UN Doc. A/55/305-S/2000/809, par. 80; Wendy S. Bretts, Scott N. Carlson, and Gregory Gisvold, "The Post-Conflict Transitional Administration of Kosovo and the Lessons Learned in Efforts to Establish a Judiciary and Rule of Law," *Michigan Journal of International Law* 22 (2000/01): 373–376.

5. On peace maintenance, see Jarat Chopra, *Peace Maintenance: The Evolution of International Political Authority* (London and New York, Routledge,1999); on the administration's accountability to the local population, see, for example, Michael Bothe and Thilo Marauhn, "UN Administration of Kosovo and East Timor: Concept, Legality and Limitations of Security Council-Mandated Trusteeship Administration," in Christian Tomuschat, ed., *Kosovo and the International Community* (The Hague: Kluwer Law International, 2002), pp. 235–239; Leopold von Carlowitz, "UNMIK Lawmaking Between Effective Peace Support and Internal Self-determination," *Archiv des Völkerrechts* (Archive of public international law) 41, no. 3 (2003): 336–393.

6. On the functional duality of international territorial administrations, see Ralph Wilde, "The Complex Role of the Legal Adviser when International Organizations Administer Territory," *ASIL Proceedings* 95, no. 251 (2001): 253; Joel C. Beauvais, "Benevolent Despotism: A Critique of U.N. State-building in East Timor," *New York University Journal of International Law and Politics* 33, no. 4 (2001): 1007–1119.

7. On the debate surrounding the concept of global governance in relation to domestic governance, see Antonio Franceschet, "Justice and International Organization: Two Models of Global Governance," *Global Governance* 8, no. 1 (2002): 19–34; Thomas G. Weiss, "Governance, Global Governance, Good Governance: Conceptual and Actual Challenges," *Third World Quarterly* 21 (2000): 795–814; James N. Rosenau, "Governance in the Twenty-first Century," *Global Governance* 1, no. 1 (1995): 13–43; Lawrence S. Finkelstein, "What Is Global Governance?" *Global Governance* 1, no. 3 (1995): 367–372; Dieter Senghaas, "Global Governance: How Could It Be Conceived?" *Security Dialogue* 24 (1993): 247–256; and Roland Paris, "Broadening the Study of Peace Operations," *International Studies Review* 2 (2000): 27–44.

8. With the establishment of the JIAS, the first pillar was dissolved, leaving UNHCR outside the UNMIK structure. In May 2001, a new UN–led Pillar I for police and justice was created to strengthen the law enforcement and criminal justice systems. Each pillar is headed by a deputy special representative of the secretary-general (DSRSG); all are coordinated by the SRSG and his principal deputy.

9. See the chart "Residential Housing Damage: June 1999" contained in Humanitarian Community Information Centre et al., *Kosovo Atlas 2*, September 2000.

10. Habitat, "Housing and Property in Kosovo: Rights, Law and Justice: Proposals for a Comprehensive Plan of Action for the Promotion and Protection of Housing and Property Rights in Kosovo," 30 August 1999.

11. Social ownership was a special property right in the former socialist Yugoslavia. Companies gave their employees an occupancy right for a socially owned apartment. This right was stronger than a tenancy right but less than full ownership. For more detail, see Elena Popovic, "The Impact of International Human Rights Law on the Property Law of Bosnia and Herzegovina," in Michael O'Flaherty and Gregory Gisvald, eds., *Post-War Protection of Human Rights in Bosnia and Herzegovina* (The Hague, London, and Boston: Martin Nijhoff, 1998), pp. 141–156.

12. Scott Leckie, "Resolving Kosovo's Housing Crisis: Challenges for the UN Housing and Property Directorate," *Forced Migration Review* 7 (2000): 12–13.

13. Compare UN/ECE, Annex 3 of draft report "Development Strategy on Land Administration in Kosovo," 31 August 1999, pp. 21–22.

14. Habitat, "Housing and Property in Kosovo."

15. UNMIK Regulations are printed in the Official Gazette, available online at www.unmikonline.org/regulations/index.htm.

16. Telephone interview with responsible UNMIK official, 8 April 2002.

17. UNMIK Regulation No. 1999/2, Prevention of Access by Individuals and Their Removal to Secure Public Peace and Order, 12 August 1999, sec. 1.2.c.

18. UNMIK Regulation No. 1999/1, Authority of the Interim Administration in Kosovo, 25 July 1999, sec. 6. This provision was later amended to also include socially owned property; see UNMIK Regulation No. 2000/54 Amending UNMIK Regulation No. 1999/1, as Amended, on the Authority of the Interim Administration in Kosovo, 27 September 2000, sec. 6.

19. On corresponding KFOR and CIVPOL practice, see Richard Büllesbach, "Aufgaben öffentlicher Sicherheit für KFOR-Soldaten im Kosovo" (Public security challenges for KFOR soldiers in Kosovo), *Humanitäres Völkerrecht* 2 (2001): 87.

20. Draft Regulation on Temporary Residence in Residential Property, August 1999 (on file with the author).

21. International Crisis Group, "Waiting for UNMIK: Local Administration in Kosovo," *ICG Balkans Report No. 79*, 18 October 1999.

22. UNMIK Civil Administration, Guidelines for the Allocation of Vacant Housing on Humanitarian Grounds, 23 November 1999.

23. Official Gazette of the Republic of Serbia, 22/91, 18 April 1991.

24. Official Gazette of the Republic of Serbia, 43/91, 20 July 1991.

25. Ibid., art. 3.

26. On the JAC's functions, see Lawyers Committee for Human Rights, "A Fragile Peace: Laying the Foundations for Justice in Kosovo," October 1999.

27. On 23 March 1989, the Serbian government had unilaterally ended Kosovo's status as an autonomous province of Serbia. Noel Malcolm, *Kosovo: A Short History* (New York: New York University Press, 1998), p. 344.

28. 23 March 1999 was the day before NATO started bombing Yugoslavia. See UNMIK Regulation No. 1999/23, Establishment of the Housing and Property Directorate and the Housing and Property Claims Commission, 15 November 1999, sec. 1.2.

29. On the mandate and work of the commission, see Hans Van Houtte, "The Property Claims Commission in Bosnia-Herzegovina—A New Path to Restore Real Estate Rights in Post-War Societies?" in Karl Wellens, ed., *International Law: Theory and Practice, Essays in Honour of Eric Suy* (The Hague: Martinus Nijhoff, 1998), pp. 549–564.

30. On UNMIK's approach to reinstall the judicial system, see Report of the Secretary-General on the United Nations Interim Administration in Kosovo, 23 December 1999, UN Doc. S/1999/1250, pars. 57–60, 70–78, 84, 111.

31. UNMIK Regulation No. 2000/1, Kosovo Joint Interim Administrative Structure, 14 January 2000, sec. 3.1.

32. Ibid., sec. 6.

33. HPD/CC, "Resolving Disputes on Residential Property. Principles of Law, Evidence and Procedure for the Housing and Property Directorate and Claims Commission," April 2000; Habitat and HPD/CC, *Collection of Basic Texts: Housing and Property Rights in Kosovo*, 1st, 2nd eds., December 1999, March 2000.

34. UNMIK Regulation No. 1999/24, Applicable Law in Kosovo, 12 December 1999, sec. 1.1. This decision was prompted by a refusal of the Albanian judges to apply postautonomy legislation that was viewed to be oppressive by the ethnic Albanian majority.

35. UNMIK Regulation No. 2000/60, Residential Property Claims and the Rules of Procedure and Evidence of the Housing and Property Directorate and the Housing and Property Claims Commission, 31 October 2000, secs. 2–4, 13.

36. Minutes of IAC meeting, 26 September and 3 October 2000.

37. JIAS Department of Justice, Statistical Report, "Preliminary Analysis of Judicial Acitivity: Statistics for the Period January–August 2000," 4 October 2000 (on file with the author).

38. Letter from the SRSG to the Civil Panel of the Pristina District Court, 28 November 2000.

39. Clarification by the SRSG of UNMIK Regulation No. 2000/60, 31 October 2000, Residential Property Claims and the Rules of Procedure and Evidence of the Housing and Property Directorate and Housing and Property Claims Commission; Document UNMIK/REG/2000/60-Clarification, 12 April 2001; Joint Working Group on Overlapping Jurisdiction, Draft Terms of Reference, October 2001.

40. In civil law systems, the cadastre is a land register that provides geodetic data and indicates the use of a plot of land. In many countries, the cadastre serves as the underlying technical basis for a property title register.

41. For example, an inventory of all cadastral offices and aerial photography over Kosovo.

42. The activities were organized by the Swedish development agency SIDA. Other donor countries were Switzerland and Norway. For an overview of the scope of the KCA's work, see Programme Document, "Kosovo Cadastral Support Programme," May 2000.

43. Compare UNMIK Regulation No. 2000/12, Establishment of the Administrative Department of Public Services, 14 March 2000, sec. 5.

44. Compare UNMIK Office of the Legal Adviser, Procedures for Preparation and Promulgation of UNMIK Legislative Issuances, 12 February 2001.

45. Administrative Direction No. 2000/14 Implementing UNMIK Regulation No. 2000/12, Establishment of the Administrative Department of Public Services, 7 June 2000, secs. 1.2, 2.

46. Xavier Forneris, Charles Caldwell, and Allen Shinn, "Legal Reform in Post-Conflict Circumstances: The Case of Kosovo," paper presented at the World Bank conference "Empowerment, Security and Opportunity Through Law and Justice," St. Petersburg, Russia, 8–12 July 2001, p. 9, available online at www.worldbank.org/legal/ljr_01/doc/IRIS.pdf.

47. Minutes of meeting of interpillar working group on property issues, 7 June 2001.

48. In the *tapia* system, legal title is established by deeds issued by a court to the individual titleholder. A central title register does not exist.

49. JIAS Department of Public Services, Research Paper, "Social, State and Private Ownership on Immovable Objects in Kosovo," 22 August 2001.

50. Compare HPD/CC, "Resolving Disputes on Residential Property," p. 10.

51. UNMIK Civil Administration, Guidelines for the Preparation of UNMIK Legislation, 31 May 2001.

52. UNMIK Civil Administration, concept paper "Issues to Be Addressed in Property Law Reform," 5 September 2001.

53. Besides the KCA, the working group consisted of representatives of the Department of Public Services (Pillar II, for civil administration), the Department of Trade and Industry (Pillar IV, for reconstruction and development), the Department of Judicial Affairs (Pillar I, for police and justice), and the OSCE (Pillar III, for democratization and institution building).

54. Memorandum by the Kosovo Cadastral Agency to the Legal Adviser regarding the Administrative Direction on the Establishment of a Property Rights Register, 12 October 2001.

55. Ibid.

56. On the "Serbification" of Kosovo's public institutions after 1989, see Wolfgang Petritsch, Karl Kaser, and Robert Pichler, *Kosovo/Kosova: Mythen, Daten, Fakten* (Kosovo/Kosova: myths, dates, facts) (Vienna: Wieser Verlagplace, 1999), p. 183ff.

57. See Central Fiscal Authority, "Budget Wage Assumptions," 10 January 2000.

58. The UN Transitional Administration in East Timor experienced similar difficulties in its attempts to "Timorize" the transitional administration. See Jarat Chopra, "The UN's Kingdom of East Timor," *Survival* 42, no. 3 (2000): 32.

59. Brahimi Report, pars. 127–145.

60. Wilde, "The Complex Role of the Legal Adviser," p. 252.

61. Compare ibid., pp. 254–255.

62. See, for example, Ngaire Woods, "Good Governance in International Organizations," *Global Governance* 5, no. 1 (1999): 43–44; Rama Mani, "Conflict Resolution, Justice and the Law: Rebuilding the Rule of Law in the Aftermath of Complex Political Emergencies," *International Peacekeeping* 5 (1998): 7–8; Ann Seidman, Robert B. Seidman, and Thomas Wälde, "Building Sound National Legal Frameworks for Development and Social Change," in Ann Seidman, Robert B. Seidman, and Thomas Wälde, eds., *Making Development Work: Legislative Reform for Institutional Transformation and Good Governance* (The Hague: Kluwer Law International, 1999), pp. 4–7.

63. JIAS Department of Public Services, concept paper "Kosovo Expert Support Programme," 8 March 2001. The program was conducted together with the Department of Non-resident Affairs and took into account experiences of

similar projects of UNDP and the International Organization for Migration (IOM). An active search for suitable candidates for certain projects was carried out by maintaining contacts with diaspora networks and creating corresponding databases.

64. The secretary-general of the UN Conference on Trade and Development (UNCTAD), R. Recupero, called international migration the "missing link between globalization and development." See IOM, strategy paper "The Link Between Migration and Development in the Least Developed Countries," available online at www.iom.int.

65. On the role of culture in peace operations, see Tamara Duffy, "Cultural Issues in Contemporary Peacekeeping," in Tom Woodhouse and Oliver Ramsbotham, eds., *Peacekeeping and Conflict Transformation* (London: Frank Cass, 2000), pp. 149–153, 165.

66. In particular, the Departments of Public Services and Judicial Affairs made use of such candidates.

67. See, for example, Report of the Secretary-General on the United Nations Interim Administration Mission in Kosovo, 13 March 2001, UN Doc. S/2001/218, par.18.

68. Minutes of the meeting, 1 November 2000 (on file with the author).

69. First Protocol to the European Convention on Human Rights, art. 1 (1).

70. UNMIK Recommendation Paper on Inter-Ethnic Sales of Property, 5 June 2001 (on file with the author).

71. The fear existed that efforts to establish a provisional self-government in a multiethnic Kosovo would have been seriously undermined if the Yugoslav or Serb authorities had called for a Serb boycott of the provincial elections to be held in November 2002.

72. The alternative approach chosen by the SRSG was nevertheless heavily criticized for property-related human rights violations. See, for example, Ombudsperson Institution in Kosovo, Special Report No. 5 on Certain Aspects of UNMIK Regulation No. 2001/17 on the Registration of Contracts for the Sale of Real Property in Specific Geographical Areas of Kosovo, 29 October 2001.

73. *Travaux préparatoires* for UNMIK Regulation No. 2001/17 on the Registration of Contracts for the Sale of Real Property in Specific Geographical Areas in Kosovo, June 2001 (on file with the author).

74. For example, *Koha Ditore* (Albanian newspaper), "There Was a Time When Serb Property Was Sold in Kosovo" (translation), 8 July 2001; *Zëri* (Albanian newspaper), "Haekkerup's Complicated Law on Property Sales" (translation), 3 August 2001.

75. Minutes of JAC meeting, 20 July 2001 (on file with the author).

76. Comments of IAC members, 19–20 July 2001 (on file with the author).

77. Administrative Direction No. 2001/16 Implementing UNMIK Regulation No. 2001/17 on the Registration of Contracts for the Sale of Real Property in Specific Geographical Areas in Kosovo, 19 October 2001.

78. Compare Michael Pugh, "Introduction: The Ownership of Regeneration and Peacebuilding," in Michael Pugh, ed., *The Regeneration of War-Torn Societies* (London: Macmillan, 2000), p. 3. On how to measure the success of peace operations in general, see D. Bratt, "Assessing the Success of UN Peacekeeping Operations," in Michael Pugh, ed., *The UN, Peace and Force* (London: Frank Cass, 1997), pp. 64–81.

79. On the danger of creating legal pluralism when external legal intervention is not based on local legal traditions, see Rama Mani, "The Rule of Law or the Rule of Might? Restoring Legal Justice in the Aftermath of Conflict," in Pugh, *Regeneration of War-Torn Societies,* p. 104.

80. Preliminary List of UNMIK Regulations Prior to Transition, 30 May 2001 (on file with the author).

81. The above-mentioned preparatory work concerning the introduction of a property rights register was one example. Another example was a program by the European Union–led Pillar IV to develop a market-oriented legal system within which relevant Yugoslav legislation was analyzed and a roundtable discussion was held with the local legal community in December 2001.

82. Paris, "Broadening the Study of Peace Operations," pp. 42–43; Outi Korhonen, "International Governance in Post-Conflict Situations," *Leiden Journal of International Law* 14, no. 3 (2001): 524–528.

[24]

TO WAIVE OR NOT TO WAIVE: IMMUNITY AND ACCOUNTABILITY IN U.N. PEACEKEEPING OPERATIONS

*Frederick Rawski**

To recognize the existence of a general and unrestricted immunity from suit or prosecution on the part of the personnel of the United Nations, so long as the individual be performing in his official capacity, even though the individual's function has no relation to the importance or the success of the organization's deliberations, is carrying the principle of immunity completely out of bounds. To establish such a principle would in effect create a large preferred class within our borders who would be immune to punishment on identical facts for which the average American would be subject to punishment. Any such theory does violence to and is repugnant to the American sense of fairness and justice and flouts the very basic principle of the United Nations itself, which in its preamble to its charter affirms that it is created to give substance to the principle that the rights of all men and women are equal.

Judge Rubin of the City Court of New Rochelle, November 1946.[1]

[T]he main purpose of granting immunity to international organizations is to protect them against the unilateral interference by the individual government of the state in which they are located. The rationale . . . does not apply to the circumstances prevailing in Kosovo, where the interim civilian administration . . . acts as a surrogate state . . . . [T]here is no need for a government to be protected against itself. . . . [N]o democratic state operating under the rule of law accords itself total immunity from any administrative, civil or criminal responsibility. Such a blanket lack of accountability paves the way for the impunity of the state.

Marek Antoni Nowicki, Ombudsperson in Kosovo, April 2001.[2]

* Frederick Rawski graduated from the New York University School of Law in May 2002. From May to December of 2000, he was an international staff member in the Human Rights Unit of the United Nations Transitional Administration in East Timor [UNTAET]. Special thanks to Professors Thomas Franck and David Malone. Thanks also to Simon Chesterman for comments on an earlier draft.

1. Westchester County v. Ranollo, 67 N.Y.S.2d 31, 34 (New Rochelle City Ct. 1946), submitted to the 6th Committee on November 6, 1949 as U.N. Doc. A/C.6/57 (1946).
2. OMBUDSPERSON INSTITUTION IN KOSOVO, SPECIAL REPORT NO. 1 ON THE COMPATIBILITY WITH RECOGNIZED INTERNATIONAL STANDARDS OF UNMIK REGULATION NO. 2000/47 ON THE STATUS,

104   **CONNECTICUT JOURNAL OF INT'L LAW**   Vol. 18:103

This proves that in East Timor, no one is above the law.

Sergio Viera de Mello, Special Representative of the Secretary-General in East Timor, announcing that immunity would not protect two civilian police officers suspected of rape, July 2001.[3]

I.   INTRODUCTION

Immunity protections are particularly important in peacekeeping operations where the UN is often intervening in an unstable political environment and where normal institutions of law and order are not functioning. With the rapid expansion of UN peacekeeping since the early 1990s, the General Assembly has regularly passed resolutions calling on states to respect the privileges and immunities necessary for the organization to achieve its objectives in difficult field environments.[4] Immunity has been invoked by the UN not only to protect its personnel from harassment, but to protect itself from suit for institutional negligence, such as its failure to act while genocide was taking place in Rwanda.[5] In recent years, however, in response to a number of highly publicized cases of misbehavior,[6] the UN has taken steps to make peacekeeping staff and

---

PRIVILEGES AND IMMUNITIES OF KFOR AND UNMIK AND THEIR PERSONNEL IN KOSOVO (18 AUGUST 2000) AND ON THE IMPLEMENTATION OF THE ABOVE REGULATION § 23 (2001).

3.   Daily Briefing, UNTAET, Two UN Police Officers Detained in Connection with Rape (July 6, 2001), *available at* http://www.un.org/peace/etimor/DB/Db060701.htm.

4.   Beginning with G.A. Res. 76(I), U.N. Doc. A/RES/76(I) (1946). *See also* U.N. GAOR, 43d Sess., 84th plen. mtg., U.N. Doc. A/RES/43/225 (1988); U.N. GAOR, 47th Sess., 72d plen. mtg., U.N. Doc. A/RES/47/28 (1992); U.N. GAOR, 50th Sess., 99th plen. mtg., U.N. Doc. A/RES/49/238 (1995); U.N. GAOR, 52d Sess., 73d plen. mtg., U.N. Doc. A/RES/52/167 (1997); U.N. GAOR, 52d Sess., 70th plen. mtg., U.N. Doc. A/RES/52/126 (1997); U.N. GAOR, 53d Sess., Agenda Item 20, U.N. Doc. A/RES/53/87 (1999); U.N. GAOR, 54th Sess., Agenda Item 20, U.N. Doc. A/RES/54/192 (2000); U.N. GAOR, 55th Sess., Agenda Item 20, U.N. Doc. A/RES/55/175 (2001).

5.   In January 2000, two Australian lawyers announced that they would initiate a lawsuit against the UN for failing to act when it had knowledge months in advance that genocide was imminent in Rwanda. The lawsuit was to be brought on behalf of two Rwandan women whose families were killed in the 1994 genocide. When the announcement was made, the UN in turn announced that the UN would invoke its immunity to protect it from lawsuit if necessary. The Spokesman for the Secretary-General, Fred Eckhard, remarked that to allow peacekeepers to be brought to court for such a suit would mean "the end of peacekeeping." Mark Riley, *UN to Seek Immunity on Rwanda*, SYDNEY MORNING HERALD, January 2000, *available at* http://www.igc.org/globalpolicy/security/issues/rwanda /unsued.htm.

6.   For instance, troops deployed to Somalia in the early 1990s were accused of sexual assault, rape, torture, deaths in custody and the defacing of local cultural objects. Press Release, UNIFEM, Women Tell UN Security Council of Abuses During War (Oct. 23, 2000), *available at* http://www.unifem.undp.org/pr_unseccoun.html. An Italian soldier allegedly tortured a Somali thief by applying electricity to his testicles. Canadian peacekeepers were accused of beating to death a Somali teenager in custody. Numerous allegations of child prostitution and black-marketeering by UN personnel in Eritrea and Bosnia have also surfaced. Manfred Gerstenfeld, *The UN's Own Abuses*, JERUSALEM POST, August 30, 2001, sec. Opinion, at 6. In 1999, troops deployed to Sierra Leone as part of ECOMOG were accused of an array of human rights violations. *See* Letter from Peter Takirambudde, Executive Director, Africa Division, and Joanna Weschler, U.N. Representative, Human Rights Watch, to Ambassador Greenstock (Oct. 4, 2000), *available at* http://www.hrw.org/press/2000/10/sl-brief-ltr.htm. In early 2001, there were allegations of rape and extortion by Jordanian peacekeepers in East Timor. *See UN Inquiry into Allegations of Staff*

administrations more accountable, including issuing an executive order requiring peacekeeping troops to abide by the Geneva conventions,[7] and denying immunity protection when a serious breach of law is implicated. The issue of immunity for peacekeepers arose most recently in June 2002 when the United States threatened to veto the extension of current peacekeeping operations in the Security Council unless U.S. personnel were granted a blanket immunity from prosecution by the International Criminal Court.[8]

While some senior United Nations officials enjoy the benefits of full diplomatic immunity and military personnel are regularly granted complete immunity in Status of Forces Agreements, most United Nations staff and field personnel are protected by a more ambiguous 'functional' or 'official capacity' immunity. The expansive mandates of transitional administrations such as UNMIK [United Nations Interim Administration Mission in Kosovo] and UNTAET [United Nations Transitional Administration in East Timor] present special problems for determining the scope of this immunity. Where the UN itself acts as the government, the normal rationale for immunity, shielding the organization from state interference, makes little sense. Broad staff immunity in such cases may violate the principles of democratic accountability and human rights at the core of these missions' mandates. This paper will attempt to draw some preliminary conclusions on current immunity practice in transitional administrations, and try to reconcile that practice with current and emerging law on immunity and human rights.

The paper will begin by setting out the basic legal texts and jurisprudence upon which claims of functional immunity are based, and reviewing current procedures for handling allegations of abuse in the field. It will then examine in some detail the ways in which issues of immunity have been dealt with in Kosovo and East Timor, and suggest that even a limited immunity may be inappropriate where the UN is acting as a government. Finally, it will discuss how the conflict between immunity protections and institutional accountability reflect a larger conflict between the human rights and peace and security functions of UN governance operations.

II. Immunity from Process for UN Peacekeeping Staff: Legal and Historical Bases

Misconduct in East Timor, World News from Radio Australia, June 24, 2001, *available at* http://www.intellnet.org/news/2001/06/24/5123-1.htm.

7.   *Observance by United Nations Forces of International Humanitarian Law,* Secretary-General's Bulletin sec. 8, U.N. Doc. ST/SGB/1999/13 (1999). The order was widely criticized by human rights groups, which called for the establishment of some kind of civilian body to investigate human rights violations allegedly committed by UN personnel. *See* Barbara Crossette, *Global Rules Now Apply to Peacekeepers, U.N. Chief Declares,* N.Y. Times, August 12, 1999, at A8.

8.   James Dao, *Solitaire; One Nation Plays the Great Game Alone,* N.Y. Times, July 7, 2002, § 4, at 1.

106   CONNECTICUT JOURNAL OF INT'L LAW   [Vol. 18:103

Diplomatic immunity from legal process has been called "the oldest established rule of diplomatic law."[9] The principles of immunity from process and personal inviolability are enshrined in the Vienna Convention,[10] and have been reiterated by the International Court of Justice as recently as February 2002.[11] Reciprocal recognition by states of the inviolability of other states' representatives is part of the very foundation of international relations.[12] While this immunity was historically based on the principle that an injury to a state's representative constitutes an injury to the state itself,[13] it has always been understood to serve an indispensable function. Immunity creates a protected space necessary for diplomats to fulfill their functions independently and free from interference by the government of the state in which they are posted. This principle of 'functional necessity' later became the basis for UN staff immunities, reflected in the UN Charter and the Convention on the Privileges and Immunities of the United Nations. The immunity of international organizations and their representatives is now so ingrained in international practice as to approach the status of customary international law.[14]

There are a number of foundational and operational documents that set forth the scope of immunity for the UN and its staff on mission. The most important of these include the UN Charter, the Convention on the Privileges and Immunities of the United Nations, Status of Forces Agreements, Security Council Resolutions, and intra-mission Regulations.

A. UN Charter

Immunity protections are intended to safeguard the efficient functioning of an organization. . They are not meant to benefit any particular individual.[15] In

---

9.   EILEEN DENZA, DIPLOMATIC LAW: A COMMENTARY ON THE VIENNA CONVENTION ON DIPLOMATIC RELATIONS 210 (Oxford University Press 1998) (1976).

10.   "The person of a diplomatic agent shall be inviolable. He shall not be liable to any form of arrest or detention . . . ." Vienna Convention on Diplomatic Relations, Apr. 18, 1961, art. 29, 7310 U.N.T.S. 96, 110. "A diplomatic agent shall enjoy immunity from the criminal jurisdiction of the receiving State . . . ." *Id.* art. 31, at 112.

11.   Concerning the Arrest Warrant of 11 April 2000 (Congo v. Belg.), 2002 I.C.J. 121, para. 52 (Feb. 14), *available at* http://www.icj-cij.org/icjwww/idocket/iCOBE/icobejudgment/icobe_ijudgment _20020214.PDF [hereinafter Arrest Warrant].

12.   See, for instance, the articulation of this principle in official US government documents. U.S. DEP'T OF STATE, DIPLOMATIC AND CONSULAR IMMUNITY: GUIDANCE FOR LAW ENFORCEMENT AND JUDICIAL AUTHORITIES (1998).

13.   The history of the 'representative character' theory goes back to Vattel, and has been reaffirmed multiple times by the International Court of Justice and the Permanent Court of International Justice. *See* J. CRAIG BARKER, THE ABUSE OF DIPLOMATIC PRIVILEGES AND IMMUNITIES: A NECESSARY EVIL? 35 (1996).

14.   While stopping short of declaring immunity for international organizations a part of customary international law, the European Court of Human Rights has recognized that immunity from jurisdiction for international organizations is "a long standing practice" with the "legitimate objective" of ensuring the "proper functioning of such organisations free from unilateral interference by individual governments." Waite and Kennedy v. F.R.G. [GC], App. No. 26083/94, Eur. Ct. H.R. 1999-I, para. 61, 63 (1999). *See also* RESTATEMENT (SECOND) OF THE FOREIGN RELATIONS LAW OF THE UNITED STATES § 83 (1965).

15.   This principle is enshrined in the Preamble to the Vienna Convention: "Realizing that the purpose of such privileges and immunities is not to benefit individuals but to ensure the efficient

accordance with this principle, the Charter gives the UN and its officials a limited 'functional' immunity. Under Article 105 the organization enjoys immunities "as are necessary for the fulfillment of its purposes," and its members enjoy immunity "necessary for the independent exercise of their functions."[16] Identical articulations of functional immunity are found in the constitutional instruments of numerous other international agencies.[17]

B. Convention on the Privileges and Immunities of the United Nations

The Convention on the Privileges and Immunities of the United Nations [hereinafter Immunities Convention][18] defines the scope of the functional immunity granted by the Charter. Article II, section 2 of the Convention states that the United Nations "shall enjoy immunity from *every* form of legal process except insofar as . . . it has expressly waived its immunity" (emphasis added). Article V, Section 19 grants full diplomatic immunity to the Secretary-General, Asst. Secretary-Generals and their families. Section 18 gives civilian staff immunity from legal process "in respect of words spoken or written and all acts performed by them in their official capacity."[19] Under Section 22, 'experts' on mission, which include Civilian Police

---

performance of the functions of diplomatic missions as representing States . . . ." Vienna Convention on Diplomatic Relations, *supra* note 10.

16. The use of 'necessary,' and the avoidance of a direct invocation of diplomatic immunity suggests that UN staff were never intended to receive the level of protection accorded diplomats. An examination of the Fourth Committee's deliberations supports this conclusion. *See* AUGUST REINISCH, INTERNATIONAL ORGANIZATIONS BEFORE NATIONAL COURTS 364 n.177 (2000).

17. For instance, Article 40(1) of the International Labor Organization Constitution, Article 67(a) of the World Health Organization Constitution, Article XV of the International Atomic Energy Agency Statute, and Article 139 of the Organization of American States Charter. REINISCH, *supra* note 16, at 140 n.542.

18. Convention on the Privileges and Immunities of the United Nations, Feb. 13, 1946, 1 U.N.T.S. 15 [hereinafter Immunities Convention]. Early on, the 1946 Sixth Committee decided that a Convention, rather than a series of recommendations, would be the most appropriate and effective way to actualize the rights enshrined in Article 105 of the Charter. The drafters felt that the goal of uniform treatment of UN staff by all states would be best served by the creation of a convention "which was as precise as possible." *See* Proceedings of the Sixth Committee, Sub-Committee on Immunities and Privileges, at 2 (January 25, 1946).

19. Immunities Convention, *supra* note 18. The distinction in Sections 18 and 19 between absolute immunity for senior staff and functional immunity for other officials is also found in Article V, Sections 15 and 16 of the Convention of July 1, 1946 between the United Nations and Switzerland. Interestingly, the Headquarters Agreement between the United States and the United Nations of June 26, 1946 does not contain a section on immunities, though the Charter would apply. This issue is addressed in U.S. national legislation by § 288d of the International Organizations Immunities Act of 1945. *See* BENEDETTO CONFORTI, THE LAW AND PRACTICE OF THE UNITED NATIONS 110-11 (1996).

[UNCIVPOL],[20] are immune "in respect of words spoken or written and acts done by them in the course of the performance of their mission."[21]

Under the Convention, the Secretary-General (hereinafter SG) has the sole ability to waive the immunity of UN personnel. Not only that, under Sections 20 and 23, the SG has "the right and the *duty* to waive immunity of any official in any case where, *in his opinion*, the immunity would *impede the course of justice* and it can be waived *without prejudice to the interests* of the United Nations."[22] In addition, the UN Office of Legal Affairs has acknowledged that the ICJ has the authority to review the SG's waiver decisions.[23] Finally, Article VIII Section 29(b) of the Convention requires the UN to provide for "appropriate modes of settlement" in civil cases against the organization and in cases in which official immunity is not waived.

C. Status of Forces Agreements

While military personnel are not covered by the 1946 Convention, they are usually granted immunities under Status of Forces agreements. In the cases of East Timor and Kosovo, where there is no host state, these guarantees are contained in agreements negotiated between the contributing states and the UN. Under the terms of Status of Forces or Military Technical Agreements, military forces in peacekeeping operations remain under the jurisdiction of the sending States, which retain the sole authority to waive immunity.[24] In addition to the immunities granted to officials and experts under the Convention, individual agreements for Civilian Police [UNCIVPOL] are often negotiated between the sending State and the UN,

---

20. A United Nations Model Status of Forces Agreement classifies military observers, UNCIVPOL and civilian peacekeeping personnel as 'experts' under the Immunities Convention. *Model Status of Forces Agreement for Peacekeeping Operations: Report of the Secretary-General*, U.N. GAOR, 45th Sess., Agenda Item 76, at 8, U.N. Doc. A/45/594 (1990) [hereinafter Model SOFA]. For relevant excerpts and analysis, see also Washington Working Group on the International Criminal Court, *US Efforts to Obtain Exemption for UN Peacekeepers: Relevant International Law*, at http://www.wfa.org/issues/wicc/UNSClaw.html (last visited Sept. 13, 2002).

21. Immunities Convention, *supra* note 18. The International Court of Justice has had occasion to define 'expert,' though not in the context of peacekeeping operations. The ICJ has held that Special Rapporteurs are to be considered 'experts on mission.' *See* Advisory Opinion of 15 December 1989 on the Applicability of Article VI, Section 22, of the Convention on the Privileges and Immunities of the United Nations (1989), *available at* http://www.icj-cij.org/icjwww/idecisions/isummaries/iecosoc summary891215.htm (last visited Aug. 19, 2002) [hereinafter Mazilu]; *see also* Advisory Opinion of 29 April 1999 on the Difference Relating to Immunity from Legal Process of a Special Rapporteur of the Commission on Human Rights (1999), *available at* http://www.icj-cij.org/icjwww/idocket/inuma/ inumaframe.htm (last visited Aug. 19, 2002) [hereinafter Cumaraswamy].

22. Immunities Convention, *supra* note 18, at Section 20 and 23. (emphasis added). An identical provision articulating a duty to waive is found in the Convention on the Privileges and Immunities of Specialized Agencies. Convention on the Privileges and Immunities of the Specialized Agencies, November 21, 1947, art. V, sec. 16, 33 U.N.T.S. 261, 272.

23. *See* Charles H. Brower, II, *International Immunities: Some Dissident Views on the Role of Municipal Courts*, 41 VA. J. INT'L L. 1, 30-31 (2000) (citing Cumaraswamy, *supra* note 21).

24. *See* Model SOFA, *supra* note 20, para. 47(b).

which grant them additional immunity protections, up to and including absolute immunity.[25]

D. Security Council Resolutions and Intra-Mission Regulations

If an operation is authorized under a Chapter VII resolution, immunity protections could be modified directly by the Security Council.[26] In the context of peacekeeping operations with broad local law making powers, such as UNMIK and UNTAET, it seems that the ability to enhance immunities is included in the power delegated by the Council to the SRSG. The most striking example of this is UNMIK Regulation 2000/47, discussed further below, which grants absolute immunity to KFOR personnel in Kosovo, and absolves UNMIK and its staff from all liability arising out of acts of "operational necessity."[27]

III. OPERATIONALIZING IMMUNITY

While the UN is not technically a State party to the Convention, the UN takes the position that the Convention is the governing law on immunity issues when the UN is the governing authority, as in East Timor and Kosovo. Status of Forces agreements will also generally reiterate that the Immunities Convention applies to peacekeeping personnel of a particular mission.[28] A determination of whether or not immunity protections attach in a particular case will depend to some extent on the relationship of the specific individual to the United Nations.

A. Types of Immunity

1. Senior Staff – Diplomatic Immunity

The Special-Representative of the Secretary General (hereinafter SRSG) and his Deputies enjoy full diplomatic immunity in accordance with Article V Section 19 of the Immunities Convention.[29] While in recent years there has been a

---

25. For instance, the Dayton Agreement gave UNCIVPOL, who were part of the International Police Task Force, "absolute immunity from criminal jurisdiction." The General Framework Agreement for Peace in Bosnia and Herzegovina, Dec. 14, 1995, Annex 11, art. II, *available at* http://www.oscebih.org/essentials/gfap/eng/annex11.asp (last visited Aug. 19, 2002).

26. In addition, under the Immunities Convention, only the Security Council can waive the Secretary-General's immunity. Immunities Convention, *supra* note 18, art. V, sec. 20.

27. *On the Status, Privileges and Immunities of KFOR and UNMIK and their Personnel in Kosovo*, UNMIK Reg. No. 2000/47, U.N. Doc. UNMIK/REG/2000/47 (2000), *available at* http://www.unmikonline.org/regulations/2000/reg47-00.htm (last visited Aug. 19, 2002).

28. Even where a host state is not a party to the Convention. *See* Model SOFA, *supra* note 20, para. 15.

29. Immunities Convention, *supra* note 18. Under Article V, Section 17, the Secretary-General is empowered to extend full diplomatic immunity protections to other officials. In the case of Kosovo, UNMIK Reg. 2000/47 further empowers the UNMIK SRSG to extend diplomatic immunity to high-ranking officials at his discretion. *See* UNMIK Reg. 2000/47, *supra* note 27, sec. 3.2.

discernable trend in national. courts towards restricting absolute immunity to exclude criminal activities unrelated to the representative's official activities,[30] the ICJ recently refused to use a distinction between 'private' and 'official' acts to limit the scope of jurisdictional immunity of a Foreign Minister.[31] Therefore, the question of defining 'official' activity, so central to the debate on the scope of functional immunity, is less relevant where senior staff carrying UN diplomatic passports are the alleged perpetrators of a criminal act.

2. Peacekeepers – Absolute Immunity

Where peacekeeping forces are working within a 'blue-helmet' operation under the command and control of the United Nations, they would presumably be entitled to the immunity protections afforded other UN staff. As a practical matter, absolute immunity protections are usually included in Status of Forces agreements.[32] Under these agreements contributing countries are given exclusive jurisdiction to try members of their own armed forces. To remove any ambiguity about the status of KFOR personnel, UNMIK Regulation 2000/47 Section 2.4 explicitly granted the force absolute immunity.[33]

3. Civilian Staff – Functional Immunity

The vast majority of United Nations civilian personnel recruited by the Department of Peacekeeping Operations and deployed to the field enjoy only the limited immunity granted under Immunities Convention Article V Section 18. This includes all internationally recruited civilian professional staff. As 'experts on mission,' UNCIVPOL would be covered by the language of Section 22.[34] Since the purpose of immunity as articulated in the Convention is to protect the interests of the organization, a reasonable interpretation would allow the UN to invoke immunity on behalf of locally-recruited staff, as it has done on occasion.[35] Under the model SOFA, "locally recruited personnel" are protected by the Convention.[36] In a transitional administration context, where a large number of indigenous

---

30. *See generally* REINISCH, *supra* note 16; *see also* Michael Singer, *Jurisdictional Immunity of International Organizations: Human Rights and Functional Necessity Concerns*, 36 VA. J. INT'L L. 53 (1995).
31. *See* Arrest Warrant, *supra* note 11, para. 51, 55.
32. *See* Model SOFA, *supra* note 20, para. 47(b).
33. *Supra* note 27.
34. Under the model SOFA, both UNCIVPOL and civilian peacekeeping staff are considered 'experts.' *See* Model SOFA, *supra* note 20, at para. 26.
35. When the Secretary-General in his 1998 report found that the arrest of Rwandan UN staff violated their immunity protections, the Rwandan government protested that the report failed to note that some locally-recruited UN staff members had been involved in genocidal activities. Rwanda representative to the Fifth Committee Jeanne-Pierre Ubalijoro: "Had a genocidal mindset been a prerequisite for United Nations recruitment in Rwanda before the 1994 genocide?" Press Release, United Nations, Many UN Staff from Rwanda Currently Under Arrest are Suspected of Participating in 1994 Genocide, Fifth Committee Told (Dec. 7, 1998), U.N. Doc. GA/AB/3277 (1998), *available at* http://www.un.org/News/Press/docs/1998/19981207.gaab3277.htm.
36. *See* Model SOFA, *supra* note 20, at para. 46.

workers are under contract with the UN, the question becomes increasingly complex.[37]

4. The Organization

While the UN Charter Article 105 explicitly limits immunities to a functional necessity standard, the Immunities Convention seems to expand the organization's immunity. Under Article II section 2, the organization enjoys immunity from "every form of legal process" unless there is an express waiver. The Convention in essence undermines the functional necessity standard of the Charter by granting the organization absolute immunity from both civil and criminal suits. Therefore, in cases of suit against the organization itself, prosecution is only possible if immunity is waived by the SG. In addition, Article 20 and 23's duty to waive only seems to apply to waiver by the SG of the immunity of a UN official or expert, not the organization itself.[38]

B. The Scope of Functional Immunity

Whether a staff member is protected by immunity is likely to hinge on the interpretation of Charter Article 105's "necessary for the independent exercise of their functions," Immunities Convention Section 18's "in their official capacity," and Section 22's "course of the performance of their mission." An interpretation that makes any activity in the field *de facto* 'official' would offer the most rigorous protection. A narrower interpretation would provide protection only for those actions, which could reasonably be considered 'official' or 'necessary.'

The drafters of the Immunities Convention almost certainly intended protections to be broad. The Sixth Committee considered and rejected interpretations of Charter Article 105 that would narrow protections to those actions "indispensable to achieving the organization's purposes."[39] The Office of Legal

---

37. In East Timor, there was the additional complication of distinguishing between UNTAET local staff and ETTA (East Timorese Transitional Administration) staff, who worked under different contracts and whose salaries were funded from different sources. In Kosovo, Section 3.3 of UNMIK Reg. 2000/47 eliminates any ambiguity by inserting "including locally recruited personnel" in its articulation of UNMIK staff immunities. UNMIK Reg. 2000/47, *supra* note 27, sec. 3.3. Section 2.3 gives functional immunity to local staff in "tasks exclusively related to their services to KFOR." UNMIK Reg. 2000/47, *supra* note 27, sec. 2.3. The "exclusively" language seems to indicate a narrower protection for KFOR versus UNMIK local staff though it is difficult to discern what this difference might entail.

38. In practice, this may not be an insurmountable obstacle, since an individual defendant could be joined and the individual's actions imputed to the organization. Brower argues that the UN would have a good-faith responsibility to waive any unnecessary immunities. *See* Brower, *supra* note 23, at 31-33.

39. The most notable being the interpretation of the judge in Donnelly v. Ranollo, a case in the City Court of New Rochelle, New York, predating the Convention. The chauffer of then Secretary-General Trygve Lie was stopped for a speeding violation. Immunity was claimed based on Article 105 of the Charter. The Court interpreted the Charter language narrowly and held that immunity should only be granted to personnel "whose activities are such as to be necessary to the actual execution of the purposes and deliberations of the United Nations," a reading which did not include chauffers and

112   CONNECTICUT JOURNAL OF INT'L LAW   [Vol. 18:103]

Affairs has also rejected an interpretation of the Convention that would deny immunity protection where staff violated the Standard of Conduct of International Civil Servants by participating in political activity.[40] There is also reason to believe that the International Court of Justice would interpret the Convention's provisions to provide maximum protection. For instance, in *Mazilu*, the Court interpreted Article 105 of the Charter and Section 22 of the Convention as protecting all "tasks entrusted to the person" regardless of whether they occurred on an official mission.[41] This is consistent with the Court's conservative approach to diplomatic immunity generally.[42] Since maintaining international peace and security is a core function of the United Nations, general peacekeeping and peace-building related activities are both 'official' and 'necessary.'[43]

1. Who Decides What Constitutes 'Official Duties'?

While it is clear that the Secretary-General has the sole authority to waive immunity, it is not so clear whether the SG alone can make the determination of whether immunity initially applies. In *Cumaraswamy*, while affirming the authority of the Secretary-General to waive immunity when it applies, the ICJ stated that the SG "has the <u>primary</u> responsibility and authority to assess whether its agents . . . acted within the scope of their functions."[44] Nonetheless, the Court indicated that the SG's determination is "pivotal" and that a national court could only set aside

---

household servants at all. Westchester County v. Ranollo, 67 N.Y.S.2d 31, 35 (New Rochelle City Ct. 1946). Notably, the Court also cited the fact that while diplomats who claim immunity are subject to trial and punishment in their home country, the United Nations does not have a tribunal to punish its own personnel who are protected by immunity. *See id.* at 34. The Sixth Committee took the case into account when making recommendations on the draft of the 1946 Convention.

40. In 1998, when the government of Ethiopia requested that locally recruited Eritrean UN staff accused of spying leave the country, the Office of Legal Affairs made it clear that any action against those staff would be a violation of UN privileges and immunities. *See* Press Release, United Nations, System Rewarding Merit, Achievement to Replace Seniority-Based Advancement Assistant Secretary-General for Human Resources tells Fifth Committee (Dec. 1, 1998), U.N. Doc. GA/AB/3275 (1998), *available at* http://www.un.org/News/Press/docs/1998/19981201.gaab3275.html. Ethiopia claimed that the staff in question were spying on behalf of Eritrean clandestine networks and that privileges and immunities did not apply when the members' activities violated the Standard of Conduct in International Civil Service ban on political activities. Press Release, *supra* note 35, *available at* http://www.un.org/News/Press/docs/1998/19981207.gaab3277.htm.

41. Mazilu, *supra* note 21.

42. In the Arrest Warrant case, the Court held that the threat of any criminal prosecution would be an impediment to the performance of a Minister's 'official functions,' and therefore violate his immunity protections under both treaty law and customary international law. *See* Arrest Warrant, *supra* note 11, para. 51-55.

43. The rhetoric of the judge in the opening quotation notwithstanding, even US Courts have recognized peacekeeping in general as constituting an 'official act' protected by immunity. In one case, a federal court refused to exercise jurisdiction over a claim against the UN in the peacekeeping context, stating that the UN enjoyed immunity from suit, and even if it did not enjoy absolute immunity, peacekeeping activities including the repossession of land, constituted official action. Abdi Hosh Askir v. Boutros-Ghali, 933 F. Supp. 368, 372 (S.D.N.Y. 1996).

44. Press Communiqué 99/16, International Court of Justice, Difference Relating to Immunity from Legal Process of a Special Rapporteur of the Commission on Human Rights (April 26, 1999), *available at* http://www.icj-cij.org/icjwww/ipresscom/iPress1999/ipresscom9916_inuma_19990429.htm.

those findings "for the most compelling reasons."[45] While this arguably creates a presumption in favor of the SG's findings,[46] it leaves open the possibility of a determination by a delegate of the SG, the Security Council, or the court. In practice, judicial determinations of the 'official duties' question are increasingly common, and in some countries, required.[47]

2. Can a Serious Human Rights Violation Constitute 'Official' Action?

Despite current practice in the field (examined below), involvement in serious crimes does not seem to constitute a *per se* 'unofficial' act. Recent ICJ jurisprudence indicates that there has not yet developed a customary international law 'exception' to jurisdictional immunity even in cases of gross human rights violations if an alternative forum for prosecution exists or may exist in the future.[48] In addition, cases implicating serious human rights violations are not necessarily clear-cut. For instance, an UNMIK staff member was accused of participating in genocide by separating Hutus from Tutsis while on security duty and officially charged with organizing the evacuation of the UN compound in Rwanda.[49] In any case, the Special Committee on Peacekeeping Operations and the Secretary-General's office have indicated that when a person is accused of having committed "gross misconduct," or an act of child abuse, an investigation should be conducted.[50]

C. *The Duty to Waive*

---

45.   Cumaraswamy, *supra* note 21, para. 50, 61.
46.   *See* Brower, *supra* note 23, at 52.
47.   In his recent study, August Reinisch documents in detail, and on a global scale, the growing role of the judiciary in the interpretation of functional immunities of international organizations. *See generally* REINISCH, *supra* note 16. For instance, the American Foreign Sovereign Immunities Act makes a federal court's determination on immunity binding on the State Department. *See* Jerrold L. Mallory, *Resolving the Confusion over Head of State Immunity: The Defined Rights of Kings*, 86 COLUM. L. REV. 169, 169 (1986). On the other hand, under the United States International Organizations Immunities Act of December 29, 1945, the privileges and immunities of UN workers can be withheld, withdrawn, conditioned or limited by Executive Order of the President. *See* United States International Organizations Immunities Act, Pub. L. No. 291-79, Title I (1945), *available at* http://www.un.int/usa/host_io.htm (last visited Sept. 16, 2002).
48.   While the ICJ in the Arrest Warrant case phrased the opinion narrowly to address the issue of the absolute immunity of an incumbent Foreign Minister before a national court, the Court was unwilling to recognize a customary international law norm denying 'official immunity' protections in the case of serious crimes. Arrest Warrant, *supra* note 11, para. 58. Importantly, the judgment distinguishes between jurisdictional and substantive immunity, stating "Jurisdictional immunity may well bar prosecution for a certain period or for certain offenses; it cannot exonerate the person to whom it applies from all criminal responsibility." *Id.* at para. 60.
49.   *See infra* note 76.
50.   Regardless of the civilian or military status of the personnel involved. *See Report of the Special Committee on Peacekeeping Operations on Comprehensive review of the whole question of peacekeeping operations in all their aspects*, U.N. GAOR, 54th Sess., Agenda Item 90, para. 66, U.N. Doc A/54/839 (2000) [hereinafter *Comprehensive review*]; *see also Report of the Secretary-General on Children and armed conflict*, U.N. SCOR, 56th Sess., Item 127 of the Provisional Agenda, para. 36-37, U.N. Doc. A/56/342-S/2001/852 (2001) [hereinafter *Children and armed conflict*].

Even where the SG has made a determination that a particular act constitutes 'official' duty and is covered by functional immunity protections, there remains the question of waiver. Under the Immunities Convention Sections 20 and 23, the SG is under a duty to waive when, *in his opinion,* failure to do so would *impede justice* without *prejudicing the interests* of the UN. Some hold that international human rights law constitutes a "superior norm" to the law on immunity of international organizations, and as a consequence, waiver is required in all cases of serious human rights violations.[51] Others set the threshold lower, arguing that the UN is under a good faith obligation "not to interfere with the normal judicial processes of member states unless necessary to maintain the integrity of its operations."[52] While there has been no comprehensive statement from the SG's office about when waiver is *obligatory,* recent rhetoric in SG reports and in the General Assembly, and recent practice in the field suggest that in cases of "serious breaches" of international law, refusal to waive immunity would violate Sections 20 and 23.[53] A failure to waive in such a case is in theory reviewable by the ICJ, but unlikely given the Court's deference to the SG in *Cumaraswamy.*

D. *Determining the Underlying Facts – Boards of Inquiry*

The SG has indicated that in certain serious cases an investigation is required, and that waiver in child abuse cases is obligatory, when an internal investigation has determined that the accused is "guilty."[54] Clearly, with so much discretion wielded by the SG in immunity matters, the actual facts of each particular case could have an enormous influence on waiver or scope of immunity decisions. In the context of a transitional administration, where the judicial system is dysfunctional, or under UN-supervision, an investigation into the underlying facts of an allegation are most often conducted by a UN-convened Board of Inquiry (hereinafter BOI).

A BOI generally consists of a small number of international staff appointed by a civilian commissioner.[55] When the accused is an UNCIVPOL or professional staff member, a BOI may make a recommendation about immunity to the SRSG who, if the facts warrant, would pass that finding on to the Secretary-General.[56] In the past, when military personnel have been implicated, UN practice has been to

---

51. Singer, *supra* note 30, at 94.
52. Brower, *supra* note 23, at 73.
53. When the draft of the Chemical Weapons Convention was circulated in the General Assembly, at least one working paper pointed out that the absence of a duty to waive in the case of 'serious breaches' would be inconsistent with international law. *See Working Paper submitted by Japan,* U.N. GAOR, 3d Sess., sec. II 2 (2), U.N. Doc. BWC/AD HOC GROUP/WP.52 (1995), *available at* http://www.bradford.ac.uk/acad/sbtwc/ahg29wp/wp052.pdf (last visited Sept. 5, 2002).
54. *See Children and armed conflict, supra* note 50, para. 36.
55. If military personnel are involved, it must include a representative from the military police of the contingent of which the alleged perpetrator is a member, bearing in mind "the desirability of justice being done in all such cases." *Comprehensive review, supra* note 50, para. 66.
56. The model SOFA reads "If the accused person is a member of the civilian component or a civilian member of the military component, the Special Representative/Commander shall conduct any necessary supplementary inquiry and then agree with the Government whether or not criminal proceedings should be instituted." Model SOFA, *supra* note 20, para. 47(a).

leave all investigation to the national contingent command.[57] However, the Special Committee has recently indicated that because it is "the responsibility of the head of mission to ensure that personnel under his or her command behave in accordance [with] United Nations codes of conduct," the SRSG has the authority to form a board of inquiry "if warranted," and make a recommendation about immunity or repatriation to the Department of Peacekeeping Operations, which will follow-up with the member state.[58]

E. 'Appropriate Modes of Settlement' – Ombudsperson

Once the Organization conducts an investigation, makes a determination that functional immunity protections apply, and refuses to waive immunity, there remains the question of whether an alternative forum is available to resolve the dispute. Section 29 of the Convention calls for an "appropriate mode of settlement" in disputes "of a private law character to which the United Nations is a party," and those "involving any official of the United Nations who by reason of his official position enjoys immunity, if immunity has not been waived by the Secretary-General."[59] This has been read to require the United Nations to provide for some separate forum in which the dispute can be resolved when a staff member is accused of criminal or tortious activity.[60] This is consistent with international jurisprudence on diplomatic law generally. In *Arrest Warrant*, the availability of an alternative forum was a significant factor in the Court's upholding of jurisdictional immunity.[61] The European Court of Human Rights has also held that "a reasonable alternative means" of protecting a right is a "material factor" in determining the permissibility

---

57. The national contingent command has "the sole authority" to take disciplinary action *See Comprehensive review, supra* note 50, para. 65-66. The model SOFA reads "Military members of the military component of the United Nations peace-keeping operation shall be subject to the exclusive jurisdiction of their respective participating States in respect of any criminal offences which may be committed by them." Model SOFA, *supra* note 20, para. 47(b). The SG has also requested that troop contributing nations inform the Secretariat of the steps taken to investigate and prosecute personnel alleged to have violated international humanitarian law. *Report of the Secretary-General on Children and armed conflict,* U.N. SCOR, 55th Sess., Item 112 of the Provisional Agenda, Recommendation 37, U.N. Doc. A/55/163-S/2000/712 (2000); *Report of the Secretary-General to the Security Council on the Protection of Civilians in Armed Conflict,* Recommendation 32, U.N. Doc. S/1999/957 (1999), *available at* http://www.reliefweb.int/library/documents/civilian.html (last visited Aug. 19, 2002) [hereinafter *Protection of Civilians*].

58. *Report of the Secretary-General on Implementation of the recommendations of the Special Committee on Peacekeeping Operations,* U.N. GAOR, 54th Sess., Agenda Item 90, para. 16, U.N. Doc. A/54/670 (2000). In at least one incident in East Timor, a Board of Inquiry was formed by the SRSG to investigate allegations of child abuse by Jordanian peacekeeping forces, rather than leave the issue in the hands of the Jordanian contingent. *See* Daily Briefing, UNTAET, Investigation Launched Into Alleged PKF Sexual Misconduct (August 3, 2001), *available at* http://www.un.org/peace/etimor/DB/d b030801.htm; *see also Allegations against Jordanian peacekeepers* (Australian Broadcasting Corporation, June 25, 2001), *available at* http://www.abc.net.au/am/s317953.htm.

59. Article 29 comes into play *after* a request for a waiver has been denied. Therefore, establishment of an alternative dispute mechanism does not release the SG from the duty to waive under Sections 20 and 23. There are indications, however, that the Office of Legal Affairs interprets Article 29 as an alternative to the duty to waive. For a full discussion, *see* Brower, *supra* note 23, at 72.

60. *Id.* at 70.

61. *See* Arrest Warrant, *supra* note 11, para. 61.

116 CONNECTICUT JOURNAL OF INT'L LAW [Vol. 18:103

of immunity.[62] In the context of a peacekeeping operation, and particularly a transitional administration with a UN-run judiciary, the provision of an alternative forum becomes a key issue, which may have implications for the legality of staff immunities in general.

Partly in response to growing concerns about abuses by UN staff and the lack of transparency of UN field missions generally, Ombudsperson offices have been the main vehicle established at the mission level to resolve claims of abuse.[63] In recent years, both the SG[64] and DPKO's Lessons Learned Unit[65] have consistently recommended the establishment of an Ombudsperson office as an essential part of current and future missions. In theory, these institutions ensure that the mission as a whole acts in a way that is consistent with its mandate, and with international human rights standards generally.[66] The offices in both Kosovo and East Timor became focal points where local citizens lodged complaints of unfair treatment or discriminatory policy. However, a lack of enforcement power and material support at the mission level have made the Ombudsperson an ineffective institution.[67] Like a Board of Inquiry, the Ombudsperson lacks enforcement power as its findings are only recommendations to the SRSG, or peacekeeping command.[68] Whether the

---

62. *See* Waite and Kennedy v. F.R.G. [GC], App. No. 26083/94, Eur. Ct. H.R. 1999-I, para. 68 (1999).

63. The Lessons Learned Unit in its evaluation of UNOSOM found that the lack of transparency and non-existence of a complaints mechanism led to the perception among the local population that mission personnel were above the law. *See The Comprehensive Report on Lessons Learned from United Nations Operation in Somalia (UNOSOM), April 1992 – March 1995*, Dept. of Peacekeeping Operations, para. 57, *available at* http://www.un.org/Depts/dpko/lessons/account.htm (last visited Aug. 19, 2002).

64. In a 1999 report, the SG recommended that the Security Council "[s]upport a public 'ombudsman' within all peacekeeping operations to deal with complaints from the general public . . . and establish an ad hoc fact-finding commission, as necessary, to examine reports on alleged breaches of international humanitarian and human rights law . . . ." *Protection of Civilians, supra* note 57, Recommendation 31.

65. *See UNOSOM, supra* note 63; *see also Multidisciplinary Peacekeeping: Lessons From Recent Experience*, Dept. of Peacekeeping Operations, Ch. O, para. 2, *available at* http://www.un.org/Depts/dpko/lessons/handbuk.htm (last visited Sept. 4, 2002).

66. Under UNMIK Reg. 2000/38, the Ombudspersons Institution in Kosovo was given a broad mandate but no enforcement power. *See On the Establishment of the Ombudsperson Insitution in Kosovo*, UNMIK Reg. No. 2000/38, U.N. Doc. UNMIK/REG/2000/38 (2000), *available at* http://www.unmikonline.org/regulations/2000/reg38-00.htm (last visited Aug. 8, 2002) [hereinafter UNMIK Reg. 2000/38]. Its mandate was "to investigate and mediate complaints from individuals, groups and organizations about possible abuses of power by international and local authorities . . . giv[ing] particular priority to allegations of severer [sic] or systematic violations and those based on discrimination." Press Release, UNMIK, Polish Human Rights Lawyer Appointed as Ombudsperson (July 12, 2000), U.N. Doc. UNMIK/PR 289, *available at* http://www.unmikonline.org/press/press/pr 289.html.

67. The establishment of an Ombudsperson was considered by UNTAET as early as Winter 2000. A draft regulation tabled by the Human Rights Unit which empowered the Ombudsperson to overturn administrative decisions that violated international human rights law was rejected by the SRSG's office. An Ombudsperson was finally appointed in the Spring of 2001. After his arrival in Dili, however, the Cabinet decided not to promulgate a public regulation establishing an independent office (as in Kosovo). Instead, restrictive terms of reference were set forth by the SRSG. Personal communication, UNTAET staff.

68. UNMIK Reg. 2000/38 makes clear that the office of the Ombudsperson is not a court, and while the office may intervene with authorities and recommend the suspension of administrative

institution of the Ombudsperson can satisfy the requirements of Article 29 will be an important element when evaluating the lawfulness of broad staff immunity protections in the context of transitional administration.

The paper will now examine the ways in which the UN has dealt with the misbehavior of peacekeeping staff and with issues of immunity in Kosovo and East Timor in order to determine how actual practice conforms or diverges from the current state of the law and policy.

IV. IMMUNITY AND ACCOUNTABILITY IN TRANSITIONAL ADMINISTRATIONS

With the possible exception of UNTEA in the early 1960s,[69] it has been only slightly more than a decade that the United Nations Department of Peacekeeping Operations has been engaged in transitional governance operations. In the early 1990s, under a Chapter VI Security Council mandate, UNTAC was given the responsibility to maintain law and order and establish a civil administration in Cambodia.[70] The mission to Cambodia set the stage for the subsequent establishment of the Chapter VII mandated transitional administrations in Kosovo and East Timor in 1999.

In their initial stages, both UNMIK and UNTAET, as governing authorities, wielded absolute legislative, police and judicial power. The Legal Affairs section of the mission drafted new regulations, UNCIVPOL enforced the regulations, and international judges on UN salaries applied the regulations in court. The Chapter VII Security Council resolutions and UN regulations establishing the framework for each of those missions granted the Special Representative of the Secretary-General vast powers, including the power to enact, amend and repeal laws.[71] Even in the later stages of these missions, after indigenous consultative bodies had been elected

---

decisions, its power ultimately rests in the ability to make recommendations to the SRSG. *See generally* UNMIK Reg. 2000/38, *supra* note 66. The Ombudsperson can recommend that an administrative decision be suspended only where there is a danger of "irreparable prejudice." *Id.* sec. 4.6. If these recommendations are ignored without good reason, the office's only recourse is to "draw the Special Representative of the Secretary-General's attention to the matter." *Id.* sec. 4.11. The SRSG can refuse the Ombudsperson access to UN files. *Id.* sec. 4.7. And the SRSG may remove the Ombudsperson for such ambiguous reasons as "failure in the execution of his or her functions" and "having been placed . . . in a position incompatible with the due exercise of his or her functions." *Id.* sec. 8.2.

69.   In 1962, the General Assembly ratified an agreement between Indonesia and the Netherlands, which established the United Nations Temporary Executive Authority (UNTEA). The UN authority attempted to administer the western half of New Guinea, pending a transfer of power from the Dutch to the Indonesian government. *See Agreement Between the Republic of Indonesia and the Kingdom of the Netherlands Concerning West New Guinea (West Irian) / West Papua*, August 15, 1962, *available at* http://www.koteka.net/nyag.htm.

70.   *See* S.C. Res. 745, U.N. SCOR, 47th Sess., 3057th mtg., U.N. Doc. S/RES/745 (1992).

71.   "[T]he Transitional Administrator, will . . . have the power to enact new laws and regulations and to amend, suspend, or repeal existing ones." S.C. Res. 1272, U.N. SCOR, 54th Sess., 4057th mtg., para. 6, U.N. Doc. S/RES/1272 (1999). "All legislative and executive authority with respect to Kosovo, including the administration of the judiciary, is vested in UNMIK and is exercised by the Special Representative of the Secretary-General." UNMIK Regulation No. 1999/1, U.N. Doc. UNMIK REG/1999/1 (1999), *available at* http://www.unmikonline.org/regulations/1999/reg01-99.htm. Security Council Resolution 1244 authorized the establishment of UNMIK. *See* S.C. Res. 1244, U.N. SCOR, 54th Session, 4011th mtg., U.N. Doc. S/RES/1244 (1999).

118   *CONNECTICUT JOURNAL OF INT'L LAW*   [Vol. 18:103

and local courts set up, the SRSG still maintained a veto power over legislative and judicial decisions. The expansive powers of UNMIK and UNTAET present special problems for the issue of immunity, which we will explore after briefly examining idiosyncrasies in the law and practice of both missions.

A. Law: Immunity According To UNMIK and UNTAET

The issue of the scope of immunity was directly and publicly confronted in Kosovo when on August 18, 2000, UNMIK SRSG Bernard Kouchner signed into law Regulation 2000/47 On the Status, Privileges and Immunities of KFOR and UNMIK and their Personnel in Kosovo. The regulation gave all international KFOR personnel absolute immunity (2.4), extended absolute immunity to the SRSG and the four DSRSGs (3.2), and empowered the SRSG to further extend absolute immunity to other high-ranking officials. Section 3.3 gave functional immunity to both international and local UNMIK personnel, removing any ambiguity about the status of local UN employees. The regulation granted the UN complete immunity from suit where a repossession or injury arises out of 'operational necessity.' Section 2.4 gave exclusive jurisdiction over disputes with KFOR to the sending state of the KFOR person in question. Where UNMIK personnel are involved, Section 7 granted exclusive jurisdiction over any claims which reach the 'operational necessity' standard to a then-non-existent Claims Commission.[72]

Unlike UNMIK, UNTAET did not promulgate a regulation defining the privileges and immunities of UNTAET staff. However, the Principal Legal Advisor to the SRSG of UNTAET has indicated that the Convention on the Privileges and Immunities of the United Nations applies fully to the staff of UNTAET, and therefore, all staff members have, at the very least, a functional immunity from criminal process in the courts of East Timor, and are immune from arrest by either UNCIVPOL or the Timorese police force.[73]

B. Practice: Under What Circumstances has Immunity been Waived, Invoked or Denied?

An examination of several instances in which immunity has been at issue in Kosovo and East Timor indicates that the UN is likely to waive or deny immunity protections to individual staff members when they are implicated in serious human rights violations or other serious crimes. In contrast, both UNMIK and UNTAET

---

72.   Other relevant provisions include the following: Sections 4.1 and 4.2 give UNMIK contractors functional immunity in matters related to their contracts. UNMIK Reg. No. 2000/47, *supra* note 27. A separate UNMIK regulation granted similar immunities to representatives of the World Bank, who under Section 6.1 are to enjoy immunities "not less favourable than those accorded to officials of comparable rank of other international organizations." *On the Privileges and Immunities of the World Bank Group and it's Officials in Kosovo*, UNMIK Reg. No. 2000/44, U.N. Doc. UNMIK/REG/2000/44 (2000), *available at* http://www.unmikonline.org/regulations/2000/reg44-00.htm (last visited Aug. 19, 2002). Under Section 7.2, requests for waiver should be addressed to the President of the World Bank by the SRSG. *Id.*

73.   Personal communication, UNTAET official.

have invoked or threatened to invoke immunity where there was a question of whether the rights of Timorese or Kosovar citizens have systematically been violated as a consequence of the implementation of mission policy.

1. Serious Crimes

In both Kosovo and East Timor, UN staff have been denied immunity protections after evidence of involvement in serious crimes has come to light. In Kosovo, while there have been a number of complaints of unlawful property damage, sexual harassment and embezzlement, immunity has been waived where murder, rape or genocide has been involved. [74] Similarly, in East Timor, two of the three cases of waiver examined here involved rape and child sexual abuse.

In Kosovo, in the past year, UNCIVPOL accused of rape in Mitrovica and murder in Pristina have had immunity protections waived. [75] In a high profile case, an UNMIK staff member was denied immunity after allegations had emerged of his possible involvement in the Rwandan genocide. [76] He was eventually turned over to Supreme Court of Kosovo, which ruled that there was insufficient evidence to extradite him to Rwanda for trial. [77] According to UNMIK staff, there was serious

---

74. The determination of what constitutes a 'serious crime' has been controversial. One UNMIK staff member felt that at least 10 allegations against UNCIVPOL should have resulted in a denial of immunity. Personal communication, UNMIK staff.

75. Personal communication, UNMIK staff.

76. On April 11, 2001, a Rwandan computer specialist working for the United Nations Development Program (UNDP) in Kosovo was arrested by UNCIVPOL following allegations that he had been an informant for the Interahamwe during the Rwandan Genocide in 1994. Although the allegations emerged while Mbarushimana was working for the UN in Rwanda, he continued his contract there, and completed a subsequent contract in Angola. He was finally transferred to UNDP in Kosovo, where he was posted as a Unit Chief. Measures seem to have been taken by the UN only after the Rwandan government requested Mbarushimana's extradition, nearly seven years after the alleged acts took place. The Secretary-General waived Mbarushimana's immunity. *See* UNWIRE, *Rwanda: War Crimes Suspect, A UN Employee, Arrested in Kosovo* (April 13, 2001), at 19, *available at* http://www.unfoundation.org/unwire/archives/UNWIRE010413.asp#19; United Nations Daily Highlights, Highlights from the Noon Briefing by the Spokesman of the Secretary-General, *Rwandan UN Staffer Arrested in Kosovo on Murder Allegations* (April 16, 2001), *available at* http://www.hri.org/news/world/undh/2001/01-04-16.undh.html; UN Forum, *Rwanda suspect in Kosovo operation: Who helped him?* (April 25, 2001), *available at* http://www.unforum.com/Unarchivesinsid er10.htm; United Nations Daily Highlights, Highlights from the Noon Briefing by the Spokesman of the Secretary-General, *Rwandan UN Staffer Arrested in Kosovo on Murder Allegations* (April 19, 2001), *available at* http://www.hri.org/news/world/undh/2001/01-04-19.undh.html.

77. On June 6, 2001, a Danish judge recommended to the Supreme Court of Kosovo that the extradition request be denied. On June 19, the Court, composed of international and Kosovar judges, rejected the request and made a recommendation to the SRSG that Mbarushimana be released. The Court based its decision on three factors. Firstly, it found that the Rwandan prosecutor's office did not set forth sufficient evidence to establish that Mbarushimana had been responsible for any act of violence. Secondly, the Court found that the Rwandan government's promise that Mbarushimana would not be subject to the death penalty was an insufficient guarantee as a matter of law; and thirdly, that there was a likelihood that Mbarushimana would be subject to torture and inhumane treatment if turned over to the Rwandan authorities. Mbarushimana was subsequently released. *See* Thierry Cruvellier, *Instruction au Kosovo*, DIPLOMATIE JUDICIARE, May 15, 2001, *available at* http://www.diplomatiejudiciare.com/Rwanda/Mbarushimana1.html; Thierry Cruvellier, *Entre la Liberte et le TPIR*, DIPLOMATIE JUDICIARE, June 9, 2001, *available at* http://www.diplomatiejudiciare

disagreement over whether a waiver was necessary. Although the question eventually went to the SG's office, senior UNMIK staff were confused as to whether the activity was beyond the protection of immunity, or whether immunity was waived. A similar controversy over the necessity of waiver was subsequently debated in the case of an Egyptian UNCIVPOL arrested for murder.[78]

In East Timor, the issue of immunity first arose in the fall of 2000 when a Finnish civilian staff member killed a 72 year-old Timorese woman in a hit-and-run car accident. UNTAET's initial refusal to waive immunity led to a heated discussion in the Timorese consultative body, the National Council,[79] over whether immunity for UN staff was compatible with the principles of accountability that UNTAET had been teaching Timorese civil-servants-to-be. Shortly afterward, the SRSG announced that the man's immunity would be lifted, though he was subsequently released and allowed to return to Finland.[80] In July 2000, when two Jordanian UNCIVPOL were arrested for allegedly raping an East Timorese woman employed as a cleaner in a hotel in the Timorese capital of Dili, the SRSG, one day after the arrest, announced that the officers would not enjoy immunity from legal process and would be tried in East Timorese courts.[81] After a BOI investigation, the SRSG decided that rape could not be construed as an 'official' or 'necessary' act and that consequently, a waiver from the SG was unnecessary because immunity did not attach.[82] On August 21, 2001, the officers were indicted by the East Timor Prosecutor General.[83] In June 2001, when allegations emerged that Jordanian peacekeepers in the enclave of Oecussi had been involved in child sexual abuse, the

.com/Rwanda/Mbarushimana3.htm; *Kosovo Court Refuses to Extradite Genocide Suspect*, UN INTEGRATED REGIONAL INFORMATION NETWORKS, June 21, 2001, *available at* http://allafrica.com/stories/200106210010.html.

78.   Personal communication, UNMIK staff.

79.   The National Council was a proto-parliamentary body set up by UNTAET consisting of 33 Timorese, including representatives from various 'interest' groups (including NGOs, women, labor, and each of the political parties). *See* Daily Briefing, UNTAET, Transfer of Political Responsibilities (May 30, 2000), *available at* http://www.un.org/peace/etimor/DB/DB300500.HTM. For a summary and analysis of the development of consultative bodies in East Timor, see Joel C. Beauvais, *Benevolent Despotism: A Critique of U.N. State-Building in East Timor*, 33 N.Y.U. J. INT'L L. & POL. 1101 (2001).

80.   Following the accident, the staff member was placed in police custody and his laissez-passer was confiscated. When he did not show up for a hearing scheduled in Dili district court on January 10, 2001, it was discovered that he had actually left the country. Somehow, reported a police spokesman, he had been released from prison, had his passport returned to him, and been boarded on a flight out of Dili. According to one press report, the staff member held a going away party at the airport before his departure. *See* Finnish hit-and-run driver flees East Timor, THE INDEP., January 23, 2001, *available at* http://www.independent.co.uk/story.jsp?story=51738.

81.   A spokesman for the Secretary-General in New York subsequently explained that the SG would waive the immunity of the UNCIVPOL, and that because they were not peacekeepers, he could do so without the approval of the Jordanian government. *See U.N. policeman charged with rape in East Timor*, AGENCE FRANCE-PRESSE, August 24, 2001, *available at* 2001 WL 24997447.

82.   This decision came only after an internal debate within the mission, in which sections argued that the UNCIVPOL were covered by the Convention's immunity provisions during their entire time on mission, that immunity protection is not contingent on the nature of the particular act in question, and that the arrests were therefore unlawful. Personal communication, UNTAET staff.

83.   *See* Two UN Police Officers Detained in Connection with Rape, *supra* note 3; Daily Briefing, UNTAET, Jordanian Civilian Police Indicted on Rape Charges (August 24, 2001), http://www.un.org/peace/etimor/DB/db240801.htm.

SRSG formed a BOI,[84] which eventually made a recommendation that legal action be taken against the soldiers.[85]

2. Institutional Abuse

In contrast, when the UN administration itself has been implicated in wrongdoing, both UNTAET and UNMIK have invoked or threatened to invoke immunity. UNMIK has threatened to invoke immunity protections to protect UNMIK police accused of trafficking in women and soliciting prostitutes.[86] KFOR has also invoked the immunity granted under Regulation 2000/47 in cases involving the confiscation of property and the impounding of vehicles.[87] Officials from the Political Affairs section of UNTAET intimated that UNTAET would invoke immunity to claims against UNTAET in the Dili district court.[88]

Issues of institutional immunity from suit have emerged in both East Timor and Kosovo in the context of land dispossession. In Kosovo, both KFOR and UNMIK have been responsible for the destruction and the repossession of privately-owned buildings and parcels of land. An early regulation took the issue of property re-possession out of the jurisdiction of local courts even before the promulgation of Regulation 2000/47, leaving no venue at all in which to claim that property had been re-possessed unlawfully.[89] In East Timor, UNTAET assigned development rights to public land without any significant consultation with the public and without a mechanism of appeal or petition for those who felt that they had been dispossessed. UNTAET eventually abandoned plans to establish an elaborate system of land courts in favor of an ad hoc system of granting long-term leases, which gave UN administrators enormous discretion in resolving land disputes.[90]

The practice of issuing executive orders of detention has also been widely criticized as violative of international human rights standards.[91] Kosovar citizens

84. In accordance with the protocol set forth in the last section of this paper, the Board of Inquiry consisted of one representative from the Jordanian battalion and two non-Jordanian PKF investigators and reported directly to the Secretariat in New York. Personal communication, UNTAET staff.

85. Mark Dodd, *UN troops face sex counts*, THE AGE, August 4, 2001, *available at* http://www.theage.com.au/news/world/2001/08/04/FFXA5FOUWPC.html. As discussed earlier in the paper, such civilian-led Boards of Inquiry are unusual. In fact, in early 2001, when allegations that Jordanian peacekeepers in Oecussi first arose, the Jordanian contingent command was asked to conduct an investigation, in accordance with traditional practice, ultimately sending one soldier home. *Id.*

86. Personal communication, UNMIK staff.

87. *Id.*

88. Personal communication, UNTAET staff.

89. NORWEGIAN REFUGEE COUNCIL, REPORT OF JUNE 7, 2001, at 8-9, *available at* http://www.db.idpproject.org/Sites/idpSurvey.nsf/wViewSingleEnv/E4AAEF766FFB579CC1256A7A0 0505393/$file/NRC+Statement+7+June+2001.pdf.

90. This often disadvantaged indigenous land owners and returning refugees vis-à-vis more influential constituencies, such as businesses related to the Portuguese military, Australian entrepreneurs, and comparatively wealthy Timorese émigrés from Portugal, Mozambique, Australia and elsewhere. *See* Masalah Tanah, *Daur Ulang Warisan Kolonial*, TALITAKUM, October 4-11, 2000, at 12.

91. Amnesty International, the OSCE Legal Systems Monitoring Section in Kosovo (LSMS) and the Ombudsperson's office all condemned UNMIK's practice of issuing executive orders of detention.

122   **CONNECTICUT JOURNAL OF INT'L LAW**   [Vol. 18:103

could not challenge the orders or seek compensation in Kosovo courts because under Regulation 2000/47's 'operational necessity' standard, those courts did not have jurisdiction. In the *Gashi* case, three Kosovar men were detained under an Executive Order issued by the SRSG even after a panel of international judges ordered their release.[92] After more than a year, all charges were dropped, the men were released and the UNMIK Claims Commission made an undisclosed offer of compensation.[93] East Timor's first criminal procedure code similarly came under fire for allowing the SRSG to detain a suspect for an unlimited period of pre-trial detention.[94] An ineffective Ombudsperson Office was the only avenue by which an unlawfully detained Timorese or the family of someone who died in detention could seek redress.

In response to issues such as executive detention and particularly, property dispossession, the Ombudsperson in Kosovo, Marek Antoni Nowicki, released a report highly critical of the immunities granted by Regulation 2000/47.[95] The report found the regulation incompatible with current human rights standards in that it failed to "protect the individual against arbitrary exercises of governmental authority and the provision of adequate control by independent legislative and/ or judicial authorities over the exercise of powers by the executive."[96] The Ombudsperson found the regulation violative of a number of provisions of the

---

See Amnesty International, *Amnesty International calls for an end to Executive Orders of detention,* AI Index # EUR 70/017/2001 (Aug. 3, 2001), *at* http://web.amnesty.org/802568F7005C4453/print/EUR7 00172001?OpenDocument; Organisation for Security and Co-operation in Europe Legal Systems Monitoring Section in Kosovo, *Kosovo: A Review of the Criminal Justice System: Sept. 1, 2000 – Feb. 28, 2001,* at 17, 80, *available at* http://www.osce.org/kosovo/documents/reports/justice/criminal_ justice2.pdf (last visited Sept. 23, 2002) [hereinafter Organisation for Security and Co-operation in Europe]; OMBUDSPERSON INSTITUTION IN KOSOVO, SPECIAL REPORT NO. 3 ON THE CONFORMITY OF DEPRIVATIONS OF LIBERTY UNDER 'EXECUTIVE ORDERS' WITH RECOGNIZED INTERNATIONAL STANDARDS (June 29, 2001), *available at* http://www.osce.org/kosovo/documents/reports/justice/ report3.pdf [hereinafter SPECIAL REPORT NO. 3].

92.   In October 1999, three men, Lulzim, Bajram and Agim Gashi, were arrested by KFOR. The "Gashis" were detained for the 12 month period of pre-indictment detention allowed under UNMIK Reg. 1999/26. It was not until October 2000 that the investigative judge handed the case file over to the prosecutor's office at which time the prosecutor asked for a further extension. The investigative judge claimed that the reason for the delay was that he was waiting for prosecutors at the International Criminal Tribunal for the Former Yugoslavia (ICTY) to disclose evidence. The ICTY stated that they had never received a request for evidence in the case. A panel of international judges in Pristina ordered the Gashis to be released after finding insufficient evidence to hold them. The SRSG's office extended their detention by executive order after which the Ombudsperson's office recommended that the SRSG stop issuing executive orders of detention. The Legal Systems Monitoring Section also found that the Gashi detention violated the right to trial within a reasonable time as guaranteed under the European Convention of Human Rights, Article 5(3). *See* Organisation for Security and Co-operation in Europe, *supra* note 91, at 80; *see also* SPECIAL REPORT NO. 3, *supra* note 91.

93.   Organisation for Security and Co-operation in Europe, *supra* note 91, at 84-85.

94.   *On Transitional Rules of Criminal Procedure,* UNTAET Reg. No. 2000/30, U.N. Doc. UNTAET/REG/2000/30 (2000). A delegation of lawyers from Australia declared that the document was "inconsistent with the [sic] UN's human rights code and could be used as an instrument of oppression." Mark Dodd, *UN Legal Code Abysmal: Lawyers,* SYDNEY MORNING HERALD, June 7, 2000, at 12, *available at* 2000 WL 21026056. Amnesty International also found that the code violated international human rights standards. *See* Amnesty International, *East Timor: Justice past, present and future,* AI Index # ASA 57/001/2001, sec. 5.5 (July 2001).

95.   *See* OMBUDSPERSON INSTITUTION IN KOSOVO, *supra* note 2.

96.   *Id.* at para. 27.

European Convention on Human Rights, including Article 6 guaranteeing "a fair and public hearing within a reasonable time by an independent and impartial tribunal."[97] The report further noted that the 'operational necessity' standard of Section 7 was unreasonably restrictive and had been abused by UNMIK to justify the appropriation of property without compensation.[98]

In summary, application of the Convention has been inconsistent and UN rhetoric has been confused. At various times, both the broad and narrow interpretations of immunity protections have been invoked, with officials sometimes calling for a waiver and other times defining certain activities outside the scope of immunity. Despite this apparent confusion over how to interpret the Convention and failure to clearly articulate the scope of protection or a duty to waive, it appears that both UNTAET and UNMIK have been willing to expose UN staff, including military personnel, to prosecution where there is evidence of involvement in a serious crime, even if that means turning them over to local courts. This contrasts with both UNMIK and UNTAET's insistence that the UN be protected from criminal and civil liability for the implementation of policy.

C. Why Immunity for Transitional Administrations Is Different

While the option of establishing a trusteeship akin to those established under UN Charter Article 77 was explicitly rejected by the UN during the planning for UNMIK and UNTAET,[99] it is undeniable that both missions look, in many ways, more like authoritarian governments than peacekeeping operations positioned in the territory of another state.[100] In this context, the normal rationales for immunity make little sense. Immunity may violate the very principles of democratic accountability and human rights at the core of these missions' mandates.

1. Principles of Functional Necessity Do Not Apply

The Charter and the Immunities Convention were explicitly concerned with ensuring 'the independent exercise of [the organization's] functions' in the context of UN personnel acting in the territory of a sovereign state. Where UN officials are working in a territory over which the UN itself has sovereign power, the traditional justifications for diplomatic immunity – protection against unilateral intervention by the host State and reciprocal respect for the integrity of a sending state's representative – become incoherent. There is no longer a need for the protections of personal inviolability when UNCIVPOL are the sole policing authority.

---

97. *Id.* at para. 52.
98. The report noted that even the Geneva Convention during times of war requires a stricter showing of 'military necessity' to justify the appropriation of property. *Id.* at para. 48.
99. *See* Astri Suhrke, *Peacekeepers as Nation-builders: Dilemmas of the UN in East Timor*, INTERNATIONAL PEACEKEEPING, Vol. 8, No. 4, Winter 2001, at 7 (describing that the U.N. rejected the option of establishing a trusteeship in part to avoid an association with the neo-colonialism of the post-war trusteeship system).
100. Sergio Viera De Mello, the Special Representative of the Secretary-General in East Timor, described his role as that of a "benevolent despot," *cited in* Beauvais, *supra* note 79, at 1101.

Similarly, there is little justification for immunity from process when the United Nations itself is writing and enforcing the laws, and the SRSG has an absolute veto over judicial decisions. As the Ombudsperson Institution in Kosovo states in the opening quotation, "there is no need for a government to be protected against itself."

2. Immunity Conflicts with Democratic Principles

Functional immunity and a standard of 'operational necessity' run counter to an emerging right to democratic governance, which requires some level of accountability by government to its people.[101]   In addition, they arguably conflict with the UNMIK and UNTAET mandates to help develop democratic institutions in preparation for self-government, as set forth in Security Council Resolutions 1244 and 1272.[102]   Both missions have gone to great lengths to socialize democratic values and establish institutions in preparation for elections.[103]   Broad ranging immunity for the entire government civil service, police force and executive authority creates a lack of accountability incompatible with that mandate.   By removing UN policy and action from the jurisdiction of the court system without establishing a viable alternate forum, immunity reinforces the absolute authority of the executive to act with impunity.   Once again, this point echoes the Ombudsperson Institution's assertion that such a scheme violates "the fundamental precept of the rule of law . . . that the executive and legislative authorities are bound by law and are not above it."[104]

3. Immunity Violates a Right to a Remedy

Granting functional immunity from the jurisdiction of the court system to the entire government is also incompatible with human rights law calling for access to an impartial court.[105]   In addition to UN Charter obligations, the Security Council resolutions and intra-mission regulations of UNMIK and UNTAET create a legal

---

101.   *See* Thomas Franck, *The Emerging Right To Democratic Governance*, 86 AM. J. INT'L L. 46, 53 (1992).

102.   *See* S.C. Res. 1272, U.N. SCOR, 54th Sess., 4057th mtg., para. 8, U.N. Doc. S/RES/1272 (1999) ("Stresses the need for UNTAET to consult and cooperate closely with the East Timorese people in order to carry out its mandate effectively with a view to the development of local democratic instiutions . . . "); *see also* S.C. Res. 1244, U.N. SCOR, 54th Sess., 4011th mtg., para. 11(c), U.N. Doc. S/RES/1272 (1999) ("Organizing and overseeing the development of provisional institutions for democratic and autonomous self-government . . . .").

103.   For instance, UNTAET's ambitious "Civic Education for Democracy Program" in preparation for the August 2001 constituent assembly elections.. The program's initial lack of consultation with East Timorese was controversial. In response to an outcry by the NGO community, the project was redesigned to be less reliant on international staffing. *See* Open Letter in Response to UNTAET's Political Affairs Document 'Civic Education Project,' East Timor National NGO Forum (March 17, 2001). (On file with author).

104.   OMBUDSPERSON INSTITUTION IN KOSOVO, *supra* note 2, para. 24.

105.   *See* UNIVERSAL DECLARATION OF HUMAN RIGHTS art. 10; INTERNATIONAL COVENANT ON CIVIL AND POLITICAL RIGHTS art. 14, para. 1; EUROPEAN CONVENTION ON HUMAN RIGHTS art. 6, para. 1.

obligation for mission personnel and the mission as a whole to observe international human rights norms.[106] Even traditional immunity theory contemplates that redress for institutional abuses would be taken up by representatives of the state against which a violation occurred,[107] and the availability of some alternative forum has been a key factor in immunity rulings of both the International Court of Justice[108] and the European Court of Human Rights.[109] In the context of East Timor and Kosovo, there is no state actor to press for a negotiated settlement. The UN does not have its own permanent criminal or civil tribunal to resolve disputes arising from the misbehavior of its personnel. While both missions have set up Ombudsperson offices, they have no enforcement powers and are not, in practice, sufficiently independent of the SRSG's office to provide a legitimate hearing.

V. HUMAN RIGHTS, PEACE AND SECURITY, AND THE FUTURE OF IMMUNITY IN UN TRANSITIONAL ADMINISTRATION

This paper has argued that immunity for a UN-run government and its staff, working as civil servants and police, is inconsistent with the spirit of emerging human rights norms and with the mandates of the missions themselves, which include the socialization of human rights and the establishment of democratic institutions with some level of accountability. While the UN has made efforts to increase the level of mission accountability through the establishment of guidelines for Boards of Inquiry and Ombudsperson offices, the broad ranging immunity established by UNMIK regulation 2000/47 and the inconsistent interpretations of the Immunities Convention by UN officials do not indicate a recognition on the part of the UN that staff immunity may conflict with the governance role of transitional administrations. With the notable exception of the Ombudsperson report, existing critiques have come primarily from NGOs and victims in East Timor and Kosovo.

This contradiction between immunity and accountability of government reflects a larger conflict between a human rights based and a state based perspective on international law. The development of multi-lateral institutions, the increased scope

---

106. All UNTAET personnel are required to observe international human rights norms as they appear in various enumerated international instruments. *On the Authority of the Transitory Administration in East Timor*, UNTAET Reg. No. 1999/1, U.N. Doc. UNTAET/REG/1999/1, art. 2 (1999), *available at* http://www.un.org/peace/kosovo/pages/regulations/reg1.html (last visited Aug. 20, 2002) [hereinafter UNTAET Reg. No. 1999/1]. Likewise, "all persons undertaking public duties or holding public office in Kosovo shall observe internationally recognized human rights standards." *Id.* sec. 2. The SG, in a report to the Security Council, further stated that "UNMIK will embed a culture of human rights in all areas of activity." *Report of the Secretary General on the United Nations Interim Administration Mission in Kosovo*, U.N. Doc. S/1999/779, para. 42 (July 12, 1999), *cited in* David Marshall, *Reviving the Judicial and Penal System in Kosovo* (unpublished draft manuscript, in possession of author).

107. When a visiting diplomat in the past has violated the laws of a host country, the main remedy has been the declaration of the diplomat as *person non grata* followed by his or her expulsion. Vienna Convention on Diplomatic Relations, *supra* note 10, art. 9, para.1. It also provided for the possibility, however remote, of prosecution in the jurisdiction of the sending state. *Id.* art. 31, para. 4.

108. *See* Arrest Warrant, *supra* note 11, para. 61.

109. *See* Waite and Kennedy v. F.R.G. [GC], App. No. 26083/94, Eur. Ct. H.R. 1999-I, para. 68 (1999).

of UN intervention and the evolution of international criminal law concepts such as individual criminal responsibility and universal jurisdiction highlight the growing importance of an individual-based rights discourse, which challenges the position that the official nature of an act can shield a person or a state from criminal responsibility. It is no longer the case that individual victims must rely solely on their government to advocate on their behalf and governments can no longer shield themselves from responsibility for violating the human rights of their own citizens.

In the context of peacekeeping operations, this tension between pragmatic state politics and the growing obligation to guarantee the rights of individuals manifests itself in the dispute over the seemingly conflicting priorities of enforcing human rights and maintaining peace and security. Some officials have stated that immunity is necessary to fulfill that security function. This is consistent with what seems to be the vision of many field staff that human rights are something to be addressed *after* security concerns have been met. Senior officials at both UNMIK and UNTAET have argued that derogation from human rights standards are necessary and expected in a peace keeping context and suggested that where there is Chapter VII authorization, a de facto 'state of emergency' exists, which justifies derogation from international human rights standards.[110] This kind of overreaction obscures the legitimate security concerns that a transitional government must face, concerns that are different than in a traditional intervention.

This rationale only makes sense when missions like UNTAET and UNMIK are viewed through the lens of a traditional peacekeeping operation. Statements by UNTAET and UNMIK personnel about immunity expose an unwillingness or inability to recognize that transitional administration brings with it a different set of legal, political and ethical realities. When UNMIK Regulation 2000/47 came before the Security Council, Assistant Secretary-General Annabi stated that in order to function "under normal conditions," staff required legal protection from "local courts," and that it was "necessary to grant them the basic privileges and immunities

---

110. One report concluded that at UNMIK "the view appears to be that a Chapter VII resolution adopted by the Security Council absolves the peacekeeping operation from certain human rights obligations." Simon Chesterman, *Kosovo in Limbo: State-Building and "Substantial Autonomy,"* INT'L PEACE ACADEMY, at 11 (August 2001), *at* http://www.ipacademy.org. The problem was so serious that the mission's own human rights unit as well as the UNMIK Department of Justice made a recommendation to the SRSG that an executive instruction be promulgated that clarifies that international human rights laws "are supreme over all other laws." No clarification was ever issued. Organisation for Security and Co-operation in Europe, *supra* note 91, at 11. Similarly, one senior political affairs officer expressed the opinion that UNTAET Reg. 1999/1's requirement of full compliance with international human rights instruments was inconsistent with state practice, and so UNTAET could not be expected to comply either. Personal communication, UNTAET official. But does this language from Reg. 1999/1 sound aspirational? "In exercising their functions, *all* persons undertaking public duties or holding public office in East Timor *shall* observe internationally recognized human rights standards, as reflected, in particular, in: The Universal Declaration on Human Rights of 10 December 1948; The International Covenant on Civil and Political Rights of 16 December 1966 and its Protocols; The International Covenant on Economic, Social and Cultural Rights of 16 December 1966; The Convention on the Elimination of All Forms of Racial Discrimination of 21 December 1965; The Convention on the Elimination of All Forms of Discrimination Against Women of 17 December 1979; The Convention Against Torture and other Cruel, Inhumane or Degrading Treatment or Punishment of 17 December 1984; The International Convention on the Rights of the Child of 20 November 1989." UNTAET Reg. No. 1999/1, *supra* note 106, art. 2 (emphasis added).

that are normally granted in such situations."[111]   Similarly, when the UNTAET SRSG and his Principal Legal Advisor were called before the Timorese National Council, they reiterated that UN peacekeeping operations and their staff are entitled to immunity under international law, regardless of the nature of the operation.[112] But as this paper has argued, transitional administrations are not normal peacekeeping operations. To characterize them as normal and to conflate the UN-supervised Kosovo and Timorese court systems with other 'local courts,' obscures the true nature of the UN's governance role and the SRSG's supervisory power over the judiciary.

When we view UN transitional administrations as government entities with similar responsibilities towards the governed as a state has towards its citizens, concepts like open-ended states of emergency and broad state immunity are no longer so easily justifiable. From such a perspective, when the UN is acting as a governing authority, vested with executive, legislative and judicial powers, a broad immunity scheme such as regulation 2000/47 would be better abandoned for a more narrow interpretation of governmental immunity coupled with a strong impartial forum for resolving allegations of criminal conduct. In the case of a legitimate state of emergency, derogation from international human rights standards can and should accord with the requirements of international human rights instruments, without crippling a mission's ability to cope with issues of peace and security.

A. *Increasing Accountability – Some Options and Recommendations*

Given the extreme conditions under which peacekeepers must work, it is not surprising that the UN has been more concerned with ensuring the protection of its staff in the field than generating legal regimes to provide for the investigation and prosecution of personnel suspected of criminal activity. First, there are compelling objections to trying staff in UN-supervised courts. In both Kosovo and East Timor, there has been a serious question as to whether the courts are capable of implementing international standards of due process.[113]   Secondly, every peacekeeping mission is the result of political negotiation and compromise and is dependent on the largesse of member states. If history is any indication, proposals to limit immunity are likely to be opposed by many member states with possible consequences for troop contributions.[114] At present, any such proposal would meet

---

111.   U.N. SCOR, 55th Sess., 4190th mtg., at 19, U.N. Doc. S/PV.4190 (2000).
112.   Author present.
113.   This rationale for denying jurisdiction to the local courts has only infrequently and selectively been invoked. This is the position that certain actors at UNTAET took in the case of the Jordanian Civpol. It is also one of the bases upon which courts in Kosovo rejected the Rwandan government's extradition request for Callixte Mbarushimana. *See* Cruvellier, *supra* note 77.
114.   At the mere suggestion by the SG that UN troops be required to comply with the Geneva Conventions, several nations announced that they would consider suspending troop contributions. Subsequently, in the Special Committee for Peacekeeping Operations, numerous Member States felt it necessary to reiterate that the order did not affect the traditional practice of trying or court-marshalling personnel in their home countries only. *Report of the Special Committee on Peacekeeping Operation on Comprehensive Review of the whole question of peacekeeping operations in all their aspects*, U.N.

with harsh opposition from the United States in the Security Council. Since UNCIVPOL would be most directly affected by any changes, a narrowing of immunity protections could seriously disturb the UN's ability to maintain a sufficient police presence in the field.

Recognizing these pragmatic concerns, this paper agrees that immunities should nonetheless be interpreted through the lens of the Charter which envisions granting only the minimum immunities necessary.[115] The UN should narrow immunities to a reasonable definition of 'official duty,' explicitly excluding serious violations of human rights and criminal law, and only invoke immunity protections when failing to do so would truly endanger the success of the mission. When a violation occurs during the conduct of official duties, the SG should consider a waiver of immunity. Most importantly, where waiver is not granted there must be an impartial and independent forum in which issues of immunity and the underlying criminal offenses can be adjudicated.

1. UN-Administered Courts

It has been suggested that in transitional administrations with UN-administered judicial systems, immunity determinations could be made and trials could be conducted in local UN-supervised courts.[116] In the past, both UNMIK and UNTAET have entrusted local court systems with the task of trying staff after immunity protections were denied. Despite the attractiveness from a justice point of view of subjecting the indigenous population and international staff to the same process,[117] trial in indigenous courts is unrealistic for reasons of resources, politics, and the potential for bias. A local court is not likely to be able to handle the additional caseload of dealing with complaints against international staff, or against the UN itself.[118] It would be unfair to try a select few transgressors in local courts,

---

GAOR, 55th Sess., Agenda Item 86, para. 21-22, U.N. Doc. A/55/1024 (2001); *Comprehensive review*, *supra* note 50, para. 29-30.

115.   Brower, *supra* note 23, at 20.

116.   These might be special tribunals consisting completely or partially of international judges similar to the special courts set up in East Timor, Kosovo, and Sierra Leone to try serious human rights violations.

117.   Perceived differences in treatment, particularly when UN jobs are restricted to a small, usually English speaking minority, can be a source of significant social unrest. *See* Tom Fawthrop, *Timorese Angered Over UN Jobs Deal*, THE AGE, March 30, 2000; Lindsay Murdoch, *Timor's social gap*, SYDNEY MORNING HERALD, April 15, 2000, at 44. Subjecting international staff to trials in the same courts as local citizens would bolster the credibility of those institutions. Sarah Pritchard has recently written that "the very authority and credibility of the UN's mission . . . is at stake in its response to the challenge of creating a fair, transparent and effective judicial system." Sarah Pritchard, *United Nations Involvement in Post-Conflict Reconstruction Efforts: New and Continuing Challenges in the Case of East Timor*, 24 U. N.S.W. L.J. 183, 189-90 (2001).

118.   Hansjorge Strohmeyer, who worked as the Head of Judicial Affairs in the early stages of both UNTAET and UNMIK, writes of the many obstacles, in particular lack of human resources, that the UN faced in establishing a functioning court system in the short-term. *See generally* Hansjoerg Strohmeyer, *Policing the Peace: Post-Conflict Judicial System Reconstruction in East Timor*, 24 U. N.S.W. L.J. 171 (2001); Hansjorge Strohmeyer, *Collapse and Reconstruction of a Judicial System: The United Nations Missions in Kosovo and East Timor*, 95 AM. J. INT'L L. 46 (2001) [hereinafter *Collapse and Reconstruction*].

and send the others home where they would likely receive no punishment. In an atmosphere where accusations of neo-colonialism abound, the potential for bias against UN staff who have committed crimes against local residents is also dangerously high. Perhaps most importantly, subjecting UN staff to local courts could have a devastating impact on staff recruitment, and in particular, the recruitment of much-needed UNCIVPOL.

2. Mission-Based Ombudsperson

The most promising reform may be the establishment of a more robust and independent mission-based Ombudsperson office. The concept of an Ombudsperson already has significant rhetorical support in the Special Committee and the General Assembly. It keeps control firmly within the UN structure. At the same time, increasing the enforcement power of current models and making the office more independent of the SRSG may make them effective alternative fora. These reforms might include giving the office a limited form of judicial review over administrative decisions, establishing a direct line of communication between the Ombudsperson and Office of Legal Affairs in New York, encouraging the dissemination of public reports, providing the Ombudsperson himself with some security of tenure and the office with access to its own source of funding.[119] The Office could be empowered to conduct its own investigations into allegations of abuse by civilian, UNCIVPOL and in serious cases, military personnel. While it will not have the power to criminally prosecute, a sufficiently competent and independent Ombudsperson's office could make both private and public recommendations to OLA in New York and to Member States on the scope of immunity, the existence of a duty to waive, and the suitability of prosecution. The Ombudsperson office should have a close relationship with any Claims Commission formed by or in association with the mission, and its judgments could be made enforceable by such a Commission.

3. International Humanitarian Ombudsperson

---

119. It has been suggested in the past that the Ombudsperson be given a soft form of judicial review – the authority to overturn or amend administrative regulations that clearly violate human rights law. This option was rejected outright by both UNMIK and UNTAET. Even narrowly construed, any power of judicial review is likely to be viewed as an unacceptable restriction on the SRSG's powers. However, even if the offices' rulings are to remain only advisory, their influence may be increased by making them answerable directly to New York, rather than via the SRSG's office. A direct line of communication between the Ombudsperson and the Office of Legal Affairs, which is theoretically required to review all mission legislation in any case, might increase the independence of the office as well as increase its influence within the mission. The Ombudsperson his/herself should be appointed by New York or Geneva, and have access to some resources separate from the mission's general budget. The SRSG should not be able to hire and fire the Ombudsperson at will, and the Ombudsperson should have some security of tenure beyond the normal professional staff contracts. Reports should be made available to the public as they have been in Kosovo, but not in East Timor. The author's ideas (for which he alone takes responsibility) in this area benefited from conversations with David Malone and Simon Chesterman of the International Peace Academy, New York.

130   *CONNECTICUT JOURNAL OF INT'L LAW*   [Vol. 18:103

A more radical option would be the establishment of an international humanitarian ombudsperson, which would handle allegations of abuse by peacekeeping staff and peacekeeping missions at the global level, and oversee the SG's waiver decisions. There would be numerous benefits of influence, independence and consistency with such a body. Given resource constraints, the need for an international mandate probably from the Security Council, and its potential impact on troop and UNCIVPOL contributions, the possibility seems unlikely. Since such a body would likely deal primarily with allegations of serious abuse by military personnel in the more traditional peacekeeping context, it would not alleviate the need for some kind of mission-based mechanism.[120]

4. International Criminal Court

Peacekeeping personnel involved in genocide or crimes against humanity could theoretically be investigated and prosecuted by the International Criminal Court. However, in July 2002, in response to US pressure, the Security Council passed a resolution prohibiting the Court from prosecuting current or former peacekeeping personnel from countries not a party to the Rome Statute for a renewable 12 month period.[121] This came after the US government threatened to withdraw US personnel from East Timor and veto the extension of the peacekeeping mission in Bosnia and Herzegovina (UNMIBH) unless US personnel were granted full immunity.[122] The current political climate, in addition to other resource issues, makes it unlikely that the ICC will be an effective check on peacekeeping abuses.

5. Boards of Inquiry

---

120. A consortium of non-government organizations including the Red Cross, Oxfam and Care have proposed a model for an international ombudsperson who would monitor NGO compliance with international humanitarian law. *See* Humanitarian Accountability Project, *at* http://www.oneworld.org /ombudsman (last visited Aug. 25, 2002).

121. Resolution 1422 reads "if a case arises involving current or former officials or personnel from a contributing State not a Party to the Rome Statute over acts or omissions relating to a United Nations established or authorized operation, [the ICC] shall for a twelve-month period starting 1 July 2002 not commence or proceed with investigation or prosecution of any such case, unless the Security Council decides otherwise." S.C. Res. 1422, U.N. SCOR, 4572d mtg., para. 1, U.N. Doc. S/RES/1422 (2002), *available at* http://www.un.org/Docs/scres/2002/sc2002.htm (last visited Sept. 23, 2002).

122. *See* Colum Lynch, *U.S. Seeks Court Immunity for E. Timor Peacekeepers,* WASH. POST, May 16, 2002, at A22; *U.N. Ends Wrangle Over U.S. Immunity,* N.Y. TIMES, July 13, 2002, at A1. The US Congress subsequently passed the American Service-Members' Protection Act which authorized the President to "use the voice and vote of the United States in the United Nations Security Council to ensure that each resolution of the Security Council authorizing any peacekeeping operation . . . exempts, at a minimum, members of the Armed Forces of the United States participating in such an operation from criminal prosecution or other assertion of jurisdiction by the International Criminal Court for actions undertaken by such personnel in connection with the operation." American Service-Members' Protection Act of 2002, H.R. 4775, 107th Cong. sec. 2005(a) (2002). For discussion on the US-UN dispute over the ICC, see Washington Working Group on the International Criminal Court, *Ambassador John D. Negroponte: Statement on the situation in Bosnia and Herzegovina, in the United Nations Security Council, at* http://www.wfa.org/issues/wicc/un-us.html (last visited Sept. 20, 2002); *see also* Human Rights Watch Statement, *U.S. Proposals to Undermine the International Criminal Court Through a U.N. Security Council Resolution* (June 25, 2002), *available at* http://www.hrw.org/ campaigns/icc/usproposal.htm.

For the near future and in all but the most serious cases, military personnel will remain outside the aegis of a local or international court or ombudsperson without the express waiver of their contributing governments. It is questionable if BOI as they currently exist are the appropriate tool to investigate the misbehavior of personnel. BOI are in no way transparent- their deliberations are not usually made public, their mandates and terms of reference are often ambiguous, and they lack independence from the mission itself. Procedures should be set into place to ensure that Boards of Inquiry are sufficiently transparent and independent including requiring the publication of investigations in a timely manner, and developing an impartial method of appointing commissioners.

6. Clarifying Current Law and Practice

The larger issue of the compatibility of international human rights law prohibiting impunity for serious crimes, and traditional legal doctrine of diplomatic immunity will have to await the further development of international jurisprudence. It is not inconceivable that someday, the courts themselves, including the ICJ, could begin to play a larger role in interpreting the scope of functional immunity. Until then, this paper further recommends that the Secretary-General's office and the Department of Peacekeeping Operations release a comprehensive bulletin on the scope of the privileges and immunities of UN staff in the field. The bulletin should set forth, among other things:

(a) the SG's interpretation of what constitutes official duty in the context of Immunities Convention Sections 18, 19 and 22, including the extent of the SG's duty to waive under Sections 20 and 23, particularly where there is evidence of involvement in serious crimes, including genocide, rape, murder, and child sexual abuse;

(b) when an explicit determination of whether immunity protections attach must be made directly by the SG's office and when, if ever, that power will be delegated to the Special Representative and/or Head of Mission;

(c) an explicit statement that where there is evidence of involvement in serious crimes, the UN will not attempt to protect individuals from prosecution in a jurisdiction where there are no other over-riding human rights concerns; and

(d) a consistent procedure for handling questions of immunity in the peacekeeping context, including a clear articulation of the role of Boards of Inquiry, Ombudsperson offices, and UN supervised courts.

7. Criminal Law 'Kits'

This paper also supports the idea of developing a general criminal law framework for future transitional administrations.[123] In addition to an interim code of criminal procedure, such a framework should include draft statutes for an internationalized tribunal, BOI and/or Ombudsperson office as well as a draft immunity statute that conforms with international human rights law. While there is always a danger of a 'quick-start package' being mis-applied in a particular local context, at the very least, it will ensure that judicial institution and capacity-building initiatives address immunity issues and provide a mechanism for adjudicating criminal transgressions by UN staff.

VI. A FINAL NOTE

While a human rights perspective on immunity in peacekeeping will no doubt constrain a UN operation more than the executive discretion associated with the traditional peace and security model, it is by no means incompatible with the maintenance of peace and the fulfillment of the traditional duties of a peacekeeping operation. This paper contends that even if international law does not yet demand a re-working of the law of official immunities generally, a more consistent and human rights-based approach would improve the credibility of future UN governance operations in the eyes of the international community and in the eyes of those populations temporarily living under the authority of UN administrations. Only by subjecting everyone to the same requirements and judging them by the same standards established by international law, will Mr. Viera de Mello be right that in East Timor, and wherever the United Nations is called to intervene in a similar manner, "no one is above the law."

---

123. Most eloquently advocated by Strohmeyer in *Collapse and Reconstruction*, *supra* note 118, at 62. The importance of establishing early a clear legal framework to structure UNCIVPOL action was also emphasized in the "Brahimi Report." *See generally Report of the Panel on United Nations Peace Operations*, U.N. GAOR, 55th Sess., Item 87 of the Provisional Agenda, U.N. Doc. A/55/305-S/2000/809 (2000).

Name Index